Make Your Family's European Vacation Special . . . Safe . . . and Problem-Free

Would you like to rock to sleep on a Parisian barge . . . or stay overnight in a *pensione* in the heart of Florence . . . or feel the mystery of a Portuguese *pousada* built in a walled city . . . or luxuriate at a beach villa in Spain's Marbella? *Innocents Abroad* gives you complete travel information to make this all happen . . . and much more. You'll find practical tips to keep children from getting bored, what foods to avoid, how to exchange homes or find a reasonable apartment, the best times to visit famous places, great detours off the beaten track, and a whole treasure house of knowledge that parents really need to keep this dream vacation from turning into a nightmare. Sample these goodies:

ENGLAND—a tricycle museum and delightful hedgerow mazes
AUSTRIA—the dancing Lippizan stallions and Punch-and-Judy shows
FRANCE—Rin Tin Tin's gravestone and a tour of the sewers of Paris
DENMARK—Legoland, with a Taj Mahal and Statue of Liberty—made out of 35 million Lego blocks!

—and literally hundreds more places to go and things to do both off the beaten track . . . and on it!

VALERIE WOLF DEUTSCH and LAURA SUTHERLAND are journalists and writers who have created, produced, and hosted many shows for a member station of National Public Radio. Both have been involved in children's activity programs. Valerie and Laura lived in Europe as children, and both are well traveled—with and without children.

INNOCENTS ABROAD

Traveling with Kids in Europe

VALERIE WOLF DEUTSCH
AND
LAURA SUTHERLAND

A PLUME BOOK

The authors have made every effort to ensure the accuracy of the travel information appearing in this book but readers should be aware that information does change. The authors and publisher can accept no responsibility for any inconvenience or injury sustained by a traveler resulting from information obtained in *Innocents Abroad: Traveling with Kids in Europe.*

PLUME
Published by the Penguin Group
Penguin Books USA Inc., 375 Hudson Street,
New York, New York 10014, U.S.A.
Penguin Books Ltd, 27 Wrights Lane,
London W8 5TZ, England
Penguin Books Australia Ltd, Ringwood,
Victoria, Australia
Penguin Books Canada Ltd, 2801 John Street,
Markham, Ontario, Canada L3R 1B4
Penguin Books (N.Z.) Ltd, 182–190 Wairau Road,
Auckland 10, New Zealand

Penguin Books Ltd, Registered Offices:
Harmondsworth, Middlesex, England

First published by Plume, an imprint of New American
Library, a division of Penguin Books USA Inc.

First Printing, March, 1991

10 9 8 7 6 5 4 3 2 1

Library of Congress Cataloging-in-Publication Data

Deutsch, Valerie Wolf.
  Innocents abroad : traveling with kids in Europe / Valerie Wolf
Deutsch and Laura Sutherland.
     p.   cm.
  1. Europe—Description and travel—1991—Guide-books.
  2. Children—Travel—Europe—Guide-books. I. Sutherland, Laura.
  II. Title.
  D909.D47   1991
  914.04'559—dc20   90-45752
                                                     CIP

Printed in the United States of America
Set in Melior
Designed by Stanley S. Drate/Folio Graphics Co. Inc.

Contents

~~~~~~~~

v

Acknowledgments

This book was inspired by our young traveling companions Madeleine, Silvie, and Walker, who enabled us to see Europe through the fresh eyes of children. Special thanks go to our talented agent Vicky Bijur, our editors Sandra Soule and Toni Rachiele, literary experts Robin Seaman and Michael S. Gant, and of course Mark Twain, who planted the seed from which our ideas grew. Marisa Ricks and Kristen Chidester served as stalwart research assistants, enduring sticky back seats, scorching summer heat, and many sleepless nights.

We are grateful to the many families who shared their experiences traveling with their children, especially to those places we did not visit with our own. Those who went beyond the call of duty were Cheryl, Paul, and Nicole Albert, Shannon Hacket, Dan Hallinan, Kathleen Hamar, Joel Leivick, Dorothy Jordon and the readers of *Family Travel Times*, Kate Neri, Janet Pollock, Dick Rahders, and Patti Schoknecht.

Many others contributed to this book, and we are indebted to them for their special assistance: Austria: Barbara Higgs, Austrian National Tourist Office; Belgium: Marlene Bervoets, Belgian Tourist Office; Denmark: Vibeka von der Hude, Lillian Hess, Danish Tourist Board; England: Reed Searle, Adrian Bevans, British Tourist Authority; France: Béraud and Diane de Vogüé; Germany: Maria Tischler; the Netherlands: Marion Gilbert, Gerrie Davis, Netherlands Board of Tourism; Portugal: Ana Maria Osorio, Portuguese National Tourist Office; Scotland: Margaret and Michael Clark; Spain: Sally Geisse, Joseph Maria Vericat; Switzerland: Monika Schumacher-Bauer. For expressing an early interest, we thank Jim Ferry, Jean Gabella, and Gerry Kelly. Our heartfelt thanks to Eadie Deutsch, Claire Miller, and Jack and Marianna Sutherland for their warm encouragement.

Our biggest support came from our husbands, Lance Linares and Richard Deutsch. Not only did they help with child care as deadlines approached, but they also endured countless take-out dinners, dragged us away from the keyboard, and listened as we talked on and on about croissants, carousels, and kilometers. This book is dedicated to you.

Introduction:
Yes, You Can Take Them
with You!

You can take your children with you on your long-awaited European vacation. Why wait? While the other moms and dads in our child-care class were hanging mobiles, we were busy arranging passport photos and airline tickets and learning how to say "crib" and "pacifier" in Italian. Instead of stockpiling diapers and baby wipes, we were shopping for the lightest umbrella stroller and solidifying our itinerary for what was to be one of the most memorable experiences of our lives as a family—a five-month trip to Europe with our young children. Granted, many of our friends thought we were out of our minds to do "Europe on Ten Diapers a Day," but we found traveling with children in a foreign land to be a joyous experience. And best of all, it was fun and easy.

Children add a new dimension to travel. We found ours open to impressions we would have most certainly overlooked. Sightseeing excursions became even more engaging when experienced through their discoveries and reactions. As a bonus, kids are the world's leading "goodwill ambassadors," and have the uncanny ability of making friends for the whole family. Trips to open-air markets took twice as long as they might have, as vendors admired our little ones and presented them with gifts of the juiciest peaches, ripest tomatoes, and most succulent figs. Any feeling of being foreign faded whenever the children were in tow.

Traveling en famille in a foreign country brings a family closer together. After all, your kids will have no one else to talk to and they'll be a captive audience for your stories, songs, jokes, and tall tales. Together you'll develop a cache of shared memories to enjoy for years to come. For many families with both parents working, vacations have become the most important block of time to spend together, and exploring a foreign culture can make that time more precious.

Traveling provides children with a tremendous educational opportunity. They learn firsthand about other people and other cultures by experiencing their food, language, history, and traditions. Classroom study simply cannot compare. Italy will no longer just be a country studied in school but a real place where they saw the Colosseum and Pompeii's massive theaters miraculously preserved under the vicious ash of Mount Vesuvius.

We'll lead you to the places children will enjoy most, from eccentric palaces to the homelands of fairy-tale characters. Denmark's Legoland, horse-drawn caravanning through the French countryside, or navigating one of Britain's challenging hedge mazes will be excursions your kids will talk about for years to come. You may not spend an afternoon listening to classical music at Salzburg's Mirabell Palace, but shooting down wooden slides into the depths of the Dürrnberg Salt Mines will be a side trip all will remember. You'll find tips on traveling abroad with different age groups and simple ideas for planning your itinerary with everyone's enjoyment in mind. We'll clue you in on what to pack, medical information, food, accommodations, and resources for preparing your kids ahead of time so they'll get the most out of your trip.

Bon voyage!

1

Planning the Trip Together

Months before the traveler's checks are purchased and the toy bags are packed comes the most important part of your adventure: planning your trip. As important as asking, "Where will we go?" is the question, "What will *each* of the different members of my family enjoy?" Get your entire family involved in deciding what to do. Have the kids write to tourist offices, visit the library to select advance reading material for each child, and talk about the foods and customs of the countries you'll be visiting. By including children in the decision-making process, you will ensure that their trip will be more meaningful.

When to Go

Europe overflows with great activities in the summer, the time when most families with school-aged children take vacations. The ideal summer month to travel is June, when sites and accommodations are less crowded. If you can't break away in June, you'll find that the locals travel with their kids in July and especially in August, and your family will experience more of a country's distinctive spirit by watching it at play. Most of Europe's summer activities take place outdoors, which means more fun for your kids. To avoid the crowds, try going to the less touristy sections of the countries you plan to visit. Visit the Highland Games in the small towns of Scotland rather than the best-known and crowded Braemar Games. Visit charming places like the medieval walled city of Lucca rather than Florence or Brittany's beaches rather than those on the French Riviera.

Bear in mind that some of the most popular sights will be favorites

1

for your kids. They'll head straight for the Mona Lisa in the Louvre, and Madame Tussaud's Wax Museum will be at the top of their list in London. When you do visit these more popular attractions, go early in the day. Sights such as the Leaning Tower of Pisa or Copenhagen's Tivoli Gardens can be packed with tourists later in the day, so be sure to get there before they look like a conference at the United Nations.

For those of you with doubts about traveling with toddlers and preschoolers, here's where you have an advantage; you'll be able to travel off-season. Late-spring and early-fall travelers will find pleasant weather throughout most of Europe along with fewer crowds, the best accommodations available, and cheaper prices. As winter approaches, some attractions can close, so be sure to note the schedule of sites that will interest your family most. It's wise to call ahead.

There are many exceptional festivals and activities off-season. In many cities February is carnival time, when you'll find parades with masked performers, fireworks, and music; Easter festivals abound all over the continent; fields of tulips burst into bloom in Holland in April and May; Monte Carlo hosts a winter Circus Festival; December Christmas fairs and pantomimes are not to be missed; and celebrations of light take place throughout the darkest winter months.

Planning Your Itinerary

Once you've made the decision to travel as a family, consider the impact children will have on your trip. Will you be able to include as many cities or countries as you'd like, or should you all stay in one place longer and get to know it better? Can you really enjoy Notre-Dame in 20 minutes, or will the stained-glass windows be a blur as you race through?

Here are some tips that may help you plan your itinerary:

- Planning your trip is like packing: For smooth traveling with kids, jot down your preferred itinerary; then cut it in half.
- Alternate big-city visits with beach, mountain, or country pursuits.
- Intersperse 1- or 2-night stops with a week or two at a home base from where you can take side trips.
- Always keep your child's perspective in mind, and plan your day's activities around your youngest child's abilities.
- Favorite activities for many kids involve heights, depths, water, unusual forms of transportation, and animals. Try to incorporate as many of these into your itinerary as possible.
- And, most importantly, **always have a park or beach close by.**

This is our tried and true secret for successful travel with kids.

Have your children write to the national tourist offices of the various countries you are thinking of visiting. Their addresses are listed in the introductory section of each country's chapter. All your child has to do is indicate an interest in visiting a chosen land or mention a specific focus such as skiing, hiking, staying on a farm, or boating and his or her mailbox will be jammed full. Your teen may be humming "Where the Boys Are" when she says, "Let's visit St. Tropez," while Dad growls and thinks about a quiet fishing trip on France's Dordogne River, but planning the trip together will ensure a meaningful experience for all.

Always Have a Park or Beach Close By

There is nothing like running in a park or swimming at a beach to rejuvenate weary young travelers. This "park" or "beach" can be as all encompassing as you wish; it is simply a place where your kids can walk barefoot, put on a swimsuit, play ball, run, or scream. For children, a daily break to run free and play will buy you countless hours of doing "adult" things. You can spend time at Paris' Musée d'Orsay or Amsterdam's Rijksmuseum if you limit your stay to a few hours and follow it with a park visit. After the chance to run and play, the kids will be ready to continue sightseeing.

Some families with young children actually plan their European holidays around easy access to beaches. Don't feel you need to limit your trip to the coastlines of Europe, but do keep a park, beach, mountain, boat, or nature trail close by, and your children will amaze you with their ability to travel happily. It is with this in mind that we have indicated the best parks and beach spots within each country's section.

Planning Tips

Babes-in-arms are a breeze, napping anywhere and content to see the sites you choose from a backpack or stroller. For the most relaxed trip, head out with them before they become really mobile; after they master crawling, you'll spend a fair amount of time chasing them.

Toddlers can be difficult to travel with, so plan your itinerary carefully. You'll be more successful if you pick one or two places to set up as a home base (which should include a kitchen) and make short trips from there.

Preschool-age children are becoming increasingly more cooperative, making short museum visits possible. The home-base approach works best with this age, too. Plan your itinerary to avoid long car trips.

School-age kids are able to take longer car journeys, so you can begin adding to your itinerary.

Teenagers, more than any other children, need a say in the types of activities planned. Adventure travel and city excitement can hold great appeal to them.

SPECIAL ORGANIZATIONS AND PUBLICATIONS

There are several organizations that specialize in assisting families who are planning a trip and a number of helpful publications:

- Travel with Your Children can provide great vacation ideas. Their publication, *Family Travel Times*, covers worldwide travel news of interest to families. Subscribers can take advantage of a phone-in travel advice service. $35 per year. For information or sample issues: 80 8th Ave., New York, NY 10011. Tel. 212-206-0688.
- Traveling with Children helps families design a successful, customized vacation to Europe. They can assist with planning an itinerary and can book airline tickets, accommodations, transportation, and entertainment. 2313 Valley St., Berkeley, CA 94702. Tel. 415-848-0929.
- Families Welcome! specializes in arranging packages for families visiting London and Paris. 21 West Colony Place, Suite 140, Durham, NC 27705. Tel. 800-326-0724 or 919-489-2555.
- Getaways is a newsletter covering vacation spots suitable for the entire family. One article per issue is devoted to European travel. P.O. Box 11511, Washington, DC 20008. Tel. 703-534-8747.
- Grandtravel has escorted two-week tours to England, France, and the Netherlands for grandparents and grandchildren (parents, aunts, and uncles are welcome, too). Prices (around $3,000 per person) include everything except airfare. 6900 Wisconsin Ave., Suite 706, Chevy Chase, MD 20815. Tel. 800-247-7651 or 301-986-0790.
- International Family Adventure sponsors five or six trips a year for twenty to thirty families to places like the Greek Islands, Switzerland, Italy, and Eastern Europe. Box 172, New Canaan, CT 06840. Tel. 203-972-3842.
- Let's Take the Kids publishes a newsletter on great places to go with children and offers escorted tours with travel nannies. They can also help arrange accommodations and make child-care recommendations. A toll-free telephone service answers questions members have about traveling with children. $35 per year.

300 W. Glenoaks Blvd., Suite 201, Glendale, CA 91202. Tel. 800-272-4377 or 213-472-4449.
- The helpful book, *Ski Europe*, by Charles Leocha and William Walker, is a comprehensive guide to skiing Europe's best resorts with detailed information about children's programs. (Published by World Leisure Corp., P.O. Box 160, Hampstead, NH 03841.)

2

"Oh Give Me a Home...": Where to Stay

Your only difficulty in finding a place to stay with your children in Europe will be choosing from the myriad of accommodations available. Beyond the traditional hotel circuit, you can rock to sleep on a Parisian barge or rest your weary feet (from trying on new shoes, of course) in a pensione in the heart of Florence. You can experience the enchantment of a Portuguese pousada built in a walled city or awaken to collect fresh eggs on an English country farm. If lounging at a beach villa in Spain's Marbella is more your style, that's available, too. It's all a matter of budget and preference. Here is an overview of the types of accommodations you'll find. Complete details are listed in the individual country chapters.

Homes, Apartments, and Villas

Rental homes, apartments, and villas provide an opportunity for families to truly taste and experience the region they are visiting. You can meet your neighbors, shop at local markets, and play in the parks. Rentals typically offer kitchens, and some have living/dining areas, grounds, and even family libraries. Relaxing in a home is much more comfortable than limiting family living to hotel bedrooms and lobbies. A vacation rental is usually more economical than staying in hotels and eating meals in restaurants. The English call this type of accommodation *self-catering*, and you will run across this term frequently.

You can rent homes, apartments, or villas by the week or month. Many organizations are available to help you locate them; in each country's chapter we provide a listing. Be sure to inquire if there will be a property manager who speaks English and which services can be supplied. Ask about all extra charges in advance, such as linens and cleaning fees. Some organizations will also arrange for babysitting or domestic help. An excellent resource is *A Traveler's Guide to Vacation Rentals in Europe* by Michael and Laura Murphy (New York: Dutton, 1990).

Hotels

Don't limit yourself to Europe's four- and five-star hotel chains. Even if you have the resources for such luxury, your children will not be that impressed unless there is a great pool or recreational activities. Save your money for a second honeymoon and find those hotels with special amenities for families.

In each country's chapter, we have listed hotels in major cities with particular family attractions, such as proximity to parks, kitchenettes, suites or connecting rooms, gardens or lawns, or supervised children's playrooms. Prices for hotels are indicated by inexpensive, moderate, expensive, and deluxe. We do not indicate specific prices; categories refer to price relationships between hotels and can be used as a rough guide.

Babies are not usually charged, whereas children sharing rooms with their parents are given reduced rates. There is often a small fee for adding a supplemental bed to a double room. Rates for children occupying their own rooms vary. If your rate includes meals, there may be a reduced price for children's portions.

Bathrooms can vary from a shared facility down the hall to complete facilities in your room. Where both options are available, rooms with private baths are more expensive. Full Pension meal plans include all meals. Half Pension or Demi Pension includes two meals (usually breakfast and dinner). Some room rates include only a light breakfast (juice, coffee or tea, milk, a roll or pastry), whereas others, such as in the Netherlands and Great Britain, provide a hearty breakfast at no extra cost.

Castles, Farmhouses, Camping, and More

Europe's guest homes and bed-and-breakfast lodgings are ideal for traveling families. You'll save money, but there are even better reasons to choose them. People who invite guests into their homes are usually friendly and eager to share their perceptions of their homeland. A long-standing British tradition, bed-and-breakfast lodgings can now be found in the Netherlands, France, Germany, and Austria. B and B's are usually small private homes with no more than a few guest rooms. You may find yourselves sharing coffee and croissants with your hosts and, perhaps, their children. We have included information on where to write for further details in each country's chapter.

In Spain and Portugal the government sponsors tourist inns, called *paradores* in Spain and *pousadas* in Portugal, in areas of natural beauty, historic significance, and traditional culture. Comprising over 100 castles, monasteries, abbeys, and villas, they are exciting places to stay. Refer to the chapters on Spain and Portugal for complete details.

A great number of privately owned castles have opened up their royal gates to overnight visitors. Staying in a castle can make history come alive for a child, and tales of knights on horseback and the lords and ladies who lived there long ago will spark many a fantasy. Ranging in price, some castles are set on large grounds with sporting activities. Refer to the chapters on Austria and Germany (Schloss), Great Britain (manor houses), and France (châteaux) for further details.

Pensiones, or *pensions*, are more casual and less expensive than hotel or castle accommodations. They range in comfort but can be well worth the memories. Many specialized guidebooks are on the market, and some national tourist offices provide listings.

Another inexpensive and charming way to go is to stay on a family farm, complete with cows, sheep, pigs, roosters, and fresh eggs. Some require a week's stay or more, but you can use the farm as a centralized base to take excursions to neighboring villages. Most provide discounted rates for children; some offer full board, others just breakfast. Information is provided in each country's chapter.

Hostels are a very inexpensive way to go; only camping is cheaper. Most guests are student-aged, but many hostels, especially in northern Europe, are now accommodating families. You'll find kitchens, small "family bedrooms," children's beds, and high chairs. Hostels are a unique way to meet travelers from all over the globe. Membership cards are available from the American Youth Hostel National Office, P.O. Box 37613, Washington, DC 20013. We have indicated where to get guides and more information in the chapters on Austria, Belgium, Denmark, Germany, the Netherlands, and Switzerland.

Born to Be Wild!: Camping

The most economical way to tour Europe is to camp. You will find campgrounds in or near almost every city and throughout the countryside. Most have showers; some have restaurants, stores, or more elaborate facilities such as pools and lakeside swimming. All are far more compact than their American counterparts. Europeans themselves are enthusiastic campers, and your kids will enjoy playing with their peers and sharing travel tales. Some countries require that you park your camper or pitch a tent only at organized campgrounds; others allow you to camp anywhere in the countryside, except on private property. An International Camping Carnet is required at some campgrounds; the card can be purchased through the National Camper's and Hiker's Association, Inc., 4804 Transit Rd., Building 2, Depew, NY 14043 (Tel. 716-668-6242), before you depart or at most European campgrounds. In each country's chapter we include where to write for further information about their regulations. Consult the helpful publication *Europa Camping and Caravanning*, available through Recreational Equipment Inc., P.O. Box C-88126, Seattle, WA 98188 (Tel. 800-426-4840), which is an annually updated catalog of European campsites. You'll find descriptions of the campgrounds in major cities in the cities sections, "Where to Stay."

Home Exchange

Exchanging your home for one abroad is an option that will take you into the heart of an area's unique charm, heritage, and customs. There are a number of organizations to help you. Most are directory services with photographic listings of homes around the globe; others take a more active role in making the match and setting up the exchange. A full range of accommodations from modest neighborhood homes to luxurious villas are available. Some include the use of cars as part of the trade. By mutual consent you can have domestic help, babysitting, or even pet care. Six such organizations are:

Global Home Exchange, P.O. Box 2015, South Burlington, VT 05403. Tel. 802-985-3825.
Home Exchange International, 22458 Ventura Blvd., Suite E, Woodland Hills, CA 91364. Tel. 818-992-8990.
Loan A Home, 2 Park Lane–6E, Mount Vernon, NY 10552. No phone.
International Home Exchange, P.O. Box 3975, San Francisco, CA 94119. Tel. 415-435-3497.
Interservice Home Exchange, Box 387, Glen Echo, MD 20812. Tel. 301-229-7567.
Vacation Exchange Club, 12006 111th Ave., Youngtown, AZ 85363. Tel. 602-972-2186.

When writing away for information about home exchanges, ask questions about the things that are important to you, such as "Is there a washing machine in the house, a play area for the kids, or a park or beach nearby?"

Nuts and Bolts

Whoever coined the familiar phrase, "easier said than done," must have spent seven hours flying over the Atlantic with kids. Unless you have the resources to fly the Concorde or the power of astral projection, fasten your seat belt because you may be in for a bumpy ride. Here are a few tips to help you.

Air Travel

Children between two and twelve pay between 50 and 75 percent of the adult fare and occupy their own seat. Consumer and medical groups are currently lobbying the Federal Aviation Administration to require use of car seats on airplanes for children under two. You will need to buy a seat for your baby, but the fare for this age group, should the law pass, has not been determined. Check with your travel agent when planning your trip.

Be sure to book your flight a month or more in advance to take advantage of the greatest possible savings. Reserve a baby bassinet ahead of time if you need one, because the supply may be limited. Be aware that most are only 27 inches long and 12.5 inches wide, so if your baby is bigger than that, you won't be able to use one. Inquire about food for children and infants when booking your flight; most airlines offer special children's meals. Some airlines supply formula and baby food, but ask in advance.

We have indicated special airline or airport facilities for families, such as infant-changing areas or supervised playrooms, in each country's "Getting There" sections. Travel with Your Children publishes a biannual *Airline Guide* as part of their newsletter, "Family Travel Times," which details what all the major airlines offer traveling families. The guide informs you which airlines provide bassinets, toy and game packets, changing tables, children's audio programs, and children's meals. To order, contact TWYCH, 80 Eighth Ave., New York, NY 10011.

UP, UP, AND AWAY! IN FLIGHT

Bulkhead? It depends. Reserving the bulkhead has traditionally been considered a must for traveling families. Since there are no seats in front of you, there is more space for wiggling feet. But, it's a trade-off. There is no convenient place to stow your many carry-on bags filled with toys and games, so you will have to fetch them from overhead compartments. Furthermore, most armrests don't move on the bulkhead seats to allow for a child to rest on your lap, and it's hard to view movies.

It takes approximately 7 hours from the East Coast and 12 from the West to fly nonstop to Europe, which is quite a long stretch for small-fry. Adopt the Scout's motto "Be Prepared" during this trans-Atlantic crossing. Bring snacks, games, toys, books, extra diapers, and formula to keep those little fidgeters busy and content. Flying during the night can help as small passengers seem to have an easier time sleeping in flight than adults. Dressing in layers is a good idea, as airline temperatures can range from subtropical to positively glacial.

Airlines will let you use your stroller right up to the door of the plane. If you have an umbrella stroller, they may even let you take it on board, stashing it in the wardrobe closet. This makes stopovers and eating at airline snack bars easy, especially if baby is sleeping.

Car seats used on board must meet Federal Aviation Administration regulations. Look for two stickers on the bottom of your car seat, one indicating FAA approval and the other complying with federal motor vehicle safety standards. The FAA also recommends using the window seat for your car seat, for the convenience of other passengers. The car seat can't be used in the emergency exit rows or in the rows just in front of or in back of them. It must be properly secured to the child's seat during the flight even when your child is not sitting in it.

Most in-flight ear problems occur when a plane is changing altitude, especially when it's descending. Small children are more prone to discomfort, as their eustachian tubes are narrow. If a cold or stuffy nose is present, be sure to administer a decongestant at least an hour before taking off, and have your children drink plenty of fluids during the flight. Have infants nurse or suck on a bottle or pacifier during takeoff and landing to reduce ear pressure. Older kids can chew gum or suck on lollipops.

Gift wrap some small toys or favorite munchies and hand them out periodically when the kids get extra fidgety on the condition that they continue to play quietly. Airlines may offer a variety of amenities that can be fun for kids such as packets of little toys, games, and puzzles. Whatever they are, kids seem to delight in their novelty. Silly collections can be initiated in flight. One traveling parent (no names, please) developed her interesting collection of airsick bags on her own preteen flights to Europe. Stereo and movies provide a distraction for some kids. Bring a Walkman in case the airline selection is "bo-o-o-ring." Help your kids space their activities so that they don't become excruciatingly restless, i.e., intersperse books with art projects, meals with games, aisle sightseeing with movie viewing.

Once there, some European airports provide nursery areas with cribs, playpens, changing tables, and play equipment. These facilities are often located near the women's restroom and lounge area. They are available at the airports in Amsterdam, Geneva, Zurich, Copenhagen, London, and other cities. Check with your travel agent or at the airport when you initiate your flight.

Passports and Important Documents

All U.S. citizens, including infants, must have passports to visit Europe. Passport applications are accepted at a U.S. Passport Agency office or your local courthouse. You can apply for a child under 13 without having the child present. Passports are valid for 5 years for children under 18 and 10 years for adults. It is advised that you apply for your passport early, as it can take six weeks (or longer) during peak travel seasons.

Obtaining a passport is simple. Arrange for a passport photographer to take the photos you'll need. Adults will need extra copies for an International Driver's License and train or subway passes. Bring a certified copy of each family member's birth certificate (that's the one with the raised state seal) and your photographs when applying. Adults also need a driver's license or some form of picture and signature identification. Passports can be renewed through your local post office.

Your local auto club can tell you if the countries you are visiting require an international insurance certificate or international driver's permit and can issue the permit to you. This takes several weeks and is very inexpensive.

Foreign Currency

Make sure you obtain a small amount of the currency of the country in which you will be landing before you depart. Airports usually have a *bureau de change* where you can exchange money, but they may be closed or crowded when you arrive. You'll need some foreign money for renting luggage carts, tipping, and cab fares, and it will be one less thing to think about in your jet-lagged state.

European Telephones

Most European pay phones have instructions in English. To avoid weighing yourself down with coins, make long-distance calls from post offices. Avoid calling long distance from your hotel room; most hotels add exorbitant surcharges. To place an international call, first dial the international access code (usually listed in the phone booth or available from an international operator), then the country code (we list them in each country's chapter), and then the telephone number. When dialing from outside the area, the telephone number must include the telephone area code. If you are calling from outside the country, omit the zero preceding the area code.

We have indicated each major city's telephone area code in the introduction to that city; telephone area codes for smaller cities are indicated in parentheses in the phone numbers of their sites. France and Denmark are an exception. Their telephone area codes are included in their countrywide eight-digit numbers. Refer to their respective chapters for details.

Medical Matters

Few situations frighten a parent more than a sick child in unfamiliar surroundings. Remember that there are millions of men, women, and children in Europe who suffer from the same colds and flus as you and I. Rest assured that Europe has well-trained doctors (we wanted to transport our Rome pediatrician to California) and excellent public health services. Most major European cities have 24-hour pharmacies.

Your kids will be delighted to hear that no immunization shots are required to travel in Europe. If you plan to be there for an extended period of time and your kids will need their regular immunization booster shots, you will find that most European children are on the same schedule as Americans for DPT, tetanus, etc.

Should any medical or dental care be necessary, the American Embassy or Consulate nearest you can provide the names of local English-speaking physicians. IAMAT (International Association for

Medical Assistance to Travelers), 736 Center St., Lewiston, NY 14092, sends its members a free listing of English-speaking doctors and locations of hospitals in 450 cities and 200 countries. Likewise, Intermedic, 777 Third Ave., New York, NY 10017, offers annual family memberships and provides access to physicians in 200 cities and 90 countries.

Before you leave, check with your medical insurance carrier for the extent of your coverage. If your coverage is limited to illnesses or accidents occurring in the U.S., you can purchase insurance to cover your trip from private agencies such as Health Care Abroad, 243 Church St. West, Vienna, VA 22180 (Tel. 708-281-9500 or 800-237-6615); Europe Assistance, 1133 5th St., NW, Suite 400, Washington, DC 20005 (Tel. 202-347-2025 or 800-821-2828)—request "Travel Assistance International"; or WorldCare Travel Assistance Association, Inc., 2000 Pennsylvania Ave., NW, Suite 7600, Washington, DC 20077 (Tel. 202-293-0335).

Before departure, schedule medical and dental checkups for the entire family, especially if you suspect any health problems. If your child has a cold, have his or her ears checked, as even a slight infection can cause severe ear pain in flight. If your youngster is prone to certain illnesses, ask your doctor to prescribe an appropriate medication for you to take along.

FIRST-AID KIT

Although all of the following are available in European pharmacies, you may want to pack some of them to save valuable vacation time:

- Band-Aids, adhesive tape, sterilized pads, packets of antiseptic
- Thermometer
- Acetaminophen (such as Tylenol)
- Dramamine (for car and motion sickness)
- Children's decongestant and antihistimine (for hayfever and/or insect bites)
- Syrup of Ipecac (to induce vomiting in case of poisoning)
- Insect repellent, a mosquito net for baby's crib (a must in Southern Europe in the summer), and sunscreen lotion, etc., depending on your destination
- Tweezers and needle for the inevitable splinter
- Your favorite child-care book
- Prescription medications and the prescriptions for them
- Telephone numbers of your doctors at home

If you do get stuck without a fever thermometer and have to buy a centigrade thermometer abroad, remember that 37 degrees corresponds to our normal and that 39 degrees is about 102 degrees.

TUMMY UPSETS?

Some people get diarrhea when their diet changes. Ways to preclude problems include:

- Drink bottled water in small villages or rural areas. Most European cities have safe drinking water on tap. Bottled water is readily found everywhere.
- Mix baby formula with bottled water or water boiled for 10 to 15 minutes. It's a good idea to bring along enough ready-to-serve formula to feed your baby until you have time to find a good source of bottled water.
- Drink only pasteurized milk and milk products. Boxed, unrefrigerated milk is common in Europe and is safe to drink, but many children do not care for its taste. It needs refrigeration after opening.

Treatment of diarrhea begins with clear liquids. Juices or flat sodas can be given to older kids, and breast-fed babies should continue to nurse. Next, binding foods such as bananas, rice, applesauce, and toast (better known as the BRAT diet) can be introduced. Milk and medications should be avoided. Even if it isn't serious, tummy upsets can sour a vacation. Cuddle up with a favorite book and slow down until recovered.

4

From the Beginning: Preparing Your Kids

"Once Upon a Time . . . ": Books

Your children may never want to read the Middle English version of the *Canterbury Tales* and may accompany you to the Vatican Museum only if bribed with a lemon gelato. But, our 3-year-old friend Eva eagerly allowed her parents to explore the architecture of the Italian hill town Collodi because it was home to Pinocchio. Seven-year-old Ben searched Switzerland high and low for Heidi's house, and 14-year-old Amy was moved to tears by a visit to Anne Frank's house in Amsterdam. Picture books can set the stage for little ones, and Europe will be more relevant for older children and teens if they scratch the surface of a culture ahead of time by exploring some of its history and customs through literature.

One of the joys of traveling is reading about a place while you are there. Keep in mind that your pace will be slower with your children and that evening activities may be somewhat curtailed. You will have time to read during the afternoon siesta in some countries, late at night, and on trains and planes. Do take as many books as you can squeeze into your bags. You can replenish your supplies by shopping in bookstores carrying English-language titles, but these publications are quite expensive.

Where to begin? Visit the library. Two helpful library reference guides are *A to Zoo: Subject Access to Children's Picture Books* by Carolyn W. Lima and the standard *Subject Guide to Children's Books in Print*, which provides the recommended grade level of the reading

16

materials listed. Simply look under the countries you plan to visit or under a specific topic (i.e., museums, theater, etc.), and you'll find a listing of everything available. In each country's chapter we provide a reading list of books for a variety of ages.

There are several series we especially like. *We Live In . . .*, which covers most of Europe by different authors, has photos and a story about one family and their daily lives. Another series, Chris Fairclough's *Take a Trip to . . .* (England, Holland, Italy, etc.), and *Anno in . . .* (Britain, Italy, and around the globe) by Matsumasa Anno, make wonderful pretrip reading. Another series, *Families the World Over*, includes titles such as *A Family in Norway* and *A Family in Ireland*. They cover most of the Western European countries, with lively text and photographs, and can be read to children as young as 5 and by school children and preteens. Jane Yolam's *Favorite Folktales from Around the World* has tales from Ireland, Norway, Italy, Wales, England, France, and Scandinavia. In the *Adventures of Mickey, Taggy, Puppo and Cica* Kati Rekai has written several engaging stories about the travels of three dogs and a cat who travel to Switzerland, France, Vienna, and the Netherlands. You can order them and their companion puzzles through Canadian Stage and Arts Publications, 263 Adelaide St., West, Toronto, Ontario M5H1Y2, Canada (Tel. 416-971-9516).

Just One Look: Museums

Museum visits can be fun for your children if their interest is stimulated ahead of time. Even the most reluctant young museumgoer will enjoy the following light-hearted books: *Let's Go to the Museum* by Virginia K. Levy (a workbook for 6- to 12-year-olds), *Visiting the Art Museum* by Laurie K. Brown and Marc Brown (with animated characters and full-color art reproductions), *Great Painters* by Piero Ventura, *Visiting the Art Museum, Mommy It's a Renoir!* (art postcards in a book) by Aline D. Wolf, or Ernest Raboff's *Art for Children* series on great artists such as Picasso, da Vinci, van Gogh, Velásquez, Klee, and Cézanne (ages 6 and up). Most libraries have art history collections. Check out a book on an artist or a museum you plan to visit; children as young as 3 or 4 can pick out their favorite paintings or sculptures to look for later. Very young children will enjoy the "Sesame Street" video *Please Don't Eat the Pictures*.

Name That Tune: Music

A typical scenario: The windows in your rented Renault are full to the brim with colorforms, the memory scrapbooks are bulging, and solving the puzzles of global license plates has lost its novelty. "When are we going to get there?" whines from the sticky backseat every 2 minutes. And you start wondering the same. Time to pull out the Walkman cassette players; they are lifesavers for the backseat blues.

Recorded literature (stories from Babar to the Greek myths) in addition to a wealth of music, songs, and rhymes from around the world are available on cassettes. They make great pretrip listening, and we found our kid's sweet (well, we think they are sweet!) voices singing "De Colores," "Sur Le Pont d'Avignon" and "By the Bonnie Bonnie Banks of Loch Lomond" a true cultural enhancement to the scenery. Be sure to pick up music cassettes from each country as you travel.

Along with stores and libraries, the following companies sell a variety of excellent multicultural cassettes and books by mail. Both of them have many more titles in their store than they list in their catalogs, and they are happy to consult over the phone:

Children's Book & Music Center, 2500 Santa Monica Blvd., Santa Monica, CA. Tel. 800-443-1856 or 213-829-0215 (inside California). Their catalog lists books, cassettes, and videos.

The Children's Book Store, 604 Markham St., Toronto, Ontario, Canada M6G 2L8. Tel. 416-535-7011. Request either the book or audio catalog, or both. The oral tradition is one of their specialties.

Videos

Your kids can preview the Swiss Alps and the canals of Venice or have European storybook classics come alive in your living room before you leave. A great guide for discovering specialized videos is *The Video Source Book*, published by the National Video Clearinghouse in Syosett, NY, and found at most library reference desks. Along with a listing of all available videos, coded by subject, it will tell you how to acquire the cassettes if local video shops have slim collections.

Save It for a Rainy Day: Projects

Introduce your child to maps and atlases. For young children, you can use a tiny car or airplane to illustrate how you'll cover the distances from here to there. Plot the route on a map and leave it in the room of the older kids. Discuss weather, customs, and language differences, and begin introducing kids to a few foreign words and expressions. Talk about the differences the kids will encounter, and start making lists of what may be different and what may be the same.

Children of all ages enjoy putting together a scrapbook filled with the mementos of their trip. You can get them started before you go by providing a few pictures of the places you plan to visit. Take the scrapbook with you (so choose its size carefully) and include a couple of glue sticks so the kids can busy themselves en route. Even the dullest ticket stub or boarding pass becomes a rich reminder of their time abroad. Kids will find amazing things to include, such as imprinted sugar wrappers, napkins, postcards, paper coasters, and newspaper clippings. The scrapbook can help kids while away many hours carefully arranging and pasting and reliving the places they have just visited.

Older children can be encouraged to select and keep a journal throughout Europe. One 15-year-old friend, Kate, wrote her deepest thoughts and most profound impressions on the back of numerous chocolate bar wrappers collected during her trip. Needless to say, her writing experience was richly inspired as she popped one chocolate morsel after another into her mouth.

Children are natural pack rats. If your child has already shown an interest in bringing home everything from bottle caps to bird nests, then he or she will have unlimited opportunities to collect foreign stamps, coins, posters, postcards, little imprinted plates, special erasers, dolls, miniatures, matches, or lead soldiers. Our 8-year-old friend Nicole collected colorful and ornate examples of the paper used to wrap oranges in Italy. You can talk about collection ideas before you go and have each child start thinking about the one or two things he or she might like to collect. Encourage the smaller, lighter items. After all, travel motto #1 states, "All you collect, you carry."

Pen Pals

There are a number of organizations that match youngsters as pen pals. Ask your reference librarian for a list or write: International Friendship League, 55 Mount Vernon St., Boston, MA 02108. Be sure to ask the age group they serve; a number of groups require that children be a minimum of 12 years old. If you know far enough in advance that you will be traveling abroad and set up a pen pal for your child in advance, you may be able to arrange a visit between the two pals.

English Muffins and Irish Stew

While McDonald's and Burger King have made worldwide inroads and typical American fare can be found at the larger hotels, the standard European diet is somewhat different from the American one. You may relish the opportunity to eat escargots in France or barbequed anchovies in Portugal, but your youngsters may get downright squeamish at the idea.

Children will often try new foods if they see you try them. It's a good idea to look up food translations before you order somewhat randomly, or you may end up with a rather stunned and hungry child sneering into a bowl of *angulas* (baby eels in boiling oil—a delicacy in Spain). Some national dishes, such as the Scottish *haggis* (sheep's bladder, lard, and oatmeal) are best avoided for the younger set.

"You know how pacifying food is," adds Linda, who used food to enhance her trip while traveling by car with her 8- and 10-year-olds (now confirmed gourmets). They made food a central part of their experience in every country, stopping for tea at 4 o'clock every day in Britain, selecting pastries in France, chocolate in Switzerland, and cheeses in Denmark. Each country had a special treat, and every day they searched for the best possible place to stop and sample it. This became a kind of treasure hunt for the kids and a fun and delicious break for the whole family.

Breakfast, Lunch, and Dinner

Most European countries offer a continental breakfast of rolls with butter and jam, coffee, and milk or juice. It's a great opportunity for adults to indulge in their love of espresso and pastry, but if you're worried about building strong bodies twelve ways, you can easily supplement the standard continental breakfast with foods you pick up.

Shopping for a picnic can be a fun way for kids to experience the local marketplace while they practice foreign tongues and currency exchanges. First, shop for the native cuisine at the corner store or open-air market—fresh mozzarella cheese in Italy, shortbread in Scotland, quiche lorraine in France. Then stop and enjoy the scenery while you eat. Be sure to bring a Swiss Army knife!

If you're traveling by car and picnicking along the way, avoid salty foods that make kids thirsty. To further cut down on bathroom stops, take bottled water instead of soft drinks or juice; kids will drink when they're thirsty rather than because they enjoy the taste.

In southern Europe, it is customary to eat the big meal during the middle of the day and have a light supper late at night, usually around 8 PM or later. Some restaurants welcome kids at noon but not at night. You can always eat in a restaurant for the main repast and picnic in your hotel or in a park that evening.

The fixed-price menu in many restaurants is usually the most economical. If you want a bit more variety and you're keeping an eye on your pocketbook, seek out the trattorias, pubs, bistros, and cafes. Don't forget that a neighborhood restaurant off the beaten track can be a delicious surprise and a lot of fun. Children's portions or smaller portions are available in some restaurants at a reduced price, or you can order à la carte for the kids. High chairs can be hard to find on the Continent.

For the very pickiest of eaters, you can do a few things before searching for the nearest golden arches. Omelets can be ordered in just about every country, as can delicious soups and custards. Juices are available everywhere, as are fruits, vegetables, great cheeses, and delicious fresh and wholesome breads if you shop in the local marketplace.

Formula au Vin: Infants and Toddlers

If you're a nursing Mom planning to travel with baby, postpone weaning until *after* the trip. You'll have no formula to mix or bottles to carry. Find a private spot to nurse, as customs vary country to country. Formula (including soy) is readily available throughout Europe, and you can count on buying it in pharmacies if you don't find it in grocery stores or supermarkets. Commercial baby foods are readily available, too; bring a small quantity to get you started, and buy the rest there. In each country's chapter, you'll find tips on the specifics of baby food and formula.

Toddlers will enjoy familiar foods. Successful travelers Mark and Janet purchased Rice Krispies along the way (yes, Kellogg *has* descended upon Europe) for their 3-year-old; the daily routine of a familiar cereal in the morning set her up for being adventurous the rest of the day. Many children don't care for the boxed, unrefrigerated milk in Europe, and cereal is a good way for them to get it down. Many families pack a Tupperware container of peanut butter (hard to find abroad) and pull it out to regularly supplement lunchtime picnic fare.

Packing—Lug It or Leave It

You've heard it before, "Pack light! Then go back and eliminate half." This is the most important pearl of wisdom we can share, especially when you're traveling *en famille*. Somehow *you* always end up carrying the extra toy bag or ten pounds of snacks and bottled water. The trip will be easier and happier if you keep your load light.

Gearing Up—Luggage

Your suitcase should be light when it's empty because you and yours will do an excellent job of filling it. It should have a few pockets, and it should be tough, with industrial-strength zippers. Most families (ours included) prefer softside luggage, because a surprising amount can fit into it, and it can be more easily maneuvered into the nooks and crannies of your car's tiny trunk or a crowded overhead train compartment. If you're traveling with older kids, each one should have his or her own bag to carry. Mark your family's luggage with colorful tape so you can spot it quickly as it comes off the airline luggage carousel.

Mom's purse or Dad's carry-on bag is an important one, as it will be carrying everything from toys and phrasebooks to maps and money. This bag transforms into a beach tote at the shore, a picnic basket in the country, and an entertainment center during long hauls. If you're traveling with older children, have each one take a carry-on bag or backpack. It's a good idea to bring a lightweight duffel bag or folding bag for the inevitable collection of souvenirs which strain the seams of your already bulging suitcase. You can use it as an overnight bag when making short stops to avoid dragging everything out of the car over and over again.

Don't Forget Blankie!: What to Take

There are a few simple packing guidelines you can follow to make your journey as uncomplicated and laundry-free as possible:

Select clothes that are easily laundered. If your family is traveling first class, you can have the hotel do your laundry. If not, plan to supplement visits to a laundromat with hand washing. Naturally you will select clothes that rinse out easily, dry quickly, and do not need ironing. Pack a travel clothesline and some plastic bags for damp clothes. Inflatable hangers can help speed up the drying process.

Select dark-colored clothing. Small prints, plaids, or stripes work better than solid colors for camouflaging stains. Select pieces that will mix and match. Because Europeans tend to dress up, especially in cities, pack some of your better things so you won't look like you saved for your plane fare by shopping at the local thrift shop.

Select clothing that can be layered. Be prepared for any kind of weather, from the steamy heat of southern Europe in summer to the Arctic freeze of an airplane at 30,000 feet.

Take comfortable multipurpose clothing. If you buy new shoes, do so well in advance so you or the kids can break them in. Avoid tight clothing; you want clothes that will allow you and the kids to curl up anywhere, anytime. Try to pack items that can do the job of two or three. Pack with style, flexibility, and, above all, comfort in mind.

Pack clothing in clear plastic zipper bags. This method makes it easier to locate specific items, especially if more than one person is sharing a suitcase.

A FEW REMINDERS

- If you must take an electrical appliance, you'll need an electrical transformer (they're heavy!) to convert to European amperage, plus a variety of adaptor plugs.
- Take a towel along if you're traveling by car for that quick stop to dip in the lake.
- After you've figured out the clothing, be sure to pack: first-aid kit, safety pins, travel towelettes, sunscreen, batteries (they're expensive abroad), travel alarm clock, Swiss Army knife, sewing kit, folding umbrella, and pocket flashlight.
- Absolute musts: passports, plane tickets, car rental papers, tip packs of currency of the country you land in, and swimsuits!

And remember, you can always buy it there if you leave it at home. In fact, foreign products make great collections.

Europe on Ten Diapers a Day: Babes in Arms

Blanket sleepers can cut down on the number of blankets you may need to pack if you're traveling to cool climates. A good supply of bibs means fewer changes of clothes and less hand washing. Head to any well-equipped baby store for a glimpse of the clever, lightweight, and convertible gear available for tiny ones. A front or back pack is handy, and a lightweight collapsible stroller sturdy enough to traverse the cobblestone streets and sidewalks is essential. Consider a lightweight hook-on seat if baby is eating solids. If you plan to travel by car, either bring a car seat or make advance arrangements to rent one from your car rental agency. Some countries' rental cars do not have back seat belts. Be sure to ask when you make arrangements.

Throughout the Continent, higher-priced hotels provide cribs and bedding. For most other accommodations, you will need to bring a Portacrib. If your baby is small and not yet mobile, there are clever diaper bags that convert into beds, and baby baskets with handles. Or, you can make do as 4-month-old Madeleine did by sleeping in converted dresser drawers or little nests made in the corner of our room. If your baby starts to climb during your vacation, you can always buy a Portacrib in Europe. Their babies visit Nana for long weekends, too.

Disposable diapers are available throughout Europe in pharmacies, supermarkets, or department stores. It's handy to pack a several days' supply so you won't have to search in desperation the day you arrive. Although often more costly, many of the brands you know and love here are available there. Since Europe is on the metric system, it's handy to know the pound–kilo conversion: 1 kilo = 2.2 pounds and 10 kilos = 22 pounds.

Little Rascals: Toddlers and Preschoolers

As toddlers can get grubby fast, select dark clothes that wash out easily and dry quickly. A stroller and a car seat are essential items for this age group, too. If your toddler is born to wander (aren't they all?), you'll need to take along a Portacrib unless you're staying in higher-priced hotels. Even if your toddler is toilet trained, you should take along or buy a small supply of diapers. Many youngsters will revert back to pre-potty-trained behavior when their routine is disrupted, so it pays to be safe.

Be sure to take your child's favorite soft animal or special blanket, as a familiar and well-loved object can feather the nest and make any strange room feel like home. Every parent we interviewed mentioned the Walkman as an essential piece of equipment for the traveling child. For young children, songs and stories on cassettes can provide the grounding that kids seem to thrive on, not to mention the hours of uninterrupted quiet for Mom and Dad. Two-year-olds are not too young to enjoy them. Other easily portable diversions include inflatable balls, sticker books, miniature cars, markers or crayons and coloring books, hand puppets, books, and paper dolls. Take a glance at the list for older kids, too, as your precocious youngster may enjoy some of their toys.

Little Bon Vivants: School-age Children

Have kids pack their own travel tote or backpack, using the sensible rule "If you carry it, you can bring it." Your child should carry his or her pack for a half hour at home to really feel how heavy it is. You may want to bring an umbrella stroller for a 4-year-old.

A Walkman is still an essential take-along, especially one with a built-in radio, which may allow your child to catch a word or two in a foreign language and to become familiar with different music. Other packable diversions include colorforms, magic slate, Etch-A-Sketch, Silly Putty, crayons and paper, coloring books, Frisbee or Aerobee, inflatable balls, a jump rope, small magnetized travel games, playing cards, sewing cards, comic books, puppets, paper dolls, pipe cleaners, jacks, and origami. Action toys will help work off the boundless energy that sitting on trains or cars builds up.

Too Many Clothes for Comfort: Preteens and Teens

If your rule states, "You pack it, you carry it," and your teen insists on taking her electric hair dryer, hot rollers, and transformer, then encourage her to take up weight lifting, too. With children in this age group it is important to give subtle guidance while encouraging them to pack as little as possible.

Backpacks are practical, as teens can carry their own entertainment items and use them for the beach or for carrying their souvenirs. Be sure to bring a Walkman and a built-in radio. Teens enjoy hearing what their European peers are listening to. Preteens and teens relish their own guidebooks. They seem to get hours of pleasure reading about where they're going and where they've just been. They may also benefit from a camera and film, phrasebooks, a calculator, and their own flashlight, travel clock, and toiletry kit. Other portable diversions include electronic pocket games, travel games, crossword puzzles, drawing materials, books, diaries or journals, letter-writing materials, midget dictionaries, Frisbees, or Aerobees.

Hit the Road, Jacques!: Getting Around

Children love boat trips, pony treks, gondolas, and horse-drawn cart excursions. Be sure to take advantage of any opportunities you have for unusual or quirky excursions. You may feel like a ridiculous spectacle touring the streets of Vienna in a horse-drawn carriage, but your kids will remember it far into the future.

All Aboard! Travel by Train

Trains are the preferred mode of transportation for Europeans. They run regularly and frequently, traveling to the smallest towns and villages. Children are free to roam the train and stretch their legs, meet other kids, and munch in the snack bar or dining car. Train travel offers spectacular views of the countryside. And people watching, meeting fellow travelers, or just listening to the lilt of a foreign tongue is a great way to absorb another culture.

Be sure to reserve seats in advance in either first- or second-class compartments. If you travel off-season or in first class, you can often get an entire compartment to yourselves. There are smoking and nonsmoking cars, so you needn't be cooped up in a compartment full of Gauloise smoke if it's not your fancy. If you're traveling overnight, you can relax in a sleeper, or *couchette*, but you must book it in advance. Plan to bring no more luggage than you can handle by yourselves, as porters or luggage carts are often unavailable.

If you plan to do a lot of train travel, the Eurailpass is a good value as it gives you unlimited first-class rail travel through 16 countries.

Eurailpasses are issued for 15 days, 21 days or for 1, 2, or 3 months. A boon for families is the Eurail Saverpass for three or more people traveling together. It allows unlimited first-class travel for 15 days. For both passes, children under 12 are half-fare, and those under 4 ride free. There are additional charges for reserved seats and sleeping berths. You must buy the Eurailpass in the U.S. or Canada *before* you leave because they are not sold in Europe; it's valid from the first day of use. Your Eurailpass is also good on certain boats and ferries. Write: Eurailpass, Box 325, Old Greenwich, CT 06870, or contact your travel agent. If you plan to travel in only one country, consider the national rail passes available in most of the countries we cover.

ON THE RIGHT TRACK: A FEW TIPS

Keep all your tickets with you until you are off the train for good, because in some countries you must turn tickets in at the end of a journey. It's a good idea to keep your passports handy, in case you cross borders or *frontiers* in the middle of the night.

Remember that European trains often purposefully break apart in transit and head in different directions. The front will continue to your destination, Zurich, while the middle heads toward Geneva and the rear eventually separates and heads toward Paris. Make sure that you and all the children are in the car that will take you where you want to go.

A trip to the dining car or snack bar can break up the trip and be a fun diversion for little ones; some dining cars require reservations. Dining and snack cars can close quite early, so it is best to be prepared with lots of drinks, snacks, and bottled water.

The Long and Winding Road: Travel by Car

Traveling by car affords you the freedom to explore areas off the beaten track and can give you tremendous flexibility to stop any time, any where the mood strikes. A quick dip in a stream or a pause to admire a herd of Swiss cows can give a trip the spontaneity that will make it truly memorable.

Driving in Europe is made simple by the use of international road signs. Once you master the signs in one country, you've mastered them all. And to make things even simpler, you don't need to understand foreign languages, for the signs have pictures on them. If you forget a few, rely on your children to come to your aid. They love this kind of guessing game.

Take your time. Kids do best when you stop every couple of hours for a picnic, a good stretch, or an excursion. Most families we interviewed said a 4- to 5-hour drive was absolute maximum. More than several days in a row of driving at this pace is not advisable. Plan to travel in the morning or at nap time and end your day early. You'll have time to explore and adjust to your new surroundings and have a leisurely dinner and a calm (well, relatively calm) evening.

The toys you and your children have selected to take are directly related to the hours of peace and quiet you will enjoy in your car. Keep your swim gear together and handy if you're traveling in warm weather, for there is nothing more refreshing than an unexpected dip.

A FEW TIPS

Kids love to be assigned important navigator jobs. Give older kids maps and directions, and let them be your guide. Bring highlighter markers and have them follow along on their maps as you travel. Let the kids choose some of the stop and stretch spots. Fighting in the backseat can sabotage an otherwise perfect vacation, and boredom is often the main culprit. Be sure to stop often, and don't forget the Walkman—one for each child—and plenty of tapes.

Some countries have regulations about kids in the front seat, and others have tollbooths every hundred miles or so, so be prepared for some idiosyncrasies. Be aware that legal requirements and a car's standard features will vary country to country. For example, no Portuguese cars, including rentals, have back seat belts, and Austria requires that you carry a first-aid kit and a red safety triangle in your vehicle at all times. We've mentioned other significant differences in each country's chapter, but check with your auto club or rental agency before you go.

Driving in Europe's major metropolitan areas can be a nightmarish ordeal and parking is often worse. Once there, rely on buses, subways, trolleys, or canalboats. The use of public transportation will inevitably lead you to another delightful form of transportation—walking. There is simply no better way to see any city, no matter what its size.

CAR RENTALS, LEASING, AND PURCHASE/BUYBACK PROGRAMS

It is usually less expensive to arrange for car rentals from North America before you depart. All European car rentals are subject to a value added tax (VAT), which varies country to country, in addition to their base price. Prices can vary greatly for the same type of car in the same country, so it pays to shop around. If you pick up a car in one country, you may drop it off in another, for an extra fee. We were pleased with Avis' program because of their many (over 3,000 in Europe) convenient pickup and drop-off sites. We picked up the car in Spain and returned it in Calais, France, before heading across the

Channel to London. Large agencies, like Avis, have English-speaking staff and 24-hour hotlines to call if you have any problems along the road. Ask your travel agent or contact the following companies, which handle rentals throughout Europe:

Avis: 800-331-1084 (U.S.) or 800-268-2310 (Canada)
Budget: 800-472-3325
Hertz "Affordable Europe Plan": 800-654-3001
National (Europcar): 800-Car-Euro
Auto Europe: 800-223-5555 (U.S.), 800-458-9503 (Canada)

If you're traveling for 23 days or more, but less than 6 months, it is more economical to enter into a purchase/buyback agreement offered by the French auto manufacturers Renault, Peugeot, and Citröen. You purchase a new car, pay basic charges in advance, and sign a promissory note for the balance, which is discharged upon return of the car in good condition. The basic charge includes unlimited mileage, taxes, guarantee, registration, and insurance. The cost to you is the difference between the purchase price and the buyback price. Cars are picked up at any of several locations, and you can drive them anywhere in western Europe. When we traveled in France, we arranged through Renault USA Inc. to pick up a new car in Nice, traveled for 10 weeks, and returned the car in Paris. The car was roomy enough for a family of five, had back seat belts, a cassette player to play our collection of French children's music, and a huge trunk. A few companies handling purchase/buyback programs include:

Renault USA Inc. (Eurodrive includes family vans): 212-532-1221 or 800-221-1052
France Auto Vacances (Peugeot): 800-234-1426
Europe by Car (Renault, Peugeot, Citröen): 212-581-3040 or 800-223-1516
Foremost Euro-Car Inc. (Renault, Peugeot): 800-423-3111 (USA), 800-272-3299 (CA), or 818-786-1960

Purchasing a European car can save you money if you would otherwise be leasing one for an extended period of time. Check with your local dealerships as you can make arrangements through them to buy, pick up, and then ship your car back home.

Additional costs to consider when driving are the higher prices of gas in Europe and the toll freeways in countries such as Italy, France, and Spain. Unless your family is large, arrange for a small car; you'll save on gas expenses and have an easier time on narrow village roads.

The Young and the Restless: Planning a Great Day

Always Have a Park or Beach Close By

When traveling with children, schedule at least 2 hours each day for free exercise at a park or beach. If the kids have been cooped up in museums, palaces, and cathedrals for hours on end, you will be arranging for an immediate flight home. Walking from one site to another doesn't count; that kind of exercise exhausts, while running along a tree-studded pathway or playing in a playground energizes.

A daily break will help you to bargain: "After we take a pedal boat ride in the lake in Madrid's Parque del Retiro, let's go to the Prado to find the strange Hieronymus Bosch paintings." If you're driving, regular exercise breaks will prevent fights and encourage quiet play once you're back in the car.

Many sites have opportunities for physical exercise built in. Cathedrals and churches often have climbable tall towers that lead to beautiful views and invigorated children. Palaces, castles, and some museums often sit on beautifully landscaped grounds, and many quaint medieval towns are surrounded by city walls or ramparts that can be climbed and explored. Build these into each day's plan to ensure success.

Just One Look: Sightseeing

Scenery does not fascinate most children until they reach the teenage years (and not for long even then). Remember this when you're driving along the wild coastline of Cornwall. Rather than sharing your enchantment over the colorful fishing villages, the kids, eyes closed and headphones on, are tapping their feet to the local top-40.

Let your children help you plan the day's activities. Veteran travelers Dan and Wendy chose the plan for each morning and let the kids choose the afternoon's activity. Other parents alternate. They select the activities one day, and the kids make the selection the next.

Infants will usually let you see much of what you want to, if you don't overdo it. They can sleep nestled in a frontpack, backpack, or reclining stroller while you walk the streets of the city. For babies needing two naps per day, we found it worked best to allow them to catch one nap on the run and one back at the room.

Attention span and patience are not part of a toddler's vocabulary, so lengthy visits to cathedrals or other activities requiring concentration can be disastrous. Don't eliminate them; simply think about shorter stays. Changing the pace or type of activity may help. Follow something that requires being attentive and quiet with something active. First an hour in a room at the Louvre and then a few hours at the adjoining park, the Jardin des Tuileries. Napping on the run will only work for a few days at a time, so plan a few quiet afternoons in your hotel, apartment, or cottage. Schedule extended drives for nap time.

Our friend Kathleen created themes with her traveling preschoolers. They threw coins and made wishes at each fountain, rode every park carousel, and searched for storybook characters each time they entered a new country. As preschoolers grow more attuned to differences in people, a European adventure will have more meaning to them. You may also find that they are able to bargain with you a bit more. We cursed the scrumptious-looking ice cream posters all through Portugal, but the promise of a cold treat did provide us with more time to see the treasures in Lisbon's Gulbenkian Museum.

For school-age children, travel may at last be termed broadening in the adult sense. Cultural differences are handled better, and meeting people from different places helps children learn more about themselves and others. At this age, kids will make suggestions and look for experiences that can often lead the whole family into memorable adventures. Museums or activities that require waiting become increasingly feasible.

When things get a little too close for comfort, we suggest you allow your teenagers to go off on their own, exploring their own interests while the rest of you head in another direction. They may also seek out opportunities to make friends their own age, so try to include activities such as swimming or skiing where new friendships can develop in a safe and relaxed setting. At this age, kids become more aware of different value systems and cultures, and may find themselves fascinated with Europe's rich history.

Do Only the Strong Survive?

Suppose you are several weeks into your adventure and it's clear no one is having a good time. Are you trying to accomplish too much, in too short a time? If small changes fail, cut something out of the schedule. It will be worth it in the long run.

Bring It On Home to Me: Souvenirs

Set limits on how many souvenirs little ones can have in each country to avoid hearing the relentless chant "Mom, can I have this?" With older children, you can try giving them a budget with simple guidelines such as, "Everything you purchase, you carry." When they control the purse strings they often become conservative shoppers. A wallet of foreign money can be thrilling for many kids, and you may find your older children far speedier with on-the-spot money exchanges than their weary parents.

Mommy, What's That Funny-Looking Toilet?: Bathrooms

It's probably a good idea to brief your kids ahead of time about European bathrooms, for some children are troubled by the unfamiliar. Explain that function, not soft toilet paper, is most important. In most countries the only thing different will be the presence of the bidet (designed for hygiene and not commonly found in the United States). Most kids will fiddle around with it, but the novelty wears off shortly. Now and then you will encounter a Turkish-style toilet, which is a hole in the floor.

When you hear your little one insistently announce, "Mommy, I have to go NOW!," don't ask for a bathroom. Europeans will think you want a bath. "Toilette" or "WC" will lead you to the right door. Finding a bathroom is no problem, simply head for the nearest cafe, child in tow, and ask to use the WC. It's a good idea to have small change on hand to tip attendants in airports, train stations, department stores, and bigger hotels.

Just One Look: Museum Visits

Search-and-find games are often fun for budding young art critics and can help you make museum visits more enjoyable for all. Challenge your kids to find the Picasso they saw in one of their books, a sculpture that looks most like Dad, or the oldest work of art in the gallery. Other tried and true tips: Take the children to the museum bookshop and let them choose a few favorite postcards. Then challenge them to locate the works as you all wander through. Seasoned art afficionados recommend staying no more than 1 to 2 hours with children. Many European museums are located in parklike settings, so you can always have the young and the restless run free, providing one parent with quiet viewing time.

Bathing Suits and Birthday Suits

Many Europeans go for an all-over tan, while others want at least a bronze upper body, be they male or female. Women go topless at beaches and pools all over Europe, and both men and women sunbathe completely nude in parts of Northern Europe. Age and figure type don't seem to matter here; going au naturel is done more in appreciation of fresh air and sunshine rather than an exhibition of one's perfect physique. You'll see senior citizens and families in the buff alongside college kids and body beautifuls.

What Is Different? What Is the Same?

Many families who travel successfully enjoy discussing what is different and what is the same while exploring Europe. Children gain a better understanding of another culture by noticing the subtle differences in a country's "accessories," such as mailboxes, sirens, toilets and their flushing mechanisms (always a favorite), money, or police. If you make a game of uncovering the differences, you'll be surprised at how adept your children become at observing small details, whether you're in the car, on a train, or walking the streets.

Austria

Amidst the pristine beauty of the Alps, Austria beckons those in search of outdoor pursuits. Two-thirds of the country is covered by majestic mountains, and, not surprisingly, Austria was the birthplace of the modern sport of skiing. In fact, many children learn to ski as soon as they can walk, and most ski areas offer "Ski Kindergarten" for little ones. Visit in winter to ski, ice-skate, or toboggan. Come in the summer to walk or hike in the Alps, pick wildflowers, swim in the many lakes, or scale rugged mountains in cable cars and funiculars.

Austrian cities are rich with extraordinary sites for children. Don't miss the crazy trick fountains of Salzburg's 17th-century Hellbrunn Palace, a performance of Vienna's snow-white Lippizan stallions, the chance to don a miner's costume and slide down long wooden chutes for a tour of Hallstatt's subterranean salt mine, or a visit to Innsbruck's alpine zoo, with a collection of rare high-altitude animals.

The arts will undoubtedly make a strong impression on your children, as Austria was homeland to Mozart, Schubert, Haydn, Beethoven, Mahler, and Klimt. A sweeter impression will be made by the country's rich and exquisite pastries that are as beautiful as they are delicious. *Konditorei*, the word for pastry shop, may very well be your children's first native word. Souvenir pins are found in every alpine village. A Tirolian hat that your children decorate with pins purchased during your journey will make a treasured Austrian memento.

Gute Reise . . . Have a great trip!

Preparing Your Kids: Books and Music

Younger children: *Away Went Wolfgang* by Virginia Kahl.

Older children: *The Devil in Vienna* by Doris Orgel, *The Adventures of Mickey, Taggy, Puppo and Cica and How They Discover Vienna* by Kati Rekai.

Music: The *Music Masters* series offers audio cassettes of the lives and music of various Austrian composers such as Mozart, Schubert, and Haydn for ages 6 to 10. They are available through the Children's Book and Music Center. UNICEF's *Sing Children Sing* series has "Songs of Austria" by the Children's Choir of the Viennese Conservatory. See Chapter 4 for information on ordering books and music.

Wha'd'ya Wanna Do?

For general and specialized information on vacationing in Austria, contact the extremely helpful national tourist offices.

AUSTRIAN NATIONAL TOURIST OFFICES

U.S.A.–Chicago: Austrian National Tourist Office, 500 N. Michigan Ave., Suite 544, Chicago, IL 60611. Tel. 312-644-5556.

U.S.A.–Houston: Austrian National Tourist Office, 4800 San Felipe, Suite 500, Houston, TX 77056. Tel. 713-850-9999.

U.S.A.–Los Angeles: Austrian National Tourist Office, 11601 Wilshire Blvd., Suite 2480, Los Angeles, CA 90025. Tel. 213-477-3332.

U.S.A.–New York: Austrian National Tourist Office, 500 Fifth Ave., New York, NY 10110. Tel. 212-944-6880.

Canada–Montreal: Austrian National Tourist Office, 1010 Sherbrooke St., W., Suite 1410, Montreal, Quebec H3A 2R7. Tel. 514-849-3709.

Canada–Toronto: Austrian National Tourist Office, 2 Bloor St., E., Suite 3330, Toronto, Ontario M4W 1A8. Tel. 416-967-3381.

Helpful local tourist offices, called *Verkehrsamt* or *Verkehrsverein,* are found in all big cities and most small towns.

In addition to skiing, skating, and tobogganing, don't miss the chance to hike and walk in the Alps; there are 30,000 miles of well-marked and maintained trails. Avoid the paths marked *Für Geübte,* which are for expert climbers only. Teens may want to take a mountain-climbing course from one of the many mountaineering schools in the Tirol. The national tourist office can send you a brochure with a listing of names and addresses. In addition to courses, they offer guided climbing tours and specialty courses such as ice climbing.

If the prospect of watching the spectacular Lippizan stallions of the Spanish riding school inspires your kids to canter through the countryside, horseback-riding information is available from the tourist office. Ask for their booklet "Equestrian Sports in Austria."

Faschingsumzüge processions welcome the coming of spring with people in masks, traditional costumes, and crowns of flowers as they parade through the town. The best are in Nassereith, Telfts, and Imst; check with the tourist offices for dates, as the celebrations often take place every other year.

December 5 marks the beginning of the **Christmas celebrations** with St. Niklaus going door to door passing out apples, nuts, and cakes to "good" children. A display of carved wooden cribs in houses and churches follows. Festive Christmas open-air markets are held in Austria's larger towns.

Lights Out! Special Austrian Accommodations

Homes, apartments, or **chalets** are available for rent by the week, and there are a number of agencies in North America that handle Austrian rental properties:

Europa-Let, P.O. Box 3537, Ashland, OR 97520. Tel. 800-462-4486, 503-482-5806.

Interhome, Inc. USA, 36 Carlos Dr., Fairfield, NJ 07006. Tel. 201-882-6864.

Rent A Home International (Innsbruck, Salzburg, and Vienna and throughout the country), 7200 34th Ave., NW, Seattle, WA 98117. Tel. 206-789-9377.

Rent A Vacation Everywhere (Vienna, Innsbruck, Salzburg), 328 Main St., E., Suite 526, Rochester, NY 14604. Tel. 716-454-6440.

Vacation Home Rentals Worldwide (Tirol, Innsbruck, Voralberg, Vienna), 235 Kensington Ave., Norwood, NJ 07648. Tel. 800-633-3284 or 201-767-9393.

Villas International (Vienna, Salzburg, Innsbruck, and resort areas), 71 West 23rd St., New York, NY 10010. Tel. 800-221-2260 or 212-929-7585.

The tourist office in many cities will help you book accommodations, usually for a small fee. They can provide suggestions of campgrounds, and many have listings with descriptions and color photographs of accommodations especially suited for families. Austrian "family hotels" generally have extras such as pools, playgrounds, playrooms, or child-care services.

Prices for accommodations vary considerably between the cities and chic winter resorts, and the country's more rural areas. A simple hotel room in Vienna or Kitzbühel often costs twice as much as a comparable room in a smaller town. Most of the newer hotel rooms in Austria have bathrooms with showers, while the less expensive, older hotels have baths down the hall. We have recommended hotels in Vienna and Salzburg that are located near parks and have kitchens or other amenities for families. Some hotels accommodate children under 6 free of charge, with kids between 7 and 12 half-price. Be sure to ask. A number of hotels in resort areas have been set up with special facilities for children. The local tourist offices can provide you with a listing. In the country, a *Gasthof* is a hotel with a restaurant; a *Frühstücks-Pension* is a guest house that offers breakfast. The sign *Zimmer-frei* outside of a private home indicates rooms to let.

Schlosshotels (Castle hotels) are scattered throughout the country, and the national tourist office can send you a booklet describing them. Most of them fall into the deluxe or expensive price categories, but staying in a 16th-century castle or a royal hunting lodge with modern amenities such as tennis courts, swimming pools, and riding facilities can be a worthwhile splurge.

Farm accommodations are perfect for families, with both self-catering units and bed-and-breakfast rooms available. Very popular with Europeans, it's a delightful way to participate in Austrian family life. Send for an English brochure with descriptions and photos from the national tourist office.

Request the brochure *Youth Hostels in Austria* for a listing of youth hostels with family rooms, kitchens, pools, and sports facilities. Many hostels have 3, 4, 5, and 6-bedded rooms.

Camping is a popular way to go, and the tourist office offers an information sheet/map, called "Camping and Caravanning," that lists campgrounds and their amenities.

Getting Around

Car travelers take note that seat belts are compulsory in front seats and children under 12 are not allowed to ride in the front seat. Austria's traffic regulations specify that no right turn is allowed on a red light, no passing is allowed on the right on expressways, and that a first-aid kit and red emergency triangle or marker are compulsory in your car. Some cities require that parking vouchers be displayed on your car's windshield in specially marked parking areas. These are purchased at banks, gas stations, and some tobacco shops. Some roads in Austria are toll roads. Avoid driving in Vienna, as its complex system of one-way streets is hard on strangers, and parking is quite limited.

Austria has an excellent **train** system running throughout the country. Some trains have cars on which you can load your automobile (the Vienna to Innsbruck or Salzburg train is popular). Children under 6 who sit on your lap ride free, and kids from 6 to 15 travel at half the adult fare. The Eurailpass is valid in Austria, and you can purchase an Austrian Rail Pass, the Rabbit Card, which is valid for 4 days worth of train travel within 10 days of purchase. **Bus** service is complete and extensive, and connects many small villages not on a rail line with the nearest railroad stations.

Boats travel from the German-Austrian border at Passau all the way up the Danube River to Vienna. You can take your car on some of the Danube steamers. **Cable cars,** funiculars, aerial trams, and gondolas are a great way to ascend the Alps. By all means, take advantage of them as kids adore this offbeat form of transportation. A restaurant or cafe is often found at the summit in addition to breathtaking views.

Over 120 Austrian railway stations rent **bicycles** by the day from April to the end of October. Bikes can be returned to any of the participating stations; the tourist office can send you a listing. Unless your children are seasoned cyclists, stick to the flatter eastern part of the country. Many of the larger cities offer **horse-drawn carriage** rides on *Fiakers*. Some cities, such as Vienna, use them as a supplement to taxis.

Nuts and Bolts

Does anyone care what time it is? Most stores are open from 8 or 9 AM to 6 PM. Some take a 1- or 2-hour lunch break in the middle of the day, especially in the more rural areas. Shops in small towns often close for the day on Saturdays at noon or 1 PM, while in resort areas and larger towns they reopen again after lunch. Stores are closed on Sundays.

National holidays: January 1, Epiphany (January 6), Easter Monday, May Day (May 1), Ascension Day, Whit Monday, Corpus Christi, Assumption Day, National Day (October 26), All Saints Day (November 1), Immaculate Conception (December 8), Christmas Day, and St. Stephan's Day (December 26).

Can I have my allowance? The unit of currency is the Austrian *schilling* (AS), and bills come in 1,000-, 500-, 100-, 50-, and 20-schilling notes. Schillings are divided into 100 *groschen*, which come in 20, 10, 5, and 2 coin denominations.

Telephones: The country code for Austria is 43. Both coin- and card-using phone booths are found throughout the country. Cards can be purchased at the post office. Some of the older telephones require that you push the red button when your party answers.

Useful nationwide telephone numbers: The operator is 09. Emergency first aid is 144, police is 133, and auto emergency is 120. If you need to call the U.S., dial 09 and ask for the AT&T operator.

Embassies and consulates: The U.S. Consulate is at Gartenbaupromenade 2, Vienna [Tel. (01) 51451]. The Canadian High Commission is at Dr. Karl Lueger-Ring 10, Vienna [Tel. (01) 533691].

Let's Eat!

Decorative and luscious Austrian desserts are world-famous, and your kids will do anything for you if you promise them a serving of their favorite cake covered with *Schlagobers* (whipped cream). Adults can sip one of the country's delicious coffee drinks (coffee was introduced to the Western world through Austria) and perhaps even read undisturbed while kids plow through a delectable pastry and a cup of hot chocolate. Flaky strudels are usually fruit-filled; the cream puffs and ice cream are also wonderful. *Torten* (cakes) are an Austrian specialty: *Sachertorte* is a rich chocolate cake filled with chocolate icing and jam; *Linzertorte* has almond-paste filling; *Doboschtorte* has many layers; *Guglhupf* is a light sponge cake. *Palatschinken* are crepes rolled around stuffings of jam, fruit, nuts, or other fillings. *Salzburger Nockerl*, a famous Austrian dessert, is a delicious soufflé omelette. Konditorei also sell nourishing snacks such as sandwiches, but you will have to leave your kids outside if that is all you plan to pick.

Lunch or dinner main-course specialties that most kids like include *Wiener Schnitzel* (veal steak, well pounded and dipped in flour, eggs, crumbs, and fried until golden brown), *Backhendl* (fried chicken), and sausages. Frankfurters are called *Wiener* except in Vienna. *Suppe* (soup) is delicious and inexpensive, and noodle or dumpling soups are a specialty. Fresh fish from lakes and rivers are tasty choices, and odd game dishes such as wild boar, pheasant, hare, quail, and partridge are surprisingly delicious. *Gulyas* (goulash), of Hungarian origin, is usually made from highly seasoned beef and is often served with potatoes. Stuffed green peppers and stuffed cabbage in tomato sauce are also Hungarian or Balkan inspired. Austrian slaw is like our cole slaw. Austrian bread is excellent, available at a *Bäckerei*. Note that cakes and pastries are available at a pastry shop, and bread in a bakery. *Apfelsaft* (apple juice), available everywhere, is a popular Austrian drink.

A few restaurants have high chairs, called *Hochstuhl*. Fancy restaurants discourage children, but most establishments welcome them. Many have a *Kindermenue* that features smaller portions.

Formula and Baby Food, Diapers and Baby Gear

Diapers, formula, and baby food are readily available in supermarkets, drugstores, and pharmacies, and the term *diaper* is used along with the German word *Windel*. Hipp and Milupa are the two most common brands of baby food. A crib is a *Krippe*, and a stroller is called *Kindersportwagen*.

Sidewalk Talk

Austria's official tongue is German; see page 171 for a list of useful words and phrases.

The Lay of the Land

Austria is located in the heart of the Continent and is divided into nine provinces. The Alps dominate in the provinces of Vorarlberg, Tirol, and Salzburg, in the western part of the country. Eastern Austria has wide river valleys and lakes. The countryside around Vienna has gently rising and falling hills. At the eastern end of Austria sits Lake Neusiedl, surrounded by flatlands, gentle hills with vineyards, and craggy wooded hills. We profile Vienna and the surrounding Lower Austria province and move roughly east to west, describing the sites and attractions in each of the nine provinces, with the southernmost province of Carinthia last.

VIENNA

Romantic baroque Vienna, home of the famed snow-white Lippizan stallions, the exquisite Vienna Boys Choir, and a world-famous amusement park offers families a culturally rich and fun-filled experience. Beethoven, Schubert, and Mozart have left an important artistic legacy, and music continues to play a role of tremendous importance to the Viennese, with scores of musical events taking place throughout the year. Horse-drawn carriages are easy to find for tours of the old part of the city, as are wonderful cafes and architectural jewels from many eras.

Wha'd'ya Wanna Do?

Pick up a copy of the inexpensive and helpful booklet "Vienna from A to Z" at one of the tourist offices. Among its many helpful entries are addresses for the homes of Beethoven, Schubert, Mozart, and other famous composers. National museums offer free admission on the first Sunday of the month, and municipal museums are free on Friday mornings.

The gleaming white **Lippizan stallions of the Spanish Riding School** are one of Vienna's best-loved attractions for most kids. Imported from Spain in 1562, the breed was used in battle as well as for the complicated stepping maneuvers that you can see them perform today. The intricate caprioles, pirouettes, courbettes, and canters are said to be based on the animals' natural movements. For a schedule and tickets to the performances, contact your travel agent or write to the Spanish Reitschule, Hofburg, 1010 Vienna. The training sessions can be visited mid-Feb.–June, Sept.–mid-Oct., and mid-Nov.–mid-Dec., Tues.–Fri. There are no reservations needed for the training sessions; purchase tickets at Gate 2 on Josefsplatz in Vienna on the day you want to attend from about 8:30 AM on.

The **Wiener Sängerknaben (Vienna Boys Choir)** is world-famous for its sweet high-voiced sound. Once a choir member's voice begins to change, he can no longer sing with the group. Performances are from mid-September to late June; tickets are not available during July and August when the choir is on vacation. Book through your travel agent or write Hofmusikkapelle, Hofburg, 1010 Vienna. Once in Vienna, tickets are sold at the box office of the Burgkapelle every Friday starting at 5 PM, and you may only buy two tickets per person. Get there early to stand in line. Standing room is free. Vienna's **tourist information offices,** called *Fremdenverkehrsverband für Wien,* are located at: Kinderspitalgasse 5 (Tel. 431608); on Kärntnerstrasse 38, West Bahnhof entrance hall on the ground floor; Südbahnhof entrance hall on the ground floor; airport arrivals hall opposite the baggage carousels. Vienna'a **telephone area code** is 01.

The Lay of the City

In the mid-19th century, the Emperor replaced the town's medieval walls with a wide, tree-lined boulevard called the Ringstrasse, or The Ring, which completely encompasses Old Vienna. Vienna is divided into twenty-three numbered districts. District 1 is everything inside The Ring, and districts 2 through 9 are arranged clockwise around it. Any number above 9 is farther out. Most street addresses are preceded by their district number.

Getting Around

Vienna's modern subway, the **U-Bahn,** uses an easy-to-follow color-coded system. Streetcars, buses, and a city railway supplement the U-Bahn. Children under 7 travel free on the city's public transportation throughout the year. During school holidays (July 1 through the end of August), children under 16 travel free provided they have a valid school ID card. The *24-Stunden-Netzkarte,* a pass for unlimited travel during a 24-hour period, and week-long passes are available at tourist offices, tobacco shops, and transit authority offices. These venues also sell a family ticket, called the *8-Tage-Streifenkarte,* which enables two people to travel for 4 days or four people to travel for 2 days. Passport photos are required for the week-long passes.

Tour Vienna during the late spring and summer in a jaunty red **trolley car** that leaves from the Otto Wagner Pavilion at Karlsplatz; tours last 2 hours. Contact the Vienna Transit Authority's information service in the Karlsplatz Underground Station. You can take **sightseeing boat tours** along the Danube Canal and the main Danube from the Danube Shipping Company (DDSG) (Tel. 21750, ext. 450). They depart from Schwedenbrück, at the edge of the old city on the canal (near subway stop Schwedenplatz).

Horses and carriage rides, departing from a number of places along the Ringstrasse, are a favorite with kids. Vienna Guides (Tel. 2206620 or 36570333) lead English-language **walking tours** such as "Unknown Underground Vienna," "Walls, Towers, and Bastions of Old Vienna," and "Vienna's Highlights by Bike."

Where to Stay

Accommodations in Vienna can be expensive and hard to find in peak season. If you plan to stay a week or more, consider renting an apartment from one of the agencies listed in "Lights Out" at the beginning of the chapter. Tourist offices will book you a room in a hotel or private home for a fee.

HOTELS

The *Vienna Intercontinental* overlooks the Stadtpark and is close to the Hofburg. An ice-skating rink is adjacent to the hotel. Johannesgasse 28. Tel. 711220 or from U.S. 800-327-0200. **Deluxe.**

The *Marriot* is across from Stadtpark and has an indoor pool. Parkring 12A. Tel. 515180 or from U.S. 800-228-9290. **Deluxe.**

Josefshof is a small, elegant hotel with a flowered courtyard and large rooms, some of which have kitchenettes. 1080, Josefsgasse 4. Tel. 438901. **Expensive.**

Clima Villenhotel has an indoor pool, a big yard where children can play, hotel rooms, apartments with small kitchens, and family bungalows with private terraces. Nussberggasse 2c. Tel. 371516 and 371349. **Expensive.**

Hotel Albatros has an indoor pool, sauna, and garage, and includes a buffet breakfast. 1090, Liechtensteinstr. 89. Tel. 343508. **Moderate.**

Hotel Schild is in a large ornamental garden overlooking the Vienna Woods about 5 miles out of the city center. Neustift am Walde 97-99. Tel. 4421910. **Moderate.**

Pension Columbia is a lovely hotel out of the center of town but accessible by tram #5. Triple rooms are available, and breakfast is included. 8 Kochgasse 9. Tel. 426757. **Inexpensive.**

Pension Kraml has three- and four-person "family" rooms, and breakfast is included. It's popular, so reserve in advance. 6 Brauergasse 5, off Gumpendorferst. Tel. 5878588. **Inexpensive.**

Even less expensive are the plain but serviceable 4-person bungalows for rent in the campground *Wien-West II,* open late June to early September. Hüttelbergstr. 80, 6 km. from the center of town. Tel. 942314. **Inexpensive.**

CAMPGROUNDS

Wein-West I and II campgrounds are open late June to early September. Hüttelbergstr. 40 and 80. Tel. 94149 or 942314.

Detour! What to See and Do

WITHIN THE RING

In the center of town in Stephansplatz is **Stephansdom (St. Stephen's Cathedral),** first built in 1147 and added on to ever since. Climb the 343 spiraling steps of its south tower for a breathtaking view of the city. Nicknamed "Steffl," this 450-foot-high tower dominates the Viennese skyline. Inside the cathedral's north tower is Die Pummerin, or the Boomer, an enormous bell. First cast from the metal in cannons captured from the Turks in 1711, it fell during a fire in 1945 and was replaced 7 years later. Spanning 10 feet and weighing 22 tons, the bell is rung at midnight on New Year's Eve and on other special occasions. The north tower and its bell can be visited by express elevator. Next to the elevator, enter the catacombs, which contain the bones and skulls of plague victims and partial remains of the Hapsburgs. Take your kids around to the cathedral's east side to see the torso of Our Man of Sorrows, also known as Our Lord of the Toothache because of his grimace. Subway excavations below the cathedral revealed Roman remains and old bones, and you can see a chamber with the contents of this excavation in the subway ticket hall. 1st District, Stephanplatz. Catacombs: daily 10–11:30 and 2–4:30; North Tower (elevator): daily 9–5:30; South Tower stairs: daily 9–5 Mar.–Nov. 15 and Dec. 15–Jan. 7.

Head around the Ring to the city's first public park, the **Stadtpark,** in a *Fiaker* (horse-drawn carriage) or on streetcar 1 or 2. You'll enjoy old-style open-air cafes and restaurants, outdoor concerts in the summer, statues of composers scattered about, and a small artificial lake in its center.

Not far from Stadtpark on the edge of the Ring near Schwartzenbergplatz is **Belvedere Palace,** originally built as a summer palace outside the city walls. The Lower Belvedere was first used as a home by the prince, who commissioned the building in the early 1700s, and now contains the **Baroque Museum** and the **Museum of Medieval Austrian Art.** Large formal gardens link the Lower Belvedere with the Upper Belvedere. Originally used for galas and official festivities, the Upper Belvedere contains the **Austrian Gallery of the 19th and 20th Centuries,** which houses an outstanding Art Nouveau and Austrian Expressionism collection as well as works by contemporary Austrian artists. Even if you can't convince the kids to spend time in the museums, walk through the gardens to the terrace at the top for a magnificent view. Fee. Both open Tues.–Sun. 10–4. Tel. 784158.

Each day at noon, larger-than-life figures parade across the face of the 1911 **Ankeruhr (Anker Clock)** to the accompaniment of music. Hoher Markt 10-11. Guides activate many clocks with movements and music at the **Uhrenmuseum.** Many of the collection's 3,000 timepieces perform on the hour. You'll see clocks from as far back as 1440; favorites were the clock with a real running waterfall set against a painted landscape and the clock whose pendulum was in the shape of a swinging child. Be sure to cover all three floors. 1st District. Schulhof 2. Tues.–Sun. 9–12:15 and 1–4:30. Tel. 5332265.

The **Kunsthistorisches Museum** has an outstanding collection of fine art, including the most comprehensive collection of the works of Pieter Bruegel the Elder, whose lively paintings of life in centuries past are very accessible to children. Peek in on the 2nd floor's coin collection. Fee. 1st District. Burgring 5 and 7. Apr.–Oct. Tues.–Fri. 10–6, Sat.–Sun. 9–6; Nov.–Mar. Tues.–Fri. 10–4, Sat.–Sun. 9–4. Tel. 934541.

The **Naturhistorisches Museum,** next to the Kunsthistorisches Museum, has a special children's corner, skeletons of prehistoric animals and fossils, a famous fertility figurine, the Venus of Villendorf, and Maria Theresa's bouquet made of precious stones. Fee. 1st District. Maria-Theresien-Platz. Daily, except Tues., 9–5. Tel. 934541.

If you're in need of a breath of fresh air, stop at the **Burgarten** or the **Volksgarten** before going into the palatial Hofburg complex. A rose- and flower-filled park adjacent to the Hofburg, the Volksgarten has fountains, statues, and the Theseus Temple, which is occasionally used for exhibitions. The Burgarten flanks the Hofburg on the other side. 1st District Dr.-Karl-Renner-Ring, next to the Burgtheater.

THE HOFBURG

The **Hofburg,** within the Ring, was the central palace of the Austrian Empire. Built in the 13th century, it is more a city than a palace, and you could spend a week exploring it. Among its attractions are numerous museums, the royal apartments, and the Spanish Riding School. Its **Schatzkammer** is a treasure chest containing enormous keys, hoods for falcons, the Imperial crown encrusted with gems from around 962, beautiful robes, vestments, objects made from "unicorn horn" (actually narwhal horn), and an elaborate baby cradle made for an infant king. Mon. and Wed.–Fri. 10–4, Sat.–Sun. 9–4; until 6 Apr.–Oct. Tel. 5337931.

The Hofburg's **Neue Hofburg** houses four museums: The **Musikinstrumentensammlung** is worth seeing, especially if your children have ever taken piano lessons, for the pianos of many famous com-

posers are on view. There is an excellent collection of early keyboard
instruments, pianos made to look like castles, a harp in the form of a
harpooned fish, and other whimsical instruments. The **Ephesos Museum** displays treasures uncovered at the archaeological dig at
Ephesus. The **Waffensammlung** has an excellent collection of armor
from all over Europe, plus swords, crossbows, and old guns. Be sure
to look for its collection of children's armor. The **Museum für Völkerkunde**'s greatest prize is Montezuma's quetzal-feather headdress
and cape, allegedly presented by Montezuma to Cortés. All four
museums: 1st District, Neue Burg, Heldenplatz (entrance close to
Burgring). Mon. and Thurs.–Sat. 10–1, Wed. 10–5, Sun. 9–1. Tel.
934541.

The lovely **Augustinerkirche** contains the hearts of the Hapsburgs,
fascinating to budding anatomy students. Look for all fifty-four of
them in the little urns in the Chapel of St. George. The **Spanische
Reitschule** is where the magnificent snow-white Lippizan stallions
train and perform fancy postures. This baroque building was created
to give the horses a chance to exercise and practice during the winter
months. For ticket information, see beginning of chapter. The
Stallburg houses the Lippizan stallions of the Spanish Riding School
and is separated from the indoor riding school by a glass passageway.

The Vienna Boys Choir performs in the Hofburg's **Burgkapelle** on
Sundays and Catholic feast days, with the exception of summer
months, when they're on vacation. See the beginning of this chapter
for ticket information.

OUTSIDE OF THE RING

The **Museum für Volkskunde** shows charming Austrian costumes
from the past and gives viewers insight into the life-styles and
customs of the Austrian people throughout the country. 8th District,
Laudongasse 15-19. Tel. 438905.

Schönbrunn Palace, to the west of town, was the summer residence
of the Hapsburgs; their winters were usually spent at the Hofburg.
The palace itself has 1,441 rooms, but only 45 of them can be visited.
Many are in the same condition as when royalty lived there. The
Wagenburg (Imperial Coach Collection) contains ceremonial state
coaches, sleighs, sedan chairs, hearses, a few baby carriages, and the
lavishly decorated imperial coronation coach. Behind the palace is a
large formal park with spectacular fountains, ponds, ruins, pools,
and grottos. During summer months climb to the top of the Gloriette,
where you can take in the view from an observation platform. One of
Europe's oldest zoos is housed in the park (see below). Stop for lunch
or a snack at the outdoor cafe close to the Meidling Gate. 13th
District, Schönbrunner Schloss-Str. Park: daily 6 AM to dusk; gala

rooms (guided tours only) and wagenburg: Apr.–Oct. 8:30–5:30, Nov.–Mar. 9–4; Gloriette: May–Oct. daily 8–6. Tel. 833646.

Kids will enjoy the railroad display with steam locomotives, toy train sets, and a model of a mountain railway at the **Technisches Museum für Industrie und Gewerbe.** Fee. 14th District, Mariahilfer Str. 212. Tues.–Fri. and Sun. 9–4; Sat. 9–1. Tel. 833618.

On display at the **Wiener Strassenbahnmuseum** are forty-two historical streetcars, from an 1871 horse-drawn trolley to a train from the 1950s. 3rd District, Erdbergstr. 109. May–Sept. Sat., Sun., and holidays 9–4. Sightseeing tours on an old-timer tram take place May–Oct. Sat. 2:30, Sun. 10. Tel. 5873186.

The **Zirkus und Clownmuseum** has costumes, old clown suits, posters, programs, photos, and exhibits related to the history of the circus and famous clowns. Free. 2nd District, Karmelitergasse 9. Wed. 5:30–7, Sat. 2:30–5, Sun. 10–noon. Tel. 3468615.

Where the Sidewalk Ends: Zoos and More Parks

Donaupark, right by the Danube, is famous for its colorful flower gardens. In addition to walking and cycling paths, a chair lift, miniature railway, and children's playground, it has the 826-foot **Donauturm,** or **Danube Tower.** Ascend the tower on express elevators to a platform 492 feet up for a great view and then continue up to the revolving cafe and restaurant. The park's Danube Park Hall has ice-skating during the winter months. 22nd District, Wagramer Str./Arbeiterstrandbadstr./Danauturmstr. **Kurpark Oberlaa** contains ponds, playgrounds, walking paths, restaurants, and a natural hot spring used in an adjoining treatment center. 10th District, Kurbadstr./Laaer-Brg-Str./Filmteichstr.

The beloved **Prater Park** has been home to Vienna's amusement park since 1766. Once the court game preserve, it is now a public park with the **Wurstelprater** amusement park, jogging and biking trails, and lakes with rowboat rentals. The Wurstelprater has a giant 19th-century ferris wheel, called the Riesenrad, made famous by the film *The Third Man,* which revolves to a top height of 212 feet. A narrow-gauge railway will escort kids around on a tiny train, and other amusements include a tunnel of love, merry-go-rounds, roller coasters, bumper cars, and more. The **Prater Museum** contains carousel animals, posters, and mementoes of the amusement park from decades past, such as a penny theater, ventriloquist, photos of old rides, and a program from a flea circus. Other attractions in the park include a racetrack, planetarium, golf course, and swimming pool. 2nd District. Amusements operate from late Feb. through Oct. and around the New Year.

The **Tiergarten Schönbrunn,** created in 1752, has animal houses designed in the baroque style, highly popular in the 18th century. Today most of the animals in the zoo are housed in more spacious, modern enclosures, but the old zoo has been preserved because of its architectural interest. It now houses only those animals who are old or crippled and can be made comfortable in smaller quarters. 13th district, Schönbrunner Schlosspark (near the Hietzinger Tor entrance). Daily 9 AM to dusk or 6, whichever is earlier. Tel. 821236.

Türkenschanzpark, the largest wooded park within the city, is located on the site of the Turkish fortification during the siege of Vienna. Peacocks wander about its immaculate lawns, and there are playgrounds, a few caged animals, ponds, and monuments. 18th District, Hasenauerstr./Gregor-Mendel-Str. Next to the School of Agriculture.

The **Vienna Woods,** or **Wienerwald,** is actually a range of low wooded hills, crisscrossed by pathways and roads along Vienna's western side. The woods extend far beyond the edge of Vienna to near the Alps. The Viennese make full use of it on weekends, and in the summer the national sports of hiking and climbing are practiced by many a city dweller. Within the woods, about 5 miles from the center of the city, is **Lainzer Tiergarten,** a natural game park where deer, boar, elk, and mouflon (an animal similar to the Rocky Mountain bighorn) roam freely. The park takes several hours to walk across and is car-free. In its center is the Hermes Villa, which has exhibitions and a restaurant with indoor and outdoor eating. Marked paths lead the way, and there are playgrounds. Free. Apr.–Oct. Wed.–Sun. 8 AM to 1 hour before dusk.

Sports

Bicycling is easy in Vienna as there are more than 155 miles of cycle paths and a number of rental firms. You can take your bikes on the Vienna Schnellbahn and subway for free except during the rush hour. Bike firms can be found at: 1020, Vivariumstrasse 8 (Tel. 266644); Praterstern Station (Tel. 268557); or Franz Josefs-Kai by the Salztorbrücke on the Danube Canal. Rowing **boats** up, down, and across the Danube can be a fun way to blow off steam; rent them near the Wagramerstrasse bridge on the left bank of the Old Danube. **Ice-skating** is popular; the tourist office can give you a list of the fifty rinks. For **swimming,** try the open-air pool in Prater Park's Stadium Pool. One of the prettiest is the Krapfenwald pool in Grinzing, overlooking the city. The enormous Amalienbad pool, in Reumannplatz, has an Art Nouveau and Art Deco setting. Most **water sports** can be found at Donauinsel, a large recreation area on an artificial island in the Danube with a long bathing beach, surfing, water skiing, boating, wind surfing, water slides, and children's play areas. Car or subway to U1 Station Donauinsel.

LOWER AUSTRIA

The largest of Austria's provinces, this castle-filled region occupies the northeastern corner of the country and is cut by the Danube on its way to Hungary.

Safari Park Gänserndorf has elephants, monkeys, lions, tigers, zebras, and more roaming through its spacious grounds. An adventure playground and animal shows will make it a day. Tel. (02282) 72610. *Gänserndorf* city has horseback riding, miniature golf, and lots of other recreational activities.

About an hour from Vienna in *St. Pölten* is 15th-century **Pottenbrunn Castle,** with a moat, ponds, beautiful parks, and a **Tin-Soldier Museum** in the middle of its English garden. Over 35,000 handmade and hand-painted miniature soldiers pose in fifty glass cases holding dioramas of famous battles. Tiny landscapes, castles, villages, animals, and many other Lilliputian details complete the scenes. Fee. Summers 9–5.

Rappsottenstein's medieval castle-fortress has Austria's best-preserved torture chamber. There is swimming and good fishing in the river, hiking, bicycling, and nearby skiing at Kirchbach in winter.

Gmünd, along the Czech border, has an interesting glass-making museum and the **Naturpark Blockheide Eibenstein,** with observation towers, deer, and huge boulders to try to climb. Some of these rounded granite boulders, called *rocking stones*, can keep your supermen and wonderwomen busy as they learn to rock them back and forth. Free. In the Waldviertel. Open year-round.

BURGENLAND

Part of Hungary until 1918, this province starts near Vienna and runs east to Hungary, north to Czechoslovakia, and south to Yugoslavia.

The *Neusiedler See,* a lake containing many interesting forms of bird life, is surrounded by wildlife sanctuaries, lovely villages, and recreational opportunities. Look for the chimney nests of the famous Rust storks of storybook fame in the towns circling the lake, especially the towns of *Oggau, Rust,* and *Mörbisch.* Rust is known as the stork capital of the world. You can spot nests even if the storks aren't in them, and boat trips for bird-watchers are available. Some of the birds found amidst the reeds surrounding parts of the shallow lake include herons, egrets, wild geese, sea eagles, and a wide variety of ducks. Every village near the lake has a small bathing beach. **Podersdorf** has especially good swimming, windsurfing, and horseback riding. **Seewinkel** is an area of wildlife sanctuaries, with one supported in part by the World Wildlife Fund. In the northeast corner of the lake is the **baroque castle** at **Kittsee.**

UPPER AUSTRIA AND THE SALZKAMMERGUT

Flowing through upper Austria is the Danube River, the route of many boat trips that start at Passau, just across the West German border. To the north sits Czechoslovakia. In the corner is the Bohemian forest and the beautiful lake district of Salzkammergut. To the south is the mountainous Pyhrn district.

The salt-rich Salzkammergut District between Salzburg and Linz has sparkling lakes and majestic mountains. Many lakes, salt mines, and caves make this a rich summer retreat. You'll find riding, water sports, children's playgrounds, wildlife parks, hiking, cycling, and cable cars available throughout the region. The town of **Mondsee** is not particularly outstanding, but there is good swimming around its lovely crescent-shaped lake, which has the warmest waters in the area. Try the local cheese specialty, also known as Mondsee. **Attersee** has boat trips, great fishing, and sailing. During summer months **Traunsee** has tours of the lake on the *Gisela,* a restored 19th-century paddle steamer.

The town of **Gmunden,** on its north shore, has a double castle connected by a causeway: **Landschloss** on the shore and **Seeschloss** on an island in the lake. Once a favorite haunt of artists and poets, the town is now a center for water sports and fishing. Walk along the lakeshore on its mile-long esplanade through chestnut trees and flowers to the beach in one direction or to the river in the other.

Bad Ischl, in the heart of the Salzkammergut, became the preferred 19th-century spa of the court, fashionable composers, and artists. Traces of its opulent era can still be seen throughout the town. Its **salt mine** has fast wooden slides down into the inner workings of the mine. Visitors are provided with funny miner's suits and hats before you head down. Mid-May–mid-Sept. Mon.–Sat. 10–6. Tel. (06132) 4231.

LINZ AND ENVIRONS

Linz, the capital of Upper Austria, is an important river port and rail center. Its old town is centered around the **Hauptplatz,** or main square. Several blocks away is the castle, which now houses the **Oberösterreichisches Landesmuseum,** with a collection of interiors of historic houses, peasant furniture, models of farmhouses, folk costumes, weapons, and traditional nativity scenes. The castle ramparts have been turned into a park with views of the Danube and the hills beyond. Across the river from the main square is the suburb of Urfahr, originally a separate town. Take the mountain train (one of Europe's steepest) up to the twin-spired pilgrimage church at the crest of Pöstlingberg Hill for an expansive view. Kids will head straight for the Grottenbahn, a small, dragon-headed train that takes them through **Fairy-Tale Wonderworld,** with life-size characters from the most popular fairy tales. They'll see Little Red Riding Hood, Sleeping Beauty, Hansel and Gretel, and more, plus plenty of tiny gnomes and dwarves, as they wind their way through grottoes and caves. Just northwest of Linz is the **Altenfelden Game Park,** in the *Mühlviertwl,* in the foothills of the Bohemian forest. In addition to its collection of indigenous species of game, it has a number of rare stags, pony rides for children, and a petting zoo. Fee. Daily 8–5.

Each year at Christmas, the Austrian post office sets up a special branch at *Christkindl,* whose name means Baby Jesus. From this little church near *Steyr,* anyone can send Christmas messages to friends around the globe during the month of December with the postmark Christkindl (address: Christmas Post Office, A-4411 Christkindl, Austria). The post office also answers all letters sent by children asking for gifts as long as they enclose an Austrian stamp. Steyr is a 1,000-year-old city with many recreational activities such as ice-skating in the winter, an indoor pool, hiking, riding, and miniature golf.

STYRIA

Rich with forests and iron ore mined since Celtic and Roman times, this province is home to the Lippizan stallions and many old folk traditions.

GRAZ

The **Landeszeughaus** has a world-famous collection of armor and old objects of war. There are jousting suits and lances, maces, muskets, swords, and armor for knights and horses, some of which have exquisite inlay work and engraving. In 1749, Empress Maria Theresa requested that this 30,000-piece collection be maintained in its original condition, which is how you see it. Fee. Herrengasse 16. Apr.– Oct. Mon., Tues., Thurs. 9–12, 2–5.

The **Schlossberg,** Graz's famous castle, overlooks the town from atop a rocky outcropping. Take the red cable railway (leaves from Kaiser-Franz-Josef-Kai) up to it, or if you're feeling energetic, climb the stairs that zigzag along its steep and rocky west side. The only part left of its original fortification is its famous bell tower with a huge clock on its front. The surrounding well-kept Herberstein Gardens are perfect for a picnic, or a stop for a snack at the restaurant with an outdoor terrace.

Young ones will like the **Grottenbahn** (Fairyland Railway) beneath the Schlossberg (entrance at Schlossbergplatz) open during the summer. Graz is known for its beautiful parks. The **Stadtpark** has an elaborate fountain and lots of room to stretch and run. Within it, the Burggarten (castle garden) is lovely.

NEAR GRAZ

Take a **gondola ride** from a station in nearby *St. Radegund* to the summit of the **Schöckel,** a 4,750-foot-high mountain for views extending from the Alps to the Hungarian plain. From there, travel on a chair lift up to Jägerwirt, a restaurant near Semriach. The hearty can hike down (it takes about 3 hours) through the charming small villages of Puch and Kalkeitenmöstl.

Lurgrotte, about 20 kilometers from Graz, between Semriach and Peggau, is a stalactite cave with eerie illuminated formations, an underground lake, and artificial pathways through its grottoes and gorges. Depending on the weather, you can tour the entire cave, which descends 7 kilometers below ground. Fee. Accessible on the A-9 or S35. Apr.–Oct. Tues.–Sun. 10–4. Tel. (03127) 2580.

The **stables of Piber Castle** are where the white Lippizan stallions are bred. The stud farm was transferred from the Yugoslavian town of Lippiza after World War I, but the horses are originally from Arabia and Spain. The colts are born black and slowly change to white between ages 2 and 7. You can see the young ones on mountain pastures in this area during the summer. Only a select few make it to the performance hall of the Spanish Riding School. Visitors to the stud farm can greet each horse in its stall and watch the horses run free and play during their afternoon romp in the pasture. Fee. Daily Apr.–Nov. 9–11, 2–4; hourly guided tours. Tel. (03144) 3323.

The **Österreichisches Freilichtmuseum (Austrian Open-Air Museum)** at *Stübing* is set on 100 acres in a wooded valley. Its rustic thatched-roof farmhouses, mills, and other buildings from all of the Austrian provinces were carefully taken down and reconstructed in their original form. Animals wander through the fields and flowers, and the interiors are authentic, with spinning wheels, decorated chests, and other household objects. Fee. 16 km. north of Graz. Apr.–Oct. Tues.–Sun. 9–5. Tel. (03124) 22431.

Take a swim in **Lake Stubenberg** and then proceed to **Schloss Herberstein,** northeast of Graz. The castle contains armor and a family museum, and the grounds contain an adventure playground and the **Herberstein Wildlife Preserve,** where chamois, ibex, deer, badger, wolves, marmots, and exotic wild animals can be observed in natural surroundings. Fee. Daily year-round. Tel. (03176) 2250 or 2810.

SALZBURG

The city of Salzburg, magnificently situated on the banks of the Salzach River, is nestled between two mountains near the West German border. In addition to exploring this intriguing town, plan an extra couple of days to visit the Hellbrunn Pleasure Castle and the Dürnnburg Salt Mines (see page 57), all easy day trips your kids will thoroughly enjoy. If you have the time, the Eisriesenwelt Ice Caves are a memorable spectacle.

Mozartkugeln (Mozart balls), Salzburg's sweet specialty, are pistachio-flavored marzipan rolled in nougat cream and then dipped in dark chocolate and wrapped in foil bearing the composer's likeness. You can buy them along **Getreidegasse,** one of the main streets of Old Salzburg. Mozart lived at #9, now a museum. Other buildings along the street are graced with carved window frames and quaint wrought-iron signs. Horse-drawn cabs called *Fiakers* are a popular way to tour the town and can be found on the **Residenzplatz,** the center of the old city. **Bikes** can be rented at the train station, and the bus system is excellent.

Popular with kids is the **Sound of Music Tour,** which starts with a short look at downtown Salzburg, followed by visits to the movie's locations, including the elaborate mansion, the lovely wedding church, and the "hills-are-alive" countryside of the Salzkammergut Lake District. For information, call Panorama Tours Company at 74029.

The celestial **Salzburg Festival** takes place from the end of July through the month of August, and tickets for all concerts except a few of those held outdoors are only available if you book well in advance. Many of the performances are held in Salzburg's palaces and historical buildings. Salzburger Festspiele, Postfach 140, Salzburg (Tel. 842541). **Folklore evenings** take place at Stieglkeller. Contact the **tourist office** at Auerspergstr. 7 (Tel. 80720) for more information. Salzburg's **telephone area code** is 0662.

Where to Stay

Salzburg's hotel's and pensions are filled from the end of July through August for the festival, so be sure to make advance reservations if you visit during that time.

HOTELS

The Salzburg Tourist Office has a three-page list of hotels and pensions with facilities for children. Our list includes just a few of them.

Haus Ingeborg, surrounded by forests and meadows, is 5 minutes from the city center. Rooms or apartments are available, and it has a pool. Sonnleitenweg 6, A-5020. Tel. from U.S. 800-736-4912. **Deluxe.**

Hotel Schloss Mönchstein is a luxury hotel in a private park near Mönchsmountain overlooking the city. Mönchsbergpark 26, A-5020. Tel. 848559 or from U.S. 212-696-1323. **Deluxe.**

Maria-Theresien-Schlössl is a small castle with parklike grounds about 4 kilometers from the city center near Hellbrunn. A buffet breakfast is included. Morzgerstr. 87, A-5020. Tel. 841244. **Expensive.**

Hotel Fondachhof is outside of the city center in a lovely park with expansive lawns and gardens, and a heated swimming pool. Several rooms have communicating doors, and rates include breakfast. The hotel sells bus tickets to simplify your quick journey into town. Gaisbergstr. 46-48. Tel. 20906 and 20907. **Expensive.**

Pension Trumer Stube has rooms for three and four people, and is well located near Mirabell Gardens and many other sites in the old city. Bergstr. 6. Tel. 74776. **Moderate.**

Hotel Blaue Gans is near the city center; children under 6 are free. Getreidesgasse 43 and Sigmundsplatz 3. Tel. 841317 and 842491. **Moderate.**

The *Haus Lindner*, set in gardens with a small playground, is run by two sisters with seven children between them. Take the 10-minute train ride into the city. Rooms for three to four people are available, and breakfast is included. Kasern Berg 64. Tel. 533254 and 533554. **Inexpensive.**

Detour! What to See and Do

THE OLD CITY

High above this beautiful baroque city sits its chief landmark, the great fortress-castle **Festung Hohensalzburg.** Built in 1077, it is accessible by cable railway or a vigorous walk up a zigzag trail. In the summer, try to time your visit to hear the 200-pipe hand-operated barrel organ built in 1502 which plays daily at 7 AM, 11 AM, and 6 PM. Walk around the castle to see old cannons, weapons, a medieval torture chamber, and superb views from the ramparts. The entire castle is floodlit during the festival. Its museum contains displays on the history of the fortress. Fee. Open daily; guided 1-hour tours 9–5. English brochure available. Tel. 80422123. Between the hill on which the fortress sits and the river lies the enchanting old town, which is just the right size for walking tours.

Along one side of the Residenzplatz is the **Glockenspiel Tower.** Its thirty-five bells ring out the works of Mozart, Haydn, and Weber at 7 AM, 11 AM, and 6 PM. The square's 40-foot-high fountain is illuminated on summer nights. Around the corner from the Residenzplatz is **Alter Markt,** the town's old marketplace, with flower stands and the Salzburg specialty *Gewürzsträusserl,* which are fragrant clusters of spices arranged to look like floral bouquets. Locals hang them in their kitchens and use the spices as needed.

The **Mozart-Museum's** collection includes mementoes of his life such as the tiny violin and the clavichord he used as a child. Getreidegasse 9. Mid-May–mid-Oct. 9–6. Tel. 844313.

The **Haus der Natur's** most famous resident is a mummified Ice Age rhinoceros, always a hit with kids. This is no ordinary natural history museum; its fourth floor has stuffed freak animals, giant insects, and enough other oddities to seem more like a circus sideshow. The second floor has a biological laboratory for children and a reptile zoo. A third-floor terrace cafe is a great place for a refreshing break. Fee. Guided tours in English if requested in advance. Museumplatz 5. Daily 9–5. Tel. 842653.

The **Spielzeugmuseum** features toys spanning three centuries, handicrafts, and musical instruments. A fully equipped playroom and interactive science exhibits keep kids happy. **Punch and Judy** perform on Wednesdays and Fridays. Fee. Bürgerspitalgasse 2, in the old Municipal Hospital. Tues.–Sun. 9–5. Tel. 847560.

The **Catacombs of Petersfriedhof** were hidden in the churchyard until a landslide in 1669 revealed the stone chambers that had been hollowed out of a rock wall. Fee. St. Peter-Bezirk 1. May–Sept. 10–5; Oct.–Apr. 11–12, 1:30–3:30. Tel. 844578.

For a splendid view of the city and the chance to wander along shady paths, take the Mönchsberg elevator from Gstättengasse 13 to the top of **Mönchsberg,** a hilly park that runs along one edge of the city. If you have lots of young energy to walk off, you can saunter all the way to the fortress-castle Festung Hohensalzburg.

ALONG THE RIVER'S RIGHT BANK

Schloss Mirabell and its gardens were built in 1606 by Wolf Dietrich for his true love. You can tour the home with its grandiose Angel Staircase, but kids will prefer the lavish gardens with baroque flowerbeds, open-air hedge theater, lush lawns, and the Dwarf's Garden, with its statues of Dietrich's beloved midgets.

Mozart's family also lived in **Tanzmeistersaal** at Makartplatz 8, which has been turned into a museum with an audiovisual show.

Chamber-music concerts are held here in July and August, and young music buffs will enjoy listening to a concert in the musician's living room. June–Sept. Mon.–Sat. 10–5; Oct.–May Mon.–Sat. 10–4. Tel. 71776.

Sports

Bikes may be rented at Krois-Schmidler, Ignaz Harrer Str. 8, from May to September, from Zweirad-Center Frey, Linzergasse 12, and from the main railway station. A special bike path map is available from the tourist office. For **horseback riding,** try Reitstall Doktorbauer, Eberlinggasse 5 (Tel. 845785) or Reiterhof Moos, Moosstr. 135 (Tel. 842791). **Ice-skating rinks** can be found at the Volksgarten, Hermann-Bahr-Promenade 2 (open Sept.–Mar.), and Rupertgasse 11. **Swimming pools** are found throughout the city. The grounds of Leopoldskron and Klessheim castles have pools; there is an indoor pool in the Kurhaus on the edge of Schloss Mirabell; and the Volksgarten has several pools. There is **skiing** and **tobogganing** 16 kilometers from the city center at Gaisberg Mountain.

Performing Arts

The world-famous **Salzburg Marionettes** perform at the **Marionetten Theater.** Professor Herman Aicher's family has been making these puppets for 200 years. Choose your performances carefully, as the performances range from Nutcracker ballets to full-scale Mozart operas. Schwarzstrasse 24, on the river's right bank. Apr.–Sept., Christmas, and New Year's. Tel. 882141. The **puppet theater, La Parapluie,** performs Punch and Judy and fairytales for little ones and has literary and cabaret performances for teenagers and adults. A puppet festival is held in July. Fee. Elisabethstrasse 53a. Tel. 53574.

EASY EXCURSIONS FROM SALZBURG

Lustschlosss Hellbrunn (Hellbrunn Pleasure Castle), 5 kilometers south of the center of Salzburg, was built in the early 17th century for Bishop Marcus Sitticus. Any child who has giggled at a trick water-squirting corsage will adore the castle and its water gardens. Water jets and fountains are hidden where you least expect them: on chair seats, statues, or in garden beds. The most famous is the outdoor table where the bishop would dine with his friends. Each seat contained a small hole through which a jet of water could be activated when the mood struck him. Be prepared to get wet in order to really experience it. In the Birdsong Grotto birds chirp and gypsies and bears dance, all using water to power them. The 18th-century Mechanical Theater shows life in a baroque city. Tiny people bustle about their business, completely powered by water alone. If you have time, visit Hellbrunn's zoo and the Salzburg Folklore Museum. Water garden: guided tour only April–October. In July and August, you can catch an evening concert and enjoy the illuminated fountains on Wednesday and Saturday evenings. The Hellbrunn Festival takes place in August with a program of music, dance, comedy, opera, and a fireworks display. Fees. May–Aug. 8–5:30; Apr., Sept., Oct. 9–4. Tel. 841696.

Touring the **Dürrnberg Salt Mines** above *Hallein* will top any kid's list of Austrian favorites. They'll don an old-fashioned miner's suit complete with a leather patch on the behind and fezlike red hat, straddle benches on a miniature train, and head down toward the center of the earth. The train drops them off down under, from where they must slide even deeper down long, fast, wooden slides through the dark. The first slide is 120 feet long and takes them 75 feet down. The next slide is 200 feet long and takes them down another 90 feet, where they'll visit a salt lake circled with winking lights. If you're there off-season, you may get to boat across the lake on a raft and head into a huge cavern. More slides await you on this tour, but don't worry, a car will take you back to the top. "*Glück auf!*" is the old miner's greeting for, "May you have the good luck to come up again." The German tour takes about 1-1/2 hours, and an English brochure is available. Fee. Min. age 5. Apr.–Sept. 9–5; Oct. 10–2. Tel. (06245) 27.

The **Eisriesenwelt Ice Caves** near *Werfen* are Europe's largest known complex of ice caves, domes, and halls. It has frozen water-falls and bizarre ice formations made from trickling water freezing in place. You must drive or take a bus to the cable-car station for a lift up to the ticket office, from where you take a 20-minute walk along a mountain path with spectacular views. The caves are cleverly lit to enhance their magnificent icy architecture as you wander past strange formations and walls of ice to a cave called the Ice Palace. Dress warmly, and be prepared to do some walking. Guided tours take about 2 hours. Caves open May–Sept. 9:30–3:30; until 4:30 July and Aug.

HALLSTATT AND ENVIRONS

The ancient and picturesque town of Hallstatt is set on Hallstätter See against a backdrop of rugged mountains and a rushing waterfall. About 60 kilometers southeast of Salzburg, off the main road to Graz, the small town of under 2,000 people is the longest continuously inhabited village in Europe. Many archaeological treasures from the early Iron Age have been uncovered here. Recreational opportunities on the lake abound. You can fish, hire rowboats, or ride a steamer across to Obertraun, where a cable car zips you up the mountain for exhilarating vistas.

As Hallstatt's cemetery is quite small, skulls and bones have been moved to Beinhaus (charnel house) of the **Chapel of St. Michel** since the 1600s. Among the 1,200 skulls and countless bones are skulls with information painted on them pertinent to the deceased and others that have been ornately decorated.

The local **prehistoric museum** contains relics from the Iron Age, and collections of folklore, such as nativity cribs, can be found at the **folk museum**. Both: Fee. Summer 9:30–6; winter 9:30–4.

Hallstatt also boasts the oldest working **salt mine** in the world, another favorite for your kids. After putting on protective overalls and a silly hat, slide down two long and exhilarating wooden slides to a beautifully illuminated salt lake. Don't worry, a little train takes you back to daylight. To get there, take the cable car from the village up the mountain and then walk 10 minutes further to get to the entrance. Fee. Summer 9:30–6; rest of year 9:30–4. Tel. (06134) 252.

Nearby, the **Ice Caves** at *Dachstein* have 1-hour guided tours in English that show off crisply lit curtains and towers of ice, hanging icicle spears, the icy chambers of "King Arthur's Cathedral," and the "Great Ice Chapel." Fee. May–Oct. 9–3:20; until 4:20 mid-June–mid-Sept. A combined ticket will allow you to enter the **Mammoth's Cave,** part of a huge subterranean network of giant domed halls and tunnels. Fee. Mid-May–mid Oct. 10–2. A ticket to either of the caves will admit you to the **Dachstein Museum,** which has a 3-D model of the entire 23-mile-long Mammoth's Cave, examples of modern equipment used by cave explorers, specimens of eyeless cave bugs, and a movie. The caves can be reached from the middle station of the Dachstein Cableway. Wear warm clothes and sturdy shoes. Tel. for caves (06131) 362.

Skiing in this region is excellent, but there are few facilities for children under 4. For older children, there are ski schools (which will take them for the entire day), horse-drawn sleigh rides, and ice-skating rinks in Rohrmoos and Haus/Ennstal.

LAND SALZBURG

Known for its excellent skiing, the province Land Salzburg is filled with rugged mountains, crystal clear blue lakes, and lush forests.

Radstadt, southeast of Eisriesenwelt, retains some of its 13th-century walls and is a center for winter sports and summer resort activities, with little lakes, Alpine wildflowers, and pure fresh air. The town has mountain bikes for rent with suggested tours for all abilities, playgrounds, swimming pools, miniature golf, and more.

Badgastein, at the southern edge of Land Salzburg, has hot springs, breathtaking mountain scenery, and a rushing waterfall, right in the middle of town. Its large indoor swimming pool has been carved out of a rock and is filled with water from the hot springs. Excellent skiing with many good intermediate runs is found here in winter. There are child-care facilities on the slopes for children ages 3 years and above. In summer you can take a number of rides to mountains surrounding Badgastein, but one of the best is the ride to Stubnerkogel. The area also has trails for hiking.

Zell am See, in the **Middle Pinzgau,** is a popular winter ski resort with many excellent intermediate runs, a children's ski school, and child care for young ones. In the summer you can swim or boat on its sparkling blue lake or ride one of the many cable cars which travel up to exhilarating heights for breathtaking views. Year-round skiing is available on its nearby glaciers.

Not far is *Kaprun,* where a three-part aerial cable car will take you across glaciers to an elevation of 9,935 feet for year-round skiing. This ski area is excellent for both intermediates and expert skiers. The **Kessel waterfall** is the highest in Europe, dropping 1,250 feet in three stages. On summer evenings it's illuminated on Wednesdays, weather permitting.

Mayrhofen, in the Ziller Valley, is a typical Austrian village with narrow streets and timbered houses. It's known for its world-famous ski school for children, the first of its kind in Austria. The ski school provides day care and ski instruction as well as entertainment during nonskiing times. Puppet shows are staged each week in the village, and children's games are offered one night each week. Contact the **tourist office** [Tel. (05285) 2305].

The tiny village of *St. Martin bei Lofer,* about an hour's drive from Salzburg, has many interesting caves. The most famous is **Lamprechtsofenlochhöhle Cave,** with spectacular domed ceilings and waterfalls. Wear sturdy shoes and a sweater for this underground excursion past colorful icicles and a cave called the "Pearl Grounds," which appears to be filled with icy jewels. Legend has it that buried treasure lies somewhere in this maze of passages. At one time, a castle belonging to the notorious robber, Knight Lamprecht, sat above the caves. When he died, one of his daughters cheated her sister out of her inheritance. As punishment, she was abandoned deep in the bottom of the cave with her dog and treasures. She made it out, thanks to her faithful hound, but left the money and jewels down under. Neither she nor anyone else has been able to find them since. Fee.

TIROL

This mountainous province with remote little villages is one of the best winter sports and ski areas in the world. In summer it is a destination for hikers, mountain climbers, and glacier skiers. Many Tirolean villages and towns have marked hiking trails. If you plan a hiking excursion, stick to trails marked with a blue triangle, as they are safe and intended for children. Be sure to wear your sturdiest shoes!

INNSBRUCK

Innsbruck, the Tirol's 800-year-old capital and site of the 1964 and 1976 Winter Olympics, stands within the sheer faces of the Alps. More than 150 cable cars and chair lifts extend from Innsbruck into some of the Alps' most breathtaking scenery for skiing. You can bobsled, luge, take a horse-drawn sleigh ride, or ice-skate; drop by the **tourist office** at Burggraben 3 (Tel. 53560) for details. In summer, cable cars and chair lifts operate for hikers and sightseers, and Tirolean brass bands play throughout the city. Innsbruck's **telephone area code** is 0512.

Detour! What to See and Do

THE OLD CITY
Innsbruck's "old city" lies cn the right bank of the Inn River. **Goldenes Dachl,** with its golden roof, is one of Innsbruck's most famous monuments, and many pictures of the town feature this ornate mansion. The folktale of its origin will fascinate your children, even if they are only mildly interested in its rich and colorful surface detail. Legend has it that Friedrich the Penniless, Duke of the Tirol in the early 15th century, was sick and tired of the jokes about his poverty, so he had this little roof covered with gold coins. Inside, the **Olympiamuseum** has films in English and exhibits from the 1964 and 1976 winter games, including a collection of international Olympic Games stamps. Fee; a combined ticket to the city tower can be purchased. In the **Goldenes Dachl.** Daily 10–5:30. Tel. 20948. The 15th-century **Stadturm** tower, next to the old town hall, has a wonderful view from its top. Fee. Herzog-Friedrich-Str. 21. Daily Mar.–Oct. 10–5; July and Aug. 10–6. Tel. 35962.

Not far is the **Hofburg Palace,** with an impressive English-style garden and paintings of the Empress Maria Theresa's children in the Giant's Hall. Fee. Rennweg and Hoffegasse. Mon.–Sat. 9–4. Next door, the **Hofgarten** is a graceful public park with lovely little lakes and weeping willow trees. Evening concerts and outdoor chess games using giant, ornately carved, wooden chess pieces take place in summer months.

Of all of the Tirolean folk art in the **Tiroler Volkskunstmuseum,** kids like the Christmas cribs best. Other favorites in the collection are charming carved and painted folk furniture, peasant costumes, musical instruments, games, tools, and farmhouse interiors from the Gothic to rococo periods. Fee. Universitätsstr. 2. Daily 9–12, 2–5; Sun. and holidays 9–12.

In summer, you can hear real **Tirolean yodeling** and see Tirolean dances performed daily at Gasthof Adambräu (Heilig-Geiststr. 16, at 9 PM) and Gasthof Sailer. For more information, contact the tourist office. For a fine view of the Tirolean Alps, take a cog railway trip to **Hungerberg** and then further up to the mountain station at **Hafelekar.** Cars leave for Hungerberg from the Mühlauer Innbrücke and from Hungerburg for Hafelekar every 15 to 30 minutes. Fee.

BEYOND THE OLD CITY

The **Alpenzoo** at Weiherburg above Innsbruck houses a variety of alpine animals. As Europe's highest zoo, it is home to bearded vultures, bald ibis, lynx, snow rabbits, beavers, bears, wolves, and otters, plus alpine birds and an aquarium full of alpine fish. Take the cog railway, the Alpenzoo-Hungerburgbahn, which departs every 20 minutes from the valley station adjacent to the Rundgemälde. Fee. Daily 9 AM to dusk or 6 PM. Tel. 892323

NEAR INNSBRUCK

There are five major **ski areas** around Innsbruck: Hungerburg-Seegrube, Axamer-Lizum, Tulfes, Igls, and Mutters. Child care for a variety of ages and ski schools for ages 4 and up are available in all ski resorts. Hungerburg has the most challenging runs, and Igls has a bobsled course you can try. Mutters is good intermediate territory.

Near *Zirl,* walk along the **Ehnback-Klamm,** a pathway that was blasted through a rocky gorge. The village of *Igls* is filled with quaint chalets and has a small lake for swimming. Take its cog railway to the mountaintop with a well-marked trail at the summit called the **Zirbenweg.** It has been a popular resort with a wealthy clientele for many years.

Schloss Tratzberg, about 45 kilometers northwest of Innsbruck, may not have the fairy-tale facade that so impresses the kids, but its plain exterior hides many fascinating treasures within. Be sure your children find the secret passageway through one of the bedroom closets and have a look at the knight's armor. The sheer beauty of a carved mahogany ceiling in the Queen's room may interest you, while your children, especially 7-year-olds, will appreciate its building trivia. It took seven carpenters and seven apprentices seven years and seven months to carve it. Fee. Near Stans. Daily Easter–Aug. 10–3.

There is year-round skiing on the **Stubai** and **Tuxer** glaciers and on glaciers in Rettenbachferner, above *Sölden*. Site of Austria's highest cable car, Sölden has excellent beginning and intermediate skiing as well as a ski kindergarten for children 3 to 8 years old for a full or half day with meals. The resort of *Hochstubai*, on the Stubai glacier, has four lifts that are always open plus many indoor swimming pools; it's easily reached via the Brenner motorway. Ski equipment is for rent at the top of the gondola year-round. Nearby, *Obergurgl*, Austria's highest village, offers excellent skiing, and is the take-off point for more year-round glacier skiing at *Hochgurgl*. Horse-drawn sleigh rides are available. Contact the **tourist office** for information in Sölden [Tel. (05254) 2212] or in Obergurgl [Tel. (05256) 0258].

KITZBÜHEL AREA

The *Kitzbühel Alps* have miles of cross-country and downhill ski trails, ice-skating, and indoor swimming pools. The town of *Kitzbühel*, a very chic winter sports center, still preserves its small walled-town atmosphere. Like other towns in the area, many of its houses are often graced with exterior paintings. Over fifty ski runs serve the area; you can choose between trams, chair lifts, cross-country trails, and night skiing. Ski kindergarten is available for children ages 2 1/2 to 5 and ski school for those 5 and over. Visit in summer months for superb hiking amidst alpine wildflowers and breathtaking vistas. Kitzbühel is lively (but expensive) at Christmas with an annual Christmas market and holiday festivities. Call the **tourist office** for details [Tel. (05356) 2155]. Three miles south of town is the **Kitzbühel-Aurach Game Park,** where visitors can see stags, deer, Tibetan yaks, foxes, alpine ibex, marmots, and a variety of aquatic animals. Fee. Daily 9 AM to dusk.

IMST AND LANDECK

Imst, a small market town, is known for its **Schemenlaufen,** a masked procession at Fasching, where cowbells ring continuously. The **Imst Museum** contains examples of the beautifully carved masks of both grotesque and handsome characters.

Landeck is famous for its **Christmas spectacle** where bonfires are lit atop cliffs and mountains surrounding the town, and huge pieces of burning pine-tar-covered wooden wheels are rolled down the cliffs to the valley below. It is an ancient and thrilling rite, and as the burning wheels race down the mountain side, village boys and girls carrying torches ski down in an attempt to beat the fireballs. Landeck's neighboring Tirolean villages are very pretty and worth a visit.

THE ARLBERG REGION

This mountainous region is in both the Tirol and Vorarlberg provinces, linked by the Arlberg pass. The 8-mile Arlberg tunnel, open summer and winter, charges a toll.

Arlberg is one of the world's most famous ski centers, as it was here that Hannes Schneider perfected the modern way to ski. *St. Anton am Arlberg* (in Tirol) is a haunt for high-society skiers, and its slopes are good for all abilities. The local **museum** shows the history of skiing. Summers are tranquil with meadows that overflow with alpine wildflowers, playgrounds, miniature golf, open-air chess, and curling. Take an aerial cable car to the top of **Valluga** for superb views of the Alps. Other towns such as *Stuben, Zürs,* and *Lech* also offer excellent skiing, and Lech has a children's mountain-climbing course in summer. All resorts have ski schools for children ages 5 and up and child care (called *Kindergarten*) for children ages 2 and older.

VORARLBERG

The tiny province of Vorarlberg, adjacent to the Swiss border at the western edge of Austria, is also filled with great winter skiing and robust open-air summertime pursuits such as walking and hiking.

Bregenz, its government seat, overlooks Bodensee (Lake Constance). The newer part of town near the lakeshore bustles with vacationers and features a flower-filled promenade, a jetty along the shore, and many recreational opportunities. The quieter old town has narrow, cobblestone streets worth exploring. A **music festival** held for 4 weeks in July and August takes place on a floating stage; concertgoers watch from the shore. Take the **Pfänderbahn** funicular ride from the center of town up to the summit of **Pfänder Mountain** for an international view of Austria, Germany, and Switzerland. Fee. Open year-round, except Nov. 1–15. Right next to the cable-car mountain station is the **Alpenwildpark Pfänder** where alpine ibex, stags, wild boars, and small animals are in enclosures. There is also a children's playground and nature study path. Free. Open daily year-round.

The **Bregenzerwald region** is as beautiful in summer as it is in winter, with glorious wooded walks, cow-filled pastures, and quaint villages where residents still dress in traditional costumes. It is a popular destination for family ski vacations because the slopes satisfy beginners as well as experienced skiers.

Explore the medieval city of *Feldkirch,* south of Bregenz, and its 12th-century castle, the **Schattenberg,** which towers over the town.

Inside the castle-fortress you'll find a museum and restaurant; the platform of the keep offers a breathtaking view. Displays of folk dancing in traditional costumes and concerts take place here during the summer months. Hiking trails are plentiful, and there is swimming, horseback riding, and many other recreational opportunities in this picturesque town at the foot of the Alps. Above the city, on the slopes of the Ardetzenberg, the **Feldkirch Game Park** has deer, mountain goats, marmots, wild boar, snow rabbits, and mouflons. Free. Open year-round.

CARINTHIA

Carinthia is a lake-filled province surrounded by high mountain peaks. *Friesach,* an important market town since the 11th century, has three ruined castles, many old churches, and the remains of fortifications with water-filled moats still in place. In the Middle Ages, huge tournaments were held in one of its castles with hundreds of knights competing.

KLANGENFURT AND ENVIRONS

Klangenfurt, founded in the 12th century, is the capital of Carinthia. The town's emblem is a dragon fountain that sits in the old part of town in Neuer Platz. The **Landesmuseum** has a broad collection of folk costumes, period folk furnishings, prehistoric collections, natural history, and a mosaic floor from nearby Roman excavations. Museumgasse 2. Tues.–Sat. 9–4, Sun. 10–1.

Minimundus has over 150 models in miniature at a scale of 1/25. It's loaded with perfect copies of the world's most famous buildings and structures, such as the Eiffel Tower and the Kremlin. Model ships crowd a tiny harbor, and a miniature train runs throughout this little world. Fee. On the Wörthersee, Villacherstr. 241. May–Sept. Tel. (04222) 21194. The **Klangenfurt Reptile Zoo,** next to Minimundus, has over 300 animals from all over the world, including cobras, mambas, pythons, and tortoises. Fee. Daily 9 AM to dusk. Take a **boat ride** around the Wörthersee; many of the boats have restaurants on board. For more information contact Wörthersee und Lendkanal-Schiffahrt, St. Veiter Str. 31 (Tel. (0463) 21155).

Hochosterwitz Castle, near Klangenfurt, is perhaps Austria's most beautiful castle; it claims to be Walt Disney's inspiration for the castle in the tale of *Snow White and the Seven Dwarfs.* Perched atop a steep hill, it was protected by more than twelve arched-tower gateways and drawbridges, all of which you walk through on your way up. View the castle's armor and historical collections, and have a bite to eat at the terrace restaurant while enjoying views of the countryside. Each June, the castle stages a medieval knight's tournament. May–Oct. 9–6. Tel. (04213) 2020 or 2010.

Thermal springs warm the waters of **Wörthersee,** a picturesque lake that small steamers crisscross during summer months. A popular summer resort, little towns rest along its shore, offering the spectrum of recreational activities. In winter, the frozen parts of the lake are made available for ice-skating.

The **Riehl Puppenmuseum** in **Winklern,** near Villach, is filled with the handmade dolls of the late Elli Riehl. Over 600 dolls are on display, each one different and lovingly created with local farm children as inspiration. In the Berger House. Daily Apr.–May 2–6; June–mid.-Sept. 9–12 and 2–6; mid-Sept–mid Oct. 2–6. Tel. (04248) 2395. Forty kilometers northwest of Villach is **Spittal an der Drau,** whose castle, **Schloss Porcia,** stands in a lush park in the center of town. Nearby is lake **Millstättersee,** surrounded by lovely towns with water-sports activities in the summer.

The **Lieser-Malta region** prides itself on being the family center of Carinthia, with fifteen hotels that cater to families with young children. Older kids can rock climb, canoe, river raft, and hike. Once a week in the summer, a hay wagon takes riders up to alpine pastures for a meal served by costumed "dairymaids." The trip leaves from **Rennweg.**

The **Lavanttal Valley** Cider Trail is dotted with little farms where you can help with cider pressing. Your reward is a cider certificate and a bottle of freshly pressed juice. Throughout this area are many farmhouse inns that welcome overnight guests.

10

Belgium

Belgium may often be overlooked by those visiting Europe, but you'll find that the country offers children a special welcome. Brussels' Children's Museum is one of the best of its kind, and the vast Antwerp Zoo sets the standard for zoos worldwide. In coastal resort towns such as De Panne, wind-driven sail-carts speed kids along the sand. Elaborate playgrounds are an important part of most parks and tourist facilities, and some of the finest puppet theaters as well as elaborate puppet operas are found in cities such as Bruges, Ghent, and Brussels. Windmills, canalboat rides, nature walks, carillon bell concerts, and colorful festivals, such as Ypres' Cat Festival, with its parade of giant cats, abound throughout the country. And, Belgium is small enough so you can get to all of its regions in just a few hours.

Dutch (often called Flemish) is spoken in the northern half of the country. French (often called Walloon) is spoken in the south. Metropolitan Brussels uses both languages. There is a small German-speaking area along the eastern border, and English is commonly spoken by those who come into regular contact with travelers.

Bon Voyage! Goede Reis!

Preparing Your Kids: Art

Painters such as Hieronymus Bosch, Pieter Bruegel the Elder, Pieter Bruegel the Younger, James Ensor, René Magritte, Hans Memling, Peter Paul Rubens, and Jan Van Eyck played an important role in the history and development of Western art and feature prominently in

Belgium's museums. Your library should carry books with photographs of their works.

Wha'd'ya Wanna Do?

Belgium's tourist office can fill your mailbox with a wide variety of booklets and brochures:

BELGIAN NATIONAL TOURIST OFFICES
   U.S.A.–New York: Belgian National Tourist Office, 745 Fifth Ave., New York, NY 10151. Tel. 212-758-8130.
   Canada–Montreal: Belgian National Tourist Office, P.O. Box 760, Succursale NDG, Montreal, Quebec 44A 352. Tel. 514-843-9028.

Bell ringing is a much-practiced art, and Belgium is famous for its **carillons,** which are sets of bells that have been chromatically tuned and readied to play musical works. Many cities, particularly Mechelen, have carillon concerts throughout the summer; a few have concerts year-round. Other popular carillons are in Antwerp, Bruges, Ghent, and Leuven. We have indicated performance information in the appropriate cities.
   Bicycles can be rented from nearly 61 railway stations throughout the country. Bikes can be returned to any of 148 stations along your route. The country is flat, and clearly marked bike paths are found throughout. When there are two paths along a street, the outer one is for motorbikes and bicycles, and the inner path is for pedestrians.
   Belgium's **Carnival** in February is world famous in Binche, but the cities of Mons, Tournai, Malmedy, Stavelot, Hasselt, Aalst, and Maaseik are among the many others with wild and colorful parades and antics. Diest has a children's carnival parade.

Lights Out! Special Belgian Accommodations

There is a good range of **villas, apartments,** and **bungalows** available for rent, particularly along the coast. The Belgian Tourist Office has a list of areas and rental agents. Local tourist offices can supply names and addresses, too.
   Hotels are expensive in Belgium. You can make reservations for hotel rooms, free of charge, through the Belgian Tourist Reservation Office, PB 41, 1000 Brussels 23 [Tel. (02)2305029]. We list a few hotels or apartment hotels in Brussels that are located near parks or have special amenities for families, such as kitchenettes or swimming pools.
   Family **hostels** are found throughout Belgium. With 3-, 4-, and 6-bedded rooms, they offer simple accommodations to families on a

budget. The tourist office can provide you with a listing, and we have listed several in Brussels.

Camping is well-organized throughout the country. The national tourist office can send you their "Camping Guide," which has a map and an extensive listing of campsites. Campgrounds come in four categories according to facilities, comfort, and quality, and some have bungalows for rent. It is forbidden to camp anywhere except official sites.

Getting Around

If you are traveling by **car,** you can use your American or Canadian driver's license in Belgium, but be sure to have an insurance green card with you at all times. Road signs can be in both Flemish and French. Express highways exist throughout the country. Children under 12 are not allowed in the front seats, and front passengers must wear seat belts at all times. You must carry a red emergency triangle in your car.

Belgium's network of **trains** is efficient and comprehensive. Both Eurail and Interail passes are valid on all Belgian trains and intercity buses. The Benelux-Tourrail Pass is good for 5 days travel in Belgium, the Netherlands, and Luxembourg during a 17-day period. A half-fare card for 1 month is also available.

Nuts and Bolts

Does anyone care what time it is? Belgium's shops are generally open from 9 AM, to 6 PM. Smaller stores often close between noon and 2 PM, but remain open in the evening until 8 PM. Many stores stay open until 9 PM one evening a week, usually on Friday. Banks are open weekdays from 9 AM to no later than 3 PM. Some banks are open on Saturday mornings.

National holidays: New Year's Day, Easter Monday, Labor Day (May 1), Ascension Day (the 6th Thursday following Easter), Whit Monday (the 7th Monday after Easter), Belgian National Day (July 21), August 15, All Saints Day (November 1), Armistice Day (November 11), and Christmas Day.

Can I have my allowance? The monetary unit is the *franc*, with notes issued in denominations of 100, 500, 1,000, and 5,000 francs. Coins are issued in 1, 5, 20, and 50 francs and 50 *centimes* (100 centimes = 1 franc; centimes are not commonly used due to inflation).

Telephones: Belgium's country code is 32. Direct-dial international calls can be made from any public phone, but you'll need many coins or a Telecard, purchased at any post office and many newsstands. If you call from a telephone and telegraph office (RTT), you can pay after you finish.

Useful nationwide phone numbers: The domestic operator is 1307; international operator is 1304 (within Europe) or 1322 (outside Europe); emergency medical service or fire is 100; police is 101.

Embassies and consulates: U.S. Embassy, 27 bd. du Régent, Brussels [Tel (02) 5133830]. Canada, 2, av. Telvurel, Brussels [Tel. (02) 7356040].

Let's Eat

Breakfast is usually continental, with coffee, tea, hot chocolate and rolls with butter and jam. Lunch is relatively light; if you want a quick bite, seek out the many snack bars and *fritures*. All restaurants serve excellent *potage du jour* (soup of the day). For a quick snack, *frites* (french fries) are at numerous outdoor stands, served in paper cones topped with mayonnaise or one of several other sauces ranging from tomato to curry.

Dinner is substantial, and a *menu pour enfants* or *kinder menu* (children's menu) is often available, usually offering chicken or burgers with applesauce and mashed potatoes or french fries. High chairs and booster seats are more commonly found in restaurants here than in the rest of Europe. *Boudin* (sausages) are delicious as are the little shrimps stuffed into hollowed-out tomatoes and served cold (*tomates aux crevettes*). *Biftec* (steak) is popular and always served with fries. Your kids will probably adore the *gaufres* or *wafels* (waffles baked in front of you in cast-iron molds in street stalls). *Brusselse wafels* are served with sugar, fresh cream, and fruit. Crêpes can be purchased from sidewalk stands, as can *glace* (ice cream). Belgian chocolates are among the best in the world.

Formula and Baby Food, Diapers and Baby Gear

See the chapter on the Netherlands for more information on Dutch translations, and France for more detailed information on French translations. Disposable diapers are readily available, and Pampers is a very common brand; buy them in supermarkets, grocery stores, or pharmacies. Baby food is available in pharmacies and some large supermarkets; Bambix is a popular brand. Cribs are readily available in hotels. Request them when you make your reservation.

Sidewalk Talk

See France for French and the Netherlands for Dutch words and phrases.

The Lay of the Land

Belgium's sandy coastline faces the North Sea, while the soft rolling hills of the Ardennes lie at its other end. From the capital city Brussels, in the center, you can easily reach all parts of the country in a few hours. The famous cities of Bruges, Ghent, and Antwerp are no more than an hour away.

BRUSSELS

Brussels, a town that loves to eat, has restaurants and sidewalk cafes everywhere. The world capital for the sinuous Art Nouveau style, the city displays graceful curved ornamentation and flowery details on many of its buildings. Brussels is a bilingual city, with street signs, menus, posters, and advertisements in both French and Dutch. "What's On," available at the tourist office, lists activities and events around the city. Their "Brussels' Guide and Map" is also helpful. "What's On" is also available bound into the English magazine, The Bulletin, at newsstands. The **National Tourist Information Office** is on Rue Marché aux Herbes (near the Grand' Place) (Tel. 5123030). They will make hotel reservations for you anywhere in Belgium. **Brussels' tourist office** is in the town hall on the Grand' Place. Brussels' **telephone area code** is 02.

The Lay of the City

A heart-shaped boulevard encloses the city's central district, with the railroad stations Nord and Midi at either end. The boulevard's name changes every few blocks; to make it easy, locals call it the Petite Ceinture (little belt). The Grand' Place (square) is at the heart of the central city.

Brussels' fast and efficient subway system is worth riding just to see the exceptional artworks that grace its stations. In 1969, when the system was built, 2 percent of the budget was set aside for public art; today over one-half of the stations possess murals, paintings, or sculpture, many by artists of international stature. Pick up a leaflet on the subject at the tourist office.

Where to Stay

HOTELS

The Hotel Stéphanie has an indoor pool, and children under 16 can stay free in their parents' room. 91-93, av. Louise. Tel. 5390240 or from U.S. 800-448-8355. **Deluxe.**

At the *Sofitel Hotel,* children stay free on weekends between July 1 and Aug. 31 and Dec. 23 through Jan. 6. The second room for up to three kids is free. There is no age limit on children. Avenue Toison D'Or 40. Book well in advance. Tel. from U.S. 800-221-4542. **Deluxe.**

The futuristic *Arcade Stephanie* has an indoor pool and is near parks. 91, av. Louise. Tel. 5388060. **Expensive.**

The *Marie-José* is a 5-minute walk from the Parc de Bruxelles. rue du Commerce 73. Tel. 5120842. **Moderate.**

The *Hôtel-Résidence Manos* has triple and quadruple apartments with kitchenettes. 100, Chaussée Charleroi. Tel. 5379682. **Moderate.**

The *Arcade Sainte-Catherine* is a real find, with a children's play area downstairs and triple and quadruple rooms made up by pulling down upper bunks fitted into the wall. Near the Grand' Place. Place Ste. Catherine. Tel. 5137620. **Inexpensive.**

FAMILY HOSTELS

Two of the city's youth hostels are among the nicest in Europe and accommodate families in triple, quadruple, or six-bedded rooms. The prices are rock bottom and include breakfast. Both of the following can be crowded during the summer, so reserve in advance: Jacques Brel International Accommodations Center (they also have high chairs and cribs upon request, a cafeteria, and a snack bar), 30, rue de la Sablonnière, Place des Barricades (Tel. 2180187); The J. H. Bruegel (near the Grand' Place with a restaurant), 2 rue St. Esprit (Tel. 5110436).

CAMPGROUNDS

There are no campgrounds in Brussels' metropolitan area.

Detour! What to See and Do

AROUND THE GRAND' PLACE

The ornate and gilded 17th-century **Grand' Place** is truly one of Europe's most breathtaking squares. Traffic is not allowed in the square. A flower market is held daily and a bird market is held on Sunday morning. The square is illuminated with colored lights on weekends and Tuesday nights in summer. The tangle of carefully preserved streets surrounding the Grand' Place, known as the **L'llot Sacré,** are filled with souvenir shops, boutiques, and restaurants.

Trouble with toilet training? **Manneken Pis** will provide a role model your kids will never forget. Brussels' beloved statue and local hero stands on the southwestern corner of the Grand' Place on the rue de l'Etuve. During certain holidays he is dressed in special uniforms. Conflicting legends tell why the statue was created in such an indiscreet pose: One says that the statue honors a clever little boy who saved the city by extinguishing a threatening fire; the other has it that the king promised to build a statue of his lost son in the precise position in which he was found. His female counterpart, installed in 1987 at the end of Impasse de la Fidelité, is called **Jeanneke-Pis.** All donations she earns go to fighting cancer and AIDS.

The King's House contains the **Musée Communal,** with a collection relating to Brussels' history as well as the various costumes worn by the Manneken Pis. You'll see the attire he wore when dressed as a soccer player, Mickey Mouse, an Arab sheik, and many more. Fee. Grand' Place. Apr.–Sept. Mon.–Fri. 10–5, weekends 10–1; Oct.–Mar. Mon.–Fri. 10–4, weekends 10–12. Tel. 5112742.

Just One Look: Museums

The **Cinquantenaire** is a huge park containing several museums. Stroll through the history of the automobile in **Autoworld Brussels,** the largest collection of automobiles in Europe. Beautifully restored "old-timers" from 1886 to the 1970s are in its impressive collection. Fee. Palais Mondial, Parc du Cinquantenaire 11. Apr.–Sept. 10–6; rest of year 10–5. Tel. 7364165. Nearby, the **Musée Royal de l'Armée et del Histoire Militaire** displays uniforms, cannons, tanks, warplanes, and other relics of military history. Free. Parc du Cinquantenaire. Tues.–Sun. 9–12 and 1–4:45 in summer; until 4 in winter.

The **Historium Wax Museum** relates 2,000 years of Belgium's history in wax. Figures are placed in elaborate settings with visual tricks and sound effects. Fee. Anspach Center, Place de la Monnaie. Daily 10–6. Tel. 2176023.

The name **Musée d'Art Ancien** sounds deadly for kids, right? Not necessarily. This museum contains a magnificent collection of the works of Pieter Bruegel the Elder, a man who painted the daily life of humble people, often with an earthy sense of humor and irreverence that even the most "bored" 14-year-old can enjoy. His son, Pieter Bruegel the Younger, has paintings here, too. Many other Flemish masterworks by Rubens, Frans Hals, and such are hung in this excellent museum. Children will appreciate the wildly surrealistic *Temptation of St. Anthony* by 15th-century Hieronymus Bosch. The Musée d'Art Ancien is housed in the same complex as the Musée de l'Art Moderne. Free. Rue de la Régence 3. Tues.–Sun. 10–12 and 1–5. Tel. 5139630. **Musée de l'Art Moderne** picks up where the Musée d'Art Ancien leaves off. Built below the museum plaza, it showcases 19th- and 20th-century works. Head straight for the paintings by René Magritte, the 20th-century Belgian surrealist who has been likened to a painterly Lewis Carroll. His paintings delight children with odd juxtapositions of scenes and objects. Free. Place Royal 1–2. Hours and telephone same as those for Ancient Art Museum.

At the **Musée des Enfants** the signs read, "Please do touch!" In a museum designed just for them, children can milk a pretend Belgian cow (with water instead of milk flowing from its udders), develop pictures in a dark room, or make wheat into flour. A real tractor and trolley car wait for children to clamber aboard and work the buttons and levers to "make it go." Kids can dress in a dentist's white coat complete with head mirror and practice dental work with real dental tools. There is a library of children's books, a theater, and live animals. Fee. 32, rue de Benbosch or rue du Bourgemestre 15. Mon., Tues., Thurs., Fri. 9:30–11:45 and 1:30–3:30; Wed., Sat., and Sun. 2:30–5. Closed August.

The **Musée Instrumental**'s musical instrument collection is so large (over 5,000 rare instruments from around the world) that only 1,200 instruments are on display at any one time. The private collection of Adolphe Sax, the Belgian who invented the saxophone, is here. On alternating Wednesdays, concerts are held in the concert hall using instruments from the museum's collection. Free. In the Royal Conservatory of Music, rue de la Regence. Tues., Thurs., Sat. 2–4; Sun. 10:30–12:30; and Wed. 6–8. Tel. 5120848.

It's a small world in the **Musée International de la Figurine Historique,** where thousands of elaborately costumed tiny people are placed in dioramas, illustrating different events in world history, particularly Belgian. Free. In the Jette suburb north of downtown, rue J. Tibackx 14, in the Abbot's House. Tues.–Fri. 10–12 and 2–4. Tel. 4790052.

Stamp collectors may want to visit the **Museum of Posts and Telecommunications** and pore over their extensive collection. 40, pl. du Grand Sablon. Tues.–Sat. 10–4, Sun. 10–12:30.

THE ATOMIUM AND BRUPARK

The **Atomium,** which resembles a giant metal molecule, was built for the 1958 Brussels World's Fair. You can actually enter it and ride escalators to lookout points, a restaurant, and exhibits in its "atomic balls." Plan to make a day of it when you visit the Atomium as there are other kid-pleasing sights next door in Brupark. Square Atomium, bd. du Centenaire. Tel. 4770977.

Brupark's **Oceadium** is the biggest water leisure center in Belgium with indoor and outdoor swimming pools, wave pools, water slides, and a "beach" (Tel. 4784320). **The Village** is a replica of Old Brussels with restaurants and shops (Tel. 4770377). **Imax Cinema** has an enormous wraparound screen which shows space adventures (Tel. 4786161). Call each for hours. **Mini-Europe** is a charming miniature village where you can visit twelve European countries in just a few hours. The Leaning Tower of Pisa, Acropolis, Gondoliers of Venice, Arc de Triomphe, and even the Grand' Place of Brussels are just a few. Many roads, seaports, and airports have animated models in their 1/25 scale. Fee. Apr.–Dec. daily 10–6; July and Aug. Mon.–Fri. 10–8, weekends 10–9. Tel. 4780550.

Where the Sidewalk Ends: Zoos and More Parks

Bois de la Cambre forms the northern extension of the Forest of Soignes. Laid out in the last century, it contains a large lake, a playground, and broad green spaces crossed by many walking paths. **Chalet Robinson** is an island in the lake that is accessible by ferry. Once there, rent rowboats or pedal boats or enjoy the puppet theater, rides, or games for children. Fee. Daily Apr.–Nov. 15; weekends rest of year. Tel. 3743013. The **Fôret de la Soignes,** an immense wooded park that extends all the way to Waterloo, has boating lakes, walking and riding trails, restaurants, racetracks, and more. **Parc de Bruxelles** is in the center of the city next to the Royal Palace with fountain-filled lakes and beautiful walkways.

Performing Arts and Special Events

The **Toone Puppet Theater** has performances, a museum of Belgium's folklore, and puppets from the past. Its puppet theater performs Tues.–Fri. at 8:30 PM and Sat. at 4 PM. Museum: daily from noon. 21, Petite rue des Bouchers. Tel. 5117137 or 5135486. If your kids are suffering from movie withdrawals, head to the **Cinema Museum,** where silent movies are often shown with musical accompaniment. 9, rue Baron Horta. Tel. 5134155. Summertime **outdoor concerts** are held in Parc de Bruxelles, the Grand' Place, and Place de la Monnai. Check with the tourist office for details.

People in ornate historical costumes lead the parade during the **Ommegang Pageant** in early July. Acrobats, dancers, and other performers add to the fun; the festival culminates in a human chess game in the Grand' Place.

NEAR BRUSSELS

Dr. Livingstone, I presume? On display at the **Koninklijk Museum voor Midden Africa** are maps and mementoes from Stanley's and Livingstone's jungle expeditions as well as masks, canoes, costumes, and dwellings from the former Belgian Congo, now Zaire. Free. 13 Leuvensesteenweg, in the outskirts of the city on the grounds of Tervuren park. Mid-Mar.–mid.-Oct. 9–5:30; until 4:30 rest of the year.

Need a break from the Flemish masters? Head to **Walibi and Aqualibi,** an amusement and water-park complex with absolutely no educational value. Excursions on The Rapido and through The Palace of Ali Baba, and the parrot, sea lion, magic, and doll shows will thoroughly entertain your kids. Costumed characters wander about, and there are plenty of kiddie rides for little ones. Be sure to bring your swimsuits for Aqualibi, with its waterslides, wavepool, and crazy river. Fee. 22 km. from Brussels; take E411 to exit 6 for Wavre. Rue Joseph Deschamps 9, Limal. Apr.–Sept. 10–6. Tel. (010) 414466.

We know families who have made a special trip to the town of **Silly,** southwest of Brussels between Ath and Enghien, just to get a postcard and a postmark. Sound silly?

To get the most from **Waterloo,** be sure to prepare your children ahead of time by filling them in on its historical significance, or it will look only like a green pasture with a few displays. Climb the 226 steps up the **Lion Mound** for a view of the entire battlefield. At the foot of the lion's mount stands the huge circular painting *Panorama of the Battle,* painted at the end of the 19th century. A circular viewing platform helps you take it all in, and model soldiers, horses, and cannons make it a bit more realistic. A reenactment of the battle takes place on June 15 with 1,000 volunteers. The "battle" ends with a sound and light show and a fireworks display. Daily 9:30–6. Tel. 3843139.

BINCHE AND ENVIRONS

Binche is famous for its **Mardi Gras** in February, an annual event that starts on Sunday and culminates on Shrove Tuesday with the **March of the Gilles.** Men dress in gold, black, white, and red suits with big bells around their waists and lavishly plumed headdresses nearly 3 feet tall. These costumes have been worn for Carnival since the 14th century. The parades start on Sunday and continue practically nonstop with brass bands providing lively entertainment. It gets a bit rough as participants throw inflated sheep's bladders and oranges at the crowds as they pass. Wear a crazy hat or red nose; you may be skipped by those tossing the oranges and bladders. Yes, the shopkeepers board up their windows for the event. Contact the tourist office in the Hôtel de Ville, Grand Place [Tel. (064) 333721] for details.

If you miss the carnival, you can see some of the costumes at the fascinating **Musée International du Carnaval et du Masque.** In addition to the lively local attire, the museum has assembled costumes, masks, and accessories from carnivals throughout western and eastern Europe as well as Latin America, Africa, Asia, and Oceania.

Mannequins and dolls dressed in bizarre costumes, crazy hats, scary masks, and puppets dripping with ornamentation are presented. A 20-minute audio-visual presentation shows you more. Your children will never be at a loss for Halloween costumes after you visit this fascinating museum. Fee. Rue de l'Eglise. Apr.–Nov. 15 Mon.–Thurs. 10–12 and 2–6; Feb.–Mar. Sun. 2–6. Tel. (064) 335741.

Northwest of Binche between Mons and Tournai is the **Beloeil Estate,** with a castle set in a beautiful park. The castle contains a collection of objets d'art ranging from the 15th to the 19th century. Its enormous grounds are laid out in a formal French manner with flower-bordered paths and impressive hedgerows. Children will head straight to **Minibel,** a magical reproduction of Belgium's most interesting architectural treasures and curiosities done at 1/25 scale. A train ride, theater, and restaurant make it a day. Fees. rue du Château 11, Beloeil. Apr.–Oct. 10–7. Tel. (069) 689426 or 689655.

ANTWERP

Legend has it that Antwerp got its name from the giant Druon Antigon, who charged a stiff toll from boatsmen who passed his castle on the river Scheld. He cut off a hand if they didn't pay. Finally a Roman soldier killed the giant, cut off his hand, and threw it in the river. The word *hand-werpen* means "throwing of the hand!" Known as the diamond capital of the world, the city is a gem in itself. Children especially enjoy its world-famous zoo. The **tourist office** is in front of the central station on Koningin Astridplein (Tel. 2330570) and at Grote Markt 15 (Tel. 2320103). Antwerp's **telephone area code** is 03.

Detour! What to See and Do

The **Het Wiel Museum** has all kinds of things related to the wheel—old bicycles, go-carts, carriages, motorcycles, and odd rolling curiosities. Fee. Hopland 17. Wed., Fri., Sat. 10–5 and Sun. 9:30–2:30. Tel. 2326274.

While the world's largest collection of paintings by Antwerp resident Peter Paul Rubens in the **Koninklijk Museum voor Schone Kunsten** may not top your kids' list of what to see, you can pay a visit to this outstanding museum with the promise of taking them to the famous Antwerp zoo afterward. Many other world-class works by the more modern Belgian James Ensor as well as paintings by the Flemish masters and other European greats are on display. Choose what you want to see carefully to get the most out of this bountiful museum. Leopold de Waelplaats. Tues.–Sun. 10–5.

The **Museum of Folklore** contains an interesting collection of folk art, including puppets and old magic implements. Fee. Gilde-kamersstraat 2–6, Tues.–Sun. 10–5. Tel. 2311690, ext. 383.

With the third-largest port in the world, Antwerp's highly regarded **Nationaal Scheepvaartmuseum** awaits those with an interest in the sea. Precise and detailed model boats, paintings, and ship's equipment are on display in the **Steen,** the city's 10th-century castle. Next to the museum is the barge *Lauranda.* Fee. Steenplein 1. Daily 10–5. Tel. 2320850

The **Plantin-Moretus Museum** is a 16th-century town house housing a lively museum on the history of printing. You can view the living quarters of the family that lived and worked there as well as priceless manuscripts, old presses, and type. This workshop is where the world's first atlas and newspaper were created, in addition to scores of important translations and classics. Fee. 22 Vrijdagmarkt. Daily 10–5. Tel. 2330294.

Your children will enjoy the period furnishings and household objects scattered throughout Rubens' home, while a visit to the **Rubenshuis** will engage you with exquisite paintings. It can be crowded during July and August. Fee; under 12 free. Wapperq. Daily 10–5.

Where the Sidewalk Ends: Zoos and Parks

The famous **Antwerp Zoo** is one of Europe's largest and best. Its broad collection of animals, aquarium, planetarium, dolphin shows, and a museum of natural history make it a full-day excursion. Be sure to see the Nocturama designed for viewing nocturnal creatures, and the reptile building with its tropical storm. Many animal displays lack moats and bars, and have ingenious trick "fences," such as blasts of cold air, to keep the reptiles in and dramatically changing light to keep the birds from flying away. A number of the zoo's original buildings, such as Greek and Egyptian temples, still stand; the zoo's founding fathers believed that the animals should be housed in architecture evocative of their native countries. You can take a tour of the zoo "behind the scenes" between October and March to see how the animals are fed and cared for. Fee. Koningin Astridplein 24. Summer 8:30–6:30; until 5:30 in winter. Tel. 2311640.

Antwerp Miniature City was under construction at the time of this writing and should have many more attractions by now, in addition to its pond with remote-controlled boats, steam train rides, and a fun children's playground. Fee. Hanger 15, Cockerillkaai (opposite Scheldstraat). Daily 10–5.

The **Rivierenhof Provincial Park,** with the magnificent **Sterckshof Castle and Museum,** is at **Deurne** on the edge of Antwerp's metropolitan area. The castle houses a Museum of Arts and Crafts, and the park has boating lakes, a maze, aviaries, children's play areas, a children's farm, miniature golf, a fairy-tale house, and more. Turnhoutsebaan 246. Tel. 3245170.

NEAR ANTWERP

Mechelen, between Brussels and Antwerp, is known as Belgium's city of the carillon, boasting a carillon school and a number of **performing carillons.** Climb the tower of the Cathedral of St. Rombout and notice the stained glass and paintings by Van Dyck on the way. Climbs can be made at 2:15 and 7 on weekends. Bell recitals are held every Monday and Saturday at 12 and 2, Sunday at 11:30, and Monday evenings at 8:30. Other carillon concerts are held at the Busleyden House and Our Lady over-the Dijle. Contact the **tourist office** in the town hall, Naamsestraat 1A [Tel. (015) 211873] for details. **Horse-drawn carriages** leave from the tourist office for tours of the city.

The **Center for Toys and Folklore** has a historic survey of games and toys with plenty of materials for children and adults to play with. Fee. Nekkerspoelstraat 21. Tues.–Sun. 2–5. Tel. (015) 200386. Take a canalboat ride from Mechelen to Planckendael, where the Antwerp zoo has established a **breeding station** for rare and endangered animal species. An excellent playground will keep young ones entertained. For information, call (015) 413268.

TURNHOUT

Fans of old maid, fish, hearts, and other card games will appreciate a visit to the **National Museum van de Speelkaart** in the city of Turnhout, east of Antwerp. It contains rare examples of early playing cards, including those painted by hand and printed on wood blocks before the invention of the printing press. Early machines on which the first playing cards were made are on display. The city itself prints more playing cards than any other city in the world. Fee. Begijnenstraat 28. Sun. 10–12 and 2–5; Wed. and Fri. 2–5. Tel. (014) 415621. The town's **tourist office** is in the town hall, Grand Place 1 [Tel. (014) 418941]. Turnhout's extensive town park has a swimming pool, miniature golf, a lake, and a small zoo.

Bobbejaanland is a first-rate amusement park with a roller coaster, stage shows, cowboy town, cowboy and Indian museum, carousels, carnival rides, train, motorboats, puppet theater, two water rides, and a time tunnel. One price entitles you to unlimited rides. Olensteenweg 45, Lichtaart-Kasterlee (not too far from Turnhout). Daily May–Sept. and Easter week. Tel. (014) 557815.

GHENT

The medieval manufacturing city of Ghent had its heyday in the 14th century but retains much of its charm to this day. **Horse-drawn cabs** can be hired to tour the town, and 35-minute **canalboat excursions** will take you sightseeing. A town of **puppet shows,** Ghent boasts eight different marionette theater companies performing throughout the year. Ask the tourist office for a list of names and addresses and try to catch one of the frequent performances. The city's historic buildings are illuminated from sunset to midnight from May through September; walk through the old section of town after dark to experience this truly magical spectacle. During the rest of the year they are illuminated on Friday and Saturday nights. Its **tourist office** is in the crypt of the town hall on Botermarkt (Tel. 253641). Ghent's **telephone area code** is 091.

The **Gravensteen Castle** is a medieval fortress with walls 6 feet thick. Climb the ramparts for a view of the rooftops of Ghent and be prepared to linger over the extensive medieval torture museum, simultaneously fascinating and repelling to children. Fee. Better behave; guides will point out the *oubliettes*, or holes, in the floor used for getting rid of troublemakers. Daily Apr.–Sept. 9–6:15; Oct.–Mar. until 4:15. Tel. 259306. There are several **Historical theme banquets** with entertainment: The Bruegel offers an enormous 13th-century feast; the Medieval has singing troubadours, jesters, and magicians; the Belle Epoque has music and dance from the turn of the century; and Dances through the Centuries has music and dance from many eras. For more information, call 218615 or 239745. **Zoologisch Park Gent** has typical zoo animals, a playground, and an outdoor cafe. Fee. Twaalf Roeden 10. Apr.–Oct. 10–7. Tel. 530790.

BRUGES AND ENVIRONS

Bruges, the beautiful city of the past, has somehow been untouched by "progress" since the Middle Ages. Peaceful canals with arched bridges and weeping willows, gabled houses, and narrow cobblestone streets speak of times past. From the 13th to the 15th century, Bruges was a thriving commercial center. When its river silted up, its economy declined, and it lay untouched; the way it looks today is largely as it looked centuries ago. Bruges, along with Siena, Italy, has the strictest building regulations of any city in Europe. The best way to enjoy its many medieval subtleties is to walk. If young feet get tired, hire a **horse-drawn cab,** departing daily from the Burg or on Wednesdays from the Markt. The **tourist office,** at Burg 11 (Tel. 448686), has a schedule of local events called the "Agenda Brugge." Bruges' **telephone area code** is 050.

Don't miss the chance to take a **canalboat cruise** around Bruges. The 40-minute tours take you past swans and ducks, under arched bridges, and past medieval treasures. Guides speak English, French, German, and Flemish. Several touring companies operate, and all offer similar routes, prices, and service. The tourist office can provide you with departure points; many are near the Burg. Fee. Mar.–Nov.

At the town's center is the Markt, a square dominated by the 13th-century **Belfort.** Climb the belfry's 366-step narrow spiral staircase for a panorama of the city and all of Flanders, but go early in summer to avoid crowds. Its carillon bells (there are forty-seven of them) chime briefly every 15 minutes and play special hour-long concerts at midday on weekends, Wednesdays, and on many summer evenings. Fee for climb. Daily Mar.–Nov. 9:30–12:30 and 1:30–6; until 5 Oct.–Mar.

Be sure to visit one of the city's **windmills.** Three of them are off Langestraat on Kruisvest; you can visit the interior of St. Janshuys windmill. Fee. Daily May–Sept. 9:30–12 and 1–6. The **Marionette Theater** produces elaborate puppet operas June–Sept. Fee. Tickets are available at the theater or the tourist office, St.-Jacobstraat 36 (Tel. 334760). **Koningin Astridpark,** also popularly called Den Botanieken Hof, was the first city park of Bruges. Adjacent to it is a fun playground.

The city's amusement park complex, **Boudewijnpark,** has a brand-new Dolphinarium with performances, underwater viewing areas, and an educational exhibition. Other attractions include bumper cars, a ferris wheel, and all kinds of other rides, plus ice- and roller-skating, pony rides, skateboarding, animal shows, and an elaborate playground. Fee. A. De Baeckestraat 12. Tel. 382343.

The residents of the historic city of *Ypres,* southwest of Bruges, have a **Cat Festival and Parade** for which locals dress in cat suits and medieval costumes, while parades with floats and giant cats commemorate their beloved felines. The town's jester throws stuffed velvet cats from the town's belfry into the crowds below. Every even-numbered year on the second Sunday in May. Contact the **tourist office** for more information: Stadhuis, Grote Markt [Tel. (057) 202623].

THE BELGIAN COAST

With broad sandy beaches and shallow water, perfect for safe swimming for young ones, Belgium's coastal resorts are ideal for families. In July and August they have many children's activities and games, including miniature golf, horseback riding, windsurfing, pedal boats, pony and donkey rides, trampolines, and puppet shows. A tram service runs the entire length of the coast, and cars are not allowed behind the wide beach promenades. A few beaches do have crosscurrents, so be aware of the system of flags used on the beaches: Green means a lifeguard is on duty and swimming is safe; red means swimming is unsafe; and a yellow flag means swimming is risky but lifeguards are on duty. If you base yourselves here, you can make day trips to Bruges, Antwerp, Brussels, the Ardennes, and even Paris and Amsterdam. For information about renting holiday accommodations, ask for the brochure "The Belgian Coast" from the national tourist office.

De Panne has the widest beach on the Belgian coast, with a broad area of sand dunes and a nature reserve nearby. On the west side of the beach, older kids can rent a seat on a **wind-driven sail-cart** and go sailing along the sand. De Panne has several sand-yachting clubs: De Krab [Tel. (058) 411545], Oiseau Bleu [Tel. (058) 411236], and Sand-yachting [Tel. (058) 411206]. **Meli-Park** is a traditional leisure park in a natural woodland setting. It offers over thirty different rides and attractions such as a fairyland, animal park, parrot circus, ghost train, flying carpet, slides, funfair, maze, and a magic show. Fee, one price entitles you to all activities. De Pannelaan 68. Tel. (058) 412555. **Fireworks** are a regular summer feature along the promenade. *Oostduinkerke* has a huge beach and a large open-air saltwater swimming pool (heated!) in its middle. Sail-carts can be rented and horseback riding is popular. Playgrounds are scattered throughout the town.

Blankenberge is a lively resort with a long wide beach, amusement park, wildlife and nature reserve, donkey and pony rides, and the **Lustige Velodroom,** a huge outdoor wooden bicycle track to ride around next to the beach. The town explodes in a profusion of colorful blooms for the **International Festival of Flowers** on the last Sunday in August. Contact the **tourist office** at Stedelijke Sportdienst, A. Van Ackersquare 1 [Tel. (050) 415634].

LIMBURG PROVINCE

Limburg has one of the world's best open-air museums, **Provinciaal Openluchtmuseum Bokrijk,** in *Bokrijk,* between the cities of *Hasselt* and *Genk.* Village buildings and old farmhouses have been carefully reconstructed and filled with rustic peasant furniture and old kitchen implements. It is one of Europe's largest open-air museums, set in a vast nature reserve filled with marshes, ponds, heathery hillsides, and pine forests. Children will particularly enjoy the areas with medieval games and toys which they can play with. Restaurants and taverns re-create old-style feasts, or you can picnic. Fee. Apr.–mid-Oct. 10–6. Contact the **tourist office** at Domein Bokrijk, 3600 Genk [Tel. (011) 222958], for more information.

DINANT AND ENVIRONS

Many canoeing and kayaking tours on the rivers Meuse and Lesse begin around **Dinant.** Mountain biking is easy to arrange; the tourist office provides trail maps. The town's **amusement park** has modern attractions, the prehistoric caves of Monfat, and an adjacent hanging rock garden. **La Merveilleuse Cave** has delicate white stalactites and stalagmites and cascading waterfalls. Fee. Entrance on the left bank of the river Meuse, past the Dinant bridge. Apr.–Sept. Tel. (082) 222210. South of Dinant are the spectacular **Caves of Han-sur-Lesse.** Enter the caves by train; wander amongst highly colored formations through rooms with names such as the Mosque, Trophy, and the Dome, and leave via a boat ride on a subterranean river. There's a large playground as you exit. Above the hill sheltering the caves is the **Reserve for Animals,** a park with deer, boars, bears, bison, and wild horses. A safari bus escorts you through. Fee: A combined ticket is available for both caves and reserve. Both open Easter–Oct. 9:30–5, until 6 in July and Aug; Nov.–Easter 9:30–3:30. Closed Jan. and Feb. Tel. (084) 377212.

Twenty-eight kilometers from Dinant, **Namur** has many of the same attractions: caves, canoeing, kayaking, an amusement park, and mountaineering. In the **citadelle** above the town is a museum of weapons; there is also an amusement park with go-carts and miniature golf on the grounds. Take a cable car to it from Pied-du-Château Square. Horseback riding is widely available.

Annevoie has one of Europe's most beautiful water gardens. Fountains, cascades, canals, pools, waterfalls, and grottoes are found amidst green trees, statues, leafy arbors, and flowers. Ducks swim throughout the many waterways, while swallows and kingfishers dart above. Fee. In the Château d'Annevoie. Easter–Oct. 10–7.

Denmark

Legoland, Hans Christian Andersen's birthplace of Odense, and Copenhagen's magical amusement park, Tivoli Gardens, are the most popular Danish destinations for children and shouldn't be missed. Legoland celebrates the Danish invention most children have played with—the Lego block. Using 35 million of these plastic building bricks, the Danes have created an entire toyland with realistic models of the Taj Mahal and the Statue of Liberty. *Lego* comes from the Danish words for "play well," and your children most certainly will in Denmark.

The life story and legacy of Denmark's beloved storyteller Hans Christian Andersen is best portrayed in Odense. An awkward and nonconforming child, he was taunted by his peers and consequently quit school at age 11. To escape his loneliness, Hans delved into the world of puppets and created elaborate fantasy characters from his observations of the world. As in his tale of *The Ugly Duckling*, Andersen grew up to become one of Denmark's most honored citizens and has since delighted all of us with his marvelous tales. Odense has opened up his home to visitors, and its museum allows children to listen to Andersen's stories told in many languages on special telephones. Local children stage one of his fairy tales during the annual Hans Christian Andersen Festival.

Tivoli Gardens is the world's most dazzling amusement park; no "honky tonk" here, but a commedia dell'arte pantomime theater, twinkling lights, fireworks, acrobats, jugglers, marionettes, carousels, and fun-filled rides.

Do try to see some of the more humbler and rural parts of the country that Andersen loved so well. The haunting Viking territory of Jutland, the charming islands of Ærø and Funen filled with moated castles, great beaches, and thatched-roofed cottages where storks nest on chimney tops, all contrast greatly with the sleek and modern Scandinavian city. Follow Andersen's words, "To travel is to live." *God tur . . .* Have a great trip!

Preparing Your Children: Books

All children: Stories such as *The Tinderbox, Thumbelina, The Nightingale, The Princess and the Pea, The Snow Queen,* and *The Ugly Duckling* by Hans Christian Andersen.

Older children: *We Live in Denmark* by Ulla Andersen; *Take a Trip to Denmark* by Keith Lye.

Wha'd'ya Wanna Do?

Denmark's **national tourist offices** can provide touring maps, information on vacation cottages, camping, and farm holidays. Once in Denmark, local tourist offices, known as **turistbureauet,** have English-speaking staff who can book holiday homes and hotels or help plan activities such as caravanning by horse-drawn carriage, sailing on fjords, horseback riding, cycling, angling, wind surfing, canoeing, parachuting, and even holidays with your dog!

DANISH NATIONAL TOURIST OFFICES
  U.S.A.–New York: Danish National Tourist Office, 655 Third Avenue, New York, NY 10017. Tel. 212-949-2333.
  Canada–Toronto: Danish National Tourist Office, Box 115, Station N, Toronto, Ontario M8V, 3S4 Canada. Tel. 416-823-9620.

Throughout the country there are fascinating remnants of **Viking** civilization, such as large fortifications in Zealand's Trelleborg or Jutland's Fyrkat, the Viking boats in Roskilde, or the stone ships near Ålborg. Rollicking Viking festivals are staged every year in or around July in Frederikssund in Zealand and Jels in South Jutland.

Open-air museums in Copenhagen, Odense, Århus, and Hjerl Hede have reconstructed the surroundings of Danish life before the 20th century. **Stone Age communities** are unique to Denmark, especially the Lejre Center, outside of Roskilde, where prehistoric living conditions are simulated by people who have committed to live like Iron and Stone Age people. Children can join in and grind wheat berries, bake a simple cake over a fire, row a canoe in the lagoon, or chop logs using Iron Age axes.

Throughout Denmark there are recreation parks called **sommerlands** ("summer lands"), many with a **dyreparken** (zoo), a **dyrehaven** (deer park), and rides. Children's traffic parks are as integral to Danish amusement parks as they are to the Dutch; kids can even take a driving test and receive a driver's license at Legoland.

Refer to Copenhagen's introductory section on how to obtain the free brochure "Hei" with coupons for free admittance to kid's attractions throughout the country.

Lights Out! Special Danish Accommodations

Denmark has a wide choice of **vacation cottages, holiday homes,** and **apartments.** Prices range from $200 to $650 per week high-season. Request the brochure "Vacation Cottages in Denmark" from the national tourist office.

We have selected a few **hotels** in Copenhagen that are near parks, have a kitchen, or offer special amenities for families such as suites, connecting rooms, or apartments. Hotel prices in Copenhagen can be as much as 50 percent higher than the rest of Denmark. A chain of **family hotels** are found throughout the countryside. For a listing, write Danske Familie-Hoteller, Gormsgade 15, DK-7300 Jelling (Tel. 75872577).

Kro are charming stagecoach inns found in villages and are less expensive than hotels. Many include hearty meals. For a countrywide listing contact Dansk Kroferie, Horsens Tourist Office, Søndergade 31, DK-8700, Horsens (Tel. 75623544).

There are two ways to stay on a Danish **farm.** The national tourist office can send you information on what they call "farm holidays." These provide a guest room in a farmhouse where there are often animals and meals are eaten with your hosts. Rates are inexpensive; children under 3 receive 25 percent off, and those 4–11 receive a 75 percent discount. Their "self-catering country holidays" enable you to rent a separate cottage on a farm. Rates start at about $200 per week during the summer.

Throughout Denmark, there are very inexpensive **family hostels** (*vandrerhjem*) offering family rooms with two to six beds, a communal kitchen, and laundry facilities. Children under 2 stay free. Many are set in recreation areas, and children can meet youngsters from other countries. Membership cards are available from the American Youth Hostel National Office (see Chapter 2) or an International Youth Hostel Card can be obtained in Denmark. For a countrywide listing, request the brochure "Family Hostels" from the national tourist office.

Denmark has approximately 500 well-equipped **campgrounds** situated along its coastline, in rural areas, or on the outskirts of cities.

Campgrounds are officially classified from one to three stars, based on amenities. You should have a valid International Camping Carnet, or a Danish carnet, which you can buy at individual sites. It is possible to rent fully equipped trailers or cabins at many campsites; during peak season they are often rented by the week. Camping in unofficial sites is forbidden. For a list of sites request the pamphlet "Camping" from the national tourist office.

Getting Around

Car travelers need a valid driver's license. Seat belts are required for front-seat passengers; car seats are mandatory. Bridges connect many of the islands and are toll-free. Ferries on inland routes are also free; there is a small fare for interisland ferries. To drive from Denmark's northern to southern border takes about 4 hours.

If you intend to travel by **train** only in Denmark, the Danish State Railways (DSB) sells economical tickets for families traveling together; inquire at any Danish rail station. The Scanrail pass, valid for travel anywhere within Scandinavia, can be used from 4 to 14 days; children under 4 travel free, and those between 4 and 11 pay half-fare. Passes are available from travel agents or at major Danish rail stations.

Good **bicycle** paths and flat roads make Denmark an ideal place to cycle. You can rent bikes for about $5 a day at a number of places, including rail stations; local tourist offices can direct you. Bikes can be sent as baggage between most train and ferry stations.

Nuts and Bolts

Does anyone care what time it is? Stores are open weekdays 9 to 5:30, Fridays to 7 or 8 PM, and Saturdays until noon or 2 PM. On the first Saturday of each month, some shops remain open until 5 PM. Banks are open weekdays 9:30 to 4, Thursdays to 6 PM.

National holidays: New Year's Day, Easter, Common Prayer, Ascension Day, Whit Sunday, Constitution Day (June 5), Christmas Eve, and Christmas Day.

Can I have my allowance? The monetary unit in Denmark is the krone (KR), which consists of 100 øre. Bills come in 100, 50, and 30 krone. Coins come in 10, 5, and 1 krone and 25, 10, and 5 øre.

Telephones: The country code for Denmark is 45. Direct calls, including international calls, can be made from all telephone booths and post offices. For English information on how to use the phones, dial 0030. As of 1990, Denmark has a new system of eight-digit numbers; you must dial the whole number regardless of where you are calling from.

Useful nationwide phone numbers: Directory information is 0030; emergency is 000.

Embassies and consulates: U.S. Embassy, Dag Hammarskjölds Allé, Copenhagen (Tel. 31423144); Canadian Embassy, Kristen Bernikowsgade 1, Copenhagen (Tel. 33122299).

Let's Eat!

Meals are served generally at the same time as in the United States, and dinner is the main meal of the day. You'll find high chairs available in most restaurants. Dairy foods play a big role in the Danish diet, and fresh milk is readily available. For breakfast your children can choose from many varieties of flavorful yogurts and delicious cereals, such as *havregryn* (oatmeal), which is served hot or cold with milk.

For lunch, a popular treat for children is *røde pølser* (hot dogs) sold from sidewalk stands. The *smørrebrød* (open-faced sandwich) is a national institution with elaborate toppings such as salmon, shrimp, lobster, eggs, roast beef, and turkey lavishly prepared on hearty *rugbrød* (ryebread), which kids may find too dense. Smørrebrød served in restaurants may have too much butter or mayonnaise to appeal to children; make your own by marketplace shopping. Danish cheeses, such as Havarti, Danbo, and Samsø are wonderful. You'll easily be able to detect those mild enough for children; look for those marked *mild or skoleost* (for school use). For dinner ask for *frikadeller* (meatballs); most children love them. You can buy them premixed in markets to prepare on your own. *Hakkebøf* (hamburger) is hamburger cooked with onions. *Stegt rødspætte med frites* (fish and chips) are another safe choice for kids.

The popular buttery pastry called "danish" here is called *wienerbrød* (Vienna bread) in Denmark. Other kid-pleasing desserts include *kræmmerhuse med flødeskum*, a cone-shaped cookie filled with chocolate, whipped creme, and fruit, and *rødgrød med fløde*, a pudding made with raspberries.

Formula and Baby Food, Diapers and Baby Gear

Disposable diapers (*papir bleer*) are biodegradable in Denmark and are found in supermarkets, as are familiar brands of baby food, including Gerber, and formula. In Copenhagen, the chain called Irma has a well-stocked line of baby goods. Even campgrounds have changing rooms for babies; some are so up-to-date that you'll find a shared room between the women's and men's bathrooms so either mom or dad can change baby.

Sidewalk Talk

Most Danes speak English and one or two other languages.

beach *strand*	park *parken*
bicycle *cykel*	playground *lejeplads*
goodbye *farvel*	yes and please *ja tak*
hello *hei*	pleasant, cozy *hyggelig**
ice cream *is*	Shall we play *Skal vi lege?*
no, thank you *nej tak*	

*(A very common expression)

The Lay of the Land

Denmark is a sea-faring country made up of nearly 500 islands. Copenhagen, Denmark's capital, sits on the far eastern edge of the country, on the island of Zealand. We will begin our tour in Copenhagen and its surrounding area of North Zealand, head to South Zealand, then to the central islands of Funen and Ærø, and on to Jutland, which is the country's largest peninsula and the only part connected to continental Europe.

ZEALAND

COPENHAGEN

Go to Florence or Paris for art, but visit Copenhagen for pure fun. The city's fortifications from a bygone age have been turned into large, centrally located parks with playgrounds; the old city moats are now lakes. Tivoli Gardens, Copenhagen's fabulous amusement park, is actually part of the old bastions. It was in Copenhagen that Hans Christian Andersen wrote over 100 of his fairy tales.

Wha'd'ya Wanna Do?

Visit the city's tourist office for the free English booklet "Hei." It presents the history of Denmark in an entertaining fashion, suggests tours of Copenhagen, lists safety tips for the beach, and provides coupons to admit kids free into many attractions throughout the country. Its travel games and projects will keep your children entertained en route. "Copenhagen This Week," also available from the tourist office, lists sports, baby-sitting services and all events. Copenhagen's **tourist office** is located at H. C. Andersens Blvd. 22 (Tel. 33111325). **Huset** (Use It), at Rådhusstraede 13 (Tel. 33156518), provides assistance to college students and other young travelers; their guide "Playtime," may be of interest to your teens.

Weekly **children's festivals** with entertainment convene at Tivoli on Tuesdays, Bakken on Wednesdays (see "Near Copenhagen"), and Sophienholm in Lyngby on Sundays from late June to early August.

Getting Around

Copenhagen is a compact city and easy to get around on foot. The heart of the city is a maze of pedestrian streets which form a triangular area dominated by the square of Rådhuspladsen to the west, Kongens Nytorv to the east, and Nørreport Station to the north. As you emerge from Rådhuspladsen, a left turn takes you to Tivoli Gardens. **Bicycles** are regularly used on specially marked bike lanes. **Buses and trains** cover the city and environs. Discount tickets are available from bus drivers and at rail stations. Children under 12 pay half-price and those under 6 ride free. The economical Copenhagen Card, valid for 1 to 3 days, provides unlimited travel throughout North Zealand, as well as free admission to Tivoli Gardens and more than forty museums. It is available at rail stations, tourist offices, and travel agents. Children ages 5–11 receive a 50 percent reduction on the pass.

Canal and harbor **boat tours** include a trip out to the park and promenade at Langeline, where the statue of The Little Mermaid (from Hans Christian Andersen's story) is perched on the water's edge. Boats depart from Gammel Strand every half hour from 10 AM. Tours under the city's twelve bridges depart from Kongens Nytorv every 30 minutes from 10 AM. Hire a rowboat from Christianshavn, a charming old section of the city, to row along the canals, or sail on the sound aboard Denmark's oldest schooner, the Isefjord, which makes a 4-hour journey on the open waters with lunch or dinner served. Departs from the Admiral Hotel, Tolbodgade 24 (Tel. 33151729). **Horse-drawn carriage rides** are available in the city center and at Dyrehaven deer park (see "Near Copenhagen").

Where to Stay

HOTELS
The Plaza is an elegant hotel right across from Tivoli Gardens. Bernstorffsgade 4, DK-1577. Tel. 31551433. **Deluxe.**

SAS Globetrotter, near the beach and 10 minutes from downtown, has a tropical pool area with a children's pool and indoor sports. Engvej 171, DK-2300. Tel. 31558145. **Deluxe.**

Hotel Dragør Kro has weekly apartment rentals. Strandgade 30, DK-2791, Dragør. Tel. 31530187. **Expensive.**

Hotel Neptune is centrally located near Kongens Have park with apartment facilities. Skt. Annæ Plads 14–20, DK-1250. Tel. 33138900. **Expensive.**

Hotel Marina is near the beach, 30 minutes from Copenhagen. Apartment facilities are available. Vedbæk Strandvej 391, DK-2950 Vedbæk. Tel. 42891711. **Moderate.**

Scandic Hotel has an indoor pool and is very "child-friendly." Kettevej 4, DK-2650 Hvidovre. Tel. 31498282. **Moderate.**

Hotel Vestersøhus, with balconies facing the lake, has apartment facilities or family rooms with kitchens and is 10 minutes from Tivoli and the zoo. Vestersøgade 58, DK-1601. Tel. 33113870. **Moderate.**

Skovshoved, just north of Copenhagen, near the beach and Bakken amusement and deer park, has large rooms and children's meals. Stradvejen 267, DK-2920 Charlottenlund. Tel. 31640028. **Inexpensive.**

FAMILY HOSTELS
Storkøbenhavns Vandrerhjem is a modern hostel with laundry and kitchen facilities. Sjællandsbroen 55. Tel. 32522908. Closed Christmas week.

Københavns Vandrerhjem, in a park with a small lake, is 20 minutes from the town center. It has laundry facilities but no kitchen. Herbergvejen 8, Bellahøj. Tel. 31289715.

CAMPGROUNDS
Absalon Camping, west of the city, has cabins, bicycles, and laundry facilities. Korsdalsvej 132. Tel. 31410600.

Detour! What to See and Do

AROUND RÅDHUSPLADSEN
Rådhuspladsen (Town Hall Square) is the city's center. From the green-roofed tower of its town hall, there is a great view of the city and the sea. Fee. Tower tours Mon.–Fri. 11, 2; Sat. at 2.

Tivoli spelled backward reads "I lov' it," and your children certainly will! Built in 1843, this dazzling 20-acre amusement park has something for all ages. The renowned Pantomime Theater features a commedia dell'arte performance with Pjerrot, Harlequin, and Columbine; Hans Christian Andersen himself often watched it. There are acrobats and jugglers, pony rides, marionette and children's theaters, and numerous other outdoor performances. The park boasts many rides such as the thrilling Comet roller coaster, a circus carousel, a flying carpet, and boat rides on a beautiful lake where kids are the captains. A free supervised children's playground is open 10–6. The best time to visit Tivoli is at night when over 100,000 lamps magically illuminate the grounds and shine on its fountains. Spectacular fireworks are part of the evening's show. On weekends the Tivoli Boy's Guard marches through to their own music. Fee. 30 percent discount before 1 PM. Some Wed. afternoons children can ride amusements for free. May–mid-Sept. daily 10 AM.–midnight. Children's amusements open at 11:30.

Next to Tivoli the **Glyptotek Museum's** collection ranges from ancient art to Impressionism and was donated to the city by Carlsberg brewery magnate Carl Jacobsen. Look for the marble babies falling over their mother in the outdoor sculpture garden; the piece is aptly titled *Watermother.* Fee. Free on Sun. and Wed. May–Aug. daily 10–4; Sept.–Apr. Tues.–Sat. 12–3, Sun. 10–4.

West of Rådhuspladsen the new **Tycho Brahe Planetarium,** named after the famous Danish astronomer, is western Europe's largest. Its computer-controlled projector displays 9,000 stars and a night sky of planets, galaxies, and comets. The complex also stages films and permanent exhibitions of astronomical topics. In 1572, Brahe discovered new stars at a time when the universe was thought to be unchangeable. Fee. Gammel Kongevej 10, on the lake. Daily 10:30–9.

North of Rådhuspladsen, the **Runde Tårn (Round Tower)** is a former 17th-century astronomical observatory. Climb its spiral ramp to the top; at 350 feet there's a sweeping view. Legend has it that Peter the Great drove up to the top in a horse-drawn carriage in 1716. Fee. Købmagergade. Daily June–Aug. 10–5; Apr., May, Sept., Oct. Mon.–Sat. 10–5, Sun. 12–4. Tel. 33936660.

SLOTSHOLMEN (CASTLE ISLAND)

Castle Island, with its building-lined canals, looks a bit like Amsterdam or Venice. This is where Denmark has been ruled for more than 500 years; long ago it was scene of many pirate wars led by the Bishop of Absalon. Visit the **Theatrical Museum,** which was once the court theater in the palace of **Christiansborg Slot.** Fee. English tours June–Aug. Tues.–Sun. 11, 1, and 3; Sept.–May at 2. Museum: June–Sept. Wed., Fri., and Sun. 2–4; winter Wed. and Sun. 2–4. To the side of the Royal Library, set in an idyllic garden, is the **Tøjhusmuseet (Arms and Armor Museum),** which displays battle flags from around the globe, armor, and weapons. Free. Tøjhusgade 3. May–Sept. Tues.–Sat. 1–4, Sun. 10–4; Oct.–Apr. Tues.–Sat. 1–3, Sun. 11–4. Tel. 33116037. Peer up at the **Børsen (Stock Exchange),** on the other side of the library. Four dragons standing on their heads with twisted tails form its spire.

NORTH OF RÅDHUSPLADSEN

The **Langeline Promenade** is a popular strolling ground for local families on Sunday afternoons. About halfway along is the **Kastellet,** an old fortress turned into a park where you can see *Den lille Havfrue (The Little Mermaid)* of Hans Christian Andersen's fairy tale sitting on the water's edge. Park open daily 6 AM–10 PM. The park is close to the **Frihedsmuseet (Liberty Museum)**, which has a moving display of the Danish resistance during World War II. Free. Esplanaden. May–mid-Sept. Tues.–Sat. 11–3, Sun. 10–5; mid-Sept.–Apr. Tues.–Sat. 11–3, Sun. 11–4.

Walking back to the town center along the water, you'll come to the **Amalienborg Palace,** where there is an elaborate performance of the changing of the guard. The ancient pageantry, with precision marching and flashing of swords, is great fun to watch. Held daily at noon, when the Queen is in residence.

Andersen wrote his first fairy tale at #20 along the **Nyhavn** canal, a street lined with boats and paintbox-colored buildings. Kids can explore the 19th-century ship, *Fyrskib XVII,* permanently moored at Nyhavn 10. Open when the gangplank is down.

Just One Look: More Museums

Jernbanemuseet focuses on the history of the Danish railways with some elaborate model trains. Free. Sølvgade 40. Sat. 12–7. Tel. 33140400.

The **Legetøjsmuseet** displays toys from the mid-19th to the mid-20th century with special films at 11 and 2. A highlight is one of the world's oldest Noah's arks from the late 1700s. There are mechanical toys, dolls, children's books, and old Christmas tree ornaments, including exquisite candlestick holders from the 1800s. Fee. 13 Valkendorfsgade. Mon.–Thurs. and weekends 9–3. Tel. 33141009.

Other toy museums include the **Dukkemuseet,** with antique dolls and doll houses (Fee. 6 Kronprinsessegade. Mon., Thurs., and Sat. 1–3. Tel. 33930111) and the **Dukketeatermuseet,** with an international collection of toy theaters (Fee. Købmagergade 52. Mon., Wed.–Fri. 12-5. Tel. 33151579).

At the **Musikhistorisk Museum** children can press a button to hear the old and fascinating musical instruments from its collection. Fee. Åbenrå 30. Tues. Wed. 10–1, Fri.–Sun. 1–4. Tel. 33112726.

Louis Tussaud's **Wax Museum** is what you'd expect: Danish personalities modeled in wax and a chilling chamber of horrors, which is not recommended for the very young. Fee. Enter from City Hall Square or from Tivoli. Daily 10–8. Tel. 33142922.

Where the Sidewalk Ends: Zoos and More Parks

In the area around Østervoldgade and Sølvgade there are beautiful parks. Children play around the statue of Hans Christian Andersen in

Kongens Have (Kings Gardens), in whose center sits the **Rosenborg Palace,** a Renaissance castle where lovers of royal fables can see the dazzling Danish Crown jewels. Fee. Østervoldgade 4a. June–Aug. daily 10–3; May–Oct. daily 11–3. Nearby is the **Statens Museum for Kunst (National Art Gallery)** also in beautiful gardens.

West of the town center, the **Zoological Gardens,** overlooking the city close to **Frederiksberg Slot (Frederiksberg Castle),** surround the **Zoologisk Have.** The zoo has a special children's section with animals to feed and ride, a tower to climb with a view as far as Sweden, and a family garden for picnics. Strollers are available. Fee. 32 Roskildevej. Daily 9–5; winter until 4. Tel. 31302555. The gardens are adjacent to two more city parks: **Sondmarken** and **Frederiksberg Have.** The latter has a playground, a pond for sailing model boats and feeding ducks, wading pools, and rowboat rides on the canal.

Sports and Performing Arts

The tourist office's free brochure "Copenhagen This Week" can inform you of local sports facilities, including swimming pools, skating rinks, bowling, and tennis.

Benneweis, Europe's oldest circus, has a colorful cavalcade of international artists, animals, clowns, and lots of merriment in the Circusbuilding, in the heart of the city. Apr.–Oct. Tel. 33142192.

NEAR COPENHAGEN: NORTH ZEALAND

In north and northeast Zealand, you will find miles of lovely beaches. The best near Copenhagen are *Amager* **Strandpark** (8 kilometers south), *Bellevue*'s popular artificial beach (10 kilometers north), and *Køge Bugt* **Strandpark** (10 kilometers south), which has many recreational activities. The quaint fishing village of *Dragør,* on the southern tip of the Amager Island and 12 kilometers south of Copenhagen, has a shallow beach backed by meadows that is ideal for young kids.

In *Klampenborg,* 10 kilometers northwest of Copenhagen, you can play at the beach, ride the thrilling roller coaster at the amusement park **Bakken,** or ride in a horse-drawn carriage through lovely **Dyrehaven,** a large deer park. Two thousand deer and their young roam the grounds, side by side with Copenhageners who escape the city to walk, ride bikes, or laze in the sun. At the edge of the park is 400-year-old Bakken, the world's oldest amusement park. Rides are its specialty, with a stomach-churning water switchback, a haunted house for thrill-seekers, and charming merry-go-rounds for little ones. The fire-eating clown Pjerrot gives free performances three times daily, and there are many open-air shows with international performers. Families flock here to enjoy the enormous ice cream cones and equally huge sausages. A fun way to enter the amusement park is by horse-drawn carriage through the deer park. Fee for Bakken. Deer park reached by S-train or Bus 21. Park open daily 10–sunset; Bakken open late Mar.–Aug. daily 2 PM–midnight.

Further northwest, along the same train line at *Lyngby*, is the **Frilandsmuseet**, a 40-acre open-air museum of rural Danish life. Houses from all over Denmark have been resurrected, with every room, nook, and cranny intact. During the summer, folkdancing (weekends only), sheep shearing and weaving demonstrations are held. Fee. 100 Kongevejan. S-train to Sorgenfri. Mid.-Apr.–Sept. Tues.–Sun. 10–5; Oct. 1–14 Tues.–Sun. 10–3; Oct. 15–mid-Apr. Sun. 10–3.

Denmark's most spectacular castle is the **Frederiksborg Slot**, in *Hillerød*, at the end of the Lyngby train line. Rising from an island in a lake surrounded by forests, the castle's double moats, gardens, and ramparts resemble a page torn from a storybook. On the castle's lake there are boat trips during the summer from Torvet to Frederiksborg Slot and returning. Castle: daily May–Sept. 10–5; Oct. 10–4; Nov.–Mar. 11–3; Apr. 11–4. At the **Dukker i Dragter (Dolls in Costume)** you'll find 70 dolls dressed in handmade miniature costumes. Inspired by paintings and books on the history of dress, they show the development of attire from the Middle Ages to the present. Queen Victoria was a favorite. Fee. Kildeporatvej 31, Nødebo. Bus 324 from Hillerød. Easter and July Tues.–Sun. 1–4.

Also north of Copenhagen is *Helsingør* **(Elsinore),** famous for **Kronborg Slot,** said to be Hamlet's castle in the Shakespearean play. Kids can climb the inner and outer ramparts and visit the cavernous dungeon where the Danish hero Holger Danske lies. Legend tells us that danger will come to the country if he ever wakes up. Parents may want to take in an evening performance of Hamlet, in English, held at the castle in August. Past performers have included Richard Burton and Claire Bloom. Daily May–Sept. 10–5; Apr. and Oct. 11–4; Nov.–Mar. Tues.–Sun. 11–3. Not far from the castle, the **Øresund Aquarium** has touch tanks for children with sea urchins, anemone, and starfish. Fee. June 20–Aug. 10 daily 12–4. Tel. 49213772. Kids can climb into old fire engines at the **Danmarks Tekniske Museum (Danish Technical Museum).** Fee. Year-round daily 10–5. On summer Sundays, an **old steam train** departing from Helsingør tours the north coast of Zealand. Contact the Helsingør **tourist office** at Havnepladsen 3 (Tel. 49211333).

Closer to Copenhagen, *Humlebæk's* **Louisiana Museum of Modern Art** is in a grand park that slopes down to the Øresund (Sound) and Humlebæk Sø (Lake). The museum often holds workshops where kids can paint and sculpt. Calder, Moore, and Arp sculptures line the park. Children free. Year-round Thurs.–Tues. 10–5, Wed. 10–10.

ROSKILDE

Roskilde, west of Copenhagen, is filled with Viking relics, such as the recently found remains of five Viking ships sunk in the Roskilde Fjord in A.D. 1000 which have been meticulously reassembled. Housing the ships is the **Vikingeskibshallen,** which overlooks the fjord where they sank. English films tell their story. Fee. Daily Apr.–Oct. 9–5; Nov.–Mar. 10–4. Tel. 42356555. Look up at the mechanical figures that grace the 500-year-old clock on the town's **Domkirke.** Each hour, St. George on horseback attacks a roaring dragon, causing a figure to move crazily and strike the hour. The **Spilkammeret (Playing Card Museum)** displays over 2,000 decks, including children's playing cards from around the world. Fee. Sct. Hansgade 20. Mid-June–mid-Sept. Wed. 3–6, Sun. 1–6. Tel. 42352009. The veteran **steamship s/s *Skjelskør*** cruises from Roskilde on the fjord late June through mid-August on weekends. Contact the **tourist office,** right near the cathedral (Tel. 42352700).

NEAR ROSKILDE

Roskilde Familieland is an animal reserve and amusement park, south of town in *Vindinge.* Kids can ride horses amongst rare deer in its Western town or glide in swan-shaped boats. Fee. Follow signs from Roskilde. May–June weekends 10–7; June–mid-Aug. daily 10–7; mid-Aug.–late Aug. weekends 10–7. Tel. 42372966.

In *Oldtidsbyen,* just west of Roskilde, the **Lejre Research Center** is an extraordinary Stone-Age community where prehistoric living conditions have been reconstructed. People volunteer to live, work, and eat as their predecessors did; they even dress as though they were from the Stone and Iron ages. It's all part of an experimental open-air laboratory which was the idea of 15-year-old Hans-Ole Hansen in 1954. In the center's Fire Valley kids can grind wheat berries, bake a simple cake over a fire, row a canoe in the lagoon, or chop logs using Iron Age axes. Fee. Slangealleen 2. Apr.–Sept. daily 9–5. Tel. 42380245.

North of Roskilde, the pleasant fjord town of *Frederikssund* stages an annual **Viking Play and Pageant** from late June through early July. Old tales are performed, and there's lots of fun-filled action; over 200 locals take part. After the performances, there is a giant Viking banquet with enormous portions. Contact the Roskilde tourist office listed above.

SOUTH ZEALAND

The islands of **Lolland, Møn,** and **Falster** in South Zealand have many wide, sandy beaches with sheltering dunes on the clear Baltic Sea. Møn is especially noteworthy for its magnificent beaches and ancient chalk cliffs, which tower above the sea along its eastern coast. For information about holiday cottages, farmhouse stays, family hostels, camping, and resorts, contact the Tourist Association, Storstrøm County, Østergåde 9,1. DK-4800 Nykøbing F., Denmark.

The town of *Nysted,* in eastern Lolland, has the 900-year old castle of **Ålholm Slot.** Set on a 62-acre estate, it has a steam locomotive from 1850 to transport you around the estate and down to the sea. The estate's **Automobile Museum** exhibits 250 vintage cars from 1896 to 1930 and a magnificent model electric train. Inside the castle, you'll see the dungeon where former resident King Kristoffer II was poisoned, a vast kitchen where the stove's smoke runs horizontally, and funny toilets suspended over the moat. Just west of Nysted on the Rødby Road. Parkvej 7. Park: year-round; car museum and model railway: Apr. 12–May 27 and Sept.–Oct. 14 weekends 10–6; June–Aug. daily 10–6; castle: June–Aug. daily 11–6. Tel. 53871509.

On summer weekends, a vintage train called the **Museumsbanen** will take you along the northern coast from *Maribo* to *Bandholm* through the parklands of Lolland's **Knuthenborg Manor.** Among its 1,500 acres is the **Knuthenborg Safari Park,** with tigers, rhinos, monkeys, zebras, giraffes, a deer park, and a children's zoo. Fee. May–mid-Sept. daily 9–6. Tel. 53888088. The park's amusement area, **Småland,** has a miniature island with radio-controlled boats. Park: Daily May–Sept. 9–6. Tel. 53888088. Train: Tel. 53888545.

CENTRAL DENMARK

ISLAND OF FUNEN: ODENSE

Hans Christian Andersen was born on the island of Funen. The thatched-roof houses graced with colorful flowers, gentle rolling hills, crystal-clear lakes, and castles dotting the countryside look as though they jumped off the pages of his books. The storyteller's hometown is 1,000-year-old Odense, Denmark's largest city. A tour of **Andersen's childhood home** reveals the storyteller's interests as a youth. Fee. Munkemøllestraede 3–5. Apr.–Sept. daily 10–5; Oct.–Mar. daily 12–3. The **Andersen Museum** is built around a lovely duck pond, perhaps in honor of his tale *The Ugly Duckling.* You'll find books of his stories in hundreds of languages; children can settle into comfortable couches, pick up a telephone, and hear tape recordings of his stories, from the Snow Queen to Thumbelina. Fee. Hans Jensens Straede 39–43. Apr.–May and Sept. daily 10–5; June–Aug. daily 9–6. Oct.–Mar. daily 10–3. Andersen's statue sits in Odense's **Fairy-tale Gardens** in the city park.

From mid-July to early August, local children stage one of Andersen's fairy tales at **Den Fynske Landsby (Funen Village)**, south of Odense, during the **Hans Christian Andersen Festival.** The village is composed of an open-air museum with farm animals, craft workshops, an old school, a poorhouse, and the delightful outdoor children's theater set in the woods. Fee. Sejerskovvej 20. Apr.–May and Sept.–Oct. daily 9–4; June–Aug. daily 9–6:30; Nov.–March Sundays 10–4. Tel. 66131372. You can return to Odense by boat.

The **tourist office** at city hall, DK-5000 (Tel. 66127520), has an economical Odense Adventure Pass, which provides access to local museums, including the fun **DBR Railway Museum,** with a model track at Dannebrogsgade 24; the **Odense Zoo,** at Sdr. Boulevard 320; the **Funen Tivoli** amusement park, at Sdr. Boulevard 304; five indoor swimming pools; and the Hans Christian Andersen plays. Children will enjoy cruising the Odense River in swan-shaped boats that depart daily from Munke Mose to the Odense Zoo. The tourist office's program "Meet the Danes" enables you to meet and spend an evening with a Danish family. The office can also provide you with information about all the Funen Island resorts, from accommodations to sports.

NEAR ODENSE

North of Odense in *Ladby,* a 1,100-year-old Viking ship was found in a burial mound in the 1930s. A museum and an air-conditioned encasement have been built around the boat. Inside, a Viking chief is buried amidst his weapons, armor, hunting dogs, and horses. Fee. Vikingevej 123. May–Sept. Tues.–Sun. 10–6; Oct.–Apr. Tues.–Sun. 10–3.

West of Odense, in *Årup,* is **Fyns Sommerland,** a recreation park with pony rides, swan-shaped boats, jumping areas, and more. Fee. Fjellemosevej 3. Off Road 161 from Odense west. Mid-May–June Tues. and Thurs. 9–4; weekends 10–6; July–mid-Aug. daily 10–7; mid-Aug.–Sept. Tues. and Thurs. 9–4, weekends 10–6. Tel. 64881750. Other easy excursions from Odense include the **Terrarium** in Vissenbjerg, with snakes and crocodiles, and the **Funen Aquarium** in *Rold,* with huge tanks of man-eating sharks.

South of Odense, in *Kværndrup,* is the dramatic 16th-century castle **Egeskov Slot,** which is built on a foundation of oak trunks rising from the center of a lake. With towers, a moat, and a drawbridge, it is one of Europe's best-preserved island castles. As legend goes, if the wooden doll buried under one of the turrets is moved, the castle will sink into the moat at Christmas. The castle has a museum of vintage cars and aircraft, all set in a beautiful baroque park with lifelike topiary animals and an enormous labyrinth made of bamboo plants. Fee. June–Aug. 9–6, castle 10–5; May and Sept. daily 10–5. Tel. 62271625 or 62271074.

ISLAND OF FUNEN: SVENDBORG AND ENVIRONS

Further south on the sound is Svendborg, with charming half-timbered houses and popular beach resorts. **Vejelegården's Familie-land** has an enchanting mechanical doll museum where kids can activate dolls. The park also has a clown museum and inflated castle trampolines. Fee. Søren Lolksvej 26. Apr.–mid-June, late Aug.–Sept. daily 10–5; mid-June–mid-Aug. daily 10–7. From Svendborg you can take a ferry to the island of Ærø or cross a bridge to the island of Tåsinge and Langeland. East of Svendborg, *Fåborg* has a delightful **Legetømuseum,** with dolls, a large electric train circuit, and colorful carts. Fee. Assensvej 279 Apr.–Aug. daily 9–6. Tel. 62619014

LANGELAND ISLAND

Rent a **prairie schooner,** a covered wagon pulled by horses, for a week and travel on specially designed trails. The wagons accommodate up to four people and come with beds, cooking and eating utensils, a small refrigerator, and a stove. Write Destination Langeland, DK-5935m, Bagenkop (Tel. 62561493). At the island's **Ye Olde Apothecary** see dragon's blood, pulverized mummy, and other time-honored medicinal remedies used in times past. Fee. Brogade 15. June 15–Jan. Mon.–Fri. 1–5.

ÆRØ ISLAND

Ærø is a great holiday island with calm, shallow beaches safe for children. *Ærsøkøbing,* with quaint meandering streets and half-timbered homes with flower boxes, is capital of the island and one of the most delightful and well-preserved towns in all of Denmark. The town is illuminated at night by cast-iron gas lamps. Ærøskøbing's **Flaskeskibssamlingen** boasts 1,600 miniature ship models, including elaborate five-masted schooners, all inserted inside narrow bottles by a very clever Peter Jacobsen, called "Bottle Peter" in his day. Fee. Smedegade 22, near the water. May–Sept. daily 9–5; Oct.–Apr. daily 10–4. For camping, family hostels, and holiday cottages, contact the **tourist office,** DK-5970, Ærøskøbing (Tel. 62521300).

JUTLAND

Jutland is Denmark's largest peninsula and the only part of the country attached to continental Europe. Children will find Legoland its most important site, but haunting Viking funeral mounds and ritual sites abound. Dunes and sandy beaches stretch along 250 miles of Jutland's west coast, while forests and fjords line the east coast.

LEGOLAND AND ENVIRONS

In the town of *Billund,* west of Fredericia on Jutland's east coast, is Denmark's prized **Legoland,** which celebrates the well-loved Lego block. Several different attractions make up Legoland: Miniland, where world landmarks have been constructed out of Legos; an amusement park; a lavish miniature palace; and a doll and toy museum.

Using 35 million of these small plastic building bricks, craftsmen have created realistic models of the Taj Mahal, the Acropolis, the Statue of Liberty, Sitting Bull, and more. Village life in England, Austria, Denmark, Norway, Holland, and Germany has been created in miniature, with every detail in place, from tiny Lego dresses in an Amsterdam clothing store to Lego ships in Copenhagen's harbor. There's even an Arabian City constructed faithfully from *A Thousand and One Nights.* The complexity of these constructions of world landmarks is no more evident than in Mount Rushmore, built with 1.5 million Legos. All details are exact. These creations can be found in the park's Miniland.

The amusement park has rides modeled after Lego toys. A highlight for 8- to 13-year-olds is its traffic school, with a challenging highway of hairpin turns, driving lessons, and a driving test that culminates in a driver's license. Legoredo Town, not the park's highlight, is a commercial Wild West town with cowboys, Indians, horses, and gold digging. Lego Safari has elephants, giraffes, and zebras all made from, you guessed it, Lego bricks. Kids can journey through on trains made of black and white zebra-patterned Legos.

A lavish 19th-century miniature mansion called Titania's Palace is an enchanting creation with every detail in place, down to the minuscule mother-of-pearl hairbrushes on nightstands. It is the result of 20 years of work by an eccentric Englishman, Sir Neville Wilkinson, whose young daughter claimed to see the Fairy Queen Titania in their garden. Her father built this masterpiece for her imaginary friend. If that were not enough, the park has a magnificent doll collection with antique dolls and moving toys from all over the world, a marionette theater, and changing exhibits of elaborately built Lego models. Fee. West of Vejle. Outdoor season: May–third Sun. of Sept. 10–8; until 9 from mid-July–mid-Aug. Indoor exhibitions: Easter–third Sun. of Dec. 10–5. Tel. 75331333.

Although the car ferry from Korsor to Billund makes 24 hourly trips a day, it is wise to make a reservation: Tel. 53571233.

East of Billund, near Vejle, drive through the **Løvenparken Zoo (Lion Park Zoo)** in *Givskud*, a 500-acre park where lions, elephants, camels, giraffes, and rhinos bask in the sun. There's a children's farm filled with pets and 100 talking parrots. Fee. 20 km. from Vejle. May–Sept. 10 AM to sunset. Tel. 75730222.

RØMØ AND RIBE

Rømø is the largest and southernmost of Jutland's western islands, accessible by a causeway from the mainland. The best beaches for children are on the island's west side. A number of supervised children's activities, such as beach tours to collect treasures that have washed ashore, art projects with shells, folk dancing, and an island specialty—polishing amber stones—are held in summer. Contact the **tourist office** at Havnebyvej 30, Tvismark, DK-6791 (Tel. 74755130). The island has a **sommerland,** with giant trampolines, water rides, and horseback riding. Fee. Borrebjergvej, Havneby. Daily May–mid-Sept. 10:30–dusk.

Medieval and quaint *Ribe,* Denmark's oldest town, is now preserved by the National Trust. Be sure to look for stork nests on chimney tops. From May through mid-September, a **night watchman** makes the rounds daily at 10 PM, strolling the streets, making sure all is well. Meet him at the town center at 10 PM if you'd like to accompany him on his rounds. Ribe's 14th-century **cathedral** is known for its "Cat-Head Door," adorned with a cat's head ornament to show that it was reserved for the devil to enter at night.

ALONG THE WESTERN COAST

On the moors of **Hjerl Hede** in *Vinderup* there is a fascinating **Stone Age Open-Air Museum.** A whole village with a church, school, mill, farms, and houses has been brought to life. One hundred people dressed in old costumes show how corn is milled, wool is carded, and how trading went on in times past. Fee. Apr.–Oct. daily 9–5; Dec. weekends.

Nykøbing Mors lies on the idyllic Limfjord, Denmark's longest fjord. Its bizarre **Lødderup Bottle Museum** has a collection of bottles, ball-point pens, and plastic bags. Free. 52 Harrehøjvej. Daily late June–early Aug. 10–11, 2–5. Tel. 97721834. South of Nykøbing Mors is **Jesperhus Blomsterpark (Jesperhus Flower Park),** with 500,000 flowers planted in intricate patterns, a bird zoo, a tropical aquarium, and a butterfly hall. There's an adjoining adventure playground and campsite with a swimming pool, trampolines, go-carts, giant air cushions, and pony rides. Fee. Mid-May–mid-Sept. daily 9–6; July daily 8–9. Tel. 97723200.

Back along the North Sea coast, **Saltum's Fårup Sommerland,** near Lønstrup, is one of the country's most popular "summer lands" with a water switchback, giant air cushions, trampolines, a giant play tower, canoes, sailboats, and horseback riding. One fee covers all. May– early Sept. daily 10–6; July until 7. Tel. 98881600.

In the far north of Jutland, around the tip of the peninsula where the North Sea merges with Kattegat, is *Frederikshavn,* a major port for crossings to Sweden and Norway. The *Eventyrbadet* has tropi- cal wave pools, a water chute, bubble pools, a waterfall, and water cannons. Fee. 14 Tordenskjoldsgade. Daily year-round 9–9. Tel. 98433233. On the **Island of Laesø,** off the coast of Frederikshavn, there are riding holidays for children and adults on Iceland ponies. The program includes tours through the woods, beaches, and mead- ows of the island for beginners and experienced riders in addition to swimming, singing, and games. Weekend and week-long excursions are available in summer. Contact Krogbækgård, DK-9440 Byrum (Tel. 98491505).

ÅRHUS, SILKEBORG AND ENVIRONS

Århus, the country's second largest city, is a student and cultural center that makes a lively base for exploring the neighboring Danish lake district. Its **Den gamle By** is one of the country's best-known open-air museums, with a special focus on urban life; you'll see merchants' shops and workshops from the 16th century. Fee. Jan.– Feb. weekdays 11–2, Sun. 11–3; Mar. daily 11–3; Apr. and Oct. weekdays 10–4, Sun. 10–5; May and Sept. daily 10–5; June–Aug. daily 9–5; Nov. weekdays 11–3; Dec. weekdays 11–4, Sun. 10–3. Climb the **city hall tower** for a great view. Open June–Sept. weekdays 12–3. The **Det dansk Brandværns Museum** has over eighty fire en- gines, many of them manually operated or horse-drawn. Children will enjoy the playroom, with a small fire brigade pump and fire hoses to squirt. Fee. Dalgas Avenue 56. Apr.–Oct. daily 10–5. **Tivoli Friheden,** the city's popular amusement park adjoining the Mar- selisborg Woods, offers merry-go-rounds, swing boats, and many out- door performances. Fee. Mid-Apr.–mid-Aug. daily. On summer weekends, free entertainment is held for children at the **Botanisk Have og Væksthusene (Botanical Gardens and Greenhouses)** in the middle of the city. Contact the **tourist office** in the city hall (Tel. 86121600); the office also runs a "Meet the Danes" program enabling you to spend time with a Danish family. Ask about local family hostels, sports and camping.

East of Århus, around the peninsula, enchanting *Ebeltoft,* with its crooked old houses and cobblestone streets, resembles a page from *Hansel and Gretel.* Its town hall, by Torvepladsen Square, is known as a "doll-house town hall" because of its low ceilings. Resounding in the town's streets during the summer is the call of the night watchman bidding all good night.

About 28 kilometers west of Århus is beautiful *Silkeborg,* the center of the lake district. Horror-movie fans will want to visit the **Silkeborg Museum**'s "Tollund Man," displayed in a glass case. He died more than 2,000 years ago in a ritualized death ceremony and was discovered perfectly preserved in peat bog in 1950. Even his skin is intact, although strangely colored from the acid in the bog. Fee. Hovegårdsvej. Apr. 15–late Oct. daily 10–12; late Oct.–mid-Apr. Wed. and weekends 12–4. Tel. 86821578. Canoes, rowboats, flat-bottomed boats, or paddle steamers are available to follow the surrounding river through woods and heather. Among them, the 100-year-old paddle steamer *Hjejlen,* meanders in the summer through the chain of lakes for a 90-minute cruise (Tel. 86820766). The **tourist office,** at Torvet 9, DK-8600 Silkeborg (Tel. 86821911), can inform you of summer cottages, farm holidays, and sports in the lake district.

Nearby in the forest south of Århus is *Moesgård's* **Forhistorisk Museum,** which displays the "Grauballe Man," who died more than 2,000 years ago. Like the Tollund Man, he too was found preserved in peat bog. He has miraculously survived the ravages of time; you can see his skin, hair, nails and teeth as well as the throat marks he received when sacrificed to an ancient fertility god. Two hundred fifty acres of parkland adjoin the museum. A "prehistoric" path running for several miles through the park past a series of re-created settlements from the Stone Age and the Bronze Age leads to a nice swimming beach. A bus will take you back. Apr.–mid-Sept. daily 10–5; mid-Sept.–Mar. Tues.–Sun. 10–5.

AROUND VIBORG

Near Viborg, in *Mønsted,* are the **Kalkgruber,** limestone caves originally hewn by Vikings and extending to the area near *Daubjerg,* which now hold tons and tons of aging Danish cheese! Some of the cave's bats are now stuffed and housed in Mønsted's **Bat Museum,** alongside the cave. Fee. 10 Kalkværksvej. Apr.–Oct. daily 10–4; June–July daily 10–6; off-season by appointment. Tel. 86646002. Daubjerg is mentioned in many myths and legends as the home of a gang of robbers in the 13th century; 400 years later a witch was burned nearby. English tours of the ancient underground **Daubjerg Mines** tell the tales; the presence of bats contribute to the eerie atmosphere. Fee. Late Mar.–Oct. daily 10–4; summers daily 9–6. 15 Dybdalsvej, Daubjerg. Tel. 97548333.·

AROUND RANDERS

Randers is known for storks. You'll see their nests on many chimney tops in the medieval section of town. The storks arrive in early May to nest and depart for warmer lands in late August. The town's **Museum of Dolls and Toys** has tin soldiers, steam engines, and doll houses from the time of our great-grandparents.

East of Viborg, between Randers and Grenå, **Djurs Sommerland** in *Djursland* has a children's science center, gold prospecting, canoe and rowboat rides on the Djurs River, a mini-train, pony rides, trampolines, and a giant hopping ride with air cushions. Fee. Randersvej 17. Late May–late June daily 10–6; late June–early Aug. daily 10–8; early Aug.–late Aug. daily 10–6. Tel. 86398400.

North of Randers, near Hobro, at *Klejtrup Lake,* you can see the whole world in grass at your feet. An unusual **World Map Garden** created by a local folk artist features an accurate model of the world's oceans and continents, which has been carved into a grassy peninsula over the lake. You can walk from land to land. Fee. Lake Klejtrup. May–Aug. daily 9–8; Sept. until 6. Tel. 98546132.

12

France

After our first week in France, we were taken aback by the country's pervasive sophistication. Cities are ingeniously planned, food is exquisitely prepared, and music and theater for children is of exceptional quality. French youngsters, for the most part, are immaculately clothed and conduct themselves with total poise, even at the local playground. Dogs are welcome to recline alongside their owners at many four-star restaurants; there's even a snack bar especially for beloved canines on the Riviera.

No wonder the French grow up to be so civilized! You won't find an abundance of theme parks here. In fact, they are a failing novelty, suffering from food boycotts by highbrow tastebuds. To the dismay of foreign park owners, most French don't snack but eat an elaborate multicourse meal at exactly 12:30.

Who needs theme parks when your kids can see art painted by prehistoric cavemen one day and masterpieces of Impressionism the next, learn to "read" the stained-glass windows at Chartres Cathedral, or climb the towers of the castle that inspired the fairytale *Sleeping Beauty*. Magical jeweled carousels with hand-painted coaches, elephants, and swans are found in most city plazas and parks. French parks are glorious, many with remarkable marionette theaters, lakes for sailing model boats, pony rides, inventive play equipment, and tree-lined promenades.

The French are known for being ungracious to American visitors, but this was not our experience. When we looked lost, strangers walked us to the correct métro stop, even in the pouring rain. We stopped counting the times our little one was called *mignonne*, an affectionate term for darling pet.

Bon Voyage!

Preparing Your Children: Books and Art

Younger children: *Paris in the Rain with Jean & Jacqueline* by Thea Bergere, *Madeline* books by Ludwig Bemelman, *Babar* books by Jean de Brunhoff, *The House From Morning to Night* by Daniele Bour, *Harlequin and the Gift of Many Colors* by Remy Charlip, and books by Francoise Seignobosc, such as *Jeanne Marie in Gay Paris*.

Older children: *Linnea in Monet's Garden* by Christina Björk, *The Hunchback of Notre-Dame* by Victor Hugo, *Madame Bovary* by Gustave Flaubert, *The Adventures of Mickey, Taggy, Puppo and Cica and How They Discover France* by Kati Rekai (see Chapter 4), *Le Petite Prince* by Antoine de St-Exupéry.

Art: Your children will encounter works by French artists such as Bonnard, Braque, Cézanne, Chagall, Delacroix, Gauguin, Léger, Matisse, Monet, Renoir, Rodin, and Rousseau. Although not native to France, Picasso's works are also widely represented. Your library should have books with photographs of their works.

Getting There

Most international airlines fly from North America into Paris's Roissy–Charles de Gaulle or Orly airports. Nice's international airport services flights from Paris, New York, and other major cities. To immediately experience the feeling of being abroad consider flying a French airline, whose food and the majority of whose passengers are French. Air France was appealing to us because its direct night flights (10½ hours from the West Coast, 7 hours from the East) allowed us to sleep. In true French fashion, we shared our row with a small dog. (We learned later that one out of every three French families has a dog and that dogs can do no wrong.)

Wha'd'ya Wanna Do?

The **French Government Tourist Office (FGTO)** can provide general information about accommodations and activities particular to a whole province. All major French cities have a well-marked **Office de Tourisme,** and smaller cities that are tourist destinations have **Syndicat d'Initiatives** who can inform you of specific local attractions, accommodations, sports, and special events.

FRENCH GOVERNMENT TOURIST OFFICES (FGTO)
USA–*Chicago:* French Government Tourist Office, 645 N. Michigan Ave., Suite 630, Chicago, Ill. 60611. Tel. 312-337-6301.
USA–*Dallas:* French Government Tourist Office, World Trade Center No. 103, 2050 Stemmons Freeway, Box 58610, Dallas, TX 75258. Tel. 214-720-4010.

USA–*Los Angeles:* French Government Tourist Office, 9401 Wilshire Blvd., Suite 314, Beverly Hills, CA 90212. Tel. 213-271-6665.
USA–*New York:* French Government Tourist Office, 610 Fifth Ave., New York, NY 10020. Tel. 212-757-1125.
Canada–Montreal: French Government Tourist Office, 1981 Ave. McGill College, Suite 490, Montreal, Quebec H3A 2W9. Tel. 514-288-4264.
Canada–Toronto: French Government Tourist Office, 1 Dundas St. West, Suite 2405, P.O. Box 8, Toronto, Ontario M5G 1Z3. Tel. 416-593-4717.

Lights Out! Special French Accommodations

France offers a wide variety of accommodations, from hotels, 16th-century castles, and country houses, to farm holidays, campgrounds, or simple *chambre d'hôtes* (bed and breakfast) overnights.

If you plan to headquarter in one place for a week or more, it is most economical to rent a **self-catering home,** large or small, in the French countryside or an **apartment** in a big city. Prices start as low as $400 per week. Many agencies handle home and apartment rentals; the FGTO publishes a brochure, "Packages & Tours," which lists about twenty. Those that we've found who work particularly well with families include:

B & D de Vogüé International Inc./Château Program, 1830 S. Mooney Blvd., Suite 203, Visalia, CA 93277. Tel. 209-733-7119 or 800-727-4748.
Chez Vous, 220 Redwood Hwy., Suite 129E, Mill Valley, CA 94941. Tel. 415-331-2535.
Families Abroad, Inc., 194 Riverside Dr., New York, NY 10025. Tel. 212-787-2434 or 718-768-6185.

The official French system grades **hotels,** from four-star deluxe to one-star, according to amenities and price. Most hotels charge you by the room, rather than by the person—a benefit for families. When three people share a double room, a supplemental bed may often be added for an additional charge of approximately $10 to $20. Residence hotels with kitchens are found in resorts, ski areas, and major cities.

We have selected hotels in Paris that are near parks, have a *cuisinette* (kitchenette), or offer special amenities for families. Also mentioned are reasonably priced hotels in other cities that we found to be quite good with families. **Sofitel Hotels,** a major chain with fifty-seven first-class hotels throughout France, offers reduced rates to families. An adjoining room or a second room for up to three children is free from July 1 through August 31, from December 23 through January 6, and every weekend all year long. The offer does not apply to their two resorts in Quiberon, Brittany. There is no age limit for children; adults traveling with their parents even qualify! Reserve well in advance from the U.S. by calling 800-221-4542.

Logis de France, one- and two-star family-run inns with home-style cooking, are found in the countryside. Write La Féderation Nationale des Logis de France, 25, rue Jean Mermoz, 75008 Paris (Tel. 43-59-86-67).

Staying as a guest in a private historic **château** is a fairy-tale experience for most kids. Accommodations vary from grand 14th-century castles with moats and towers to cozy manor houses and often include dinner with aristocratic hosts. Kids are welcome in most; be sure to check in advance. We profile a few that we found to be particularly suitable for families. Most châteaux have parklike settings with sporting activities available. Double occupancy, including breakfast, typically ranges between $80 and $250 a night, although there are more opulent offerings which cost up to $400 a night. Contact B & D de Vogüe International Inc. (see page 106). They also book barge or houseboat cruises and can arrange for baby-sitting in their home and apartment rentals.

Chambres d'hôtes are guest rooms in private country houses which also provide breakfast and sometimes dinner. Your kids can share the *table d'hôte* with your host's children. Look for green and yellow signs along the road; to book from the U.S., contact Chez Vous (see above). Many rural tourist offices keep lists of families willing to take in guests.

A **gîte de France** is a simple self-catering home in the countryside, typically rented by the week. Gîtes receive aid from the French government and are extremely economical, averaging $100 to $350 a week high-season for homes that sleep anywhere from four to twelve people. Order the annual *French Farm and Village Holiday Guide* (Hunter Publishing Inc., 300 Raritan Center Parkway, P.O. Box 7816, Edison, N.J. 08818-7816, $14.95), which has pictorial listings of over 1,200 gîtes. The book tells you how to book gîtes directly, saving you an agent's commission. Once in France, check with local tourist offices. Our gîte in Brittany was a charming old stone farmhouse with a very modern interior. With three bedrooms, a play area, laundry facilities, and a much needed espresso machine, it was much cheaper than a hotel stay for five people. **Gîte-camping à la ferme** is a camp-site on a working farm which usually also provide meals. **Gîte d'en-fants** are farm holidays for kids on their own. The Fédération Nationale des Gîtes Ruraux, 34, rue Godot-de-Mauroy, 75009 Paris, will supply regional brochures.

French **campgrounds,** like hotels, are rated by a star system. Three- and four-star sites usually have hot showers, bathrooms, and often a lake or pool. Campgrounds fill up early in August when all of France is on vacation. The *Guide Officiel Camping/Caravaning*, which lists sites and provides maps, is available from Fédération Française de Camping et Caravaning, 78, rue de Rivoli, 75004 Paris (Tel. 42-72-84-08). Regional tourist offices also provide lists.

Getting Around

An international driver's license is not required for driving a **car** but is helpful if you don't speak French. A valid driver's license from your hometown is required; the minimum driving age is 23, or 21 for credit card holders. All vehicles must be insured; if you are renting a French car, the rental agency will arrange this for you. Seat belts must be worn at all times by front-seat passengers. Kids under 12 may not sit in the front seat, and car seats are commonly used. The *autoroute-péage* (paying expressways) charge tolls and most accept Visa for long hauls. The average expressway speed is 130 kilometers per hour (80 mph), and the left lane is used only for passing. Along expressways, you'll find frequently placed rest stops with elaborate play areas and picnic tables. Look for signs, *Jeux d'Enfants / Pique-Nique.*

Renting a car is very expensive in France due to a costly (VAT) value-added tax. The most economical plan for rental periods of 23 days or more is the **Purchase/Buyback programs** offered by French car manufacturers, such as Renault's program described in Chapter 7.

In addition to the budget Eurail Saverpass (see Chapter 7), families traveling only by **train** in France can take advantage of the France Railpass and the new France Rail'n'Drive Pass. Both must be purchased in the U.S. or Canada before departing. With the France Railpass you can travel throughout the country on any 4 days over a 15-day period or on any 9 days over a 1-month period for a very economical fare. Children ages 4–11 pay 60 percent of the adult fare; children under 4 travel free. The Rail'n'Drive Pass offers varied combinations enabling you to travel by rental car and train. For both the France Railpass and the Rail'n'Drive Pass contact your travel agent or French National Railroad (SNCF), 610 Fifth Ave. New York, NY (Tel. 212-582-2816); or 1500 Stanley St., Suite 436, Montreal, Canada (Tel. 514-288-8255).

The SNCF has the world's most advanced trains. The high speed TGV (*trains à grande vitesse*), traveling more than 150 mph, have nursery cars. Some French lines have *trains-auto-couchettes,* where you can sleep in a berth while your car is carried on the same train. SNCF also offers a *carte famille,* with reductions for families traveling on "discounted" days. It entitles all but one family member to a 50 percent reduction if two or more persons of the same family travel together and is available at all rail stations or SNCF tourist offices (passport photos needed).

Nuts and Bolts

Does anyone care what time it is? Outside of Paris, most stores and services close for a midday break of at least 2 hours from 12 to 2. Food stores open around 8 AM and close at 7 or 7:30 PM; smaller grocery stores are open from 9–12 and 2–7. Typical bank hours outside of Paris are 9–12 and 2–4:45 or 5, Tuesday–Friday, with earlier 4 PM closings on Saturday. Banks that are open Monday are closed Saturday. (See Paris for its hours.)

National holidays: New Year's Day, Easter Monday, Labor Day (May 1), V.E. Day (May 8), Ascension Day, Whit Monday, Bastille Day (July 14), Assumption Day, All Saints' Day (November 1), Armistice Day (November 11), and Christmas Day. Businesses in rural areas often close for local celebrations.

Can I have my allowance? The French monetary unit is the *franc*, which is divided into 100 *centimes*. Banknotes are 10, 50, and 500 *francs*. Coins are 5, 10, or 20 *centimes* or ½, 5 and 10 *francs*.

Telephones: The country code for France is 33. The area code is included in the first two digits of the eight-digit phone number everywhere in France except for Paris. To call Paris from outside the city, dial 16, wait for another tone, then dial 1 followed by the eight-digit number. If you are making a call from Paris or the inner suburbs to a number in the same area, just dial the eight-digit number.

Useful nationwide phone numbers: Operator is 10; international operator is 19-33-11; directory information is 12; fire is 18; ambulance and police are 17.

Embassies and consulates: The U.S. Embassy is at 2, av. Gabriel, 8ème, Paris (Tel. 42-96-12-02); the U.S. Consulate is at rue St-Florentin, 1ème Paris (Tel. 42-60-14-88); the Canadian Embassy is at 35, av. Montaigne, 8ème, Paris (Tel. 47-23-01-01).

Let's Eat

Most cafés and restaurants welcome children although a certain amount of good behavior is expected. Ask for the *menu d'enfant*, or feel free to order only an appetizer for your kids. The quality of food is high in cafeterias, where you'll often find a hamburger option. The French invented "café society" to sit and watch the world go by. Join in. Kids will enjoy un *citron pressé* (freshly squeezed lemonade), un *chocolat chaud* (hot chocolate), or un *lait fraise* (milk with strawberry syrup). *Un sandwich* is typically made on a crusty *baguette* and can be made *au fromage* (of cheese), *au jambon* (of ham), or *au saucisson* (of salami). Kids' favorites are un *croque-monsieur* (grilled cheese and ham), un *croque-madame* (grilled cheese and bacon, sausage, chicken, or egg), or un *hot-dog* (guess . . .).

Street food is delicious. Try wafer-thin *crêpes* (pancakes) with sugar, honey, or jam, small quiches, or pizzas. For picnics, pick up meats at the *charcuterie*, cheese at the *fromagerie*, bread at the *boulangerie*, pastries at the *pâtisserie*. French open markets have fresh fruits and vegetables, and their supermarkets are very similar to ours. Fruit juices are much sweeter than ours; check labels for *sucre* (sugar).

The French breakfast (*petit déjeuner*) usually consists of rolls, croissants, or *pain au chocolat* (pastry filled with chocolate) served with butter, jam, and *café au lait* (bowl-sized cups of coffee with milk). Cold cereal, hot chocolate, and orange juice are often available for kids if you ask. Lunch (*déjeuner*) at 12:30–1 and dinner (*dîner*), after 7, are usually multicourse affairs. *Hors d'oeuvres* are served first. Most kids enjoy *soupe à l'oignon* (onion soup with cheese floating on top) and ours surprised us by gobbling up soup made with *cresson* (watercress) although they were squeamish to sample *les escargots* (snails). Favorite *entrées* (main courses) include *coq au vin* (chicken stewed in wine), *poulet rôti* (roast chicken served with *pommes frites* or French fries), *cassoulet* (casserole of beans and meat), and for the adventurous, *canard à l'orange* (roast duck with orange sauce). Fussy eaters can always order *une omelette* or *entrecôte* (rib steak) *avec pommes frites*. Ask for it *bien cuit*, if you don't want it rare. *Légumes* (vegetables) such as *courgettes* (zucchini) and *petits pois* (peas) are generally ordered separately from your meat or fish, *à la carte*.

The next course, *fromage* (cheese), is served before dessert. *Chèvre* is scrumptious goat cheese; *le plateau de fromages* is an assorted cheeseboard. *Désserts* are sinfully delicious, especially *mousse au chocolat* (creamy chocolate custard), *madeleine* (shell-shaped sponge cake), or *truffes* (truffles).

Formula and Baby Food, Diapers and Baby Gear

Disposable diapers (*couches à jeter*), formula, and baby food (*aliments pour bébé*) are available in supermarkets and pharmacies throughout France. Bébé-Confort has France's most extensive line of baby gear. Cribs (*lits d'enfant*) are found in most three- and four-star hotels.

Sidewalk Talk

Children should be formal with adults. Use *Monsieur* and *Madame* (Mr. and Mrs.), *s'il vous plaît* (please) and *merci* (thank you).

bathroom *toilette*

bicycle *bicyclette*

boy *garçon*

candies *des bonbons*

carousel *un mamège de chevaux de bois*

chocolate *chocolat*

comic strip *bandes dessinées*

cotton candy *barbe à papa*

doll *poupée*

girl *jeune fille*

happy birthday *joyeux anniversaire*

hello *bonjour*	okay *d'accord*
ice cream *glace*	toys *jouets*
no *non*	yes *oui*

The Lay of the Land

France is officially divided into ninety-five *départements*, numbered 1 to 95, which are always the first two numbers of the zip code for any address in that *département*. To identify areas of interest to visitors, France is informally divided into anywhere from ten to twenty-five regions. Outside of Paris, we have divided France into fifteen of the most popular vacation destinations, which are geographically placed under the broader headings, Northwest, Northeast, Central, East, Southeast, and Southwest France.

PARIS

Any parent who has heard the warning that Paris is not for children has only to look through our scrapbook and see snapshots of our little one ducking under the trunks of the kissing topiary elephants at the Jardin des Enfants or photos of her donning a hard hat and lifting foam blocks with a crane at the extraordinary Cité des Sciences. Even the city's standard tourist attractions have tremendous appeal for children. At night, the brightly lit Eiffel Tower appears to glow like a torch. It was so dazzling, our 2-year-old was afraid to step off the elevator at the top for fear that she might burn her feet. And, Paris is the home of the world's greatest museums. We'll never forget the observations of a passing 5-year-old on how Monet's water lilies, at the Musée de l'Orangerie, "looked beautiful from far away, but like blobs up close," which was precisely Monet's intention.

Wha'd'ya Wanna Do?

Pick up a copy of the weekly guide "Pariscope." Its section "Pour les jeunes" (for the young) lists everything from kids' theater, puppet shows, circuses, and zoos to sporting facilities and baby-sitters. "Pariscope" is published each Wednesday and is available at newsstands. **The Centre d'Informations Jeunesse,** 101, quai Branly, 15ème, or **the Loisirs-Jeunes,** 36, rue de Ponthieu, 8ème, also provides information on kids' activities. Each *arrondissement* has a **Maison de la Jeunesse et de la Culture (MJC)** with inexpensive sports activities and hands-on arts workshops. The Mairie (town hall) of each arrondissement can provide addresses. Les Petits Dragons has a bilingual playgroup and arranges au pair help (Tel. 42-28-56-17); the American University in Paris maintains a roster of baby-sitters (Tel. 45-55-91-73).

In Paris, most large stores are open Monday through Saturday 9:30–6:30; some are closed Monday mornings and are usually open until 9 or 10 PM one or two evenings a week. Smaller shops close between noon and 2. Museums close either Monday or Tuesday; check individual listings. Unlike the museums in smaller towns throughout France, most Parisian museums do not close midday.

Tourist offices are at 127, av. des Champs-Elysées, 8ème (Tel. 47-23-61-72), and at Champs de Mars, 7ème (Tel. 45-51-22-15). Other branches are found at the train stations Gare du Nord, Gare de L'Est, Gare de Lyon, and Gare d'Austerlitz.

The Lay of the City

The sights in Paris, a city of 40 square miles, are surprisingly close together. The Seine River divides the city into the Right Bank and the Left Bank, a division which is both geographical and social in the minds of Parisians. The Right Bank is famous for high fashion, the presidential palace, and more expensive neighborhoods, whereas the Left Bank, home to Sorbonne University, is considered more unconventional. The heart of the old city, the Île de la Cité and the Île St-Louis, are two islands which lie in the middle of the Seine.

Paris is divided into twenty *arrondissements*, or districts, which are referred to by number 1er (first), 2ème (second) 3ème (third), etc. Some streets are long and cut through more than one arrondissement, so be sure to note the street's arrondissement number. The best map of the city is "Plan de Paris par Arrondissements," which has an index of street names and clearly marks métro stops.

Getting Around

Traveling the underground **métro** is the most efficient way to get around. Most stations provide a free métro map, and all post a "Plan du Quartier," a detailed map of the surrounding neighborhood. Have your kids try the station's route planners, where the fastest route is illuminated by pushing a button indicating your final destination. Save money by buying a *carnet*, a packet of ten tickets, or the more economical weekly and monthly Carte Orange (you'll need a passport photo), available at major stations. Métro tickets are valid for all connections, buses, and the RER lines.

Although touristy, **boat trips** along the Seine in glass-covered boats offer an up-close look at major sights. Boats run all day and serve food. Children are not encouraged to take dinner trips, but you can take them at lunch. The following companies depart from the various bridges or ports indicated along the Seine and charge a fee: Bateaux-Mouches: Pont de l'Alma (Tel. 42-25-96-10); Métro: Alma-Marceau. Bateaux Parisiens: Port de la Bourdonnais (Tel. 47-05-50-00); Métro: Trocadero. Bateaux Vedettes de Paris Île-de-France: Port de Suffren (Tel. 47-05-71-29). Bateaux Vedettes: Pont-Neuf (Tel. 46-33-98-38). A 3-hour **canalboat ride** cruises along the Canal St-Martin through the city's old sections and underground waterways to Place de la Bastille. Fee. Canauxrama Canal St-Martin: Departs Parc de la Villette, 5 *bis* quai de la Loire. Métro: Jaurès. Departs Port de l'Arsenal, 50, bd. de la Bastille. Métro: Bastille. Tel. 42-39-15-00. All boat schedules are listed in "Pariscope." **Hélicap de Paris** (Tel. 45-57-75-51) and **Chanair** (Tel. 43-59-20-20) conduct **helicopter** tours over all of Paris. Rates are as high as a good French dinner, but more memorable for kids.

Where to Stay

Renting a Parisian **apartment** is the most economical option for a family planning to stay at least a week. Most apartments range from $800 to $1,000 a week for a family of four, and studio apartments start at $550 a week, compared to the $100 to $160 a night average you'll pay for double occupancy in a well-located two- or three-star hotel with additional charges for supplemental beds and dining out. Our 9ème apartment through Chez Vous (see "Lights Out!"), was adorned with turn-of-the-century ironwork from the métro, slept eight, and had both a washer/dryer and an unobstructed view of the Sacré-Coeur.

Our friends and their three children rocked to sleep on a converted **barge** moored on the Seine. With as little as a three-night minimum, barges offer an unusual alternative to hotel stays. For agents, request FGTO's "Packages and Tours."

HOTELS

NEAR THE LUXEMBOURG GARDENS: 6ème & 5ème

The *Hôtel des Saints-Pères* has apartments and double rooms (less expensive) as well as a great location. 65, rue des Saints-Pères, 75006. Tel. 45-44-50-00; fax 45-44-90-83. **Expensive.**

Select is well located on a traffic-free *place*, right by the Luxembourg Gardens. 1, pl. de la Sorbonne, 75005. Tel. 46-34-14-80. **Moderate.**

Grandes Ecoles has a garden and is comfortable and charming at a bargain price. 45, rue du Cardinal Lemoine, 75005. Tel. 43-26-79-23. **Inexpensive.**

Hôtel Marignan with rooms for up to five people, a free laundry room, and an area to bring in food, is a short walk from the Luxembourg Gardens. They can arrange baby-sitters, have cribs, will heat baby bottles, and keep baby food refrigerated. 13, rue du Sommerard, 75005. Tel. 43-54-63-81. **Inexpensive.**

LE MARAIS: 4*ème* and 3*ème:*

Marais has communicating rooms. 2 *bis,* rue Commines, 75003. Tel. 48-87-78-27. **Moderate.**

Hôtel Place des Vosges has a great location near the park of the same name. 12, rue Birague, 75004. Tel. 42-72-60-46. **Inexpensive.**

OPERA, PALAIS-ROYAL, HALLES: 1*er*

Régina has suites and two- or three-bedroom apartments facing Tuileries Gardens. 2, pl. des Pyramides, 75001. Tel. 42-60-31-10. **Deluxe.**

Family welcomes families, just as their name implies, and is a bargain for such an elegant location. 35, rue Cambon, 75001. Tel. 42-61-54-84. **Moderate.**

15*ème:*

Sofitel Paris has connecting rooms, an interior pool and gym, and a nursery. It has direct access to Aquaboulevard de Paris Sports Center, with a Polynesian waterland, toboggans, and bowling. A second room or an adjoining room for up to three children is free July 1–Aug. 31, Dec. 23–Jan. 6, and every weekend all year long. Reserve well in advance by calling 800-221-4542 or write 8, rue L.-Armand, 75015. Tel. 40-60-30-30; fax 45-57-04-22. **Expensive.**

Hôtel Plaza Mirabeau overlooks the Seine with a patio garden, kitchenettes, and one- to three-room apartments, 10, av. Emile Zola, 75015. Tel. 45-77-72-00. **Expensive.**

CAMPGROUNDS
Camping du Bois de Boulogne is the city's only campground. Laundry and warm showers. Fee. Allée du Bord de L'Eau, 16ème. daily 6 AM–2 AM Tel. 45-24-30-00. Métro: Porte Maillot.

Detour! What to See and Do

Sites are grouped by their geographic proximity within the Île de la Cité, the Right and Left Bank, the Suburbs, and Parisian Environs. Addresses are followed, where needed, by arrondissement number and the closest métro stop.

ÎLE DE LA CITÉ: WHERE PARIS BEGAN

Children who climb the worn and winding 255 spiral steps of **Notre-Dame's bell tower** will get a close look at the cathedral's fanciful gargoyles and funny devil-statues that were created to scare him away. It was here that *The Hunchback of Notre-Dame,* a tale of the beautiful Gypsy Esmerelda and the ugly bell ringer Quasimodo, was set. **Cathédrale de Notre-Dame** is one of the shining examples of Gothic architecture. Point out how the cathedral seems to float in air because of its flying buttresses, or supports, which run along the building's sides. Stand back and show your children how the building's lines draw their eyes to the sky. The 12th-century architects intended for them to look toward the heavens. Free. Daily 8–7. Tel. 43-54-22-63. Bell tower: fee; half-price Sun. and holidays. Daily 10–5:45; winter until 4:45. Tel. 43-54-22-63. Métro: Cité.

Nearby is **La Sainte-Chapelle,** a small church inside the Palais de Justice, housing Christ's Crown of Thorns. An English hands-on discovery guide to the church, "La Sainte-Chapelle for Children" is available in the gift shop. When it's sunny, you'll feel enclosed by the glow of an emerald and sapphire ring as the 7,000-square-foot expanse of green and blue stained-glass windows shimmer. The crown worn by Jesus on his last day is placed above the heads of most kids, but the nearby photographs provide a closer look. Fee; half-price Sun. and holidays. Bd. du Palais, 4ème. Daily Apr.–Sept. 9:30–7; Oct.–Mar. 10–5:45. Tel. 43-54-30-09. Métro: Cité.

The same ticket admits you to **La Conciergerie,** the prison where more than 2,500 inmates stayed before meeting the guillotine. Gruesome types will be fascinated with the barber shop where hair was cut short before the big ax fell. The exhibit's strange memorabilia includes a note that prisoner Marie-Antoinette wrote by poking holes in paper because she was prohibited access to a pencil. Obligatory French tour. Fee. 1, quai de l'Horloge. Daily Apr.–Sept. 9:30–7, Oct.–Mar. 10–5. Tel. 43-54-30-06. Métro: Cité.

Walking along the north side of the Île de la Cité from Sainte Chapelle, you arrive at Place Lépine, where a daily flower market is transformed on Sundays into a **bird and pet market.** Free. quai de la Megisserie, between Pont Neuf and Pont au Change, 1er. Métro: Pont Neuf.

RIGHT BANK
Sites are arranged from west to east to northeast.

LE MARAIS

Head off on a hunt for some of the everyday objects Picasso used in his paintings and sculptures at the extraordinary **Musée Picasso.** We found a bike seat used for the bull's head in *Tête de Taureau*, and a basket that formed the girl's belly as she jumped rope in *Petite Fille Sautant à La Corde.* According to museum officials, the art piece favored by most children is the humorous bronze sculpture of a mother pushing a baby carriage, *La Femme à la Poussette.* Stop in the museum shop to buy the excellent French kids' book *Picasso Le Minotaure,* part of Paris' Musée National d'Art Moderne's series "L'Art en Jeu." Fee, 5, rue de Thorigny, 3ème. Mon., Thur.–Sun. 9:45–5:15, Wed. 9:45–10. Tel. 42-71-25-21. Métro: St-Paul or Chemin Vert.

The **Place des Vosges,** one of the oldest and most beautiful Parisian squares, has a grassy area and small playground where local children often play. Considered a masterpiece of 17th-century architecture, it hasn't changed much since the days when it was built for Henri IV. Carriages bringing men to fatal duels once arrived here in the pre-dawn hours.

MUSÉE DU LOUVRE

A gleaming and renovated **Louvre,** crowned by I. M. Pei's tall glass pyramid, has transformed what was once a museum of many dark galleries into a light-filled experience. With more than 400,000 works of art, make several short trips concentrating on a few sections each time. Better to have your children enjoy a few paintings, than to moan from overkill. Have them pick out some favorite postcards from the selection at the Librairie du Musée (museum bookshop), and then embark on a treasure hunt.

Your kids will want to see the most famous paintings, so arrive as soon as the doors open. Avoid Sundays, when admission is free and the more popular exhibits are packed all day. There are now video screens in the main entry, the Hall Napoléon, indicating the best routes to the most popular works of art, such as *La Joconde* (Mona Lisa) and "Winged Victory." Shorter lines are found by entering the portes on quai du Louvre. Fee; free Sunday. Thur.–Sun. 9–6, Mon. and Wed. 9 AM–9:45 PM. Tel. 40-20-51-51. Métro: Palais Royal Musée du Louvre. For a real treat, walk by the Louvre at night. The pyramid and fountains are illuminated, and the contrast of the ultramodern geometric structure with the Palais du Louvre of 1871 is startling. Our family thought it looked as though a spaceship had landed.

AROUND THE JARDIN DES TUILERIES

A short walk westward from the Louvre along Rue de Rivoli brings you to the **Jardin des Tuileries,** where children can play in the playground or ride the vintage carousel, La Belle Epoque. Ponies pull carts for the very young. Running the length of the gardens along the river is a terrace that was once the playground for the royal Medici children. The carp that live in the park's pond are said to have lived there for over 100 years. Model boats can be rented by the half-hour in the afternoon. The **Théâtre de la Petite Ourse** performs marionette shows in the playhouse near the carousel every Wed., Sat., and Sun. afternoon. Check "Pariscope." Toddlers will adore the multicolored wooden rocking horses adjacent to the theater. 1er. Métro: Tuileries.

Don't miss the **Musée de l'Orangerie** at the end of the park closest to Place de la Concorde. Its treasures include works by Matisse, Rousseau, Modigliani, Monet, Renoir, and Cézanne. A small, intimate museum, the Orangerie doesn't have the crowds of the Louvre or the Orsay, so your kids can get up very close to the works of art, and it's just the right size for the attention span of most children. Suggest a hunt to find the many paintings of artists' children in the Impressionist collection upstairs. Our favorite was Renoir's son, dressed up in a red clown costume in *Claude Renoir en Clown.* Fee. 1er. Wed.–Mon. 9:45–5. Tel. 42-97-48-16. Métro: Concorde.

Homesick for **English storybooks?** Across the street from the Tuileries at 248, rue de Rivoli is W. H. Smith, an English bookshop with a wide range of children's books. Many focus on French life.

LES HALLES

Spend an afternoon at the fun-filled **Centre National d'Art et de Culture Georges-Pompidou,** better known as the Beaubourg. A highly controversial, tubular steel and glass building, the Beaubourg has become a hotbed of activity for contemporary artists in all media. Ascend the glass escalators that run *outside* the building to the fifth level for an ever-changing view of the festivities below in Plateau Beaubourg, typically a scene of street artists, fire-eaters, clowns, and mimes.

Along with numerous, frequently changing exhibits, the Beaubourg houses the **Musée National d'Art Moderne** and its selection of 20th-century art, from the Fauves to the present. Matisse's cutout gouaches were a big hit with our children, who attempted a few of their own back at our apartment with the aid of travel scissors and used maps. The museum publishes its own art education series for children, L'Art en Jeu, with French picture books on Magritte, Léger, Arp, Braque, Delaunay, Bonnard, Kandinsky, Giacometti, Picasso, and more. They also offer animated films for kids of permanent works from their collection in the series Les Mots Pour Voir L'Aventure de L'Art Moderne. Free. Wed. at 3, Sat. at 4. Meet at the museum entrance. If you are planning to be in Paris for a while, the museum offers two series of **hands-on children's workshops** in visual and performing arts, many with English-speaking attendants: (1) on five or six Wednesday afternoons at Les Mercredi de L'Art en Jeu, 6- to 12-year-olds create artwork inspired by artists from the museum's collection; (2) the Exposition Animation series allows 6- to 13-year-olds to create animated films. Fee for both. Entire Center: Fee. Tues.–Fri. noon–10 PM, weekends and holidays 10–10. Workshops: Tel. 42-77-12-33. Recorded program of events: Tel. 42-77-11-12. Métro: Rambuteau, Hôtel-de-Ville, Châtelet or Les Halles.

Don't miss the squirting skeletons, snakes, parrots, and spinning top hat in the colorful and whimsical **fountains of Jean Tinguely and Niki de Saint-Phalle,** between the Pompidou Center and Church of St-Merri. You'll get soaked if you get too close, but it's worth it.

The **Forum des Halles** is a huge subterranean multilevel complex housing some of the city's most desirable shops. It covers an enormous expanse, all below the ground. Avoid it unless your kids are suffering from "mall withdrawal" or need a fast-food fix. Amidst the boutiques is an aquarium, the **Parc Oceanique Jacques Cousteau,** with many special effects. Volcanos rumble, thunderstorms roar, coral islands are full of dayglow-colored fish. There's a three-dimensional film about giant octopuses and a learning area with English computerized games. Fee. Forum des Halles. 1er. Sat.–Thurs. 12–7, weekends and holidays 10–7:30. Tel. 40-26-13-78. Métro: Châtelet-Les-Halles.

On the street-level plaza atop the forum, landscape artist Pascal Cribier and sculptor Claude Lalanne have created an **imaginative children's play area** with topiary kissing elephants, mazes, caves, and baskets of surrealist treasures such as swinging balls and puzzles. Professional attendants will watch your 7- to 12-year-olds. Fee. St-Eustache, west of the Forum. Follow signs for **Jardin des Enfants.** If your under-7s are disappointed that they can't play in the topiary wonderland, steer them next door to a playground or to the jeweled carousel nearby.

AROUND THE ARC DE TRIOMPHE

Two hundred and eighty-four steps lead to the top of the **Arc de Triomphe,** the monument to French patriotism which stands in the garden between the Pavillon de Marsan and the Pavillon de Flore. Two-thirds of the way up is a dull museum, but there are telescopes from which your kids can marvel at the madness of Parisian drivers below. Twelve streets converge into one broad avenue, the Champs-Elysées, and even from that height you can tell that *all* drivers think they alone have the right of way. Fee. Access: underground passage on the even-numbered side of both the Champs-Elysées and Avenue de la Grande-Armée. Daily 10–5:30. Tel. 43-80-31-31. Métro: Charles-de-Gaulle/Etoile.

Parc Rond-Point is a small park on the north side of the Champs-Elysées with puppet shows held Wed., Sat. and Sun. Check "Pariscope." Further down the Champs-Elysées, the **Palais Découverte,** a touch-and-feel science museum, is devoted to each major area of natural science. English-speaking guides will help your kids discover how a telephone works, how lasers function, or why we see the colors we see. Fee. Grand Palais, facing Avenue de Franklin D. Roosevelt. Tues.–Sun. 10–6. Métro: Champs Elysées Clemenceau.

MONTMARTRE

Climb or take the funicular from rue St-Pierre up to this famed hill, which was an artistic haven for turn-of-the-century bohemians. Although touristy, Montmartre's narrow winding streets filled with musicians and portrait artists are fun to explore. The popular **Place de Tertre** is a plaza with a lively open-air market. Just east of Tertre is Montmartre's landmark, the white **Basilique de Sacré-Coeur.** Its bell tower has one of the best views of Paris. Basilique: Free. Dome: Fee. 35, rue du Cheval de la Barre, 18ème. Daily 9 AM–11:15 PM. Tel. 42-51-17-02. Métro: Château Rouge. Back down the hill near where the funicular lets out is a vintage two-tier carousel and a small local park.

Heading south toward Palais-Royal and the Opéra is the **Musée Grévin.** Here, kids can watch an old-fashioned light and magic show and view waxworks of such historical notables as Marie-Antoinette in jail. The museum's Palais des Miracles is lined with weird distorting mirrors. Fee. 10, bd. Montmartre, 9ème. Daily 1–6. Tel. 47-70-85-05. Métro: Montmartre.

BOIS DE BOULOGNE AND THE 16ème ARRONDISSEMENT

En route to the lush, 2,000-acre **Bois de Boulogne** from the Left Bank is the **Palais de Chaillot,** which contains many museums of interest to children. To get there, cross the Pont d'Iéna near the Eiffel Tower. Its **Musée de la Marine** contains models of ships, antique diving suits, and a realistic ship's bridge that kids can explore. Fee. Wed.–Mon. 10–6. Tel. 45-53-31-70. The Palais' **Musée de l'Homme** colorfully traces how we have evolved from apes, with examples of skulls and bones. Its excellent costume collection is wide-ranging and includes armor from a Samurai warrior. Kids are inevitably drawn to the collection of shrunken heads. Fee. Wed.–Mon. 9:15–5:15. Tel. 45-53-70-60. The **Aquarium du Trocadéro,** in the gardens near the Palais, is a small underground aquarium built to look like a grotto. Kids like the flesh-eating piranhas best. Fee. Palais de Chaillot, 16éme. Daily 10–5:30. Métro: Trocadéro.

Avoid the Palais de Tokyo's **Musée des Enfants,** which documents the lives of children hundreds of years ago in Paris, unless your kids have an interest in frilly frocks of the last century. Fee. 13, av. du Président-Wilson. Tues.–Sun. 10–5:40. Métro: Iéna.

The **Musée Marmottan** does not have as grand an Impressionist collection as the Orsay (see 7ème), but its manageable size and lack of crowds make up for it. Try to obtain the wonderful book by Christina Björk, *Linnea in Monet's Garden* (Rabén & Sjögren Publishers, 1985), about a young girl's experiences viewing the Monets in this museum and those at Giverny. We bought it in the Orsay's bookshop. You'll find that Monet painted not only water lilies, but trains, churches, and people. Fee. 2, rue Louis-Boilly. Tues.–Sun. 10–5. Tel. 42-24-07-02. Métro: La Muette.

The **Musée des Lunettes et Lorgnettes de Jadis** houses an historic collection of specs of the rich and famous as well as unusual glasses cleverly hidden in adornments such as perfume bottles, fans, or old canes. Free. 2, av. Mozart. Tues.–Sat. 10–12, 3–6:30. Closed August. Tel. 45-27-21-05. Métro: La Muette.

The **Musée de la Contrefaçon (Museum of Counterfeits)** displays designer "rip-offs," from clothes to candy, passed off as the real thing to naive consumers. Free. 16, rue de la Faisanderie. Mon.–Fri. 9–5. Tel. 45-01-51-11 Métro: Porte-Dauphine.

The **Bois de Boulogne,** running the length of the 16th arrondissement's west side, is perfect for unwinding after a day of sightseeing. A miniature railway from Porte Maillot will escort your young ones to the **Jardin d'Acclimatation,** an amusement park at the park's north end. Kids can ride boats down an "enchanted river," race remote-control boats, or climb through a city of large inventive sculptures. The Hall of Mirrors has some very kooky fun-house mirrors, and carnival rides include a wild Chinese dragon roller coaster. Quiet types can immerse themselves in the giant doll house or take a wide variety of workshops at the **Musée en Herbe.** A petting zoo, camel and pony rides, sea lions, Punch and Judy shows, and an *Automatons* village are sure to keep your francs flowing. The **Théâtre du Jardin pour l'Enfance et la Jeunesse** performs ballet and musical concerts at the park's theater. Check "Pariscope." Entrance plus activity fees. North of Avenue du Mahatma-Gandhi. Daily 10–6. Petite Train departs Porte Maillot Wed., weekends, and holidays 1:30. Tel. 40-67-90-82. Métro: Sablons. Just past the entrance to the Jardin is the

Musée des Arts et Traditions Populaires. Head for the rear to the magic and witchcraft exhibitions. Fee. 6, rte. du Mahatma-Gandhi. Wed.–Mon. 9:45–5. Tel. 47-47-69-80. Métro: Sablons. Rowboating out to the islands in the middle of **Lac Inférieur** can be arranged with hourly rentals. Bikes can be rented across from the rowboat dock.

EASTERN PARIS

The 12ème's park, the **Bois de Vincennes,** contains many fun-filled attractions for children. Its **Vincennes Zoo,** where animals wander uncaged in their natural habitats, is considered to be the best in France. There are wild goats, baboons, lions, tigers, bears, and an incubation room where chicken eggs hatch. Fee. Daily 9–5. Tel. 43-43-84-95. Kids can visit a real dungeon in the park's medieval fortress, **Château de Vincennes.** Fee. Daily 10–6. The park's graceful **Lac Daumesnil,** a lovely picnic site, has boats for rent. The **Foire du Trône,** a giant amusement park held the end of March through May near the park's Porte Dorée entrance, has pony rides, fun houses, side shows, and carnival rides. Kids can sample *barbe à papa* (cotton candy) or, literally, "papa's beard." Avoid it on weekends. Bois de Vincennes. Métro: Port Dorée.

Also in the 12ème, on the other side of the woods, is **Parc Floral.** A small train will take you to its playground, which has an electric car track, and there are clowns, jugglers, and magic shows on summer weekends. The park's resident troupe, Théâtre Astral, performs mime, music, and dance, so the language difference rarely matters. Check "Pariscope." Fee; under 6 free. Rte. de la Pyramide. Sun.–Fri. 9:30–8, Sat. 9:30–10; winter until 6. Métro: Château de Vincennes.

NORTHEASTERN PARIS:
19ème AND 20ème ARRONDISSEMENTS

The picture perfect **Parc des Buttes-Chaumont** has a lake with ducks, high cliffs, grassy fields, and carts led by donkeys. It's good for a picnic away from the city crowds. The Marionnettes du Parc perform Wed., Sat., and Sun. afternoons. Check "Pariscope." Angle av. Simon Bolívar et rue Botzaris, 19ème. Métro: Buttes-Chaumont.

Not quite a park, the **Père Lachaise Cemetery** has beautiful open spaces, tree-lined promenades, and paths for wandering about between the graves of such notables as Gertrude Stein, Isadora Duncan, Cyrano de Bergerac, Chopin, and Oscar Wilde. Père Lachaise has long been a meeting ground for hero-worshipers. A young friend met fellow Jim Morrison fans from as far away as Santa Barbara and New York at the rock star's grave where, alas, his gravestone had been stolen. Maps of famous gravestones at the gate. Free. 20ème. Mid-

March–Nov. 5 daily 7:30–6; rest of the year 8:30–5. Tel. 43-70-70-33. Métro: Père Lachaise.

La Cité des Sciences et de l'Industrie de la Villette is one of the world's great centers of science and technology. Within the enormous 322,000-square-foot building are exciting discovery areas for kids, such as the highly recommended **Inventorium,** where 3–6 and 6–12-year-olds explore the world of science through interactive games, workshops, and experiments. The wind blew while our preschooler completed a cloud puzzle; then she gave vegetables computer-generated faces and built a house with a crane. Six- to twelve-year-olds can examine an ant megalopolis or play games to compare their genetic identity with others. The cité also houses a **planetarium** and sections chronicling the universe, life, matter, and communication. Its famed **Géode,** a mirror-slick sphere that looks like a crystal ball, houses a movie theater with a 180-degree projection screen. Cité: Fee; discounts for families. Separate modest fee for planetarium, inventorium, and geode. 30, rue Corentin Cariou. Tues.–Sun. 10–6. Inventorium's 90-minute sessions are Tues., Thurs., Fri. 9:30 (except holidays), 11, 12:30, 2, 2:30; Wed., weekends 11, 12:30, 2, 3:30, 5. Tel. 46-42-13-13. The adjoining **Parc de la Villette** has a wacky dragon slide. Our tribe voted it the best and longest in the city. Métro: Porte de la Villette or Corentin Cariou.

LEFT BANK
Sites are arranged from west to east, followed by Montparnasse.

JARDIN DES PLANTES

The **Jardin des Plantes** park contains a **natural history museum** with fossils and dinosaur skeletons, insects, and minerals. Its **zoo** has a kid's "please touch" section and a vivarium with slimy creatures, lizards, and bats. Don't touch the deadly Green Tree Viper from Cambodia, which is said to have hidden amongst the leaves of trees and bitten the fingers off of fruit pickers. Skip the **aquarium** but don't miss the park's **botanical gardens,** a topiary labyrinth kids can find their way out of. Zoo and museum: fee. 57, rue Cuvier, 5ème. Park: daily 7 AM–8 PM. Museum: 11–5:30. Zoo: summer daily 9–6; off-season daily 9–5. Tel. 43-36-19-09. Métro: Jussieu.

LATIN QUARTER

Dragnet fans will enjoy the **Musée des Collections Historiques de la Préfecture de Police.** Among its exhibits are examples of many different types of exploding devices collected by the Parisian police, from perfume-bottle bombs to a bursting book. Free. Police Department Building: 1 *bis,* rue de Carmes, 5ème. Enter on rue de la Montagne-Ste-Geneviève. Mon.–Thur. 9–5, Fri. 9–4:30. Tel. 43-29-21-57. Métro: Maubert-Mutualité.

JARDIN DU LUXEMBOURG AND THE 6ème ARRONDISSEMENT

Kids can rent a toy boat to sail in the pond at this glorious park, or they can watch a familiar fable performed by the puppeteers, Les Marionnettes du Théâtre Luxembourg. As you wander amongst the trees past statues of poets Baudelaire and Hérédia, well-dressed nannies stroll their equally well-dressed charges. Theater critics Claire (8), John Patrick (6), and Silvie (2) all agree that the puppet theater here is the city's best. Check "Pariscope" and choose a recognizable tale from the repertoire, which includes *Blanche Neige* (Snow White), *La Belle au Bois Dormant* (Sleeping Beauty), or *Le Chat Botté* (Puss 'n' Boots). The playground (fee) adjacent to the puppet theater is the best we found in Paris; there are also pony rides and a carousel.

7ème ARRONDISSEMENT

The intimate **Musée Rodin** displays such noted sculptures as *The Kiss* and *The Cathedral,* and outdoors, alongside *The Thinker* and *The Gates of Hell,* is a rose garden frequented by local young children and ideal for picnicking. Fee for each. 77, rue de Varenne, 7ème. July–Sept. Tues.–Sun. 10–5:15; Oct.–June Tues.–Sun. 10–4:40. Tel. 47-05-01-34. Métro: Varenne.

The grand **Musée d'Orsay,** devoted to French art of the second half of the 19th and early 20th century, is housed in an immense steel and glass railway station built for the Great Exhibition of 1900. Pick up the free English guide for children at the information desk, "From Station to Museum," which has photographs of the museum in its former incarnation and leads kids on a thought-provoking museum tour. Children write or draw their responses to such inquiries as, "What color attracts your attention here the most?" or "Is the vault of the Orsay station the same shape as the roof in this painting?" Groupled activities and tours are organized for 5- to 15-year-olds in the basement's Young Visitors' Center. Kids are drawn to the miniature stage sets of the flamboyant 1875 Rossini opera *William Tell,* and the 1/100 scale model of the city's opera quarter, which is seen through a big glass window set in the 1st floor. There is also a supervised childcare center for infants, toddlers, and preschoolers with a nap area, toys, art projects, and snacks. Check at the main desk. Slight fee. Museum fee. Main entrance: 1, rue de Bellechasse, 7ème. June 20–Sept. 20 Tues., Wed., Fri., Sat., Sun. 9–6, Thur. 9 AM–9:45 PM; opens at 10 rest of year. Tel. 40-49-48-14. Young Visitors' Center: Tel. 40-49-48-69 or 40-49-49-76. Métro: Solferino.

The **Hôtel des Invalides** is where Napoleon lies in an impressive tomb. In 1815, he was banished to an island in the South Atlantic; his body was not allowed back to France until 1840. Its **Musée de l'Armée** has enough model soldiers, swords, daggers, suits of armor, and uniforms to fascinate any military buff. Fee admits to both. Apr.–Sept. 10–6; Oct.–Mar. 10–5. Hôtel open until 7. Tel. 45-55-92-30. Métro: La Tour-Maubourg, St-François Xavier.

AROUND THE EIFFEL TOWER

A visit to Paris with kids is not complete without ascending the **Eiffel Tower,** the city's most famous landmark. Go at night, when the tower is brightly illuminated. Recently refurbished for its centennial, the top 3rd level is now accessible by elevator and is a must for thrill seekers. The view of the city, from the fountains of the Palais Trocadéro to the illuminated boats cruising the Seine, is unsurpassed. During the day, arrive at least 30 minutes before it opens to avoid the long line. Different fees for levels 1–3. Daily 10 AM–11 PM. Tel. 45-55-91-11. Métro: Bir Hakeim. Across from the Eiffel Tower is the **Champ de Mars,** a park with a carousel and the Marionnettes de Champ de Mars, which perform Wed., Sat., and Sun. afternoons. Check "Pariscope."

Guided 1-hour tours by sewer workers through the tunnels of the Parisian waste disposal system **Les Egouts de Paris** follow the streets of the city. The aroma is far from Chanel No. 5 so hold your nose and wear rubber shoes. Fee. Place de la Résistance, 7ème. Wed.–Sun. 3–8. Tel. 47-05-10-29. Métro: Alma Marceau.

MONTPARNASSE

At 688 feet, the **Tour Montparnasse** is Europe's tallest skyscraper. The elevator to its 59th floor is said to be the fastest in all of the continent and the view is spectacular, especially at night. Fee. 33, av. du Maine, 14ème. Summer daily 9:30 AM–11:00 PM; off-season daily 10–10. Tel. 45-38-52-56. Métro: Montparnasse-Bienvenue.

Even fans of the macabre will get chills at the doorway of the **Catacomb Tour,** where they are greeted by the sign, "Stop! Here is the Empire of Death." The tour through the silent, underground labyrinth of Roman stone quarries passes carefully arranged piles of skulls and ribs. Why? The cemeteries of Paris were too full by the 18th and 19th centuries, so the bones of 6 million souls had to be stored. Bring a flashlight. Fee. Tours Tues.–Fri. 2–4; Sat.–Sun. 9–11, 2–4. 1, pl.

Denfert Rochereau, 14ème. Tel. 43-22-47-63. Métro: Denfert-Rochereau.

Toy boats can be rented at **Parc Montsouris** to sail alongside swans, ducks, and large fish on its beautiful pond. The *Marionnettes de Montsouris* perform regularly. Check "Pariscope." Métro: Cité-Universitaire, 14ème.

Did you know letters were once delivered by balloon? The **Musée de la Poste** is a stamp collector's paradise. It houses a collection of famous and very rare stamps and provides explanations of how stamps are made and how the postal service has developed since the Middle Ages. Fee. 34, bd. de Vaugirard, 15ème. Mon.–Sat. 10–4:45. Tel. 43-20-15-30. Métro: Montparnasse-Bienvenue.

Sports and Performing Arts

For a complete listing of *bowlings* (bowling alleys), *patinoires* (skating rinks), and *piscines* (pools), check "Pariscope" under its Guide de Paris listing.

In the Pour les Jeunes listings in "Pariscope," Enfants in "7 à Paris," or Jeunes in "L'Officiel des Spectacles," you can learn who's in town. Among the best **circuses** are Cirque d'Hiver Bouglione at 10, rue Amelot, 11ème; Cirque de Paris at 92-Nanterre, RER (bus), Nanterre Ville; Cirque Zavatta-Fils at Square du Serment de Koufra, 14ème; and Cirque Pauwels at Square de L'Amiral Bruix, 16ème.

Children's **theater** companies include Galerie 55 Underground, the English Theater of Paris, at 55, rue de Seine, 6ème (Tel. 43-26-63-51), and Théâtre Astral, in the Parc Floral de Paris, 12ème (see Parks).

Special Events

For March through May's giant amusement park, the **Foire du Trône,** refer back to Eastern Paris' Bois de Vincennes.

Waiters and waitresses must keep their formal posture while racing through the city streets, balancing a full glass and a bottle of beer on a tiny tray during the **Course des Garçons et des Serveuses de Café.** They cannot spill a drop. It usually starts and finishes at the Hôtel de Ville and takes place at the end of June.

The **Festival du Marais** includes theater, songs, mime, circuses, dance, and many children's events in courtyards of restored mansions. Many events are free. It continues through mid-July. Tel. 48-87-74-31.

June's **Fêtes du Pont Neuf** showcases street artists, musicians, and dancers on the famous bridge, which closes to all cars. Tel. 42-77-92-26.

Bastille Day, July 14, is celebrated with military parades down the Champs-Elysées, fireworks, and dancing in the streets.

The world's most grueling and prestigious bicycle race, the **Tour de France,** ends in Paris a few days after Bastille Day. Winners stream through L'Arc de Triomphe to the cheers of crowds who pack the Champs-Elysées. Bring something for your kids to stand on so they can see and pick a spot very early.

The French Communist Party's giant annual fair, the **Fête de l'Humanité,** held the second or third week of September, features international stars, food, bands, and amusement park rides. It is one of the world's largest international fairs, and visitors of all political persuasions attend. Parc de la Courneuve. Tel. 42-38-66-55.

An amusement park on the Neuilly Lawn of the Bois de Vincennes is held during the **Fête de Force Ouvrière,** the second or third week of September.

Thousands fill the church for midnight Mass on **Christmas Eve** at Notre-Dame.

THE SUBURBS OF PARIS

Le Cimetière des Chiens in *Asnières* is a cemetery with eccentric inscriptions on its tombstones for dogs, cats, birds, and other beloved pets. It is the heralded resting place of Rin Tin Tin. Free. 4, Pont de Clichy. 30 minutes northwest of central Paris. Mon.–Sat. 9–11:45, 2–5:45; Sun. and holidays 2–5:45. Tel. 47-93-87-04, Métro: Asnières.

Charenton's **Musée du Pain (Bread Museum)** is devoted to bread making and exhibits many strangely shaped loaves. Free. 25 *bis*, rue Victor-Hugo. Southeast corner of Paris. Sept.–June Tues. and Thur. 2–5. Tel. 43-68-43-60. Métro: Charenton-Ecoles.

NEAR PARIS (listed alphabetically)

Built around a grotesquely fat, 110-foot-tall statue of Gargantua, a character created by 16th-century author François Rabelais, **Mirapolis** in *Cergy St-Christophe* is France's first theme park and rather disappointing. Kids are led through the history and legends of France with an adventure land and the typical array of carnival rides. Fee. Train from Gare St-Lazare to Cergy St-Christophe. May 12–Oct. 16 Sun.–Fri. 10–7; Sat. until 9. Tel. 34-43-20-00.

Chantilly, 40 kilometers from Paris, is the setting of the lavish **Château de Chantilly** and a grand park. Horse lovers will want to visit the stables, **Grandes Ecuries,** and the **Musée du Cheval (Horse Museum),** which displays real horses, horse sculptures, and videos. Fee. Apr.–Oct. Wed.–Mon. 10:30–6; Nov.–Mar. Mon. and Wed.–Fri. 2–4:30. Budding equestrians can take a 20-minute horse-training lesson at the Cours des Chenils at 11:30, 3:30, and 5:15; Nov.–Mar. weekends at 3:30. Tel. 44-57-13-13. 35-minute train ride from Paris. SNCF: Gare du Nord.

In *Chartres,* visit the **Cathédrale de Chartres** on a sunny day to view the glowing reflections of the intricate 13th-century stainedglass windows. Our kids enjoyed the story of how the windows were dismantled during both world wars, stored piece by piece, and then reassembled. An 8-year-old friend especially enjoyed learning how to "read" the windows, courtesy of Malcolm Miller's excellent English tour. Tours Apr.–Jan. Mon.–Sat. noon, 2:45. And a climb up the north tower is exhilarating. Cathedral: Free. Winter 7:30–7; summer until 6:30. Tower: Fee. Oct.–Dec. and Feb.–Mar. Mon.–Sat. 10–11:30, 2–4:30; Sun. 2–4:30; Apr.–Sept. Mon.–Sat. 9:30–11:30, 2–5:30, Sun. 2–5:30. 50-minute train ride from Paris. SNCF: Gare Montparnasse.

Don't miss the folk-art miracle, the **Maison Picassiette (House of Mosaics),** built by Chartres cemetery worker Raymond Isidore. His entire house, including the floors and furnishings, are covered inside and out with mosaic shards. You'll see birds, people, flowers, and scenes based on the Chartres cathedral. Fee. Impasse du Repos, 22, rue de Repos. Summer Wed.–Mon. 10–12, 2–6; off-season Sat. all day, Sun. afternoons. Tel. 37-36-41-39.

Yes, Mickey, Minnie, Donald, Pluto, and Goofy are equally famous in France and are the inspiration for the newly created **Euro Disneyland,** 30 kilometers east of Paris in *Marne-la-Vallée.* Unparalleled in all of Europe, the park is one-fifth the size of the city of Paris! Americana pervades as kids enter the Magic Kingdom along La Grand'Rue, a turn-of-the-century bustling American main street, or forge their way through Le Monde de l'Ouest, America's wild frontier. A French influence is definitely felt, however, in Le Pays de la Découverte (Discoveryland), inspired by French futurist Jules Verne, and in the castle in Le Pays Imaginaire (Fantasyland), inspired by the illustrations in *Les Très Riches Heures du Duc de Berry.* Favorite Disney classics, in French, such as *Peter Pan* and the *Swiss Family Robinson,* are found throughout Le Pays de l'Aventure, the most exotic of the park's settings. Like Tokyo's and California's Disneylands and Florida's Disney World, theme hotels, campgrounds, and a championship golf course accommodate visitors. Fee varies with season and holiday prices. Off autoroute A4. Opens spring 1992. Open daily year-round.

Astérix Park, in *Plailly,* is based on the immensely popular French comic-book character, Astérix, a feisty wild boar hunter from Gaul who outfoxes the invading Romans at the time of Julius Caesar. Represented in the park are five different fun worlds, including a Gaul village and a Roman world with gladiators. Fee. 38 km. from Paris and 10 km. from Roissy. Near Charles de Gaulle Airport, on A1 heading toward Survilliers to Plailly. Daily 10–7. Tel. 44-60-60-00.

Thoiry's **game park** at the **Château de Thoiry** features more than 800 wild animals, including lions, tigers, bears, elephants, rhinoceroses, giraffes, emus, and flamingos that roam free. A favorite stop at the château is its **Musée de la Gastronomie,** where among the gastronomic delights kids can view the 16-foot-high cake. Zoo: Fee. West of Paris. Weekdays 10–5:15; weekends and holidays 10–5:45. Museum: Fee. Apr.–Sept. daily 10–5:15; Oct.–Nov. Mon., Wed., and Thur. 10–5:15. Tel. 34-87-40-67.

Self-proclaimed "Sun King" Louis XIV (1638–1715) built *Versailles,* one of the most magnificent palaces in all of Europe. If your kids can tolerate a guided tour, visit the Hall of Mirrors, where, on June 28, 1919, the famous Versailles Treaty was signed to end World War I. The surrounding classical French gardens, once the king's playground, have elaborate fountains and spectacular water shows. The tourist office can provide a current schedule for the shows, called **Les Grandes Eaux,** which generally take place Sunday afternoons from May to September. The river's edge is the least crowded spot to enjoy the summer **Fêtes de Nuit,** a 90-minute spectacle of fireworks, fountains, and light shows at Neptune's Pond. Tickets go on sale one month prior at the **tourist office** at 7, rue des Réservoirs (Tel. 39-50-36-22). Château: Fee. Tues.–Sun. 9:45–5. Beat the crowds by getting there when it opens. Tel. 30-84-74-00. 35-minute bus and train ride from Paris. RER Line C from Paris Center or Métro: Pont de Sèvres, transfer to bus 171.

THE NORTHWEST

LOIRE VALLEY

A brief history of the French **château** (castle) will increase your children's appreciation of the castle-filled Loire. Built for protection by noblemen in the Middle Ages, they stood either on hills or were surrounded by deep water-filled moats. As artillery improved, the defensive advantages of the châteaux declined, and they became country manor houses. Access to most châteaux is gained only by joining a guided tour, often in French. From Easter through October, many châteaux produce the famous **Son et Lumière programs** which are touristy historic pageants with colored lights, music, and sound effects held in the late evenings and inappropriate for young children. A schedule is available from the tourist office in the city of Tours. Tel. 47-05-58-08. **Bikes** and suggested itineraries are available at most Loire Valley train stations, such as Amboise, Blois, Chinon, Langeais, Loches, Onzain, or Azay-le-Rideau. Return bikes at any participating station.

AMBOISE AND ENVIRONS

Amboise's **Château d'Amboise** has a mechanical puppet exhibition of costumed marionettes which you can see after the mandatory French tour. Have your children imagine horse-drawn carriages arriving in the 1500s along the castle's huge ramp, the Tour des Minimes. Fee. July–Aug. daily 9–6:30; Sept.–June 9–12, 2–5. Tel. 47-57-14-47. **Clos Lucé Manor** is linked to Amboise by a tunnel. Its basement contains resident Leonardo da Vinci's working models, including a flying machine and a swingbridge. Fee. Mandatory French tour. Daily June–Sept. 9–7; Oct.–Dec. and Feb.–May 9–12, 2–5.

Near Amboise is the **Château de *Chenonceau*.** Kids will enjoy running in the spacious gardens or rowing in its lake. Packed high-season. Fee. Tour not mandatory. Mar.–Oct. daily 9–6; Nov. 1–Nov. 15 daily 9–5; Nov. 16–Feb. 15 daily 9–12, 2–4:30; Feb. 16–Feb. 28 daily 9–5:30.

BLOIS AND ENVIRONS

Willie Wonka fans, enjoy! You will know you have reached Blois by the thick smell of chocolate. The **Poulain Chocolate Factory** offers a 90-minute French tour that takes you from the cocoa bean to an ingenious wrapping machine. Kids are rewarded with samples. Fee. Rue du Docteur Desfray, near train station. Tours: Mon.–Thur. 8:45, 10, 1:30, 2:45; Fri. 8:45, 10. Tel. for reservations: 54-78-39-21. The **Château de Blois** has a **Robert Houdin Magic Museum** inside its archeology museum. Houdin was a 19th-century French magician who was the idol of American magician Erich Weiss, who renamed himself Houdini in his honor. On view are many of Houdin's magic tricks as well as fun toys and mechanized oddities. Fee. June–Sept. daily 9–6; Oct.–May daily 9:30–12, 2–6. Tel. 54-78-06-62. Across the street is the **Salon de la Magic,** with a magicians' forum and a 30-minute magic show. Fee. 23, pl. du Château. July–Aug. 1–6. Tel. 54-82-80-98.

Near Blois is ***Chambord,*** the grandest of the Loire châteaux. Its centrally planned Italian structure is attributed to Leonardo da Vinci. It has a double winding staircase where a child climbing one side can see but never meet someone climbing the other. Pick up the English booklet *Chambord for Children* (Mila Boutan, Mila Éditions, 1987) available in most castle bookshops. Through games, kids are provided with an understanding of the façade's rhythmical ornamentation, and there are fun stories about its dungeon. Chambord is a hunting reserve and you can watch large animals from observation sites. Fee. July–Aug. daily 9:30–6:30; Sept.–July daily 9:30–11:45, 2–4:45.

Walking on the château's grass at ***Cheverny,*** 9 kilometers southeast of Blois, is forbidden, and all of its rooms are roped off, making this castle a bit stuffy for kids. But, its guard room has a fascinating collection of 15th- and 16th-century armor. Its 2,500 sets of antlers and mounted animals show how important hunting has been to its owners, who still keep seventy hunting dogs. If you visit at 5 PM, you can watch the owner feed them, an elaborate ritual. Don't make a special trip for this; we did, and the dogs were off on a hunt. Fee. June–Sept. daily 9:15–6:45; Sept. 16–May daily 9:30–12, 2:15–5. Tel. 54-79-96-29.

NEAR SAUMUR

Twenty kilometers west of Saumur is **La Caverne Sculptée de Dénezé-Sous-Doué,** a cave where masons sculpted several hundred figures into the cave walls 400 years ago. You will see the first American Indian ever carved in Europe as well as messages left by the diggers. Fee. Follow signs from the village center. English tour. July–Aug. daily 10–7, Sept.–Oct. daily 2–7. Tel. 41-59-08-80.

In the quaint underground village of ***Rochemenier,*** there are subterranean farmhouses dating back to the Middle Ages; a few are still inhabited. Grass grows out of the roofs, and chimneys poke through the ground. Fee. 20 km. southwest of Saumur; 6 km. from Doué-La-Fountaine. Apr.–Sept. Tues.–Sun. 9:30–12, 2–7; July–Aug. daily 9:30–7; Oct. Tues.–Sun. 2–6; Nov.–Mar. Sat. & Sun. 2–6 only. Tel. 41-59-18-15.

TOURS AND ENVIRONS

Situated at the hub of the château region, Tours is one of the Loire's main cities. The English-speaking staff at the **tourist office,** Place Maréchal Leclerc (Tel. 47-05-58-08), can assist you with trip planning for the entire Loire.

Sorry, you cannot eat the 6-story Chinese pagoda made of frosting, the castle of sugar, or the superrealistic chocolate violin at the **Musée du Campagnonnage (Museum of Master Craftsmanship).** Showcasing the talents of craftsmen from all parts of France, the museum exhibits everything from food art to the meticulous works of ropemakers, bootmakers, and blacksmiths. Fee. 8, rue Nationale. Wed.–Mon. 9–12, 2–6. Tel. 47-61-07-93. The **Château Royal de Tours** houses the Grevin wax museum, **Historial de Touraine,** with figures depicting the history of the region. Fee. Guise Tower & Pavilon de Mars. Nov. 16–Mar. 15 daily 2–5:30; Mar. 16–June 15 and Sept. 16–Nov. 15 daily 9–11:30, 2–6:30; June 16–Sept. 15 daily 9–6:30. Tel. 47-61-02-95. The château's **Aquarium Tropical** has more than 200 species of fresh and saltwater fish. Fee. Ground floor, Pavilon de Mars. Apr.–June daily 9:30–12, 2–6; July–Aug. daily 9:30–7; Sept.–Nov. 15 daily 9:30–12, 2–6; Nov. 16–Mar. daily 2–6. Tel. 47-64-29-52. The history of costumes up to 1950 is traced with dolls dressed in children's clothes at the **Petit Musée du Costume.** A highlight is the tribute to the circus featuring characters from the circus Barnum. Fee. 54, bd. Béranger. Year-round. Guided tour Tues.–Sun. 9:30–11 and 2:30–5 by arrangement. Tel. 47-61-59-17.

The **Grottes Pétrifiantes (Petrifying Grottoes),** in *Savonnières,* about 11 kilometers southwest of Tours, stretch underground several kilometers to the castle in Villandry. Geology buffs will enjoy the glittering formations, stalactites, and the subterranean lake. Trickling water has petrified objects, creating astonishing reliefs. Fee. Feb. 8–Mar. Fri.–Wed. 9–12, 2–6:30; Apr.–Oct. 15 daily 9–7; Oct. 16–Dec. 20 Fri.–Wed. 9–12, 2–6. Tel. 47-50-00-90.

Inspired by the romantic **château** at *Ussé,* 17th-century author Charles Perrault wrote *La Belle au Bois Dormant* (Sleeping Beauty). You don't need to take the tour to see the tale told with 18th- and 19th-century costumed dolls. Simply climb the tower to the left of the château entrance. The only problem, according to our resident fairy-tale critic, is that the story is told out of order. Fee. 30 km. west of Tours. May–Sept. daily 9–12, 2–7; Mar. 15–Apr. and Oct. daily 9–12, 2–6. Tel. 47-95-54-05.

The **château** at *Valençay* has a formal garden with black swans, ducks, and peacocks. Under the great trees of the surrounding park, deer, llamas, and kangaroos roam in large enclosures. Fee. Château tour mandatory. Mar. 15–Nov. 15 daily 9–12, 2–7; off-season weekends 10–12, 1:30–4:30.

BRITTANY

Home of the thinnest, crispiest crêpes, distinctive Quimper stoneware, glorious beaches, and fascinating Breton culture, Brittany has its own distinctive flair. The Bretons are a Celtic people, a fact most evident in their folk music, folklore, and old language, called Breizh; and they work to keep this culture alive. Don't miss the chance to eat tasty buckwheat or plain flour crêpes, which can be ordered with any combination of sweet or savory fillings. Beware of the other delicious local food specialty, cider, which is 6 percent alcohol. For children many of Brittany's beaches have clubs that offer inflatable castles to bounce on, trampolines, and playground-type equipment. For a small fee you can leave your children in these supervised settings. One colorful Breton tradition you should try to see is the **Breton Pardon,** a religious procession in honor of the local patron saint, for which locals dress in traditional black with embroidered aprons and white lace headdresses and parade through the town carrying banners, statues, and candles. Each town has its own procession, and many take place throughout the summer. Check with the local tourist offices for a list of dates. Towns and villages in Brittany's interior are as intriguing as its coastal villages, and usually cheaper. Nevertheless, kids will prefer staying at the beach and venturing inland for special expeditions.

ALONG THE NORTH COAST

The *Côte d'Emeraude,* to the west of St-Malo, has spectacular jagged cliffs, quaint fishing villages, and soft, sandy beaches. Near *St-Brieuc* is the **Zoo de Trégomeur,** a wild animal park with a tiny zoo train, a free playground, and walk-through grounds with chimpanzees, zebras, ostriches, llamas, yaks, and more. Fee. Daily 9–8. Tel. 96-79-01-07. The westernmost portion of this coast, *Ceinture Dorée,* has warm sandy beaches and a mild climate. Take a boat ride from *Brest* to the *Île d'Ouessant,* an island somewhat isolated from the rest of Brittany with its own Breton subculture and thousands of migrating birds. The tourist office in *Lampaul* will provide addresses for bicycle rentals, a fun way to explore the island. Tel. 98-48-85-83. About 1 kilometer northwest of Lampaul is the **Ecomusée du Niou-Huella,** an open-air museum with old stone houses that show how life was lived in centuries past. Fee. Wed.–Mon. 2–6.

THE CROZON PENINSULA

Morgat is a delightful family resort and a great place to headquarter as there are plenty of water sports and excellent beaches. Morgat's **Marine Caverns,** with strange, unearthly rock formations, are worth a visit. Two boat companies lead tours from the Quai Kader: Vedettes Sirènes (Tel. 98-27-29-90) and Vedettes Rosmeur (Tel. 98-27-09-54).

QUIMPER AND ENVIRONS

One of Brittany's larger cities that has kept its Breton atmosphere, Quimper has many streets closed to cars and old city walls you can climb for views of the town. In the garden of the **Cathédrale St-Corentin** is the **Musée Départemental Breton,** which has a good collection of regional costumes, pottery, furniture, and carvings. Fee; free Wed. and Sun. Place St.-Corentin. June–Sept. Wed.–Mon. 10–7; Oct.–May 10–12, 2–4:30. Traditional **Breton dancing** takes place every Thursday night in summer at 9 PM in the cathedral gardens.

Kids enjoy the lively folk-art paintings of people in traditional costumes that decorate the local pottery known as **Quimperware.** Two studios are open to the public: Les Faïenceries de Quimper H. B. Henriot (Tel. 98-90-09-36), across from Notre-Dame de Locmaria, charges a fee, while Faïenceries Keraluc (Tel. 98-90-25-29), just outside of town on route de Bénodet, is free. The **Festival de Cornouaille,** Brittany's most important folk festival, is held here on the fourth Sunday in July with music, theater, parties, and films. The **tourist office** is at Place de la Resistance, tel. 98-95-04-69.

East of Quimper along the coast is *Concarneau,* a popular seaside resort and fishing town. This walled island-city is connected to the mainland by two bridges; the old city's ramparts provide a good view of the harbor. The town has decent beaches but can be crowded in summer. The city comes alive with parades that feature traditional costumes, music, and dance at the annual **Festival International,** held the last week in July. In late August, the local folk festival, **Les Filets Bleus,** has lively dancing and delicious food. The **tourist office** is at Quai d'Aiguillon (Tel. 98-97-01-44).

Further eastward along the coast is *Quiberon,* with great beaches and lots of camping sites, as thousands of tourists will agree. Its main beach, **Grande Plage,** is safe for kids, but beware of the sandy coves outside of town that look inviting but have Baignades Interdites (Swimming Forbidden) signs; the waters are surprisingly dangerous.

Belle-Île, a beautiful island off the coast of Quiberon, can be reached by ferry in 45 minutes from Quiberon's Port-Maria. You can rent bicycles to explore its wild coast, with many coves and grottoes and heather-covered inlands. Rental information is available at the **tourist office,** near the gangplank where the ferries arrive. Tel. 97-31-81-93.

East of Quimper is *Carnac,* best known for the **Alignements du Ménec,** a 2-kilometer row of megalithic standing stones that kids can run around while you marvel at their origin. Your children may not be fascinated by ancient monuments, but Carnac is a first-rate family destination with great beaches, miniature golf, crazy beachside playgrounds, and 2- to 4-seat pedal cars with canopies for rent in town. You can horseback ride, parasail, fish, wind-surf, learn to unicycle, or just relax and eat crêpes, pastries, or *beignets* (long, twisted donuts). Tour the internal passageways of the **Tumulus de St-Michel** and have a candlelit look into a funeral chamber. Fee. Guided tours Easter–Sept. 10–6. Carnac's **Musée de Préhistoire** will give you a look at some of the other items discovered long ago in the region. Fee. Easter–mid-Oct. daily 10–12, 2–4. Dozens of campgrounds are found throughout Carnac, and houses with the sign "Chambre" have rooms for rent.

ST-MALO AND ENVIRONS

St-Malo, in Brittany's northeast corner, is an ancient walled city built entirely of granite. If you enter the town from the west, follow signs to the **Rochers Sculptés,** or Carved Rocks, of Rotheneuf. Years ago, the Reverend Abbé Fouré sculpted his family's dramatic life story into these cliffs and rocks near his home. Carved steps lead you through the weathered carvings of pirates, sea monsters, children, and castles. Run as a family business, there's a small saltwater aquarium next door. Fee. Call for hours. Tel. 99-56-97-64 or 99-56-96-85.

St-Malo was originally founded as a free city in the 12th century, and its **ramparts** helped keep out French, Norman, and English invaders. Head for the old city and explore the ramparts between the sea and the city, then climb down to the beach and continue along the stone walkway to **Le Grand Bé,** an island housing the grave of the poet Chateaubriand. Be sure the tide is low so you won't get caught on the island. Nearby, the ocean has been enclosed in the **Piscine de Bon-Secours,** a safe saltwater swimming pool. The **Musée de la Ville** has pirate treasure chests, old maps, and an unsurpassed view from its turret. Fee. Near port St-Vincent. June–Sept. 9:30–12, 2–6:30; Oct.–May Wed.–Mon. 10–12, 2–6. Visit the **Musée de la Poupée** to see its three rooms of lovely old dolls. Fee. 13, rue de Toulouse. Mar. 15–Nov. 15 daily 10–12, 2–7. Tel. 99-40-15-51. Kids enjoy a ride around the old city on **Le Petit Train de St-Malo,** departing from Porte St-Vincent every 30 minutes in summer. Fee. Tel. 99-82-65-75. The **tourist office** is at Esplanade St-Vincent (Tel. 99-56-64-48), across from the old city in the port. They can provide information on the area's many types of water-sports activities.

Dinard's main beach has a promenade with cafés and beautiful views across the water to St-Malo. At one end is an open-air saltwater pool. Next door, **St-Enogat** beach has a "Club Mickey" with paddleboats and other amusements for kids.

NORMANDY

Normandy is remembered most for the D-day landings and the key role it played in World War II, although its long sandy beaches, pungent cheeses, and associations with William the Conqueror and Joan of Arc make it an alluring destination.

COTENTIN PENINSULA

The coastal resort of *Granville* has a marine aquarium complex, with attractions such as **Seashell Fairyland, Mineral Palace,** and **Butterfly Garden.** The best in coquillage is exhibited in Seashell

Fairyland, where life-size architectural columns are made of shells. A similar theme pervades the Mineral Palace, with its animals and geologic wonders made from stones. In the Butterfly Garden you'll see butterfly-wing mosaics. Fee. Pointe du Roc. Easter–Nov. daily 9–12, 2–7. Tel. 33-50-03-13. Kids will also enjoy Granville's 15th-century **Grande Porte drawbridge** and **Christian Dior's garden,** a park with beautiful ocean views and a path leading to the beach at Donville. Off av. de la Libération. Along the coast near Granville are the beautiful beaches of *Hauteille-sur-Mer* and *Coutainville.*

LE MONT SAINT-MICHEL AND ENVIRONS

The resplendent religious city of Mont Saint-Michel, perched atop a tiny island, was founded in 708 and has been a popular pilgrim and tourist spot ever since. Despite the crowds, it is still a dazzling attraction. Today's visitors need not worry about the rapidly advancing tides as did the early pilgrims, since a causeway has been built to carry them safely to Mont St-Michel. In summer, plan to visit early in the day before the crowds swarm upon it. Climb up the winding main street to the **abbey. La Merveille,** a 13th-century cloister, housed the monastery and a treadmill that prisoners walked to power the system of pulleys used to haul stones up the side of the Mont. Be sure to wander about the **ramparts** of the Mont—the best way to explore its subtleties and exhilarating views. Do not wander off the Mont onto the beach at any time as there are treacherous tides and patches of quicksand.

Near the lace-making center of *Alençon,* in the village of *Fye,* are the folk-art **Centaurs** of artist Fernand Chatelain. Since 1965, he has been building whimsical sculptures in his garden that resemble giant papier mâché preschool projects. Ask for directions in town; everyone knows the way.

ROUEN AND ENVIRONS

Cars are prohibited on Rouen's maze of medieval streets, where nothing appears to have changed for 500 years. Visit the **Cathédrale de Notre-Dame,** painted so many times by Monet, and the square where **Joan of Arc** was burned at the stake. The **Tour Jeanne d'Arc,** the remaining tower of the castle in which she was imprisoned, has an exhibit of her trial. Free. Rue de Donjon. Fri.–Wed. 10–12, 2–5. Amble down rue du Gros Horloge to see its namesake, a huge Renaissance **clock** which spans the street like a bridge. For a view of this picture-postcard city, climb the platform above the clock. Rouen's **Musée des Beaux Arts** exhibits works by noted Impressionists. Fee. Rue Thiers. Wed.–Mon. 10–12, 2–6. The grassy slopes of the adjacent

Place Verdrel are great for playing and picnics. Rouen's gracious **Jardin des Plantes** offers many shady resting spots. Off rue St-Julien. May–July daily 9–6.

Just south of Rouen, in *Louviers,* is milkman Robert Vasseur's **mosaicked house and garden,** a true folk-art spectacle. Vasseur covered his house and furnishings from top to bottom, inside and out, in shards of pottery and seashells found at the beach and around his village. 80, rue du Balchampête. Mon.–Sat. 5–9, Sun. afternoons. Tel. 32-40-22-61.

Further south, in *Giverny,* is the **Musée Claude Monet,** the artist's home/studio set in the gardens which inspired his water-lily series. During the 1-hour train ride from Paris we reread the delightful *Linnea in Monet's Garden* [Christina Björk (R & S books, 1985)], the tale of young Linnea's visit to Giverny. Children will enjoy wandering through the gardens where each row of flowers is a different color. Fee. 27620 Gasny. Museum: Apr.–Oct. Tues.–Sun. 10–12, 2–6. Gardens: 10–6. Tel. 32-51-28-21. From Paris: SNCF Gare Saint-Lazare, Paris-Rouen line to Vernon. Bikes are for rent at the train station for a lovely ride out to Giverny.

THE NORTHEAST

ALSACE

Alsace, a quiet and lush region of vineyards and castle ruins, lies between the Rhine River and the Vosges Mountains. With a mix of German and French influences, Alsace has its own culture, cooking, and language. Restaurants serve *choucroute* (sauerkraut, potatoes, ham, and sausage) along with French wine and bread.

STRASBOURG AND ENVIRONS

Straddling the German border, Strasbourg is a central point for trips through Alsace. Covered bridges and half-timbered houses grace the old part of town, which is an oval-shaped island surrounded by canals. At its western end is the city's picturesque Alsatian neighborhood, **La Petite France,** with carved wooden houses overlooking the canals. The **tourist office** is at Place de la Gare (Tel. 88-32-51-49).

The heart of the island is Strasbourg's glorious 11th- to 15th-century **Cathédrale de Notre-Dame.** Mechanized apostles and a chariot parade out of the clock face of its **Horloge Astronomique** daily at 12:30 PM. Fee. Find a spot to watch at least 30 minutes in advance. Tel. 88-35-03-00. The cathedral's **tower** was the world's tallest Christian monument until the last century; climb it for a panoramic view. Daily 9–6. Mimes and acrobats entertain crowds in the Place de la Cathédrale on summer evenings. **Open-air trolley rides** depart from the cathedral every half-hour from late March through the end of October. Passing swans and low bridges, **boats** tour the city's canals. Daily departures from Château Rohan, Pl. du Vieux-Marché-aux-Poissons, every half-hour 10:30 AM–9 PM. **Rhine cruises** operate during the summer. Contact the tourist office for details. Across town is the **Palais de l'Europe,** home to the European parliament and the ornate **Parc de l'Orangerie** with its small **zoo.** The park was created by André Le Nôtre, who designed Versailles. Free. Always open. In need of a dip? **Océade** is a water park with a river with waves, two giant water toboggan rides, and a large pool. Fee. Parc du Rhin. Call for hours (Tel. 88-61-92-30).

In June the city stages Europe's oldest **international music festival** with music, theater, ballet, and satirical cabarets. Summer brings **folk dancing** to the Château des Rohan, across from the cathedral, and free concerts to the city's **Parc des Contades** and Parc de l'Orangerie. In fall, Strasbourg hosts **Musica,** a contemporary music festival; November and December bring the **Festival Mimes et Clowns** (Tel. 88-32-74-01).

Kintzheim, at the edge of Alsace's 90-mile **Route du Vin,** has one of Europe's most renowned aviaries of birds of prey, with soaring, uncaged vultures and eagles housed in its **château.** Fee. Apr.–Sept. daily afternoons; Oct.–Nov. 11 Wed., Sat., Sun. afternoons. Outside of town, don't miss **La Montagne des Singes (Monkey Mountain),** where hundreds of free-roaming barbary apes amuse visitors with their adorable antics. Fee. Apr.–Sept. Mon.–Sat. 10–12, 1:30–7.

COLMAR AND ENVIRONS

The horse carriages hired at Colmar's city hall are a fun way to tour this storybook town with its ancient (and often crazy-angled) half-timbered houses and beautiful Gothic **Church of St-Martin.** Most of the town center has been closed to cars. The **tourist office** is at 4, rue des Unterlinden (Tel. 89-41-02-29).

Trivia fiends will get a kick out of the Statue of Liberty memorabilia at the **Frederic Bartholdi Museum,** devoted to the creator of New York's famed icon. Fee. 30, rue des Marchands. May–Oct. daily 10–12, 2–6; Nov.–Apr. Sat.–Sun. Colmar's most important site, the **Musée d'Unterlinden,** has an exquisite collection of Alsatian art from folk art to modern. Kids especially like the museum's 18th-century peasant's home, while adults find the 16th-century **Issenheim Altarpiece,** possibly the masterpiece of German art, spellbinding. Fee. Place Unterlinden. Apr.–Oct. daily 9–6; Nov.–Mar. daily 9–12, 2–6. Tel. 89-41-89-23. The best examples of half-timbered houses are in **La Petite Venise,** in the Quartier des Tanneurs. Colmar is especially lively during the first three Saturdays in September when **Les Journées de la Choucroute (Sauerkraut Days)** feature dancing, music, outdoor food, and, of course, wine. August's **Foire aux Vins et Fête Folklorique** draws people from all over Europe. If your kids are still up at 10 PM, they can hear the last night watchman pass through the quiet streets of *Turckheim* calling out the hour and proclaiming "All's well." Nightly between May and the fall grape harvest. 5 kilometers west of Colmar. Tel. 89-27-38-44.

METZ AND ENVIRONS

Metz's Gothic **Cathédrale St-Etienne** is nicknamed the Lantern of God because of its extraordinary stained-glass windows whose creators included artists from the 13th and 14th centuries to Marc Chagall. Walk along the garden of the **esplanade,** the adjoining Place de la République, or **Lac des Cygnes (Swan Lake),** near the banks of the Moselle River. The **Fête de Mirabelle** takes place in late August and early September with fireworks and a parade of carts decorated with flowers, costumed dancers, and a cherry plum queen. Metz's late November **international festival** features New Wave music. Contact the **tourist office** at Place d'Armes (Tel. 87-75-65-21).

North of Metz, in *Hagondange,* is **Big Bang Schtroumpf,** a theme park based on the cartoon and toy characters from Belgium that are called Smurfs in the U.S. Kids can explore worlds based on the earth, water, planets, and a lake upon which sits the Island of Schtroumpfs. Fee. Intersection of A4 and A31. May–Oct. daily 10–6; July–Aug. daily 10–10. Tel. 87-51-73-90.

East of Metz is *Verdun,* encircled by World War I battlefields. The **Citadelle,** near the **Cathédral,** houses a **Museum of War** and provides access to the famous tunnels that once protected the army. Visit the **Fort de Vaux** and the **Fort de Douaumont** to view gun casements and underground tunnels. Fee. Feb.–Mar. and Oct.–Dec. 10–4:30; Apr.–June and Sept. 9–6; June 15–Aug. 9–7. Artillery and models of battlefields are on exhibit at the **Mémorial-Musée de Fleury.** Fee. Open Apr.–Sept. daily 9–6; Oct.–Mar. 9–12, 2–5.

CENTRAL FRANCE

DORDOGNE

Few provinces command a more spectacular setting than the Dordogne. Sleepy country roads and quiet rivers meander through rolling green hills spotted with cows and magnificent castles, revealing the region's deeply etched history. The area is geared to English-speaking visitors because many British families spend their holidays here. The Dordogne is world famous for its well-preserved **prehistoric sites.** Caves with artwork 9,000 to 30,000 years old are hollowed from dramatic cliffs. Most require guided tours; only take your kids if they have a strong interest as the caves and group tours are very small; once you are in, it's difficult to leave.

The sites of the Dordogne can be visited in an antique **horse-drawn carriage.** Departing at 10:30 AM, the day-long trip includes a picnic with farm-fresh produce. Fee. "Le Périgord en Calèche," Mazerolles, 24550 Villefranche du Périgord. Telephone 2–3 days prior to departure (Tel. 53-29-98-99).

High-season accommodations fill up months in advance. Our Dordogne-loving neighbors arranged for their summer **gîte** the previous November through the *French Farm and Village Holiday Guide.* For a list of more than eighty **campgrounds** open from Easter–October, contact Camping Information Dordogne: B.P. 33, 24290 Montignac-Lascaux, France (Tel. 53-50-79-80). The Château program has four private châteaux in the Dordogne region, two of which we sampled. Outside of Périgueux is **Domaine de Monciaux** (open Easter–Nov. 30; moderate; including breakfast); an 18th-century, family-run château with a pool and tennis courts. There are also three inexpensive self-catering gîtes on the property which each sleep four. **Manoir de Hautegente** (open Apr. 1–Nov. 15; expensive; meals extra) is an ivy-covered manor house with a pool ideally situated near Sarlat and the Lascaux Caves. Only plan to stay if your kids are older; the food at Hautegente was the best we tasted in all of France. Châteaux: See Château Program, "Lights Out!" beginning of this chapter. Gîte: Domaine de Monciaux, Bourrou, 24110 Saint Astier (Tel. 53-81-97-69).

LES EYZIES

The prehistoric cave art at Les Eyzies is the area's most famous. The most important cave is the **Grotte de Font-de-Gaume.** Here, an enthusiastic guide leads a small group by flashlight into a dark narrow cavern to see subtle silhouette drawings in black and red of horses, bison, and reindeer the relief of whose bodies is created by the form of the cave. Fee. Mandatory 1-hour French tour. 2 km. down D47. Apr.–Sept. Wed.–Mon. 9–11:15, 2–5:15; Oct.–Mar. Wed.–Mon. 10–11:15; 2–4:15. Tel. 53-06-97-48. In summer, arrive before 8 AM for morning tickets; if you arrive later, you'll have to wait for an afternoon ticket. While waiting, take a bike ride or visit Les Eyzies' **Musée National de Préhistoire** to view tools made from ivory, bone, and antlers, cave art, and weapons. Nearby, a wild statue of Cro-Magnon man stares out from beneath the cliff. Fee. Apr.–Nov. Wed.–Mon. 9:30–12, 2–6; Dec.–Mar. Wed.–Mon. 9:30–12, 2–5. **Bike** rentals are available at the train station or at the local **tourist office** at Place de la Mairie (Tel. 53-06-97-05).

Farther down the road from Font-de-Gaume is the **Grotte des Combarelles** with detailed, naturalistic animal carvings and rarely depicted human figures. In summer, tickets go on sale at 9 for morning visits and at 2 for afternoon visits. Fee. Mandatory 1-hour French tour. Same days/hours as Font-de-Gaume. Tel. 53-06-97-72.

NEAR LES EYZIES

Stalactites and stalagmites dazzle you from the **Grotte du Grand Roc,** high in the cliffs above the Vézère River. Fee. 25-minute mandatory tour. 1.5 km. from Les Eyzies along D47. Daily 9–7. Tel. 53-06-96-76, 53-06-92-70. Human remains are evident in the cross sections of the earth's strata in the caves at the **Laugerie-Basse** and **Laugerie-Haute,** next to the Grand Roc. Fee. 35-minute mandatory tour. Laugerie-Basse: June–Sept. daily 9–6:30. Tel. 53-06-97-12. Laugerie-Haute: July–Aug. daily 9–7; Sept.–June daily 9–12, 2–6. Tel. 53-06-92-90.

The town of *Montignac* features the caves of **Lascaux II.** The original art deteriorated, and the work of the cave dwellers was completely re-created in 1983. You'll see remarkable paintings of small-headed horses and deer. In season, tickets are sold at Place Tourny in Montignac starting at 9 AM. Off-season, tickets are sold at the cave site. There is a 40-minute mandatory tour. 20 km. northeast of Les Eyzies on N704 toward Brive. July–Aug. daily 9:30–7:30; Feb.– June and Sept.–Dec. Tues.–Sun. 10–12, 2–5:30. Tel. 53-53-44-35. The **Thot Center for Prehistory** exhibits huge photographs illustrating the diverse aspects of cave painting. Animals most often painted by prehistoric men, such as wild sheep and the extremely rare Przewalski's horse, live in its outdoor park. Fee. Combined ticket with Lascaux II. In-season tickets sold at Montignac; off-season at Lascaux II. Guided tour for part of visit. July–Aug. Tues.–Sun. all day; off-season mornings and afternoons. Tel. 53-50-70-44.

Tursac's **Prehisto Park** is a highly recommended woodland park where sculptors have created realistic scenes from the daily life of Neanderthal hunters, including wild beasts, a burial ground, and a 15,000-year-old Magdalenian home with children. This is a wonderful way for your kids to absorb the past while scampering through the trees. Fee. Near Les Eyzies D706. Daily 9–7. Tel. 53-50-73-19, 53-06-96-76. Nearby, the cliff fortress of **Le Roque St-Christophe** traces the life of Neanderthal man. You'll see a kitchen and other signs of daily life 50,000 years ago. Many steep steps. Fee. Between Tursac and Le Moustier on D706. Mar.–May 30 and Sept. 11–Nov. 11 daily 10–12, 2–6; June–Sept. 10 daily 9:30–6:30. Tel. 53-50-70-45.

Accompanied **horseback rides** from 1 hour to 1 week are available through Tursac's La Baronie Equestrian Center. Tel. 53-06-93-83.

PÉRIGUEUX AND ENVIRONS

Périgueux is the principal city of the Dordogne. The English-speaking staff at the **tourist office,** 1, av. d'Aquitaine (Tel. 53-53-10-63), can provide topographical maps and lists of accommodations from farms to campsites. Head for the *vieille ville* (old city) and the tree-lined waters of L'Isle and its canal. Up from the Romanesque Eglise St-Etienne-de-la-Cité is the **Jardin des Arènes,** a park that is great for kids to play in while exploring the remains of this 1st-century Roman arena. At the **Musée du Périgord** you'll find Stone Age tools and exhibits of the Neanderthals and their ancestors. Fee; Wed. free. Allée de Tourny. Wed.–Mon. 10–12, 2–5. Tel. 53-53-16-42.

ROCAMADOUR AND ENVIRONS

Built into the face of a sheer cliff, Rocamadour commands a spectacular setting claimed by few others. Since the Middle Ages, the village has drawn countless pilgrims who climb on their knees up the 216 steps to the upper Cité Religieuse. Young legs and tired parents can take the elevator. Still higher, at the cliff's summit, is a 14th-century **château** with ramparts upon which kids can climb for extraordinary views. Fee. July–Aug. 9–7; Apr.–June and Sept.–Oct. 9–12, 1:30–8. Visit early or late at night, when the city's rock face is illuminated by lights and the stars.

A short drive away, outside *Hospitalet,* 150 monkeys roam free at the **Forêt des Singes,** a large open space similar to their North African homeland. Moms will especially appreciate how well the males take care of the babies. And, the babies! Your kids will squeal with delight at their adorable antics. The free bag of popcorn included with admission is a nice bonus. Fee. June 15–late Aug. daily 9–7; Sept. 1–Nov. 2 daily 10–12, 2–6. Tel. 65-33-62-72.

Between Rocamadour and Souillac is the **Grottes de Lacave,** whose train takes you on a mile-long underground journey to see concreations that look like people, animals, buildings, whole cities, and our favorite, the "twelve fairyland halls." Fee. One-hour guided tour. Early Apr.–mid-Oct. mornings and afternoons; Aug. daily. Tel. 65-37-87-03.

For an even more amazing subterranean voyage, visit the enormous underground caverns of the **Gouffre de Padirac,** at one time believed to be a gate to hell, 15 kilometers from Rocamadour. You'll travel in aluminum boats along a translucent underground river to see a rainfall lake and a giant stalactite that almost touches the water. Wear a raincoat. Fee. 90-minute guided tour. Apr.–July and Sept.–Oct. 11 daily 8:30–12, 2–6:30; Aug. 8–7. Tel. 65-33-64-56.

Close by is the **Parc de Vision de Gramat (Gramat Safari Park)**, a 94-acre park with wild ox, bison, and farmyard animals who live in semicaptivity in their natural environment. Fee. Just before Gramat railway station turn right and take D14 for 1 km. Easter–Oct. daily mornings and afternoons; off-season afternoons only; Sundays and holidays all day. Tel. 65-38-81-22.

SARLAT AND ENVIRONS

Wander around the narrow streets and ancient alleyways of Sarlat's *vieille ville* to find a corner of the world unchanged for centuries. **Bikes** can be rented from L'Aventure à Vélo (Tel. 53-31-24-18). Group-led **horseback** riding is available through the Centre Equestre de Vitrac (Tel. 53-59-34-31). The helpful **tourist office**, at Place de la Liberté (Tel. 53-59-27-67), can provide information on camping and canoeing. Sarlat's colorful **Saturday market** exudes an aroma of chocolate, fresh breads, and baking chestnuts. Kids can munch on walnuts while you sample the world's best *foie gras* and truffles. Follow the red fish painted on the street to Sarlat's **Musée Aquarium** with salmon, carp, and sturgeon from the Dordogne basin. Fee. Rue du Camondant Maratuel. June 15–Sept. 15 daily 10–7; off-season daily 10–12, 2–6. Tel. 53-59-27-67.

The drive along the Dordogne River from Sarlat to Domme, La Roque-Gageac, and Beynac is one of France's most beautiful. Fortified villages perch and castles huddle between the high cliffs and the tree-lined river below. Pause to swim or picnic at one of the many spots along the river. Kids will enjoy the 20-minute tour of the feudal village of *Domme* on **Le Petit Train**. Fee. Mar. 25–Nov. 15 daily 9–8. Tel. 53-28-21-16, 53-28-32-07. **Canoe** trips from Beynac to Cenac depart from Le Port de Domme. Contact Randonné Dordogne (Tel. 53-28-22-01). Domme boasts its own cave, the **Grotte de Domme**, with stalactites and crystalline formations. Fee. Place de la Halle. Fee. Guided tour. July 15–Sept. 14 daily 9:30–12, 2–7; off-season daily 9:30–12, 2–6. Tel. 53-28-37-09. Nearby is the **Musée des Arts et Traditions Populaires**, which features life-size reenactments of life in the Perigord in the 1800s. Fee. Place de la Halle. Apr.–Oct. 10–12, 2–6. Tel. 53-28-20-67.

As you approach the village of *Beynac* on D703 you won't be able to miss its 12th-century **feudal castle**. Climb to its top for a great view of the neighboring castles of Marqueyssac, Castelnaud, and Fayrac. Fee. Visit Sundays to avoid the 50-minute guided tours. Early Mar.–mid-Nov. mornings and afternoons. Every 30 minutes, **flat-bottom barges** called *gabarres* leave Beynac's parking lot by the river for a 45-

minute journey along the Dordogne. You'll see La Roque-Gageac and four of the area's most spectacular castles. Fee. July–Sept. daily 10–7. Tel. 53-59-47-48 or 53-28-51-15. Spectacular *La Roque-Gageac* has a grassy area with picnic tables along the river bank. Flatboats, canoes, and kayaks depart every 15 minutes from the town's river bank for 1-hour cruises.

LE LOT

The **Lot River Valley** is as beautiful as the Dordogne but less traveled. The 51-kilometer drive from Cahors to Conques is breathtaking with chalky canyon walls and dramatic vistas. Canoeing and kayaking down the Lot River can be arranged in Cahors; contact the tourist office (address below).

CAHORS AND ENVIRONS

For a look at the medieval town, climb the first turret of the six-arched bridge **Pont Valentré** in Cahors or cross the bridge and hike into the hills that encircle the city. The **tourist office** is at Place Aristide Briand (Tel. 65-35-09-56). From Cahors, drive the stretch to *Cabrerets, Bouzies, St-Cirq-Lapopie, Calvignac, Montbrun,* and *Conques,* all ancient villages clinging to sheer canyon walls. Visit the **Grotte du Pechmerle,** a cave discovered by two 14-year-old boys, 7 kilometers from St-Circ-Lapopie. Its vast caverns are painted with prehistoric animals and carvings and petrified imprints of a 2,000-year-old human are on view. Fee. Easter–Sept. daily 9:30–12, 2–6. Phone for off-season hours (Tel. 65-31-27-05).

BERRY AND AUVERGNE

Berry and Auvergne, the very center of France, are often bypassed by tourists who concentrate on its more popular surrounding regions. Their appeal may be subtler, but you'll be immersed in the real France where age-old traditions still exist.

BOURGES AND ENVIRONS

The magnificent **Cathédrale St-Etienne,** in Bourges, Berry's principal city, receives far fewer tourists than its rivals in Chartres or Rouen. Visit its **crypt** to see the statue of its native author, the Duc de Berry, whose *Très Riches Heures du Duc de Berry* inspired the castle in Euro Disney's Fantasyland. Crypt: Mon.–Sat. 9–11:30, 2–5:30; Sun. 2–5:30. The **Jardin de l'Hôtel de Ville,** behind the cathedral, is a lovely park. Within a 90-kilometer radius of Bourges is the châteaux-filled **Route Jacques-Coeur.** Many of these privately owned and inhabited castles contain charming personal touches such as family photographs and mementos. Unlike the grand châteaux of the Loire, which limit public viewing to the museumlike uninhabited sections, here you can tour rooms where people actually live. One château owner showed our young romantic her regal wedding photos. The Bourges **tourist office,** at 21, rue Victor Hugo (Tel. 48-24-75-33), provides a châteaux listing.

One of the several châteaux in the area that welcome overnight guests is the magnificent **La Verrerie,** a 15th-century lakeside castle in the midst of a forest. Splurge, if only for one night; you'll stay with a real count and countess. The large grounds provide tennis, canoeing, and horseback riding. Castle visits mid-Feb.–mid-Nov. daily 10–12, 2–7. Fee. 9 km. west of Aubigny-sur-Nère on D13. Accommodations moderate to expensive. See Château Program, *"Lights Out!,"* at the beginning of this chapter.

EASTERN FRANCE

BURGUNDY

Not whine, whine, whine. But, wine, wine, wine, gastronomic delights, and Romanesque architecture is what Burgundy is all about.

DIJON

We may know it for its mustard, but *Dijon* is really a town with a colorful history, a well-preserved *vieille ville,* delicious food, and many festivals. A climb up **Tour Philippe Le Bon,** near the lavish **Palais des Duc de Bourgogne,** in the town center, provides a good introductory view of the city. Mid-Apr.–mid-Sept. Wed.–Mon. 9:30–11:30, 2:30–5:30; off-season Wed. and Sun. only. The **Jardin de l'Arquebuse** is home to the **Musée d'Histoire Naturelle** and the **Botanical Gardens** with exotic trees from Asia. Daily 7–5. av. Albert 1. The beautiful **Parc de la Colombière** has lovely promenades. The **Eglise de Notre-Dame** has fanciful gargoyles and a clock, the **Horloge à Jacquemart,** with moving figures of a man and wife who strike the hours and of their son and daughter, who strike the quarter hours, resounding throughout the city. The adjacent **Musée Archéologique** has objects from prehistoric times. Fee. 5, rue Docteur Maret. Wed.–Mon. 9–12, 2–6. Mustard lovers can see the original **Grey Poupon** jars from the mid-1700s and sample mustard flavors as unusual as beer and thyme. Grey Poupon Mustard Shop, 32, rue de la Liberté. Mon.–Sat. 8:30–12, 2–7. Dijon hosts **Estivade** with performances through the streets from mid-June to mid-August. **La Fête de la Vigne,** a wine festival in early September, has colorful parades. Contact the **tourist office,** at Place Darcy (Tel. 80-43-42-12), for details.

THE RHÔNE VALLEY

LYON AND ENVIRONS

Bustling Lyon is France's second largest city. Its old section, Vieux Lyon, just below **Notre-Dame de Fourvière,** is a network of medieval churches, alleyways, and 15th- to 16th-century houses. Don't miss its **Parc de la Tête d'Or,** a botanical garden with lakes, a zoo, miniature golf, a mini-train, and pony and go-cart rides. On summer afternoons there are free puppet shows. Boulevard des Belges. Summer daily 6– 11; winter until 8. The exquisite **Musée des Beaux Arts,** with Spanish, Dutch, and Impressionist artworks, has a sculpture garden where kids can catch a breath. Place des Terreaux in the Palais St-Pierre. Free. Wed.–Sun. 10:30–6. Lyon's favorite children's museum is the **Musée des Marionnettes,** which houses a collection of internationally famous puppets. Free. Hôtel Gadagne. Wed.–Mon. 10:45–6. Puppet fever pervades at the **Festival International de la Marionnette** with puppet parades and music in the streets. First weekend in Sept. Centre Commercial Part-Dieu. Tel. 78-62-90-13. Windows lit with candles and parades mark the historic **Fête de la Vierge,** a festival held in early December. Contact the **tourist office** at Place Bellecour (Tel. 78-42-25-75). A cozy, inexpensive, centrally located family **hotel** is the **Bayard,** 23, pl. Bellecour, 69002 Lyon. Tel. 78-37-39-64. *Pérouges,* 40 kilometers northeast of Lyon, is a town pre-dating the Roman occupation with cobblestone streets, medieval food specialties, and craft demonstrations.

THE DROME

Continuing south down the Rhône valley from Lyon you'll come to ancient *Vienne* with Roman ruins. Nearby is *Hauterives* and the folk-art wonder **Palais Idéal.** Your kids won't believe it and neither will you. Possessed French mailman Joseph Ferdinand Cheval, who taught himself the craft of masonry, created an "imaginary palace" with a Hindu temple, Swiss chalet, medieval castle, and hundreds of creatures made from stones, mosaic chips, and glass fragments. 28 km. north of *Romans-sur-Isère.* It's remote but worth finding. Fee. Summer daily 8–8; winter until 6. Tel. 75-68-81-19.

The smallest region in France? Fans of miniatures will enjoy *St-Marcellin's* **Le Jardin Ferroviaire,** a French railway village at 1/23 scale. Fee. Between Romans and Grenoble. Apr.–Nov. daily. Tel. 76-38-54-55. Nearby, in **Pont-en-Royans,** is the **Grottes de Choranche,** a cave with thousands of pencil-thin stalactites. Fee. Year-round daily. Tel. 75-48-64-92.

THE ALPS

The French Alps are held in high esteem by sports enthusiasts for their extensive selection of year-round recreational activities, which include exceptional skiing in winter and hiking amidst rushing streams and glorious wildflowers in summer.

ANNECY

On a magnificent crystal-clear lake, Annecy is a popular vacation spot with castles, narrow cobblestone streets, and flower-lined canals. Pick up *Le Mois à Annecy,* a free publication that tells you what's happening in town, at the **tourist office** on 1, rue Jaurès 9 (Tel. 50-45-00-33).

All types of sports are available on **Lake Annecy,** and there are many swimming **beaches.** Plage des Marquisats and Albigny are free beaches; Impérial Plage charges a fee and has lifeguards, a water slide, and tennis. Three **parks** encircle the lake. The central **Jardin Public** is large and informal with two exceptional playgrounds. Free. Along the park's lakefront promenade, rent wind surfers, pedalboats, canoes, and rowboats. Its jeweled carousel, Manège du Paquier, decorated with embroidered beads and small lamps, was our favorite in all of France. Fee. Daily afternoon–dusk. **Champs de Mars** is Annecy's lakefront park for sunbathing and frisbee tossing. Leaving town en route to *Thônes* you'll find **Le Parc de l'Impérial,** adjacent to the beach club, with another terrific playground. **La Compagnie des Bateaux à Vapeur** offers 90-minute boat tours of the lake with frequent castle viewing stops. Fee. 2, pl. au Bois. Tel. 50-51-08-40.

In Annecy's old town, climb up to the 12th-century **château,** whose museum has a folklore and natural history display. Fee. July–Aug. daily 10–12, 2–6; off-season Wed.–Mon. 10–12, 2–6. Tel. 50-45-29-66. **Horse-drawn carriages** tour the charming *vieille ville.* June and Sept. Wed.; July–Aug. Wed., Thurs. Departs Quai du Semnoz. Reservations: Tel. 50-45-00-33. Early July's **Festival de la Vieille Ville** has parades and street performances; the **Fête du Lac,** held the first Saturday in August, features hilarious floats and fireworks.

NEAR ANNECY

Twelve kilometers west of Annecy, in *Marcellaz-Albanais,* the **Musée Arts de l'Enfance** is a small museum designed for children. Apr.–Oct. Sun., Mon., Wed., Thurs. 2–8. Tel. 50-69-73-74. The enchanting lakeside haven of *Talloire,* 13 kilometers from Annecy, has many lakefront family hotels, swimming, boating, and hiking. Just west of *Chambéry,* on D40 in *Les Avenieres,* is **Walibi,** an enormous amusement park with a roller coaster that turns completely upside down, fire divers, and a myriad of water rides. Fee. Mar.–Sept. daily 10–7. Tel. 74-33-71-80.

MONT BLANC REGION

The Mont Blanc area is a paradise for hikers and skiers, and the resulting crowds would almost make it worth skipping were not Mont Blanc, Europe's highest peak, such a spectacular site. At the foot of Mont Blanc is *Chamonix,* a family resort in the summer and a chic ski resort in the winter. For an amazing panorama of the French, Swiss, and Italian Alps, venture up the **Aiguille du Midi** *téléphérique* **(cable car),** one of the world's highest (15,700 feet), with four different places to stop en route. A 10-minute trip takes you to 7,545 feet but most people soar through the clouds to the next stop at 12,600 feet (90 minutes round-trip). If your children are seasoned walkers, stop midway down on your return trip to play in the glaciers and walk from there. The third stop of the téléphérique crosses the international border to Pointe Helbronner in Italy. You can continue to the Italian town of Courmayeur. Meeting the Italian border guards at 11,000 feet is a great journal entry. Expensive. Departs from South Chamonix station every 10 to 30 minutes. During high-season, get there early to avoid crowds and cloudy afternoons. Jan.–Dec. 8–12, 1:30–3:45; May–Sept. 8–12, 1:30–4:45; July–Aug. 6–5. Tel. 50-53-30-80.

A 20-minute cog-rail train ride will transport you up to Chamonix's **Mer de Glace,** a glacier in a panoramic bowl. From there, a cable car swings you down to **La Grotte de Glace,** a kitschy cave with ice sculptures of a piano, bed, couch, and more. Separate or combined fee. Departs from small station next to main train depot. July–Sept. daily. Tel. 50-53-12-54. **Club Med**'s winter alpine village in Chamonix has bilingual staff and provides kids' activities on and off the slopes. From the U.S. Tel. 800-CLUB-MED.

Les Grandes Montets, at *Argentière,* up the valley from Chamonix, has some of the Alps' best skiing. Close to the Swiss border is *Avoriaz,* a chic car-free ski resort. You can enter the village by sleighs drawn by horses, reindeer, or dogs, or take the funicular from Morzine. Its children's village has ski instruction and play areas. *Megève* is a *trés chic*, expensive ski resort with gentle slopes and many Maisons d'Enfants—hotels especially suited for children. The older resort of *Morzine* has sleigh rides and ice shows.

SAVOIE RESORTS

Savoie, site of the 1992 Winter Olympic games, is a region with some of the Alps' finest skiing. *Albertville,* host city of the games, is a gateway to Savoie's resorts. The city has a ski school, an ice-skating rink for 9,000 spectators, a smaller practice rink, and a large sports center. The **tourist office,** Place de la Gare, 73200 Albertville (Tel. 79-32-04-22, 79-37-49-50), can provide you with information on skiing, summer canoeing, kayaking, mountain biking, ballooning, and hiking. Overlooking Albertville is the 14th-century walled city of *Conflans,* perched on a rocky point.

Savoie's leading winter resorts, and perhaps the world's best, are *Val d'Isère* and *Lac de Tignes,* sites of the 1992 Olympic men's alpine skiing. Over the ridge is *Courchevel,* in the Trois Vallées, the largest French ski resort for all levels and a great place for families. You can rent apartments and chalets in *Méribel.* Courchevel is connected by lift to *Val Thorens,* France's highest resort, where a *téléphérique* takes you almost 7,000 feet up to the top of Mount Caron. Summer in *Tignes* offers lake sailing, swimming, and hikes into the **Vannoise National Park.**

THE SOUTHEAST

THE FRENCH RIVIERA: CÔTE D'AZUR AND MONACO

The best-known stretch of the Mediterranean coast, the Côte d'Azur starts east of Menton and ends just beyond Marseille. Here, amidst the salt air and clear skies, famous resorts line the coast: regal Cannes, bustling Nice, brash St. Tropez. The increasing overbuilding of condos and crowded summer highways has obscured some of the Riviera's charm—but not all. Families wishing to avoid the bustle should consider staying in the hills bordering Haute Provence, where small ancient villages cling to the cliffs. Mougins, Vence, St. Paul de Vence, Tourettes-sur-Loup, and Biot are less than a 20-minute drive from the beach yet seem an era away.

Accommodations, especially self-catering homes, are booked months in advance for July and August. Most resorts have a single stretch of sand, divided into a public and private section. For a fee, you get a cabana, an umbrella, and a lounge chair. Prepare your kids for the numerous topless sunbathers. Most resorts rent wind surfers and sailboats. Rent **bikes** at the train stations in Antibes, Cannes, Juan-les-Pins, and Nice. **Club Med** has recently opened its newest and most luxurious international village, **Opio,** in the hills overlooking the Riviera, 30 kilometers from Nice. The club boasts a mini-club for children 4 and older and bilingual staffs. From the U.S. Tel. 800-CLUB-MED.

MENTON AND ENVIRONS

Menton claims to be the Riviera's warmest resort. Its **Fête Internationale du Citron,** a celebration of the lemon, features floats made from this tart aromatic fruit. Late Jan.–early Feb. Housed in a 17th-century bastion, the **Musée Jean Cocteau** showcases the work of this brilliant filmmaker, writer, and sculptor. Head upstairs for his series of fantastic animals. Fee. Promenade du Soleil. Summers Wed.–Sun. 10–12, 2–6; rest of year 10–12, 2–5:30. Tel. 93-57-72-30. Ninety-minute **boat excursions** depart from Vieux Port, near the lighthouse. Fee. Tel. 93-35-58-81.

Between Menton and Monte-Carlo is the resort of *Cap Martin,* watched over by the hill town and castle keep of *Roquebrune.* Cap Martin has several quiet beaches dominated by an old village: two at Cabbé, facing southwest, and one at Carnolès, on the east side next to Menton. The ancient keep in Roquebrune is the oldest feudal castle in France. Its upper artillery platform commands a scenic view of the sea. Fee. Sat.–Thurs. mornings and afternoons. Closed mid-Nov.–mid-Dec. Tel. 93-35-07-22.

PRINCIPALITY OF MONACO

Monaco, capital of the principality, is extravagant and expensive, full of high-rise apartments and glitzy hotels. A number of family-oriented attractions make it a worthwhile day trip. Built on a rock that juts some 875 yards out to sea, the city drops dramatically to the sea on almost all sides. The **Jardin Exotique (Tropical Gardens)** offers a great view of the palace and the coast from its position above the cliffs where thousands of cacti cascade down 300 feet to the ocean. From the gardens, walk down to the **Musée d'Anthropologie Préhistorique** to see skeletons, including bones from collective burials. Further down are the **Grottes de l'Observatoire,** caves with a number of chambers adorned with stalactites and stalagmites. The entire excursion is rather steep for young legs. Combined fee for garden, museum, and caves. May–Sept. daily 9–7; Oct.–Apr. daily 9–6. Tel. 93-30-33-65/66.

In *Old Monaco,* better known as **The Rock,** leave your car in the car park and take the elevator up to the **Océanographic Museum and Aquarium,** directed by Jacques Cousteau and founded by Prince Albert I. Its aquarium has dayglow-colored fish from the Indo-Pacific and Indian Oceans, but the cases are too high to be seen by young children. The zoology hall features skeletons of large marine mammals, including a whale, sea cow, and giant turtle. Expensive. July–Aug. daily 9–9; June–Sept. daily 9–7; Oct.–May daily 9:30–7. Tel. 93-30-15-14. In front of the oceanographic museum, a small **train** departs regularly for a 15-minute tour of all major city sites, including the **palace,** where you can watch the changing of the guard at 11:55 daily. Fee. Terraced on the southwest face of the Rock is a **zoo** with mammals, birds, and monkeys.

Our young daughter raved about the **Museum of Ancient Dolls and Automatons,** a short walk from the famous casino in *Monte-Carlo,* in the National Museum. The collection of fashion and folklore dolls, clowns, and puppets includes dolls of papier mâché, wax, and wood. You'll see extravagant doll houses, music boxes, circus scenes, and even . . . Barbie, "la plus célèbre du monde." Fee. 17, av. Princesse Grace. Easter–Sept. 15 daily 10–6:30; Sept. 15–Easter daily 10–12:15, 2:30–6:30. Tel. 93-30-91-26.

Late January to early February marks the **Festival International du Cirque,** held in Monte-Carlo. Top circus acts from more than twenty countries bring excitement and thrills to the star-spangled "Big Top" where the event is held. Children judge the afternoon performances; try to get tickets for the daytime shows so your kids can select the "greatest show on earth." From the U.S. Tel. 1-800-AF-PARIS. The **International Fireworks Festival** takes place over the Monte-Carlo harbor in late July and early August. Make sure young ones take a long afternoon nap so they can enjoy this nocturnal spectacle. May's **Grand Prix of Monaco** is one of the world's most famous Formula One auto races, running through the tight turns and steep grades of Monte-Carlo's streets. Pick your spot early for the best view. For events, contact the **tourist office** 2a, bd. des Moulins (Tel. 93-50-60-88).

MONACO TO NICE

Perched 1,300 feet above the ocean on the road between Nice and Monte-Carlo is *Éze,* a beautifully preserved medieval hill town. Should you choose to join the hordes of tourists, be sure to see the 14th-century streets and the **Jardin Exotique (Tropical Gardens).** Fee. June–late Sept. daily all-day; off-season mornings and afternoons. Tel. 93-41-03-03. The best beach in this area is at *Cap d'Ail.* Its eastside beaches are dangerous for swimming, so head for the safe and sheltered beach west of the train station. **Beaulieu** is a fashionable winter resort because it is one of the warmest spots on the Riviera. Leave the sand toys at home as its beaches are gravel.

Cap Ferrat is the name of the peninsula extending from the Villefranche Road and Les Fourmis Bay toward Beaulieu. Families tend to stay here as it is less frenetic and more secluded than Cap d'Antibes. The **Plage de Passable** is a soft-sand beach facing Villefranche. View the eclectic collection ranging from Impressionist paintings to Far Eastern art at the **Ephrussi de Rothschild Foundation** while the kids romp in the gardens of this 17-acre estate. Fee; reduced for garden only. Guided 1-hour tour. Summer Tues.–Sun.; off-season Tues.–Sun. 2–6. Gardens: mornings and afternoons. Tel. 93-01-33-09. Don't miss the daily chimpanzee show at the **Zoo du Cap Ferrat,** near the former fishing village of *St-Jean Cap Ferrat.* Two chimps ride bikes, juggle, play guitars, and even brush each other's teeth. This was one of the few zoos we visited where the animals seemed quite content. Fee. Mid-June–mid-Sept. daily 9–7; off season daily 9:30–6. Tel. 93-76-04-98.

Three kilometers east of Nice is the colorful harbor town of *Villefranche.* Huge eyes and fish narrate scenes from the life of Saint Peter, the patron saint of fishermen, cover the **Chapelle St.-Pierre,** painted inside and out by surrealist Jean Cocteau. Fee. Overlooking harbor. Summer Sat.–Thurs. 9:30–12, 2:30–7; winter Sat.–Thurs. 9:30–12, 2–4:30; spring and fall Sat.–Thurs. 9–12, 2–6. Tel. 93-80-73-68.

NICE

Nice has a casual and spontaneous ambience for a big city. Its beaches, parks, museums, and major airport make it a convenient base for exploring the Côte d'Azur. Accommodations are more reasonably priced here than in the neighboring coastal resorts. An 8-year-old school chum, Nicole, highly recommended the Villa Rose, a **bed-and-breakfast** establishment. She especially liked the family atmosphere; her parents appreciated its inexpensive price and off-street parking. 43, av. Bellevue, 06100 Nice. Tel. 93-84-45-93. The staff at the **tourist office** at Gare Central, Avenue Thiers (Tel. 93-87-97-07) speak English and will provide information on everything from snorkeling to hotels with baby-sitters.

The best part of Nice is its *vieille ville,* where cars are not allowed. Tuesday through Sunday there is a huge **outdoor market** with food, flowers, and lots of colorful commotion. Try *socca,* a scrumptious street-food delicacy, also recommended by our young friend. On cour Saleya. Climb the stairs to the ruins of the **château** above the *vieille ville,* where there's a park with cacti and a grand view of the water.

The colorful **Musée Matisse** is housed in a rambling villa in

Cimiez, the site of ancient Nice. Free. 164, av. des Arènes de Cimiez.
May–Sept. Tues.–Sat. 10–12, 2:30–6:30; Dec.–Apr. Tues.–Sat. 10–
12, 2–5. Tel. 93-81-59-57. Cimiez is also home to the **Musée National
Marc Chagall.** Visitors are brought into Chagall's world of fantasy
through tapestries, paintings, sculpture, and mosaics. Our favorite
was the "Song of Songs" with dreamy figures flying over the rooftops
of sleeping villages. Fee. Av. du Docteur Ménard. July–Sept. Wed.–
Mon. 10–7; Oct.–June Wed.–Mon. 10–12:30, 2–5:30. Tel.
93-81-75-75. The **Musée International d'Art Naïf** displays brilliant
amateur art, including childish and primitive paintings from all over
the world. Fee. Château Ste.-Hélène, av. Fabron. May–Sept. Wed.–
Mon. 10–12, 2–6; off-season Wed.–Mon. 10–12, 2–5. Closed Nov.
Two aquariums and thousands of shells are on view at the **Musée
International de Malacologie.** Free. 3, cours Saleya. May–Sept.
Tues.–Sat. 10:30–1, 2–6:30; Oct. and Dec.–Apr. Tues.–Sat. 10:30–1,
2–6. Tel. 93-85-18-44. The shady **Jardin Albert 1er** provides space to
roam and a resting spot. Promenade des Anglais and quai des États-
Unis.

Nice is the place to be in February to enjoy one of the best examples
of **carnival** in all of Europe. Colorful parades with elaborate floats,
garlands, and flower displays; spectacular fireworks; and street balls
celebrate the King of the Côte d'Azur. Held mid-February. Late summer brings the **Festival de Folklore International** and **Batailles des
Fleurs** with floral parades and music along the waterfront. Late July–
early August. Contact the tourist office for both events.

NICE TO CANNES—INLAND

The hill town of *St-Paul-de-Vence* inspired us to coin the phrase
"medieval chic." Amidst the well-dressed tourists, old gentlemen in
bérets still sip their *pastis* in cafés as they watch a game of *boules.*
Visit in the late afternoon when the tour buses have departed. If you
want to expose your children to the finest in contemporary art, visit
St.-Paul's outdoor **Foundation Maeght,** with its Calders, Giacomettis,
Arps, and Légers set amidst fountains and a vast lawn. Whimsical
colorful works, such as Miró's sculpture *Jeune Fille S'Evidant,* are
tremendously appealing to children. The sweet-scented shady pines
are a good place to relax midday while other sites are closed, and the
café serves delicious pizza. Fee. July–Sept. daily 10–7; Oct.–June
daily 10–12:30, 3–6. Tel. 93-32-81-63.

The charming hill town of *Vence* provides a pleasant break from
the bustle of the coastal towns below. Highly recommended for this
expensive area is the budget **hotel** Diana, just a 20-minute drive from
Nice and the coast. Its rooms have kitchens, small balconies, and
cribs on request, and there's a parking garage, a garden pond with

goldfish, and live piano music. Av. des Poilus, 06140 Vence. Tel.
93-58-28-56.

Two minutes away is **Matisse's Chapelle du Rosaire.** Vence native
Henri Matisse decorated this chapel inside and out when he was in
his eighties. Note how the primary-colored windows reflect floral
motifs on the white marble floor. The ceramic water fountains look
like grade-school pinch pots. Fee. 46, av. Henri Matisse. Tues. and
Thurs. 10–11:30, 2:30–5:30. Closed Nov.–mid-Dec. Tel. 93-58-03-26.

The tours of the Fragonard perfume factory, 11 kilometers north of
Cannes, in *Grasse,* provide a glimpse of the entire perfume-making
process from pressing and crushing flowers and petals to dissolving
them into perfume. Free. English tour. 20 bd. Fragonard. Daily 8:30–
6:30. Tel. 93-36-44-65.

Vallauris is potteryland where kids can find delightful handmade
marionettes in the town center. It was here that Picasso was drawn to
work in clay. View his ceramics at the small **Musée Picasso.** Fee. At
Château des Moines. Daily 10–12, 2–6; off-season 10–12, 2–5.

NICE TO CANNES—COASTAL ROUTE

Câgnes-sur-Mer is a short drive toward the coast from Vence. In a
beautiful park, the **Renoir Museum** is actually the house Renoir built
in 1908. Kids are impressed by seeing the studio of a working artist,
preserved just as he left it. The museum's park has benches, plenty of
grass, and a glorious view of the Cap d'Antibes. Fee. Nov. 16–May
Wed.–Sun. 2–5; June–Oct. 14 Wed.–Sun. 10–12, 2–6. Tel.
93-20-61-07.

Biot is home to the **Musée National Fernand Léger,** where kids can
learn about cubism by viewing this artist's robotlike figures, composed of everyday objects such as bolts and tubes. Kids enjoy his
painting The Great Parade, which depicts a lively circus. Fee. Summer Wed.–Mon. 10–12, 2–6; off-season Wed.–Mon. 10–12, 2–5. Tel.
93-33-42-20. Outside of Biot, along coastal route 7, is the large
Marineland complex. It's a bit more run-down than its American
counterpart but it provides a good dose of French family life. In true
French fashion, there's even a snack bar just for dogs! Children can
view funny shows where dolphins dance, shake hands, and jump
through hoops to taped French music which is never quite in sync
with the dolphins. Shows: daily at 2:30, 4:30, and 6:30; summer late-
show 9:45 PM. Skip Marineland's dark aquarium but don't miss its
Maritime Museum, where everything from fans to boats are created
from shells, chandelier glass, and all kinds of other odd materials.
Separate fees will admit you to three more areas in the complex. In **La
Jungle des Papillons,** butterflies of every possible color and pattern
fly free in a lush tropical garden. **Aquasplash** has winding, twisting

water slides and a giant shallow pool. **Adventure Golf** has 18- and 36-hole courses. Expensive entry fees. Year-round daily 10–7. Tel. 93-35-58-81.

Cap d'Antibes, or "Le Cap," is the southern tip of the cape embracing the resorts of Antibes and Juan-les-Pins. The highlight in *Antibes* is the **Musée Picasso,** with its sculpture garden, perched on a cliff by the ocean. Don't miss his joyful and exuberant artwork, especially "La Joie de Vivre," an enormous work in cement of a plant-woman dancing among goats. Fee; free Wed. only Dec.–May. Pl. du Château. Summer Wed.–Mon. 10–12, 3–7; off-season Wed.–Mon. 10–12, 2–6. Closed Nov. Tel. 93-34-91-91. High-rises are stacked above the crowded beach of *Juan-les-Pins,* a resort with a jumping nightlife. Its clubs stay open until 4 or 5 AM.

Cannes is a cosmopolitan and expensive resort city with dazzling villas, opulent boutiques, and sandy beaches. Along its lavish promenade, **La Croisette,** are casinos, a harbor with pleasure boats, costly cafés, luxury hotels, and the famous Festival Hall, home to the Cannes Film Festival. Each year in May, Cannes becomes the film capital of the world. The **tourist office** is at 1, rue Jean Jaurès (Tel. 93-99-19-77). A small public beach, **Plage du Midi,** is at the far west end of the old harbor; **Plage Gazagnaire** is the public beach to the east of the old harbor. Between the two are expensive private beaches with imported white sand. Kids can take wind-surfing lessons at the beach past Palm Beach, on Place Franklin Roosevelt. Sailboats and motorboats can be rented at Sun Way, Port de la Napoule.

CANNES TO ST. TROPEZ

The Esterel, a stretch of coast between *La Napoule* and *St-Raphaël,* is the most breathtaking part of the Côte. From Cannes, the drive along the Esterel Cliff Road to St-Raphaël will take about half a day. Here rust-colored volcanic rocks have been carved by the wear and tear of the sea to create fantasy shapes. Small beach resorts lining the coast include *Théoule-sur-Mer, Miramar, La Trayas, Agay,* and *Boulouris.*

St-Raphaël has many public beaches and inexpensive hotels. In neighboring *Fréjus* there is an elaborate water park, **Aquatica,** with geysers, "kamikaze toboggans," and water slides, along the coast road where it intersects in the direction of St-Tropez. Fee. May–Sept. daily 10–7; July–Aug. daily until 10:30 PM. Tel. 94-52-01-01. At the 50-acre **Parc Zoologique Safari de Fréjus** you can either walk or drive amidst the great variety of wildlife, which includes vultures, elephants, yaks, and zebras. Fee. Daily. Tel. 94-40-70-65.

Off-season is probably the best time to enjoy the rich, pastel-colored beauty of *St-Tropez,* one of the most beautiful resorts in southern France. St-Tropez has the best sandy **beaches** on the entire coast; they are all 3 to 8 kilometers from the town center. In summer, the town's population swells to over 50,000. **Plage des Greniers** and **Bouillabaisse** are the best private beaches for families, while **Plage de Tahiti** is quite ritzy. **Bikes** can be rented at Peretti (2, av. du Général-LeClerc) or at Louis Mas (5, rue Quaranta). Teens get a kick out of the **tandem pedi-cars** available for rent along the rue Poste. **Wind surfing** can be arranged at the Surfing Shop also on avenue Général-LeClerc. Climb up the **citadelle** for a grand view of the gulf or step down into the dungeon of St-Tropez's **16th-century fortress,** which also houses a naval museum. Fee. Dec.–Oct. Wed.–Mon. 10–5. Closed Nov. Tel. 94-97-06-53. The **tourist office** is on the water at Quai Jean Juarès (Tel. 94-97-41-21).

MARSEILLE AND ENVIRONS

Crowded and hectic Marseille does not have a reputation as a family-oriented destination. However, the city does offer charm, ethnic variety, and many inexpensive accommodations. Take the 15-minute boat ride from the Vieux Port to the **Château d'If,** a fortress from which the Count of Monte Cristo is said to have escaped in the tale by Dumas. Fee. Daily 7–7. You can also sail out to **Île de Frioul,** an island with especially beautiful parks. Boats depart from Gare Maritime, Quai des Belges. Tel. 91-55-50-09.

Twenty kilometers north of Marseille, in *Chateauneuf-les-Martigues,* Gunsmoke fans can experience **El Dorado City,** a western theme park with cowboys and Indians, saloons, and daring stunt shows. Fee. South of 155, east of the road to Carry-le-Rouet. Mar. 16–Nov. 15 Thurs.–Sat. 10–7, Sun. 12–7; Nov. 16–Mar. 15 Sun. only 12–dusk. Tel. 42-79-86-90.

And if all the cowboy hoopla has whet your appetite, head about 20 kilometers east of Marseille to *Cuges-les-Pins,* home of the **OK Corral,** with French cowboys and a myriad of carnival rides. Fee. N8 road, 3½ km. east of town. June–Aug. daily 10:30–7:30; off-season Wed. and weekends 10:30–6:30. Tel. 42-73-80-05.

CORSICA

Perhaps the loveliest of the Mediterranean islands, Corsica, a *département* of France, is a very popular family vacation spot for those who love the outdoors and are willing to forgo some creature comforts. Its main attractions are sports, unspoiled beaches, and mountainous wilderness. Islanders speak French but prefer their own Italian-influenced dialect. Mid-June through September 15 is high-season, when prices escalate.

Corsica is accessible by Air France and Air Inter from Paris, Nice, and Marseille. The short flight from the Riviera is inexpensive. However, car rentals on the island are very expensive and public transportation is slow and infrequent. If you plan to tour the island by car, there is a 5- to 10-hour car-ferry crossing from Toulon, Nice, or Marseille and from Italy's Livorno or La Spezia (often shorter and less expensive). Sardinia, Italy, is only 10 kilometers away. Nice offers a year-round 30 percent discount for those under 26; all ports offer this discount off-season. For summer crossings, book the car-ferry well in advance.

The tourist office in Ajaccio distributes a free brochure, "Corsica, The Holiday Island," with information on train trips; car and bike rentals; accommodations, including holiday villages, gîtes, and chambres d'hôte, sailing, and horseback riding. Write to the **tourist office**, Syndicat d'Initiative d'Ajaccio, B.P. 21, Place Foch, 20176, Ajaccio (Tel. 95-21-40-87, 95-21-53-39).

AJACCIO TO BONIFACIO

Southward from Ajaccio, at the mouth of the **Gulf of Ajaccio,** are the **Îles Sanguinaires (Bloody Islands),** where boats will take you to fire-colored grottos. The beautiful beaches along the way to the Iles Sanguinaires are clean and wide. Ajaccio is the birthplace of Napoléon; older kids may enjoy a visit to his home. Fee. Off rue Bonaparte. Mon. and Wed.–Sat. 9–12, 2–6; Sun. 9–12.

At the southernmost tip of Corsica is *Bonifacio,* considered by many to be the most spectacularly situated town in the Mediterranean. It juts out from 200-foot-high rocky cliffs with houses overhanging the cliff's edge. In the **Haut Ville,** houses were built without first-floor entrances and some contain drawbridges that were pulled up during an attack. Fine sandy beaches are 8 kilometers east, in *Calalonga,* or 10 kilometers northwest, in *Tonnara.*

AJACCIO TO BASTIA

North along Corsica's western coast, twisting roads with amazing panoramas lead to the seaside resorts of *Calvi,* a chic resort, and nearby *L'Île-Rousse,* which attracts an older clientele. Along the way are Corsica's cleanest and nicest beaches, called the **Golfe de Sagone.** Among them is *Tuiccia,* with good camping and a ruined castle. Children will be thrilled with the little **train** that winds through two barely touching mountain ranges from Ajaccio to *Bastia.* The entire one-way trip takes 4 hours but you can get off and return from a number of small towns along the way. Ajaccio train station: rue Jean-Jérôme Levie (Tel. 95-23-11-03). Bastia train station: pl. de la Gare

(Tel. 95-32-60-06). The inland road between the two cities is breathtaking and extremely narrow; driving takes as long as the train.

PROVENCE: THE RHÔNE VALLEY

The fertile Rhône Valley was favored by the Romans, whose 2,000-year-old imprint can be found in the ruins of this varied region. Fields of lavender, poppies, grapevines, and olive trees embrace tiny villages perched on craggy cliffs. Cézanne, Picasso, and Van Gogh struggled to capture the region's unique luminosity. Book ahead in the summer as Provence's festivals, ranging from simple folkloric events to sophisticated artistic spectacles, are a big draw.

The 18th-century **Château de Vergières,** a 700-acre farm in the heart of Provence, on the edge of the Camargue, welcomes overnight guests. Special treats for children, high chairs, cribs, and comfort make this an idyllic family getaway. Rooms range from moderate to expensive and include breakfast. The family also operates a number of inexpensive self-catering **gîtes** nearby. See Château Program, "Lights Out!" at the beginning of this chapter. Gîtes: Madame Pincedé, Domaine de Vergières, 13310 Saint-Martin-de-Crau, Bouches-du-Rhône (Tel. 90-47-17-16).

AIX EN PROVENCE AND ENVIRONS

A visit to Aix en Provence must begin with un citron pressé (lemonade) at one of the many cafés lining shady **Cours Mirabeau,** the lively center of Aix, which drew such famous literary personalities as Emile Zola and Jean Cocteau. Your kids will enjoy the Egyptian mummies at the **Musée Granet** while you savor the eight small Cézannes. Fee. Pl. St-Jean-de-Malte. July–Aug. daily 10–12, 2–6; Sept.–June Wed.–Mon. 10–12, 2–6. Throughout his entire life, native **Paul Cézanne** celebrated Aix in his paintings. Visit his birthplace at 2 rue de l'Opéra and his **studio,** as he left it in 1906, easel, smock, and all. Fee. 9, av. Paul Cézanne. June–Sept. Wed.–Mon. 10–12, 2:30–6; Oct.–May Wed.–Mon. 10–12, 2–5. The **Musée du Vieil Aix** boasts a collection based on historic popular customs, including puppet shows and pageants. Fee. May–Oct. Tues.–Sun. 10–12, 2–6; Nov.–Jan. and Mar.–Apr. Tues.–Sun. 10–12, 2–5. Black and white op-art patterns reach from almost floor to ceiling at the **Foundation Vasarely,** dedicated to the artist's hypnotic plays with pattern, color and shape. The adjoining **park** is perfect for running or relaxing. Fee. 1, av. Marcel Pagnol, Jas de Bouffan, Vasarely. June–Sept. Wed.–Mon. 10–12, 2:30–6; Oct.–May Wed.–Mon. 10–12, 2–5.

Between Aix-en-Provence and Marseille, in *Pennes-Mirabeau,* is the **Aquacity** water park with giant toboggans, a wave pool, and rivers with rapids. Fee. Rte. de Septemes-Les Vallons. June 10–Sept. 13 daily 10–7. Tel. 91-96-12-13.

AVIGNON AND ENVIRONS

Kids will enjoy seeing the ruins of Avignon's famous 12th-century **Pont St-Bénezet (bridge)** from the popular song "Sur le Pont d'Avignon." According to folklore, a young shepherd boy, St-Bénezet, was told to build a bridge across the Rhône by a heavenly voice. All that remains today are four arches as the bridge extends halfway across the Rhône and ends abruptly. Fee. Daily 9–5. The square in front of the grand **Palais des Papes (Pope's Palace)** is always alive with musicians, skateboarders, and hungry pigeons. Visit the pope's bedroom, which is painted entirely in tempera paint, in the Angel's Tower. You'll see birds swooping among vines and squirrels jumping between oak trees. Fee. July–Aug. daily 9–6; Sept.–June daily 9–11:30, 2–5:30. A short walk up from the palace is the **Rocher des Doms,** a park with a playground and a pond full of enormous goldfish and graceful swans. Artists sit along the park's ramparts to capture the view of the Pont St-Bénezet and the fortified village of Villeneuve-lès-Avignon, where the bridge used to end. Daily 7:30 AM–9 PM.

After dinner, clowns and mimes fill the streets around **place de l'Horloge,** reached along the half-mile rue de la République extending from the city walls to the palace. Its splendid carousel, La Belle Epoque, is a must even if the figures are a bit risqué. Avignon goes wild during its notorious **Festival d'Avignon,** held mid-July through early August. Avant-garde artists, puppeteers, plays, dance, and mime fill the streets and practically all of Avignon's courtyards and buildings. Info: Bureau du Festival, BP 92, 84006, Avignon, or the **tourist office,** 41 cours Jean Jaurès (Tel. 90-86-24-43).

The castles, forts, and ramparts of medieval *Villeneuve-lès-Avignon* are straight out of a fairytale. For a view over the Rhône River towards Avignon, climb the massive **Tour de Phillippe le Bel** of 1302. It is all that remains of the little castle that defended the entrance to the bridge of St-Bénezet. Fee. Apr.–Sept. Wed.–Mon. 10–12:30, 3–7:30; Oct.–March Wed.–Mon. 10–12, 2–5. At sunset, the view of Avignon from the **Fort St-André** is memorable. Fee. Daily 9–12, 2–6:30. Be sure to wander through its adjacent garden.

ARLES AND ENVIRONS

The beautiful light, Roman ruins, and quiet landscape of Arles exercised an overpowering influence on Van Gogh and Picasso. With its many festivals and close proximity to the beach, Arles is a popular family destination. Its elliptical **Arènes** is among the most ancient arenas of the Roman world. Acoustics here are so good that when our 8-year-old friend stood at the top of the spectator stand and her 6-year-old brother stood at the bottom, they could talk in regular voices and still hear each other. Kids can walk along the arena's top rim or climb its tower, where the view is exceptional. Fee. May–Sept. daily 8:30–7; Oct.–Apr. daily 9–12, 2–5. Dance, drama, and folk festivities take place in the ruins of the nearby **Théâtre Antique.** Children will enjoy running through this picturesque stone setting, climbing the stage, and testing the acoustics. Behind the théâtre along Boulevard des Lices is the manicured **Jardin d'Eté.** Its colorful playground has a train, playhouse, and seesaw.

Groups from all over Provence participate in the **Fête de la Tradition,** held July 2 and 4, in the Arènes where a young woman is chosen to represent the region from the many dressed in local costumes. Van Gogh immortalized these costumes in numerous paintings, some of which may be seen in the **Réattu Museum.** Fee. May–Sept. daily 9–7, off-season daily 9–12, 2–5. Real chariots enter the arena at September's **Roman Festival,** which made a lasting impression on our young traveling companions. Contact the **tourist office** at Esplanade Charles de Gaulle (Tel. 90-96-29-35) for details.

Les Baux is a haunting natural fortress built into a towering rock plateau. Avoid the tourist stalls and head up to **Cité Morte.** Dominating most of the hill are moonlike, weathered ruins with ample space for children to run. Climb the narrow steps to the top of the ridge at sunset for an extraordinary view of the valley, the Camargue, and Arles. At night, spotlights illuminate the ruins. Fee. July–Aug. daily 8–8; Sept.–June daily 9–7.

The famed **Tarasque Parade** is held the last Sunday in June in *Tarascon,* a town with a sprawling castle. A 15-foot papier mâché tarasque, or bloodthirsty monster, half-lion and half-fish, marches through the streets. Legend claims he terrorized this region until Mary Magdalene's sister vanquished him in AD 48.

THE CAMARGUE

Most of the immense stretch of marshland in the Camargue is protected as a natural park because it is the home of exotic wildlife. A guided **horseback ride** (hourly, half-day or whole day, all levels) allows kids to get up close and see baby bulls, wild horses, flamingos, herons, egrets, and ducks in their natural habitat. Wear rubber boots; there's a lot of sloshing through swamps. The **tourist office,** 5, av. Van Gogh (Tel. 90-47-82-55), in the Camargue's capital, Les Saintes Maries de la Mer, will give you a list of horse rentals. Behind the office along the beach is miniature golf and a good playground.

Les Saintes Maries de la Mer, known as the "budget Riviera," is a low-key resort and a great base for exploring the Camargue. Its beaches have wide stretches of white sand and are good for shell hunts, swimming, and wind surfing. East of town are the area's **camping** sites with miles of beach and dunes. There are many **bike** trails within the Camargue's preserve. Trail maps and bike rental agencies are available at the tourist office. Children will enjoy the boat rides into the sea and the Rhône aboard the *Tiki III,* a 1-hour, 15-minute excursion to view wildlife. Fee. Tel. 90-97-81-68. **Le Parc Ornithologigue du Pont-de-Gau** is a reserve for owls, egrets, herons, vultures, and pink flamingos all in their natural habitat. The park is across the street from one of the area's horse rentals. Fee. Along D570, 4 km. from Les Stes-Maries. Mar.–mid-Nov. 9–sunset. Tel. 90-47-82-62. On May 24 and 25, during the **Pélerinages (procession) des Gitans,** Gypsies from all over the world gather in Les Stes-Maries in honor of Sarah, the patron saint. The *Gardiens* **(cowboys from the Camargue)** have a procession, there are folk dances, and Sarah's statue is carried from the church to the sea.

NÎMES AND ENVIRONS

Home to many ruins, Nîmes was built by the Romans 2,000 years ago. Its well-preserved **Amphithéâtre Romain,** where gladiator fights took place, is now used for outdoor performances. Daily 8–8. For a great climb, ascend the ancient **Tour Magne,** part of the Roman city walls. July–Aug. daily 9–7; Apr.–June and Sept. daily 9–12, 2–7; Oct.–Mar. daily 9–12, 2–5. Have a picnic in the town's ornamental park, the **Jardins de la Fontaine,** at night, when its geometrically arranged ponds are lit.

We first learned about the majestic **Pont du Gard,** a three-story 2,000-year-old Roman aqueduct, from a 7-year-old pal who enjoyed playing and swimming along its river banks. The bridge, boldly spanning the river Gard, is a technical and aesthetic masterpiece. Three levels of receding arches, placed one above the other, are completely independent of each other. Discourage young thrill seekers from walking across the aqueduct's narrow top as there are no rails separating them from the rocky river below. 20 km. from Avignon. Canoes and kayaks can be rented near the tourist office.

North of Nîmes is the spectacular, rugged canyon of the **Gorges de l'Ardèche.** Riding the rapids of the gorge's sparkling Ardèche River by canoe is crowded high-season but loads of fun, and there are lovely swimming beaches spanning the length of the canyon from Vallon-Pont-d'Arc to Pont-St-Esprit. The gorge's **Grotte de la Madeleine** is a cave with outstanding stalagmites and stalactites that resemble waterfalls. Fee. On the *route touristique,* D290. Apr.–Sept. 9:30–12, 2–6:30; July–Aug. 9:30–1, 2–6:30. The **tourist office** in Vallon Pont d'Arc (Tel. 75-88-04-01) can give you lists of campgrounds, trail maps, and canoe or kayak rentals.

A trip in the Gorges is not complete without a visit to the **Grotte d'Orgnac,** a cave with a 160-foot-high Gothic arch and two 60-foot-high stone pillars which resemble the pipes of an organ. Fee. 7 km. northwest of Orgnac on D217. Mar.–Nov. 9–12, 2–6. Tel. 75-38-62-51.

Fifty kilometers north of Nîmes, near *St-Ambroix,* is the water-filled **Grotte de la Cocalière,** a cave with stalagmites, underground lakes with crystallized sections called "cave pearls," and, believe it or not, a subterranean bike path. Accessible by a small train. Fee. On 104 and D904 between Alès (25 km.) and Aubenas (50 km.). Apr.–Oct. daily 9–12, 2–6. Tel. 66-24-01-57.

LANGUEDOC-ROUSSILLON

Languedoc-Roussillon has some of the best beaches in France, which are less expensive than the popular resorts of neighboring Provence and the Côte d'Azur. You'll find the history, language, and architecture of this highly cultured, rugged region to be as much Spanish as it is French.

ALBI AND ENVIRONS

Thirty kilometers northeast of Toulouse is Albi, a city cast in a brick-red hue. Its 13th-century red stone **Cathédrale Ste-Cécile** is a startling structure appearing more like a fortress than a church, which was indeed its intention. This authoritative exterior hides a glorious interior covered with brilliant Italian frescoes. The cathedral is illuminated nightly 8:45–10:30 PM in July and August. Concerts are held on Wednesday afternoons on its enormous organ, said to be the largest in France. Across the way is the **Palais de la Berbie,** also built to look like a fortress, which now houses the **Musée Toulouse-Lautrec.** Here you can view Albi's native son's famous posters of Montmartre's belle epoque as well as paintings he created when just a teenager. Fee. July–Sept. daily 9–12, 2–6; Oct.–June Wed.–Mon. 10–12, 2–5. The steps adjoining the palace lead to the ornamental maze-like garden, the **Jardin de la Berbie.** Its view of the Tarn River and the arched 11th-century bridge, the **Pont Vieux,** is beautiful although the manicured gardens are frustrating for active kids because they are fenced off. Children can run free in the **Parc Rochegude,** on the outskirts of the old town. Off bd. Carnot. Children will enjoy touring Albi's old section, *Vieille Albi,* in **Le Petit Train** with daily departures 1:30–6:30 and Sundays 3:30–6:30. Tel. 63-54-22-30. Albi's **tourist office,** Place Ste-Cécile (Tel. 63-54-22-30) can provide information on canoeing or kayaking along the Tarn, horseback riding, and hotels or camping.

CORDES

Twenty-five kilometers from Albi is Cordes, a tiny walled medieval city restored by artists. No cars are allowed so get ready for a good climb up to its charming, although touristy, main street lined with the studios of artisans. The **tourist office,** Place de Halle, will give you a list of craftspeople who open their studios to visitors. Children will enjoy balancing on the town walls as you ascend. Cordes is home to a favorite museum for kids, one that exhibits **artwork created from sugar,** on Place de la Bride, the town's central square. At the base of the town's walls there's a small park with tables and play equipment in the shape of fruit. Cordes comes alive on Bastille Day for the **Fête du Grand Fauconnier,** a historic celebration of the town 500 years ago. Locals surround their homes in floral garlands and there is a torchlit parade of queens, princes, and damsels in distress.

CARCASSONE

The fortified 13th-century **Cité de Carcassone** is a child's vision of how fairy-tale lands must look. This extravagant fortress of fifty-two towers and two concentric walls dates back to the Middle Ages but was restored in the 19th century. In spite of its touristy atmosphere, Carcassone emits a medieval aura and is worthy of a visit. The **tourist office,** 15, bd. Camille Pelletan, Place Gambetta (Tel. 68-25-07-04), can provide you with a list of hotels and campgrounds. There are a number of hotels within the medieval city.

At the **Port Narbonnaise,** the city entrance, children can spin in a whir of color on a beautiful carousel or ride **Le Petit Train** for a 15-minute tour of the city. May 1–Sept. 30. Walk along the grassy passages, called **lists,** between the two sets of the town's walls, which at one time were used for jousting competitions. Entrance to the lists and the outer walls of the city is free. To enter the inner walls and towers, you must pay a fee. Inside the old city, visit the grand medieval **Château Comtal,** complete with a real moat. Fee. 40-minute English tours daily 10, 2:30. Apr.–Sept. 9–12, 2–6:30; Oct.–Mar. daily 10–12, 2–5. Tel. 68-25-01-66. Escape the summer sun to the cool **Basilique St-Nazaire,** where stained-glass windows glow in the sunlight. Free. Summer 9–12, 2–7; winter 9–12, 2–5.

In June, Carcassone stages **Les Troubadours,** a festival of music and dance of the Middle Ages. Tel. 68-71-30-30. The **Festival de la Cité,** held in early July, is an explosion of music, theater, and dance held in the château, which reaches its peak on July 14 **(Bastille Day)** with singing and dancing in the streets. An amazing fireworks display lights the sky over the city's fifty-two towers. Tel. 68-71-30-30. In August, the festival of the **Médiévales** takes the city back to the Middle Ages with townsfolk dressed in historic costumes, crafts displays, and performances. Tel. 68-47-09-07.

GORGES DU TARN

Forty kilometers north of Montpellier along D986 is *Ganges,* a gateway to the spectacular landscape of the **Gorges du Tarn.** Take the underground funicular ride into the **Grotte des Demoiselles.** The biggest of its caverns, called "The Cathedral," truly lives up to its name. You'll see a statue that looks like Mary and Jesus, a church organ, and gargoyles. Fee. 5 km. south of Ganges on D986. Oct.–Mar. 9:30–12, 2–5; Apr.–Sept. 8:30–12, 2–7. Tel. 67-73-70-02.

THE SOUTHWEST

THE BASQUE COUNTRY

The nationalistic French Basques believe the Basque nation to be one country, divided between France and Spain. Awaiting visitors is an interesting heritage along with wide sandy beaches and food-filled festivals.

BAYONNE, BIARRITZ, AND ENVIRONS

To gain an introduction to Basque culture, visit *Bayonne's* **Musée Basque,** whose extensive exhibit includes a room devoted to the regional sport of *pelote* **(jai alai).** Fee. July–Sept. Mon.–Sat. 9:30–12:30, 2:30–6:30; Oct.–June Mon.–Sat. 10–12, 2:30–5:30. *Pelote* matches can be viewed in town. Contact the **tourist office** at Hôtel de Ville, Place de la Liberté (Tel. 59-59-31-31). Pick up their brochure "Programme des Fêtes" for the region's many festivals.

Called the "California of Europe," the ritzy summer resort of *Biarritz* has sandy beaches, fireworks, and festivals ranging from acrobatic water skiing to volleyball tournaments. Families crowd the calm **plage du Vieux Port.** Visit the **Aquarium** in the **Musée de la Mer** for a look at Atlantic fish and boats. Fee. Summer daily 9–7. The **tourist office,** Place d'Ixelles, can lead you to surfboard rentals and scubadiving classes.

Further south, *St-Jean de Luz,* like Biarritz, was a Basque fishing village. Pedalboats are for rent along its main promenade, Jacques Thibaud. The **Fêtes de St-Jean,** held around June 24, is the town's grandest folkloric festival; July's **Nuit de la Sardine St-Jean-Pied-de-Port** celebrates the sardine with fireworks. And if that is not enough, tuna is honored at July's festive **Fêtes du Thon.** Contact the **tourist office** at Place Foch (Tel. 59-26-03-16) for details. They can also tell you about *pelote* matches and bullfighting spoofs.

THE PYRÉNÉES

Hikers and nature-loving families are drawn to the High Pyrénées with its rare wildlife, from mountain antelope to eagles, and breathtaking vistas. *Cauterets* is a good base for exploring the impressive **Parc National des Pyrénées;** the town also has excellent downhill and cross-country skiing as do the neighboring mountain villages of *Luz St-Sauveur* and picture-perfect *Gavarnie.* Near Gavarnie is the **Cirque de Gavarnie,** a natural amphitheater circled with snow-covered mountains and plunging waterfalls. You can ride **horses** out to the Cirque, a 2- to 3-hour trip. Held here is July's **Festival des Pyrénées,** when torches light the paths back to mountain villages after evening performances.

Pau's **Castle Museum** exhibits the cradle Henri IV made from one giant turtle shell. Under 18 free. Summer daily 9:30–11:45, 2–5:45; off-season 9:30–11:45, 2–4:45. The city's **Parc Beaumont** is a lush park with a waterfall. A free funicular carries you from the train station to the Boulevard des Pyrénées for a great view of the mountains. June's **Festival de Pau** features fireworks, *pelote* competitions, and a leg of the **Tour de France.** Contact the **tourist office** at Place Royale (Tel. 59-27-27-08).

POITOU-CHARENTES

In summer, you'll share the sandy beaches of Poitou-Charentes, the sunniest stretch of coast on the French Atlantic, with the many who come in search of fine Bordeaux wine and Cognac. Cruise the Charente River along the 200 kilometers of peaceful waterways between the Atlantic estuary of *Rochefort* to just west of *Angoulême* on **houseboats,** rented by the week or weekend and equipped with kitchens, showers, and beds for two to eight people. The water is clean and safe for swimming. When you've had enough of cruising, moor by a bank and unload bikes to explore. Contact: Loisirs-Accueil Charente, Place Bouillaud, 1600 Angoulême (Tel. 45-92-24-43), or Blake's Holidays, 4939 Dempster St., Skokie, Ill. 60077 (U.S. tel. 800-628-8118).

BORDEAUX AND ENVIRONS

Bordeaux's Gothic **Cathédrale St-André** has a fanciful façade with strange gargoyles and flying buttresses. And, while adults are off sampling the famous red Medoc and Grave wines of Bordeaux, kids may want to sample the 25 acres of green in the city's **Jardin Public**. Daily 7–10. The city's **Musée des Douanes (Customs Museum)** traces the subject from ancient Roman times with exhibits of smuggling devices and photographs of famous attempts. Fee. 1, pl. de la Bourse, near Quai de la Douane. May–Sept. Tues.–Sun. 10–12, 1–6; Oct.– Apr. Tues.–Sun. 10–12, 1–5. Tel. 56-44-47-10.

About 30 kilometers east of Bordeaux is **St-Emilion**, the most enticing of the region's wine towns. Visit the strange **Eglise Monlithe**, a church carved by 8th-century monks out of a single piece of solid rock. Fee. 45-minute obligatory tour departs from the **tourist office**, Place des Créneaux, daily at 10. Tel. 57-24-72-03. In late September or early October during the medieval ritual of the **Jurade**, councilmen dressed in regal attire climb to the top of **La Tour du Roi (King's Tower)** and chant the result of the year's harvest to cries of "Hallelujah!"

Ten kilometers south of the beautiful sandy beach of *Arcachon* is *Pilat-sur-Mer,* which boasts the largest sand dune in all of Europe, the **Dune du Pilat**. Go before a long car ride! Your kids will tire themselves out by climbing up and rolling or skiing down its steep slopes. Also 10 kilometers from Arcachon is *Gujan-Mestras,* where kids can ride giant toboggans, splash in a wave pool, and ride rapids at the **Aquacity** water park. Fee. Route des Lacs. June 10–Sept. 13 daily 10–7. Tel. 56-66-39-39.

MARAIS POITEVIN

Midway between Poitiers and La Rochelle is *Niort,* a good base for visiting the curious marshlands of the Marais Poitevin. Visitors can travel this park's canals and waterways on a flat-bottomed boat from *Arçais, Coulon, La Garette, Sansais, Saint-Hilaire-la-Palud;* on a pleasure boat from Arçais; or by horse-drawn caravans. Eels, herons, snipes, and ducks populate this half-aquatic landscape. Contact the **tourist office**, Place de la Poste, 79002 Niort (Tel. 49-24-18-79).

Near Niort, in the *Forêt de Chizé,* visit **Le Monde Vivant des Insectes,** a zoo with over 5,000 butterflies and bugs. Fee. June–Aug. 10–12, 2–8. Tel. 49-09-61-14. The fôret also houses the **Zoorama Européen,** a park created as a wild animal biological study center. Rare animals such as lynx and bison roam in the wild. Fee. Villiers-en-Bois. Apr.–Sept. 9–7, Sun. and holidays until 8; Oct.–Mar. 10–12,

2–dusk, Sun. and holidays 10–dusk. Closed Tues., except May–Aug. Tel. 49-09-60-64.

NEAR POITIERS

Futuroscope Park, near *Poitiers,* is the first European amusement park devoted entirely to new technology with Space Age villages, futuristic lakes, high-tech machines, and more. In the Futuroscope Pavilion, kids are guided by Christopher Columbus on a voyage starting with the *Santa María* and ending with the space shuttle. The park's Kiddyland has over seventy inventive attractions from a pumpkin maze to computers that play international music. A teen favorite is the compact-disc room, while babies and toddlers will get a kick out of seeing their favorite Fisher Price toys on a larger-than-life scale. The park's theater, the Kinémax, is a startling metallic seven-story building with the largest flat screen in Europe. Fee. 8 km. north of Poitiers on N10, near Jaunay-Clan. May–Nov. 12 daily 9:30–7; July–Aug. daily 9:30–8:30. Tel. 49-62-30-20.

Germany

Germany is world-renowned for the beauty and quality of its toys: charming little wooden villages of barns, cottages, trees, animals, and people; the world's most elaborate toy trains; brightly painted peasant-style doll-house furnishings; exquisitely detailed dolls; and life-like Steiff animals. Better than any toy museum, the displays in toy stores can be touched and, of course, taken home. Of all the countries in Europe, Germany is the one where your children's piggy banks will be emptied.

And if you can tear your children away from the toy stores, they can get up close to an oom-pah band in one of Munich's *Biergärten* or ride a one-horse open sleigh through the snow in a small Bavarian village. Many cities are surrounded by lush forests, protected as open space, where you can hike, rent bikes, or picnic. Well-preserved half-timbered towns and villages with fantasy castles abound. Cuckoo clocks are still handmade in the Black Forest, and German traditional festivals are loads of fun. Germany's folktales are known by children throughout the world thanks to the Brothers Grimm, who made collecting and writing them down their life's work. These are brought to life in Germany's many fairy-tale parks.

Have a great trip! . . . *gute Reise.*

Preparing Your Kids: Books and Art

Your children are probably already familiar with many of the folktales compiled by the Brothers Grimm, such as *The Bremen Town Musicians, Cinderella, The Frog Prince, Hansel and Gretel, Little Red*

Riding Hood, The Pied Piper of Hamlin, Rapunzel, Rumplestiltskin, Snow White, and Tom Thumb. Pantheon Books (N.Y.) publishes a full compendium called Complete Grimm's Fairytales (1976, $9.95).

Art: Among the German artists whose works your children will encounter are Altdorfer, Cranach, Dürer, Grunewald, Holbein, Kandinsky, Marc, and Macke. Your library should have books with photographs of their works.

Wha'd'ya Wanna Do?

The **German National Tourist Office** will pack your mailbox full of brochures. Local tourist offices are found in even the tiniest village. They are called **Fremdenverkehrsamt** or simply **Verkehrsamt.**

GERMAN NATIONAL TOURIST OFFICES
>   *U.S.A.–Los Angeles:* German National Tourist Office, 444 South Flower St., Suite 2230, Los Angeles, CA 90017. Tel. 213-688-7332.
>   *U.S.A.–New York:* German National Tourist Office, 747 Third Ave., 33rd floor, New York, NY 10017. Tel. 212-308-3300.
>   *Canada–Montreal:* German National Tourist Office, Box 418, 2 Fundy Place, Place Bonaventure, Montreal, H5A 1B8. Tel. 514-878-9885.

Festivals and fairs are held in almost every city, town, and hamlet, especially from May through September. Germany has originated many of our Christmas customs. You'll find enchanting **Christmas markets** throughout the country; the most notable are held in Munich, Nuremburg, Augsberg, and Cologne. Dozens of vendors set up festive booths selling Christmas ornaments and decorations of all kinds, handmade toys, and crèches. You'll also find cider, hot mulled wine, roasted chestnuts, and gingerbread booths. **Horse-drawn sleigh rides** are commonly found in winter in smaller alpine villages.

Elaborate **Märchenparadiese** (fairy-tale paradises) and **Märchenwälder** (fairy-tale forests) are found throughout Germany. They typically have animated fairy-tale characters, some of which are wired for sound, performing in storybook stage settings. Little ones adore them. **Spielplätze** (adventure playgrounds) are found in many cities, most of them created as an alternative to the routine sandboxes and swing sets of the past. You'll find inventive climbing structures and projects for children to create under supervision.

Swimming *lidos* (lake or riverfront beaches), open-air swimming-pool complexes, or more elaborate water parks are found throughout Germany, especially in resorts.

The Germans are big on **wild West theme parks,** a far cry from our picture of medieval Europe. *Gunsmoke* fans who want a dose of cowboy and Indian Americana will have plenty of opportunities to saddle up Old Paint and wander through the OK Corral.

Lights Out! Special German Accommodations

If you'll be staying in an area for a week or more, consider renting an **apartment** or **chalet.** The tourist office can send you their booklets "Self-Catering in Germany" or "Holidays in Germany," both of which list properties and photographs. Most are found in rural or resort areas, and many have facilities for children. The only major city included in the booklet is Berlin. The following companies can also help you:

Interhome, Inc. USA, 36 Carlos Dr., Fairfield, NJ 07006. Tel. 201-882-6864.

Rent A Home International, 7200 34th Ave., NW, Seattle, WA 98117. Tel. 206-789-9377.

Hotel standards are high throughout the country. Local tourist offices will often make bookings for you at a nominal fee. Some hotels offer baby sitting, but it can be expensive; be sure to inquire about price first. We have listed a few hotels in Munich and Berlin that have special amenities for families, such as kitchenettes or proximity to parks. Schloss Hotels, or **castle hotels,** are usually found in more rural areas. The tourist office can send you a brochure with photographs and addresses.

A *Gasthof* or *Gasthaus* is a **country inn** that serves food. Prices usually include breakfast. **Guest houses,** or *Fremdenheime,* are simpler and less expensive. The sign *Zimmer frei* means a room is available in a private home, similar to Britain's popular bed-and-breakfast accommodation. **Farmhouse** holidays are popular with families. Local tourist offices, especially in Bavaria, have extensive listings of them.

Most German **youth hostels,** or *Jugendherberge,* accommodate families with school-age children. You will need a family membership card which is obtainable at most hostels; contact the tourist office for details. **Camping** facilities are excellent, and the top-graded ones have swimming pools and supermarkets. Sites in popular areas fill up quickly from June through September, so be sure to arrive early. Camping out of official grounds is *verboten* (forbidden). The tourist office's "Camping in Germany" lists campgrounds and includes a location map.

Getting Around

Start your engines! **Car** traffic on the *Autobahn* (freeway) moves *fast* and takes some getting used to. The official speed limit is 130 kilometers per hour (80.6 mph) on this excellent system of superhighways. Drivers will need an international driver's license and proof of insurance. Back and front seat belts must be worn at all times, and children under 12 may not sit in the front seat.

Train travelers will find the fast and efficient German Railway System to be one of Europe's best. The Deutsche Bundesbahn (DB) covers most of the country. Children under 4 travel free, and those between 4 and 11 travel half-fare. A EurailPass is valid in Germany, but if you plan to take the fast and comfortable IC (intercity) train, you'll have to pay a supplementary fare. The Germanrail Tourist Card offers unlimited rail travel within Germany for 4, 9, or 16 days. Contact the tourist office for more information.

Nuts and Bolts

Does anyone know what time it is? Open hours for shops are generally Monday through Friday from 9 AM to 5:30 or 6:30 PM. On Saturday most close at 2 PM. Banks are generally open weekdays 8:30 or 9 AM to 3 or 4 PM, and until 5 or 6 PM on Thursday afternoons. Some take a 1- to 2-hour midday break.

National holidays: January 1; Good Friday and Easter Monday; May Day (May 1); Ascension Day; Pentecost Monday; German Unity Day (June 17); All Saints Day (November 1); Day of Repentance (November 22), and December 25 and 26.

Can I have my allowance? The *Deutschmark* (DM) is divided into 100 *Pfennig* (pf). Bills come in DM 10, 20, 50, 100, 500, 1,000. Coins are in 1, 2, 5, 10, and 50 *Pfennigs* and 1, 2, and 5 *Marks*.

Telephones: The country code for West Germany is 49; the code for East Germany is 37. International calls can be made from public phones with the sign "Inlands and Auslandsgespräche" or from post offices.

Useful nationwide phone numbers: Police and emergencies are 110; fire is 112.

Embassies and consulates: U.S. Consulate General, Köeniginstrasse 5, Munich [Tel. (089) 23011]. Canadian Consulate, Maximiliansplatz 9, Munich [Tel. (089)558531].

Let's Eat!

Frühstück (breakfast) ranges from the continental-style coffee and *Brötchen* (roll) to a smorgasbord of cold meats and cheeses with bread, rolls, jam, cereal, and *Orangensaft* (orange juice). *Kakao* or *Schokolade* (hot chocolate) is served for children. Many bakeries have a few tables and chairs set up with coffee, tea, and chocolate available along with delicious freshly baked bread and rolls.

For *Mittagessen* (lunch), try marketplace shopping to make your own *Butterbrot* (sandwich or, literally, "buttered bread"). *Käse* (cheese), *Wurst* (sausages), or fresh *Früchte* (fruit) such as *Apfel* (apple), *Banane* (banana), *Birne* (pear), *Erdbeeren* (strawberries), *Himbeeren* (raspberries), and *Pfirsich* (peach) are delicious. For a quick bite, stop at an *Imbiss* (stand-up snack bar). Sausages, meat-balls, hamburgers, and rolls filled with cheese, meat, or fish are usually served with french fries. The more elaborate snack bars have excellent soups, salads, and roast *Huhn* (chicken).

Beer gardens are restaurants with outdoor seating, and they are great places to take kids as they often have playgrounds, rides, and other children. They are not to be mistaken as bars. Most beer gardens have food that appeals to children such as barbecued chicken, hot dogs, and french fries.

Dinner is served between 6 and 9 PM. Some higher-priced restaurants don't cater to kids, and most do not have high chairs. If your children are noisy, the manager may give you a card that reads "Please leave." Most restaurants serve delicious *Suppe* (soup), sausages cooked in a wide variety of styles, and some kind of *Gemüse* (vegetable), such as *Kartoffeln* (potatoes), *Kohl* (cabbage), *Sauerkraut*, or *Salat* (salad). Many children like German hot sauerkraut, which is nothing like the kind we get in jars; it is flavorful and somewhat sweet. *Fleischplanzel* is similar to hamburger but has more spices and breadcrumbs. Pizzerias and kebab houses provide inexpensive ethnic food. Movenpick is a chain with high chairs and good food for children. If you're desperate, hamburger fast-food joints are easily found.

Kids will find *Eis* (ice cream), *Krapfen* (donuts), and *Gebäck* (pastries) readily available for dessert. Beverages include *Milch* (milk), *Apfelsaft* (apple juice), or *Zitronenlimonade* (lemonade). Pasteurized milk is stamped with the date of production while *Vorzugsmilch* is not pasteurized. *Sterilimilch* will stay fresh for several months without refrigeration but lacks nutrients (and taste) because of its processing.

Formula and Baby Food, Diapers and Baby Gear

Baby food and formula are found in *Apotheken* (pharmacies). Gerber and Hipp are two common brands. *Windeln* (diapers) are available in markets, supermarkets, and Apotheken. Beautiful 100 percent cotton baby clothes are found in even the least expensive stores.

Sidewalk Talk

beach *Strandbad*
bicycle *Fahrrad*
candy *Bonbons*
castle *Schloss*
children *Kinder*
cotton candy *Zuckerwatte*

doll *Puppe*
fairy-tale *Märchen*
girl *Mädchen*
merry-go-round *Karussell*
playground *Spielplatz*
please *bitte*

roller skates *Rollschuhe*
rowboat *Ruderboot*
slide *Rutschbahn*
swimming pool *Schwimmbad*

swing set *Schaukeln*
thank you *danke schön*
toy shop *Spielzeugladen*

The Lay of the Land

A long and narrow country, Germany lies in the middle of Europe with the Alps at its southern border and the North Sea at its northern end. We will be focusing on southern Germany (Munich, the Bavarian Alps, Bodensee, the Black Forest, the Romantic Road, Nuremberg, and Heidelberg), on northern Germany's Fairy-tale Road, and on Berlin.

MUNICH

Once you pull your children out of the toy stores, you'll discover many wonderful places to visit with children in Munich. It is one of Germany's most beautiful cities; although upscale and expensive, you will still find oom-pah bands playing in family restaurants and a casual atmosphere in its parks and gardens. Munich's weather is very unpredictable, even in summer, but there are many indoor activities, so you'll never be at a loss for what to do. All city-run museums are free on Sundays. Beautiful countryside with little villages, hiking paths, cable cars, and mountain lakes are only a 40-minute ride from the heart of the city. Beer gardens are open throughout the city on warm days from late spring to mid-fall. Most have playgrounds or rides for children. You can bring your own picnic or purchase food there. Kids love the typical Bavarian *Krapfen* (donuts), which are traditionally served for Fasching (Mardi Gras) but are available year-round. In winter, stands sell hot roasted chestnuts to keep you warm and *Mandeln* (almonds fried in butter and brown sugar).

Pick up a copy of the monthly "Monatsprogramm" for a listing of upcoming events; it's available at hotels and many newsstands. For English information on museums and galleries, phone 239162; for information on castles and other city sights, dial 239172. The **tourist office** is in the heart of the city at Sendlingerstr. 2 (Tel. 23911). Other tourist offices are located in the Hauptbahnhof opposite platform 11 and in the Rathaus in Marienplatz. They can provide you with good English maps, detailed travel guides, lists of hotels and pensions, and can book accommodations. Munich's **telephone area code** is 089.

The Lay of the City

Marienplatz, surrounded by shops, cafes, and restaurants, is the heart of the city. A pedestrian shopping zone stretches west from Marienplatz to Karlsplatz-Stachus and north to Odeonsplatz. The U-Bahn and S-Bahn systems cross underneath Marienplatz. Leopoldstrasse runs straight through the university district and the trendy area of Schwabing, home of the German *Schickies* (yuppies). Along it you'll find plenty of chic cafes serving Italian ices and espressos. The Englischer Garten borders Schwabing to the east, while Olympiapark is at its farthest edge.

Getting Around

Downtown Munich and the city's major sites are easily covered on foot along the network of pedestrian streets around the Marienplatz. The U-Bahn is Munich's efficient **subway** system, which is supplemented by the S-Bahn suburban railway and Strassenbahn (streetcar) systems. Tickets can be purchased at the blue dispensers in U- and S-Bahn stations. Economical tickets include the Mehrfahrtenkarten (multiple-ride ticket) and the 24-stunden (24-hour) ticket, which allows unlimited travel on all public transportation for any 24-hour period.

Where to Stay

HOTELS

The *Hilton International*, across from the Englischer Garten, has an indoor pool. Am Tucherpark 7. Tel. 340051. From U.S. 800-445-8667. **Deluxe.**

The *Penta Hotel*, near the Deutsche Museum, has an indoor pool. Hochstr. 3. Tel. 445555. From U.S. 800-448-8355. **Expensive.**

Wuermtaler Haestehaus, in Munich-Graefelfing, has a children's playground. Rotenbucher Str. 55. Tel. 851281; from U.S. 800-448-8355. **Moderate.**

HOSTELS

Youth Guesthouse Thalkirchen's room sizes range from singles to triples, quadruples, and dorm style. Sheets are available, and breakfast is included in the price. Miesingstr. 4. Tel. 7236550 or 7236560. **Inexpensive (hostel).**

Wendl-Dietrch-Strasse 20 has assorted room and dorm sizes. Sheets are available and breakfast is included in the price. Tel. 131156.

CAMPGROUNDS

Thalkirchen, on the outskirts of Munich near the zoo, in the Isar River valley, is accessible by U-Bahn and bus. 1 Zentralländerstr. 49. Open mid-Mar.–Oct. Tel. 7231707.

Obermenzing Campground is near the Nymphenburg palace and park. Lochhausenerstr. 59. Open mid-Mar.–Oct. Tel. 8112235.

Detour! What to See and Do

AROUND THE MARIENPLATZ

Mechanical figures in the new town hall's **Glockenspiel Tower** in the Marienplatz perform daily. As the doors open, out pop colorfully costumed dancers, jousting knights, and crowing roosters. Performances take place at 11 AM, noon, 5 PM, and 9 PM from May to October; rest of the year at 11 AM only. Travel to the top of the tower via elevator for an expansive view of the city. Fee. Year round Mon.–Fri. 9–4; summer Sat. and Sun. only 10–7. While waiting for the Glockenspiel figures to perform, enjoy the many street artists and musicians who perform around this square. Nearby, at the **Viktualienmarkt,** the city's open-air food market, you can buy fresh fruits and vegetables, sausages, cheese, and flowers from stands with colorfully striped awnings.

Peterskirche, or Alter Peter (Old Peter), Munich's oldest and smallest parish church, offers one of the best views of the city. Climb its 300-foot tower to see as far as the Alps. Fee. Mon.–Fri. 9–5, Sat. 8:30–7, and Sun. 10–7.

The **Münchener Stadtmuseum** has historic puppets, collections of old photographs, and musical instruments. The puppet collection is one of the world's largest and includes large mechanical European puppets and folk art puppets from Asia and India. You'll see full-size vintage puppet theaters, many puppet heads, and funny and grotesque puppet characters. The photo collection includes a camera obscura, holograms, a zoetrope, and a 19th-century round 3-D viewing arcade. Some of the hands-on displays are placed low for children. Classic films are shown nightly at 8 PM; non-German films are subtitled. Breeze through the musical instrument collection for a look at old and interesting horns, string instruments, and more. Fee. St. Jakobplatz. Tues.–Sat. 9–4:30, Sun. 10–6. Tel. 2332370.

A small **Spielzeugmuseum** in the Alte Rathaus (old town hall) has a charming collection of toys from the past with dolls, Christmas tree ornaments, kaleidoscopes, a doll zoo, and many other playthings. Fee. Daily 10–5:30. Tel. 294001. The **Hofbräuhaus,** Munich's most famous beer garden, dates from 1589. It is huge and fun but smoke-

filled and noisy. Platzl 9, 2 blocks from Marienplatz. Daily 10 AM–
midnight; live Bavarian music after 7 PM.

THE ENGLISCHER GARTEN

The Englischer Garten, 3 miles long and more than a mile wide, is
Germany's largest city park. No cars are allowed, and jogging and
cycling trails wind throughout. Rent bikes at the southern entrance to
the park to pedal through at your leisure. Rowboats can be hired for
rides on the Kleinhesseloher See. Four beer gardens are found inside
the park. The beer garden near the lake has a fun steam carousel. The
Chinese Tower beer garden in the park's center is the most famous. In
summer, its ornate 100-year-old carousel entertains children, or they
can play in the adjacent sandbox. A larger playground is not far off.
Free oom-pah band concerts are held from one of the tower's plat-
forms on summer afternoons and all day long on Sundays. The tourist
office can give you a schedule. Another beer garden in the park on the
Osterwald edge serves a Bavarian brunch of little hot dogs, sweet
mustard, pretzels, and . . . beer. Children can get closer to its oom-
pah band's musicians. Nude sunbathing (a popular German pastime)
is allowed in designated areas, although it often spills into other areas
on very warm days. In winter there is free skating on the park's lakes
and ponds, cross-country skiing, and stands selling hot roasted
chestnuts.

Just One Look: Museums

Alte Pinakothek contains a stellar collection of European masters
from the 14th to the 18th centuries such as Giotto, Van Eyck, Cranach,
Rembrandt, and Rubens. The German painter Dürer is well represented. Search for Pieter Bruegel the Elder's "Land of Cockaigne,"
where boiled eggs with legs and other oddities make fun of gluttony.
Fee; free Sunday and holidays. Barerstr. 27. Tues.–Sun. 9–4:30 and
Tues. and Thurs. 7–9.

The **Neue Pinakothek,** across the street, is best known for its
collection of French Impressionist paintings, but it also exhibits 19th-
century German works. Look for the works of Carl Spitzweg, whose
scenes from everyday life are far more interesting to kids than are
works with classical or religious themes. Fee. Barerstr. 29. Tues.–Sun.
9–4:30 and Tues. 7–9 PM.

Bayerisches Nationalmuseum contains charming Christmas
crèches, Bavarian folk art, arms, and armor. Fee; children free. Prinzregentenstr. 3. Tues.–Sun. 9:30–5.

Car fanciers will enjoy the **BMW Museum and Factory Tour** where
they can see a display of old and new BMW cars and motorcycles.

The tour shows how they are made. Fee. Lerchenauerstr. 36. Daily 9–5.

Deutsches Jagd und Fischerei Museum is for fishing and hunting aficionados. Anglers will appreciate the world's largest collection of fish hooks. Students of taxidermy can look over the 500 stuffed animals; we thought it was "overkill." Fee. Neuhauserstr. 53. Daily 9:30–5; Monday 7–9.

The **Deutsches Museum** is the world's largest scientific and technological museum. Select carefully to get the most out of this outstanding museum as there are 12 miles of corridors! Pick up a copy of the English guide before you get started so you can choose in advance what you want to see. There are many hands-on exhibits with hundreds of levers to pull and buttons to push. Entire rooms cover aeronautics, photography, time measurement, writing and printing, and weights and measures. The displays of huge trains, model helicopters, airplanes, cars, and vintage submarines have been put together with great imagination. Peek through the submarine's periscope, which protrudes through an opening in the floor above. A simulated coal mine in the basement is always a favorite and the electrical show is a tingler. The planetarium is also top-notch, but most shows are in German. Fee. Museumsinsel 1. Daily 9–5.

Lenbachhaus has an outstanding collection of works by the Blaue Reiter school, such as Kandinsky, Jawlensky, Marc, and Klee. The Blaue Reiters were a group of artists whose styles were a reaction to the prettiness of Impressionism; their vivid paintings vibrate with intensity, color, and movement. Most children enjoy this gallery and its garden setting. Fee. Luisenstr. 33. Tues.–Sun. 10–6.

Staatsgalerie Moderner Kunst contains an outstanding collection of 20th-century works by Kandinsky, Nolde, Picasso, Matisse, Dalí, Magritte, and more. Many children enjoy the vivid colors and vibrant movement in these works. The Kandinsky collection is renowned. Fee. Prinzregentenstr. 1. Tues.–Sun. 9–4:30, Thurs. 7–9 PM.

OUTSIDE THE CITY CENTER

At **Schloss Nymphenburg,** a baroque and rococo summer palace, a favorite for children will be the Marstallmuseum, with one of "Mad" King Ludwig's elaborate sleighs and other highly ornate royal carriages. Also on the grounds is the Amalienburg, a rococo-style hunting lodge that resembles a wedding cake turned outside in. Be sure to see the kennel for the hunting dogs; Bowser never had it so good. Children will prefer wandering through the lovely gardens to touring the palace. Fee. Complex: Tues.–Sun. 9–12:30 and 1:30–5.

Bavaria Filmstadt, also known as "Bavarian Hollywood," offers Universal Studio-type tours of its sets. Little train cars meander

through German movie sets such as that of *Das Boot*. Fee. Bavaria
Filmplatz 7. Daily Mar.–Oct. 9–4. Tel. 649067.

Where the Sidewalk Ends: Zoos and More Parks

Hirschgarten has deer in its enclosures, a playground for the kids,
and a *Biergärten* for the adults. In the suburb of Nymphenburg, accessible on the westbound S-Bahn to Laim. **No-name City** is a Western-style town with country music, saloons, daily duels, and cowpokes. Fee. East of Munich in Poing, Gruberstr. 60a. Tues.–Sun. 9:30–6.

 Tierpark Hellabrun is a zoo with a broad collection of animals in
spacious enclosures and special areas where children can pet and
feed animals or take pony rides. There's a little train, tiny cars for very
young kids, and a playground. It's all set in a spacious, attractive
park. Fee. Number 52 bus from Marienplatz. Daily 8–6. **Westpark** has
children's play areas, summer jogging trails, cross-country ski trails,
beautiful and varied plantings, and restaurants. U-Bahn lines 3 or 6 to
West Park.

Sports

Olympiapark, the site of the 1972 Summer Olympic Games, has
jogging trails, rowboating on the Olympiasee, indoor ice-skating at
the Eissportstadion, and swimming at the Olympia-Schwimmhalle.
Bicycles can be rented at the Englischer Garten (corner of Königstr.
and Veterinärstr.). Tel. 397016. **Ice skaters** can choose from indoor
and outdoor rinks in the Eissportstadion (Spiridon-Louis-Ring 3);
indoor rinks at Prinzregenten Stadium (Prinzregentenstr. 80) and
Eisbahn-West (Agnes-Bernauerstr. 241). Outdoor skating is possible
on the lake in the Englischer Garten. Watch out for signs reading
Gefahr, meaning danger.

 Roller skaters can head to the Roll Palast in the western suburb of
Pasing, Stockackerstr. 5. **Swim** in Art Nouveau splendor at the indoor
Müllersches Volksbad. Cosima Bad's pool has waves (corner of Englschalkingerstr. and Cosimastr. in Bogenhausen).

Performing Arts

Circus Krone performs an old-fashioned show from Christmas to
the end of March. Performances take place throughout the week.
Marsstr. 43. Tel. 588166. **Münchner Theater für Kinder** is a children's
theater company using a lot of pantomime. Dachauerstr. 46. Tel.
595454 or 593858. **Münchner Marionettentheater** has regular puppet
shows of familiar fairytales. Blumenstr. 29a. Tel. 265712. **Otto Bille's**

Marionettenbühne is another respected puppet theater. Brei-terangerstr. 15. Tel. 1502168 or 3102168.

Special Events

Octoberfest, the world's largest block party, takes place at the fairgrounds with enormous beer tents, row after row of picnic tables, bushel baskets of *Wurst* and pretzels, and liters of beer. There are plenty of carnival rides for children and balloon, puppet, and toy vendors. Some of the beer tents have brass bands, although it can be hard to hear them with all of the surrounding merriment. Though great fun, it's very crowded, and the drunken masses can make it harrowing with toddlers.

The enchanting **Christkindlmarkt** on the Marienplatz runs from late November through Christmas. Beautifully illuminated booths sell Christmas decorations and nativity figures, and stands offer hot wine, apple cider, hot roasted nuts, and gingerbread. The square is trans-formed into a true winter wonderland. An "alternative" Christmas market selling crafts as well as health-food delicacies can be found in Schwabing. It has a stage with bands, clowns in the afternoon, and other special programs for children.

NEAR MUNICH

Dachau was one of the first Nazi concentration camps. Two of its barracks have been reconstructed, and a film and photo exhibition are a horrifying reminder of the Holocaust. The only buildings left stand-ing are the original gas chamber and watchtowers. The documentary film in English is shown at 11:30 and 3:30. Dachau is a very powerful and upsetting experience and is recommended only for older chil-dren who can place the experience in a historical context. Free. Tues.–Sun. 9–5.

BAVARIAN ALPS

Running south of Munich to the Austrian border are the Bavarian Alps, Germany's premier playground. Quaint villages of rustic houses with flower-filled window boxes neatly tucked below towering peaks and locals in *Lederhosen* and *Dirndl* dress create the picturebook scenery that graces many German tourist brochures. The region is a sports buff's paradise with many resorts providing a full range of winter and summer activities. Avoid the spa resorts that begin with the word *Bad* (bath), they are geared primarily for seniors rather than children. The region's **tourist office** is at Sonnenstr. 10, 8000 Munich 2 [Tel. (089) 597347].

GARMISCH-PARTENKIRCHEN AND ENVIRONS

At the foot of the **Zugspitze** is the alpine capital of *Garmisch-Partenkirchen,* the area's best-known year-round resort. Former host to the Olympic games, Garmisch-Partenkirchen is known for its extensive array of winter sports. Its ski season runs from December through May. In winter, the resort runs a **Kindergarten** for children under 3 [Tel. (08821) 52729] and the **Kinder-Skikurse** ski school for those over 4 [Tel. (08821) 4600].

Journey up the Zugspitze, Germany's highest peak, via cog railway and cable car. Its 10,000-foot summit provides a spectacular panorama. The 80-minute trip is recommended for height-lovers only. At the top, you can walk through a tunnel and cross over into Austria. Fee; discounts for families. Departs from Zugspitzbahnhof in town center.

Summer hiking in the area is spectacular. Walk up the dramatic **Partnachklamm gorge;** follow the trail behind the town's Olympic stadium. Local forest rangers will take children with them to **feed alpine deer** [Tel. (08821) 2038]. **Horse-drawn carriages** will take you through a beautiful alpine route along the Zugspitze during the summer. In winter glide through the snow on a **horse-drawn sleigh** [Tel. (08821) 55917].

One of the region's best swimming lidos, the **Alspitz Wellenbad** has seven indoor pools, including a wave pool for body surfing. [Tel. (08821) 58061 or 62]. The local **tourist office** is at Bahnhofstr. 34, 8100 Garmisch-Partenkirchen [Tel. (08821) 1806].

Northwest of Garmisch-Partenkirchen, near *Ettal,* is "Mad" King Ludwig II's country retreat, **Schloss Linderhof.** As you will see at his elaborate Neuschwanstein (see "The Romantic Road"), Ludwig had an oversized ego and indulgently built lavish Rococo-style palaces to amuse himself. He was eventually relieved of his duties as king because of the enormous sums of government money he was spending on his "edifice complex." Mildly flamboyant in comparison to his other retreats, Linderhof will still enthrall children. Its fantasy garden's artificial Grotto of Venus, based on the first act of Wagner's opera *Tannhäuser,* has a rock slide that is activated by the push of a button. Ludwig's enormous gold touring boat still sits in the grotto's illuminated subterranean lake. Fee. Apr.–Sept. 9–12:15, 2:45–5:30; Oct.–Mar. 10–12:15, 2:45–4. Tel. (08822) 512. Nearby, **Lake Plansee** is beautiful for swimming, rowing, and wind surfing.

OBERAMMERGAU AND MITTENWALD

Twenty kilometers northwest of Garmisch-Partenkirchen is the enchanting village of Oberammergau, known for its century-old wood-carving tradition and solemn Passion Play, which tells the story of the final days of Christ. Presented every 10 years, it will next be performed in 2000. At 5½ hours, it is too long for most children. Securing tickets and accommodations is very difficult.

You can observe **wood carvers at work** at the Pilatushaus, on Verlegergasse, from April through June and September through November. Children can pick up small animals and figures for souvenirs. Stop in to see the charming 18th-century wooden Christmas crèches at the town's **Heimatmuseum.** Fee. Dorfstr. 8. May 10–Oct. 15, Tues.–Sat. afternoons.

In need of a dip? Try riding the waves at Oberammergau's open-air **Wellenberg pool** [Tel. (08822) 6787]. Oberammergau is also a ski resort with apartment rentals, a children's ski school, tobogganing, horse-drawn carriage and sleigh rides through the snow, skating, and curling. The town's **tourist office** is at Eugen-Papst-Str. 9a, 8103 [Tel. (08823) 1021].

Tranquil Mittenwald, next door to Garmisch-Partenkirchen, is Germany's center of violin making and one of Bavaria's jewels. Spread along the Isar River, it is surrounded by the jagged Wetterstein-Gebirge Mountains, clear lakes, and forests. Take the cable car up to Karwendel for a stunning alpine view. **Horse-drawn carriage rides** are available in town, while the central **Kurpark** is a great place to picnic.

Swim in the nearby lake of **Ferchensee** or head north, where more lakes beckon. The dramatic glacial lakes of **Walchensee** and **Kolchelsee** have a variety of water sports, including Kolchelsee's elaborate **swimming lido** with pools and water slides. Fee. Trimini Kochel. Daily 9–8:30.

ENVIRONS OF BAD TÖLZ

Take a day trip into the famous German spa resort of **Bad Tölz** to see the **Tölz Marionette Theater** or the **Tölzer Knabenchor** boys choir. Contact the **tourist office** at Ludwigstr. 11 [Tel. (8041) 70071] for schedules. A thrilling ride is found west of Bad Tölz on the ski slopes of **Blomberg,** where kids can ascend the mountain by chair lift and whiz down Europe's longest (almost a mile) **dry toboggan run.** Fee. Open Apr.–Oct.

North of Bad Tölz, in *Wolfratshausen,* is the enchanting fairy-tale park **Märchenwald,** where familiar animated characters speak many languages as they peer out of little cottages. Young children will enjoy the park's miniature train, boat rides, rocket ride, and fun house. Fee. Daily 9–5.

East of Bad Tölz, much of the region from Tegernsee to Berchtesgaden is heavily geared to the tourist trade. **Tegernsee,** in the alpine lowlands amidst green rolling hills, offers a myriad of summer water sports and winter ice-skating. **Sleigh rides** through the snow above the lake will put apples on your children's cheeks. Contact the Bad Tölz tourist office listed above.

THE CHIMERGAU

The Chimergau region includes the large alpine lake of **Chiemsee,** the medieval town of *Rosenheim,* and a number of smaller jewellike lakes, all about an hour's drive south of Munich. Ludwig II built the ostentatious and extravagant **Schloss Herrenchiemsee** on the Chiemsee. Its dizzying Hall of Mirrors, with many optical illusions, was modeled after Versailles. The palace, set on an island, is accessible by ferry from the lakeside village of Prien. Fee. Apr.–Sept. daily 9–5; Oct.–Mar. daily 10–4.

BERCHTESGADEN AND ENVIRONS

Berchtesgaden, high in the Bavarian Alps, was a resort long before its most notorious guest, Adolf Hitler, arrived. Although somewhat tarnished by his association and by overcommercialization, the resort is still breathtaking.

History buffs interested in seeing where Adolf retreated can take the elevator or cable car up Mount Kehlstein, upon which rests the **Alderhorst (Eagle's Nest).** The elevator, lined with mirrors and Art Deco decor, ascends 300 feet up a shaft cut right into the mountain. The view of the Berchtesgaden National Park from the summit is a spectacular eagle's-eye view. Fee. Hour-long round-trip ride. Retreat open late May–early Oct.

For a change of pace, take the half-mile ride down into the depths of the **Salzbergwerk (Salt Mines).** A miniature train escorts you into the darkness of this salty mountain. You then board wooden chutes to slide further down, where there is a raft tour of the subterranean salt lake. Your kids will love it. Fee. 30-minute tour. Salzburg Road. May–mid-Oct. daily 8:30–5; mid-Oct.–Apr. Mon.–Sat. 12:30–3:30.

Berchtesgaden is known for its wooden toys; children can pick up intricately carved toy horse-drawn carriages called *Hoheitskutschen,* little wooden treasure boxes called *Spanschachteln,* or colorful dollhouse furniture. The area's **tourist office** is at Königsseer Strasse, tel. (8652) 5011.

A short distance from Berchtesgaden is the glistening **Königssee.** Surrounded by towering snow-capped peaks, it is one of the country's most beautiful and unspoiled small lakes. A cluster of hotels hug the lake's northern shore. Take the cable car from Königssee to Mt. Jenner for yet another spectacular vista. Daily 8:30–5:30.

On the glassy lakes of **Königssee** and the **Obersee,** ferries glide peacefully to the castle of St. Bartholomä or into the National Park. Fee. Königssee departures: year-round; Obersee: summers only. Or, you can rent a rowboat and explore the tranquil lake on your own.

Another lake well worth a visit is the less-crowded **Hintersee,** where the "magic forest" of Zauberwald has charmed painters for years. By the village of *Ramsau,* you'll find children's playgrounds, rowing on the lake, and wonderful hiking.

BODENSEE (LAKE CONSTANCE)

West Germany, Austria, and Switzerland all share the Bodensee, a water-sports playground graced by idyllic islands, medieval castles, and fun-filled resorts. You'll find clean and beautiful beaches, open-air pools, paddleboats, bicycling, horseback riding, tennis, and more. For resort information, contact the Bodensee's regional **tourist office** at 8990 Lindau [Tel. (08382) 5022]. Switzerland's and Austria's chapters offer additional lakefront suggestions.

Konstanz is Bodensee's largest city. Part of Konstanz, called Kreuzlingen, is in Switzerland. After climbing the **Münster's** tower in the Altstadt (fee; Mon.–Sat. 10–5, Sun. 1–5), escape to the lakefront park **Freibad Horn,** whose neighboring indoor pool complex, **Freizeitbad Jakob,** can hit the spot on a rainy day. Fee. Daily 9–9. **Boats** run daily to the park and pool from behind the train station. Boats also sail round-trip every 2 hours to Lindau, stopping at the Mainau Islands and the neighboring resort of Meersburg. Many families prefer to stay in Meersburg or in Nonnenhorn and take a side trip into Konstanz.

North of Konstanz, **Mainau Island** can also be reached by car. The island has an unusual tropical climate and is filled with peacocks and exotic plants such as flourishing bougainvillaea and hyacinth. The warm water of the lake creates this unusual habitat. Youngsters will want to look at the whimsical topiary animals that have been carefully cultivated. Each animal, from enormous ducks to elephants, requires 90,000 individual plants that are changed two and three times per season. There is also a small **playground** and **children's zoo** for the little ones. Fee; under 6 free. Daily Apr.–Oct. dawn to dusk. Get there early; the island is very popular.

Überlingen, along the lake, still has its original 13th-century towers and some of its ramparts and gates. Its former moat has been transformed into a delightful city park. North of Überlingen, *Affenburg's* **zoo** has over 200 free-roaming monkeys which children can feed. Fee. Daily mid-Mar.–Oct. 9–12, 1–6.

Meersburg is a picture-book medieval town frequented by summer vacationers. Its impressive **Altes Schloss (Old Castle)** has medieval jousting implements, an old kitchen, and a very sinister dungeon called "the Hole of Fear"; it truly lives up to its name. Fee. Daily Mar.–Oct. 9–6; Nov.–Feb. 10–5.

Near the Austrian border is *Lindau,* a tiny island-town with half-timbered houses and meandering streets that is joined to the mainland by a causeway. Climb its lighthouse, the **Neuer Leuchtturm,** for a view over the shimmering waters. Fee. Daily 9:30–6. Nearby is a 20-foot marble sculpture of a lion, Bavaria's symbol. Lindau has five lakeside **swimming lidos.** The **Eichwald,** with a long beach and a grassy area for picnics, is one of the best. The **tourist office** at Hauptbahnhof [Tel. (08382) 26000] can provide information on bike rentals, horseback riding, and water sports.

Seventy kilometers east of Lindau is the glorious mountain resort of *Oberstdorf,* with very reasonable accommodations and sports facilities that include skiing, swimming, and skating. In spring, the valley is ablaze with wildflowers, and its thick forests are filled with baby deer.

SCHWARZWALD (BLACK FOREST)

Stretching from the Rhine River all the way to Basel, the **Black Forest** is filled with dense evergreens and mountain villages where townspeople still dress in traditional folk costumes. The area is known for its lovely carved wooden toys and elaborate cuckoo clocks. Franz Ketterer created the first cuckoo clock, a simple wooden mechanism with a bird that called out the hours, in the early 1700s. The best place to see cuckoo clocks is around *Triberg,* whose **Heimat-museum** has a very impressive collection. Fee. Wallfahrstr. 4. Tel. (07722)4434. You can see Ketterer's original timepiece further south at *Furt-wangen's* **Uhrenmuseum.** Fee. Apr.–Oct. daily 10–5.

The Black Forest is very popular with vacationers. Avoid the super-chic spa resort of Baden-Baden; your children will have more fun at the Black Forest's lakes. **Titisee** is gorgeous but crowded; **Schluchsee** is a better bet. Lakeside resorts offer swimming, tennis, and bike riding. Contact the regional **tourist office** at Bertoldstr. 45, 7800 Freiburg [Tel. (076) 31317].

A magnificent view of the Black Forest awaits those who climb *Freiburg's* majestic **Gothic cathedral.** Kids will also enjoy riding the town's cable car to the top of **Schauinsland Mountain.** For uncultured fun, head for *Ettenheim's* **Europa Park** amusement park north of Freiburg or slide down the **dry toboggan ride** at *Poppeltal,* south of Wildbad.

THE ROMANTIC ROAD

The popular and very scenic **Romantische Strasse,** a route developed by the German Tourist Office, runs from northern Bavaria to the Austrian alpine hamlet of Schwangau. Exploring this delightful part of Germany will take you to enchanting castles and beautifully preserved medieval villages; if you visit off-season you'll miss the crowds. The regional **tourist office** at Fuggerstr. 9, D-9800, Augsburg [Tel. (0821) 33335], can inform you of sporting activities here such as cycling, canoeing, wind surfing, and skiing.

AROUND NEUSCHWANSTEIN CASTLE

Neuschwanstein, castle of "Mad" King Ludwig II, was the inspiration for the Disney version of Sleeping Beauty's castle, and you'll see why. The castle is one of Germany's most popular tourist attractions and highly commercialized, but worthwhile for kids. Ludwig was a self-indulgent misfit who loved building ornate and elaborate palaces for himself. He was found dead in a lake before he had the chance to see this vision of a fantasy castle come to life. The ultimate "royal castle," it drips with opulence. There's an artificial grotto next to the living room, storybook pinnacles, and exaggerated oversized rooms. *Neuschwanstein* means "new swan stone," and a swan motif is found throughout, on door handles to dinnerware. Climb the path behind the castle to the dramatic narrow **Poellat Gorge,** along the steel **Marienbrücke (Mary's Bridge),** for a view of the castle; you'll find it looks even more make-believe from a distance. **Hohenschwangau,** another fantasy castle remodeled by Ludwig, is down the hill from Neuschwanstein. Painted on its bedroom ceiling are gold stars, which were spotlit for Ludwig at night. Fee. Both open early Apr.–Sept. 9–5:30; Oct.–Mar. 10–4. Get there very early on weekdays as both castles are heavily visited, especially in high-season.

Use *Füssen* or the smaller Austrian town of *Reutte* as a base for visiting the castles. The latter is a bit farther away, but it has a good selection of accommodations and can be less crowded. Nearby, *Schongau*'s delightful **Märchenwalder (Fairy-tale Forest)** has animated fairy-tale stories, a miniature railway, and a deer park. Fee. Diessenstr. 6. Late Apr.–Oct. daily 9–7.

AUGSBURG AND ENVIRONS

Lively Augsburg, a well-preserved city that flourished during the Renaissance, was founded by the Romans in 15 B.C. One-fourth the size of Munich, the city has many music festivals and an active student scene. Try and catch a local **puppet show;** they are fun for all ages. For a city view climb the **Perlachturm,** originally the town's watchtower, next to the Rathaus. The Rathaus sits in the cobblestoned **Rathausplatz,** or central square, which is the setting for Augsburg's charming **Weihnachtsmarkt** Christmas market, held from November 23 through December 24. Next to Nuremberg and Munich, it is one of the country's best. The **tourist office** at Bahnshofstr. 7 [Tel. (0821) 502070] can inform you about the town's **medieval banquets,** replete with hearty servings of 15th- and 16th-century German dishes. For a break from tales of medieval lore, head to the open spaces of Augsburg's **Zoo.** Fee. Apr.–Sept. daily 8:30–6; Oct.–Mar. daily 8:30–5. **Rowboats** are for rent for cruises on the town moat.

About 25 kilometers east of Augsburg is **Fred Rai Western City,** a wild West theme park should your young travelers be homesick for a taste of cowboy-and-Indian–style Americana. Fee. Late Mar.–Oct. Tues.–Sun. 9–6. Tel. (08205) 225. Further east, ancient *Ulm*'s **Gothic cathedral,** with the world's tallest steeple, is also one of Europe's most beautiful. For an aerobic workout, climb the 750 steps to its top; you'll be rewarded with a magnificent view as far-reaching as the Alps and the Bodensee. The town's unusual **Deutsches Brotmuseum** shows the important role bread has played in the culture, religion, and economy of civilizations dating back to the Egyptians. Children will enjoy seeing the hundreds of oddly shaped loaves. Free. Fürsteneckerstr. 17. Sun.–Fri. 10–1, 2–5. Tel. (073) 30561.

DINKLESBÜHL

No, *Dinklesbühl* is not Disneyland's Magic Kingdom but the real thing! This medieval town, surrounded by old walls and towers, is protected by a storybook moat. Climb to the top of **St. Georg's Kirche** in *Marktplatz* for a view of the charming disarray of the city. Dinklesbühl celebrates the colorful **Kinderfest,** where local children dress in old costumes and reenact the actual incident when children saved the town from invaders during the Thirty Years' War. The week-long festival begins on the weekend before the third Monday in July. Germany's best-known boys' band, **Kanbenkapelle,** dresses like 18th-century soldiers. Contact the **tourist office** at Segringer Str. 30 [Tel. (09851) 90240] for details. Pick up the helpful **Kinderstadtplan,** a town map that indicates points of interest for children. There is also a special tourist office for children called **Das Jugendbüro "Boje,"** Spitalhof [Tel. (09851) 90277]. Their free handouts include listings of children's activities; ask them about Dinklesbühl's children's **soap box races.**

ROTHENBERG-OB-DER-TAUBER

Rothenberg-ob-der-Tauber, one of Europe's best-preserved medieval towns, is crowded with tourists in the summer. Children enjoy running completely around the city atop its **ramparts** and playing hide and seek among the half-timbered gables and clock towers. Try to find the fun entrance to the ramparts from the underground passage of **St. Wolfgang's Church.** There are dungeons to explore below the town's original **Gothic Rathaus.** A **Renaissance Rathaus** replaced much of the Gothic building and stands behind the original town hall. Its tower is the town's highest; from the top is another sweeping view. Fee. Rathauspl. Apr.–Oct. daily 9:30–12:30, 1–5. In the 17th century, after being challenged by an invading general, Rothenburg's mayor saved the town by drinking a gallon-sized mug of wine. A joyous, but crowded parade called **Der Meistertrunk** celebrates this feat every Pentecost. Held the preceding day is the **Schäfertanz,** re-creating a time when this Shepherd's Dance celebrated the end of a war or illness. It is repeated on some Sundays in July and August. The town also has a highly regarded **puppet theater.** Contact the **tourist office** at Marktplatz 1 [Tel. (09861) 40492].

Near the Rathaus, the **Puppen und Spielzeugmuseum** has Germany's largest private collection of toys and dolls. Two hundred and fifty dolls made from papier mâché, wood, and wax are on display; they date from the late 1700s to the mid-1900s. The collection's exquisite doll houses have every detail intact, from the tiniest knobs on dressers to miniature hand-painted tea sets. There's even a doll-sized schoolroom and circus. Fee. Hofbronnengasse 13. Mar.–Dec. daily 9:30–6; Jan.–Feb. daily 11–5. Tel. (09861) 7330. The **Mittelalterliches Kriminalmuseum** has a grisly display of medieval torture implements, including iron maidens, thumb screws, stocks, and chastity belts. Squeamish types may want to close their eyes until they reach the dunce caps. Fee. Burggasse 3. Apr.–Oct. daily 9:30–6; Nov.–Mar. daily 2–4. Tel. (09861) 5359.

WÜRZBURG

The beautiful baroque city of Würzburg, at the northern end of the Romantic Road, was practically wiped out in World War II and has been totally reconstructed. The **Residenz,** its dazzling baroque palace, has the world's largest ceiling fresco. Look up to see Tiepolo's rendition of the four continents. Fee; under 15 free. Apr.–Sept. Tues.–Sun. 9–5; Oct.–Mar. Tues.–Sun. 10–4. The 13th-century **Marienburg Fortress** looks over the city from a hilltop above the Main River. Its **Mainfränkische Museum** houses Renaissance sculpture by Riemenschneider, a Würzburg native, but your kids will be more

drawn to the display of vintage toys. Fortress: fee. Apr.–Sept. Tues.–
Sun. 9–12, 1–5; Oct.–Mar. Tues.–Sun. 10–12, 1–5. Museum: fee.
Apr.–Oct. daily 10–5; Nov.–Mar. daily 10–4. Children will enjoy
cruising the Main River by boat. Two companies operate cruises to
the **Veitshöchheim Castle,** a palace surrounded by a verdant public
park. Fee. Apr.–Sept. Tues.–Sun. 9–12, 1–5. For boat information,
contact the **tourist office** at Falkenhaus am Markt [Tel. (0931) 37398].

Between Würzburg and Nuremberg, off the Autobahn in *Geisel-
wind,* is the **Vogel-Pony Märchenpark Steigerwald.** Thousands of
birds create a "bird safari"; there's also a monkey zoo, adventure
playground, camel rides, fairy-tale forest, and a wild West park.

NUREMBERG (NÜRNBERG)

Nuremberg is the world's leading center for the production of children's toys. Its mechanical toys are especially coveted; children may
want to save their allowance for a tiny steam engine or Märklin train
sold in local toy shops. For an introduction to the city, walk its
ramparts. Among the moats and towers, you'll be transported to an
earlier era.

Detour! What to See and Do

THE ALTSTADT
In the summer the city's compact old section, the Altstadt, is
especially lively with theater and music performances. Central
Hauptmarkt hosts the city's dazzling **Christkindlmarkt,** held from the
end of November until Christmas Eve, said to be Germany's best
Christmas fair. The square is filled with booths offering handmade
toys of every description, *Lebkuchen* (gingerbread), and *Früchtebrot*
(fruit bread), while street poles are decorated with garlands of fir and
colored lights. An incomparable **candlelit procession** on the eve of
December 10 brings to the streets hundreds of young children holding tiny twinkling candles. Contact the **tourist office** at Frauen-
torgraben 3 [Tel. 23360]. The city's **telephone area code** is 0911.

At other times of the year Hauptmarkt hosts Nuremberg's colorful
outdoor market, with fruit, flowers, and knickknacks. The **Männ-
leinlaufen,** a 16th-century clock which graces the **Frauenkirche,** has
performances daily at noon. Seven princes bow and pound drums
honoring Emperor Karl IV as the hour is struck. Nearby is the fountain of the **Schönner Brunnen** in the Hauptmarkt; if you stroke the
gold ring next to it, it will bring you good luck. Children will enjoy
watching the artisans working as they did in the Middle Ages at the
Handwerkerhof by the Königstor (King's Gate). Craftsmen make tin

soldiers and dolls, weave baskets, and pound pewter. Don't forget to taste the *Lebkuchen* made here.

Above the city, the **Kaiserburg** is a lavish 11th-century fortress, once the residence of the Holy Roman emperors. Tours include a visit to the Knight's Hall and Throne Room; kids will prefer a climb up its **Sinwellturm (Round Tower).** Fee. Guided German tour. Apr.–Sept. daily 9–12, 12:45–5; Oct.–Mar. daily 9:30–12, 12:45–4. With summertime musicians and street vendors, the area around the **Tiergärten Tor,** next to the Kaiserburg, is one of the nicest parts of the Altstadt. Nuremberg's **zoo** is nearby; a big hit is its dolphinarium. Fee. Am Tiergärten 30. Daily 9 AM–sunset. Next door to the Kaiserburg, stop in at **Albrecht Dürer**'s medieval home. His detailed woodcuts tell the story of life in Germany in the early 1500s; compare them with the real house's furnishings. Even the kitchen utensils date back to the late Middle Ages. Fee. Albrecht-Dürer Str. 39. Mar.–Oct. Tues., Thurs.–Sun. 10–5, Wed. 5–9; Nov.–Feb. Tues., Thurs., Fri. 10–5, Wed. 9–1. East of the Dürer house is the **Lochgefängnisse,** an underground labyrinth with a medieval dungeon and torture chamber below the **Altes Rathaus.** Each minuscule prison cell had room only for tiny air holes and a wooden bed. Stretching racks and spiked clamps will add still more haunting journal entries to the gruesome tour. Fee. Behind St. Sebaldus Church. German tour. May–Sept. Mon.–Fri. 10–4, weekends 10–1.

Just One Look: Museums

The **Germanisches Nationalmuseum** is one of Germany's greatest museums; it has been compared to London's British Museum. Its old weapons, musical instruments, and toys are sure to captivate your children while you admire the Renaissance treasures. Fee; Sun. free. Kornmarkt. Tues., Thurs.–Sun. 9–5, Wed. 9–5, 8–9:30.

Near the Dürer house is the exceptional **Spielzeug Museum,** with antique dolls and doll houses, whimsical mechanical carnivals, and elaborate model trains. Fee. Sigmundstr. 220. Tues., Thurs.–Sun. 10–5, Wed. 10–9. The city holds an **international toy fair** in February.

The city's **Verkehrsmuseum** has the country's first train parked in the exhibition hall, 19th-century royal trains, mail coaches, and moving model trains. Fee. Lessinstr. 6. Apr.–Sept. Mon.–Sat. 10–5, Sun. 10–4; Oct.–Mar. daily 10–4.

NEAR NUREMBERG

Southeast of Nuremberg is *Regensburg,* a storybook medieval city on the Danube. Its Gothic **Altes Rathaus,** a melange of half-timbered buildings, once held important meetings of the Holy Roman Empire.

Fans of horror movies will undoubtedly want to see its torture chamber and execution room. Fee. Tours April–Oct. Mon.–Sat. every 30 minutes from 9:30 to 4; Sun. hourly 10–12; Nov.–Mar. Mon.–Sat. hourly 9:30–11:30, 2–4, Sun. 10–12. The town's **Figurentheater** hosts puppet shows on weekends from May through September. Try to hear a concert featuring the **Domspatzen (Cathedral Sparrows)** in the beautiful Gothic cathedral. They are Germany's most famous youth choir. Contact the **tourist office** in the Altes Rathaus [Tel. (0941) 5072141].

About 20 kilometers north of Nuremberg is the bewitching 17th-century castle of **Schloss Thurn.** Your children will be equally excited by the elaborate **Erlebnispark** adventure park built around the castle. The park has a fairy-tale forest, a deer park, petting zoo, a square to safely reenact medieval jousts, the typical array of stomach-churning rides, and a very unmedieval wild West city. Fee. Park open Easter–mid-Sept. daily 9–6. Tel. (09190) 555.

HEIDELBERG

Ancient Heidelberg, home to Germany's oldest university, is the quintessential German college town and one of Germany's most beautiful cities. In summer, hundreds of tourists are drawn here; the best time to savor the city is in the fall. The **tourist office** is at Friedrich-Ebert-Anlage 2 [Tel. 10821]; the city's **telephone area code** is 06221.

Detour! What to See and Do

AROUND THE CASTLE

Take the **Königstuhl funicular** up to the Königstuhl heights above the city; it stops at the ruins of the magnificent **Heidelberg castle.** There's also a trail leading up to it if you feel ambitious or should your kids choose to run down. The castle complex was begun in the early 13th century and evolved into a powerful medieval fortress. In summer, the castle is illuminated to commemorate its burning in 1693, and there are beautiful fireworks the first Saturday evening of June, July, and September. During August, the **Castle Festival** includes performances of Sigmund Romberg's musical The Student Prince in the castle courtyard. Children will be impressed with the castle's reconstructed 18th-century pharmaceutical laboratory in the **Apothekenmuseum.** It may sound dull until they hear that there's a mummy with long hair, dried insects, and frogs among the rows of utensils and vessels. Also in the castle is the enormous **Heidelberger Fass,** a wine barrel made from over 100 oak trees. It once held 50,000 gallons of wine, all of which had been paid as a tax. It is the biggest barrel your kids will ever see! The barrel was guarded by a dwarf court jester whose statue is now nearby. One fee admits you to the castle's obligatory guided tour and Heidelberger Fass. Daily 9–5. Separate fee for Apothekenmuseum. Daily 10–5. Expect long lines in summer. The castle's terraces provide spectacular views of the city and Necker Valley. Funicular departs near Kornmarkt [Tel. 22796]. Also on the Königstuhl heights is the **Märchen-paradies**, with animated storybook characters, a miniature train, and an adventure playground. Fee. Mar.–Oct. daily 10–6. Tel. 23416.

THE UNIVERSITY

Kids will feel lucky when they realize how kindly our students are treated today. The old **Alte Universität** had a student jail, called the **Studentenkarzer**. From the early 1700s through the early 1900s those who misbehaved were locked in for up to 2 weeks. The naughty acts were typically drunkenness and other *Animal House*-style pranks. You can still see graffiti and student self-portraits on the jail walls. Fee. Augustinerstr. Mon.–Sat. year-round 9–5. More haunting tales of the past are found in the **New University** built into the old city ramparts. Witches from the Middle Ages were incarcerated in its **Hexenturm (Witches' Tower)**. Universitätsplatz.

More to See and Do

Head next to the pedestrians-only old heart of the city and stroll by elegant Hauptstrasse for a look at the **Haus zum Riesen (Giant's House)**, which sports a giant-sized statue of its 18th-century builder over the front door. Witches were burned by the 15th-century **Hercules Fountain** at Marktplatz.

The **Kurpfälzisches Museum (Electoral Palatinate Museum)** relates the city's history; kids will be drawn to the replica of the jaw of the Heidelberg Man, one of the oldest human beings found. You'll get a glimpse of how humans looked 500,000 years ago. Fee. Hauptstr. 97. Tues.–Sun. year-round 10–5, Thurs. 10–9. Tel. 583402.

The city's **zoo** is on the banks of the Necker River and has horseback riding (Tel. 412728) and miniature golf. Zoo: fee. Tiergartenstr. Apr.–Sept. Mon.–Thurs. and Sat. 9–7, Fri. 9–9, Sun. 10–6; Oct.–Mar. Mon.–Sat. 9–5. Tel. 480041. There is a **swimming pool complex** in the gardens near the zoo at Klausenpfad or in Vangerow-Str.

NEAR HEIDELBERG

Boats cruise the Necker for a 3-hour ride up to *Neckarsteinach*, home to four 12th- and 13th-century castles and a departure point for Germany's Castle Road. Boats depart below Stadthalle (convention hall) from May through September (Tel. 20181). Pedal boats, rowboats, and sailboats can be hired to cruise the river.

A few kilometers west of the city in **Schwetzingen,** take a minitour of the world's major sites at **Schwetzingen Castle Park.** You'll see very realistic models of a Greek temple, the grounds of Versailles, and Roman ruins. Fee. Year-round daily 7 AM–8 PM. Tel. (06202) 4933.

Holiday Park, one of Europe's largest amusement parks, is about 50 kilometers west of Heidelberg near **Hassloch.** A Lilliputian city, the heart-pounding Super Whirl, rides on the rapids of the Thunder River, magic show, and a lion and a dolphin show will thoroughly entertain children. Fee. Early Apr.–early Oct. daily 9–6. Tel. (06324) 5993.

MÄRCHENSTRASSE (FAIRY-TALE ROAD)

The Fairy-tale Road running east of Frankfurt to Bremen for over 600 kilometers is the German countryside that inspired the brothers Jacob and Wilhelm Grimm to record their stories of kings and queens, magic and witchcraft, and dwarfs and elves in the early 1800s. The brothers carefully wrote down stories and legends told to them by good friends and family. Tales such as *Cinderella, Hansel and Gretel, Little Red Riding Hood, Sleeping Beauty,* and *Snow White* continue to captivate children all over the world today.

The Fairy-tale Road is actually a route developed in 1985 by the tourist office to draw visitors to northern Germany. Those we interviewed provided mixed reactions to the route. Some felt, "It was enchanting every step of the way"; others commented, "It is a well-trod, highly professional tourist trap." The entire road is a long journey, so pick and choose accordingly. Contact the road's **tourist office** for a map at Box 120420, Humboldstr. 26, 3500 Kassel [Tel. (0561) 1003288].

HANAU TOWARD KASSEL

The brothers Grimm were born in Hanau, near Frankfurt, in the 1780s. Their statue graces the Neustädter Marktplatz. Stop in to see the delightful marionette performances at Hanau's **Puppenmuseum.** Contact the **tourist office** at Altstädter Markt 1 [Tel. (06181) 252400].

Twenty kilometers away is the small, ancient hamlet of **Steinau,** where the brothers spent most of their childhood and first heard the stories from their family friend Frau Viemann. Its cobblestone streets, teetering half-timbered houses, and castle with moats, towers, and turrets appear to be illustrations from their tales. Inside the castle, the **Grimm Museum** has memorabilia from their formative years. Nearby is the **Amtshaus,** the turreted manor where the family lived. It also exhibits mementos of their childhood. Fee for both. Castle: Mar.–Oct. Tues.–Sun. 10–11:30, 1–4:30. Amtshaus: Mon.–Fri. 8–12, 1–5. **Die Holzkuppe** marionette theater performs enchanting renditions of familiar Grimm fairytales in the castle's stables. The **tourist office** can provide a schedule of performances [Tel. (06663) 6336].

Medieval *Lauterbach*'s **Schloss Hohhaus** was the setting for the Grimms' tale of the "little scallywag" who lost his socks. Children can pick up tiny gnomes produced by artisans in town. Further north, in enchanting *Alsfeld,* stop to see the statue of **Little Red Riding Hood,** who supposedly made her home here. Picture-postcard **Rotkäppchenland (Little Red Riding Hood Country)** starts here and follows the Schwalm River; somewhere in its deep forests lurks the big bad wolf! *Schwalmstadt* is the proclaimed capital of Little Red Riding Hood Country; visit its **Schwalm Museum** to see colorful folk costumes. Near Marburg, in the 13th-century village of *Neustadt,* you can see the tall circular tower where **Rapunzel** let down her golden hair.

KASSEL

The Grimm brothers worked as librarians in Kassel, where they collected the majority of their folktales and legends. Copies of their books, drawings, and manuscripts are exhibited at the **Brüder Grimm Museum** in the town center. Most young children find it too scholarly. Free. Schloss Bellevue, Schöne Aussicht 2. Tues.–Sun. 10–5. Kassel is an industrial town, although you will find lovely parks and one of Germany's leading art museums, the **Staatliche Kunstsammlung,** with works by Dürer and Rubens. The city is most famous for its multimedia event, **Documenta,** which covers everything from painting to video and takes over the entire city every 4–5 years. The next event will be in 1992. Past participants have included Yoko Ono, the late Joseph Beuys, and the late Rainer Werner Fassbinder.

Kids will get a kick out of climbing up to and inside the colossal 30-foot-high **Statue of Hercules,** symbol of the city. The giant can be found behind the castle Schloss Wilhelmshöhe, above the city in the baroque **Bergpark Wilhelmshöhe** park. A 250-meter-long, 885-tiered cascading waterfall tumbles from below Hercules down the hillside in the summer, on Sundays and Wednesdays. Fee to enter Hercules. Open Tues.–Sun. The park also has grottoes and the re-created ruins of the medieval **Löwenburg** castle, complete with an artificial drawbridge. The park's **Schloss Wilhelmshöhe** contains the **Staatliche Kunstsammlung Kassel,** an exquisite art collection with works by Rembrandt, Rubens, Titian, and Tintoretto. Children can play in this elegant, expansive park when they tire of viewing art. Free. Summer Tues.–Sun. 10–5; winter until 4. If you are leaving Kassel on the Autobahn to Frankfurt, make a stop at Baron Dornberg's **leisure park,** which has a wonderful *Kinderspieldorf* (children's play village) accessible by cable car. There are towers to climb, games, forts, trampolines, and a small zoo. Contact Kassel's **tourist office** at Hauptbahnhof [Tel. (0561) 13443].

NORTH TO HAMLIN

A statue of The Little Goose Girl graces the central square in the university town of *Göttingen.* She is called "the most kissed girl in the world," as every new graduate has to kiss her bronze mouth. The town's **Junges Theater** offers performances for children and puppet plays. Outside of town, in *Bremke,* Grimm's fairytales are performed in a charming woodland theater. Contact Göttingen's **tourist office** at Altes Rathaus, Markt 9 [Tel. (0551) 54000].

Hidden deep in the dense woods of the Reinhardswald, north of the beautiful village of Münden, in *Veckerhagen,* is **Sababurg.** The castle, now a hotel, has been designated Sleeping Beauty's haunt to promote tourism. A few animals roam in the depressing zoo in front of the castle. Booths selling Sleeping Beauty stickers and tacky souvenirs led us to conclude that the French Sleeping Beauty's castle in the Loire Valley, which inspired Perrault to write the original tale, is far more authentic.

Bodenwerder was the home of the peculiar liar Lügenbaron (Lying Baron) von Münchhausen. The tales of his exploits fighting the Russians and the Turks in the 1700s grew into hilarious English and German adventure stories. The **Münchhausen Museum** has a cannonball he claimed to have ridden to the moon and trick chairs. Fee. In the Rathaus. Tel. tourist bureau (05533) 40541.

Hamelin (Hameln) is home to the Pied Piper, a tale told in the Grimms' book *German Legends,* based on a 13th-century event. A flute-player pretending to be a rat catcher claimed he could free the town of a plague of mice and rats for a large fee. By playing trancelike melodies, he led the rodents to the Weser River, where they perished. The townspeople refused to pay the piper upon completion of his task. In retaliation, he returned and sounded his pipes once again. One hundred and thirty children responded to his tune and never returned. To this day, it has not been possible to find an exact explanation for their disappearance. A statue of the Piper sits in the town center, and the **Rattenfängerhaus (Rat Catcher's House)** is open to visitors at Osterstrasse 28. A 30-minute version of the story is performed by nearly 100 local children and adults in front of the

Hochzeitshaus (Wedding House), also on Osterstrasse, at noon on Sundays from mid-May through September. The piper, dressed in green, with two long feathers in his hat, toots his flute as he struts along the Weser River. Children dressed as little rats prance behind him and disappear. Free. Hochzeitshaus' carillon rings out a Pied Piper tune daily at 8:35 and 11:05, and mechanical figures reenact the tale on its clock at 1:05, 3:35, and 5:35. Kids can pick up fun souvenirs such as rats and mice made out of baked bread that have been shellacked.

The municipal gardens of **Bürgergarten** have a *Kinderspielplatz* (playground) and chess games with human-scale pieces. Children can operate the fountain of **Wasserspiele** in Pferdemarkt by turning the water on and off. **Play afternoons** for children convene in summer at the indoor pool on Hafenstrasse. Contact the **tourist office** in the Bürgergarten [Tel. (05151) 65081].

Verden lies on the river Aller. Seven fairytales are represented in its **Freizeitpark Verden (Storybook Holiday Park),** where mechanical figures speak and act out familiar tales. Its Hansel and Gretel gingerbread house is so realistic that kids may want to bite off a scrumptious corner of the door. Fee. Daily Apr.–Oct. 9–6. Tel. (04231) 61744.

BREMEN

The Bremen Town Musicians came to seek their fortune; today you can visit to share in more of the brothers Grimm's tales. Sculptures of the donkey, dog, cat, and rooster are found throughout this bustling port city. Head for the elaborate Rathaus and Gothic cathedral where a bronze statue of the quartet by Gerhard Marcks, stacked one on top of another, graces the lovely market square. A windmill stands close to the center of town. Did you know that the teeth of the Greenland whale reach higher than the ceiling of a normal-sized room? In the **Focke-Museum,** children can learn about the daring days of whaling in the last century with educational guides prepared just for them. There's also a section called "Children's Lives, Children's Games." Fee. Outskirts of town center at Schwarchhauser Heerstr. 240. Tues.–Sun. 10–6. **Bürgerpark** is one of city's largest spots of green with ornate carousels.

Near Bremen, in the busy fishing port of *Bremerhaven,* children can stand on the helm of a fully rigged ship in the open-air section of the **Deutsches Schiffahrtsmuseum,** one of the country's leading maritime museums. Fee. Van-Ronzelen-Str. Tues.–Sun. 10–6.

BERLIN

Berlin is an energetic open-minded city with a many-sided cultural scene. Almost one-third of the city is devoted to parks, forests, rivers, lakes, meadowland, or farmland, with over sixty city parks alone. With the wall down, Berlin is now finally able to enjoy a free flow of traffic, both in and out. For a long time, the "Berlin Green," as the open space is called, was essential to the well-being of its citizens. Plenty of activities designed just for kids are found throughout the city: children's sections in its famous museums, excellent children's theater, elaborate adventure playgrounds, and animal farms. Now that the borders of Eastern Europe have been opened, it is possible to travel freely throughout the entire city. The contrast between the eastern and western parts of the city is still quite striking.

Wha'd'ya Wanna Do?

You could spend weeks with your children in Berlin and still not cover all there is for children to do. The tourist office offers a German book, *Berlin Tut Gut,* describing attractions for children. Have the tourist office point out the activities that fit your areas of interest. More than forty **Spielplätze** (adventure playgrounds) are found throughout the city, most of them created as an alternative to the routine sandboxes and climbing bars of earlier years. They now have elaborate wooden climbing structures and projects for children to build under supervision. They are generally open Monday through Saturday from 1 PM to 8 PM; the tourist office can give you the address of one nearest your hotel or apartment. The book also lists baby-sitting services in Berlin.

Available for children from mid-June to mid-August is a special vacation pass called the **Schülerferienpass,** which gives children access to various swimming pools plus one free admission to the zoo, the aquarium, botanical gardens, and horse races as well as discounted entrance fees at miniature golf, theaters, concerts, and boating lakes. It is available at swimming-pool offices or through the Senator für Jugend und Familie, Am Karlsbad 8-10 (Tel. 26041). The publication "Berlin Turns On," available from the tourist office, can give you general information on the city.

The main **tourist office** is in the Europa-Center (entrance on Budapester Str.) (Tel. 2626031). Other tourist offices are located at the airports, at the Bahnhof Zoo train station, and at the Alexanderplatz. Tourist offices will help you book hotels and lodgings in private homes. Berlin's **telephone area code** is 030.

The Lay of the City

Berlin is an expansive city with broad boulevards running through the eastern and western sections. Now that the wall is down, Unter den Linden runs through the Brandenburg Gate, becoming Strasse des 17 Juni, running past the Siegeshaüle, and branching out into other avenues. Potsdamer Platz is still the heart of Berlin. Debate currently rages on how to resurrect this former "no man's land" where the wall once stood. Some would like to see its former glory restored, while others would like to create a modern, new square.

Kurfürstendamm, called the Ku'damm, is a chic shopping boulevard that runs through the city center in the western side of the city. Nearby are the Zoologischer Garten and Tiergarten park. Zoo Station is an important transportation hub where the U-Bahn, S-Bahn, and train lines meet. The Berlin Green, as the open spaces are known, are found throughout the city.

Getting Around

An extensive system of buses and U-Bahn and S-Bahn trains cover the city, both above and below ground. A special family pass, *Familientageskarte*, can be purchased for weekends and holidays. Most economical for those wanting to cover much of the city is the 24-hour Berlin Ticket, which is good for all trains and buses. Children ages 6 through 14 travel half-price; passes are available from the main ticket offices at the Bahnhof Zoo station and the Kleistpark U-Bahn station. All other tickets are available from vending machines at any station. Bikes may be taken on the S-Bahn and U-Bahn. Many of Berlin's buses are double-decker, providing fun rides and great views for your children.

Canalboat tours leave from the Kottbusser Bridge in Kreuzberg. For a whale of a time, tour the waterways on the **Moby Dick** (the boat looks like a whale). Your best bet is to ride it for a shorter cruise around the Wannsee, or from the Wannsee to Tegelsee via the canal. Contact the **tourist office** for a list of canal boat rides through former East Berlin.

Where to Stay

Accommodations in Berlin may be difficult to find due to the many people visiting the city now that its border has disappeared. Book as far ahead as possible. Berlin's agencies, called *Mitwohnzentrale*, can always help you find a room or apartment. Contact: Mitwohnzentrale, 3rd floor, Ku-damm Eck, Kurfürstendamm 227-8 (Tel. 8226694) or Mitwohnzentrale, Holsteinischestr. 55 (Tel. 8618222).

HOTELS
The *Schweizerhof* is near the zoo and has an indoor pool. One child under 11 is free with two paying adults. Budapesterstr. 21-23. Tel. 26960. From U.S. 800-448-8355. **Deluxe.**

The *Ambassador Berlin* has a baby-sitting service, and children under 11 are free with two paying adults. Bayreutherstr. 42-43. Tel. 219020. From U.S. 800-448-8355. **Expensive.**

Hamburg Hotel is near the Tiergarten. Landgrafenstr. 4. Tel. 269161; from U.S. 800-448-8355. **Expensive.**

Landhaus Schlachtensee is very close to two lakes that offer boating and swimming. Bogotastr. 9. Tel. 8160060. **Moderate.**

Econotel, near Schloss Charlottenburg and its beautiful park, is popular with families. Sommeringstr. 24. Tel. 344001. **Inexpensive.**

Ravenna is near the Botanical Garden; a few rooms have kitchenettes. Grunewaldstr. 8-9. Tel. 7928031. **Inexpensive.**

CAMPGROUNDS
Camping Haselhorst is near the Havel Lakes. Pulvermühlenweg. Tel. 3345955.

Camping Kladow has a free nursery. Krampnitzer Weg 111-117. Tel. 3652797.

Detour! What to See and Do

AROUND KURFÜRSTENDAMM AND THE TIERGARTEN
Many tourists start their exploration of Berlin by wandering along Ku'damm to enjoy street musicians and sidewalk artists or people watching at one of the eighty sidewalk cafes. Ku'damm is the city's best-known shopping area, with outdoor sculpture installations and lots of hustle and bustle. Children over 6 can get a quick overview of the city from the audiovisual show **"Story of a Great City"** at the Multivision Berlin, on the first floor of the **Europa-Center.** Fee. Daily 8–6. While there, head up to the 22nd floor for a telescope view of Ku'damm, the Zoo district, Tiergarten, and surrounding area, or stop at the center's **ice rink.** The Europa-Center has shops, businesses, cafes, and a globe fountain nicknamed The Wet Dumpling.

KaDaWe Department Store is the largest department store on the continent; the gourmet floor/delicatessen has to be seen to be believed. While browsing through the delicacies, your kids will be transfixed by the vast sweets displays. Tauentzienstr. near Wittenbergplatz. Be sure to stop for a snack or meal at the enormous **Loretta im Garten** outdoor restaurant, which seats up to 1,000 people. There is a small ferris wheel and tree houses for children to play in. It's open summer afternoons and evenings the rest of the year. Just off Ku'damm on sidestreet Lietzenburger Str. and Knesebeckstr.

The **Uhr der fliessenden Zeit** is a three-story water clock in which colored water flows through a system of pipes and cascades over falls to show the time. The **Tiergarten** is the city's lovely downtown park, with boats to rent for cruising its little lakes. Tiergarten is the biggest and most beautiful of the inner-city parks with playgrounds scattered throughout the city. Climb the 285 steps of the **Siegessäule** in the middle of the park for a view over the Tiergarten and beyond. Fee. Tues.–Sun. 10–5:30. Mon. 1–5:30.

The **Berlin Zoo** on one edge of the Tiergarten has 13,000 animals. Most popular is Bao Bao, the giant panda. Other attractions include a very modern bird house, a nocturnal center, children's zoo, playgrounds, a crocodile house, and a cliff compound for monkeys. The **aquarium** has fish, snakes, crocodiles, unusual reptiles, and insects. Enter through the zoo or on Budapester Str. Combined or separate tickets available. Zoo and aquarium open daily 9–7 in summer; until 6 in winter.

Just One Look: Museums

The **Berlin Museum** focuses on local history, with works by the famous caricaturist Zille, who captured the life of the Berlin people in his earthy and humorous works. Children will also enjoy the display of toys, dolls, puppets, and costumes. Lindestr. 14. Tues.–Sun. 11–6. Tel. 25860.

MUSEUM ISLAND (in former East Berlin)

The **Nationalgalerie** contains East Berlin's largest art collections. Head for the 20th-century German Expressionist section, with colorful works by the groups Die Brücke and Der Blaue Reiter. Fee. Wed.–Sun. 9–6; Fri. 10–6. The **Pergamonmuseum** houses treasures from the ancient world, most famous of which is the enormous Pergamon Altar, dating back to 180 B.C. and discovered in what is now Turkey. Fee. Hours same as those of Nationalgalerie. The **Bodemuseum** houses several large collections. Kids will like the coin collection and the Egyptian Museum/Papyrus Collection, with mummies, weapons, and grave artifacts. A special children's gallery aimed at 6- to 10-year-olds has special exhibitions. Fee. Wed.–Sun. 9–6; Fri. 10–6; hours change frequently.

Checkpoint Charlie Museum shows the methods used in the past to get across the wall that once separated the city. One man invented a tiny submarine powered by a tiny scooter motor which carried him to freedom. Another dodged the barricades by driving a "low-rider" sports car under the border bar, ducking as he sped through. Once a family escaped on a line and pulley. Many other ingenious methods were used and are on display. Thirty people never made it. Friedrichstr. 44. Daily 9 AM–10 PM.

In the southwestern part of the city, the **Dahlem Museums Complex** houses the **Gemäldegalerie,** with paintings and drawings from early medieval to late 18th-century periods. Its collection of German masters such as Dürer, Cranach, and Holbein is exceptional, and Rembrandt and the Dutch and Italian masters are well represented. Free. Arnimallee 23-27. Tues.–Sun. 9–5. Tel. 83011. The extraordinary and internationally famous **Museum für Völkerkunde** contains a collection of ethnographic articles from ancient America, Africa, Asia, and the South Seas. Children should head for the junior museum, with specialized exhibitions and performances. Free. Lansstr. 8. Tues.– Sun. 9–5. Tel. 83011.

The **Museum für Verkehr und Technik** has buttons to push and levers to pull. Kids can play with computers and old machinery, view examples of the world's classic forms of transportation, from steam trains to planes, and participate in practical experiments. Fee. Trebbiner Str. 9. Tues.–Fri. 9–6, Sat. and Sun. 10–6. Tel. 254840.

Museumsdorf Düppel is an open-air museum dedicated to Berlin's early history, with demonstrations of weaving, pottery, carving, and other crafts. Set in the little town of Düppel, children can ride through the reconstructed village on ox carts. Clauerstr. 37 May–Oct. Sun. 10–1. Tel. 8026671.

Musikinstrumenten Museum contains musical instruments from the 15th century to the present. Children can listen to tapes of sounds the instruments make. Free. In the Tiergarten Museum complex. Tues.–Sun. 9–5. Tel. 254810.

Neue Nationalgalerie, in a building designed by Mies van der Rohe, has a permanent collection of Impressionists, German Romantics, Expressionists, and Surrealists. Main collection free; fee for special exhibitions. Potsdamer Str. 50. Tues.–Fri. 9–5. Tel 2666.

SCHLOSS CHARLOTTENBURG AND SURROUNDING AREA

Schloss Charlottenburg was originally built in 1695, destroyed in World War II, and meticulously reconstructed. Its gardens, open daily, offer beautiful walks and lovely lakes. Sections of the Schloss are used for special exhibitions; there is also a Schlossgarten cafe and an outdoor restaurant in the summer. Park and garden free. Mandatory guided tours of its historical rooms are available only in German.

Just south of the Schloss is the **Ägyptisches Museum,** which boasts the Bust of Queen Nefertiti, one of the best-known early Egyptian sculptures from about 1350 B.C., and other treasures from the days of the Pharaohs. Kids inevitably linger over the mummies. Free. Schloss Str. 70. Tues.–Fri. 9–5. Tel. 3209111.

Where the Sidewalk Ends: Zoos and More Parks

Between the Dahlem and Wilmersdorf suburbs is the **Grunewald**, Berlin's largest wooded area, with three lakes. You can rent bicycles, including tandems, at the S-Bahn Grunewald station to tour the park. Climb Grunewaldturm's 204 steps for a magnificent view across the Grunewald and Havel of villages on the opposite bank and beyond. Daily 10 AM–dark; closed winter. Teufelsberg is an artificial hill made out of rubble from the World War II bombings. In winter it's a popular place, with a ski slope and toboggan run; the rest of the year, it offers beautiful walks. Glienicke castle and park are other lovely destinations in the Grunewald.

Strandbad Wannsee, Berlin's longest bathing beach, had its sand imported from far away Timmendorf, in Schleswig-Holstein. It has a good children's playground and an outdoor swimming pool nearby.

The protected island of **Pfaueninsel** is perfect for walks. A ferry runs between the island and the mainland. The artificial ruins of an 18th-century castle, peacocks, birds, swans, and ducks are found amidst the weeping willows and majestic oaks.

Tegelsee has lots of water sports and lovely beaches; it's not as crowded a green space as the popular Grunewald.

Freizeitpark Tegel has trampolines, huge drums children can run in as they turn, Ping-Pong, volleyball, and more. Campestr. 11. Tel. 7913040.

Freizeitpark Lübars mit Jugendfarm in the village of Lübars, in north Berlin, is one of the city's best children's farms. There is pony and bike riding, a playground, a winter sledding course and ski run, and farm animals. Blacksmithing, bread making, and beekeeping demonstrations are given, and you can attend a Farmer's Breakfast on Sunday mornings. Fee. Quickborner Str. Tues.–Fri. 9–7, Sun. 10–5. Tel. 4157027.

Tierpark Berlin is on the grounds of the former palace park in former East Berlin. The polar bear enclosure and deer collection are among the wild animal park's best collections; many of the species roam in the open. Daily 7 AM; 8 AM in winter. Tel. 5100111.

Treptower Park is on the Spree River in former East Berlin, and in summer its fireworks show, "Treptow in Flames," is performed on the Liebensinsel Bridge. Sculptures are placed throughout the park, and 5,000 rose bushes bloom. Boats will carry you from the Spree to the **Müggelsee,** a popular lake for water sports and hiking expeditions. The **Pioneer Park** in Wuhlheide has carousel rides and a playground.

The **Fernsehturm** TV tower in former East Berlin provides a fantastic view, although the visibility at the top is often blocked by clouds. You may have to wait your turn in line to go up. The **Tele-Café** above the observation platform turns on its own axis once an hour. Young people skateboard on the sidewalks below the tower. Tower open May–Sept. daily 8 AM–11 PM; Oct.–Apr. 9 AM–11 PM. Fee. Alexander Platz. The **tourist office** is in the tower.

Sports and Performing Arts

Refer to the tourist office's publication on attractions for children for a listing of the many different sports activities and facilities available.

The excellent and highly political **Grips-Theater** has performances geared for older kids. Topics they tackle include teen employment and race issues. Language may not be a problem as pantomime is an important element. Altonaer Str. 22. Tel. 3933012. **Klecks-Theater's** puppet shows for little ones feature original puppets. Schinkestr. 8-9. Tel. 6937731. **Berliner Figurentheater** also has puppet shows for younger children. Yorckstr. 59. Tel. 7869815.

The **Tempodrome** has highly inventive circus performances in which children can participate. John-Foster-Dulles-Allee (Tiergarten). Tel. 3944045. The popular **UFA-Zirkus** has special circus performances for children. They pride themselves on developing new alternatives to the traditional circus. UFA-Fabrik, 42, Viktoriastr. 13. Tel. 7528085. For information on other circuses that regularly tour during the summer, contact the Zirkusdirektorenverband, 15, Xantener Strasse 9 (Tel. 8814660).

Be on the look out for magic shows by popular **Igor Jedlin,** and try to go to a family concert in the **Waldbühne,** one of Europe's most beautiful open-air concert halls. For more information on concerts, contact the concert office at Haupstrasse 83 (Tel. 8524080).

Special Events

Berlin loves a celebration. The long season of folk festivals begins as soon as the winter frost has melted. Most festivals have merry-go-rounds and other children's rides, booths, and delicious food. Neighborhood street festivals take place throughout the spring and summer and offer a good opportunity to experience the real Berlin. The tourist office can provide you with a full schedule. Some of the most noteworthy celebrations include:

Grüne Woche Berlin (Green Week), in early February, is like a huge county fair, with agricultural products, animals, food tents, and carnival rides. Everyone takes their kids. At the Funkturm.

Berlin's famous **International Film Festival,** held in middle to late February, includes a Children's Film Festival.

The **Berliner Drehorgelfest,** in July, is an international meeting of barrel organ players.

September's **Berliner Festwochen** is a large arts festival with music, theater, dance, and exhibits.

Octoberfest in Berlin is a lively celebration with food, beer, bands, and carnival rides.

For four weekends before Christmas, Berlin hosts several enchanting **Christmas markets.** The entire little village of Spandau, on the edge of West Berlin, is magically transformed with booths, rides, concerts in churches, and theater programs. One street is turned into "Fairy-tale Street," with puppet shows, art projects, and other fun activities for young ones. The inner city's Christmas market has carousels, arts and crafts projects, puppet theaters, and choirs in addition to food and Christmas decoration and toy booths.

Great Britain: England, Wales, Scotland

Great Britain is made up of **England, Scotland,** and **Wales.** Separated from the rest of the European continent by the English Channel and the North Sea, these three countries along with Northern Ireland (covered separately) share a monarchy, monetary system, and government.

Wha'd'ya Wanna Do?

The **British Tourist Authority (BTA)** is one of the most helpful in the business and will send you bushels of material on all kinds of topics. Ask for specialty information on activities just for kids, game-fishing holidays, special walking and biking paths, golf holidays, and more. Their free booklet "Family Fun in Britain" lists a few of Britain's many attractions for children. They also publish a list of books and pamphlets you can order for a small fee.

BRITISH TOURIST AUTHORITY (BTA) OFFICES
U.S.A.–Chicago: British Tourist Authority, John Hancock Center, Suite 3320, 875 N. Michigan Ave., Chicago, IL. 60611. Tel: 312-787-0490.
U.S.A.–Los Angeles: British Tourist Authority, World Trade Center, 350 S. Figueroa St., Suite 450, Los Angeles, CA 90071. Tel: 213-628-3525.
U.S.A.–New York: British Tourist Authority, 40 West 57th St., New York, NY 10019. Tel: 212-581-4700.
Canada–Toronto: British Tourist Authority, 94 Cumberland St., Suite 60, Toronto, Ontario, M5R 3N3. Tel: 416-926-6326.

Many tourist attractions have **adventure playgrounds** on their premises. You'll find them on the grounds of castles and historic manor houses, and alongside safari parks and open-air museums. They are usually much like a typical playground with slides and swings but can include more elaborate and challenging structures such as free-fall slides or extra-fancy climbing structures with ropes and nets, sliding poles, and more. They are a wonderful way to combine sightseeing with run-around time.

Less common, but even more exciting are the full-size **hedge mazes** found on castle grounds and at other sites. The maze walls are thick, tall hedges, and kids absolutely adore negotiating the many twists and turns to find their way to the middle and out again. Young ones may need the help of a parent or older sibling as most are surprisingly difficult. Most of the larger ones have attendants to assist those who are hopelessly lost.

Many cathedrals and churches have memorial brasses from which **brass rubbings** can be made for a small fee; they make great souvenirs. The procedure is as simple as that of putting a piece of paper over a coin and rubbing with a lead pencil, only the brasses are bigger and much more elaborate. Churches that offer brass rubbing often sell the necessary equipment needed to do it; if not, you can pick up the simple ingredients (masking tape, drafting paper, and a lumber crayon) at any art store.

Britain is one of the most **well-trod** areas in the world. Thousands of miles of paths and trails exist for walkers, cyclists, and horseback riders; maps are available from local tourist offices. Bookstores carry dozens of titles on great walks and hikes, and sell the ordinance survey map system, which will take you anywhere. Some walks take several hours; others take days or even weeks, with overnight stops at suggested bed-and-breakfast establishments. If your children are old enough, hiking through the countryside's small villages and hamlets is a delightful way to experience the country. **Orienteering** is popular in Britain. Simply put, you go into the middle of a forest equipped with a compass and a map and try to find your way out. Some resorts and parks have challenging yet safe orienteering courses for children.

Christmas pantomimes are a tradition in many larger towns, especially in England. Women dress like men and vice versa in the plays, which are often based on a familiar fairytale. They're slapstick and corny, but kids love them because they have an opportunity to respond to the actors and actresses.

We have listed hundreds of great places to visit with kids, but there are hundreds more. Once there, the tourist offices found in every city and region can provide you with more ideas.

Lights Out! Special British Accommodations

England, Scotland, and Wales offer a wide variety of accommodations, from first-class hotels to furnished farm cottages and from 13th-century castles to simple bed-and-breakfast (B & B) overnights. The BTA can send you several free brochures, including "Stay on a Farm," "Stay with a British Family," "Holiday Homes," and "Camping and Caravan Parks." Once there, many of the tourist offices in the larger cities will book hotels or B & B's for a small fee.

If you plan to stay in one place for a week or more, the following businesses can find you cozy cottages in the countryside, Gothic castles with butlers, or practical flats in London, Edinburgh, and other cities. Some have such family-oriented features as working farms, game rooms, or swimming pools. Priced by the week, there are choices that sleep from two to twenty. Some charge a small fee for their catalog. We have listed a few that handle properties in both England and Scotland.

Castles, Cottages and Flats of Ireland and the U.K., P. O. Box 261, Westwood, MA 02090. Tel. 617-329-4680.

Families Abroad, 194 Riverside Dr., New York, NY 10025. Tel. 212-787-2434 or 718-766-6185.

Hearthstone Holidays, P.O. Box 8625, Station L, Edmonton, Alberta T6C4J4, Canada. Tel. 403-465-2874.

Hideaways International, 15 Goldsmith St., Box 1270, Littleton, MA 01460. Tel. 800-843-4433 or 617-486-8955.

Livingstone Holidays, 1720 E. Garry Ave., Suite 204, Santa Ana, CA 92705. Tel. 714-476-2823.

British **hotels** often have baby-listening services: You leave your room phone off the hook, go to the hotel bar or restaurant, and keep track of the activity in your room. The desk clerk can listen in for you, or you can call into your room. Unlike much of the rest of Europe, most British hotels, no matter how small or inexpensive, can supply baby cribs called "cots." Of the thousands of hotels in London and the many in Edinburgh, we have recommended only a few with special amenities for families, such as kitchenettes, swimming pools, and proximity to parks.

Many private homes display **Bed-and-Breakfast** signs. They are what they say, a room with a bed, and a home-cooked English breakfast. They won't offer all of the services of a hotel, but they are a less-expensive, charming, and more personal alternative. Many of them have a lower price for children, especially if they sleep in your room.

During the peak of the Industrial Revolution, a network of canals was created throughout Britain to float its goods to markets and port cities. Two thousand miles of inland waterways still exist, and you can rent a **narrowboat** to tour about. They're said to be easier to learn to drive than a car (well, maybe not a right-hand-drive car), and come with bathroom, kitchen, heating, and more. Hotel boat cruises are another option where all your needs are taken care of. Request the BTA's brochures, "Holidays on Inland Waterways," "Self-Skippered Canal Cruises" or "Blakes Boating in Britain."

Camping is a popular pastime in Britain and sites are plentiful. The BTA publishes "Camping and Caravan Parks in Britain," which lists campsites, their amenities, and prices. Trailers are called "caravans," trailer parks are "caravan parks," and campsites are "pitches."

Getting Around

If you're traveling by **car**, you can use your U.S. or Canadian driver's license for up to 12 months, or an International Driver's Permit. There are many American-based rental car agencies to choose from. It's often significantly cheaper to book from home; we made arrangements through Avis before we left, and they have just as many pickup and drop-off sites in Britain as they do in the states. Rental cars have front and rear seat belts, and car seats are regularly used for babies; be sure to request one when reserving your car. It takes several days of driving to get used to right-hand drive. Remember to yield to traffic coming from the right in a roundabout, or traffic circle, and you'll do fine. Avoid driving in London, especially at rush hour.

British **trains** offer a fast and easy way to travel, as distances are relatively short. A high-speed train trip from London to Edinburgh, Scotland, takes just 4 hours and 50 minutes. Those who intend to do a lot of train travel should investigate the Britrail Pass. It offers unlimited travel throughout England, Scotland, and Wales, and is available for 4, 8, 15, 22 days, or 1 month. Children 5 to 15 pay one-half the adult fare, and the Britrail Youth Pass offers savings for 16- to 25-year-olds. Book in advance from North America through your travel agent.

Nuts and Bolts

Does anyone care what time it is? Most stores are open from 9AM to 5 or 5:30 PM. A few of the larger department stores in big cities are open one evening a week, usually Wednesday or Thursday; stores are open on Saturday but closed on Sunday. Banks are generally open from 9:30 AM to 3:30 PM on weekdays. A few are open on Saturday mornings.

National holidays: New Year's Day, Good Friday, Easter Monday, May Day (May 1), Christmas Day, and Boxing Day (December 26). Bank holidays occur seasonally, one in winter, spring, summer, and fall, and most businesses are closed while tourist attractions are usually open.

Can I have my allowance? The monetary unit is the pound sterling, and bank notes come in denominations of 5, 10, 20, and 50. The pound is divided into 100 pence (p); coins come in 1 pound, 50p, 20p, 10p, and 5p; 2p and 1p are in bronze. The old 2-shilling piece is worth 10p, and 1 shilling is worth 5p. Scotland also uses the Scottish pound note, which is identical in value to the pound sterling.

Telephones: The country code for Britain is 44. Both coin-operated and card-using phone booths are located throughout. Plastic credit-card-like phone cards can be purchased at post offices, news kiosks, rail station bars, and shops where the green Cardphone sign is displayed.

Useful nationwide phone numbers: Operator is 100; information is 192; international operator is 155; and emergency police, fire, or ambulance is 999.

Embassies and consulates: The U.S. Embassy is at 24 Grosvenor Square, London W1 (Tel. 071-499-9000), and 3 Regent Terrace, Edinburgh (Tel. 031-556-8315). The Canadian High Commission is at Canada House, Trafalger Square, London SW1 (Tel. 071-629-9492).

Let's Eat!

The English, Scottish, and Welsh start their day with a "full breakfast," and that is exactly what's included in the price of a room in many inns, hotels, and, of course, bed-and-breakfast establishments. Juice, cereal (both the cornflakes variety and "porridge" or creamy oatmeal), eggs, bacon, sausage, grilled tomatoes and mushrooms, fried bread, and toast with butter and marmalade are the standard fare. The more daring can try kippers (smoked herring) but watch for the little bones.

Restaurants in Britain usually have high chairs and booster seats on the premises. Many restaurants and pubs have children's menus of "fish fingers" (fish sticks), sausages, or hamburgers with "chips" (french fries). Potato chips are "crisps." Fish and chips are popular, and the Wimpy Burger chain is as widespread as our McDonald's, which are also found everywhere. Pizza is another easy-to-find favorite. Food "to go" is called food "to take away," and many cities have Indian, Chinese, and Greek take-away establishments. The greasy spoons, or little neighborhood places where workmen eat, are surprisingly good and inexpensive, too. Vegetables can be scarce and unappetizing in family-style restaurants. We purchase them at local markets and serve them for picnic lunches. Many kids like the more traditional fare, such as meat pies, pasties, and bangers (sausages). The British call our 7-Up lemonade; "squashes" are fruit-flavored drinks. Children really enjoy the variety of cheeses; a favorite for two veteran kid travelers was Cotswold cheese.

Many pubs have "bar meals," meaning simple lunch or supper

dishes, and they are a very good value. A "ploughman's lunch" of cheese, sausage, fruit or salad, and rolls was popular with our kids. Some pubs have rooms just for families or adjacent play yards, especially in the smaller towns and in the more rural areas. Other pubs do not allow children at all, so be sure to inquire first.

Teatime is fun for kids, with scones served with clotted cream and strawberry jam, sweet pancakes, and all kinds of sweet biscuits (cookies). "High tea" is generally served a bit later than the 4 o'clock tea and has sandwiches, boiled eggs, and other more substantial food. It can take the place of supper, although it is not as commonly found as it used to be. And for the pudding (dessert), most kids will love the cream cakes, trifles, puddings, and other sweets.

Formula and Baby Food, Diapers and Baby Gear

Formula and baby food are found in larger grocery stores, supermarkets, and chemists (drugstores) throughout Great Britain. The Boots the Chemist chain has a huge selection of baby foods and all kinds of paraphernalia. Much of the baby food comes without sugar, and there are a few very British selections, such as steak and kidney, pureed and in a jar. The British call diapers "nappies," and you will get a blank look if you ask for diapers. Many brands are available in neighborhood grocery stores, chemists, and large supermarkets. Wipes are also readily available wherever you find nappies. Cribs are called "cots" in Britain, and most inns, hotels, and bed-and-breakfast establishments have them. A baby carriage is a "pram," a stroller is a "push-chair," and a pacifier is a "dummy."

ENGLAND

Robin Hood, Winnie the Pooh, King Arthur, Peter Rabbit, Paddington Bear, and other best-loved characters from literature and history have given many children a glimpse of the life and landscape of England. Nursery rhymes, myths, and stories of the pageantry and pomp of kings, queens, princesses, and princes continue to capture their imaginations. The shared language makes England an easy country to visit, and many families test their travel wings here where communication is never difficult.

England has been extensively developed for tourism, and you'll find adventure playgrounds and full-size hedge mazes on the grounds of historic castles and manor houses, and fun children's trails in museums. The many miniature model villages, puppet theaters, rare animal breeding farms, drive-through safari parks, boat rides, and pony-trekking opportunities found throughout the country will enchant your little ones for weeks.

London has many marvelous things to do with kids, but don't miss the more rural parts of England. Spend a week or two in London and then rent a thatched cottage or stay in a bed-and-breakfast farmhouse in the Cotswolds, Devon, or elsewhere in the English countryside. There, you can take your time wandering through quaint villages, ride on little steam trains, stop for a cream tea, or visit one of the hundreds of other family attractions.

Preparing Your Kids: Books and Art

Younger children: *Madeline in London* by Ludwig Bemelman; *Alice in Wonderland* by Lewis Carroll; *Bernard of Scotland Yard* by Berneice Freschet; any of the following by John S. Goodall: *An Edwardian Christmas*, *The Story of an English Village*, *The Story of a Farm*, or *The Story of a Castle*; *A Day in London* by Lesley Anne Ivory; The Paddington Bear books; any of the Mother Goose Nursery Rhymes or *Tales of Beatrix Potter*; *Prep the Little Pigeon of Trafalger Square* by Milton Shulman.

Older children: *The Secret Garden* by Frances Burnett; *Canterbury Tales* by Chaucer; works by Charles Dickens; *Dr. Doolittle* by H. Lofting; Winnie the Pooh books by A. A. Milne; *A Family in England* by Jetty St. John; stories about Robin Hood and King Arthur; and *Kidding Around London*, published by John Muir (Santa Fe, NM).

Art: Among the best-known English artists are Blake, Constable, Gainsborough, Hogarth, Reynolds, and Turner. Children particularly enjoy the paintings and prints of William Hogarth, whose depictions of English life have great wit and sarcasm. Your library should carry books with photographs of their works.

Getting There

Most international airlines fly to London Heathrow or Gatwick airports. The British Airways Terminal 4 at Heathrow Airport houses **Volvo's Playcare Centre**, where trained nurses look after up to thirty-five 2- to 8-year-olds in a brightly decorated room. There are toys, books in a variety of languages, a home corner, climbing structures, trampolines, and little tables and chairs. Next door, at the Babycare Playroom, under-2s can be looked after by their parents. It is open daily 6 AM to 10 PM and 7 AM to 9 PM on Sunday and is free of charge.

Sidewalk Talk

Although we share a common language, many terms are different:

bathroom	*loo*	line of people	*queue*
busker	*street performer*	napkins	*serviettes*
checkers	*draughts*	pants	*trousers*
cotton candy	*candy floss*	Ping-Pong paddle	*bat*
custom made	*bespoke*	popsickle	*ice lolly*
flashlight	*torch*	raisin	*sultana*
friend	*mate*	sweater	*jumper*
hamburger meat	*mince*	tic-tac-toe	*naughts and crosses*
jungle gym	*climbing frame*	underpants	*knickers*

The Lay of the Land

Most people who plan a trip to England visit London, but from there, anything goes. We start with London, followed by attractions near London, and then profile the Southeast, the South, the West, the Heart of England, East Anglia, York, North of York, the Lake District, and the Borders.

LONDON

Covering over 600 square miles, London is the biggest city in Europe, and it contains enough attractions for the entire family to fill a several-month stay. Specialty tours for kids with interests such as stamp collecting, horseback riding, Egyptian mummies, or dinosaurs can be easily arranged. Many museums are set up for children with special "children's trails" and provide printed ideas for helping children get the most out of museum in an entertaining way. And London contains many of England's National Museums, most of which are free of charge.

Both *City Limits* and *Time Out,* London's weekly entertainment magazines, have special children's listings. Several publications on activities for kids are available at the **tourist offices** run by the London Tourist Board. They are located at: Victoria Station Forecourt SW1 (on one side of Victoria Station); Harrods, Brompton Road, SW1 (fourth floor); Selfridges Dept. Store, Oxford St., W1 (Basement); H. M. Tower of London (West Gate). London has two **telephone area codes**, 071 and 081.

Getting Around

London is a city of small winding streets that change names at every turn, and it can be difficult to find your way around. Pick up a copy of the detailed map book, London AZ (Z is pronounced "Zed") and get a good city map. The map provides a general orientation and shows relationships, while the book shows specific streets.

London's famous red double decker buses, the mode of transportation favored by kids, offers excellent views from the upper deck. The **Original London Transport Sightseeing Tour** departs hourly from Grosvenor Gardens near Victoria Station, Haymarket, Baker Street Station and Marble Arch (Tel. 071-222-1234; they'll answer other transportation questions as well). Teens may enjoy the 2-hour **Rock Tour of London** aboard a bus with stereo sound, video, and live commentary. Book through the tourist office at Victoria Station or through Ticketmaster (Tel. 071-379-4444).

The extensive **underground** subway system (often called "the tube") is the best way to travel when you want to cover territory fast. Day passes or passes that are good for 1 to 7 days (you'll need a passport-size photo for the 7-day pass), are also good for buses and some of the trains that supplement the subway system.

There are frequent **boat tours** up the Thames River to Kew, Hampton Court and down to Greenwich, and all of them are great fun. The trip to Hampton Court takes several hours, which may be too long for younger children. One of the most popular excursions is the round-trip tour starting at Westminster pier down to Tower Bridge and back in less than an hour. You can also take a night cruise along the Thames. Most run in spring and summer only. River Boat Information Service: 071-730-4812 or 071-480-7716.

Canalboat trips run during the summer along the "backwaters" of the Grand Union and the Regent's Canal. The narrow boats are brightly painted and travel through the canals' most picturesque parts. Get off at the London Zoo, if you like, or at several other interesting destinations. London Waterbus Company: Tel. 071-482-2550; Jason's Trip: Tel. 071-286-3428; or Jenny Wren Cruises: Tel. 071-485-4433/6210.

One of the best ways to explore London is **on foot.** There are a number of walking tours kids will love, such as Ghost Walks, The Buried City, and Dickens's London. City Walks of London: Tel. 071-937-4281; John Mufty Historical Tours: Tel. 081-668-4019; London Walks: Tel. 081-882-2763; or Junior Jaunts: Tel. 071-235-4750. And, if you tire, shiny black **taxi cabs** are everywhere. Kids especially like riding on their jump seats.

Where to Stay

Request the brochure "Apartments in London" from the British Tourist Authority, or check the beginning of this chapter to find out where to book apartments or flats if you plan to stay for a week or longer.

HOTELS

Dolphin Square is a luxury unit with fully equipped apartments, indoor pool, tennis courts, health club, restaurants, grocery stores, and lovely gardens. Reserve well in advance in summer months. Dolphin Square, London SW1V 3LX. Tel. 071-834-9134. **Expensive.**

Grosvenor House overlooks Hyde Park and has connecting suites as well as a pool, a gym, 3 restaurants, and baby sitting if prearranged. Park Lane, London W1A 3AA. Tel. 071-499-6363. **Expensive.**

The *Regent Crest* is near Regents Park and allows children 13 and under to stay free in their parents' room. Carburton St. Tel. 071-388-2300, or from U.S. 800-548-2323. **Expensive.**

Fairlawn Apartments have one- to four-room fully equipped apartments, with cribs, strollers, and high chairs available. 109 Elgin Crescent, London W11. Tel. 071-229-5006 (booking office). **Moderate.**

The *Park Court Hotel*, right across from Hyde Park, has a lovely outdoor cafe. 75 Lancaster Gate, London W23NN. Tel. 071-402-4272. **Moderate.**

Hotel Kensington Close has an indoor pool, sauna, small gym, and a children's menu. There are connecting rooms; it's a 10-minute walk from Kensington Gardens. Wrights Lane, London W85SP. Tel. 071-937-8170. **Moderate.**

Clearlake Hotel is an apartment hotel with studios, one-, two-, and three-bedroom apartments in a quiet neighborhood near Kensington Gardens. Reserve in advance. Prince of Wales Terrace, London W8. Tel. 071-937-3274. **Inexpensive.**

Rent-a-Suite has plain furnished apartments of various sizes. 17 Sloane Gardens, Sloane Square, London. Tel. 071-730-4847. **Inexpensive.**

The *Caring Hotel*, near Hyde Park, includes a full English breakfast. Their family room has a double bed and two singles. 24 Craven Hill Gardens, Hyde Park, London W2 3EA. Tel. 071-262-8708. **Inexpensive.**

CAMPGROUNDS

There are no campgrounds in central London, but a few are not too far out. Try *Picketts Lock,* part of the Picketts Lock Sports and Leisure Centre, Picketts Lock Lane, Edmonton, London N9 (Tel. 081-803-4756). It has 200 "pitches" (campsites), a shop, cafe, laundry facilities, and the sports centre next door. You can take the bus and underground into the city.

Detour! What to See and Do

A KID'S TOP FIVE

The **Changing of the Guard** ceremony tops any child's list. There are two daily ceremonies, one at Buckingham Palace, the other at Whitehall. Arrive at 11 AM for the 11:30 Buckingham Palace ceremony to get a good seat on the top steps of the Queen Victoria monument. In winter months it's held on alternate days. Call the tourist office (Tel. 071-730-3488) for the schedule. At Whitehall, the Changing of the Guard Horseguards Parade is daily at 11 AM, except Sunday, when it's held at 10 AM. Both ceremonies take about 30 minutes. Underground: Victoria, St. James Park, or Green Park for Buckingham Palace; Westminster, Embankment, or Charing Cross for Whitehall.

Madame Tussaud's is the world's oldest, largest, and most famous waxworks. French-born Marie Tussaud, an accomplished wax sculptor, opened the exhibition in London in 1835. Figures from English history, rock stars, sports heros, murderers, thieves, presidents, film stars, and figures from fairytales are among the 350 wax models on display. Every detail is on target, from clothes, buttons, and shoelaces to facial expressions. Children love to be surprised by the stiff guard who at first appears like a wax model but turns out to be real. A planetarium is next door; you can purchase a joint ticket. Fee. Mon.–Fri. 10–5:30; Sat., Sun., and bank holidays 9:30–5:30. Marylebone Road, NW1 Tel. 071-935-6861. Underground: Baker Street.

The **Tower of London** was built by William the Conquerer in 1078. The foundations he laid were placed on fortifications that were over 1,000 years old then. Go first to the History Gallery, which tells the tale of the tower from its beginnings. The main tower, called the "White Tower," is surrounded by fifteen smaller towers, and it contains arms, armor, and torture instruments. The Bloody Tower is a popular spot for kids as here prisoners were held captive and tortured. Tower Green, which was the site of many executions, now houses the famous black ravens. Legend has it that if the ravens leave, the tower will collapse and the British Empire will come to an end. Good thing their wings are clipped. One cell, called "Little Ease," was so small that inmates couldn't stand, lie down, or even sit. The crown jewels are housed in the Jewel House along with other treasures used in coronations. The Royal Armories contains a set of armor made for an Indian elephant as well as armor for a dwarf and a giant. The tower is still used by the military, and you can often see Beefeaters or Yeoman Warders in Tudor-style uniforms. Fee. Tower Hill, EC3. Mar.–Oct. Mon.–Sat. 9:30–5:45, Sun. 2–5:45; Nov.–Feb. Mon.–Sat. 9:30–5:30, closed Sun. Last admission 45 minutes before closing. Tel. 071-709-0765. Underground: Tower Hill.

Both the **British Museum** and the **British Library** in the same building have educational pamphlets on topics such as "Animals in Ancient Egypt" and "Cuneiform Writing" as well as "children's trails" through the museum. Ask for them at the main information desk. And don't miss the **mummies**! All kids seem to be fascinated by the Egyptian collection, with painted coffins, burial blankets, and the mummified people and animals. The Elgin marbles, a clock room, coin and medal collections, and the Assyrian armor and weapons are interesting to many kids. Structure your time at the British Library carefully and look for odd bits in the collection: a letter written in Balinese on a sheet of pure gold, the miniature books from Persia with tiny Arabic script known as ghubar (dust) devised for pigeon post, Beatles memorabilia, and the magnificent stamp collection. Free. Great Russell St., WC1. Mon.–Sat. 10–5, Sun. 2:30–6. Tel. 071-636-1555. Underground: Russell Square, Holborn or Tottenham Court Rd.

The **Maze at Hampton Court.** Ten miles outside of London in a park by the Thames, Hampton Court has fabulous ornamental gardens, a giant hedge maze, and a palace inhabited by royal ghosts. You can tour the rooms and view fine art, but the maze will be tops with the young set. It's surprisingly difficult. People stationed in towers along the way help those who become hopelessly lost. Fee for palace and maze; gardens free. Apr.–Sept. Mon.–Sat. 9:30–6, Sun. 11–6; Oct.–Mar. until 5:00. Maze open Mar.–Oct. 10–5. Last admission 30 minutes before closing. Hampton, Middlesex, KT8 9AU. Tel. 081-977-8441. British Rail to Hampton Court or accessible by bus or by a 3- or 4-hour boat ride from London.

More to See and Do

Big Ben, London's most famous landmark, is the name of the bell, not the clock. It is 320 feet high and was cast at Whitechapel in 1858. Its tolling is broadcast to the entire nation. Underground: Westminster.

Buckingham Palace is the residence of the Queen. The royal standard flies from the roof when she is in residence. The palace is open to invited guests only, but a few sections are open to visitors. The **Royal Mews** has the glass coach that Princess Diana and Prince Charles rode in on their wedding day and other royal coaches right out of a storybook. Fee. Wed.–Thurs. 2–4. There are 40 acres of private gardens at Buckingham Palace; the public St. James Park is nearby.

The **Cabinet War Rooms,** restored wartime headquarters of Winston Churchill, are hidden 10 feet beneath the streets of Westminster. The Cabinet Room, where Churchill and his war cabinet met over 100 times between 1940 and 1945, still contains the red and green lamps used to indicate air raids and other wartime memorabilia. There is a transatlantic telephone room where Churchill could call Roosevelt and much more. Fee. Daily 10–5:50. Underground: Westminster.

Covent Garden, originally a flower, fruit, and vegetable market, has recently turned into a rather upscale and trendy shopping area. There are cafes, shops, and galleries along with the The Royal Opera House and St. Paul's Church, with its memorials to actors and actresses. Inside and outside the Covent Garden Central Market are street musicians, jugglers, magicians, and mimes. A crafts fair is held on weekends, an antique market on Mondays, and an old-fashioned fair at Christmas. While there, don't miss the **Caberet Mechanical Theatre**, a fun exhibition of automata that move with the push of a button, the turn of a crank, or the pull of a lever. Fee. Summer 10–7; winter until 6:30. 33–34 The Market, Covent Garden WC2. Tel. 071-379-7961. The **London Transport Museum** is in the old flower market building of Covent Garden. (See "Museums.") Underground: Covent Garden.

The **Guinness World of Records** brings the book to life using videos, models, and dioramas. You'll see models of 8'11" Robert Wadlow, the world's tallest man; the world's heaviest man (1,076 pounds); and the most tattooed woman. Television broadcasts of records being set include the largest number of tumbling dominoes and the highest shallow dive into water. Exhibits such as The Human World, Animal World, Planet Earth, Machines, Sports, Entertainment, and Great British Achievements are found, along with a kitschy gift shop. Fee. Daily 10–9:30. The Trocadero Centre, Piccadilly Circus W1. Tel. 071-439-7331/5. Underground: Piccadilly Circus.

Hamley's Toy Store is one of the biggest toy stores in the world. With six floors of toys and a cafe in the basement, you decide if you want to turn your kids loose here. 200 Regent St. W1. Tel. 071-734-3161. Underground: Oxford Circus.

If you're traveling with teens, don't forget the **Hard Rock Cafe**; it may be their favorite memory. They can pick up a tee shirt or sweatshirt while you wait (and you will) for a table. Elton John's glitzy glasses are here along with David Bowie's jeans, Jimi Hendrix's guitar, and lots of other rock memorabilia. 15 Old Park Lane. Underground: Hyde Park Corner.

The **London Dungeon** is a true-to-life exhibit of the gruesome and gory side of life, and older kids love it. You will see people who were boiled, beheaded, hanged, drawn and quartered, or just plain tortured. Voices cry out in the darkness, victims of plague suffer the ravages of disease, a monster glares and snarls. Not for children under 10 or the squeamish. Fee. Apr.–Sept. 10–6:30; Oct.–Mar. 10–5:30. 34 Tooley St., SE1. Tel. 071-403-0606. Underground: London Bridge.

The **London Brass Rubbing Centre**, in St. Martin-in-the-Field's Church, has a selection of 70 replica brasses to select from. Children of all ages can create a lasting memento; materials and instructions are supplied for a small fee. Medieval music plays while you work. Trafalger Square. Mon.–Sat. 10–6, Sun. 12–6. Tel. 071-437-6023. Underground: Charing Cross, Leicester Square, or Embankment.

The Monument, a 17th-century hollow column designed by Christopher Wren, commemorates the Great Fire of London. It is 202 feet high because it stands 202 feet from the site where the fire that destroyed much of London in 1666 began. Climb the 311 steps for an expansive view. Fee. Monument St., EC3. Open hours vary considerably; call first. Tel. 071-626-2717. Underground: Monument.

The **Rock Circus** in the London Pavilion at Piccadilly Circus is a new exhibition on the story of rock and pop from the 1950s to the present. Daily 10 AM to 10 PM.

Spaceniks will enjoy **Space Adventure**, which simulates a real trip through the solar system that launches you "from the heart of London to the edge of the universe." Fee. 64-66 Tooley St. May–Oct. 10:30–6; Nov.–Apr. 10:30–5. Tel. 071-378-1405. Underground: London Bridge.

Another panoramic view of London is offered those who climb the 600 steps to the classical dome of **St. Paul's Cathedral.** Kids will like the Whispering Gallery down below; what is whispered close to the wall on one side can be heard on the gallery's other side. Cathedral nave free. Mon.–Fri. 10–4:15, Sat. 11–4:15. Underground: St. Paul's.

Tower Bridge, one of London's best-known landmarks, was built in 1894. You can cross the glassed-in walkways between the upper floors of the two towers for a superb view of London on a clear day. Each tower holds a different exhibition on the bridge's history and design, and a museum housed below shows steam-pumping engines and massive boilers. Kids will like the walk best. Fee. Tower Bridge, SE 1. Apr.–Oct. 10–6:30; Nov.–Mar. until 4:45. Last admission 45 minutes before closing. Tel. 071-407-0922. Underground: Tower Hill.

Many rallies and political meetings take place around Nelson's Column in the middle of **Trafalger Square**. The **National Gallery** (see "Museums") sits on the north side of the square with the **National Portrait Gallery** (see "Museums") just around the corner. You can buy bird seed from street vendors to feed the masses of pigeons who will settle on your arm, head, or finger to be fed.

The scene of coronations for the last 900 years, **Westminster Abbey** has been the burial place of kings and queens of England and many other heros, artists, and statesmen. Children might enjoy the Poets Corner, the Chapel of the Innocents in the tower of Henry the VII's Chapel, and the museum in the cloisters containing wooden and wax effigies of historic figures and royalty. Nave and cloister free; fee for everything else. Broad Sanctuary, SW1. Daily 8–6; Wed. until 8. Tel. 071-222-5152. Underground: St. James Park, Westminster. At the **Brass Rubbing Centre, Westminster Abbey,** kids can create their own brass rubbing of knights, ladies, priests, children, or many other subjects from the centre's collection of medieval and Tudor brasses. Small fee, materials available. Tel. 071-222-2928.

Just One Look: Museums

The **Bethnal Green Museum of Childhood** houses the Victoria and Albert Museum's famous collection of toys, dolls, children's costumes, and other relics of childhood. There are charming doll houses, hand-painted wooden toys from Germany, toy theaters, soldiers, historical costumes, optical toys, and teddy bears. An Art Room downstairs is open on Saturdays. One child we know insisted on going twice to take it all in. Free. Cambridge Heath Rd., E2. Mon.–Thurs. and Sat. 10–6, Sun. 2:30–6. Tel. 081-980-2415. Underground: Bethnal Green.

The **Geffrye Museum** contains furniture and decorative arts displayed in period room settings. There is an 18th-century woodworking shop, an open kitchen hearth, and more. Kids can pick up great worksheets and puzzles linked to the collection. Free. Kingsland Rd., E2. Tues.–Sat. 10–5, Sun. 2–5. Tel. 071-739-9893. Underground: Liverpool St., then bus 22, 48, or 67.

If your kids can't get enough of old planes, try the **Imperial War Museum,** which has planes, tanks, submarines, and memorabilia from World War I and World War II. It also has a bomb shelter that you can enter and a simulated air raid—bombs explode, sirens go off, lights flash. Free. Lambeth Rd., SE1. Mon.–Sat. 10–5:30, Sun. 2–5:30. Tel. 071-735-8922.

A 10-minute walk from Kew Gardens is the **Kew Bridge Steam Museum,** with the world's largest steam-powered engines used from the Victorian era to the mid-20th century, a working forge, a railway, and other engines. Engines operate on weekends. Fee. Green Dragon Lane, Brentford, Middlesex. Daily 11–5. Tel. 081-568-4757. Underground: Gunnersbury, then 10-minute walk.

The **London Toy and Model Museum,** another museum of childhood, has a large garden with a running model railroad, a railway for children, a carousel, and a vintage bus. Other highlights include a charming postcard collection, tin toy collections, and a fire engine room. Fee. 23 Craven Hill, W2. Tues.–Sat. 10–5:30, Sun. 11–5:30. Tel. 071-262-9450. Underground: Bayswater, Paddington, or Queensway.

The **London Transport Museum** is a delight for kids who love trains, buses, and trolleys. You'll see the development of the London public transportation system, starting with horse-drawn omnibuses.

There are video displays, activity sheets, and even a simulated ride in the driver's seat of the underground. Fee. Covent Garden, WC2. Daily 10–6. Tel. 071-379-6344. Underground: Covent Garden or Leicester Square.

The **Museum of London** traces the history of London chronologically, from prehistoric times to the present. The displays begin with the Stone Age and take you through life in Roman London, the Great Fire of London, the 18th and 19th centuries, and, finally, the 20th century, with suffragettes, zeppelins, and World War II. You'll see what life was like in a Roman kitchen, an 18th-century prison cell, a 19th-century grocery store, and much more. Free. London Wall, EC2. Tues.–Sat. 10–6, Sun. 2–6. Tel. 071-600-3699. Underground: Moorgate.

The **Museum of Mankind** has changing displays on the life and culture of people from all over the world. Films show Tuesday through Friday. Children's worksheets are available at the information desk. Free. Administered by the Ethnography Department of the British Museum, it is housed in a separate location. Burlington Gardens, W1. Mon.–Sat. 10–5, Sun. 2:30–6. Tel. 071-437-2224. Underground: Piccadilly Circus or Green Park.

Don't miss the exceptional **Museum of the Moving Image (MOMI)**, a relatively new, interactive museum, and any kid who loves video, movies, or TV could easily spend a day here. Kids will learn about everything from cinema's earliest experiments to modern animation techniques. They can host a newscast, edit some footage, create their own cartoons for a Zoetrope, and find out what it feels like to fly through the skies of London like Peter Pan. Even the bathroom is an experience; it has music from the movie *Jaws*. Get there early to avoid the crowds. Fee. South Banks Art Centre, Waterloo, SE1. Tues.–Sat. 10–8, Sun. until 6. Tel. 071-401-2636. Underground: Waterloo or Embankment.

The **Musical Museum** was founded in 1963 to allow the public to hear player pianos, but the collection now includes self-playing instruments of all types, with 20,000 music rolls for the piano, self-playing violins, pipe organs, and music boxes, to name a few. Fee. 369 High St., Brentford. Apr.–Oct. Sat. and Sun. 2–5. Tel. 081-560-8108. Underground: Gunnersbury, then 20-minute walk.

The **National Army Museum** relates the history of the British Army from 1485, with arms, armor, uniforms, and the skeleton of Napoleon's poor horse Marengo. Other kids' favorites are the colorful old banners, horse costumes, bayonets, and pikes. There are summer activities for kids in model making and drawing as well as films and children's worksheets. Free. Royal Hospital Rd., SW3. Mon.–Sat. 10–5:30, Sun. 2–5:30. Tel. 071-730-0717. Underground: Sloane Square.

The **National Gallery** houses one of the world's great collections of

European art, with outstanding paintings from all of the major schools from the 13th to the early 20th century. The information desk has children's illustrated worksheets on themes common to many of the paintings, each of which takes about an hour to complete. One sheet on mythology for 5- and 6-year-olds has them searching through the collections for golden apples. Free. Trafalger Square, WC2. Mon.–Sat. 10–6, Sun. 2–6. Tel. 071-839-3321/3526. Underground: Charing Cross.

Just around the corner from the National Gallery is the **National Portrait Gallery,** where you can see pictures of the famous and infamous from all stages of history. If your child is a Winnie-the-Pooh fan, look for the portrait of A. A. Milne with Christopher Robin and Pooh Bear. Quiz and worksheets are available. Fee. St. Martin's Pl., WC2. Mon.–Fri. 10–5, Sat. 10–6, Sun. 2–6. Tel. 071-930-1552. Underground: Charing Cross.

The **Natural History Museum,** next door to the Victoria and Albert, contains a popular dinosaur exhibition, lots of hands-on activities, videos, odd fossils, and interactive machines. A family center is open during summers and school holidays, and the information desk has a wide range of activity sheets for children. Fee. Cromwell Rd., South Kensington SW7. Mon.–Sat. 10–6, Sun. 3–6. Tel. 071-589-6323. Underground: South Kensington.

Pollack's Toy Museum is known for its toy theaters; a toy shop downstairs sells several designs that are still made. Other charming toys from all over the world are on display. Fee. 1 Scala St. Mon.–Sat. 10–5. Tel. 071-636-3452. Underground: Goodge Street.

The **Royal Air Force Museum, Battle of Britain Museum** and **Bomber Command Museum** are all in the same location in Hendon. The Royal Air Force Museum has real planes and scale models of all aircraft ever flown by the RAF. Free. The Battle of Britain Museum has planes that fought in that battle plus other related memorabilia. Fee. The Bomber Command Museum has displays of bomber aircraft. Fee. All located at Grahame Park Way, Hendon NW9. All open Mon.–Sat. 10–6, Sun. 2–6. Tel. 081-205-2266. Underground: Colindale, then 15-minute walk.

Near the Victoria and Albert and Natural History museums is the **Science Museum**, with push button machines and models, famous locomotives, old carriages, cars, airplanes, and exhibitions on space and the history of medicine. A favorite is the launch pad area, which offers lots of fun hands-on opportunities. The Children's Gallery in the rear of the basement is a good place to explore, too. Free. Exhibition Rd., SW7. Mon.–Sat. 10–6, Sun. 2:30–6. Tel. 071-589-3456. Underground: South Kensington.

The **Tate Gallery** houses a world-famous art collection. Try to restrict your visit to viewing the national collection, which includes works by Hogarth, Blake, Turner, and Constable. Children can appreciate William Hogarth's rowdy depictions of life in centuries past and funny caricatures and the dreamy visions of Blake. Free. Millbank St. Mon.–Sat. 10–5:50, Sun. 2–5:50. Underground: Pimlico.

The history of theater, ballet and dance, rock and pop, the circus, puppetry, opera, and the musical stage is found at the **Theatre Museum.** The exhibits, from the Victoria and Albert Museum's collection, include costumes, props, playbills, and more. Fee. 1E Tavistock St. (public entrance on Russell St.), Covent Garden WC2. Tues.–Sun. 11–7. Tel. 071-836-7891. Underground: Covent Garden.

The **Victoria and Albert Museum** is a museum of decorative and fine arts with costumes, furniture, jewelry, medieval art, armor, and musical instruments. Be selective to get the most out of it. This museum has one of the best period costume collections in the world; kids enjoy it because it is put together with a sense of humor. The loud ties, wire-frame bustles, weird shoes, and hair ornaments will have them giggling. Other highlights for most kids seem to be the musical instrument gallery, with the odd giraffe piano, and the Great Bed of Ware, big enough to hold eight adults. Free. Cromwell Rd., South Kensington. Mon.–Sat. 10–5:50, Sun. 2:30–5:50. Tel. 071-589-6371. Underground: South Kensington.

Where the Sidewalk Ends: Zoos and Parks

Battersea Park is a riverside park with a boating lake, playground, sports facilities, beautiful gardens, and a children's petting zoo with pony rides. Puppet shows, band concerts, and other entertainment and special events are held during the summer months. You can picnic in the park or eat at a lakeside cafeteria. Tel. 081-871-7530. Underground: Sloane Square, then bus 137.

Crystal Palace Park has large-scale models of dinosaurs on an island in the boating lake, a playground, a children's zoo, and a fun fair open during the summer. Its National Sports Centre has many facilities, including an artificial ski slope. Tel. 081-778-7148. British Rail: Crystal Palace Station.

Hampstead Heath consists of hundreds of acres of wild parkland about 4 miles from the center of London. In addition to invigorating nature walks, children can watch model boats being sailed in Whitestone Pond, stroll past deer and other animals, and play in the playgrounds. There's a paddling pool, special children's shows, and open-air band concerts in the summer. Tel. 071-0730-3488. Underground: Hampstead.

Hyde Park and the adjoining Kensington Gardens cover 636 acres in central London, making it one of the world's largest city parks. You can row in the Serpentine, a 41-acre lake that runs between Hyde and

Kensington parks or listen to a band concert during summer months. Speakers Corner, inside the gates at Marble Arch, is best on Sundays, when some people still stand to speak on soapboxes. Only treason and obscenity are taboo subjects. Tel. 071-262-5484. Underground: Hyde Park Corner or Marble Arch.

Kensington Gardens contains the famous statue of Peter Pan, who reputedly lived on an island in the Serpentine. A favorite place for children is Round Pond, where you can sail small boats, and the playground in the northwest section with swings donated by Peter's creator. The Elfin Oak is a tree stump with lumps and bumps fashioned into animals, elves, and pixies. There's lots of space to fly kites, plus a pet cemetery and many puppet shows, especially in August. Tel. 071-937-4848. Underground: Queensway or Bayswater for north side of gardens; High Street, Kensington for south side.

Nine miles southwest of London, at Kew, are the Royal Botanic Gardens, known as **Kew Gardens.** In addition to thousands of varieties of plants, Kew Gardens contains lakes, greenhouses, museums, and garden pavilions. Children's quizzes are available. You can travel to Kew in the summer along the Thames by boat or take the subway. Small fee. Daily from 9:30. Closing hours vary from 4:30 to 8, depending on time of sunset. Tel. 081-940-1171. Underground: Kew Gardens.

Regents Park contains the Zoological Gardens, four children's playgrounds, ponds, lakes with canoes and rowboats for hire (summers only, call 071-486-4759), and sporting facilities. There are puppet shows in July and August (check *Time Out* and *City Limits* for listings) as well as military band concerts. The zoo's animal houses each have a distinct architectural style. The canal barge along the Regent's Canal travels through the zoo. Tel. 071-486-7905. Underground: Regents Park, then bus 74.

St. James Park, near Buckingham Palace, has a small children's playground and a large lake with birds and pelicans. There are military band concerts here in the summer, and it's a great park for strolling and running. Tel. 071-930-1793. Underground: St. James Park.

The **London Zoo** is one of the world's great zoos. It houses some 8,000 animals, most famous of which is Chia-Chia, the giant panda. Kids shouldn't miss the bird-eating spider in the insect house and the Sobell Pavilion for Apes and Monkeys. Day and night are reversed in Moonlight World, where kids can view nocturnal creatures going about their nightly habits. The Children's Zoo Farm has animals that are kept as pets, and small children can ride on diminutive Shetland ponies. Fee. Summer 9–6 or dusk; winter 10–dusk. Tel. 071-722-3333. Underground: Baker St., then bus 74Z or Z1.

Whipsnade Park Zoo is the "country home" for some of the animals from the London Zoo. Tour it via the Whipsnade and Umfolozi

Railway through huge paddocks to see the animals close up, or walk around. Many endangered animals are also housed here in open-air exhibits arranged geographically. The children's zoo has a baby-penguin rearing unit. Fee Dunstable, Bedfordshire. Daily 10–6 or sunset, whichever is earlier. Tel. (0582) 872171.

Sports

Watch a game of **cricket** on Sunday afternoons at the Lord's Cricket Ground, St. John's Wood; there is also a Cricket museum (Tel. 071-289-1611). Ask the Londoner next to you to explain the rules. Games are also held at The Oval, Kennington SE11 (Tel. 071-582-6660). For **horseback riding** on Rotten Row, a 2½-mile track in Hyde Park, try Bathurst Riding Stables, 63 Bathurst Mews, W2 (Tel. 071-723-2813) (minimum age 6), or Ross Nye's Riding Establishment, 8 Bathurst Mews, W2 (Tel. 071-262-3791) (minimum age 8). **Ice-skating** rinks are open year-round at the Queen's Ice Skating Club, Queensway W2 (Tel. 071-229-0172) or Silver Blades Ice Rink, 386 Streatham High Rd. (Tel. 081-769-7861). **Rugby** season is autumn through spring at the Rugby Football Ground, Whitton Rd., Twickenham (Tel. 081-892-8161). The **soccer** (called football) season runs fall to spring, and the most popular ball clubs are the Arsenal, Highbury Stadium, Avenell Rd., N5 (Tel. 071-359-0131); the Chelsea at Stamford Bridge, Fulham Rd., SW6 (Tel. 071-381-0111); and West Ham United, Boleyn Ground, Green St., E13 (Tel. 081-470-1325). Good indoor **swimming pools** are Swiss Cottage Centre, Adelaide Rd., NW3 (Tel. 071-586-5989); Putney Swimming Baths, 376 Upper Richmond Rd., SW15 (Tel. 081-789-1124); and The Oasis, 167 High Holborn, WC1 (Tel. 071-836-9555).

Performing Arts

London is known for its theater. Try to find a play the whole family can enjoy. Kids will surprise you with their sophistication; one 8-year-old boy we know loved *Phantom of the Opera*. London is also a town of theater just for kids. There are excellent puppet/marionette troupes in or near London and many Punch and Judy shows in parks, especially in the summer. Check *Time Out* and *City Limits* for specifics.

Little Angel Marionette Theatre has performances for a variety of age groups in one of London's most beautiful little theaters. Reserve by phone for weekend performances. 14 Dagmar Passage, Cross St. N1 (Tel. 071-226-1787). Underground: Angel or Highbury and Islington. The **Polka Children's Theatre** combines puppets and live actors, and has a lovely large theater with changing plays, a garden playground, and an exhibition of puppets and marionettes from around the world. 240 The Broadway, Wimbledon, London SW19. Tel. 081-543-4888. Underground: Wimbledon.

NEAR LONDON

About an hour's train ride from London, in *Maidstone,* is **Leeds Castle.** One of the most beautiful castles in England, it stands in the middle of a lake surrounded by 500 acres of parkland and gardens. It has a funny **dog collar museum** with a 500-year-old collar, gold and silver collars, and other medieval-era collars. Tops with the young set will be the maze, made of 3,000 yew trees, with a secret underground grotto at the center. There is an **Easter egg hunt** on the grounds at Easter, a **country fayre** in April, the **International Hot Air Balloon Fiesta** in June, concerts throughout the summer, and a **fireworks display** in November. Fee. Four miles east of Maidstone. Apr.–Oct. daily 11–6; Nov.–Mar. weekends 12–5. Tel. (0622) 65400.

Hever Castle has a terrific clipped-hedge maze for kids, an adventure playground, beautiful gardens with odd topiary hedges, and a formal Italian garden with classical sculpture. Parents can tour the moated castle, but bring the kids along for a tour of the torture and execution instruments in the gatehouse. Fee. 3 miles SE of Edenbridge. Follow signs from M25 and A21 Sevenoaks turnoff. Easter–Oct. daily 12–5; grounds 11–5. Tel. (0732) 865224.

GREENWICH

Greenwich has a number of sites to make it a delightful day trip out of the city. Take a boat along the Thames (several-hour trip), a bus, or a train to get there. The *Cutty Sark* is the famous clipper ship built in 1869 for the Far East tea trade, and its interior has been restored to that of its famous sailing days. It has a fascinating collection of ship's figureheads, but be sure to notice the one decorating her own bow. *Cutty Sark* means "short shirt" or "short chemise," and that is exactly what she is wearing. Fee. King William Walk, Greenwich Pier. Apr.–Sept. Mon.–Sat. 10–6; Oct.–Mar. Mon.–Sat. 10–5, Sun. 12–5. Tel. 081-858-3445. Right next to the *Cutty Sark* is another boat, the *Gipsy Moth IV,* in which Francis Chichester sailed around the world solo in 1966. Fee. Mon.–Sat. 10:30–6, Sun. 12–6. Tel. 081-858-3445.

The **National Maritime Museum** is the world's largest museum of its kind. You can see ancient boats and royal barges, or climb aboard an old paddle steamer. Displays trace the development of the ship through the ages, from prehistoric log boats to the high-tech Amercia's Cup yachts. You'll see the world's largest ship in a bottle, model ships, swords, medals, maps, and old ship's logs. Stroll up the rolling green from the ships to the **Royal Observatory** and see the Time Ball drop at 1 PM while you stand with one foot in each hemisphere. There are also sundials, an atomic clock, and astronomical and navigational instruments on display. Fee. Romney Rd. Mon.–Sat. 10–6 (winter until 5); Sun. 2–6. Tel. 081-858-4422, ext. 221.

WINDSOR

Windsor and **Windsor Castle** are accessible by a 35-minute train ride from Paddington Station. The Royal Family still resides in the Castle part-time, as have English rulers for the past 900 years. A must-see is Queen Mary's Dollhouse, considered to be the world's best. It has electric lights, tiny keys that open tiny locks, elevators from floor to floor, and a library of tiny books. You can also visit the State Apartments when the royal family isn't there and see the changing of the guards. Small fee. May–Aug. daily, except Sun. at 11. Grounds: daily 10–7:15. Doll house: daily 10:45–7:15. Tel. (0753) 868286.

Windsor Great Park is one of the world's oldest parks; it was mentioned in the *Domesday Book of 1086*. It's a real beauty with lots to discover; take the Long Walk to the top of Snow's Hill for a spectacular view.

Windsor Safari Park, once a royal hunting ground, now houses drive-through animal enclosures for viewing the animals up close. Other attractions for kids include a "Noah's Ark" adventure play center, an alpine toboggan run, animal shows, and a chimpanzee enclosure. Get there when it opens in July and August. Fee. Winkfield Rd. Daily from 10. Tel. (0753) 830886.

Royalty and Empire is housed in the restored railway station that was built in 1897 for Queen Victoria's Diamond Jubilee. Madame Tussaud's is responsible for the superb animated tableaux in which 130 figures re-create the exact moment when Queen Victoria and her entourage stepped off the train to begin celebrating the Diamond Jubilee. Fee. Summer 9:30–5:30; winter until 4:30. Tel. (0753) 857837

THE SOUTHEAST

Counties Kent, East Sussex, West Sussex, and Surrey are within easy access of London with some "delightfully English" villages and beach resorts.

CANTERBURY

Canterbury retains much of its Old World atmosphere, with narrow streets, crumbling walls, old churches, historic inns, and the famous **West Gateway** under whose arch Chaucer's knight, nun, squire, and merchant traveled and told their tales. You can reach Canterbury in about 1½ hours by train from London's Victoria Station.

The walls that once surrounded the city are still standing in some places. Children can climb the **Westgate Tower** for a magnificent view and then tour its museum, filled with arms, armor, shackles, manacles, and instruments of torture. Fee. St. Peter's St. Apr.–Sept. daily, except Sun., 10–1, 2–5; Oct.–Mar. 2–4. Tel. (0227) 452747.

Canterbury Cathedral was England's first Gothic cathedral, and its stained-glass windows are exceptionally beautiful. It was here that Thomas Beckett was dramatically murdered by four knights in 1170 because he refused to put the demands of the king above those of the church. Twelve stained-glass windows tell his life story. Evensong masses take place Mon.–Fri. at 5:30 and Sat.–Sun. at 3:15. Free. Cathedral open Mon.–Sat. 9–5 (summer until 6); Sun. 12:30–2:30, 4:30–5:30. Tel. (0227) 762862.

Join 14th-century pilgrims on their journey to Canterbury at the **Canterbury Pilgrim's Way,** housed in the shell of medieval St. Margaret's Church. As the sun rises, you begin your pilgrimage at the Tabard Inn in London. Traveling along, listen to the tales of the courtly Knight, the Wife of Bath, the Pardoner, and more. Wax figures, real people dressed in costumes, slides, and moving sets are used to tell its tale of medieval adventure and chivalry. Fee. St. Margaret's St. Apr.–Oct. daily 9–7; Nov.–Mar. 9–5:30. Tel. (0227) 454888.

The **Canterbury Festival of the Arts** begins in late September with a costume parade and stage performances in the cathedral and historic buildings. Contact the Canterbury Festival, 59 Ivy Ln., Canterbury. Booking agency is Forwood Bookings, 37 Palace St. Tel. (0227) 55600.

DOVER AND ENVIRONS

Dover and its famous white cliffs have welcomed tourists to and from England for years. **Dover Castle,** built in the 12th century, sits on a cliff on the eastern side of the city. You can wander for hours around the towers, keep, and underground passages leading into the cliffs. The exhibition "All the Queen's Men" traces the history of the British army. **The Pharos,** a Roman lighthouse, has stood alongside the castle for over 1,900 years. Fee. Castle Rd. Apr.–Sept. daily 10–6; Oct.–Dec. 10–4. Tel. (0304) 201628. On the opposite hill from Dover Castle is the **Grand Shaft,** a 140-foot triple spiral staircase cut into the white cliffs on Snargate Street. Built in 1804, it was part of a series of Napoleonic fortifications. Small fee. May–Sept. 2–5; winter months by arrangement. Tel. (0304) 201066.

Most beaches along the southeast coast north of Dover, such as those in *Broadstairs* and *Ramsgate*, have children's play areas with trampolines, ice cream kiosks, Punch and Judy theaters, and amusement arcades. Broadstairs is famous as the home of Charles Dickens, and the **Dickens House Museum,** which contains personal belongings and letters, is located along its main seafront. *Margate* has an underground shell grotto, Bembom's Theme Park, and lots of children's facilities on its sandy beaches. *New Romney* is an historic old smugglers' town with a good beach.

THE COAST BETWEEN DOVER AND PORTSMOUTH

Folkestone is the site of the Eurotunnel, which will connect England with the rest of the European continent in 1993. The **Eurotunnel Exhibition Centre** has a display of the plans for the Channel tunnel. There is a model railroad exhibit of tunnels and terminals, a full-size mock-up of a section of a tunnel train, and a viewing tower. Fee. Cheriton High St. Summer Tues.–Sun. 10–6; winter until 5. Tel. (0303) 70111.

Hastings is a seaside town with a ruined castle, underground caves, and a fisherman's quarter. The **Smugglers Adventure at St. Clement's Caves** offers a fun tour of inland caves that served as headquarters for smugglers for hundreds of years. Victorians used the caves as a romantic, candle-lit ballroom. Now a smugglers museum, sights and sounds recall the time of the cave's smuggling heyday. Fee. West Hill. Apr.–June 10–6; July–Aug. 10–8; Sept.–Oct. 10–6. Tel. (0424) 422964). The **National Town Criers' Championships** are held here each August.

Eastbourne has all the diversions of a seaside resort, with a 3-mile-long seafront, pier, gardens, bandstand, fort, nature reserve, and wind surfing. Its children's adventure playground, **Treasure Island,** has models of Long John Silver, Jim Hawkins, and jungle animals. There are also paddling pools, slides, and go carts. Small fee. Along the Royal Parade. Apr.–mid.-Oct. 10–6. Tel. (0323) 411077. At the eastern end of the seafront is the **Sovereign Centre,** offering all-day, all-weather family fun with swimming pools, slides, a toddlers' play area, and other facilities. Fee.

Brighton, directly south of London, is a lively resort town with two piers, a huge fun fair with rides for all ages, colorful lights, beach chairs, three indoor swimming pools, crazy water slides, and everything to make it a memorable stop for the kids. A trolley/train called **Volk's Electric Railway** takes you up and down the beach, stopping half way at **Peter Pan's Playground,** the seafront amusement area. The steep beaches here are pebbly rather than sandy, so leave your sand buckets and shovels behind. Kids will want to taste Brighton Rock, a rainbow-colored candy stick with the word *Brighton* spelled out in red sugar all the way through. Cars are not allowed in **The Lanes,** a 1-square-mile area of narrow winding streets filled with shops, pubs, and restaurants, in the middle of which is Brighton Square, with open-air cafes. The **Royal Pavilion** is an exotic and ornate Indian-style building that your kids will think is right out of the Arabian nights. **Brighton Aquarium Entertainment Centre** has dolphin shows, sharks, sea lions, and all of the other standard features of an aquarium, plus an indoor playground called The Pirates' Deep for kids 2–14. Fee. On the seafront. Daily 9–5. Tel. (0273) 604234. The **Brighton Festival,** held in May, encompasses music of all kinds, theater, opera, poetry, and fireworks as well as more offbeat performances.

Arundel, a medieval town west of Brighton, has the large Norman **Arundel Castle** and a huge **cathedral.** Its **Toy and Military Museum** has a good collection of toy soldiers and dolls, doll houses, and teddy bears housed in a small Georgian cottage. Be sure to see the collection of pocillery (egg cups). Fee. 23 High St. Jun.–Aug. 10:30–5; Sat. and Sun. 12–5 rest of year. Tel. (0903) 883101.

Near Arundel is *Amberley* and its **Chalk Pits Museum,** with an exhibition on industrial history. It's set in 36 acres of a former chalk quarry and limeworks with a narrow-gauge railway. Kids who appreciate vintage objects will enjoy the old radios and lawn mowers. Resident craftsmen demonstrate their skills in boat building, blacksmithing, printing, pottery, and wood turning. Nature trails show off a collection of woodland plants and views of the Arun Valley. Fee. Houghton Bridge. Apr.–Oct. Wed.–Sun. 10–5; daily during summer school holidays. Tel. (0798) 831370.

Bognor Regis has a nice beach with children's play areas, pedalboats, ice cream and snacks, a miniature railway, and special holiday activities for children. Each April, an **International Clown Convention** takes place in the town center [Tel. (0903) 716133 for information].

Long a navy town and important seaport, *Portsmouth* has many seafaring-related attractions, all in the Portsmouth Naval Heritage Area. Nelson's flagship, **HMS *Victory,*** is open for exploring in Portsmouth's historic dockyard, where she has been meticulously restored to her appearance before the Battle of Trafalger. Fee. #2 Drydock. HM Naval Base. Mon.–Sat. 10:30–5:30, Sun. 1–5:30. Tel. (0705) 819604. The **Royal Naval Museum,** devoted to the history of the Navy, contains models of ships, uniforms, and medals. Fee. HM Naval Base. Daily 10:30–5. Tel. (0705) 733060. The *Mary Rose,* built in the 16th century for Henry VIII, keeled over and sank for no known reason in 1545. She was miraculously raised from the deep in 1982, and you can see the restoration work in progress from specially constructed viewing galleries and visit an exhibition of relics found with her. Fee. College Rd., HM Naval Base. Daily 10:30–5. Tel. (0705) 750521. **Portsmouth Fort** has subterranean passages and lovely views.

The town of *Southsea,* right next to Portsmouth, is a popular seaside resort with good beaches and amusements. Enough of historical sites? Visit **The Pyramids,** an indoor resort with pools with rolling waves, two superflumes, fountain bubblers, and geysers. Then dry off and explore Mr. Chuckles Fun Factory, with its maze of towers, ladders, walkways, and games. Fee. Clarence Esplanade. Call for hours. Tel. (0705) 294444.

THE SOUTH—ALONG THE COAST FROM SOUTHAMPTON TO WEYMOUTH

SOUTHAMPTON

Southampton, an important port since the Middle Ages, was the port from which the *Mayflower* set sail. Near Southampton is **Paultons Park,** a place to visit when your kids need a break from historical sites. One admission price allows you to visit an elaborate adventure playground and the Kids Kingdom; see owls, peacocks, flamingos, emus, and other exotic wildlife; bounce on crazy trampolines; go on rides, ride the Rio Grande railway; and more. Fee. Off exit 2 on the M27. Mid-Mar.–Oct. 10–6:30. Tel. (0703) 814442.

THE ISLE OF WIGHT

Children love the short ferry crossing to the *Isle of Wight.* Although touristy in the summer, it has the reputation of being one of the sunniest places in England with many attractions for families. The best towns for kids are **Ryde, Seaview, St. Helens, Sandown,** and **Lake.** There are many more attractions than those mentioned here, such as butterfly parks, pirate's ships, windmills, aquariums, bird parks, and children's fun parks. Tourist brochures listing them are readily available everywhere.

Osborne House was used by Queen Victoria as a retreat. Children love the Swiss Cottage in the gardens, which was built as a playroom for the royal children. Fee. East Cowes. Apr.–Oct. daily 10–5. Tel. (0983) 200022.

Once a prison for King Charles I, **Carisbrooke Castle** now houses the **Isle of Wight Museum.** A favorite with kids is the Well House, where donkeys take turns treading a large wooden wheel which draws up buckets of water. Fee. Two miles southwest of Newport. Mar.–Oct. 9:30–6:30 (winter until 4), Sun. 2–6. Tel. (0983) 522107.

The **Model Village** in Godshill has charming tiny thatched cottages, stone churches, miniature gardens, trees, and tiny figures. In Old Vicarage Gardens. Apr.–Sept. Mon.–Sat. 10–5:30, Sun. 2–5:30. Tel. (0983) 840270. Kids love the touristy **Blackgang Chine Fantasy Theme Park**, with a wild West town, sawmill, model village, jungleland, nurseryland, smugglers cave, giant dinosaur models, and more. Originally opened in 1843, the park has been run by the same family ever since. It's illuminated at night during the summer. Fee. Blackgang. Apr.–Oct. 10–5; Jun.–Sept. 10–10. Tel. (0983) 730330. In the same vein, The **Robin Hill Adventure and Zoological Park** has a section called "Freeriderland," where kids can ride BMX bikes, play on paddleboats and grass sledges, or try their hands at archery. The zoo has about 100 species of animals in large walk-through enclosures. Woodland walks through the park's 80 acres are available. Fee. Downend, near Arreton. Mar.–Oct. daily 10–6. Tel. (0983) 527352.

BOURNEMOUTH AND ENVIRONS

Bournemouth is a large Victorian resort town known for its beautiful parks and gardens. It has a bandstand, two amusement piers, and 7 miles of sandy beaches. Four times a year during the summer, children light 21,000 candles in the lower gardens. Each candle sits in a colored jar and makes part of a picture within a frame: animals, flowers, ships, etc. Dates can be obtained from the Bournemouth **tourist office** at Westover Road, Bournemouth BH1 2BU [Tel (0202) 291715]. You can see one of the illuminations during the **Regatta and Carnival** in August along with fireworks and other festivities. All the sporting facilities of a resort town can be found here, too: miniature or "crazy" golf; indoor and outdoor swimming pools, including one with a wave-making machine; ice-skating; tennis; and nature trails. There is even a free children's beach club between the two piers during summer holidays, and a special children's week in late August with Punch and Judy shows, parachuting teddy bears, kite flying, and more.

One mile east of Bournemouth is *Christchurch,* which has an odd little **Tricycle Museum** containing a collection of adult's and children's trikes from the past several hundred years. Fee. Quay Rd. Easter–Oct. 10–5:30; weekends only the rest of the year. Tel. (0202) 479849.

Southwest of Bournemouth are the romantic ruins of **Corfe Castle.** Nearby, and of greater interest to kids, is the **Corfe Castle Model Village,** which shows what Corfe Castle looked like before it was laid to ruin by Oliver Cromwell and his men in 1645. The miniature model village is alive with horses, wagons, and tiny people from the castle's heyday. Fee. Easter–Sept. daily 10–6; Oct. Sun.–Thurs. 11–4. Tel. (0929) 481234 or 423700.

An attraction also within easy driving distance of Bournemouth is the **Dorset Heavy Horse Centre.** On the edge of the New Forest, it has examples of many huge horses, such as Shires, Clydesdales, Ardennes, Percheron, and Suffolk Punch. For those who don't think big is better, a collection of miniature and toy ponies has been added over the last couple of years. There is a playground, displays of farm carts and farming implements, daily parades, and harnessing demonstrations. Fee. Brambles Farm, Edmonsham. Easter–Oct. daily 10–6. Tel. (0202) 824040.

Weymouth is another popular seaside resort to the west of Bournemouth. In addition to many typical British resort facilities, it has an old man who creates sand sculptures on the main beach and then paints them. Each lasts about 2 to 4 weeks. Chesal Beach, west of Weymouth, has 15 miles of pebbly beaches and a famous swannery. The famous Weymouth Kite Festival takes place in June. Contact the **tourist office** for details [Tel. (0305) 772444].

THE SOUTH: INLAND

Winchester, once the political and religious capital of England, is one of England's most ancient cities. The **Great Hall of Winchester Castle** houses what is claimed to be King Arthur's Round Table, which is 18 feet in diameter and is believed to be 700 years old. Free. Castle Ave. off High St. Daily 10–5; Nov.–Feb. until 4. Six miles south of Winchester is **Marwell Zoological Park,** a wildlife conservation and breeding center. Besides herds of rare species and many typical zoo animals, there are train rides through the park, a children's farmyard, play area, and picnic sites. Fee. Bishop's Waltham Rd. Daily from 10. Tel. (096 274) 406.

NEW FOREST

New Forest is a 90,000-acre wildlife preserve whose name was chosen by William the Conquerer when he claimed it as a hunting preserve. Many small picturesque towns and villages are sprinkled through it, and wild horses and ponies, deer, badgers, and other animals wander about. Ponies have the right of way on roads in the area, and visitors are asked not to feed them. Pony trekking and riding on tame horses is popular here, and it is easy to find places to rent them. Walking is popular, too. You can see the New Forest by taking a horse-drawn wagon from Balmer Lawn Road, near Brockenhurst, into peaceful wooded enclosures.

Beaulieu sits in the heart of the New Forest and is the home of **Beaulieu Abbey and Palace House.** On the palace grounds is the **National Motor Museum,** which contains an exceptional collection of vintage to modern cars and motorcycles. A special exhibition, called **Wheels,** takes you on a journey in a little electric car through the history of the automobile. There are car and bike rides for kids, radio-controlled model cars, and a miniature railway world. One fee admits you to the palace, gardens, abbey, museum, and one ride. Apr.–Oct. daily 10–6; Nov.–Mar. until 5. Tel. (0590)612123. On the western edge of the New Forest is **Breamore House,** an Elizabethan manor house noted for its collection of tapestries. There's medieval jousting, two mazes, a carriage museum, and a countryside museum. Fee. In Breamore, near Fordingbridge. Open hours vary; call for schedule. Tel. (0725) 22233.

THE WEST: SOMERSET, AVON, AND DORSET COUNTIES

BATH

About an hour's high-speed train ride southwest of London, *Bath* is an ancient Roman resort town and a city made for strolling. Much of it was built when Bath was a very fashionable spa retreat for 18th-century Londoners. As you wander through the streets filled with shops selling antiques and books, you feel part of a different era. Several families we interviewed used Bath as their headquarters to tour London as well as the English countryside.

Kids may enjoy a quick visit through the **Roman Baths and Pump Room** for a picture of life in Roman Britain. The bath (from which the city gets its name) is lined with its original lead sheets, now almost 2,000 years old. The pump room upstairs has morning and afternoon concerts; you can sip a glass of cloudy water while you listen, or opt for Bath buns and tea. The museum contains a wide variety of archaeological finds from the Roman period as well as Victorian objects. Fee. Abbey Churchyard. Mar.–Jun. and Sept.–Oct. daily 10–6; July and Aug. 9–7; Nov.–Feb. Mon.–Sat. 9–5; Sun. 10–5. Tel. (0225) 61111. Housed in the Assembly Rooms, the **Museum of Costume** contains four centuries of fashion, with each period in its own room. Take the guided tour, it's full of funny trivia and facts. Fee. Bennett St. Hours and phone same as Roman Baths.

If the kids are homesick, take them to the **American Museum,** 2½ miles east of town. Billed as the first American museum outside of the U.S., kids will undoubtedly appreciate the "teas with American cookies" more than the rooms full of historical furnishings. Other hits with the young are the Hopi kachina dolls, teepees, and Conestoga wagon. Fee. Claverton Manor. Mar.–Oct. Tues.–Sun. 2–5. Tel. (0225) 60503.

For 17 days in May and June, Bath hosts the **International Festival,** one of Europe's most prestigious music and arts festivals. Concerts take place in some of the city's most fascinating buildings. Reservations required. Bath Festival Office, Linley House, 1 Pierrepont Pl. Bath, BA1 1JY. Tel. (0225) 62231.

NEAR BATH

Not too far from Bath is **Longleat House,** the home of the 6th Marquess of Bath, whose son, Lord Weymouth, turned the 16th-century family estate into many attractions. You can buy a ticket for all fifteen attractions, which include a visit to the estate, a drive-through safari park, the world's largest maze, a children's adventure playground with a daring free-fall slide, butterfly house, safari boats, a small train ride, doll house, and more. Go early in the summer to avoid the crowds. Fee. A portion of the proceeds goes to the World Wildlife Fund. Midway between Bath and Salisbury on the A362. Mar.–Oct. 11–6. Tel. (09853) 551.

Littlecote Park is a magnificent Tudor manor in a large garden. There are daily falconry displays and jousting, plus an adventure playground, rare-breeds farm, steam train, car collection, and more. Many special events are held on summer weekends. Fee. Near Hungerford/Marlborough off the M4 and A4. Mid-Mar.–Oct. 10–6. Tel. (0488) 84000.

Stonehenge is the best-known example of a Druid's Circle, which is a group of ancient stones. It has recently been fenced off because of hordes of visitors, so you can't get up close, but you can get a good view from a distance. How the stones got there and how they were put in position is a mystery which kids find most fascinating. Fee. On the A303. For more information, call the **West Country Tourist Board** [Tel. (0392) 76351].

Avebury is a monument consisting of huge stone circles set inside banks and ditches, while a mile-long row of stones lead off to Oveton Hill, a small village with a museum. Most people who are interested in henge monuments like Avebury best. Eighteen miles from Stonehenge off the A4 between Marlborough and Calne. For more information call West Country **Tourist Board.**

BRISTOL

Bristol, just 10 miles west of Bath, has been an important port city since the Middle Ages. An exhibit of its maritime history can be seen in the **Bristol Maritime Heritage Centre.** The SS *Great Britain,* the world's first luxury liner and iron steamship, sits next door. Fee. Great Western Dock, Gas Ferry Rd. off Cumberland Rd. Both open 10–5; summer until 6. Tel. (0272) 260680. Walk along 17th-century King Street for a taste of old Bristol. Stop for a bite at **Ye Llandoger Trow,** an inn where pirates used to carouse and where Daniel Defoe met the man who inspired the tale *Robinson Crusoe.* Bristol has a number of odd specialty museums such as the **National Lifeboat Museum** and **Dauphine's Theatrical and Historical Costume Collection,** with its historical display on the fashion wig. In August, the skies are filled with the vibrant colors of hot-air balloons flying in the **Bristol International Balloon Fiesta.** Ashton Court Estate. For dates, contact the Park Dept. [Tel. (0272) 266031]. Four miles northwest of Bristol, in *Henbury,* is the **Blaise Castle House Museum,** with a collection of historical folk toys, costumes, crafts, and memorabilia. There are walkways and attractions for children. Fee. Wed.–Sat. 2–5. Tel. (0272) 506789.

NEAR BRISTOL

South of Bristol is *Wells,* a town with a beautiful English **Gothic cathedral** containing a well-preserved clock with performing figures. Every 15 minutes, four knights on horseback joust while Jack Bladiver rings bells with his hands and feet. Inside the cathedral, kids can hunt for carved figures showing life as it was in the 12th and 13th centuries, such as a man suffering from a toothache, another with a thorn in his foot, and a farmer chasing a fox. The effigies of knights in armor are especially good. Famous bell-ringing swans live at the **Bishop's Palace,** next door to the cathedral. The swans swim the moat, and when they want to be fed, they pull on a rope attached to the wall.

At **Wookey Hole Caves and Mill,** two miles from Wells, you'll find some of the most spectacular caves in Britain. Walk along high, suspended catwalks while you tour the brightly illuminated caves, then watch the Victorian Paper Mills produce handmade paper, play games in the Edwardian penny arcade, and tour the old-time "Fairground by Night" exhibition. Wookey Hole, Wells, Somerset. Summer daily 9:30–5:30; winter 10:30–4:30. Tel. (0749) 72243.

A 15-minute drive from Wookey Hole are the **Cheddar Showcaves,** within Cheddar Gorge. Visitors walk along ½ mile of easy trails through passages and chambers in Gough's Cave, passing elaborate stalactite and stalagmites, pools of still water, and glistening rocks and minerals. Accompanied by an experienced guide, adventurous kids over 12 can try caving through dark tunnels and hard-to-reach places. Wear sturdy clothes and shoes; helmets, caver's lamps, and boiler suits are supplied. Advance booking recommended. Outside,

climb the 322 steps to the top of Prospect Tower for a view of the
Mendip Hills, sample the Beginning Orienteering Course, or stroll
through Gough's Cave Museum, with Paleolithic tools and the skeleton of 9,000-year-old Cheddar Man. Fee. On the A371. Daily 10–
5:30; winter 10:30–4:30. Tel. (0934) 742343.

On the Devon and Dorset county border is the tiny beach resort and
fishing village of **Lyme Regis.** The cliffs above the beach contain
fossils, which fall down on the beach so your young ones can collect
them. This charming 18th-century town was the setting for John
Fowles's novel and the film *The French Lieutenant's Woman.*

THE WEST: DEVON COUNTY

Devon is about a 5-hour drive from London. Its Atlantic coast is
rugged and brisk, with cliffs and sandy beaches, whereas the southern coastline is milder, with red cliffs and lovely bays. ***Dartmoor
National Park's*** heather-covered hills are in the southern part of the
county. Prehistoric sites abound, and it is a wonderful place for the
hiker or walker. The tors, or granite outcroppings at the top of hills
are frequently shrouded in fog and mist, giving them an eerie feel.
Conan Doyle's *Hound of the Baskervilles* was set here. ***Widecomb-in-
the-Moor*** is a small picturesque village in the moors nearby. Although it can be crowded in the summer, it's absolutely charming.
There are many places to rent horses; most stables are licensed and
guides accompany you on your trek.

ALONG THE SOUTHERN DEVON COAST

Exeter Maritime Museum has an enormous collection of English
and foreign boats; its larger boats moored in the canal basin can be
boarded. You'll see canoes, junks from Hong Kong, Arab *dhows*, and
the oldest working steamboat. During the summer you can rent one of
five Portuguese *chatas* and cruise along the 3 miles of navigable water
on the canal. Fee. Haven. Sept.–June daily 10–5; July–Aug. 10–6.
Tel. (0392) 58075. Eleven miles southeast of Exeter is the town of
Exmouth, home of **À la Ronde,** a 16-sided home decorated by two
Victorian ladies with rows and rows of seashells placed in beautiful
patterns. Fee. Two miles north of town on Summer Lane. Easter–Oct.
Mon.–Sat. 10–6, Sun. 2–7. Tel. (0395) 265514.

Paignton is a beach town made popular by Victorians. Its beaches
have paddleboats; Paignton Beach has a pier with an amusement
arcade. Many festivals take place during the summer, including **Children's Week** in August, with competitions for the best sidewalk art,
donkey rides, brass bands, fireworks, and sandcastle competitions.

Fifteen miles west of Plymouth is the **Monkey Sanctuary** in *Looe,* where rare South American woolly monkeys are bred. You can walk through their habitat and observe them happily going about their business. Not recommended for kids under 4. Fee. July–Aug. Sun.–Thurs. 10:30–5; mid-Apr.–June and Sept. Sun., Wed., Thurs. 10:30–5. Tel. (05036) 2532.

THE WEST: CORNWALL

The southernmost county of England, often called "the toe," Cornwall was once a favorite haunt of smugglers and pirates. A mild climate and beautiful beaches make it a popular summer vacation spot. A Celtic culture, rather than an Anglo-Saxon one, predominates here. The northern side is wild and rugged; the southern coastline is warm. This is King Arthur country, and myths and legends abound. Cornwall is also the surf center of England. While teenagers familiar with the surf in Malibu may turn up their noses, wet-suited surfers can be seen in Newquay, St. Ives, Widemouth Bay, and Bude.

NORTH CORNWALL

In *Bolventor* kids will get a kick out of Victorian taxidermist Walter Potter's **Museum of Curiosity,** with its stuffed animals in nursery-rhyme settings such as the Guinea Pig's Cricket Match and the Kitten's Tea Party, with thirty-seven kittens dressed in the clothes of the day playing croquet and taking tea. Other oddball displays include a church made from pigeon feathers, an authentic cannibal's fork, and the largest shoe in the world, made to fit a giant in 1851. Fee. In the Jamaica Inn in Bolventor (10 miles east of Bodmin). Daily 10–6. Tel. (0566) 86250.

Tintagel is supposedly the birthplace of King Arthur, and you can view the ruins of the castle where he was born. The castle and its setting are most impressive; you can almost hear the hooves of Arthur's and Lancelot's horses thunder past. Your young knights in shining armor can rent horses from the local stables to explore the area. Walk along the moors here; it is truly inspiring.

MID-CORNWALL

Newquay, with its 7 miles of beaches, is the premier resort on this coast. Most of the beaches have fun castles and kids' play areas along with deck chairs for weary parents, snack bars, and ice-cream stands. Some have amusement arcades and surf boards to rent. **Tunnels Through Time,** sort of a kitsch wax museum, contains scenarios related to Cornwall's history. Kids will like the Dungeon of Despair, with its torture scenes. Fee. St. Michael's Road. Easter–Oct. 10–dusk. Tel. (0637) 873379.

Goonhavern has the **World in Miniature,** where in one afternoon you can see all the sights of the world. Twenty perfect miniature models of sights such as the Leaning Tower of Pisa, the Taj Mahal, the Pyramids, and the Statue of Liberty stand amidst 11 acres of gardens. There is also a wild West town and an adventure dome with a 3-D film experience. Fee. On the B3285. Mid-Mar.–Oct. 9:30–dusk. Tel. (0872) 572828.

WEST CORNWALL

Penzance, warmer than many other places in England, is popular as a year-round resort. The town is a bit touristy but has many activities just for kids as well as an interesting old town. From Penzance you can go to **St. Michael's Mount,** which rises out of the sea to a height of 230 feet. Just like its sister of the same name in France, you can walk across at low tide to the island.

Helston has **Flambards Triple Theme Park,** with thrilling children's rides and amusements such as the Demon Dropslide and Bumper Boats. Its authentic Victorian village has period shops, fashions, and carriages. **Britain in the Blitz** is a popular re-creation of the Blitz experience. **Aeropark** has a Battle of Britain War Gallery, helicopters, Concorde flight deck, and 3D superscreen. Fee. Easter–Oct. daily 10–5; later in July and Aug. Tel. (0326) 573404.

THE HEART OF ENGLAND: FROM STRATFORD TO THE WELSH BORDER

This area encompasses the counties of Gloucestershire, Herefordshire, Shropshire, Worcestershire, West Midlands, Warwickshire, and Staffordshire.

STRATFORD-UPON-AVON

Visit **Shakespeare's Birthplace** and see a period kitchen and the bedroom where England's greatest writer was born. A small museum chronicles his life. Fee. Henley St. Open daily. Tel. (0789) 204016. The **Royal Shakespeare Company** performances are one of the main attractions in Stratford. Arrange for tickets in advance from your travel agent. Most performances take place in the **Royal Shakespeare Theatre,** which also has an interesting collection of costumes, props, and staging devices used for Shakespeare's plays through the ages. Budding young actors and actresses will always remember the backstage tours, booked in advance. Small fee. The collection is open

Mon.–Sat. 9:15–6:30, Sun. 12–5. Tel. (0789) 296655, ext. 215. The **Royal Shakespeare Collection,** housed at the Swan Theatre, in back of the Royal Shakespeare, has costumes, wigs, and helmets kids can try on. When your kids need a change of pace, rent a **rowboat** or **punt,** on the Avon River. As you float along, swans glide past you while cows and weeping willows grace the banks. The enchanting **Teddy Bear Museum,** housed in a beautiful 16th-century Elizabethan house, has hundreds of cleverly displayed bears from all around the world, including famous storybook bears and bears owned by celebrities. Fee. 19 Greenhill St. Daily 9:30–6. Tel. (0789) 293160. **Stratford-upon-Avon Butterfly and Jungle Safari** may not have tremendous historical significance, but it can provide a welcome break after too much Shakespeare. Don't miss Insect City, which has a particularly gruesome selection of bugs. Fee. Open daily; call for times. Tel. (0789) 299288.

NEAR STRATFORD

Warwick, between Stratford and Coventry, contains the popular and much visited **Warwick Castle,** a 14th-century fortress with a 17th-century mansion inside. It was beautifully restored in the 1970s by the owners of Madame Tussaud's. Don't miss the tour of the private apartments in which a 19th-century party is going on; life-size figures and sound effects allow you to feel like a fly on the wall. Kids will also enjoy the dungeon and torture chamber, towers, and peacocks roaming the beautiful grounds. Live entertainment and colorful pageants are held throughout the year. Considered one of England's finest medieval castles, it can be quite crowded during the summer. Visit the castle early in the day and then visit the grounds after the tour buses arrive. Fee. Mar.–Oct. daily, 10–5:30; Nov.–Feb. 10–4:30. Tel. (0926) 495421.

Ragley Hall, 8 miles from Stratford, is a restored 17th-century Palladian home containing magnificent family treasures and beautifully landscaped gardens. Kids will enjoy the adventure playground, maze, snakes and ladders, cricket pitch, and farm and woodland walks. You can picnic by the sailing lake, get a home-baked meal at the bakeshop, and wander through the stables or carriage collection. Fee. Two miles from Alcester on the A435. Park: Apr.–Sept. Tues.–Thurs., Sat., Sun. 10–5:30. House: Apr., May, Sept. Tues.–Thurs., Sat., Sun. 12–5; June–Aug. 10–5. Tel. (0789) 762090.

COVENTRY

Coventry is the town where Lady Godiva made her famous au naturel ride. Now principally an industrial town where cars and motorcycles are manufactured, it's home to the **Museum of British Road Transport,** which contains the largest municipally owned vehicle collection in the U.K. You'll see the Thrust 2, which holds the land-speed record, a 1910 taxi driven over 1 million miles, royal limos, bicycles, and more. Small fee. St. Agnes Lane. Hale St. Apr.–Sept. Mon.–Fri. 10–4, Sat. and Sun. 10–5:30; Oct.–Mar. Fri. 9:30–4, Sat. and Sun. 10–5. Tel. (0203) 832425.

The original **Coventry Cathedral** was largely destroyed during World War II, and it is in ruins today. The new and somewhat controversial cathedral features exceptional modern tapestry and stained-glass work. It may be one of the only modern cathedrals your children will get to see. In the undercroft of the cathedral is an exhibit called **The Spirit of Coventry** with an exciting walkway of holograms where you walk through sound, light, and special effects. Fee for guided cathedral tours and special exhibit. 7 Priory Row. Open daily. Tel. (0203) 27597.

The **Coventry Toy Museum** contains dolls, trains, games, and dollhouses from about 1750 to 1951. Small fee. Much Street Park. Daily 2–5. Tel. (0203) 27560.

THE COTSWOLDS

The Cotswolds, a region of gently rolling hills and medieval towns, is filled with homes and buildings made from the soft golden-colored stone mined from the Cotswold Hills. Many families we know make this their base from which to explore the charming villages with plenty of engaging activities for children. Some of the most picturesque towns include Stow-on-the-Wold, Lower and Upper Slaughter, Chipping Camden, Bibury, and Castle Combe (the town where the film *Dr. Dolittle* was shot). Ask the BTA to send you a thick brochure called "Places to Visit in the Heart of England," which lists castles, nature trails, stately homes, farms, and carriage collections in this area.

Fifteenth-century **Royal Sudeley Castle** is 6 miles northeast of *Cheltenham.* Its notable art collection includes works by Constable, Turner, Rubens, and Van Eyck; children will enjoy its collection of dolls and toys. Outside, peacocks wander through its formal gardens, and there is an adventure playground and falconry exhibition. Local artisans work on the grounds producing marbled paper, stained glass, wooden furniture, and leather articles. Fee. Winchcombe off A46. Mid-Mar.–Oct. noon–5. Tel. (0242) 602308.

Burford, a charming, unspoiled medieval town, was once the center of the wool trade. Its **Cotswold Wildlife Park** has safari-park animals, an adventure playground, a narrow-gauge railroad, falconry displays, and a brass-rubbing center. Fee. Just off the A40 and A361 junction. Daily 10–6. Tel. (099) 3823006.

Cotswold Farm Park and Rare Breeds Centre, a five-star site with both kids and parents, contains the country's most comprehensive collection of rare breeds of British farm animals, plus an adventure playground, pets' corner, and farm trails. You'll see rams with four horns, red-wooled sheep, bristly striped prehistoric pigs, and other strange-looking cows, goats, and chickens. Fee. Near Guiting Power off the B4077. Easter–Sept. daily 10:30–6. Tel. (04515) 307.

Bourton-on-the-Water boasts a number of unusual attractions for families. The **Old New Inn,** built in 1709, has an enchanting miniature **model village** in its garden. One 9-year-old we know insists on visiting it every year during her family's annual trek to the Cotswolds. The model village is a miniature copy of Bourton-on-the-Water, and it's created from the same honey-colored stone. Trees are bonzaied, and music emanates from the 3-foot-high church. Visit the real town first and then check out the same shops and buildings in small scale. Of particular appeal is the model of the model village itself. Daily 9–6; winter 10–4. Tel. (0451) 20467. Nearby, **Birdland/Windrush Trout Farm** has animals that fly or swim. Birdland has 1,200 birds on display, including everything from penguins to hummingbirds, while the Trout Farm has fish to view and fish to catch. Small fee. Rissington Rd. Mar.–Nov. 10:30–6. Tel. (0451) 20480. The **Cotswold Perfumery** has an exhibition of perfumery and a perfume garden with the amusing "smelly-vision" in a specially constructed theater. Small fee. Jan.–Dec. Mon.–Sat. 9–5, Sun. 10–5, later in summer. Tel. (0451) 20698.

Alton has one of Europe's leading leisure parks, **Alton Towers,** with five theme areas and over 100 rides and attractions set in 300 acres of some of the most beautiful 19th-century gardens in Europe. Among the major attractions are a Chinese temple, rock gardens, and pagoda fountain. Take your kids here when they won't put up with another historic site and let them run loose while you enjoy the gardens. Fee. On highway B5032. Mid-Mar.–Oct. 10–6. Tel. (0528) 702200.

Gloucester is a charming little half-timbered town built on the lines of a Roman city. Next to its beautiful cathedral is the **Beatrix Potter Museum.** Beatrix Potter lived there while she wrote *The Tailor of Gloucester,* and your children will recognize it as the house depicted in the book. The **Jubilee Maze and Maze Museum** is 18 miles west of Gloucester, in *Symonds Yat.* Here you'll find a huge hedge maze to get lost in and a museum devoted to displays about real mazes. Small fee. Off the A40. Apr.–Oct. 11–5:30. Tel. (0600) 890360.

EAST ANGLIA

This section of England is made up of the counties of Norfolk, Suffolk, and part of Cambridgeshire and Essex. It juts out into the North Sea and is flat and filled with marshes loaded with birdlife.

Not too far from **Norwich** is the **Thursford Collection** of steam engines and organs. Kids will head straight for the old musical organs with moving figures, stacks of windpipes, and colorful decorations. They play every day at 3. Outside is a children's play area, a Venetian gondola switchback ride with an organ, and a steam railway, called The Cackler, that runs during the summer months. Fee. Off the A148 at Thursford Green. Easter–Oct. 2–5:30. Tel. (0328) 77238. South of Norwich, in **Easton,** is the **Easton Farm Park,** where cows are milked each afternoon and farm animals wander. There is vintage farm machinery, a nature trail, an adventure playground, and a pet paddock filled with small animals. Fee. Near Wickham Market. Easter–Oct. 10:30–6. Tel. (0728) 746475.

Great Yarmouth, a popular British family beach resort, is home to one of the largest open-air marketplaces in England. It has 15 miles of sandy beaches backed by dunes, some of which have children's playgrounds with trampolines, ice-cream stands, snacks, and fun fairs. There are pony rides on the promenade, many children's playgrounds in the town, roller skating, indoor and outdoor swimming pools, and the children's Joyland. Pleasure Beach has an amusement park.

CAMBRIDGE

Cambridge is a university town with many historic buildings throughout the city. You might take your kids to tour **King's College,** founded in 1441, or any of the other twenty-nine colleges making up Cambridge University, but remember, Cambridge's colleges are for students and are not to be disrupted by tourists, although thousands visit the town each year. Don't miss the chance to **"punt along the Cam,"** a popular student pastime. A punt is a large, flat-bottomed boat that is steered and propelled by a long pole. Scudamore's Boatyard will rent punts, rowboats, or canoes by the hour and has two locations: one at Quayside off Bridge Street and one at Mill Lane near Silver Street. Kids can just pole around the Cam or go up the river to Grantchester for tea. Among Cambridge's famous bookstores is one devoted to children's books, **Heff's Children's Bookshop,** at 30 Trinity St. Other fun things to do include feeding the ducks at Mill Pond, or watching the university's rowing teams practice on the Cam while the coach rides a bike alongside, shouting instructions through a megaphone.

About 20 miles from Cambridge along the A11 is Newmarket, the center of English horseracing, where you'll find the **National Horse-racing Museum.** In addition to showing the history of racing, the museum offers tours of the town that include watching morning exercise on the heath, the Jockey Club Rooms, training operations, and statues of famous horses. Fee. 99 High St. Mar.–Nov. Tues.–Sat. 10–5, Sun. 2–5. Tel. (0638) 667333.

THE HEART OF ENGLAND: NORTH OF BIRMINGHAM

Ironbridge Gorge was considered the birthplace of the Industrial Revolution, as it was here in 1709 that the technique of smelting iron ore with coke was discovered. In commemoration, a series of open-air museums were opened, the most interesting of which is the **Blists Hill Open-Air Museum.** It re-creates a 19th-century village with vivid details of the harsh conditions for workers, including the young children who worked 600 feet down in the mines. On a lighter note, the museum's Victorian sweetshop is a child's fantasyland. Fee. 35 miles west of Birmingham. Apr.–Oct. daily 10–6; Nov.–Mar. 10–5. Tel. (0952) 453522.

Nottingham is an industrial town, but its **castle,** perched high above the town, has dungeons where Robin Hood was thrown, only to be daringly rescued by his merry men. Be sure to tour **Mortimer's Hole,** the castle's secret entrance, and the underground passages carved out of soft sandstone. Small fee. Apr.–Sept. daily 10–5:45; Oct.–Mar. 10–4:45. Tel. (0602) 483504. Visit **The Tales of Robin Hood,** not far away on Maid Marian Way, to learn more about the life and times of this elusive outlaw and experience "A Flight to Adventure," which explores the Robin Hood stories and legends. Fee. Easter–Sept. daily 10–6; Oct.–Easter until 5. Tel. (0602) 414414. Nottingham also is home to Britain's oldest pub, **Ye Olde Jerusalem.** The current building dates from 1760, but an alehouse has been on the premises since 1168, as have the cellar and foundation. 2 Castle Rd.

Homesick? The **American Adventure,** 5 miles west of Nottingham in *Ilkeston,* has plenty of attractions to satisfy your little one's longings for home. Visit Kool Hand Luke's Ice Cream Shop, Medicine Man Island with teepees and totem poles, the San Francisco Wharf, the Tennessee Tentacles Octopus Ride, and more. Fee. Jun.–Sept. 10–6. Tel. (0773) 769931.

Sherwood Forest in Nottinghamshire is Robin Hood country. Although there are few trees left in the "forest," you can visit the **Major Oak** on whose branches Robin Hood sat. It's next to the **Sherwood Forest Visitors' Centre** in Sherwood Forest Country Park, at Edwinstowe near Mansfield. The centre has life-size replicas of Robin and his entourage as well as a little shop. Tel. (0623) 823202. Nearby, **Sherwood Forest Amusement Park** has a ghost train, dodg'ems, a bouncy castle, and more. Fee. In Sherwood Forest Country Park. Mid-Mar.–Oct. 10 to dusk. Tel. (0623) 823536.

The **Acton Scott Working Farms Museum** employs farming methods used at the turn of the century before electricity and gas-powered engines. Work is carried out by hand or heavy horse, and there are cider-making and craft exhibitions. Wenlock Lodge, off A49. Apr.–Oct. Mon.–Sat. 10–5, Sun. 10–6. Tel. (0696) 306/7.

Your young reptile enthusiast may want to go to *Weston-Under-Lizard* to get a postmark on a piece of mail, but the entire family will enjoy **Weston Park,** a 17th-century house with tapestries, furniture, art, nature trails, a miniature railway, adventure playground, aquarium, and museum of country bygones. Fee. Park: June and July Tues.–Thurs., Sat., Sun. 11–5; Aug. daily 11–5. House: June and July Tues.–Thurs., Sat., Sun., 1–5; April, May, and Sept. Sat. and Sun. 1–5. Tel. (095) 276207.

LIVERPOOL

An important fishing city since the 12th century, Liverpool is still a great commercial shipping port. It has recently realized that tourism can be an important source of funds and has begun to develop its waterfront. **Albert Dock Village** has been renovated and includes cafes, restaurants, and shops in addition to the **Merseyside Maritime Museum,** with its floating exhibits, special events, and working displays. Fee. Daily 10:30–5:30. Tel. (051) 7091551. Surrounding the museum is a maritime park perfect for a break from viewing.

Liverpool is also noted for its famed Liverpudlians **The Beatles,** and there are plenty of opportunities to find out about the Fab Four. The Cavern Club is no longer there (they performed there over 300 times), but in its place, the **Cavern Walks,** a shopping complex with a statue of the Beatles, has been decorated by John's former wife, Cynthia Lennon. Down the street is the Beatles' Shop. There are minibus tours of various Beatles sites, self-guided tours, and **Beatle City,** a permanent exhibition of Beatlemania re-creating the sounds and sights of the 1960s. Fee. Seel St. Daily 10:30–8:30. Tel. (051) 7090117.

Festival Park is filled with giant backyard objects. The 8-foot-tall mushrooms, giant pitchforks and shovels, and 30-foot-high sunflowers may be a welcome break from all the miniature worlds you've seen. Kids can climb in a full-scale model of the Beatles' yellow submarine. Fee. Sefton St. June–Aug. 11–6. Tel. (051) 7289888.

North of Liverpool, in *Blackpool,* is the popular **Blackpool Pleasure Beach.** It has 150 rides and attractions, with over thirty of them under cover in case it rains, and it often does. Younger kids will enjoy Funshineland, and there are lots of thriller attractions for the older kids plus ice-skating, comedy shows, restaurants, and its own British Rail station. Admission to park is free; fee for individual rides. 525 The Promenade, South Shore, Blackpool. Tel. (0253) 41033.

YORK

Considered one of England's best-preserved medieval cities, York has many other claims to fame, including being the birthplace of Yorkshire Pudding. The **tourist office** is in the De Grey Rooms, Exhibition Square [Tel. (0904) 643700]. Walk around the old city's **walls,** especially exciting in the places that are only 3 feet wide and don't have handrails. Climb the lookout towers for a view of the city. Look for a break in the walls with a staircase leading up, or a turreted "bar" to climb. Fortified walls are open for exploring from dawn until dusk. The **Shambles** is a narrow street filled with houses with medieval timbered gables so close together that one could lean out a window and pass a neighbor a taste of mutton stew.

Visit the **Jorvik Viking Centre** to see one of the best-preserved Viking cities in Europe. Board a "time car" and move backward through 1,000 years of vividly presented English history until you reach Viking York. Here, in the year 948, you enter a Viking scene complete with re-created sounds and smells. The little electric time cars whiz you away to reconstructions of the original archaeological dig which shows layers of excavated dirt and the objects found there. The layers of damp, peat-rich soil helped preserve plant and insect remains along with those of humans. It is a very well-done and popular exhibit, so get there before it opens to ensure a short wait to get in. Fee. Coppergate. Apr.–Oct. 9–7, Nov.–Mar. 9–5:30. Tel. (0904) 643211.

In the imaginative folk museum, **York Castle Museum,** you'll see displays on the evolution of valentines, musical instruments, charming reconstructed Victorian streets, and something called "Every home should have one"—a collection of domestic gadgets from the past 100 years. Mom may want to encourage the kids to linger over the display on the history of the vacuum cleaner, but the kids will be more fascinated by the evolution of the toilet. Fee. Tower St. Daily. Tel. (0904) 653611.

The **National Railway Museum,** housed in the city's old depot, illustrates the importance of rail travel in Britain. One of the few national museums outside London, it features real locomotives and carriages, including Queen Victoria's lavish Pullman carriage. Free. Leeman Rd. Mon.–Sat. 10–6, Sun. 11–6. Tel. (0904) 621261.

Friargate Museum brings history to life with over sixty life-size models of kings and queens, statesmen, and famous personalities. They wear authentically reproduced costumes and are displayed in special sets with lighting and sound effects intended to give a realistic atmosphere. There is a brass-rubbing center here, too. Fee. Lower Friargate in center of city. Feb.–Dec. 10–5. Tel. (0904) 658775.

Kids and cathedrals don't often mix, but **York Minster,** the largest Gothic cathedral in Britain, has some of the most beautiful stained glass in the British Isles. It was completed in 1480, having taken 250 years to build. The minster has 130 glass windows, with some 50 feet tall and 5 feet wide. The windows were all removed in 1939 to avoid damage during World War II, and it took 20 years to painstakingly replace them. A beautiful choral presentation, Evensong, is held on weekdays at 5 and Sundays at 4. Donation. Daily 7 AM–8:30 PM. Tel. (0904) 664426.

The **Jorvik Viking Festival** takes place in February. Longships race along the river, Viking battles take place in the streets, and there are glorious fireworks displays.

NORTH OF YORK

If you want to go to **Scarborough Fair,** then find your way to *Scarborough* sometime in early June for a festival of theater, concerts, parades and a traditional street market. Telephone the **tourist office** for details. [Tel. (0723) 373333].

In the town of *Stanley,* in Durham county, is the **Beamish Open-Air Museum.** People wearing turn-of-the-century costumes welcome you to Old Town Street, a working farm with animals, and to a Victorian fairground with rides in the summer. Old cottages and shops to wander through are scattered throughout this delightful museum, which has won both the "British Museum of the Year" and the "European Museum of the Year" awards. Fee. Apr.–Oct. 10–6, Nov.–Mar. 10–5. Tel. (0207) 231811.

THE LAKE DISTRICT

Cascading waterfalls, lakes, lush green mountains, and deep valleys make up this area, which contains a large national park. It is a very popular summer destination, with wonderful walks anytime of year, and fishing, sailing, rowing, and waterskiing in the summer. In winter, when the lakes are frozen, you can ice-skate or practice the sport of curling. Steamships operate on the two largest lakes, Windemere and Ullswater. **Dry stone walling** is an unusual summer activity for older kids. Participants learn about the old craft of building stone walls by helping rebuild or repair damaged walls in the area.

Days when visitors can help are numerous and are scattered throughout the summer. **Rush bearing** dates from the days when church floors were bare earth and covered each year with freshly cut rushes. The tradition continues throughout the summer in different lake district villages. You'll see little girls wearing flower and rush crowns, parading bands, children's sports, and more. **Sheep dog trials** take place here during the month of August. If your kids are "doggy," it's a fun activity. The national park offers special **children's activities** throughout the summer. For information on any of the above, get in touch with the Lake District National Park Office or The Visitor's Centre at Brockhole in Windemere [Tel. (09662) 5555]. They can also provide you with the helpful publication "Places to Visit and Things to Do in Cumbria."

The charming towns of *Windemere* and *Bowness,* on the eastern shore of Lake Windemere, are popular and are good spots to head-quarter. The **Windemere Steamboat Museum and Motorboat Collection** contains historical boats used on the lake, including Beatrix Potter's rowboat and early ferry boats used to transport horses and carriages across the lake. You can ride one of them, the *Osprey,* around the lake. Fee. Rayrigg Rd. Easter–Oct. from 10. Tel. (09662) 5565.

In the town of *Near Sawrey,* at the other end of Lake Windemere from Windemere Village, you can tour Beatrix Potter's cottage at **Hill Top Farm.** Many of the scenes painted in her stories are from in and around her home, and kids who are familiar with her books will recognize the landing with the red curtain from the *Tale of Tom Kitten,* and other scenes from *Peter Rabbit* and *Jemima Puddle-Duck.* Go early to avoid the crowds. Fee. Apr.–Oct. daily, except Fri.

Acorn Bank Garden, in *Penrith,* on the edge of the Lake District along the M6 Motorway, is the National Trust's most comprehensive collection of medieval and culinary herbs. Kids can sniff and guess herbs, and older kids can learn about the different uses for the herbs. Small fee. Apr.–Oct. 10–6. Tel. (05394) 33883.

Just east of Penrith, near *Appleby,* is the **Holesfoot Ancestral Research and Leisure Centre,** which has brass rubbing, heraldry exhibits, and other fun ways to experience history. Kids can learn how to trace their own family tree, bake bread in the Victorian bake house, sled down grassy slopes, get lost in the giant maze, roller skate, ride bikes down a bike course, or play giant board games. Fee. Open summers 10:30–5. Tel. (07683) 51458.

The **Ravenglass and Eskdale Miniature Railway** starts at Ravenglass along the coast. Popular with children, it runs 7 miles inland through beautiful scenery to Eskdale. Fee. Apr.–Oct. daily; reduced service all winter. Tel. (0765) 86333.

The **Beatrix Potter Gallery,** in *Hawkshead,* has an exhibition of her original drawings and illustrations, plus a display on her life. Fee. Main St. Apr.–Oct. Wed.–Sun. 11–5. Tel. (09666) 355.

Levens Hall Topiary Gardens are just outside of *Kendal,* a town often called "The Gateway to the Lake District." It contains a quirky collection of topiary created in 1692 by the famous French topiary artist Beaumont. There are birds, horses, mushrooms, donuts, and much more, all out of trimmed hedges. Fee. Five miles south of town on the A6. Easter–Oct. Sun.–Thurs. 11–5. Tel. (05395) 60321.

Keswick, in the center of the Lake District and next to Lake Derwentwater, is famous for yet another oddball English museum, **The Pencil Museum.** It boasts the world's longest pencil, a wartime pencil display, the history of graphite mining, brass rubbing, and a children's drawing corner, plus video shows of pencil making and artistic techniques. Small fee. Southey Works, Greta Bridge. Mar.–Oct. Mon.–Fri. 9:30–4, Sat.–Sun. 2–4:30; Nov.–Feb. daily 10–4. Tel. (07687) 73626. **Keswick Launch** rents rowboats and motorboats from Keswick and Lodore landings, and offers an hour-long narrated cruise around the lake. Tel. (07687) 72263 for details.

WALES

Wales is right next to the heart of England and shares with Britain its government and monarchy, but its people and culture are decidedly Celtic. Many natives speak Welsh and English, and street signs are in both languages. In fact, Welsh is Europe's oldest spoken language, and the importance of the spoken word and music can be seen throughout the country. It is most evident in the country's many festivals of music, poetry, and dance, called *eisteddfod* (pronounced "eye-steth-vod," just one of many tongue twisters you'll encounter). The most famous is the International Eisteddfodau Festival held in Llangollen in July.

Wales is filled with massive castles. Its northern region is largely scenic and pastoral, with rugged mountains and lush countryside, whereas much of the south has been scarred by its industrial past. The discovery of coal in the 19th century led to a mining economy with all of its accompanying horrors. Slate mines followed. Both industries have waned in the last century, and the economy of Wales has consequently suffered. Some of the abandoned mines have been transformed into tourist attractions where kids can wander through the long dark tunnels. They'll be glad that they aren't the children whose sad, smudged faces fill the photo collections of mining museums.

Getting Around

Road and rail links with most of Britain's main areas of population are good. Motorways (like our freeways) connect London with Cardiff and the northern border of Wales. Two-lane roads cover the rest of the country. They can be crowded with slow cars pulling trailers during the summer months, particularly in the north. British Rail's 125 InterCity Service makes the London to Cardiff run in less than 2 hours, and rail travel within Wales is scenic and widespread.

Let's Eat!

Traditional Welsh dishes include Welsh *rarebit* (often called "rabbit"), buttered toast topped with a cheese and egg mixture; *crempog*, or griddle cakes, made with sour cream and slathered with butter; and a wide selection of hearty breads. Your kids will either love or hate laver bread, made with seaweed and fried with bacon.

NORTHERN WALES

SNOWDONIA NATIONAL PARK

Snowdonia covers 840 square miles of mountains, forests, waterfalls, and coastline in the northwestern corner of Wales. The glaciers of the Ice Age molded its landscape, and its attractions are many for lovers of the out-of-doors. Visitors can enjoy fishing, pony trekking, canoeing, skiing, sailing, hiking in the mountains, or meandering along a country lane.

Llanberis, once the center of the slate industry, is a compact little town on the northwestern edge of the park with beautiful walks to nearby waterfalls, lovely parks, and castle ruins. The **Snowdon Mountain Railway** has been in operation for almost 100 years; take its coal-fired train from Llanberis to the summit of Mount Snowdon. Call for schedules [Tel. [0286] 8702231]. The **Padarn Country Park** houses a number of attractions. The **Llanberis Lake Railway** provides a 40-minute trip with magnificent views of Snowdonia along Lake Padarn's shore. Fee. Easter–Oct. Mon.–Thurs. (first two months), Sun.–Fri. rest of season. Tel. (0286) 870549. Canoes and rowboats are available for hire. Housed in the former State Quarry Workshops is the **Welsh Slate Museum,** where visitors can see the largest waterwheel in Wales and the technology once used to extract slate. Landrover trips depart from the museum throughout the day to explore the quarries nearby. Easter–Sept. 9:30–5. Tel. (0286) 870549. **Craft workshops** in clay, copper, slate, and wood are open for view. Mar.–Oct. 10–6. Nature trails and picnic sites abound. Admission to the park is free, but attractions within the park are individually priced. Park open dawn to dusk. Tel. (0286) 870892. Not far from Llanberis on the A4085 is the town of **Beddgelert,** which translates as Gelert's Grave. According to Welsh legend, Gelert was the faithful wolfhound of the 13th-century Prince of Llewelyn. Upon returning home, the prince found his son missing and his bedsheets red with blood. The prince discovered Gelert also covered with blood and promptly killed him. Shortly thereafter, the prince found his baby hiding near the wolf that Gelert killed to save the child. Story has it that the prince never smiled again. Gelert is buried near the charming town, which is a good base for hiking in Snowdonia. The **Sygan Copper Mine** has guided tours of the old mine with winding tunnels, large chambers, magnificent stalactite and stalagmite formations, and copper ore veins with traces of gold and silver. Tours take about 40 minutes, and there are stairs to climb. Fee. Mar.–Sept. 10–5 (until 4 on Sat.); Oct. 11–4. Tel. (0766) 86595.

Porthmadog, on the very edge of Snowdonia, is the gateway to the Llyn Peninsula and the starting point for the **Ffestiniog Railway,** a narrow-gauge railway traveling through some of the most beautiful and remote parts of Snowdonia National Park. Kids like the buffet and observation cars. Fee depends on distance traveled; Blaenau Ffestiniog is the final destination. Apr.–Nov. daily; Mar. weekends. Tel. (0766) 512340. **Porthmadog Pottery** makes traditional Welsh pottery. With instruction kids can paint or turn a pot on a potter's wheel; boxes are supplied for you to carry home your pieces. Small fee. Snowdon St. Mar.–Oct. Mon.–Fri. 9–5:30. Tel. (0766) 512137.

Just southeast of Porthmadog is *Portmeiron,* the fantasy creation of architect Sir Clough Williams-Ellis, who wanted to build his own Utopia. Roughly based on the Italian village of Portofino, the village is perched on a rock amidst woodlands and gardens crisscrossed with walking paths. Its lovely beach is fine for sunbathing but not for swimming as the current is treacherous. The cult TV series The Prisoner was filmed here, and there is a Prisoner Information Centre in town. Fee to enter the village; Prisoner fans will find it well worth it. Village open Easter–Oct. 9:30–5:30; grounds open year-round. Tel. (0766) 770228.

Dolgellau, in the southern part of Snowdonia Park, has **Tal-y-Waen Farm Trail,** an award-winning Welsh hill farm. Walk the farm trail and see farm animals and wildlife at work and play. There is also a pets' corner, an adventure playground, pony rides, a little museum, and a picnic area. Fee. May–Oct. Sun.–Fri. 10–5. Tel. (0341) 422580.

Blaenau Ffestiniog, in the heart of Snowdonia, is the home of **Llechwedd Slate Caverns.** You can choose between two tours: "The Miners Underground Tramway Tour" takes you through floodlit tunnels and caverns to a part of the mine where Victorian working conditions have been re-created. On the "Deep Mine Tour," you descend on a railway into the depths of the mine where tales of miners' lives are recounted as you explore the huge caverns and underground lake. Fee. On the A470. Easter–Sept. 10–5:15; Oct. until 4:15. Tel. (0766) 830306.

Betws-Y-Coed, northeast of Blaenau Ffestiniog, is one of the most charming Welsh villages. Thousands of tourists will agree, especially in July and August. Nevertheless, it is an excellent base for exploring Snowdon. Nearby are Swallow Falls, the magical Fairy Glen, and Conwy Falls, plus interesting bridges in the village.

The **Pen-y-Pass Youth Hostel** offers family packages and will arrange canoeing, pony trekking, and mountain walking for you and your children. A "Mountain Centre" operates from the hostel and offers daily and weekly courses in rock climbing, canoeing, orienteering, sailing, photography, and more. If the kids aren't exhausted by evening, they can play in the hostel's game room. Pen-y-Pass, Nant Gwynant, Caernarfon, Gwynedd LL554NY.

LLANDUDNO

Wales' largest beach resort, *Llandudno,* is on the northern shore of Wales, and has both a north- and west-facing seashore. The north shore has most of the action, with donkey rides and a **Victorian Punch and Judy Theater,** called "Professor Codman's Wooden-Headed Follies." A **fun pier** reaches 2,296 feet out into the bay; its amusements include the **Llandudno dungeon waxworks,** cafes, and summer shows. The west shore is quieter and has a statue of the **White Rabbit** from Lewis Carroll's *Alice in Wonderland,* in commemoration of Carroll's 1862 visit to the family of Alice Liddell, the little girl for whom the story was invented. The statue sits next to the model boat pond. On the lower slopes of Great Orme, a limestone headland, is **Happy Valley,** with gardens, miniature golf, a children's playground, and summer fireworks shows. Great Orme, a country park with beautiful walks, towers over Llandudno and its bays. A tramway/cable car operates between several different points in the town and the top of Great Orme between April and September. A **Doll Museum** contains more than 1,000 dolls and their accessories plus model trains. Fee. Masonic St. Apr.–Sept. daily 10–5, Sun. 2–5. Tel. (0492) 76312.

NEAR LLANDUDNO

Conwy, an ancient walled town near Llandudno, has 13th-century **Conwy Castle,** with 15-foot walls and eight drum towers. Small fee. Mid-Mar.–mid-Oct. daily 9:30–6:30; mid-Oct.–mid-Mar. Mon.–Sat.

9:30–4. Conwy also has Britain's tiniest (6 feet across) house, **Ty Bach.** Tiniest fee. July–Aug. 9:30–9:30; May, June, Sept., Oct. 10–6. Tel. (0492) 3484. The **Welsh Mountain Zoo** has elephants, chimpanzees, lions, bear, penguins, free-flying eagles, and a Jungle Adventure Land and Tarzan Trail. During summer months there are displays of falconry and sea-lion feeding. Fee. Off the A55. Daily 9:30–5. Tel. (0492) 532938. *Rhyl,* to the east of Llandudno, has golden sand beaches and amusements for children such as Skateworld, Cyclorama, a fun fair, and crazy boat rides. The **Rhyl Suncentre** along the promenade is an indoor entertainment center for poor weather. Its "tropical island setting" is always 80 degrees (the water, too) and offers swimming, surfing, slides, rides, a monorail, and evening entertainment. Fee. Apr.–Sept. daily 10 AM–11 PM; Oct.–Nov. Fri.–Sun. 10 AM–11 PM. Tel. (0745) 31771.

LLANGOLLEN

Llangollen is inland and close to the English border. It is the site of the **Llangollen International Eisteddfod,** an international music festival in the traditional style of a Welsh Eisteddfod. Thousands of singers and dancers travel from all over the world to compete in friendly rivalry in folk dance, song, and instrumental works in the first week in July. Book tickets months in advance through the Eisteddfod Office, Llangollen, Clwd, Wales LL208NG [Tel. (0978) 861 804]. For a list of accommodations, send a separate inquiry to the Private Accommodation Secretary. The **Canal Museum** offers a 45-minute horse-drawn canalboat ride. The museum uses models, pictures, and slides to explain the history and importance of the canals in Britain. Fee. Museum: Easter–Sept. daily 10:30–5. Horse-drawn boat trips: Easter–Sept. Sat. and Sun. afternoons; July and Aug. daily afternoons. Tel. (0978) 860702.

ISLE OF ANGLESEY AND THE MENAI STRAIT

The **Menai Suspension Bridge** connects Bangor on the mainland with the island of Anglesey. *Bangor* is the site of the grandiose 19th-century **Penrhyn Castle,** built far too late to have any defensive purpose. The museum of dolls (over 1,000 in the collection) is always a hit, as is the old train museum, the Victorian walled garden, and the castle's weird heavy slate furniture. A special children's "Adventure Audio Tour" is available. Fee. On A5122. Apr.–Oct. Wed.–Mon. noon–5. Tel. (0248) 353084.

Anglesey Island has popular beaches and resorts. The island's city of *Beaumaris* has a **castle** that is surrounded by a water-filled moat and still has its original small dock, where supplies were brought to the castle by sea. Walk the ramparts for a view of the entire castle. Mid-Mar.–mid-Oct. Mon.–Sat. 9:30–6:30, Sun. 2–6:30; mid-Oct.–mid-Mar. Mon.–Sat. 9:30–4, Sun. 2–4. Tel. (0248) 810361. **Starida Sea Services,** in Beaumaris, operates cruises to Puffin Island, the Penmon Lighthouse, or around Beaumaris Bay. Fee. Off Rosemary Lane. Daily trips Easter–Oct. Tel. (0248) 810251. The **Anglesey Sea Zoo** lets visitors wander through a real shipwreck with fish swimming all around them. Touch tanks, a children's play area with model boats, and the "Aquablaster" water game are some of its highlights. Fee. Brynsiencyn. Follow signs from Britannia Bridge. Mid-Feb.–Oct. 10–5. The town of *Menai Bridge* on the island has a lovely **Museum of Childhood** with dolls, clockworks, toys, music boxes, and piggy banks. Fee. Water St. off Uxbridge Square. Easter–Oct. Tel. (0248) 712498.

The town of *Llanfairpwllgwyngyllgogerychwyrndrobwll Llantysiliogogogoch* has been thankfully nicknamed Llanfair P.G. So named as a publicity gimmick in the 19th century, it has the longest name of any town in Britain and probably the world! Take a train ride here as your ticket will be stamped with the entire name, making a great souvenir.

Plas Newydd is an elegant 18th-century house nestled along the banks of the strait. Its Military Museum houses relics from the Battle of Waterloo, and it offers idyllic walks, lovely gardens, and a children's adventure playground. Fee. Apr.–Sept. Sun.–Fri. 12–5; Oct.–Nov. Fri. and Sun. 12–5. Tel. (0248) 714795. *Caernarfon's* castle, back on the mainland along the Menai Strait, was built in the 13th century. Walk along its ramparts, climb the Eagle Tower for a view of the whole castle and surrounding countryside, and be sure to explore its intricate passageways and vaulted chambers. Fee. Mid-Mar.–mid Oct. daily 9:30–6:30; mid-Oct.–mid-Mar. Mon.–Sat. 9:30–4. Tel. (0286) 77617.

SOUTHERN WALES

CARDIFF

The capital city of Cardiff is the largest and most urban city in Wales. **Cardiff Castle** has traces of Roman walls and a Norman keep, but it is the lavish and extravagant 19th-century additions by the rich 3rd Marquis of Bute that give it its character today. Peacocks and other birds wander through the grounds, and a military tattoo performs in August. Fee. Castle St. May–Sept. daily 10–12:30, 2–5; less frequently rest of year. Tel. (0222) 822083. The **National Museum of Wales** relates the story of Wales, and it can be a good quick overview of the country. An exceptional collection of French Impressionists will captivate art lovers. Free. Museum Ave., Cathays Park, City Centre. Tues.–Sat. 10–5, Sun. 2:30–5. Tel. (0222) 397951. The **Welsh Folk Museum** has reassembled buildings with authentic furnishings carefully moved from rural parts of Wales. Wander through to see how the Welsh lived and worked in years past. Farm animals and craft demonstrations such as blacksmithing, hand weaving, leather tanning, and saddle making make it all the more vivid. A gallery displays a number of objects, including Welsh love spoons, which are carved wooden spoons made by romantic young men for their *cariads* (sweethearts). The more elaborate the carving, the more passionate the suitor. Fee. St. Fagans. Mon.–Sat. 10–5. Tel. (0222) 569441.

NEAR CARDIFF

Caerphilly Castle, about 8 miles north of Cardiff, in *Caerphilly,* is Europe's second largest fortress. At one time its thick castle walls had kept out invading armies. When they were no longer effective, a novel concentric defense design with moats was constructed in the 13th century. In later years, the water was drained and some of the towers were destroyed. One of the few towers that did not fall was the Leaning Tower of Caerphilly, which now tilts about 9 feet off the perpendicular. Small fee. Mid-Mar.–mid-Oct. daily 9:30–6:30; rest of year Mon.–Sat. 9:30–4, Sun. 2–4. Tel. (0222) 465511.

Southwest along the coast toward Swansea is *Margam Park,* in *Margam,* West Glamorgan. An 850-acre country park, it has a castle, an abbey, a large hedge maze, an unusual sculpture park, pony rides, putting, an adventure playground, "Fairy-tale Land," and beautiful walks. Small fee. East of M4 junction 38. Apr.–Sept. 9:30–7; Oct.–Mar. Wed.–Sun. 9:30–5. Tel. (0639) 881 635.

Tredegar House and Country Park, in *Newport,* just northeast of Cardiff, is set in 90 acres of parkland. The house has tours of elaborate state rooms, intimate family rooms, and much plainer servants' quarters. Craft workshops, carriage rides, boating, an adventure play farm, and nature trails will keep children busy. Grounds: year-round. House: Easter–Sept. Wed.–Sun. Tel. (0633) 815880.

PEMBROKESHIRE COAST NATIONAL PARK

The **Pembrokeshire Coast National Park,** one of Wales' three national parks, juts out into the Irish Sea in the country's southwestern corner. It is spectacular, with rugged cliffs, sheltered coves, sandy beaches, and wild moorlands. A 167-mile footpath runs through the park from Amroth in the south, around to St. Dogmaels in the north. *Tenby,* on its southwestern coast, is often called the "Welsh Riviera" as its wide sandy beaches are sun-drenched in the summer. The Victorian town has all of the extras of a good English beach resort: a heated indoor pool, miniature golf, children's gardens, Punch and Judy theater, pony trekking, bowling, and a seaside promenade. The **Tenby Museum and Picture Gallery** has an extensive bird's egg collection. Small fee. Apr.–Oct. 10–6. A few miles offshore is *Caldy Island,* home to many different kinds of seabirds. Monks make perfume, chocolate, and woven goods at its monastery; a shop on the islands sells their wares. You can grab a ride from **Caldy Boats** at the harbor. They leave every 15 minutes May–Sept. Mon.–Fri. 9:45–5:30.

Inland from Tenby, the **Oakwood Adventure and Leisure Park,** in *Narberth,* has 80 acres of fun activities for children such as a BMX bike course, boating lakes, go carts, bobsledding, a miniature railway, and an orienteering course. Activities designed for those under age 10 include a dry ball pool and nature walks. A miniature train runs between the attractions. Fee. Apr.–Oct. daily 10–6. Tel. (0834) 85373. Heading west along the coast from Tenby brings you to *Pembroke* and its 12th- and 13th-century **Pembroke Castle.** Kids find this castle very impressive, especially its moat and its underground passage to the harbor. Small fee. Apr.–Sept. daily 9:30–6; Oct.–Mar. Mon.–Sat. 10–4.

ABERYSTWYTH

Further north along the west coast is *Aberystwyth,* a Victorian Era resort town and deep-sea fishing center. **Aberystwyth Cliff Railway,** running up Constitution Hill, offers a smashing view of the town and bay. A camera obscura and tearooms are at the top. Departs from the northern end of the promenade. Easter–Oct. daily 10–6. Tel. (0907) 617642. Don't miss the **Vale of Rheidol Railway,** which will escort you 12 miles up the river to Devil's Bridge. Here, three bridges from the 13th, 18th, and 20th centuries are stacked one on top of the other. You can cross a raging waterfall on a footbridge, follow the steps of Jacob's Ladder into a gorge, or take a more subdued nature trail for some magnificent views of the bridges and river below. Narrow-gauge steam trains leave five times each day in July and August, twice daily the rest of the year, from the main Aberystwyth Railroad Station on Alexandra Road. Fee. Tel. (0970) 612378. Eleven miles east of town is the **Llywernog Silver-Lead Mine.** Underground tunnels, waterfalls, a floodlit cavern, and a slide show of the miners' lives and their harsh mining conditions makes this a favorite with kids. Fee. Easter–Aug. 10–6; Sept. 10–5; Oct. 11–4. In Ponterwyd on the A44. Tel. (0970) 85620.

BRECON BEACONS NATIONAL PARK

In the middle of southern Wales, **Brecon Beacons National Park** is an area of sharp contrasts with massive crags, sweeping valleys, heather-covered hillsides, and high moorlands. Sheep and Welsh mountain ponies roam freely. The two main towns in this area are Brecon and Abergavenny, and both are good bases from which to explore. *Brecon* is an old market town with the ruins of a medieval castle and a part-13th-century castle. The **Brecknock Museum**'s collection includes the old town stocks, which kids can try out. Free. Mon.–Sat. 10–5. Tel. (0874) 4121. *Abergavenny* has plenty of buildings dating back to Tudor times, the ruins of an 11th-century castle, and, like Brecon, many opportunities for arranging pony trekking, walking, and fishing.

Five miles southwest of Abergavenny, in *Blaenavon,* is the **Big Pit Mining Museum,** where, outfitted with helmet, lamp, and emergency air supply, you descend 300 feet for a fascinating tour through the cold and narrow tunnels of the mine. Tour guides tell grim mining stories. Remind your children that youngsters often worked long hours in the mines the next time they complain about sharing the backseat. Back on the surface, a renovated miner's cottage, workshop, and special exhibition complete the story. Under-5s not admitted; dress warmly and wear walking shoes. Fee. Mar.–Dec. 10–3:30. Tel. (0495) 790311. A short walk away is **Mr. Puzzle's Jigsaw World,** where children can try to cut a wooden jigsaw puzzle or watch a video describing how a puzzle is made. There is a huge selection of puzzles to admire or purchase at the gift shop. Free. Easter–Sept. daily 9:30–5:30; Feb.–Easter and Oct.–Dec. weekends only. Tel. (0495) 791140.

Three miles north of *Abercraf,* near the park's southern border, are the illuminated caves of **Dan-yr-ogof** with underground lakes and stalagmites and stalactites. One of the largest showcave complexes in western Europe, it also has a dinosaur park and dry ski slope. Fee. On the A4067. Easter–Oct. daily from 10. Tel. (0639) 730284. West of Abercraf, 3 miles north of *Merthyr Tydfil,* is the **Brecon Mountain Railway,** whose vintage steam locomotive will take you on a 4-mile trip through beautiful scenery into the Brecon Beacons Park. Each paying adult can take one child free. Easter–Oct.; call for timetable. Tel. (0685) 4854.

SCOTLAND

The sight of clansmen in full dress wearing kilts, *sporrans,* and *skean dhu* daggers, and the haunting, moody sound of their bagpipes stopped my kids in their tracks. They were silent and still for many minutes, taking it all in. As the Scots Guard marched by, the children followed, listening and watching with total absorption. Scotland was a favorite country, and the exhilarating piping and drumming by kilt-clad Scotsmen was one of the reasons why.

The Scots possess great warmth and charm, and your bonnie wee lassies and bonnie wee laddies are the recipients of this hearty and heart-felt welcome. Whether you opt to stay in sophisticated Edinburgh for the Edinburgh International Festival or head to the Highlands to catch a glimpse of the Loch Ness Monster, you will encounter hospitality of the highest order. If you visit in the summer, plan to see one of the many Highland games as this is the kind of experience you bring your kids to Europe to have. The games are engaging and fun spectacles that combine sport and cultural expression. They are not historic revivals but an important tradition that a community looks forward to each year.

Scotland is the northernmost of the three countries that make up the island of Great Britain. While joined constitutionally with England since 1707 and sharing a monarchy, it has its own legal system, its own currency (although the British pound is valid as legal tender and has the same value), and a strong, independent national identity.

Preparing Your Kids: Books

Younger children: The Runaway Brownie by Mary Calhoun; Old Man of Lochnager by Charles, Prince of Wales; The Wee Wee Mannie and the Big Big Coo by Marcia Seawall; Argyle by Barbara Brooks Wallace; books by Leclaire Alger, such as Kellyburn Braes; and any of the Katie Morag books by Mairi Hedderwick.

Older children: A Dog Called Porridge by William Mackeller, Kidnapped by Robert Louis Stevenson, Mystery at Loch Ness by Rosy Wandelmaier, and books by Mollie Hunter or Eileen Dunlop.

Wha'd'ya Wanna Do?

The British Tourist Authority (BTA) can send you information as most of their publications cover Scotland; see page 203 for addresses. Once in Scotland, you will find excellent tourist offices in all regions.

Highland games and gatherings take place on summer weekends throughout Scotland. You can watch brawny clansmen toss the caber and throw the hammer while Highlanders dance to Scottish folk music. It's colorful, nonstop entertainment for kids with tug-of-wars, athletics, bands, and lots of glorious, noisy bagpipers. The Braemar Games are the biggest of the Highland games, with the Royal Family and lots of other people in attendance. Book in advance; tickets are sold at the local bank. Cowal's Games feature 1,000 pipers playing and parading, but the smaller gatherings are just as much fun, as you are so much closer to the action. Be sure to arrive in time for the caber toss, an event in which a huge tree trunk is tossed for distance. Each game has its own particular caber; the world-famous Braemar Caber measures 19 feet, 9 inches and weighs 192 pounds.

The tourist office publishes a list of all games. Get one before leaving, or drop by a local tourist office for a list. A few are listed here to help you plan:

June: Aberdeen, Grantown-on-Spey
July: Dufftown, Dundee, Elgin, Forres, Kenmore, Inverary, Inverness, Ft. William, Lochearnhead, Dingwall
August: Mallaig, Aberfeldy, Glasgow, Perth, Crieff, Oban, Dunoon, Birnam, Strathpeffer, Aboyne, Rothesay (Bute), Portree (Skye)
September: Braemar, Pitlochry.

Try to take your kids to see a game of the **Scottish sport of curling,** known as the "Roarin' Game" because play is accompanied by much loud exhortation. It's much more difficult than it looks. Imagine a cross between bowling with big granite stones and brooms on slick ice and Mickey's frantic sweeping in the *Sorcerer's Apprentice,* and you have a picture of the game. It tends to be a winter game, although many cities now have year-round indoor rinks.

Getting Around

If you travel by **car,** pick up a Michelin map or a copy of the tourist office's "Scotland Touring Map." Take advantage of the many rest stops with views and picnic tables. Some roads in the Highlands are one-lane with passing pullouts. In the more remote west coast areas and islands, gas stations are few and far between and are usually closed on Sundays. **Train** routes in the Scottish Lowlands are extensive, while routes in the Highlands are not as wide-ranging. **Buses** run throughout the entire country. **Ferry service** to the islands is good, and the timetable/map "Getting Around the Highlands and Islands" can help you plan your route. Be sure to make a reservation if you are taking your car across during high-season, particularly on weekends.

Sidewalk Talk

The lilting Scottish tongue has a few words all its own:

bleak and dreary, esp. weather *dreich*
children *bairns*

fancy or complicated *fantoosh*
fine or good *braw*
hill *brae*

mob of rowdy people *clamjamfry*	party with singing and
offensively dirty	dancing *ceilidh*
person *ramscallion*	pocket *pooch*
pants *breeks*	Scottish drinking cup *quaich*

Let's Eat!

The Scots make wonderful soups. Try scotch broth, a rich broth with barley, various vegetables, and bits of meat; or cock-a-leekie soup, a chicken broth with vegetables. Common fish are haddock, cod, and mackerel, and a classic is finnan haddie (smoked haddock). Haggis is eaten on Burns' night, and can be ordered at other times of the year, too. Don't tell your kids that it's made from a sheep's bladder or stomach filled with animal organs, oatmeal, and suet. Teatime will have your children sipping tea and nibbling a sweet pick-me-up. Scottish shortbread leaves our Lorna Doons in the dust. Their oatcakes come sweetened and plain, and both are delicious. Pancakes are often served at teatime, as are scones. As for the basic food groups, it helps to know that mince is ground beef, tatties are potatoes, and neeps are turnips. Delicious desserts with great names include flummery, clootie dumplings, and trifle.

The Lay of the Land

Scotland's two major cities are its capital, Edinburgh, and Glasgow, the third largest city in Britain. The country is divided into the Lowlands and the Highlands, and many islands are scattered along the west and north coasts. We profile Edinburgh; the Borders area, which lies along the English border; Central Scotland, which includes Glasgow; the Northeast, including cities such as Aberdeen; the Cairngorm Mountains area; the Highlands; the Northern Highlands; and the islands.

EDINBURGH

An elegant city of manageable size, Edinburgh is dominated by its castle, which rests on a dramatic outcropping of rock in the middle of the city. It has been the capital of Scotland since 1500 and is affectionately known as "Auld Reekie" (Old Smelly) from the stench created by the coalfires of the past. The Royal Mile runs between the castle and Holyrood Palace, through the old part of town. In the "old days," the Royal Mile didn't have sewers. Chamber pots and their contents were thrown from fourth- and fifth-floor windows with the shout, "Gardy-loo!" A number of these houses can still be seen along the Royal Mile, but reassure your kids that the plumbing is 20th century.

Edinburgh hosts the Edinburgh International Festival, Europe's largest festival of the arts. Along with its companion festivals, the Festival Fringe, Film Festival, and Jazz Festival, Edinburgh is the place to be for music, dance, theater, and film in August and early September. Some of the entertainment is decidedly highbrow and not for most kids, but there are plenty of clowns, pantomimes, and puppet shows. Our children thoroughly enjoyed the city's street musicians. They are often seen in full-dress kilts playing Scottish ballads on bagpipes or accordions. Be sure to consult *What's On*, a weekly paper whose listings include events and activities in Edinburgh. The city's **tourist office** is at Waverly Market, 3 Princes St. (Tel. 557-2727). Edinburgh's **telephone area code** is 031.

Getting Around

Lothian Regional Transport provides bus service within the city. Have exact change ready. Private car parking is scarce and expensive, especially in the city center. Start your visit with a **city walk**. There are different choices, such as Ghosts and Witches, Georgian Edinburgh, or The Royal Mile: Old Town. Call 661–0125 or 557-3443 for information and reservations.

Where to Stay

See "Lights Out!" in Great Britain for information on booking apartments or flats.

HOTELS

The *Caledonian Hotel,* an elegant old hotel at the west end of Princes Street on the edge of Princes Street Gardens, has rooms with communicating doors and several dining rooms. Princes St. and Lothian Rd. Tel. 225-2433. **Expensive.**

Near the Edinburgh Zoo is *The Trusthouse Forte Post House Hotel* with special prices for children. Fifteen minutes by taxi to Princes Street Garden, it has several restaurants and baby-listening services. Corstorphine Rd. Tel. 334-8221. Tel. from US 800-225-5843. **Expensive.**

The *Thrums Private Hotel* has several family rooms and its own garden and car park. A full Scottish breakfast is included in the price. 14 Minto St. Tel. 667-5545. **Moderate.**

Teviotdale House is a small hotel that is a 10-minute ride from the city center. All rooms have baths, and an exceptionally good breakfast is included. 53 Grange Loan. Tel. 667-4376. **Moderate.**

West End Apartments, near the west end of Princes Street, have studios and one- or two-bedroom apartments that can be rented by the day or week. 2 Learmouth Terrace. Tel. 332-0717. **Inexpensive.**

Glen House Apartments, also near the west end of Princes Street, have apartments for two to six people with a minimum stay of three nights. 22 Glen St. Tel. 2284043. **Inexpensive.**

Craig Mon, close to Princes Street and the city center, has family rooms if you'd all like to be together in one room. Otherwise, ask for two doubles. Not all rooms have showers. Reduction for children under 12. 62 Pilrig St. Tel. 554-3885. **Inexpensive.**

Detour! What to See and Do

ALONG THE ROYAL MILE

The **Royal Mile** is made up of four consecutive streets: Castle Hill, the Lawnmarket, High Street, and the Canongate, which descend the rocky ridge from the Castle to Holyrood Palace. **Royal Mile Banquets** gives your family a taste of foods from a bygone era while entertainers sing songs and perform dramas from the past. Reservations are required; children of all ages are welcome. 9 Victoria St. Tel. 220-1708. **Edinburgh Castle** sits overlooking the city on Castle Rock, a dramatic outcropping of volcanic rock. Be sure to find "Mons Meg," the enormous 15th-century siege cannon used to batter down walls of castles and towns. The biggest "gun" in its day, the cannonballs were 18 inches across and weighed 330 pounds. The prison was added in 1842. At that time, the number of lashes handed out for punishment was reduced to a "humane" maximum of 200, a fact your kids will appreciate. Peek down at the tiny cemetery for soldiers' dogs near St. Mary's Chapel. The military museums have a display of military memorabilia including the tall black feathered officers' "bonnets," and Bob, the stuffed military dog. The Crown Room has the Crown Jewels of Scotland, a gem-and-pearl-encrusted crown, scepter, and sword. Soldiers stationed on the castle grounds can be seen wearing kilts or tartan trousers. Fee. Summer Mon.–Sat. 9:30–5, Sun. 11–5; winter Mon.–Sat. 9:30–4:15, Sun. 12:30–3:30. Tel. 225-9846.

Next to the castle is the **Camera Obscura,** installed in the 1850s by Edinburgh optician Maria Theresa Short. Climb to the top of the narrow building, stopping on each floor to view holography exhibits and pinhole cameras made from soft-drink cans and candy tins. At the very top is the camera obscura, which is actually a periscope projecting views of the city onto a rounded disk in front of you. A lively history of the city is presented both visually and by a humorous Scottish guide. A small gift shop at the bottom sells books on how to build your own camera obscura. Fee. Top of the Royal Mile next to the castle. Daily 9:30–evening. Tel. 226-3709. The oldest surviving house along the Royal Mile is **Gladstone's Land,** at 483 Lawnmarket. Furnishings are just as they might have been in 1620, when this six-story tenement was built. June–Sept. Mon.–Sat. 10–6; rest of year until 5. Tel. 225-2424, ext. 6593. Seventeenth-century **Lady Stair's House** contains a collection of mementos from Robert Louis Stevenson, Robert Burns, and Sir Walter Scott, three of Scotland's most famous literary figures. Free. June–Sept. Mon.–Sat. 10–6. Greyfriars Kirk has a statue of **Greyfriars Bobby,** the loyal Scottish Terrier who stayed by his master's grave for 13 years.

Have a set of bagpipes or *skean dhu* (literally "black dirk," the dagger that is worn in the sock of a man wearing a kilt) made to order at **Clan Bagpipes,** 13a James Court, Lawnmarket. The real thing is expensive but exquisite. The **Museum of Childhood** is a treasure house of toys and other objects associated with children. Housed on five different light-filled floors of a tall narrow building, it displays over 100,000 toys, including doll houses, cars, tea sets, automata, and puppets. Free. 38 High St. Mon.–Sat. 10–6, Sun. 2–5. Tel. 225-2424. The **Edinburgh Wax Museum** contains life-size wax figures of Scottish celebrities and people from Scottish history. Kids particularly like the characters from *Peter Pan* by Scottish author J. M. Barrie, and the Chamber of Horrors. A holography exhibition is in the same building. Fee. 142 High St. Daily Oct.–Mar. 10–5, Apr.–Sept. 10–7. Tel. 226-4445. At the **Scottish Stone and Brass Rubbing Centre,** kids can create their own rubbings of any of the brasses or stones on display. All the materials they need to create a lasting souvenir are provided for a fee. Closed Sundays. Tel. 225-1131. Another brass rubbing center is the **Trinity Apse Brass Rubbing Centre,** on Chalmers Close, right off High St. Mon.–Sat. 10–5. Tel. 225-2424 ext. 6638.

The **Palace of Holyroodhouse** was the ancient home of the Stuarts and is the official Scottish residence of the queen. By the side of the palace are the ruins of Holyrood Abbey and Queen Mary's Bath House, where Queen Mary was said to have bathed in red wine. Fee. Apr.–Sept. Mon.–Sat. 9:30–5:15, Sun. 10:30–4:30; Nov.–Mar. Mon.–Sat. 9:30–3:30. Tel. 556-7371. Holyrood Park, adjacent to the palace, was once described by Sir Walter Scott as "a little piece of Highlands within the city." Walk behind the palace up the steep path to **Arthur's Seat** for a magnificent view across the city.

Just One Look: More Museums

The **National Gallery of Scotland** is on The Mound in the middle of Princes Street Garden. It is a small museum with a carefully selected collection containing outstanding works from the Renaissance to post-Impressionism. The national collection of Scottish art is worth touring for a glimpse of Scottish life as it once was. Outside the museum, talented artists often create their own masterpieces in chalk while street musicians perform. Next door, the **Scottish National Portrait Gallery** contains portraits of significant and beloved Scots done in many different media. Both free. Mon.–Sat. 10–5, Sun. 2–5. Tel. 556-8921.

Where the Sidewalk Ends: Zoos and More Parks

Below the castle, where the castle's moat once stood, is **Princes Street Gardens.** During summer months there are open-air performances for children, displays of Scottish country dancing, afternoon and evening band concerts, and competitions in Ross Open-Air Theatre. In the East Princes Garden is a flower clock, replanted every spring. The West Princes Garden has a children's playground and an outdoor cafe open during summer months.

The **Edinburgh Zoo**'s most popular summer exhibit is the group of comical penguins who parade every afternoon. Its children's farm has many of the same animals you'll find in any children's zoo, but the working miniatures of hay wagons, ploughs, and other farming equipment will enchant your youngsters. Fee. 2½ miles west of the city on Corstorphine Rd. Mon.–Sat. 9–6 (or dusk), Sun. open at 9:30. Tel. 334-9171.

The Edinburgh International Festival

With music, drama, dance, and exhibitions, Europe's biggest cultural festival runs from mid-August to early September. On stage are the world's best-known and most accomplished performers in theater, dance, music, and opera. Kids especially like the **Edinburgh Military Tattoo,** when massed bands of pipes and drums in full Highland dress play on the castle esplanade. Don't miss the festival's spectacular last-night fireworks. The **Festival Fringe** has close to fifty performances just for kids that include puppetry, storytelling, and mime plus clowns, jugglers, and strolling musicians. For adults, there are hundreds of plays, dozens of orchestral concerts, many traditional music concerts plus jazz, blues, rock, poetry readings, performance art, exhibitions, and circuses. Also coinciding with the festival are the **Edinburgh International Film Festival** and the **Edinburgh International Jazz Festival,** both a bit more informal than the other two festivals. Book tickets, especially for the Tattoo, as far in advance as possible from International Festival Box Office, 21 Market St.,

Edinburgh EH1 1BW; the Tattoo Office, 22 Market St., Edinburgh EH1 1BW; or the Edinburgh Festival Fringe Society, 180 High St., Edinburgh EH1 1QS. The BTA should have a listing of festival performers by May.

Sports

Marco's Leisure Centre has "Little Marco's" programs for kids. If the weather's been bad and your kids need to blow off some steam, take them here to crawl through tunnels and a maze, slide down bumpy slides, bounce on the "fantasy forest," and swim in the giant ball crawl. The centre also has squash, saunas, a gym, and aerobics classes for the adults. Fee. 51-95 Grove St. Call for times available to the general public. Tel. 228-2141.

Central Cycle Hire will rent **bicycles,** bike seats, and helmets for tiny ones. Ask and they will show you Edinburgh's off-road cycle routes. 13 Lochrin Pl., Tollcross. Tel. 228-6333. **Ice-skating** is offered at Murrayfield Ice Rink on Riverdale Crescent. The rink opens at 10 AM weekends and 2:30 weekdays. **Hillend Ski Centre,** in Pentland Hills, outside of town, has artificial snow and a chair lift that offers beautiful views from the top. Fee. Daily 9:30 AM–10 PM. Tel. 445-4433. For **swimming,** try the Royal Commonwealth Swimming Pool. Fee. 21 Dalkeith Rd. Weekdays 9–9, weekends 10–4. Tel. 627-7211.

NEAR EDINBURGH

Edinburgh Butterfly and Insect World has hundreds of rare butterflies in an indoor tropical setting plus tarantulas, praying mantises and scorpions, an adventure playground, picnic area, and tropical fish shop. Fee. Near Dalkeith on the A7. Apr.–Oct. 10–5:30. Tel. (031) 663-4932.

Dalhousie Courte Banquets re-creates a period feast in a candlelit setting with singing, music, and skits performed by actors and actresses in traditional costume. Dalhousie Courte, Cockpen, Bonnyrigg. Tel. (031) 663-5155 for essential advance booking.

At the **Union Canal Museum,** in *Linlithgow,* you can take a canal trip in a re-created steamboat, rent a rowboat or canoe, and see an exhibition on the Edinburgh-Glasgow canal. Fee. Manse Road Basin. Easter–Sept. Sat. and Sun. 2–5. Tel. (0506) 842575. **Linlithgow Palace,** the birthplace of Mary, Queen of Scots, is missing its roof, but it is still stately and impressive. There is a large children's play area below the castle, known as "The Peel," with swings, climbers, and a small pool. Call for open hours. Tel. (0506) 842896. **Beercraigs Coun-**

try Park, 2 miles south of Linlithgow, has a trout farm, deer farm, archery, canoeing, orienteering, fishing, rock climbing, and picnic areas. Open daily. Tel. (0506) 844516.

Traquair House, 1 mile south of *Innerleithen,* is famous as the oldest continuously inhabited house in Scotland with strong associations to Mary, Queen of Scots. The house contains many fine treasures, including a secret staircase, five craft workshops, an 18th-century brewery that still brews real ale plus a children's play area and a new maze. Fee. Easter–mid-Oct. 1:30–5:30, Jul.–Aug. 11:30–5:30. Tel. (0896) 830323.

THE BORDERS

In *Melrose* is **Melrose Abbey,** at one time the richest abbey in Scotland, made famous by Sir Walter Scott. Look for the pig gargoyle playing the bagpipes on the roof. Buried in the abbey is the famous 12th-century magician/alchemist Michael Scott, who is the wizard in Sir Walter's book *Lay of the Last Minstrel.* His recipe for making gold called for the blood from the finger of a ruddy man, a red owl, saffron, alum, and cucumber juice. Fee. Apr.–Sept. Mon.–Sat. 9:30–7, Sun. 2–7; Oct.–Mar. Mon.–Sat. 9:30–4, Sun. 2–4. Tel. (0896) 822562. The **Melrose Motor Museum** has old cars, bicycles, motorcycles, and more. Fee. Newstead Rd. May–Oct. daily 10:30–5:30. Tel. (0835) 22356.

Bowhill, 3 miles west of *Selkirk* off the A708, is the lovely home of the Scott Clan Chiefs. It has the typical collection of an historic home plus an adventure playground, pony trekking, nature walks, and mountain bike rentals. Fee. House and grounds: July–Aug. Mon.–Sat. 1–4:30, Sun. 2–6. Grounds: Apr.–Aug. daily (except Fri.) 12–5. Tel. (0750) 20732

Nearby, at *Jedburgh,* the 19th-century **Jedburgh Jail** stands on the site of the original castle. The jail has been turned into a museum with re-created scenes in the original cells. Small fee. Easter–Sept. Mon.–Sat. Mon.–Sat. 10–12 and 1–5, Sun. 2–5. Tel. (0835) 63254. The **Woodland Visitor Centre** has an adventure playground, children's games, and woodland exhibits. Three miles north of Jedburgh near junction of A68 and B6400. June–Sept. daily 10:30–5:30. Tel. (08353) 306.

CENTRAL SCOTLAND

GLASGOW

In Gaelic, *Glasgow* means "the dear green place," and given its 260 parks (more per capita than any other European city), it's easy to see why. Gracious Victorian buildings surround the dear green places, and an artistic vitality is felt throughout the city. People from Glasgow are called "Glaswegians," and you may need to pay close attention when chatting with them, as they have some of the thickest brogues in Scotland. The river Clyde cuts through the city. Circling the center of the city is an underground subway with trains running approximately every 5 minutes. Glasgow's **tourist office** is at 35 St. Vincent Place (Tel. 227-4880). The **telephone area code** is 041.

Detour! What to See and Do

The **Museum of Transport,** a must-see for kids, has streetcars, horse-drawn vehicles, bicycles, buses, model ships, the history of the Scottish automobile industry, and an old subway station. The one-horse open sleigh and the oldest bicycle in the world were our favorites. Free. Kelvin Hall, Bunhouse Rd. Mon.–Sat. 10–5, Sun. 2–5. Tel. 357-3929. Next door is the **Kelvin Hall International Sports Complex,** with an indoor track, table tennis, badminton, and more. Reserve in advance; kids must be accompanied by an adult. Tel. 337-1806.

Hagg's Castle, a 16th-century house near Pollok Park, is geared to children. Treasure-hunt cards and imaginative booklets help kids imagine Scottish domestic life from the 1560s to Victorian times and guide them through a 16th-century kitchen, a 17th-century bedroom and a Victorian nursery. There are kids' activities such as butter making, spinning, and weaving on Saturday afternoons. Free. 100 St. Andrew's Dr. Daily 10–5 and Sun. 2–5. Tel. 427-2725.

The **People's Palace Museum** traces Glasgow's history, particularly the city's 19th-century life and industry, although there are objects from every century. Its oddball collection has things kids are sure to love. Free. Glasgow Green. Mon.–Sat. 10–5, Sun. 2–5. Tel. 554-0223.

Glasgow Green is Europe's oldest public park. Once the site of Glasgow's public "laundry," washerwomen brought their tubs and dirty clothes to the park to stomp and squeeze out the dirt while they socialized. Today more civilized pastimes are pursued. If it's been raining cats and dogs and the kids are getting a bit jumpy, take them to **Marco's Leisure Centre,** where they have "Little Marco's" activities to tire them out. They can swim through a sea of balls, jump on trampolines, or play on slides. Call for days and times for the general public. Fee. Templeton Business Centre, Templeton St. Tel. 554-7184, ext. 240 or 241.

Glasgow has recently added a few festivals of its own. May's **Mayfest** offers a program of Scottish theater and music, and, in July, the **Glasgow International Folk Festival** has outstanding traditional music. Each August, Glasgow hosts the **World Pipe Band Championships.**

SOUTH OF GLASGOW

Langbank has **Finlaystone Country Estate,** an interesting historic home. Of greater interest to your kids will be the collection of dolls, the adventure playground, and the pony-trekking opportunities found there. Other outdoor attractions include woodland walks and formal gardens. Small fee. House: Apr.–Aug. Sun. 2:30–4:30. Gardens: daily year-round.

Southwest of Glasgow is *Kilmarnock* and **Dean Castle,** ancestral home of the Boyd family. This 14th- and 15th-century castle contains an outstanding collection of medieval armor and arms, musical instruments, and tapestries. The 200-acre park has an adventure play-ground, riding school, nature trails, aviary, and gardens. Fee for castle, children under 16 free; park free. Dean Rd. Castle: daily 12–5. Park: dawn–dusk. Tel. (0563) 26401, ext. 36.

The **Kelburn Country Centre,** 2 miles south of *Largs* along the west coast, has the feeling of an old village square with 18th-century farm buildings converted into craft shops, an old stockade, adventure course, and pony trekking plus beautiful gardens with waterfalls and nature walks. Fee. Easter–Sept. 10–6; Oct.–mid-Feb. Sun. 11–5; mid-Feb.–Easter weekends 11–5. Tel. (0475) 56685.

Continuing down the west coast, you'll reach *Ayr,* a popular seaside resort and the site of the annual **Robert Burns Festival.** Held during the third week of June, it features recitations and celebrations in honor of Burns. The **Tam o'Shanter Inn,** from Burns' best-known narrative poem, "Tam O'Shanter," is still in the town. Two miles south of Ayr is *Alloway,* birthplace of Burns and site of the **Land o'Burns Centre,** and the **Burns Cottage. Belleisle Park** has a small zoo and nature trail. Two miles of sandy beaches offer traditional seaside pastimes, and early strollers along the shore may see racehorses being exercised as Ayr is Scotland's racing center. Twelve miles south of Ayr is **Culzean Castle and Country Park,** the most visited castle in Scotland. There are 563 acres of gardens to explore, including an adventure playground, deer park, walled garden, aviary, swan pond, and orange and camellia house. Fee. Castle: May–Sept. 10–6; Apr., Oct. 12–5. Park: year-round. Tel. (065) 556274.

NORTH OF GLASGOW

Just northeast of Glasgow is **Stirling,** historic gateway city to the Highlands, dominated by its **castle,** perched above the city on a steep crag. Nearby, the **Blair Drummond Safari and Leisure Park** lets you drive through in your car to get a view of free-ranging zebras, camels, bison, monkeys, and elephants, to name a few. If you don't have a car or are driving a convertible, you can take a bus through the park. There is an adventure playground, sea lion performances, petting zoo, and barbecue and picnic facilities. Fee. Along A873 and A84. Apr.–Sept. daily 10–4:30. Tel. (0786) 841456.

The **Dunmore Pineapple** in *Airth* is an 18th-century "folly" that was originally a residence built for an 18th-century noblewoman. Now owned by the National Trust, it's a 40-foot carved-stone pineapple on top of a house available for overnight rental. Grounds: daily 10 AM–sunset. Near Stirling on the A905. For rental information contact Landmark Trust, Shottesbrook, Maidenhead, Berks. [Tel. (0628) 825920].

Between Edinburgh and Stirling is the **Scottish Railway Preservation Society** in *Bo'ness,* with its collection of old trains and a refurbished station. Steam trains run along the Bo'ness o' Kinneil track. There is a visitor center with the "Buffer-Stop Cafe." Union St. April–mid-Sept. weekend afternoons. Tel. (0506) 824318.

You take the high road and I'll take the low road to *Loch Lomond,* northwest of Glasgow. Cruise the largest expanse of fresh water in Great Britain on one of the boats run by **Maid of the Loch** in *Dumbartonshire.* Tel. (0389) 52044.

AROUND ST. ANDREWS

Along the North Sea between Edinburgh and Perth is the famous golfing town of St. Andrews. Considered the home of the sport, which Scotland originated, fairways there used to be hand-cut with scythes. **Old, New, Eden,** and **Jubilee** are courses in town that are open to visitors, but there can be a wait for a game. The town has manufactured golf balls for over 100 years. To reserve tee times, contact the Secretary, Links Management Committee, Golf Place, St. Andrews [Tel. (0334) 75757]. St. Andrews is also a popular beach resort with a swimming pool on the North Sea. The **Lammas Fair,** a re-creation of a medieval fair, is held in August. For more information contact the **tourist office** on South St. [Tel. (0334) 72021]. **St. Andrews Castle,** a 13th-century fortress with a bottle-shaped dungeon, secret passageways, and a museum is fun for the kids. Fee. Daily Mar.–Oct. 9:30–6:30; rest of year Sun. 2–6:30 Tel. (0334) 77196. **Earlshall Castle Gardens,** 6 miles north of St. Andrews, has topiary chessmen and a secret garden. Fee. Easter weekend–Sept. Thur.–Sun. 2–6. Tel.

(0334) 83205. The *East Neuk* is Scotland's beachy resort area, about a half hour's drive from St. Andrew's. Not quite the Côte d'Azur when it comes to sun and sand, the James V "golden fringe" and the little fishing villages possess great charm and character. The town of *Largo,* with a new Robinson Crusoe museum just opened, is popular with kids.

THE NORTHEAST

PERTH

For a view of the city that calls itself the heart of Scotland, climb to the top of Kinnoull Hill, where there is a tower and a stone table once used for dining. Two historic open spaces flank Perth, **South Inch** and **North Inch.** North Inch has a golf course and the Bells Sports Centre. South Inch has a fun park with a boating pond, paddling pools, and miniature golf. There is salmon fishing (permits needed; apply in advance at the tourist office) and boating in the Tay River. For 400 years **Scone Palace** was the place where the kings of Scotland were crowned. The current palace was built largely in the 1800s, but its importance goes back as far as the 9th century. The Stone of Scone, or Stone of Destiny, was once used for coronations; the original is now in Westminster Abbey and a replica is in its place. The palace has a great collection of rare objects, including French papier mâché objets d'art. The beautiful grounds have an adventure playground and a picnic park. Fee. Apr.–Sept. Mon.–Sat. 9:30–5, Sun. 1:30–5. Tel. (0738) 52300. From a special viewing gallery at **Caithness Glass** visitors watch paperweights being made. Free. Inveralmond Industrial Estate. Shop: Mon.–Sat. 9–5, Sun. 1–5. Glass making: Mon.–Fri. only. Tel. (0738) 37373. **Fairways Heavy Horse Centre** is a breeding center for the enormous Clydesdale horses, and late summer is the time to see the foals. Kids can take a ride in a wagon pulled by these huge but gentle horses, see a display of old farm implements, or on weekends watch a blacksmith at work. Fee. Two miles from Perth, at Kinfaun's. Apr.–Sept. daily 10–5. Tel. (0738) 25931.

NEAR PERTH

Crieff, to the west of Perth, has beautiful **Drummond Castle,** which offers nature trails and gardens. **Highland Horse Holidays** operates horse-drawn gypsy wagon holidays for families. They can set up your itinerary to insure the most scenic route. For more information, contact Gipsy Caravans, Bennybeg, Muthill Rd., Crieff, PH7 3 HQ [Tel. (0764) 2490].

South of Perth is *Dunfermline,* the birthplace of Andrew Carnegie. Thanks to Andy, its **Pittencrieff Glen Park** is one of the most generously endowed parks in Britain. There are 76 acres of formal gardens, nature walks, an aviary, animals, and a maze. Kids can enjoy the model traffic area, playground, outdoor theater, and pug engine. Open year-round during daylight hours. The public park in Dunfermline has trampolines, tennis, and a children's play area. Dunfermline Loch has wind surfing, canoeing, and sailing. Seven miles west of Dunfermline is *Culross,* a lovely town saved by the National Trust for Scotland, which restored its houses and cobblestone lanes. Little has changed in the last 300 years.

ABERDEEN AND ENVIRONS

The busy seaport of *Aberdeen* has one of the liveliest fish markets in Scotland. Its beach has an adventure playground with a fishing village theme. An amusement arcade and fun fair are open during spring and summer months, and its Beach Leisure Center is the place to be on a rainy day. **Hazelhead Park and Zoo** is an expansive park whose beautiful rose gardens are famous throughout Britain. The zoo has domestic animals and birds, and there is a playground and maze, trampolines in July and August, and nature walks year-round. You can rent horses at the Hayfield Riding School but you must book 24 hours in advance. Tel. (0224) 315703. Nearby is a leisure center with a swimming pool. **Duthie Park and Winter Gardens** has a boating pond, carved wooden animals, and playgrounds. Special children's entertainment and trampolines are available in July and August. The gardens have greenhouses with birds, fish, and turtles. Daily 10 AM–dusk. Polmuir Rd. and Riverside Dr.

A hit with the wee ones is **Storybook Glen,** with larger-than-life nursery rhyme characters set in a lovely garden and children's playgrounds scattered throughout. Fee. Five miles west of Aberdeen off South Deeside Rd. Daily Mar.–Oct. 10–6, Nov.–Feb. Sat. and Sun. 11–4. Tel. (0224) 732941.

Aberdeen is the center of "**castle country,**" and there are many castles within easy driving distance of the city. It has been called the land of fairy-tale castles, among the most enchanting of which is **Craigievar.** Many of the area's castles have educational brochures for children. **Crathes Castle and Gardens,** 2 miles east of Banchory, feature exceptionally beautiful painted ceilings, 300-year-old yew hedges, nature trails, an adventure playground, and wayfaring course. Fee. Daily May–Sept. 2–6. Tel. (033044) 525. **Drum Castle,** 10 miles from Aberdeen, has a massive stone tower, adventure playground, wayfaring course, farmland, and woodland areas. Fee. Castle: Daily May–Sept. 2–6. Grounds: year-round 9:30–dusk. Tel. (03308) 204. Queen Victoria bought **Balmoral Castle** in 1847 and enlarged it to accommodate the Royal Family as a country getaway. You can visit the grounds and the castle ballroom, but the rest of the castle is off limits. The grounds have a 100-foot tower, pony trekking, and lovely country walks. Fee. May–June Mon.–Sat. 10–5. Tel. (03384) 334.

INVERNESS AREA

Loch Ness is one of the largest freshwater lochs (lakes) in Scotland and its changing shadows from the trees along the shorelines and swirling mists make it the perfect place to search for Nessie, the Loch Ness Monster. Nessie was first sighted in the 6th century, and sightings continued intermittently over the years until the 1930s, when a road was built around the Loch and the sightings increased. Most sightings have been near **Urqhart Castle,** about 16 miles from Inverness, near the little town of *Drumnadrochit.* The castle is a ruined beauty with a tower and a spiral staircase from which there are stunning views on a clear day. You can climb all over the castle; it's surrounded by grassy slopes. Fee. Apr.–Sept. Mon.–Sat. 9:30–7, Sun. 2–7, Oct.–Mar. Mon.–Fri. 9:30–4, Sun. 2–4. Drumnadrochit's **Loch Ness Centre** is a rather expensive tourist trap, but kids love it. The new high-tech exhibition consists of photos of Nessie taken throughout the years, video documentaries about searches for her, and some models of the little darlin'; it may be over the heads of "wee ones." Its gift shops are large and have every kind of Nessie item under the sun. Daily June–Aug. 9 AM–9:30 PM. Spring, Fall 9:30–6:15. Tel. (04562) 573. Drumnadrochit and nearby *Lewistown* are farming communities with lots of bed-and-breakfast establishments if you want to stay overnight to continue your monster hunt. **Borlum Farm** rents farm cottages for up to six people for a reasonable price, and they also have pony trekking. Tel. (04562) 358.

Cawdor Castle, built in the 14th century, is best known for its romantic link with Shakespeare's Macbeth. Tour the castle and look for the tiny living room in the tower, the dungeon, and the kitchens. There are nature trails, a putting green, miniature golf, ducks to feed, swings, picnic areas, and snacks. Fee. Between Inverness and Nairn on B9090. Daily May–Oct. 10–5:30. Tel. (06677) 615.

THE CAIRNGORM MOUNTAINS

The **Highland Wildlife Park,** in *Kincraig,* is operated by the Royal Zoological Society of Scotland and has animals that once roamed the Scottish Highlands, including brown bear, elk, arctic fox, and lynx. You'll also see shaggy long-horned Highland cattle, wild sheep, horses, goats, bison, and deer. The park is renowned for its collection of Scottish birds. Fee. Between Aviemore and Kingussie on the B9152. Apr.–Oct. Mon.–Sat. 10–6, Sun. 2–6; Nov.–Mar. Mon.–Fri.

10–3. Tel. (05404) 270. The **Highland Folk Museum,** in *Kingussie,* recreates life in the Highlands throughout the ages. An open-air museum includes a turf house, clack mill, and salmon smokehouse. Indoor attractions include examples of domestic interiors from the past and a farming museum. Fee. Duke St. Apr.–Oct. Mon.–Sat. 10–6, Sun. 2–6; Nov.–Mar. Mon.–Fri. 10–3. Tel. (05402) 307.

The fun-filled **Landmark Visitor Centre,** in *Carrbridge,* between Inverness and Aviemore on the A9, has an adventure playground with a 50-foot tube slide, tarzan swings, and a giant woodland maze. Its Tree Top Trail leads children through the pines to a height of 20 feet. Climb to the special viewing tower above the trees for a panorama of the surrounding countryside. Active kids can roam around the Highland Sculpture Park which has works by Britain's best-known sculptors in wood, bronze, stone, and steel, or they can accompany you to the exhibition and audiovisual show documenting the Highland clans' struggle for survival. Fee. Summer 9:30–9:30; winter 9:30–5. Tel. (047984) 614.

THE HIGHLANDS

Oban, about 50 miles south of Fort William, is a popular coastal resort with lots of ruined castles nearby. It offers pony trekking, sailing, fishing, sandy beaches, and evening entertainment with a Scottish flavor. It's called "The Gateway to the Islands" as it is an important ferry port. A **Highland music festival** takes place in May. Special events in July include a **puppet festival** and **Highland games.** For more information, contact the **tourist office,** Boswell House, Argyll Square [Tel. (0631) 63122].

Blair Castle, in *Blair Atholl,* dates from the 13th century. Its beautiful grounds contain a deer park, nature trails, and pony trekking, while the castle has an interesting collection of arms, toys, and treasures. Fee. Northwest of Perth on the A9. Apr.–mid-Oct. Mon.–Sat. 10–6, Sun. 2–6; Jul. and Aug. Sun. 12–6. Tel. (079681) 232. The **Atholl Country Collection** shows how villagers lived in the 19th century. Kids can touch and examine the artifacts from the blacksmith's shop, crofter's stable, and school. Fee. June–mid Oct. daily 1:30–5:30; Jul. and Aug. 9:30–5:30. Tel. (079681) 207.

THE NORTHERN HIGHLANDS

Heading northwest into the Highlands, you'll come to the 18th-century fishing village of *Ullapool,* on the shore of saltwater Loch Broom. It's a charming little town and a good base for fishing, pony trekking, canoeing, sailing, or hiking. Your best bet here is to stay at the child-friendly **Ceilidh Place** at 14 Argyll Pl. (Tel. (0854) 2103). It contains a congenial hotel, a great bookshop with a children's section, and cafe with nightly Scottish music jam sessions. The staff will help arrange your recreational activities.

Northwest from Ullapool is *Lochinver,* a quaint town with some of Scotland's most beautiful scenery. Nearby there are magnificent white-sand **beaches;** a particular favorite was Achmelvich. North of Lochinver, in *Durness,* is **Smoo Cave,** a limestone cave set in the seacliff wall with three large rooms hollowed out by the ocean. You can enter one of the rooms by land. The Scottish **National Surfing Championships** are held in *Thurso,* on the northernmost coast of the Highlands. California kids might sniff at a Scottish surf championship, but this one is quite tricky because of the reefs the surfers must avoid while competing.

THE ISLANDS

ARRAN

The scenic *Isle of Arran* is primarily a holiday island, and the coastal road around it is dotted with hotels and tearooms, tourist shops and playgrounds. Its mountain-capped interior is as wild as any part of the Highlands, and you can ride ponies, canoe, or fish without seeing the crowds hovering along the shore. The island's major site is the 13th-century **Brodick Castle,** historic home of the Duke of Hamilton, and now owned by the National Trust. Kids can explore the gardens and country park with its adventure playground while adults savor the excellent collection of antiques. Fee. Castle: May–Sept. daily 1–5. Gardens: year-round 10–5. Tel. (0770) 2202.

ISLE OF SKYE

This 48-mile-long island offers spectacular mountain scenery, old castles, and little villages. It has good climbing and hiking trails plus pony trekking, fishing, and boat trips. The Isle of Skye is a quick ferry ride from mainland Scotland if you leave from Kyle of Lochalsh, and there are ferries from other mainland towns and islands. **Dunvegan**'s moated **castle,** the oldest inhabited dwelling in Scotland, was the home of the McLeods for 700 years. It contains a fairy flag called "Bratach Sith," believed to have magical properties. Fee. May–Sept. Mon.–Sat. 10:30–5:30; Apr. and Oct. 2–5. Several miles north of Dunvegan is the **Piping Centre** at *Boreraig,* which will tell the history of the Highland bagpipe and its music.

The **Skye Museum of Island Life,** in *Kilmuir,* has five thatched cottages that give a glimpse of Highland life in centuries past. One of the tiny cottages was once inhabited by 12 children, parents, and grandparents. Small fee. On the A855. Mid-May–Oct. Mon.–Sat. 9–6.

The **Clan Donald Centre** has 40 acres of woodland gardens and nature trails, the ruins of **Armdale Castle,** and a restaurant in a restored stable with authentic Scottish food. Fee. At *Armdale,* just north of Armdale pier. Easter–Oct. 10–5:30. Tel. (04714) 305.

Ireland

Nicknamed the Emerald Isle, Ireland brings to mind a mossy green countryside covered in mists, shiny green shamrocks, and the forest-green waistcoats of leprechauns and little people. Its past is filled with tales of fairies, changelings, banshees, giants, and other friendly and fierce inhabitants of the spirit world.

The Irish have large families, and their "little people" are welcome everywhere. Children accompany their parents to pubs, social events, and fancy restaurants. "The more the merrier" is the attitude of the Irish when it comes to children. Irish courtesy, wit, and hospitality are even more pronounced when you take the kids.

When asked what they like most about Ireland, young travelers inevitably reply, "Playing with the Irish kids." Meeting other people and making friends "on the road" creates some of the most treasured memories for adults as well as children. Families go back again and again to enjoy Ireland's warm welcome.

Preparing Your Kids: Books

Younger children: *Leprechauns Never Lie* by Lorna Balian, *Clancy's Coat* by Eve Bunting, *The Hungry Leprechaun* by Mary Calhoun, *Animal Tales from Ireland* by M. Grant Cormack; *Fin M'Coul* by Tomie De Paola; *The Leprechaun's Story* by Richard Kennedy; *To Sing a Song as Big as Ireland* by Nathan Zimelman.

Older children: *A Fine, Soft Day* by Jane Forman, *A Family in Ireland* by Tom Moran, *Finn MacCool and the Small Men of Deeds* by Pat O'Shea, *The Lost Legend of Finn* by Mary Tannen, *Trouble at Mrs. Porkwines* by John Wood, and books on Irish illuminated manuscripts containing examples such as the *Book of Kells*.

Wha'd'ya Wanna Do?

Structure your trip loosely so that your kids can have time to play with the locals when the opportunity arises. If you have a particular interest, you can plan a specialized vacation with the help of the Irish Tourist Board. Request a checklist of their wide variety of brochures.

IRISH TOURIST BOARD
> *U.S.A.:* Irish Tourist Board, 757 Third Ave., New York, NY 10017. Tel: 212-418-0800.
> *Canada:* Irish Tourist Board, 150 King St., East, Toronto, Ontario M5C 1C3. Tel. 416-364-1301.

Ireland has local tourist boards, referred to as **Bord Fáilte,** in large cities and most medium-sized villages.

If it is an **out-of-doors holiday** that you seek, request brochures such as "Angling Ireland," "Cycling Ireland," "Equestrian Ireland," "Sailing Ireland," and "Walking Ireland." If your children are older and you want part of your trip to have an **educational focus,** a brochure called "Live and Learn Ireland" or "Outdoor Pursuits Centres: Adventure Sports" can help you choose a summer-school experience in the arts, traditional music, canoeing, or mountaineering. Both residential and nonresidential schools are available, and the length of the session ranges from 1 day to several weeks.

The Irish love a good party, and their sense of fun is at its best during the week of March 17, when they honor their beloved patron saint on **St. Patrick's Day.** Colorful theme parades march through the cities' streets, with the largest celebration held in Dublin. If that's not enough of an eyeful, be sure to catch the dog shows, horse races, folk dancing, and Gaelic games held throughout Dublin and all of Ireland.

Throughout the country there are hundreds of small **traditional music and dance festivals,** and most of them take place during the late spring and summer months. The tourist board's pamphlet "Calendar of Events" has information about a great many of them. Informal music festivals, called *Fleadhanna,* where traditional musicians gather to play, eat, and chat, take place throughout the summer. They are free of charge.

Don't miss the chance to enjoy a **medieval banquet** at Bunratty or one of the other castles that offer them. While you feast on medieval specialties, entertainers amuse you with the lively music, dance, and the oral tradition of the Ireland of centuries past. **Kissing the Blarney Stone** in Cork has always been a favorite for many children who visit Ireland, as is taking a **pony cart ride through the Gap of Dunloe.**

Gaelic games are great fun to watch. They take place every Sunday afternoon throughout the summer somewhere in Ireland. The local tourist offices can give you a schedule. **Point-to-point races,** which are local horse races that are often run in the field, from one point to another, are a very Irish tradition and take place all over the country from spring to fall.

Lights Out! Special Irish Accommodations

The Irish Tourist Board's *Self-Catering Accommodation Guide* and *Irish Cottage Holiday Homes* publication can tell you all about renting a traditional Irish cottage equipped with modern facilities. The following businesses can also arrange a cottage or apartment for you:

> Castles, Cottages and Flats of Ireland and the U.K. (Counties Cork and Galway), P.O. Box 261, Westwood, MA 02090. Tel. 617-329-4680 or 617-326-6762.
>
> Families Abroad (Dublin, Galway, and Sligo), 194 Riverside Dr., New York, NY 10025. Tel. 212-787-2434 or 718-766-6185.
>
> Hideaways International (countrywide), P.O. Box 1464, Littleton, MA 01460. Tel. 800-843-4433 or 617-486-8955.
>
> Lismore Travel (countrywide), 106 East 31st St., New York, NY 10016. Tel. 800-547-6673 or 212-685-0100.
>
> Lynott Tours (the southwest), 350 Fifth Ave., Suite 2619, New York, NY 10018. Tel. 800-221-2474 or 212-760-0101.

For information on **hotels,** the national tourist board can send you their *Hotels and Guesthouses Illustrated Guide*. **Guest houses** are a less expensive option. Many hotels and guest houses have family rooms with three, four, or more beds in the same room; children are often given special discounts. In many cities and towns, the local tourist office will book a room for you for a very small fee. We have listed a few hotels in Dublin with special features for families such as kitchenettes, swimming pools, or proximity to parks.

Bed-and-Breakfast establishments are as common in Ireland as they are in Britain and offer accommodations in city or country homes or in farmhouses. Many of them are run by people with children, and staying in B and B's is a good way to experience what it's like to live like the Irish. A list is available from the national tourist board.

Families are welcome in all **hostels** operated by An Óige, the Irish Youth Hostel Association. Some hostels are more suitable for families than others. Contact the head office for information and advice. 39 Mountjoy Square, Dublin 1. Tel. (01) 363111.

Horse-drawn caravans are available for hire. They usually sleep four people and have a tiny galley (kitchen). You can sleep in them or park the caravan and opt for a B and B. Here again, the national tourist board can be of help.

Camping should be attempted in camper vans only as the frequent rain can put a damper on family fun. Request the brochure "Caravan and Camping Parks" from the national tourist board for a list of official campsites. You can camp almost anywhere, but be sure to ask the local farmer for permission before you park and set up camp on his property.

Getting Around

Touring Ireland by **car** is the most popular way of getting around. A few areas in the west have signs in Gaelic while maps are in English, making navigating a bit tricky.

Irish Rail operates **trains** to all major cities. Irish Bus has a nationwide network of **buses** serving all the major cities outside the Dublin area. There is an interlink service connecting those cities to small towns and villages. Ireland is a member of the Eurail network, and Eurailpasses are valid for bus and train travel in Ireland, excluding city services. Irish ferries from Le Havre and Cherbourg in France to Rosslare, Ireland, provide a free ferry link for Eurailpass holders. The Emerald Isle Card is good for unlimited travel on rail services of Irish Rail and Northern Ireland Railways, long-distance buses, and city buses. Passes are available for 8 days of travel within a 15-day period with discounts for children. Contact the national tourist board for details.

Ferry boat services operate to many islands from the mainland. The Irish Tourist Board can supply you with information and schedules. If a family **bicycling** tour is on your agenda, the national tourist board can give you a list of the 76 Raleigh "Rent-a-Bike" dealers throughout the country.

Nuts and Bolts

Does anyone care what time it is? Most shops are open from 9 AM to 5:30 or 6:00 PM Monday through Saturday. In many smaller towns, they close at 1 PM, 1 day per week (usually Wednesday, Thursday, or Friday).

National holidays: New Year's Day, St. Patrick's Day (March 17), Good Friday, Easter Monday, the first Mondays in June and August, the last Monday in October, Christmas Day, and St. Stephen's Day (December 26).

Can I have my allowance? Ireland uses the Irish pound, or "poont," as it is sometimes pronounced. It is a currency separate from the British pound sterling, although it is often close to the same value and is divided into 100 pence. Notes used are 1, 5, 10, 20, 50, and 100. Coins are in the following denominations: 50p, 20p, 10p, 5p, and 1p.

Telephones: Post offices, with green fronts and the Irish name *Oifig an Phoist*, are convenient for making long-distance calls.

Useful nationwide phone numbers: Ireland's country code is 353. The operator is 10; directory assistance is 190; and all emergencies are 999.

Embassies and consulates: The U.S. Embassy is at 42 Elgin Road, Dublin 4, Ireland [tel. (01) 688777]. The Canadian Embassy is at 65/68 Street, Stephen's Green, Dublin 2 [Tel. (01) 781988].

Let's Eat!

Breakfast is hearty with lots of "porridge," eggs, bacon, sausage, toast, tea, coffee, and juice. Irish cooking is for the most part plain with boiling and stewing the two most common ways of cooking. Milk is widely available. The miles of coastline mean lots of delicious, fresh "normal"-looking fish; fish and chips is a national institution. Potatoes are still a very important part of the Irish diet and you can find them baked, boiled, sliced, fried, or made into potato pancakes. Be sure to try *colcannon*, a dish of diced potatoes fried in butter with onions and cabbage and topped with cream. Irish soda bread and brown bread are delicious paired with Irish cheddar cheese. In Dublin taste the *coddle* (boiled sausages and bacon with potatoes). Limerick ham, which is smoked over oak chips, is delicious. Lamb, pork, and beef are high quality, and pheasant is popular.

Formula and Baby Food, Diapers and Baby Gear

Formula and baby food are found in larger grocery stores and chemists (drugstores) throughout Ireland. Much of the baby food comes without sugar. Diapers are called "nappies," and they are available in neighborhood grocery stores, chemists, and large supermarkets. Wipes are also readily available wherever you find "nappies." Cribs are called "cots," and most hotels and bed-and-breakfast establishments have them. A baby carriage is a "pram," a stroller is a "push chair," and a pacifier is a "dummy." Rental cars have front and rear seat belts, and car seats are regularly used for babies.

Sidewalk Talk

The country's official tongue is Irish, a Gaelic langauge that was spoken nationwide until the mid-19th century. There are still over 79,000 native Gaelic speakers, mostly in the west. With over 40 million Americans and Canadians of Irish descent, tracing one's ancestry has become a popular pastime.

The Lay of the Land

The Island of Ireland is divided into thirty-two counties, twenty-six of which make up the Republic of Ireland. The other six form Northern Ireland, which is part of the United Kingdom. We will begin our tour of Ireland in Dublin and then travel out from there.

DUBLIN

Founded by the Vikings over 1,000 years ago, Dublin has a very youthful population and children are seen everywhere. It is a city of talkers and storytellers; your children may not appreciate that its prolific output of the written word has produced three Nobel Prize winners for literature (George Bernard Shaw, William Butler Yeats, and Samuel Beckett), but the output of the spoken word in tall tales and yarns will delight them. Be sure to pick up a copy of the city magazine In Dublin to know what's happening. The **tourist board** is at 14 Upper O'Connell St. (Tel. 747733) and Baggot St. Bridge (Tel. 765871). Dublin's **telephone area code** is 01.

Public buses, some of them double decker, cover the city. Get a free route map at the tourist board. Weekly passes offering unlimited rides are available. The DART (Dublin Area Rapid Transit) is an electric commuter train that travels from the Connolly and Pearse railway stations in the city center to outlying areas.

Where to Stay

HOTELS

The *Shelbourne Hotel,* next to St. Stephen's Green, is part of the child-friendly Trusthouse Forte chain. Many rooms have interconnecting doors and baby-sitting can be easily arranged. 27 St. Stephens Green. Tel. 766471. From U.S. 800-225-5843. **Expensive.**

The *Georgian House* is close to St. Stephen's Green and has reduced rates for children sharing their parents' room. Prices include a full Irish breakfast, and a good restaurant serves dinner. 20 Lower Baggot St. Dublin 2. Tel. 618832. **Moderate.**

Saint Aiden's Guesthouse, a refurbished Victorian guest house, has five family rooms with special rates for children and baby-sitting services by advance request. 32 Brighton Rd., Rathgar, Dublin 6. Tel. 906178/902011. **Inexpensive.**

Kellys Hotel is a centrally located family-run hotel near St. Stephen's Green and the castle. Six family rooms are available, and a full Irish breakfast is included. 36 S. Great George's St. Dublin 2. Tel. 779277. **Inexpensive.**

CAMPING

Cromlech Caravan and Camping Park is off N11 at Ballybrack village. Tel. 685512.

Shankill Caravan and Camping Park is on route N11. In addition to trailer and campsites, it has sixteen trailers (called caravans) you can rent on-site. Tel. 820011.

The Lay of the City

Many of the sights in Dublin are in close proximity in the center of the city to the south of the river Liffey, which cuts through the town. Most are within walking distance of each other.

Detour! What to See and Do

TRINITY COLLEGE AND THE OLD TOWN

Trinity College, in the center of town, was founded by Elizabeth I in 1591. Its library receives a free copy of any book published in Ireland or Britain, and there are currently about 2.5 million volumes housed here. Needless to say, it is Ireland's largest collection of books, and half a mile of shelves are added every year! Remind your kids that before the invention of the printing press, books were hand-printed using carved wooden blocks; before that they were written entirely by hand. Show them the library's greatest treasure, *The Book of Kells,* a detailed illuminated manuscript from the 8th century embellished with designs and illustrations in gold, silver, and bright colors. Two volumes are on display along with other examples of early illuminated manuscripts. Fee; under 18 free. Mon.–Fri. 9:30–4:45, Sat. 9:30–12:45.

Head down Dame Street and then St. Edward Street to **Dublin Castle,** where families of Irish descent can trace their ancestry at its Heraldic Museum. Started in 1205 and rebuilt in 1228 and 1361, the castle held the Courts of Justice where "Trials by Ordeals" were fought gladiator-style. The accused and the accuser fought with sword and shield; whoever remained alive was declared innocent.

Down Kildare Street from Trinity College is the **National Museum,** which houses a collection of Irish antiquities dating from as far back as 6,000 B.C. and other items from the present day. Most famous is the 8th-century Tara brooch, but kids will like the "live" leprechaun. The Music Room contains many Irish-made musical instruments, such as harps, pipes, and odd string instruments. Fee; under 18 free. Tues.–Sat. 10–5, Sun. 2–5. Tel. 618811.

Continue down Kildare Street until you reach **St. Stephen's Green,** a refreshing public park in the middle of the city with an artificial lake with ducks, waterfalls, fountains, a "smell garden" for the blind, a children's playground, and flower gardens. Outdoor performances are given during the summer months near the old bandstand.

ACROSS THE RIVER

St. Michan's Church has vaults with open coffins revealing mummified bodies; some are hundreds of years old. Enter the vaults through a metal trap door on the outside of the church. Their clothing has long ago vanished, but the bodies' leathery skin, fingernails, teeth, and other features are remarkably well-preserved due to the dry air, constant temperature, and the natural methane gas being released by what's left of the rotting oak forest beneath the church. Not for the squeamish. Fee. Vaults: Mon.–Fri. 10–12:45, 2–4:45.

The **Hugh Lane Municipal Gallery of Modern Art** has a Saturday morning children's program from 11:30 to 12:30 where children can do hands-on art projects. Children 5 to 12 are welcome; those under 7 must be accompanied by a parent. The museum's collection includes French Impressionists and 19th- and 20th-century Irish artists. Kids program free. Parnell Square. Tel. 741903.

Nearby, the **National Wax Museum** has a "Children's World" of fairytales brought to life, music and film stars, and characters from Irish history. Most kids will insist on visiting the creepy Chamber of Horrors. Fee. Granby Row, Parnell Square. Mon.–Sat. 10–5:30, Sun. 1–5:30. Tel. 726340.

The **Museum of Childhood** in Dublin has a collection of beautifully made toys from the past. Of particular interest are the doll houses with their exquisitely detailed miniature furnishings, the antique dolls, and the rocking horses. Small fee. 20 Palmerston Park, Rathmines. Jul. and Aug. 2–5:30; rest of year Sun. 2–5:30. Closed Oct. Tel. 741903.

Where the Sidewalk Ends: Zoos and More Parks

Phoenix Park is Europe's largest enclosed city park; here deer roam through the trees as they have since the 17th century. There are pony and pony-cart rides, an amusement park, lakes, a racetrack, ball grounds, and a lakefront coffeeshop. Polo games and an open-air market take place on Sunday mornings.

Dublin Zoo, in Phoenix Park, is the world's third oldest zoological gardens, famous for its lion-breeding program and birthplace of the MGM lion. In the movies, he was, in fact, only yawning and another lion's roaring voice was superimposed over his. Other special attractions for kids include a pets' corner, zoo train, and pony rides. Fee. Tel. 771425.

Sports

Bicycles can be rented at Rent-A-Bike, 58 Lower Gardiner St. (Tel. 725931). **Hurling** is a popular sport in Ireland. Similar to field hockey, in that sticks are used, the ball can be hit in the air as well as on the ground. The women's version of hurling is called **camogie.** Games are played throughout the year. If you need an indoor activity, try **ice-skating** at the Dublin Ice Rink, Dolphins Barn, Dublin 8 (Tel. 532170), or Silver Skate Ice Rink, 376 N. Circular Rd., Dublin 7 (Tel. 307355/ 301263). The **rugby** season starts in October with home games played in Lansdowne Stadium.

Performing Arts

The **Lambert Mews Puppet Theatre** is 5 miles from the center of Dublin, in Monkstown; the Dart train will take you within 100 yards of it. Its marionette or rod puppet performances are held in a 300-seat theater on most Saturdays at 3:30. Call to find out the program. Fee. Clifden Lane. Tel. 800974. The **Olympia Theatre,** on Dame Street, has everything from vaudeville shows to dramatic works, pantomimes to concerts. *In Dublin* will let you know what is being performed at this classic example of a Victorian music hall. 72 Dame St. Tel. 778962.

NEAR DUBLIN

TO THE SOUTH

Glendalough, called "the valley of the two lakes," is a beautiful steep-sided valley with ruined abbeys and hiking trails. At one time a monastic city existed here, but today all that remains are three sets of ruins. Because it is only 30 miles south of Dublin, it is often filled with tourists. The Upper Lake up to Wicklow Gap is less visited; you can hire boats to take you across to visit the ruins of a church and a cave used as a place of solitude. The Lower Lake has the remains of a monastic settlement along its shores.

Bray was a Victorian seaside resort and is still one of Ireland's biggest and most popular beach towns. Built in the 1850s, it has a wide promenade, a beautiful park, miniature golf, a bandstand, and amusement park fare such as carnival rides and games. Rowboats can be hired on the promenade. **Bray Head** rises steeply from the sea to a height of 791 feet. The side facing town is a public park; walk to its top from the end of the promenade on a path known as the Great White Way. **Kilruddery House and Gardens** has canals, fountains, ponds, and a garden theater. Apr.–Oct. by appointment. Tel. 01-683405.

TO THE NORTH

Malahide Castle, in *Malahide,* contains a collection of paintings that depict Irish life in the old days. Its collection of Irish period furniture is one of the best in the country. Have your kids keep an eye out for the two ghosts, Puck and the White Lady, who are said to roam the halls. Puck is a dwarf from medieval times and the White Lady is said to step out of her portrait in the Great Hall and wander about at night. There are 270 acres of grounds with Irish railway models from the 1840s and 1850s and beautiful gardens. Fee. Apr.–Oct. Mon.–Fri. 10–12:45 and 2–6, Sat. 11–6, Sun. 2–6; Nov.–Mar. Mon.–Fri. 10–12:45 and 2–5, Sat.–Sun. 2–5. Tel. 452655.

THE SOUTHEAST

COUNTY WICKLOW

Wicklow Town has the least rainfall of any city or town in Ireland; good thing there are decent beaches nearby. East of town are the ruins of the 12th-century **Black Castle.** Slightly inland from Wicklow, in *Rathdrum,* is **Avondale Forest Park,** a 523-acre forest park with nature trails and a river walk. Open year-round. Three miles from Rathdrum is the **Clara-Lara Fun Park,** an outdoor adventure park with boating, rafting, nature walks, fishing, and adventure playgrounds. Fee. Apr.–Oct. daily 10:30–6:30. Tel. (0404) 46161. **Powerscourt Gardens** are on a hillside with a natural lake and magnificent view of the Wicklow Hills. Its lavish formal gardens cover 14,000 acres with the highest waterfall in Ireland, a wishing well, deer park, Japanese garden, sundials, and statuary. Easter–Oct. daily 10–5:30. Twelve miles south of Dublin outside of Enniskerry.

COUNTY KILKENNY

Kilkenny is a medieval city whose buildings are made of a distinctive limestone rock quarried in the area. When the stone is polished, it turns black; you'll often hear people refer to Kilkenny as the marble city. The **tourist office** is on Rose Inn St. [Tel. (056) 21755]. The beautifully restored 12th-century **Kilkenny Castle** is the most-visited historic building in Ireland. Its landscaped grounds include a children's play area. The tearoom in the old castle kitchen is also a kid's favorite. Fee. Mid-June–mid-Sept. 10–7; mid-Sept.–mid-June Tues.–Sun. 10–5. Tel. (056) 21450. **Kilkenny Design Workshops,** housed in the castle's stables, are worth a visit if you are interested in seeing the best in modern Irish design in ceramics, woven and printed textiles, silver and metalwork, and woodturning. Apr.–Dec. Mon.–Sat. 9–6; Jan.–Mar. Mon.–Sat. 10–6. **Kyteler's Inn,** one of Ireland's oldest houses, was the home of wealthy Dame Alice Kyteler (born in 1280), who gained prominence as a banker and money lender. She was accused of witchcraft in 1324 and of poisoning her four husbands. She escaped in the nick of time, but her poor maid Petronilla was convicted and burned at the stake. The house is now a restaurant and bar. The city comes to life in late August with **Kilkenny Arts Week,** which brings a great outpouring of music from chamber orchestras to pub entertainment, theater, and the spoken word.

Dunmore Cave, 7 miles north of Kilkenny, is an outstanding example of a natural limestone cave. Head down 200 steps into the cave where illuminated walkways allow you to admire the elaborate stalactite and stalagmite formations. Most famous is the "Market Cross" stalagmite, which is over 20 feet high. Fee. Mid-Mar.–mid-June Tues.–Sat. 10–4:15, Sun. 2–4:15; mid-June–mid-Sept. daily 10–6:15. Tel. (056) 67726.

COUNTY WEXFORD

This county is known for its good beaches, particularly Courtown, Curracloe, Rosslare, and Duncannon. *Wexford,* an ancient town of narrow winding streets, can be explored on foot. Its **tourist board** is on Crescent Quay [Tel. (053) 23111]. The **Wexford Maritime Museum** is on a ship in Kinmore Quay. Catch a horse race at **Bettyville Races** for a raucous good time. The **Wexford Wildfowl Reserve** has screened approaches and an observation tower from which you can see many varieties of ducks and geese. Half of the population of Greenland's white-fronted geese winter here. A display of animals found on the reserve is near the reception area. Three miles south of Wexford is **Johnstown Castle,** which contains the **Irish Agricultural Museum** on its grounds. Here, reconstructed stables, authentic cottage interiors, and a dairy as well as collections of farming implements and agricultural tools bring Ireland's past to life. June–Aug. Mon.–Fri. 9–5, Sat. and Sun. 2–5; rest of year 9:30–12:30 and 1:30–5. Tel. (053) 42888. The **Irish National Heritage Park** is 2 miles from Wexford, at *Ferrycarrig.* Opened in 1988, this open-air museum has full-scale replicas of a Viking ship, stone circles, homesteads, burial sites, and places of worship. Its exhibits cover 9,000 years of Irish history. Fee. Tel. 053-41733.

COUNTY WATERFORD

Remains of **Waterford's** old Norman city walls are found near the railway station and Castle Street, where you can visit some of the old defensive towers. Tour **Reginald's Tower,** an ancient fortification with 10-foot-thick walls, which was a dank prison in the 19th century. Erected in 1003, it was a target during Waterford's many sieges; its walls still bear the scars of cannon shots. The **tourist board** is at 41 The Quay [Tel. (051) 75788]. Keep your hands to yourself! The **Waterford Crystal Factory,** now the largest crystal factory in the world, offers tours and items for sale. Tours are conducted Monday through Friday; call the tourist office for times. Free. Cork Road, 2 miles out of the city. Nine miles south of Waterford is **Tramore,** a family resort with 3 miles of sandy beaches. On a hillside overlooking Tramore Bay, it has lots of entertaining seaside activities for kids. In addition to miniature golf and swimming, there is an enormous **amusement park** with a miniature railway, paddle steamer, boating lake, and adventure island. Walk the long seaside promenade to the **Burrows,** an odd group of sand hills about a mile long to the east of town. Old ruins are speckled throughout the area.

COUNTY TIPPERARY

Cahir Castle, in the picturesque town of **Cahir,** is Ireland's largest 15th-century castle. You may recognize it from the movies *Excalibur* and *Barry Lyndon,* which were filmed there. A 20-minute audiovisual presentation, short enough to keep the kids' attention, tells about Irish architecture and sites in the area. Fee. June–Aug. 10–7:30; Sept.–May 10–5:30. Tel. (052) 41011. About 10 miles from Cahir is the **Fetchard Folk Farm and Transport Museum** with displays of 2,000 items from folk and farm life. Kids will especially enjoy the old baby carriages, bicycles, and tricycles. There is a well-equipped playground and a picnic area outside. Fee. Fetchard. May–Sept. Mon.– Sat. 10–6, Sun. 1:30–6. Tel. (052) 31516. The **Mitchelstown Caves,** southwest of Cahir, are filled with extraordinary limestone formations aptly named "The Cathedral," "The House of Commons," and "The Organ." They were discovered by accident in 1833 and are privately owned by farmers. Guided half-mile tours are flood-lit. Fee. Burncourt. Daily 10–6. Tel. (052) 67246.

The **Rock of Cashel,** north of the town of **Cashel,** supports an impressive complex of medieval buildings and monuments perched atop the dark limestone rock. Illuminated at night, it is truly an eerie and impressive sight. Saint Patrick said one of his first masses here, and legend has it that he used a shamrock to explain the concept of three-in-one divinity. From that moment, Ireland's emblem was born. Cashel Cathedral, the tallest of the ruins, is connected to a 15th-century castle. A small museum at the entrance to the complex contains St. Patrick's cross. Be sure the kids see the elaborately decorated sarcophagus in the 12th-century Cormac's Chapel. Small fee. June–Sept. 9–7:30; Oct.–May 10–4:30. Cashel's **tourist board** is in the town hall [Tel. (062) 61333]. **Cashel Folk Village** is a re-creation of a 19th-century town with a forge, schoolhouse, pub, blacksmith, and butcher. Fee. Dominic St. Mid-Mar.–Oct. 10–6. Tel. (062) 61947.

THE SOUTHWEST

To the west of Dublin is horse country. Highway N7 cuts through the center of the Irish racing world. Visit **Currgh Racecourse** (where the Irish Derby is run) in the town of *Naas* to see lots of racehorse training activity. Get there early in the day to watch. In *Tully,* the **Irish National Stud and Horse Museum** traces the history of Irish horses and breeding since early times.

COUNTY CORK

Road bowling, played on quiet country lanes, is still found here. The game is a contest between two players to see who can throw a heavy iron ball a distance of 3 miles with the smallest number of throws. The rules are a bit complicated, and there is much betting and blarney and a lively celebration after the game at the local pub.

Cork City is a big, bustling industrial town with a lively marketplace at the top of Patrick Street. The open-air **Coal Quay Market** is a flea market of sorts, while the **English Market** is an old-style covered market with produce, fruits, and vegetables. If your kids appreciate rhythms slightly more complex than rock and roll, head to Cork for the **Guinness Jazz Festival** in late October. A great outpouring of jazz in every style imaginable can be heard all over the city. The **tourist office** is on Grand Parade [Tel. (021) 23251].

Kiss the Blarney Stone! Five miles from Cork in the ruins of Blarney Castle is a tourist sight your children will not want to miss. Legend has it that if you kiss the Blarney Stone, you will be forever blessed with the gift of gab. (When you return from your trip you may have to install a second phone line!) According to the same legend, Cormac McDermott McCarthy, the King of Munster, once saved the life of a drowning woman. She turned out to be a kindly witch who rewarded him by telling him the secret of the Blarney Stone. When kissing the stone, you must twist into an awkward posture (which makes it all the more exciting for kids) and pucker up. Don't worry Mom, it's disinfected four times daily, and there is an attendant to keep you from falling the four stories to the ground below. Fee. June–July Mon.–Sat. 9–8:30; Aug. Mon.–Sat. 9–7:30; Sept. 9–6:30; Oct.–Apr. Mon.–Sat. 9–sundown; May Mon.–Sat. 9–7. Sun. in summer 9:30–5:30; rest of year 9:30–sundown. The town of Blarney is touristy with lots of shops offering Irish crafts, but the prices are quite competitive for souvenir shopping.

Eight miles east of Cork is **Fota Island,** one of Cork's newest and most popular tourist attractions, which has 750 acres of park and farmland with an arboretum and a wildlife park that is home to a prospering colony of wallabies. **Fota House,** a restored 18th-century hunting lodge, contains an important collection of Irish landscape paintings from the 18th and 19th centuries.

Youghal, about an hour out of Cork, is a charming beach town with an interesting old fishing quarter, sandy beaches, a big amusement park, and good seafood restaurants.

Kinsale, to the west of Cork, is a walled city and a popular deep-sea fishing site. Two miles out of the town is **Charles Fort,** said to be one of the best-preserved examples of the "star fort" (a fort in a star shape) in Europe. Built in 1611, it held over 2,000 inhabitants within its walls, which enclosed 12 acres of land and moats. Hourly guided tours. Mid-June–mid-Sept. 10–6:30; mid-Sept.–mid-Apr. Mon.–Fri. 8–4:30; mid-Apr.–mid-June Tues.–Sat. 1–5, Sun. 2–5.

COUNTY KERRY

Killarney is a busy town, but its surrounding countryside is one of Ireland's most beautiful areas. Many families rent a cottage in this vicinity for a week or two and tour about. The area's tourist board is in the town hall [Tel. (064) 31633]. Killarney's **Transport and Treasure Museum** has a collection of old modes of transportation such as cars, bikes, and trikes. Small fee. East Avenue Rd. Tel. (056) 32638.

Killarney National Park contains the lakes of Killarney and lovely forested mountains. In the heart of the park, 3 miles from Killarney, is **Muckross Estate,** where you can rent a bike to pedal around the grounds. Better yet, hire a ride from a two-wheeled horse-drawn cart called a "jaunting car." The **Kerry Folklife Centre,** in the basement of 19th-century **Muckross House,** has blacksmiths, weavers, potters, and basket makers who demonstrate their craft. An exhibition of Irish poetry and music, and a restaurant are on the premises. The gardens are ablaze with color in spring, when hundreds of azaleas and rhododendrons are in bloom. Fee. Jul.–Aug. 9–7; Sept.–Oct. and Mar.–June 9–6; Nov.–Feb. Tues.–Sun. 11–5. Tel. (064) 31440. The beautiful lakefront walk, Lovers Lane, runs halfway from Muckross Abbey to Muckross House. The islands in the lake are said to still hold the abbey's buried treasures, hidden in 1589 to avoid plunder.

Don't miss the chance to journey by pony or pony-cart through the **Gap of Dunloe,** about 10 miles from Muckross. Hire them at the gap's entrance for a 7-mile ride through this romantic mountain pass where massive rocks rise on either side of the valley. Be sure your children test the gap's legendary echo abilities. You can make a day of it and pick up a bus outside the tourist board office in Killarney. First you tour Kate Kearney's cottage and then take a pony-cart or ride a pony through the gap. Next, you continue by boat across three beautifully scenic lakes while your boatman entertains you with tales and legends. The boat ends its journey at Ross Castle, a well-preserved 14th-century ruin. Contact Killarney's tourist board for details. For more information on other pony rides throughout the area, contact the Ballydowney Riding School [Tel. (064) 31686]. **Ross Castle** was the 16th-century stronghold of the O'Donoghue clan. Hire rowboats to explore its lake and **Innisfallen Island,** where you'll find the remains of a 7th-century abbey. Boatmen are available to lead you. Riverboat cruises of the area's lakes are available from here as well.

The beautiful *Dingle Peninsula* can be explored in a figure-eight loop by bike or car, or you can base yourselves here and explore at a slower pace. Its western end is an important *Gaeltacht*, an Irish-speaking region where the government has helped preserve Irish culture. Be sure to ask the friendly inhabitants for a singing Gaelic pub for dinner and entertainment, as music and crafts are an important part of life. Bring raincoats to outwit the rain, fog, and mist common here. There are many fishing communities along this coast, many of which use *currachs*, boats made of a wooden framework covered with tarred canvas. Peculiar to the west of Ireland, their high prows are designed to safely ride the waves. *Ballydavid Village* is a town where currachs are made.

Ballybunion is a popular family resort on the northwest coast of County Kerry. Sea caves, rugged cliffs, coves, and beaches are some of its natural offerings. You can walk through any of the caves in the cliffs on the north side of town during low tide. A path runs along the cliff.

Teach Siamsa, near *Listowel,* is a rural folk-theater workshop run by the National Folk Theatre of Ireland. Story telling, poetry, music, dance, and drama are held in an old-time Irish kitchen. July and Aug. Tues. and Thurs. at 3 and Wed. at 9. Reservations: Tel. (066) 23055.

COUNTIES CLARE, SHANNON, AND LIMERICK

This region boasts 900 castles, fascinating caves along the Atlantic coast, and long sandy beaches. Crafts are an important source of the area's income. **Bunratty Castle,** outside of Shannon, has been restored to its medieval splendor. Have your young explorers pick up its "Young Visitors Guide." Children are most welcome at the castle's famous nightly medieval banquet. Seated at long tables, you'll all put on bibs and enjoy a feast of treats based on authentic medieval recipes. Adults drink from a beaker of honey mead while children sip juice. Every now and then a "serving lass" in 15th-century dress will stop to sing a ballad or pluck the strings of the harp. While one family we know was there, the "maids" took the kids on a quick tour of the castle's dungeons so the parents could more leisurely enjoy their dinner. Be sure to book banquets well in advance as this castle is the most authentic and best-preserved in Ireland, and the banquets are often booked ahead by tour groups. Dinners at 6 and 9. Tel. (061) 61788. **Bunratty Folk Park,** behind the castle, is a re-creation of turn-of-the-century Irish village life. Wander through a little village of thatched cottages, farmhouses, shops, and mills which have been reconstructed and furnished in period decor. You'll see people making butter by hand, soda bread baking on an open turf fire, and lace making. Twice nightly between May and September, a céilí (party) with Irish meals and traditional Irish music, song, and dance is held. Folk Park: Fee. Daily 9:30–5. Tel. (061) 361511. Céilí: shows at 5:45 and 9:00. Reservations: Tel. (061) 61788.

Several other castles offer medieval banquets. **Knappogue Castle,** at *Quin,* 8 miles from Bunratty, also offers an entertaining pageant (Information: Tel. (061) 61788; reservations for the twice nightly banquets: Tel. (061) 71103). Not far from Quin is the 16th-century **Craggaunowen Castle,** which boasts a reconstructed Bronze Age lake settlement, including a ring fort and a *crannog* (a lake dwelling) on its grounds. Also on display is the *Brendan,* a replica of a 6th-century leather-covered boat which actually sailed across the Atlantic in 1976. The leather covering was useful in centuries past as it could be easily patched if a sharp piece of North Sea ice pierced the boat's hull. A special guide for children to the entire complex is available. Tel. (061) 72178.

The *Clare coast* has sandy beaches, dramatic limestone caves, and golf courses. The area is famous for its fiddlers, step dancers, and singing pubs. *Kilkee* offers safe swimming at all stages of the tide, plus fishing, an amusement park, tennis, handball, miniature golf, and Ping-Pong. *Lahinch* has an entertainment center with a children's pool and playground, game room, tennis courts, and a saltwater swimming pool. *Doolin* is the departure site for ferries to the Aran Islands, and its reputation for folk music spreads far beyond the Irish borders.

Ireland's famous 5-day festival of traditional entertainment, **Fleadh Nua**, takes place in *Ennis* in late July. For more information: Tel. (065) 27115; or the **tourist office:** Tel. (065) 28366.

Lisdoonvarna, a spa town, hosts the **Lisdoonvarna Matchmaking Festival** with folk music, dancing, and a "carnival of romance" in late August or early September. Nearby, in the northwest corner of County Clare, is the *Burren,* a region of extensive and odd rock formations and rugged terrain. Appearing something like the surface of the moon, this barren 100-square-mile area is filled with spectacular caves, streams, potholes, seasonal lakes, stone forts, and prehistoric burial sites. Formed millions of years ago, **Aillwee Cave** is the only cave out of the many in the area that has been made available for public tours. Along its illuminated paved pathways you travel 1,120 yards down into its depths. Ancient hollows carved out by bears can still be seen. Guided tour. Fee. 2 miles southeast of Ballyvaughan. Mar.–Oct. 10–6; until 7 in summer. Tel. (065) 77036. The **Burren Display Center** at *Kilfenora* uses film and music to tell the story of prehistoric life in the region and how the strange geology of the Burren was formed.

Don't get too close to the edge! There is nothing between you and the 700-foot vertical drop to the ocean of the dramatic **Cliffs of Moher,** one of Ireland's top tourist attractions because of its scenic splendor. Climb the highest cliff to O'Brian's Tower, constructed as a viewpoint for Victorian tourists. From its exceptional vantage point you can view the Clare coastline, Aran Islands, and far-away mountains. Tower: daily May–Sept. 10–5:30. Tel. (065) 81171. There is a visitor's center with a tearoom and a souvenir shop nearby, open 10–6.

To the west of Galway City is the *Connemara,* popular for fishing. Many of the Connemara's inhabitants speak Gaelic; the region's schools teach the old language while a radio station broadcasts in it. *Clifden* is a picturesque family vacation spot, ideal as a base for exploring the region's glorious scenery. About 1 mile from town there is an excellent swimming beach with riding, boating, and fishing. The little fishing village of *Inishbofin* also has nice beaches. *Spiddal,* in the heart of the Irish-speaking area, has a noteworthy crafts center. A curragh race is held here during the second week of June.

On the shores of Galway Bay in the seaport village of *Kinvara* stands the majestic 16th-century **Dunguaire Castle.** Between May and September there are nightly medieval banquet feasts followed by Irish music, dance, and readings from Irish writers. Tel. (091) 37108 or (061) 61788.

THE NORTHWEST

People in this lovely remote area of Ireland still speak Gaelic, and you'll find many road signs written in it. William Butler Yeats was born in the northwest, an area famous for its golf courses and seaside resorts.

COUNTY DONEGAL

The ever-changing landscapes and seascapes of Donegal are set against a backdrop of mountains and moors. The most northwestern of all the counties, its terrain is rugged and sea winds blow relentlessly. There is a thick mist that obscures visibility but like the rain and the sun, it descends and leaves very quickly. Donegal has the largest Irish-speaking population in Ireland.

The seaside resort of *Bundoran,* at the southwesternmost corner of the county, has an excellent sandy beach, a leisure center, water sports, and traditional music. The action of the sea has shaped some of its rocks into curious formations. Look for "The Fairy Bridge" and "The Wishing Chair." *Letterkenny,* 31 miles north of the city of Donegal, has an August folk festival that brings musicians and dancers from all corners of the globe. For specifics contact the **tourist office** [Tel. (074) 21160]. **Glenveagh National Park,** in the northwestern part of the county, is home to Ireland's largest herd of red deer, rugged mountains, moorland, crystal clear lakes, and tranquil woods. No cars are allowed in the park, and it is a great place to walk and hike. **Glenveagh Castle** stands on top of a promontory that juts out into Lake Veagh. Park at the visitors centre and take the minibus to the castle.

COUNTIES MAYO AND SLIGO

Croagh Patrick, near Westport in Mayo, is the mountain top where St. Patrick prayed and fasted for 40 days and nights in 441. One legend says that he rang a bell here to make all of Ireland's snakes cast themselves over the precipice, thereby ridding the country of all snakes. There are good beaches in this area. *Sligo* town, encircled by mountains except on its sea-facing side, has ruins, pony trekking, horseback riding, miniature golf and boats for hire. Lough Gill has summer cruises. Contact the tourist board on Temple Street [Tel. (071) 61201] for details. If you enjoy traditional music, the **South Sligo Traditional Music Festival** takes place in July. An **arts festival** the last week of September has more traditional music, crafts, classical music, theater, and recitations. Many of the pubs also have live music year-round. Yeats fans of all ages attend the **Yeats International Summer School** in August. Three miles north of town is the **Sculpture Trail at Hazelwood,** which features wooden sculpture by modern artists. Surfing in Ireland? Five miles from Sligo is the seaside resort of ***Strandhill,*** with long sandy beaches and excellent surfing. Irish surfers may not be winning international championships, but they are respected for their skill and ability to handle challenging waves.

16

Italy

Italians treasure children. Sophisticated career women kiss and coddle little ones on the street, crusty old farmers gush as school kids stroll past; even teenage boys pause to admire a sleeping baby. Again and again, families are greeted with the proverbial blessing *auguri*, wishing them well. The warmth and conviviality for which Italians are known heightens when children are about. And you as their escorts will reap the benefits.

With such hospitality, how can your kids help but adore Italy? They'll love the mild climate, the food, and the people. The pace is slow, the atmosphere relaxed. While your children may not appreciate long museum visits, they will delight in discovering an ancient Roman aqueduct still gushing water or an out-of-the-way cobblestone pattern upon which to play a game of hopscotch. And there are plenty of compelling sites for them to explore in addition to the three not-to-miss cities, Florence, Venice, and Rome.

Buon Viaggio!

Preparing Your Children: Books and Art

Younger children: *Anno's Italy* by Mitsumasa Anno; *Piccolina and the Easter Bells* by Lorna Balian; books by Tomie De Paola, such as *Strega Nona*; *Pantaloni* by Bettina Erlich; *Looking for Daniela* by Steven Kroll; *Little Leo* by Leo Politi; and *Grumpus and the Venetian Cat* by Rosalie Seidler.

Older children: *Chichibo and the Crane* by Giovanni Boccaccio; *A Roman Soldier* by Giovanni Caselli; *Pinocchio* by Carlo Collodi (many translations available); *Take a Trip to Italy* by Chris Fairclough; *A Bell for Adano* by John Hersey.

Art: Your children will encounter artwork by Italian artists such as Fra Angelico, Bernini, Botticelli, Caravaggio, Leonardo da Vinci, Donatello, Piero della Francesca, Ghiberti, Giotto, Modigliani, Raphael, and Tintoretto. Your library should have books with photographs of their works.

Wha'd'ya Wanna Do?

The **Italian Government Tourist Office**'s most helpful free booklets include "General Information for Travelers in Italy," "Art in Italy," and "An Italian Year," which lists all traditional special events. Large cities have a **local tourist office,** called an Ente Provinciale per Turismo (EPT). In smaller cities, where they are called Azienda Autonoma di Soggiorno e Turismo, you can stop en route to learn about local attractions, accommodations, sports, and special events.

ITALIAN GOVERNMENT TOURIST OFFICES (ENIT)
  USA–*Chicago:* Italian Government Tourist Office, 500 N. Michigan Ave., Chicago, IL 60611. Tel. 312-644-0990.
  USA–*New York:* Italian Government Tourist Office, 630 Fifth Ave., New York, NY 10111. Tel. 212-245-4822.
  USA–*San Francisco:* Italian Government Tourist Office, 360 Post St., San Francisco, CA 94108. Tel. 415-392-6206.
  Canada–*Montreal:* Italian Government Tourist Office, 1 Pl. Ville Marie, Suite 2414, Montreal, Quebec H3B 3M9. Tel. 514-866-7667.

Shhh! Your kids may only choose to enter **cathedrals** and churches to avoid the sweltering summer heat. Remind them that people will be praying and that they need to keep voices down. Most churches have a dress code and shorts are not permitted.

For general planning, be aware that some **beaches** are polluted and swimming should be avoided in the Ligurian coast (from San Remo to Livorno), and in the immediate areas near Rome, Venice, Naples, Salerno, and Palermo. Nevertheless, you'll see swarms of Italian families enjoying these beaches, and Italy is spending countless lire trying to clean up its pollution problem. The cleanest beaches are found in Sardinia, Calabria, Apulia, Basilicata and the Gargano peninsula, Elba, parts of Capri and Ischia, and the south and west coasts of Sicily. Beaches near tourist meccas are usually private and you must pay for a changing cabin, shower, deck chair, and umbrella.

In the early evening, around 5 or 6 PM, many families go out for a *passeggiata* (stroll). Head for the nearest park or *piazza* to find kids playing, moms comparing notes, and dads showing off their well-dressed infants.

Italy abounds in colorful traditional **festivals,** and we have listed some of the best. In order to avoid disappointments, reconfirm dates by contacting ENIT before departing or the local tourist office once there. Keep your eye out for posters or check with the local EPT for a gastronomic festival called a *sagra* or a *festa*, held generally in the fall, when the whole village celebrates their local food specialty. They range from the more common *funghi* (mushroom), *polenta*, and *salsicce* (sausages) to offbeat festivals of the *cippolla* (onion), *anguilla* (eel), or *lardo* (lard).

Lights Out! Special Italian Accommodations

Italy offers a wide variety of accommodations, from hotels and villas to farmhouses, campgrounds, and alpine huts. If you plan to headquarter in one place for a week or more, it is most economical to rent a **self-catering villa** (Italians call homes villas), large or small, either in the Italian countryside or near the major city you plan to visit. Apartments within the center of a city are harder to come by. Many agencies handle villa rentals. ENIT's booklet "General Information for Travelers in Italy" lists about twenty agencies.

One of the most reliable agencies for families from ENIT's listing is the Italian/Swiss company Cuendet, which handles villas, farmhouses, castles, and apartments in Tuscany, Umbria, Sicily, and villas just outside of Rome and Venice. Our stone villa in Umbria had a picture-postcard view of the Basilica of St. Francis, a charming neighbor who brought us fresh eggs, and all the modern amenities we could ask for. Cuendet rates all their properties in five comfort categories based on such things as views, gardens, cleanliness, quality of beds, and the type of bathroom. Prices start at about $350 per week off-season and $500 per week high-season for a two-bedroom apartment in a rural villa. Contact them in December or January for the upcoming summer.

Cuendet: Suzanne T. Pidduck, 1742 Calle Corva, Camarillo, CA 93010. Tel. 805-987-5278, 800-726-6702.

Another very reliable agency is Vacanza Bella, a small company that specializes in hard-to-locate city apartments in Rome and Florence as well as rural villas on the Amalfi Coast and Lake Garda and in Tuscany and Umbria.

Vacanza Bella: Daniel Morneau, 2443 Fillmore St., Suite 228, San Francisco, CA 94114. Tel. 415-821-9345

For villas in other areas of Italy, refer to ENIT's comprehensive listing.

Italian **hotels** are officially classified from two stars to five stars. Hotel prices, especially in major cities, are very high. *Pensioni* (small two- through four-star hotels) or *locande* (one-star hotels) are a less expensive option, although in Italy, you usually get what you pay for. When traveling with children we found many pensioni and locande to be quite uncomfortable because of their tiny rooms, terrible beds, poor ventilation, and street noise. However, exceptions do exist; it's worth hunting around.

We have selected a few hotels, pensioni, and locande in Rome, Florence, and Venice that are near parks, have a kitchen, or offer special amenities for families such as gardens or terraces. An extra bed or *culla* (crib) can often be placed in a room for a slight additional charge. Rates are usually lower from November through March in major cities, towns, and resort centers and from April through May and September through November at ski resorts.

Farmhouses are an ideal family getaway. For information, contact the head office of Agriturist, Corso V. Emanuele 101, 00186 Rome, or write to your nearest ENIT office for a complete listing of the twenty-five provincial offices that arrange farm and cottage rentals.

A free list of **camping** sites with maps is issued free by the Federazione Italiana del Campeggio e del Caravanning (Federcampeggio). Copies are available by contacting your nearest ENIT office or from Federcampeggio, Via V. Emanuele, 11, Casella Postale 23, 50041, Calenzano (Florence).

Getting Around

Cars are a must for exploring the countryside or out-of-the-way hill towns. City driving is often nerve racking with wildly gesticulating drivers, one-way streets, and difficult parking. Lanes, as we know them, don't seem to exist. All foreigners must have a "green card," or International Insurance Certificate. U.S. or Canadian driver's licenses are valid for those driving their own cars but they must be accompanied by a translation, available from the Automobile Club d'Italia, C. Colombo 261, 00185, Rome. An international driver's license (no translation necessary) is required for those driving rental cars. Contact ENIT for up-to-date details of their special discount packs, which include a savings on gas (15 percent) and tolls. It must be purchased in advance from the Italian Auto Club at the border. The Italian *autostrade* are toll roads, and you pay according to the distance covered. Only a few gas stations are open on Sundays and most close for a few hours midday. Those on the autostrade are open 24 hours. Car seats are gaining more popularity in Italy.

In addition to honoring the Eurail Saverpass (see Chapter 7), the Italian State Railway offers "Go Anywhere" **train** tickets in both first and second-class for 8, 15, 21, and 30 days. Passes may be purchased in advance from the Italian State Railway in New York at 666 Fifth

Avenue, New York, NY 10013 (Tel. 212-397-2667). Children under 12 are charged half-fare, and those under 4 travel free. Discounts are available for families with four or more members. In Italy, you can purchase family tickets where four or more members of the same family traveling together get 30 percent off both the adult and children's fares. There are four kinds of Italian trains: the *locale*, *diretto*, *espresso*, and *rapido*. The *locale* stops at every station along the line.

Nuts and Bolts

Does anyone care what time it is? Store and museum hours vary considerably. Don't let it frustrate you. The secret of successful travel in Italy is to relax. Most stores and museums are open from 9 to 1 and from 4 to 8. Italy is on a "toddler's schedule," where people rest after lunch. Some museums do not reopen, so be sure to check ahead. Most museums are closed Mondays. Shops are closed Sundays and retail stores close Monday or Saturday afternoon. Banks are generally open from 8:30 to 1:30 and 2:30 to 4 and are closed weekends and holidays.

National holidays: New Year's Day, Epiphany (January 6), Easter Sunday and Monday, Liberation Day (April 25), Labor Day (May 1), Republic Day (June 2), Assumption (August 15), All Saints' Day (November 1), Day of Immaculate Conception (December 8), Christmas Day, Santo Stefano (December 26). Businesses also close for local saints' days and festivals; ENIT can provide you with a listing.

What, you can't divide by 1250? money: Pay attention to your bills as it is easy to misplace the odd zero at the end of a number, and Italian waiters have been known to make "mistakes." Notes are issued for 1,000, 2,000, 5,000, 20,000, 50,000, and 100,000 *lire*.

Telephones: The country code for Italy is 39. When direct-dialing international calls, dial two zeros, the country code (1 for U.S. and Canada), followed by the phone number.

Useful nationwide phone numbers: Police is 112; Emergency is 113; Fire Department is 115; Road Assistance is 116. The Italian Automobile Club's number is 4212 (prefix 06 for calls outside of Rome); they provide English information about traffic, road conditions, weather, and motorway tolls.

Embassies and consulates: The U.S. Embassy is at Via Vittoria Veneto, 119a, Rome 00187 [Tel. (06) 4674]; one of the six U.S. Consulates is at Lungarno Amerigo Vespucci, 38, 50123 Florence [Tel. (055) 298276]. The Canadian Embassy is at Via Zara, 30, Rome [Tel. (06) 4403028]; the Canadian Consulate is at Via Vittorio Pisani, 19, Milan [Tel. (02) 6697451].

Mangia, Mangia! Let's Eat

Mealtime is important to the Italians as both sustenance and a social family occasion. Their delicious pizza and pastas with scrumptious sauces and enchanting shapes will tempt even your most finicky eater. Your whole family will not be able to resist the incomparable *gelato* (ice cream). Italians start the day with a light breakfast of *caffè* (coffee) served *espresso* (black) or *cappuccino* (with steamed milk), and a *cornetto* (roll), which you can supplement with your own *latte* (milk), *frutta* (fruit), and *formaggio* (cheese). Lunch tends to be the important meal of the day, when schoolchildren come home and restaurants are packed. If you plan to picnic, remember that markets and stores close from 1 to 4 PM, so get your *formaggio*, *prosciutto* (ham), and *panini* (bread) early. Dinner is usually eaten around 8 PM and tends to be much lighter than lunch.

The full meal, whether it's lunch or dinner, begins with an *antipasto* (appetizer). The first course, *il primo*, consists of *pasta* or *risotto* (rice casserole). The second and main course, *il secondo*, is usually *pesce* (fish) or *carne* (meat) with *contorno* (vegetable) and is followed by salad, fruit and/or cheese, and dessert. Ask about the *piatto del giorno* (dish of the day) and for *mezzo* (half) portions for your kids. Don't feel pressured to consume a four-course meal. We often ordered an *antipasto*, a variety of pastas from the *primo course*, and dessert. For a smaller meal go to a *tavola calda* (literally "hot table"), *rosticceria*, *trattoria*, or a *pizzeria*. All, of course, welcome children.

Favorite pastas for kids include *fettucine al ragù* (ribbonlike noodles with a tomato and meat sauce), *ravioli* (small stuffed pillows), *manicotti* (pipes stuffed with cheese and a creamy sauce), *cappelletti* (little hats stuffed with different fillings), and *lasagne*. Pizzas can be ordered at street stands or at more expensive sit-down establishments. The local *forno* (bakery) often sells it by the slice. Kids can't resist *pizza margherita* (cheese, tomatos, and basil), *ai funghi* (with mushrooms), and *bianca* (olive oil and herbs). Try *calzone*, which are puffed dough pastries stuffed with cheese, vegetables, and meats.

Amaretti (macaroons), *monte bianco* (meringue, whipped cream, and pureed chestnuts), *zucotto* (cake filled with chocolate ice cream and whipped cream), and *torrone* (nougat candy) are among the delicious desserts. The Italians make the best *gelato* (ice cream) in the world, and your kids will most likely remember it more than the ruins of Pompeii or Da Vinci's *Last Supper*. *Gelato* can be ordered *con panna* (with whipped cream) and in a *cono* (cone) or *coppa* (cup).

Integral to Italian society is the bar—really a cafe—where many sit for hours. You can order small pizzas and sandwiches at bars or *spremuta d'arancia* (freshly squeezed orange juice), *frullatti* (fresh fruit shakes), or fruit *granite* (flavored ices). At the market, you will use the metric system: *etto* = one quarter lb., *mezzo kilo* = aprox. 1 lb., *kilo* = 2 lb. 2 oz., *litro* = 1.065 qt. Waiting on line goes against the grain of even the sweetest Italian grandmother. She may kiss and coddle your baby, but she'll push you out of the way at the food counter.

Expect this and stand your ground. Don't squeeze the *frutta* or *verdure* (vegetables) as you shop; you're likely to get a scolding from the shopkeeper. *Rosticcerie* (grills) offer delicious roast meats and take-out pasta dishes. *Pollo arrosto* (roast chicken) will feed a family inexpensively.

Formula and Baby Food, Diapers and Baby Gear

Alimento per bambini (baby food) can be found in pharmacies, supermarkets, and some department stores (UPIM, Standa). Gerber products are often stocked in larger cities. Most fruit juices packaged for babies have *zucchero* (sugar) in them. Formula, including soy, is purchased in pharmacies. *Pannolini di carta* (disposable diapers) are available in pharmacies, department stores, most supermarkets, and stores specializing in children's goods. The most popular brand is *Linas*. Imported Pampers and their equivalent are available but not easily located. Italian baby gear is high quality and beautifully designed. *PreNatal*, a chain of children's stores found in most cities, stocks all types of baby gear, including the noted *Chicco* line of equipment and toys.

Sidewalk Talk

Italians greet each other with *buon giorno* (good day) until 2 PM; goodbye is *arrivederci* if they know you or *arrivederla* if you've just met. *Ciao* is a greeting used with friends.

Hi! *Ciao*
See you later. *Ci vediamo.*
Please *Prego, per favore*
Thank you *Grazie*
Okay *Va bene.*
What are you doing, what's happening? *Che cosa fai?*

Bathroom *il gabinetto*
Beach *la spiaggia*
Doll *la bambola*
Ice cream shop *la gelateria*
Swimming pool *la piscina*
That's enough. *Basta così.*

A KID'S GUIDE TO GELATO

chocolate and nuts *bacio*
banana *banana*
chocolate *cioccalata*
coconut *cocco*
cream *crema*
strawberry *fragola*
fruit salad *fruitti di bosco*
kiwi *kiwi*
raspberry *lampone*

lemon *limone*
rum raisin *malaga*
mint chocolate *mentacioccolata*
berry *mirtillo*
blackberry *mora*
pistachio *pistacchio*
rice *riso*
chocolate chip *stracciatella*

The Lay of the Land

Italy is a bootlike peninsula jutting out into the Mediterranean Sea. The country is divided into twenty diverse regions, each with a capital city. Each region is divided into provinces. We have described Italy under the broader headings of Central, Northern, and Southern Italy, and Sicily.

CENTRAL ITALY

ROME

As legend tells us, the jealous brother of a princess threw her twin sons into the Tiber River out of spite. A "she wolf" found the boys on the shore, and suckled them and kept them warm. Raised by a shepherd, Romulus and Remus grew up to build the great city of Rome. Cats, not wolves, are now Rome's specialty. You will see them everywhere, from the posh streets off the Via Condotti to the massive ruins of the Forum. They are fed every day by caring residents. This adoration is unique to Rome; elsewhere in Italy they wander unloved.

Children will be enchanted with the city's fountains, found at almost every turn, and the lively parks and piazzas, each with its own mood and amusements. For a major city, Rome still retains the feeling of an overgrown village. Turn off a busy street of darting buses and screeching Fiats and you'll immediately hear nothing but the slow trickle of a fountain and the laughing and splashing of playing children.

The most comprehensive English listing of events is the monthly guide "This Week in Rome," available at newsstands. From Rome's **tourist office** (EPT) at Via Parigi, 5 (Tel. 463748), pick up the free publications "Young Rome," and "Here Rome," which list attractions for children. (Their mailing address is Via Parigi, 11.) The EPT also publishes a free listing of monthly events. Rome's **telephone area code** is 06.

The Lay of the City

The river Tiber cuts through the middle of the city. Most major sites are to its east. The enormous Vittorio Emanuele monument, which looks like a giant wedding cake, is the city's most visible landmark. Ancient Rome with the Forum and the Colosseum are southwest of Vittorio Emanuele. To its west is the compact *centro storico*, Rome's historical center with the Pantheon, Piazza Navona, and the colorful Campo dei Fiori. To its northwest are the popular Spanish Steps and the Piazza del Popolo, above which sits Rome's largest park, the Villa

Borghese. To the west of the Tiber is the Vatican and the Trastevere quarter. Most of the Catacombs are outside the city walls.

Getting Around

Rome is a city for walking. Many streets, piazzas, or entire areas are completely closed off to traffic. These pedestrian zones include Piazza Navona, Piazza Farnese, and the areas around the Pantheon and the Spanish Steps. The city's **bus** system, which is excellent, offers weekly and half-day passes available at the ATAC office, via Volturno 65, and at Piazza dei Cinquecento. Individual tickets and bus maps are sold at tobacco shops and newsstands. The Roman **metropolitana** (subway) is a very efficient means of crossing town quickly. Tickets are available from machines in the stations, and at tobacco shops and newsstands. **Horse-and-carriage** rides are available at the major tourist sites, and there are a few summer **riverboat tours** along the Tiber River. Contact the EPT for schedules.

Where to Stay

Apartments in Rome can be hard to locate; try Vacanza Bella, listed at the beginning of this chapter. Rome has many **residential hotels,** which are furnished two- and three-room apartments with hotel services and minimum stays of usually 1 week to 1 month. A listing of over fifty is available in the free booklet "Here's Rome," available by writing Rome's EPT.

HOTELS

The luxurious *Hassler-Villa Medici*'s backyard is the Villa Borghese. Piazza Trinità dei Monti, 6. Tel. 6782651. **Deluxe.**

The *Hotel Forum* is across the street from the 2,000-year-old Forum. Apartments (deluxe) are available. Via Tor de' Conte, 25. Tel. 6792446. Fax 6799337. **Expensive.**

La Residenza, next to Via Veneto and Villa Borghese, is popular with diplomatic families. Rates include breakfast. Via Emilia, 22-24, 00187. Tel. 460789. **Expensive.**

Sant'Anselmo is a bed-and-breakfast establishment in a garden on the Aventino hill with doubles and a family room for four people. Piazza Sant'Anselmo, 2. Tel. 5745231. **Moderate.**

La Scalinata di Spagna, a small pension at the top of the Spanish Steps, has family rooms, a big terrace, and is a short walk from Villa Borghese. Piazza Trinità dei Monti, 17. Tel. 6793006. **Moderate.**

Palazzo al Velabro, in Piazza Bocca dell Verità, is an apartment hotel with kitchenettes and maid service. Rates include breakfast;

cribs available. One-week minimum stay. Via del Velabro, 16, 00186. Tel. 6792758. **Moderate.**

Residence Guiggioli, near the Vatican, is a small pension with large suites. Via Germanico. Tel. 315209. **Inexpensive.**

Residence Alimandi, a stone's throw from the Vatican Museum, has a beautiful garden and roof terrace but uncomfortable beds. Triples are available. Via Tunisi, 8, 00192. Tel. 6799343. **Inexpensive.**

CAMPGROUNDS
Campsites are all located outside the city: *Camping Roma,* via Aurelia, 831 (8 km. away), Tel. 6223018; *Camping Flaminio,* Via Flaminia Nuova (8 km. away), Tel. 3279006; *Camping Capitol,* via Castelfusano, 195 (in Ostia), has a pool and tennis courts, Tel. 5662720.

Detour! What to See and Do

ANCIENT ROME

ALONG THE VIA DEI FORI IMPERIALI

The **Capitoline Hill** looms above Piazza Venezia's **monument to Vittorio Emanuele II,** nicknamed "The Wedding Cake" or "The White Typewriter." Temples and monuments surrounded the hill from 78 B.C. until Rome fell from power. Its central **Piazza Campidolgio** became the site of bloody executions. In the mid-16th century Michelangelo was asked to redesign it and restore its splendor. Climb his magnificent broad staircase, the *Cordonata,* to the hill's summit and piazza. On the Campidolgio is the **Palazzo dei Conservatori,** where you can view the Etruscan *Capitoline Wolf,* a sculpture of the wolf who rescued Romulus and Remus from their death. Look for the *Boy with a Thorn,* a sculpture of a young lad removing a splinter from his foot. Also on the Campidolgio is the **Musei Capitolini,** the world's oldest museum, with a collection of classical sculpture. Fee; free last Sun. of the month. Museums: Wed. and Fri. 9–1:30; Tues. and Thurs. 9–1:30, 5–8, Sat. 9–1:30, 8–11; Sun. 9–1. Tel. 67101. Just above the piazza is **Santa Maria d'Aracoeli,** a pagan temple built around 600 A.D. containing the *Bambino,* a world-famous statue of the Holy Child. During the Christmas season until January 6, young children recite carefully prepared poetry in front of him. Open daily 7–12, 3:30–sunset. As you descend the Capitoline Hill on the way to the Forum, you'll come to the **Mamertine,** an ancient prison now used as a chapel. Prisoners were thrown into its pit to starve, and legend has it that St. Peter escaped through its sewer drain. Donation. Via dei Falegnami at Forum. May–Sept. Wed.–Mon. 9–5; Oct.–Apr. Wed.– Mon. 9–4.

The **Forum** was the main center of Roman life. With temples, shops, and government buildings glistening with gold, imagine what it was like when toga-clad bankers haggled at the **Basilica Amelelia,** shoppers gossiped in front of the local butcher shop and fish market, judges set the law at the **Basilica Guilia,** and the senate met at the ancient **Curia.** Climb up to the **Altar of Vulcan** for a view of the Capitoline Hill. Rome's oldest street, Via Sacra, leads to the restored **Temple of Vesta,** where for over 1,000 years six young girls known as the Vestal Virgins tended a sacred fire and were endowed with great power. If they failed to keep the fire burning, they were buried alive. There is ample space for running and wandering in the Forum and many quiet picnic spots. Fee. Enter Forum on via dei Fori Imperiali. Mon. and Wed.–Sat. 9–sunset, Sun. 9–1. At the end of Via Sacra, you can climb up the **Palatine Hill,** which was once home to noble Roman families. Today its grassy fields are a relaxing escape from the stark ruins of the Forum and the congestion of Rome. According to the legend, the "she wolf" took Romulus and Remus to a cave here. From the **belvedere** you can look down on the **Circus Maximus,** which was the course of the Roman empire's biggest horse and chariot race, last run in the 5th century A.D. The starting and finishing marks for the races still exist at its western end. The entrance to the Palatine is at via San Gregorio between the Arch of Constantine and the Circus Maximus. Mon.–Sat. 9–one hour before sunset; Sun. 10–one hour before sunset.

Did Roman teens hang out at a mall? Probably. Across from the Forum are the ruins of **Trajan's Market** within the **Forum of Trajan.** The market was once Rome's shopping mall with over 100 shops. Fee. Via IV Novembre, 94. Forum: Tues.–Sat. 10–5; Sun. 9–1.

The city's most famous landmark, the 2,000-year-old **Colosseum,** was a scene of gruesome spectacles. Eighty entrances allowed 50,000 spectators to take their seats in 10 minutes. The gladiators who fought in the arena had been condemned to die. They fought each other to death; if one was lucky and survived, he might someday be freed. During the persecutions of the Christians, many martyrs were thrown into the arena to be mauled by beasts who were kept in underground cages. Kids will enjoy the climb to the arena's three upper levels. Free; fee for climb. Oct.–Apr. daily 9–sunset; May–Sept. 9–7. Climb allowed until 1 hour before closing. Between the Colosseum and the Baths of Caracalla is the **Villa Celimontana,** a lush walled park perfect for a pause and a picnic. Its entrance is on Piazza della Navicella.

The **Terme di Caracalla,** built in the second century B.C., were the communal baths used by poorer Romans. Up to 1,600 people could bathe here; you can still see their little dressing rooms. Gardens, shops, and promenades surrounded the baths where townsfolk met to exchange the news of the day. Fee. Tues.–Sat. 9–5, Sun. and holidays 10–1. Opera and open-air ballet performances are held in the baths June through August. The atmosphere is informal and lighthearted with many children in attendance.

If you circle back to Piazza Venezia, you will see famous Italians from popes and inventors to musicians in wax at Rome's **Wax Museum.** Fee. Piazza Venezia, 67. Daily 9–8. Tel. 6796482. There is a second museum near the train station at Piazza della Repubblica, 12. Daily 9–9. Tel. 4751509.

EAST OF THE TIBER

CENTRO STORICO: THE HISTORICAL CENTER

The **Pantheon** was built over 2,000 years ago by Marcus Agrippa as a temple honoring all gods. Rebuilt by Emperor Hadrian in 80 A.D., it is an outstanding architectural accomplishment. You will find yourself in a vast open space with a 143-foot-diameter dome overhead. The Pantheon's only light comes through an opening in this dome. If you visit when it is raining, you'll see water pour through this opening and splatter the marble floor. Free Tues.–Sat. 9–2, Sun. and holidays 9–1. The Pantheon is on the lively **Piazza della Minerva,** a lively piazza with many cafes, gelaterias, and Bernini's wonderful elephant statue supporting an obelisk. East of the Pantheon is **Piazza del Gesù,** said to be the windiest piazza in Rome. One day when the Devil was out walking with the wind, he paused to visit the Jesuit Church. According to legend, the wind is still waiting for him to return.

Piazza Navona, Rome's most active piazza, has sidewalk artists, children playing, and people relaxing on stone benches or in cafes. In December, stalls selling Christmas cribs and toys (see "special events") fill the piazza. Three Bernini fountains grace Navona, the most magnificent among them being the **Fontana dei Fiunni,** representing the four great rivers of the world: the Ganges, the Nile, the Danube and Río della Plata.

The piazza of the **Campo dei Fiori ("Field of Flowers")** is in a dense medieval quarter across Corso Vittorio Emanuele from Piazza Navona. The campo hosts one of the world's most colorful and lively open-air markets with flowers, fresh foods of all kinds, toys, hair ornaments, kitchenware, and knickknacks. Daily, except Sundays, 6

AM to 1 PM. Taste the olive bread in the *panaderia* at the far end of the campo; it was the best we tasted in all of Italy. The streets surrounding the campo are some of the most charming in Rome.

You will inevitably pass the walled-off excavations of the **Largo Argentina** many times as this is a busy central intersection and bus stop. Try the *frulatti* (fruit ices) at Bar Pascucci near the Largo; they're mouthwatering. Directly south of Largo Argentina is the Jewish Quarter's **Piazza Mattei.** Dolphins spout water while turtles drink from the piazza's **Fontana delle Tartarughe (Turtle Fountain).** The turtles were removed for safekeeping during the German occupation as this fountain is so cherished by the Romans.

The 12th-century portico of the **Church of Santa Maria in Cosmedin** holds a huge grimacing face with an open mouth known as the **Bocca della Verità (Mouth of Truth),** a medieval lie detector! Those thought to be lying had to put their hand into this mouth. If they had lied, the mouth would close and bite off their hand. Portico daily 9–5. End of via del Teatro di Marchello in the vicinity of the Jewish quarter.

NEAR THE SPANISH STEPS

Climb the popular **Scalinata della Trinità dei Monti (Spanish Steps)** on Piazza di Spagna; the view from the top is breathtaking, especially at Easter when the steps are lined with blazing pink azaleas. It's usually crowded in high season. Nicola Salvi's **Fontana di Trevi** is easily one of the world's most famous waterworks. Tradition has it that if you hope to return to Rome, throw a coin in the fountain over your left shoulder. Young Romans are often seen fishing the coins out with magnetized fishing lines. Go at night when King Neptune and his chariot drawn by Tritons are illuminated. Via di San Vincenzo.

AROUND THE VIA VENETO AND VILLA BORGHESE

Piazza Barberini's fountain, the **Fontana del Tritone,** with conch shells and dolphins was designed by Bernini. Nearby, at the corner of via Veneto, his **Fontana dell Api** has a shell with three giant bees that drink the water. The bees honor the Barberini family; the busy bee was their family symbol. On the piazza is **Palazzo Barberini.** Up the oval circular staircase is the **Galleria Nazionale d'Arte Antica.** In its ballroom are trompe l'oeil frescoes of the buzzing Barberini family symbols. Fee. Via delle Quattro Fontane, 13. Tues.–Sun. 9:15–7. Tel. 4750184. Rome's most ghoulish site is the 17th-century **Cave dei Capuccini (Cemetery of the Capuchins)** in the church of **Santa Maria della Concezione.** Its vaults hold the bones of close to 4,000 monks which have been applied to the walls to create a decorative tableaux of arches, butterflies, bushes, shrines, and flowers. Standing, hooded skeletons spook up the scene. Donation. Via Veneto, 27. Daily 9–12, 3–6. East of Palazzo Barberini is Rome's main train station, the Termini. Downstairs is an **aquarium** with poisonous frogs, turtles, crocodiles, skeletons of snakes, and sculptures of dinosaurs. Fee. Piazza dei Cinquecento. Daily 8–9.

At the top of Via Veneto is one of Rome's most glorious and centrally located parks, the **Villa Borghese. Rowboats** are for rent on its peaceful Giardino di Lago (Lake Garden) with ducks and swans. Daily 9–12, 2–sunset. **Horseback riding** is available at the Galoppatoio, near Porto Pinciana. Nearby is a **children's movie theater** [Viale della Pineta, 15 (Tel. 863485)], bicycle and tricycle rentals, and pony and donkey rides. In the park's Pincio section, there is a carousel and a **Punch and Judy** marionette theater. Within the park is the **Museo Borghese,** a museum big enough to hold a collection of masterpieces but small enough to hold the attention of most children. The collection includes major works by Raphael, Titian, Bernini, and Caravaggio. Kids enjoy Caravaggio's painting of David slaying Goliath and Raphael's *Lady with Unicorn.* Fee. Tues.–Sat. 9–2, Sun. and holidays 9–1. Tel. 858577. Rome's **Giardino Zoologico,** on the park's fringes, has monkey, giraffes, antelopes, seals, elephants, and rare species of reptiles. Fee. Daily 8:30–one hour before sunset. Tel. 870564.

Where the Sidewalk Ends: More Parks

Villa Ada, once the private residence of a king, is a large rambling park with roller-skating and a bicycle track. Entrance on Via Salaria. Closes at sunset. **Villa Glori,** east of Villa Ada, has pony rides. West of Villa Ada is **Parco Nemorense** with a carousel, ponies, trains on a large track, and bicycle rentals.

WEST OF THE TIBER

THE VATICAN

The *Vatican* is a city-state within Rome. Its focal point, Bernini's vast colonnaded **St. Peter's Square** and **St. Peter's Basilica,** can take your breath away. The Emperor Caligula built a chariot-racing circus here in A.D. 37 and commissioned the 135-foot Egyptian obelisk in the square's center. Weighing 312 tons, it took 900 men and 140 horses to have it installed! To the right of the square is the **Apostolic Palace,** home to the Pope. Every Sunday at noon he appears at his window to bless the crowd. When he is in Rome, he addresses the crowd in the piazza Wednesdays at 11 AM.

Climb to the top of **St. Peter's Basilica**'s dome, designed by Michelangelo; thrill seekers can climb 352 feet to a gallery that runs around the lantern of the brick dome, stopping at the many view-points for glimpses of the ant-size people in the square below. The entrance to the dome is to the left of the basilica's interior entrance. Inside the basilica, don't miss Michelangelo's early-16th-century mar-ble Pietà. It is now encased, because of vandalism. Basilica: Free. Dome: summer daily 7–7; winter daily 7–6. Fee. Daily 8–dusk. Dome closed during Papal audiences.

The nine museums of the **Musei del Vaticano** can be overwhelming for children. Get an illustrated guidebook in advance and let your kids look through it for ideas of what they'd like to see. Several suggested museum tours are posted at the entrance. Choose one appropriate for the age of your kids and how much time you have. The **Sistine Chapel,** in its new state of restoration, is an astonishing achievement. Kids are intrigued with the fact that Michelangelo spent 4 years painting the frescoed ceiling all alone and flat on his back. Twenty-two years after painting the ceiling, he was asked to paint a fresco of the Last Judgment on the wall behind the altar. It caused a scandal because Christ was painted nude. Twenty-three years later another artist was given the task of painting strategic draperies on the nudes. The **Museo Gregoriano Egizio (Egyptian Museum)** is another that most kids enjoy. There are statues of Egyp-tian queens, pharaohs, gods, and goddesses, a throne belonging to Rhameses II from the 13th century B.C., and an assortment of mum-mies. Don't miss the 16th-century **Stanze di Raffaello (Raphael Rooms),** which are entire rooms painted by the artist. Among the images in his *School of Athens* is Euclid teaching geometry. All museums: Fee; no charge for kids under 1 meter tall and free last Sun. of month. Easter week and July–Sept. Mon.–Fri. 9–5, Sat. 9–2; off-season Mon.–Sat. 9–2; last Sun. of the month 9–2. Tel. 6982.

TRASTEVERE AND ALONG THE TIBER

The Trastevere is one of Rome's most vivacious quarters with tiny meandering streets, many cafes, and lively piazzas. Take the steep but worthwhile climb up to the **Gianicolo Hill** for superb views of St. Peter's, the Vatican, and all of Rome. On weekends there is a Punch and Judy show in the park plus a carousel, pony rides, and gelato stalls. Down the hill is **Villa Farnesina,** the palace from which Cleopatra fled when Cæsar was murdered. It is claimed that she was the first to have a cesarean section, named after her beloved. The villa has rooms with astonishing trompe l'oeil perspective that were frescoed by Raphael and Peruzzi. There is a small garden for picnicking. Mon.–Sat. 9–1. Tel. 650831. At the end of Via Corsini are Rome's **Botanical Gardens** with expansive lawns for strolling, running, and picnicking amongst the tropical trees and ponds. Mon.–Fri. 9–6, Sat. 9–11. Largo Cristina di Svezia.

Surrounded by peaceful gardens, the **Castel Sant'Angelo** was first built by Hadrian as his tomb and later made into a fortress. More recently it was a grim prison, and you can see ancient artillery and the cells that held inmates. Fee. Tues.–Sat. 9–1, Sun. 9–12. Tel. 6564227. Angels line the pedestrian bridge, the **Ponte Sant'Angelo,** which is the best way to get to the fortress.

The picturesque **Isola Tiberina (Tiber Island)** is shaped like a small ocean liner. The best way to get to there is via the Bridge of the Four Heads, named after four faces that look in different directions from a pillar in the bridge's center. The island's embankment is great for strolls; rock concerts are often held here on summer nights.

Where the Sidewalk Ends: More Parks

A must is **Villa Doria Pamphili,** bordering the Gianicolo. Its vast expanse of meadows, fountains, statues, and gardens of mazelike hedges are favorite spots for Sunday outings by Roman families who convene for lively day-long picnics, soccer games, jogs, and strolls. It was our favorite park for people watching.

Villa Sciarra is a gem of a neighborhood park in the Monteverde Vecchio district near Doria Pamphili. The park, with its curious clipped topiary, 18th-century statues, beautiful fountains, and playground, comes alive at 5 for the evening passeggiata. On Sundays there is a fun fair for children with rides and donkey carts.

ALONG VIA APPIA ANTICA AND THE CATACOMBS

South of the city, **Via Appia Antica** starts where the walls of Rome end. Along the route you can see vestiges of tombs and Rome's famous catacombs. Visit the **Museum of the Walls and Walks of Rome,** where kids can walk a short way along the top of the walls. Fee. Via Porta San Sebastiano. Wed. and Fri. 9–1:30, Sun. 9–1, Tues., Thurs., and Sat. 9–1:30, 4–7.

Rome has over forty **catacombs** that were giant caves where Christian burials took place. Most of them are between Via Salaria and Via Nomentana on one side of the city and off Via Appia on the other. They are fascinating rather than frightening for children as they are shrouded in mystery. No one is sure of their exact use or how the suppressed Christians found the freedom to build them. Many contain paintings of biblical tales children may know, such as the story of Noah's Ark. The best bets for kids are the **Catacomb of Santa**

Domitilla, off Via Appia, which has paintings and tombstone inscriptions (Fee. 22A Via delle Sette Chiese. Wed.–Mon. 8:30–12, 2:30–5. English guided tour.) and the **Catacomb of Priscilla,** near Villa Ada (see "East of Tiber" parks), which dates back to the 2nd century B.C. An English guide will show you lots of bones, a 3rd-century tomb with paintings of a Roman woman at her wedding, the funeral of her husband, and finally, her own funeral. Fee. Via Salaria Nuova, 430. Tues.–Sun. 8:30–12, 2:30–5.

South of the city in the city's **EUR** district is the **LunEUR,** an amusement (luna) fun fair, playground, and lake with boat rentals. Its highlights include a giant ferris wheel and the "Himalaya Railroad." Fee. Via delle Tre Fontane. Open daily year-round. Tel. 5925933. Across from the luna park is a miniature traffic park for kids.

Sports

Pick up the free publication "Here Rome" from the EPT, which lists swimming pools, riding clubs, sports centers, and nearby waterskiing, sailing, and canoeing. The nicest **swimming pool** is at the Foro Italico sports complex, on the banks of the river at Lungotevere Maresciallo Cadorna. Open June–Sept. Tel. 3601498. **Bicycles** can be rented at Via della Purificazione, 13/14 off piazza Barberini. Daily 9 AM–7:30 PM. Tel. 465485.

Performing Arts

The newspaper *La Repubblica* has a section called "Roma Teatri," which lists performances, puppet shows, and circus visits for young and old. A more complete listing can be found in its Saturday insert, "Trova Roma." Italian puppet shows are delightful, especially the **marionette theater Il Torchio,** Via Morosini, 16 (Tel. 582049). For other performances refer to the Villa Borghese.

Special Events

On the night of January 5–6, the Eve of Epiphany, Piazza Navona hosts a **toy fair.** Legend claims that a witch, Befana, brings toys to good kids and coal to those who misbehave. The coal is actually candy, so naughty kids should not fear.

February's **carnival** in Rome brings confetti and costumed children to the streets.

On **St. Joseph's Day** in mid-March there is a parade with stalls selling traditional *bignè* (cream puffs) in the Trionfale area. During the week following **Easter** there is an **international horse show** in the Piazza di Siena.

July's **Festa di Noantri,** held in the Trastevere and other local *piazze* during the last two weeks, features acrobats, fire-eaters, and lively street entertainment.

December is the busiest month for **Piazza Navona,** where kids stream in to patronize booths selling Christmas decorations and games.

LAZIO: NEAR ROME

EAST OF ROME

Tivoli is one of Italy's most fanciful parks, spilling down a terraced cliff in front of the grand 16th-century **Villa d'Este** palace. Hundreds of fountains of every imaginable shape and size line its Viale delle Centro Fontane (Avenue of a Hundred Fountains). At the lower level, the Fontana dell'Organa (Organ Fountain) is a water-infused organ that emits strange musical tones as water passes through; nursing mothers will relate to a voluptuous fountain where water sprays from, well, guess . . . The Rometta ("mini Rome") Fountain reproduces some of the city's best-known classical monuments. Visit at night to see the palace and gardens illuminated. Fee. 32 km. from Rome along the via Tiburtina; follow signs. Palace and gardens: Tues.–Sun. 9–one hour before sunset. Gardens: illuminated Easter–Sept. 9–11 PM.

Villa Adriana (Hadrian's Villa), 10 minutes away, is where Emperor Hadrian built his enormous country palace as a miniature version of all that had impressed him on his extensive travels abroad. Stop first to see the model of what it looked like in its heyday back in 120, then venture into the ruins of this giant, pleasure palace. What luxury! You'll see the ruins of his private athletic field, a lake encircled by statues, the "hospitaria" for his many guests, and underground paths so servants could not be seen or heard. The palace is set in a large pastoral landscape, ideal for a picnic. Fee. Tues.–Sun. 9-one hour before sunset. Nearby is **Villa Gregoriana,** a large park ideal for hiking and cooling off in the mists of the beautiful **Aniene Falls,** a series of cascading waterfalls. Fee. Daily 9-one hour before sunset.

NORTHWEST OF ROME

The resort of **Lake Bracciano,** 39 kilometers from the city, offers swimming, sailing, motorboating, and waterskiing. Climb up to its **Odelscalchi Castle.**

Northwest of Lake Bracciano and 80 kilometers from Rome is the walled city of *Viterbo.* The untouched medieval **San Pellegrino** quarter has churches and towers, austere cloisters, and playful fountains. Fans of the macabre should see the smiling saint's body that lies inside a metal urn inside one of Viterbo's temples, the **Sanctuary of Santa Rosa.** In early September, townsfolk celebrate the **Macchina di Santa Rosa.** A 100-foot-high, 5-ton spiraling tower with a saint at its crest is lugged on the backs of 100 robust men through Viterbo's winding streets up the steep hill from Piazza Verdi to the saint's shrine. Tel. (0761) 226161.

North of Viterbo is **Lago di Bolsena,** Italy's largest volcanic lake. Many hotels and campsites line its shores. Activities include water-skiing, swimming, and boating out to the unspoiled islands of Martana and Bisentina. In May, when the town celebrates **infiorata,** decorative designs of flower petals adorn the streets leading to the church where the miracle of Corpus Domini took place in 1263. Tel. for both: (0761) 98601.

Most of the grounds of *Bagnaia's* **Villa Lante,** 4 kilometers from Viterbo, have been turned into a public park, and kids will delight in its delightful fountains, such as the one with plump little angels blowing shells. Fee. Villa: Tues.–Sun. 9–5. Guided tours. Park: June Tues.–Sun. 9–7; July–Aug. 9–7:30; Sept. 9–6; fall and spring 9–5; winter 9–4.

For a completely different park experience, head up the same road to the **Parco dei Mostri (Monster Park),** in *Bomarzo,* named for its gigantic, surreal, and grotesque sculptures commissioned by one of the 16th century's most unusual personalities, Count Pier Francesco Orsini. Orsini's intent was to mock the formal, aristocratic Italian garden, such as the one found at Villa Lante or Tivoli. You'll find a garden of scenes carved from huge bolders that include giants, dragons, bears, a 20-foot-high stone elephant with a castle on his back crushing a Roman soldier, an enormous Hercules tormenting a poor victim, a colossal human head built into the hillside, mermaids, and more. Kids can climb into the cavernous mouth of "il Mascherone." There's a house built deliberately to lean and a small zoo. Fee. Buses depart from Viterbo daily. About 1.5 km. northwest of Bomarzo; 132 km. north of Rome. Daily 9–8.

ISLAND OF PONZA

Off the coast of *Anzio,* south of Ostia, is the volcanic island of Ponza. Ponza is in many ways the quintessential Italian island with a colorful pink and yellow town, a dramatic coastline, beautiful beaches, and delicious seafood. There are good swimming bays near the village of *La Forna.* The long curving beach of **Chiaia di Luna,** set against a vast limestone cliff, is the island's most popular beach. Although frequented by Italian families, the island has yet to draw the crowds of Capri and Ischia. A limited number of hotels ranging from inexpensive to expensive are available. Ferries depart July 15–

September 15 from Anzio; frequent planes depart from Fiumicino Airport near Rome.

TUSCANY

Tuscany's olive groves, vineyards, and forests surround well-preserved hill towns steeped in Etruscan, Roman, medieval, and Renaissance history. The region has many engaging spots for children, such as the Leaning Tower of Pisa and Collodi's Pinocchio Park, which can be visited by making side trips from Florence by train or car. With the exception of Elba, Tuscany's beaches are not clean for swimming.

FLORENCE

Florence is typically filled with visitors, especially in the summer, when the sidewalks and popular sights are shoulder to shoulder with people. Yet, wherever you walk, you confront the city's artistic legacy. Architectural monuments, sculpture, and whimsical fountains are found at every turn. The two museum giants, the Uffizi Gallery and the Pitti Palace, contain some of the Western world's greatest art. Numerous other galleries, churches, and museums make Florence a paradise for adult art lovers, but kids will find it deadly unless you structure their day carefully. Combine short museum tours with time spent running in Cascine Park, feeding pigeons in the Piazza della Signoria, and souvenir shopping at the Mercato Nuovo. Let your kids view the city and its art at their own pace and draw their own conclusions.

Wha'd'ya Wannna Do?

Florence's **tourist office (EPT),** at Via Manzoni, 16 (Tel. 2478141), publishes a helpful free pamphlet, "Florence for the Young," with listings of parks, sports facilities, and suggested itineraries for school kids. City maps and the most current information on sites is available at the **Azienda Autonoma di Turismo,** via Tournabuoni, 15 (Tel. 216544), or at the train stations' red and white tourist booth. The publication "Firenze Spettacol," available at newsstands, has listings of current entertainment. Florence's **telephone area code** is 055.

The Lay of the City

Most of the city's major attractions are within easy walking distance of one another within the old and central part of Florence, *il centro storico.* The city's principal streets extend from the Piazza San

Giovanni and its duomo. The city's main artery, Via Calzaioli, runs from here to Piazza della Signoria, home of the Uffizi. Piazza della Signoria is a short walk from the Ponte Vecchio, the bridge spanning the Arno River which leads you to the Pitti Palace. This is the Florence that floods of tourists see; to get an even better feel, allow time to wander off the main track.

Getting Around

Avoid driving in the city; park outside and walk in. Two supervised **car parks** that are convenient are at Piazza Pitti (if you enter the city from the south) and at Piazza Stazione (if you enter from the north). **Buses** are convenient and taxis available, but touring Florence *a piedi* (by foot) is the best way to experience the city. Most of the historical center of town is a pedestrian zone. When young legs get tired, hire a **horse-drawn carriage** at Piazza della Signoria.

Where to Stay

An alternative to staying in the center of Florence, with its hustle and bustle, is to select an **apartment** or **villa** in the hills around the city and take the short train or bus ride in. Nearly all the rental companies arranging for homes and apartments in Tuscany have listings outside Florence. Rates start at approximately $500 per week. Vacanza Bella has a few apartments in Florence's center that sleep from four to six. Rates start at $1000 per week, and there's a 2-week minimum stay.

HOTELS

The *Villa Cora* is an 18th-century villa above the Boboli Gardens with a suite reserved for families and a pool. Via Macchiavelli, 18, 50125. Tel. 2298451. **Deluxe.**

The *Villa Medici*, near Cascine Park, has a garden and pool. Via del Prato, 42, 50123. Tel. 261331. **Deluxe.**

The *Jolly Carlton*, located at the entrance to Cascine Park, has a 6th-floor garden and 7th-floor pool. Piazza Vittorio Veneto, 4A, 50123. Tel. 2770. **Expensive.**

Villa Villoresi, outside the city, is a 17th-century villa with apartments in a large park with a children's pool. Cribs, baby-sitters upon request, and early dinners for children provided. 50019 Colonnata di Sesto Fiorentino. Tel. 4489032. **Expensive.**

Continental has a terrace overlooking the Arno and communicating rooms or suites for up to five people. Lungarno Acciaiuoli, 2, 50123. Tel. 282392. **Moderate.**

Villa Le Rondini is in a large park with a pool, tennis, and connecting rooms. It's 15 minutes from the city center on a hill overlooking Florence. Via Bolgnese Vecchia, 224. Tel. 40081. **Moderate.**

Pensione La Scaletta, near the Boboli Gardens, sports a rooftop terrace. Via Guicciadini, 13. Tel. 283028. **Inexpensive.**

Pensione Rigatti is an old palazzo with exquisite paintings. It is well located near the Uffizi. Reserve rooms on its lush garden well in advance. Lungarno Gen. Diaz, 2, 50122. Tel. 213022. **Inexpensive.**

CAMPGROUNDS

Italiani E. Stranieri may be crowded as it accommodates 320 tent sites, but it offers a grand view of the city. Apr.–Oct. Via Michelangelo, 880. Tel. 6811977

Villa Camerata has 55 tent sites. Open year-round. Viale A. Righi. Tel. 610300.

Mugello Verde, a bit out of town, has a pool, tennis courts, horseback riding, 194 tent sites, and 38 bungalows. San Piero a Sieve in La Fortezza. Tel. 848511.

Detour! What to See and Do

Sites are arranged geographically in the order you are most likely to see them *a piedi*, on foot.

AROUND THE DUOMO

The **Piazza del Duomo** in the heart of the old city hosts the enormous **duomo (Santa Maria del Fiore).** The duomo's mosaiclike walls of green, red, and white marble and red-tiled dome make it a majestic example of the Florentine variant of Gothic architecture. While its splendor will take your breath away, your kids will be amazed by its size. They will especially appreciate that the duomo is cool inside and that it's great for hearing the echoes of their shoes. Point out that when the candlelit church was filled with people listening to a fire-and-brimstone sermon, there were no microphones. Climbing the 465 spiral steps to the top of the dome will give them a spectacular view of Baccio d'Agnolo's marble floor and the tiny spectators below. Duomo: Free. Daily 7–12, 2:30–6. Last entrance 5:30. Climb: Fee. Mon.–Sat. 8:30–12:30, 2:30–5. Last entrance 4:30. Tel. 213229.

The 14th-century **Campanile di Giotto** next door stands 296 feet high. To get to the top, climb the bell tower's 414 steps for an unparalleled view of the duomo and the red rooftops of all of Florence. As kids climb, they can peer down the bell's center rope hole or out of peep holes to see pinhole views of the duomo. Fee.

Summer daily 9–7; off-season daily 9–5. Last entrance 40 minutes before closing. In front of the duomo, in the adjoining **Piazza San Giovanni** stands the **battistero (baptistry)**, one of the city's most beautiful buildings, boasting Ghiberti's elegant bronze-and-gold doors, which took 27 years to complete. When asked why she thought it took so long, our 4-year-old friend responded, "He must have been sick a lot." Free. Daily 9–12:30, 2:30–5. The city's **Ludoteca Centrale,** a short walk from the duomo, is a free city-run library with playrooms and a toy and book library. Piazza della Santissima Annuziata, 13.

AROUND THE UFFIZI

A short walk from the duomo is the **Palazzo e Gallerie degli Uffizi,** which houses a vast collection of masterpieces from the Italian Renaissance. You'll find Botticelli, da Vinci, Raphael, Michelangelo, and Giotto, to name a few, and some exceptional examples from the Northern Renaissance, including Dürer, Rembrandt, and Rubens. Head for the Botticelli Room. His *Birth of Venus* is sublime. The goddess, her red hair flowing, stands on a seashell as she emerges from the sea. Piazzale degli Uffizi, 6. Tues.–Sat. 9–7, Sun. 9–1. Tel. 218341. Adjacent to the Uffizi is the active **Piazza della Signoria,** where tame pigeons wait patiently for bread crumbs. The piazza has a rousing array of statues, including the *Fountain of Neptune* by Ammannati and a copy of Michelangelo's *David*. Horse-and-carriages depart here for tours of the city. The city's best **gelateria,** "Perchè No!!" (Why Not?), is just off Piazza Signoria at Via Tavolini, 19.

Around Piazza Santissima Annunziata is the **Gallerie dell'Accademia,** where your children can see Michelangelo's original sculpture of *David*. In summer, get there when the museum opens. Fee. Via Ricasoli, 60. Tues.–Sat. 9–2, Sun. 9–1. Tel. 214375. A short walk in back of the Uffizi is the **Museo di Storia della Scienza,** with scientific objects assembled by the houses of Medici and Lorraini along with some of Galileo's original telescopes and compasses. The prospect of seeing Galileo's right index finger displayed in a glass case excited our young fans of the macabre and started a search for the "Gruesome Top Ten" as part of our Italian tour. Fee. Piazza dei Guidici, 1, along the rive Arno. Fee. Mon., Wed., Fri. 9:30–1, 2–5; Tues., Thurs., Sat. 9:30–1. Closed Sun. Tel. 293493.

ACROSS THE PONTE VECCHIO

Along the **banks of the Arno** are stretches of grass where you'll often see soccer games or crowds assembled to watch rowing competitions along the river. The **Ponte Vecchio,** built in 1345, is the city's oldest bridge, and the only one spared from destruction during World War II. It is one of Florence's most characteristic monuments, with three stories of touristy goldsmith's shops precariously stacked above it. The bridge is packed with people and vendors by day and street musicians by night.

Crossing the Ponte Vecchio, you reach the **Palazzo Pitti,** filled with tapestries, portraits, sculpture, and an excellent collection of 16th- and 17th-century paintings. Kids may not be able to tolerate many of the palace's 1,000 rooms and 10,000 paintings, but they will enjoy its **Museum of Coaches,** which houses carriages from earlier days. The new **Galleria del Costume,** in the palace's Museo degli Argenti, features clothing and jewelry from the past three centuries; a highlight is the two 19th-century tiaras on display. In the **Galleria Palatina,** have your kids guess which painting is Caravaggio's *Sleeping Cupid*. The young and restless can run in the adjoining **Giardini di Boboli (Boboli Gardens)** (see "Parks" below) when museum viewing gets to be too much. Fee. Galleria Palatina, Galleria d'Arte Moderna, and Royal Apartments: Tues.–Sat. 9–2, Sun. 9–1. Tel. 210032. Museo degli Argenti: Wed. and Fri. 9–2, Sun. 9–1. Tel. 212557.

Just One Look: More Museums

Horse lovers should not miss Florence's first contemporary art museum, the **Museo Marini,** in an ingeniously restored former church. Named for an Italian artist who died in 1980, the museum has a collection of his artwork that includes his 1930s sculptures of adolescent riders. Fee. June–Aug. Wed.–Sun. 10–1, 4–7; off-season 10–6. Piazza San Pancrazio. Tel. 219432.

Across town in the northern part of the city in a charming park is the **Museo Stibbert,** where kids can see 16th-century mounted knights, costumes, and armor from the Far East and western Europe. Fee. Via Federico Stibbert, 26. Fri.–Wed. 9–2. Tel. 475520.

Where the Sidewalk Ends: Parks

The **Giardini di Boboli (Boboli Gardens),** in back of the Pitti Palace, were designed in 1550 and are an exceptional example of the formal, terraced Italian garden. Don't miss the **grotto** by Buontalenti to the left of the palace. Take a seat on the delightful mosaic bench where you can pause to view the grotto's images of turtles and shells. Boboli's amphitheater, the **anfiteatro,** is lined with stone benches where visitors picnic and soak up sun. Kids must stay off the grass, but they can run off steam by climbing up the promenade to **Citadel Belvedere,** perched at the top of the hill with a great city view. Gardens and citadel free. Gardens: May–Aug. daily 9–6:30; Mar.–Apr. and Sept.–Oct. daily 9–5:30; Nov.–Feb. daily 9–4:30. Citadel: Daily 9–8. Garden Tel. 213440.

The grand **Parco delle Cascine,** to the west of the *centro storico*, stretches along the north banks of the Arno. It has a number of playgrounds with inventive equipment, and many beautiful old trees provide shade for picnics. Cascine has a pool, bikes for rent, horse-and-carriage rides, a small carnival called the "Piccolo Eden" near its pond, and a small "Piccolo Zoo." Lawns extend for miles, and there are many trails to stroll. Follow brown road signs.

Sports

Bikes can be rented in spring and summer at Ciao & Basta, Via Alamanni, near the Piazza Stazione (Tel. 213307), and in summer at Fortezza da Basso, Romito, 77 (Tel. 499319). **Horseback riding** is available through Centro Ippico Toscana, Via de Vespucci, 5/a (Tel. 372621). An indoor Olympic-sized **swimming pool** and **kiddie pool** is at Costoli, Via le Paoli (Tel. 675747). For an **outdoor pool,** try Bellariva, Lungarno Colombo, 6 (Tel. 677521). The EPT's publication "Florence for the Young" lists ice-skating rinks, canoeing, bowling, soccer, and tennis facilities.

Special Events

February's **Carnival** is celebrated in Florence with children in costumes and lots of confetti throwing.

Easter Sunday's magical **Scoppio del Carro (Explosion of the Cart)** begins when a large cart, drawn by white oxen wearing garlands of flowers, pulls into the Piazza del Duomo. At exactly noon during high mass, a mechanical dove is sent from the highest altar of the Duomo along a wire to set off a pyramid of fireworks in the cart. Firecrackers, colored smoke, twirling wheels, and unfurling banners go off while all the bells in the city ring.

Jumping Jiminy, don't miss May's **Festa del Grillo (Festival of the Crickets),** held on Ascension Day! Thousands of chirping crickets in little cages in Cascine Park bring back memories of hot summer nights. They are sold as good luck charms, and you can buy one for a song to serenade you in your hotel room.

Emperor Charles V held Florence under siege in 1530 and Florentines defied him by playing soccer under the muzzles of his cannons. Each year, the **Gioco del Calcio (Soccer Games in 16th-century Costumes)** are held in commemoration of that event, after which there is much roughhousing. Fireworks, pageantry, and a historical costume procession make this a fun way for kids to assimilate history. It is held in late June and the first Sunday in May.

Late June's **Festa del Patrono,** honoring Florence's patron saint, John the Baptist, features fireworks over the city.

The dazzling **Rificolone (Night Festival of the Lanterns)** is a children's lantern festival with a procession through the center of the city on the eve of the Virgin Mary's birth, that converges on the Ponte Vecchio. Held the first Sunday in September, hundreds of illuminated paper lanterns reflect off the Arno River.

EAST OF FLORENCE

Five kilometers out of *Pistoia* is the **Zoo Citta di Pistoia,** a lush park set amidst the verdant Tuscan hills, with fruit trees and grape arbors. A train tours the park, where you'll see panthers in cages with fresco murals, kangaroos, llamas, a bird aviary, reptiles, giraffes, and many Italian families conversing as emotively as the caged monkeys. There are little huts for picnicking and a vintage playground. Fee. Follow yellow signs. Daily 9–7. Further up the road is a public **swimming pool.** July's month-long festival, **Luglio Pistoiese,** features concerts, soccer games, foot races, arts and crafts markets, and folkloric spectacles leading up to acclaimed **Giostra dell'Orso (Bear Joust),** held the fourth Sunday in July. Recreating a 13th-century palio, twelve knights gallop around the piazza in two's, with their lances lowered, until reaching the figures of two stylized bears—their target. The winner is named "Knight, Spur of Gold, Pistoia and Countryside." Advance tickets essential. Contact the **tourist office (EPT)** at Palazzo dei Vescovi, Piazza Duomo, Pistoia. Tel. (0573) 21622.

Collodi's **Parco Monumentale di Pinocchio** pays tribute to Carlo Collodi, the author of the lively fairytale, who took his pen name from his birthplace. Upon entering, kids climb on a dancing Pinocchio and his fairy mother and then wind through a deceptively innocent-looking maze and a pirate's lair. All of the book's scenes are sculpted in bronze or depicted in mosaic. Traveling through the Land of Toys, you wind through a little village and pass between the legs of a policeman barring the way. The Shark Fountain, with double rows of teeth, bulging eyes, and skin patterned with broken glass, spurts water out of a blowhole and sprays everyone who crosses its path. Fee. About 60 km. northwest of Florence, off the Pescia-Lucca road. Daily 8–6:30. Tel. (0572) 429342.

Across the road is the historic **Villa Garzoni and Garden,** built for the Marchese Romano Garzoni during the 17th and 18th centuries. Kids enjoy running up and down the garden's steep incline to see fountains with crazy jets of water, grottoes, mazes, and bridges. At the top of the garden stands the historical palace, with its imposing steps, several ramps, and monumental facade. Fee. Daily 8–8. Don't miss the hill town of Collodi, a hidden treasure. The town's olives are delectable, and the surrounding olive groves are an ideal spot for a family picnic. On the first Sunday in September at Collodi's **Sagra of Fried Polenta**—a regional delicacy—the whole family will clean their plates.

LUCCA

The walled city of Lucca is one of the jewels of Tuscany, both for its beauty and its friendly, small-town atmosphere. Just off the main road between Pisa and Florence, Lucca has somehow escaped the throngs and has retained its elegant charm. Lucca is an "outdoor city," contained within long 16th-century walls. Cars are prohibited within the walls of the old city, the *città vecchia*.

The most dazzling church in Lucca is **San Michele in Foro,** in the **Piazza San Michele,** the lively center of the città vecchia. The facade's whimsical 13th-century ornamentation was added so often that it now looks like a child dressed up in a trunk full of clothing and costume jewelry. The piazza hosts a Wednesday morning market with toys and wine and many of the city's special festivities (see "Special Events"). In an alcove at the entrance to the **Basilica of San Frediano,** at the northern edge of the city off Piazza Scarpellini, look for **Santa Zita's Mummy.** Once a child servant to one of Lucca's wealthiest families, Zita was later canonized for her work in helping the poor. Her preserved body, draped in white lace and plastic flowers, lies in a glass case. In late April, the townspeople place her in the middle of this imposing Romanesque church and eerily stroke her withered limbs. We gawked at her sunken cheeks and gave this a high rating in the "Gruesome Top Ten." From the church, walk through the oval-shaped **Piazza Anfiteatro,** the site of a Roman amphitheater, where the tall and narrow buildings appear to tilt inward, and you'll arrive at the **Torre Guinigi,** a massive tower with gnarled oaks growing on top. Give it a climb; the view is worth every huff and puff. Fee. Summer Mon.–Sat. 9–7; off-season 10–5. Ascent of the tower: entrance in Via S. Andrea behind Via dei Guinigi.

Be sure to walk, bike, or picnic on Lucca's tree-planted 16th- and 17th-century **baluaradi** (city walls). Pick up a map at the tourist office just outside the city to find all the entrances. This broad esplanade, the longest of its kind in Europe, has shady paths, grassy parks, playgrounds, fountains, and a moat below. For **bike** rentals, contact Casermetta S. Croce (Tel. 587857).

Late July's **Feast of San Paolino** is celebrated with a torchlight parade in period costume and a ritual offering of a candle to the saint, with the blessing of the *Palio* or banner. This is followed by a crossbow contest, the **Palio della Balestra,** held between the city's three districts. Thousands of votive candles flickering in intricate wrought-iron holders shaped as trees, stars, and waves from all the town's windows illuminate Lucca for mid-September's **Luminaria di Santa Croce.** The festivities culminate in a procession in which townspeople bedecked in Renaissance costumes carry banners of velvet from the Cathedral of San Frediano to the Duomo of San Martino. The next day, a fair is held in Piazza San Michele. A tip from a veteran traveler: Try and spend the night in Lucca before the festival to avoid incoming traffic.

ALONG THE NORTHERN COAST

Carrara is the world center for quarrying and sculpting marble. What appear to be snow-capped peaks towering over the city are "glaciers" of white marble; even the town's rivers run white. To visit some of the famous quarries (there are over 500), follow signs for **Cave** (quarry). Our favorite was at the top of the winding mountain road marked Codena-Bedizzano that led us to *Colonnata,* a small village where marble was extracted for Michelangelo. On the way up you may hear explosions as marble is blasted out of the mountain and the crash of great marble blocks falling as they are cut through by tough, thin cables. Your kids can pick up souvenirs di marmo (marble) from the millions of chunks on the ground—it's all free. Forget about cholesterol for one night and join the town's quarry families at large picnic tables for barbecued sausages, ribs, and the surprisingly delicious local delicacy of cured lard at Colonnata's **Sagra del Lardo (Festival of Lard),** held in late August in the town's 14th-century medieval piazza. Tel. (0585) 318069.

You may want to avoid swimming in the beaches of the *Riviera della Versilia* as the water is not the cleanest. You'll find many facilities in the Riviera's towns for fun and amusement: miniature trains, bikes to rent, puppet shows, and carousels. From *Marina di Pietrasanta,* journey inland to the artisans' colony of *Pietrasanta,* where Michelangelo also quarried his precious marble. Kids can peek into the studios of working sculptors and see how realistic figures are formed. *Viareggio* is the Versilia's largest city and the capital of **Carnival,** when masquerades, hilarious floats, and parades with pirates and animals and dancing children pack the streets closest to the beach and on the promenade. On the final night, fireworks explode in the sky over the ocean. Contact Fondazione Carnevale, Via Saffi, 1, Viareggio (Tel. 962568).

PISA

What family's trip to Italy with children would be complete without the kids chuckling at the **Leaning Tower of Pisa**? One of the seven wonders of the world for children, it is something they know as legendary. Why does it appeal to kids of all ages? Maybe it's because it sounds like *pizza*, or maybe it's because they have all built a leaning tower of blocks only to have it topple. As a little friend of ours claimed when she heard her parents wanted to skip it, "Don't you realize it's leaning, Daddy? Any day it might fall and then we'd miss it." Get to the tower as soon as it opens at 9 AM to avoid crowds. The Leaning Tower veers about 14 feet off center because of a slight shift of land during its construction; nobody knows quite why. It continues to slide by a fraction of an inch each year despite attempts to halt the slippage. In 1990 officials determined the tower unsafe to climb.

At mid-June's **Feast Day of San Ramieri** the banks of the Arno are illuminated by torches and thousands of lit candles float downstream on corks. This occurs the night prior to the historical **Regatta of San Ramieri,** which is a rowing contest with eight oarsmen on each boat representing Pisa's city districts; all are dressed in 16th-century costume. Late June brings the annual **Gioco del Ponte (Battle of the Bridge),** for which participants parade through the streets of Pisa in 16th-century costumes, reenacting old rivalries between the Mezzogiorno and Tramontana districts, two neighborhoods separated by the Arno River. The parade begins at 4:30 PM followed by the staged battle on the Ponte di Mezzo (between Piazza Garibaldi and Piazza XX Settembre) at 6:30 PM. Tel. (050) 560464.

SAN GIMIGNANO

Time stands still in the well-preserved hill town of *San Gimignano,* with its lavish frescoes, ocher-colored churches, and expansive views of the Tuscan plain with olive groves and cypress trees. Fifteen towers dominate San Gimignano's skyline, creating a remote resemblance to medieval skyscapers. Harpists entertain from enchanting courtyards and an air of cozy containment pervades—if you avoid visiting in-season on weekends. The real heart of the city is the **Piazza della Cisterna,** named for its central 13th-century cistern. Your kids will be more impressed with its "Gelateria Joly," where little umbrellas and fish-shaped straws embellish the ice-cream wonders. Cisterna's adjacent **Piazza del Duomo** is home to the **Torre Grossa,** the town's highest tower, which is the only one you can climb. The view is stupendous. Fee (also provides access to civic museum). Daily 9:30–12:30, 3–6. The adjacent **Palazzo del Posdestà** has tunnels, *loggie,* a wonderful open-air courtyard, often the site of musicians, and frescoes of hunting scenes. Piazza del Duomo hosts an **open-air market** Thursday and Saturday mornings.

Pack up picnic supplies and head up the small road behind the duomo to the 14th-century **rocca** (fort), a large public park with olive trees and grassy lawns, built by the Florentines in 1353. The fort's pentagonal shape is made up of towers and parts of walls which kids can climb for splendid views of the Tuscan countryside. While parents are sipping the town's famous white wine, *Vernaccia di San Gimignano,* kids must try some of the local sweet specialties. *Cantucci* are nutty cookies *(biscotti),* and *panforte* are various dense fruit and nut torts. The best **pastry shop** is Bar Enoteca, Via San Matteo, 29, a short walk from the Piazza del Duomo.

SIENA

Siena's special charm resides not only in her monuments and outstanding works of art, but in the atmosphere of the place as a whole. The grand *palazzi,* steep alleyways, orchards, and the all-pervasive warm color of the brickwork, from which the color burnt sienna gets its name, should impress even the sleepiest teenager. The historic center is closed to traffic so you won't have to dodge cars; to best experience the city, go off-season to avoid shuffling around crowds, too. Pick up a free city map at the Azienda Autonoma di Turismo along Siena's main shopping street, Via di Città, 43, which circles the **Piazza del Campo,** the city's central square.

The Campo is always lively with children chasing the many pigeons who call the piazza their home. At its highest part, children converge around the **Fonte Gaia,** a pool surrounded by copies of carvings by Siena's most famous architect and sculptor, Jacopo della Quercia, to play with its faucet and to clean their pigeon feather souvenirs. Climb the piazza's old clock tower, the **Torre di Mangia (Tower of the Gluttonous Eater),** named for the food-crazy watchman in charge of striking the hours by hand. Only thirty people are allowed up at a time, so the wait can be long. A steep and narrow passage leads you up the 409 steps, but once at the top you can sit right below the giant bell, which still rings out the time, and have a 360-degree view of Siena and the countryside. Fee. Climb: Apr.–Oct. Mon.–Sat. 9–6:30, Sun. 9:30–1; Nov.–Mar. Mon.–Sat. 9:30–1:30, Sun. 9:30–1. Busy shopping streets radiate out from the piazza. In Piazza Salimberi, the gelateria Nannini sells gelato in a *cornetto paralinato,* a sinfully rich chocolate-covered cone with nuts.

Siena's immense unfinished **duomo** is breathtaking with its inlaid mosaic floor and zebra-striped black-and-white marble exterior. The north transept's famous 13th-century **pulpit,** with lions and mythological animals designed by Pisano, "looked like a carousel," according to one of our kids. The inlaid marble floor is fully uncovered only in October in order to preserve it. Other times you can see only parts of its mythological figures. Have your kids look up to the highest point in the dome, where there are painted stars of real gold—a beautiful image of a starry night. Daily Apr.–Oct. 9–7; Nov.–Mar. 8–5. Siena's main **parks, La Lizza** and its adjoining **Piazza della Libertà,** are close to the historic center.

Mid-March's **Feast of San Giuseppe** is celebrated at the Church of San Giuseppe in the city's Onda quarter. A hit for kids are the rice fritters and locally made toys sold in the nearby streets. A donkey race, a parade with floats, and an historical tournament are also featured [Tel. (0577) 42209]. In August, artists intricately replicate Italian masterworks, from da Vinci to Botticelli, in colored chalks on the sidewalks of the Piazza del Campo. The **street painting** of Siena is folk art at its finest and children love watching it slowly fade in the rain or morning dew. On July 2 and August 16 Siena is packed for the infamous **Palio di Siena** in the Piazza del Campo. No child will ever forget this spectacle, when Siena explodes in a frenzy of local rivalries, celebrating its historic Parade of the Banner. Representatives of Siena's seventeen individual *contrade* (districts) parade in medieval costume, compete in a horse race in the piazza and hold open-air feasts after the winning district has been awarded the *palio* (banner). Rooms in Siena during Palio are reserved up to at least 6 months in advance, but it's easy to commute from a nearby city such as Arezzo. For tickets, reserve in writing to the **tourist office,** Azienda Autonoma di Turismo, Via di Città, 43, 53100 Siena. Tel. (0577) 280551.

AREZZO

Sorry, kids, it wasn't Julie Andrews but Guido d'Arezzo who invented "do, re, mi" and modern musical notation. His tranquil and picturesque birthplace, Arezzo, is also close to the birthplace of Piero della Francesca, whose poignant and masterful frescoes grace Arezzo's central **Church of San Francisco** (open daily 7–12, 2:30–7) and the nearby **duomo** (open daily 7–12, 3:30–7:30). Leaving the Church of San Francisco, make a right and head down Via Cavour. Near Corso Italia, kids will delight in Arezzo's modernized version of Rome's **Bocca della Verità (Mouth of Truth),** a stone sculpture of a sun god. Kids who stick their hand in his mouth will receive a computerized printout of their fortune—in four languages, no less. Small fee.

Arezzo's central **Piazza Grande** typifies the town's tranquil small-town feel, except when the lively **Giostra del Saracino (Joust of the Saracen)** comes to town. Held the first Sunday in September, this tilting competition features horsemen who reenact a heroic battle against invading Saracens. The competition grows fierce as knights in horseback dash with lances against a revolving puppet, the Saracen, who hits them with a heavy whip if they miss his shield. All is done in medieval dress with lots of fanfare, parades, and celebration. Plan to attend only if you have purchased tickets for seats in the arena (L18,000–L40,000) in advance. Less expensive standing-room tickets are available the day of the event but you'll be on your feet for hours, packed like sardines, as you wait for the joust. We made this mistake and ended up sitting in a nearby gelateria and watched the competition on television. At least we could see! Purchase (or call to reserve) tickets at least 1 week in advance from the **tourist office (EPT)**, Piazza Risorgimento, 116 [Tel. (0575) 23952]. Arezzo's **Parco del Prato,** atop a hill by the duomo, is a large grassy space with views and the setting of the **Fiera Antiquaria (Antique Fair),** with old dolls, trains, and bricbrac the first Sunday of each month.

NEAR AREZZO

Monte San Savino, a 15-minute drive south of Arezzo, is a typical Tuscan village with a great open-air market Wednesday mornings in its medieval center. We set up base here because of its rural but central location (45 minutes from Siena, Florence, and Umbria's Perugia). The second Sunday in September brings a delicious **Sagra della Porchetta** (pork) with giant picnic tables set up to devour roast pork washed down with local wine. **Crocodile Aqua Park,** just off the autostrade A1 heading from Florence to Rome (Monte San Savino exit), is a great break from the highway. You can't miss its 100-foot-long tunnel shaped like a reclining woman in the park's open field. A cross between a mermaid, Cleopatra, and Alice in Wonderland, the mystery woman has long blond hair, a dazzling blue dress, pink shoes, and bright red fingernails. We never explored the tunnel; our kids were more fascinated with her outer appearance. Let us know what lurks within. She rests alongside other attractions in the complex's **Luna Park,** including our favorite carousel, mirrored with hand-painted Cupids and Western scenes; its horses even have real horsehair. Kids can ride in coaches or in swans. The complex also has an **Aqua Park** with a giant slide and pool and an **Aqua Zoo.** Fee. Oct.–Apr. Sat. and Sun. only 3 PM–late evening. Summer daily 5 PM–late evening.

Put your hiking shoes on! A climb awaits you in the noble hill town of *Montepulciano* south of Monte San Savino off A1. Gear up by munching the generous samples of honey cake, cheese, salami, and famous *vino nobile* available in the specialty shops as you enter the Porta al Prato, the town's main gateway. The real magnet in Montepulciano is the **Piazza Grande** at the very top of its hill, considered to be a gem of town planning. Climb the soaring tower of the 15th-century **Palazzo Comunale** for stupendous views of Monte Amiata, the nearby fortress of Radicofani, lakes, and valleys. Mon.– Sat. 9–1. History is evoked in the boisterous **Bravio (Race of the Casks)** on the second Sunday in August, held to commemorate the eight local districts that fended off the Sienese and Florentines. Tel. (0578) 716935.

Thirty-nine kilometers north of Arezzo on S70 past Bibbiena, turn onto S71 to the hill town of *Poppi* and its **Parco Zoo della Fauna Europa.** Animals are in their natural habitats amidst pine trees, ferns, and many African-style huts where you can relax and picnic. A farm section has goats, ponies, and grape arbors. Snacks are available at a small restaurant adjacent to a play area with electric motorcycles, the only fast-moving experience in this quiet refuge. Fee. Tel. (0575) 58602 or 529079.

ELBA

Elba, the third largest island in Italy, is famed for Napoleon's 10-month stay. Its miles of clean turquoise water, sandy beaches with rocky inlets, mountains, and quaint coastal towns give it tremendous appeal; vacationing families pack its beaches in August so plan ahead. *Portoferraio,* Elba's capital city, is served by ferries from a number of cities, and a 30-minute hydrofoil service frequently runs from Piombino Marittima. Bus service around the island is excellent, or you can rent a car or boat to reach inaccessible beaches. Contact the **tourist office** for information on hotels, bungalows, and camping: Azienda Autonoma di Turismo, calata Italia, 26 [Tel. (0565) 92671].

Along the south coast, in *Marina di Campo,* you can rent pedal boats, wind-surfing equipment, sailboats, and fishing gear; there is good swimming at its neighboring beaches. Near Portoferraio the best sandy beaches are La Biodola and Procchio, which boasts a wind-surfing school. For a break from beachy pursuits, take the dangling *cabonivia,* a small cage that climbs **Monte Capanne,** for a great view. Daily 10–12, 2:30–6. Visit Napoleon's house, the **Villa dei Mulini,** in Portoferraio, or his country getaway in nearby **San Martino.** In the Egyptian room you can view optical illusions of scenes from the Egyptian campaign and a wall where he scrawled, "Napoleon is happy everywhere." Fee. Both open Mon.–Sat. 9–1:30, Sun. 9–12:30.

UMBRIA

In a sweetshop in Umbria, a waiter asked our youngster, when she selected a *bacio,* if she could guess the meaning of the Italian word. The word means "kiss," but it is also the name of a flavor of the region's renowned Perugina chocolate. His face grew scarlet when she showed him she knew the word well and planted a big smack on his cheek. Made in Umbria's capital of Perugia, these sweets made a big imprint on our children as did the region's cherished amusement park, Città della Domenica. Try to attend one of Umbria's many festivals—Gubbio's Race of the Ceri, Foligno's Joust of the Quintana, or Spoleto's world-famous arts festival—the experience will be sure to make an impression, perhaps as rich as the bacio.

PERUGIA AND ENVIRONS

Head directly for Perugia's historic "Upper City," which dates from the late Middle Ages and Renaissance, perched atop a small hill overlooking the bustling "Lower City" and Umbrian plain. At the far end of Corso Vannucci, the city's main street, in the lively Piazza IV Novembre, is a magnificent 13th-century tiered fountain, the **Fontana Maggiore.** Children often come to chase the thousands of pigeons waiting here for their daily feeding at noon by a devoted local. Inside the piazza's Gothic **duomo,** lovers of romance can see the supposed wedding ring of the Virgin Mary housed in a reliquary in the first chapel on the left. Kids may only know Perugina for its chocolate, but it is also the nickname of the town's most renowned artist and teacher of Raphael, Pietro Vannucci, whose works can be seen along with those of Piero della Francesca and other Umbrian notables at the impressive **Galleria Nazionale dell'Umbria** in the piazza. Fee. Tues.–Sat. 9–2, Sun. 9–1. Tel. (075) 20316. Walk along Via Maestà delle Volte, leading off from the far end of the piazza, with its labyrinth of medieval houses and arched passageways.

The **public gardens of Giardini Carducci** have breathtaking views of the peaceful Tiber Valley, reminiscent of the graceful landscapes so often painted by the great Umbrian painters whose works are displayed in the National Gallery. Right before the Giardini, is a smaller park at **Piazza Italia,** with a fountain, flowers, and picnic benches. From the Giardini, climb down to the Rocca Paolina, a 16th-century fortress. Ask directions (it's a bit tricky) to the **Porta Marzi,** a 2nd-century Etruscan gateway through the city wall near the Giardini Carducci, which will lead you to one of Perugia's strangest streets, the **Via Baglioni Sotterranea** (subterranean). The Giardini gardens were built on top of this street, burying its 15th-century houses, and you can see their remains, which are now traversed by a high-tech escalator system connecting the upper and lower city. People scurry about with little notice to the subterranean city about them. The tunnels are used for special exhibitions; we saw contemporary sculpture on view alongside the ruins. Free. Tues.–Sat. 8–2, Sun. 9–1. Tel. (075) 23327.

Five kilometers from Perugia, in *Spanolia,* is **La Città della**

Domenica (Sunday City), an amusement park and zoo, which, as its name states, is only open on Sundays. Its zoo has lions, antelopes, zebras, a well-stocked serpentarium, and an African village. The mediocre fairyland is home to characters from fairytales, and there is an Indian Camp and Western Land, a tricky labyrinth, and cross-country cycling. Deer and big-horned sheep roam freely, especially around the picnic area, where they hovered over our pizza. Fee. Follow yellow signs from Perugia. Open last Sun. in March–Oct 9:30–sunset, Sun. only; after Nov. 1 only indoor attractions (Amusement Hall, Serpentarium). Tel. (075) 754941

Italy's largest freshwater lake, **Lake Trasimeno,** 20 kilometers west of Perugia, has clean beaches at Castiglione del Lago, Magione, and Passignano sul Trasimeno. The lake boasts numerous water sports and campgrounds. You can take a ferry out to the lake's island, Isola Maggiore, to swim and picnic. Perugia's **tourist office,** Corso Vannucci, 94A (Tel. (075) 23327), can provide information.

ASSISI AND ENVIRONS

Perched high on the slopes of Monte Subasio, Assisi draws countless devotees and tourists because of its association with St. Francis, who founded a Catholic monastic order here. Friars in long brown robes and inspired singing ensembles parade through the town's narrow streets; practically everything here in some way relates to the saint's memory. Check with the **tourist office** in the central **Piazza Communale** about the city's wealth of free outdoor performances such as folkloric dancing. Climb up Via Rufino, off of the piazza, to **Piazza Rufino,** a courtyard where local children play ball, ride bikes, and climb the animal sculptures that grace the front of its **duomo.** A hike further up Vicolo San Lorenzo leads to the **Rocca Maggiore,** a 14th-century military castle that is fun to explore, and a grand view. Fee; kids under 7 free. Apr.–Sept. 9–7:30; off-season hours vary.

A visit to Assisi is not complete without viewing its grandiose **Basilica di San Francesco,** which consists of two churches, one on top of the other, built upon a chain of huge arches. On view in town, off Piazza Communale on Via Portica, is a miniature of the basilica—a good way to first experience its grandeur. In the early 1200s St. Francis allowed another teenager, St. Clare, to organize a convent. Across town in the church of **Santa Chiara (St. Clare's Church)** fans of the macabre can gasp at her body, which lies open in a crypt, blackened over the years.

In late May, **Corpus Domini** is the occasion for **Infiorate,** a procession that passes along streets over which colorful designs of flower petals are strewn. The month-long **August Festival** has historical, folkloric, and religious events, including a parade, flag-tossing, and a crossbow contest. December 24's **Liturgical Celebrations** feature beautiful Christmas cribs exhibited at all the town's churches, in streets, and piazzas. For all events: Tel. (075) 812450.

Foligno, 18 kilometers southwest of Assisi, is famous for the **Giostra della Quintana.** On the first and second Saturday of September, knights in 17th-century costumes ride along the city's main streets to the central Piazza della Repubblica. On the second and third Sunday in September, a major tournament is held in the town's stadium, where galloping horsemen must lance a ring held in a dummy's hand. Reserve tickets (L10,000-L45,000; reduced for kids under 10) by phone: Tel. (0742) 60459. Pick up tickets at the **tourist office,** Azienda alla Promozione Turistica, Corso Cavour, 130. Be flexible; when we attended, the event was pushed forward one week due to a light rain in the stadium.

GUBBIO

Wander through the maze of narrow streets of the città vecchia of Gubbio, a tranquil hill town north of Assisi, and you'll see ochre-colored houses, palaces, towers, small piazzas, and secluded dwellings clinging to sheer cliffs. The houses often have two doors, one for everyday use and one called the **Door of Death,** for coffins. Get on your climbing shoes and head up the steep stairways to the central **Piazza della Signoria.** Kids may not choose to poke around the piazza's **Palazzo Ducale** or **Palazzo dei Consoli** for long (although its famous bronze tablets from the 3rd and 1st centuries A.D. tell us about the original language of Umbria) so plan a short stop and head out for a dangling **funicular ride** in the **Colle Eletto;** on a clear day you can see for miles. A bird cage takes you up to the heights of Monte Ignino, which has a small restaurant, ample picnic spots, and hiking trails. Fee. Off-season daily 9:30-7; in-season daily 9-9:30. Visit the **Basilica of San Ubaldo,** a short walk from where the bird cage lets off. Saint Ubaldo was Gubbio's patron saint and voyeurs of creepy sites can view his decayed remains in the church's glass case. Next to the ruins of Gubbio's well-preserved **Teatro Romano,** on Via del Teatro Romano, are tennis courts, a swimming pool, bowling, and a soccer field. Also located around the Roman theater is **Coppo,** the town's wooded **public park.**

On the second Sunday in May, Gubbio goes wild for the **Corsa dei Ceri (Race of the Ceri).** Twenty vigorous young men called *ceraioli* run in teams with extremely heavy wooden candles called *ceri* on their shoulders during a mad race through the narrow town streets and finally attempt the arduous climb to the top of the hill to the Basilica of Saint Ubaldo. The **Palio della Balestra** is a medieval crossbow contest between Gubbio and Sansepolcro held in Piazza della Signoria on the fourth Sunday in May. Highlights also include a flag-tossing contest, costumed pageant, and parades. For both festivals advance tickets are recommended by writing the **tourist office** (Azienda Autonama di Turismo), Corso Garibaldi, 6, 06024, Gubbio [Tel. (075) 9271989].

SPOLETO AND ENVIRONS

Spoleto, an austere city tempered by the grace of narrow winding alleys, palaces, and medieval buildings, has gained worldwide fame with its **Festival of Two Worlds,** held in late June and early July, which presents the latest in music, theater, painting, and sculpture. Purchase tickets well in advance from travel agents or by mail from Associazione Festival dei Due Mondi, Via Margutta, 17, 001897, Rome. Pick up picnic fare at the **open-air market** in **Piazza del Mercato** (Mon.-Sat. 8:30-1) and head to explore the **rocca,** a papal fortress high in the surrounding wooded hills. Fee. Wed.-Mon. 10-7:30. Thirteen kilometers north of Spoleto is the **Fonti del Clitunno (Source of the River Clitunno)** and its adjacent **Parco del Clitunno,** a large park with a lake, boats, and swans. Fonti: Fee; under 10 free. 9–12, 2:30–sunset.

TODI

Todi was founded on the site where a legendary eagle dropped a cloth it had whisked off a dinner table, a tale that inspired the town's insignia of an eagle with outstretched wings holding a cloth between its claws. Like Lucca, Todi has escaped the masses of tourists and remains an unspoiled Italian treasure. Look into the lofty Romanesque-Gothic Church of San Fortunato for a look at the Masolino's Madonna before climbing the pathway on the right of the church to Todi's playground, the **Parco della Rocca,** with climbing structures and well-shaded picnic tables amidst the ruins of **La Rocca,** a 14th-century castle. Peek into the nearby shop at Via dei Condutti, 4, to see the **costumes** of Maurizio Tognalini, who creates masks and fanciful regalia for the famous Venice Carnival.

EMILIA-ROMAGNA

Yum . . . *Parmegiano* cheese and *prosciutto* from Parma, *spaghetti alla bolognese,* and well, yes, even *bologna* from Bologna will tempt the pickiest of eaters and certainly the heartiest, as exemplified by Luciano Pavarotti, native son of the region of Emilia-Romagna, the food capital of Italy.

BOLOGNA AND MODENA

A visit to the region's capital of **Bologna** must start with sampling some of the city's delicious pasta specialties, such as *lasagne* or *tortellini.* You'll have no problem finding treats, for *rosticcerie, trattorie,* and *pizzerie* abound. To work off your *pranzo alla Bolognese* (Bolognese luncheon), climb the 486 steps of the 328-feet-high leaning **Torre degli Asinelli** in the city's medieval quarter for an astounding view. Fee. Daily 9-6. There were originally 200 towers in Bologna, as aristocratic families competed to build the highest and most impressive. Only two still stand, both in the **Piazza di Porta Ravegnana.** In **Piazza Maggiore,** the town center, head for the **Basilica di San Petronio** to see Italy's largest working sundial with images from the zodiac. Free. Daily 7:30–7. On **Strada Maggiore,** a street lined with Gothic and classical palaces, is the **Museo d'Arte Industriale.** In its Davia Bargellini Gallery, kids will enjoy the exhibit of 18th-century puppet theaters. Fee. Tues.-Sun. mornings only. Bologna's park, the **Parco Cavaioni,** is 5 kilometers out of the city. Also on the outskirts is the **Santuario della Madonna di San Luca,** where a colonnade made up of 660 arches and extending for 4 kilometers leads to the church and a grand city view.

More food and climbs await visitors to **Modena,** a wealthy community nestled midway between Bologna and Parma. After a picnic of *gnocco,* a type of fried-bread sandwich of meat, and the city's famous *salcicce* (sausages), climb the 14th-century bell tower **La Ghirlandina.** Mon.–Sat. 9–12:30, 3:30–7. Request admittance at the Muncipio (town hall). Take note of the duomo's marble lions and its "Fish Market Doorway" with fantasy animals. A renewal program is now underway to further improve the medieval quarter, which includes a large **park. Carnival** commences in Modena in early February with the carnival family, "the Pavironicas" (papa Sandrone, his wife Pulonia, and their son Sgorghiguelo), who come from the legend of Bosco de Sotto, arriving in an antique carriage to address the crowd from the balcony of the town hall. Contact the **tourist office** at Via Emilia, 179 [Tel. (059) 237479].

PARMA AND ENVIRONS

Of all the cities in Emilia-Romagna, Parma seems to outshine its neighbors. The city has brilliantly combined elegant architecture, art, and gardens into a small and very livable city. Apart from wandering the medieval streets and playing in its parks, you can devour Parma's renowned food sprinkled with *parmegiano* cheese. Gaze up at the "heavenly" cupola of Parma's exquisite 11th-century Romanesque **duomo** to see Corregio's famous fresco of the virgin as she ascends to heaven amidst a swirling group of pink cherubs. Free. Daily 7:30–12, 3–7. In the adjoining **battistero (baptistry)** look for Antolami's marvelous series of reliefs depicting the twelve months of the year, and have kids try to find their birth month. Fee. Apr.–June 9–12, 3–6; July–Aug. 9–12:30, 3:30–7; Sept.–Mar. 9–12, 3–5. Closed Mondays. By the river, **La Citadella,** once a military defense center, is now a city **park.** The **Ducale Garden,** in the grand **Palazzo del Giardino (Garden Palace),** is beautifully landscaped and adorned with sculpture. May–Sept. 6–midnight; Oct.–Apr. 6–dusk. During the first half of the 18th century, this Baroque park extended the whole length of Parma but was later transformed to create suburban avenues for strolling. In mid-January, Parma celebrates the **Feast of Sant'llario,** the city's patron saint. Special cookies, shaped like shoes, are reminders of legends associated with the saint. Contact the **tourist office** at Piazza del Duomo, 5 [Tel. (0521) 34735].

ALONG THE ADRIATIC

Ravenna, a small Adriatic city, is world-famous for its incandescent Byzantine mosaics, some of which date from as early as the 5th century. The biblical scenes of those found at the **Basilica di San Vitale** are easy for older kids to unfold. Free. Daily 8:30–7:30. Have kids drop coins to illuminate the brilliant mosaic flowers at the adjacent **Mausoleum di Galla Placidia.** Free. Daily 8:30–7. Ravenna's **duomo** has an enchanting pulpit covered with birds and a dome completely laden with mosaics. Free. Daily 6–12, 2–6. The most startling jewellike mosaics of images such as angels and birds are found at the 6th-century **Church of Sant' Apollinare in Classe.** The church is surrounded by the grassy lawn of the **Pineta di Classe.** Five kilometers south of the city. Free. Daily 8–12, 2–6:30. Ravenna's *pineta* (pine woods), which line its strip of **beach towns,** are where Dante apparently drew inspiration for his *Divine Comedy.* They are not as inspirational nowadays, as the 20-kilometer strip is crowded and is surrounded by Ravenna's industrial section.

The Adriatic resort of *Rimini* resembles a modern and crowded Atlantic City, but its Roman ruins and a well-preserved medieval center are evident of its age. An effort has been made to clean up its beach and the water has been deemed safe. More than 150 miniatures of the most famous monuments and aspects of Italian culture are on view at **Miniature Italy.** Fee. Daily 8:30–sunset. The world of tales and fantasy is re-created in the park of **Fiabilandia.** Fee. Rivazzurra di Rimini. For information about both parks, call the resort's **tourist office (EPT)** [Tel. (0541) 51331 or 51101].

South of Rimini is the equally bustling modern resort of *Riccione,* with waterfront hotels, vacation rentals, camping, beach clubs, water sports, and parks. Among its highlights are **Aquafan,** a huge aquatic park with swirling water slides, an enormous shallow pool, **Il Delphinarium,** where dolphins perform, and a **luna (amusement) park.** For information about the resort complex, contact Ufficio IAT Riccione, P.le Azzarita, 47036 Riccione Forli [Tel. (0541) 643489].

THE MARCHES

The region of the Marches runs between the Apennine Mountains and the Adriatic Sea and has two hilltop treasures—Urbino and Ascoli Piceno. It's best to avoid swimming along the coast between Pescara and Ancona, although farther north, near Rimini, the beach is cleaner.

URBINO

To really experience Italy, Urbino is a must, and it's an easy day trip from the resorts near Rimini. One of the most overlooked spots in the country, this walled and hidden gem was by far our favorite hill town. The magnificent **Palazzo Ducale,** originally built as a fortress by the great patron Duke Frederico da Montefeltro, is the city's central masterpiece. Up Via Raffaello, past the house where Raphael was born, is Piazzale Roma, from where it is a short climb to the public grassy garden, **Giardini Pubblici,** and its 14th-century **Fortezza Albornaz,** where kids can run. The view of the Ducale Palace from here is magnificent.

THE NORTH

LIGURIA

Liguria, the Italian Riviera, is the narrow strip of coastline that twists for 217 miles along the Mediterranean between the French border and Tuscany. The climate is mild, the air is fragrant with sweet blossoms, and there is an easy Old World ambiance. The large port of Genoa divides the region into the Riviera Ponente, to its east, and the more beautiful Riviera Levante, to its west. With the exception of the Cinque Terre, local beaches are somewhat polluted. Most of the Riviera's beach clubs and hotels have swimming pools, and there are endless activities for children.

RIVIERA DI LEVANTE: THE EASTERN RIVIERA

This is the most beautiful stretch of the Italian Riviera so be sure to book ahead in high season. The coastline is dotted with colorful villages in sheltered bays.

NERVI TO RAPALLO

The resort of *Nervi* is renowned for its beautiful parks with spectacular ocean views. Further south is *Camogli,* a colorful fishing village and tranquil resort of pastel houses that spill down to the sea has a small **aquarium.** On the second Sunday in May, the town hosts its celebrated **Sagra del Pesce (Fish Festival),** a huge feast of freshly caught fish fried in two gigantic frying pans, each 12 feet in diameter. In mid-August Camogli hosts the **Canine Fidelity Awards,** where prizes are awarded to dogs from all over Italy who have distinguished themselves for acts of courage, fidelity, and love. Tel. **tourist office:** (0185)771066.

Santa Margherita Ligure is a charming coastal city with accommodations more moderately priced than those of its neighboring resorts. The town is a stone's throw from the beautiful villages of *Portofino* and *San Fruttuoso.* Local children gather along its waterfront promenade, where there are a few rides and usually a game of hopscotch in full swing near the shell-laden statue of Christopher Columbus. The boat departs from here every 20 minutes for Portofino and San Fruttuoso. Santa Margherita has beach clubs behind its pier with swimming pools for children. Pick up picnic fare at Corso Matteoti's active **morning market** and head up to the benches and shady palm trees of the town's park, **Villa Durrazzo,** which overlooks the water.

Portofino is an up-scale, beautiful little waterfront hamlet with gaily colored houses and fancy yachts moored offshore. There are many places to walk and climb as it is surrounded by a nature reserve. Hike up to its **castle** and garden. From there, walk out to the **lighthouse.** At sunset, the views of the coast between the olive trees and sea pines are breathtaking.

San Fruttuoso is a tiny village nestled below Mount Portofino and accessible only by boat from Santa Margherita, Rapallo, or Camogli. Skin divers will be surprised to find a large underwater bronze statue of Christ sunken in the bay. Boaters can see him through the translucent waters. Save coins for the town's 11th-century **Abbey of San Fruttuoso di Capo di Monte** so your kids can activate the singing nativity scene.

Rapallo is beautifully situated at the head of the bay, east of the Portofino peninsula. En route from Santa Margherita before entering the town, you'll find the beachfront park, **Parco della Rimembranza.** Rapallo's tree-lined waterfront promenade, the **Lungomare Vittoria Veneto,** has the **Giostra,** with a carousel and rides. The beach club **Bagni Ariston** has a small pool for children. **Parco Casale,** near Villa Porticciolo, is a park with a "miniature Disneyland" and miniature golf. There is a kid's train and playground near Corso Assereto. A **funicular** travels up to the sanctuary of Montallegro for sweeping views. Fee. Off Via Betti. Excursions from Rapallo by **horse-drawn carriage** are available. Contact the **tourist office,** the Azienda Autonoma di Soggiorno e Turismo, Via Diaz, 9 [Tel. (0185) 51282]; they can also inform you of the dates of Rapallo's annual **International Show of Cartoons.**

THE CINQUE TERRE, PORTOVENERE, AND LERICI

Time stands still in the *Cinque Terre,* five villages which hover over the rugged coast north of La Spezia. With many tourists packing the Italian coastline in the summer, this stretch of beach is surprisingly unspoiled. Each village has a distinct character but all share terraced hillsides, meandering walkways, sun-bleached pastel-colored buildings, and delightful beaches.

Boats depart for the Cinque Terre from many ports such as Portovenere or Marina di Carrara from the south; a local train departs from La Spezia and stops at each village. You can visit by car on the N370, although you'll need to walk to most of the towns. All five are also interconnected by footpaths, which are the best way to see them if your kids are seasoned walkers. Coming from the south, the boat passes all the villages and stops at the most developed, *Monterosso al Mare,* which boasts a great beach, a central town park with play equipment, a range of accommodations, and scrumptious seafood cafes. Be sure to visit the strange church of **Convento dei Cappuccini,** which pays homage to the dead. Its combination of skeletons and Christmas lights are reminiscent of Mexico's Day of the Dead. Climb up to the town's **castle** for a great view. Boats can be rented by the hour at the southern end of the beach.

The other four villages are overlooked and often underbooked. From Monterosso, a 90-minute walk (a bit rough in places) leads to *Vernazza,* the most beautiful village of the five, where tall colorful houses huddle together along a sheltered cove. Neighboring *Corniglia* has a long pebbly beach. Be sure to climb the winding stairs to the actual town for the staggering view (and hearty wine). A 1-hour trail from here leads to *Manarola,* a fishing village set amidst terraced vineyards from where you can walk to medieval *Riomaggiore.* All have glorious scenery. As accommodations are limited in the villages, it is worth planning ahead, especially in August and on weekends.

Jutting out to sea, picture-postcard *Portovenere,* south of the Cinque terre, is dominated by its 12th- to 16th-century citadel. Climb up to its cliff-hanging black and white jailbird church, the **Church of San Pietro.** Boats depart from here to the offshore islands of Palmaria and its **Grotta Azzurra (blue cave),** *Tino,* and *Tinetto.* Around the cove, *Lerici* is a quaint harbor and resort with delicious seafood restaurants.

PIEDMONT AND VALLE D'AOSTA

Bordering France and Switzerland, the regions of Piedmont and the glorious Valle d'Aosta in Italy's northwest corner have magnificent alpine peaks, including Monte Bianco (Mont Blanc) and the Cervino (the Matterhorn), and valleys of incomparable beauty. Families will find the region ideal for summer pursuits, while some of the best winter skiing is found in Piedmont's mountainous valleys. Skiing here is far more economical than in the crowded neighboring Swiss and French resorts. The region's historical importance is evident in its many medieval castles.

TURIN AND ENVIRONS

Turin, the capital of Piedmont, is a lot more than just the "Detroit of Italy," although 77 percent of Italy's cars are made here. Amidst a blend of Roman and Baroque urban architecture, the city is filled with unusual museums that kids will really like. For a spectacular view of the city, take the elevator to the terrace atop the very unusual **Mole Antonelliana.** This odd building, composed of a two-story temple on top of a glass pyramid upon which sits a tall spire, shoots dramatically into the sky. Fee. Via Montebello, 20. Tues.–Sun. 9–7. Tel. (011) 8398314.

Just One Look: Museums

The **Armeria Real (Royal Armory),** which adjoins the **Palazzo Reale,** has a large collection of armor, including ancient weapons from all over the world. Fee. Piazza Castello. Tues.–Sun. 9–2. Tel. (011) 543889.

Kids into cars will love the **Museo dell'Automobile Carlo Biscaretti di Ruffia.** Turin not only produces cars but is obsessed with them and has put the finest in its museum, including an incredible array of vintage autos and their accessories. Fee. Corso Unità d'Italia, 40. Tues.–Sun. 9–12:30, 3–7. Tel. (011) 677666.

The **Museo Nazionale del Cinema** displays everything about filmmaking, including examples of the art's forerunners, such as magic lanterns, Chinese shadows, and the pantoscope. Fee. Piazza S. Giovanni, 2. Tel. (011) 510370.

The **Museo della Marionetta** has a charming display of puppets. Fee. Via Santa Teresa, 5. Weekdays 9–1, weekends 9–1, 3–5. Tel. (011) 530238.

See how rock climbers scale the alps at the **Museo Nazionale della Montagne (Mountain Museum).** Fee. Monte dei Cappuccini. Tues.–Fri. 8:30–7, Sat. 9–12:30, Sun. 9–2:45, Mon. 9–7:15. Tel. (011) 688737.

More to See and Do

Look up! Among the images in the Guarini dome of the opulent **Church of San Lorenzo** in Piazza Castello are swirling starfish. Guarini's metaphysical black marble dome in the **Cathedral of San Giovanni's Cappella della Santa Sindone (Chapel of the Holy Shroud)** is equally impressive. Above the altar is a piece of linen believed to be Jesus' shroud when he was taken off the cross. You can see the marks from his head and body impressed on the cloth. Free. Tues.–Sat. 7:30–12, 3–5:30; Sun. 9:45–12. Tel. (011) 542664.

Turin is noted for its graceful squares and parks. The most impressive is the **Parco del Valentino,** with beautifully landscaped Japanese-style gardens extending along the river Po. Our kids couldn't get over the throne that converted into a potty in the park's **Castello del Valentino,** which also contains the **borgo medioevale,** a true-to-life reconstruction of a medieval town. Fee. Tues.-Sat. 9-4, Sun. 10-4. Tel. (011) 6699372. **Row-boating** is available on the river. **Fortune-tellers** convene at Porta Pila. In April, Turin's piazzas are transformed into an **Easter Island** for children, with events and entertainment especially designed for them. In late June, Turin celebrates the **Feast of San Giovanni,** a parade in historical costumes with fireworks over the Po River. Tel. for all events: (011) 535181.

MOUNTAIN RESORTS

Strikingly beautiful valleys and tall mountain peaks cut through the region of the Valle d'Aosta. On Italy's slopes of Monte Bianco (Mont Blanc) is the ski resort of *Courmayeur,* while the resort of *Claviere* sits at the foot of the Italian portion of Monte Cervino (the Matterhorn). Courmayeur has a children's ski school. Summer skiing is possible at both resorts from June through September.

Aosta's neighboring valleys also offer a myriad of summer and winter pursuits; the **Val d'Ayas** is one of the most affordable. **Valtour-nanche's** *Breuil-Cervinia,* also at the foot of Mont Blanc, has more up-scale prices with special ski classes designed for children. Take its cable car to **Testa Grigia** on the Swiss border for a spectacular panorama. Cross-country skiing is at its best in the **Parco Nazionale del Gran Paradiso** in the **Val di Cogne.** Aosta's **tourist office** will send you ski information. Write Ufficio Informazioni Turistche, Piazza Chanoux, 8, 11100 Aosta [Tel. (0165) 35655].

LOMBARDY

Lombardy includes Italy's "lake district," with the family resorts of Como, Garda, Maggiore, and Orta. Each sparkling, clear lake has its own personality and all are within a short drive from Milan, Italy's most fashionable city.

MILAN

Milan may not top your list of Italian hot spots for kids but since many travelers to Italy arrive or depart from its major airport at Malpensa, we have listed a range of attractions that appeal to kids. Milan is competing with Paris to be the fashion capital of the world and is the home of ground-breaking contemporary design. Older kids, especially teens, will be enamored of its great sense of style. Where else can you see an exquisitely dressed youngster cavorting from a futuristic car against a medieval backdrop? Save yourself a big headache and avoid driving in the city; the metro system is very efficient for crossing town, and the historical center is easy to explore on foot. The **tourist office** is at Via Marconi, 1 [Tel. 809662]. Milan's **telephone area code** is 02.

Detour! What to See and Do

A climb or elevator ride up to the roof of Milan's enormous and lavish **duomo,** in the central **Piazza del Duomo,** is for thrill seekers only as there are no railings at the top. The view, through an array of gables, pinnacles, and statues (the cathedral has 135 pinnacles and over 2,000 statues!) is far reaching; on a clear day you can see the Alps. For an even better view, climb to the top of the Tiburia, or central tower. The duomo is the heart of Milan; it is the largest Gothic duomo in all of Italy and the third largest in the world. Fee for roof. Cathedral: daily June–Sept. 7–7. Roof: daily June–Sept. 9–5; Oct.–May 9–4:30. The piazza's **Museo del Duomo** has an interesting display of how the cathedral was created; it took nearly 500 years to complete. Fee. Tues.–Sun. 9:30–12:30, 3–6. Tel. 8603588. Close by is the **Teatro alla Scala (La Scala),** the glamorous opera house said to have perfect acoustics. Among the mementos on display in its **museum** are plaster castings of the hands of renowned conductors and composers and some strands of Mozart's and Bellini's hair. Fee. Mon.–Fri. 9–12, 2–6; Sat. 9–12, 2–4. Closed Sun. **Carnival** in Milan is a week-long celebration in early February. Shows and festive events for children take place on Tuesday and Thursday with parades of floats and figures in the costume of the local folk characters Meneghin and Cecca. Early June brings the **Navigli Festival** to the two navigli (canals) of the city with swimming meets and water games. Tel. for both: 809662.

Just One Look: Museums

Leonardo da Vinci's famous dramatic fresco *The Last Supper* is in the **Cenacolo Vinciano** next to the entrance of the **Church of Santa Maria delle Grazie.** Our favorite kid's comment was, "It's amazing how they can make the postcard look so big." Fee. Mon.–Sat. 9–1:30, 2–6:30; Sun. 9–3. Tel. 4987588.

The **Museum of Ancient Weapons,** in the **Pusterla di Sant'Ambrogio,** has arms, armor, and swords from the 16th and 17th centuries and 15th-century horse trappings. Fee. Via San Vittore, corner of Via Carducci.

The **Museo Nazionale della Scienza e della Tecnica Leonardo da Vinci** has drawings and wooden models of his brilliant inventions as well as exhibits on the history of motors, trains, space, and the ocean. Fee. Via San Vittore, 21. Tues.–Sun. 9–5. Tel. 462709.

Your kids will enjoy the **Poldi Pezzoli Museum**'s 200 sundials from the 16th to 20th centuries while you gaze at the works by Botticelli. Fee. Via Manzoni, 12. Tues.–Sat. 9:30–12:30, 2:30–5:30; Sun. 9:30–12:30; additional hours Thurs. 9 PM–11 PM. Tel. 794889.

LAKE GARDA

Lake Garda is the most popular of the lakes in Italy's "lake district" because of its balmy weather, recreational opportunities, and proximity to the art treasures of Verona, Trento, and Brescia. Kids will enjoy taking the lake steamers, ferries, or hydrofoils. Contact the Navigazione sul Lago, 2 Piazza Matteotti, Desenzano sul Garda, for schedules.

Stretching out along the lake is *Sirmione's* 13th-century turreted castle, **Rocca Scaligera,** which has a moat and great views from its tower. Fee. Summer daily 9–8; winter Mon. 9–12, Tues.–Sat 9–12, 3–8. Boats are for rent by the castle bridge. The public beach off Via Catullo is good for young kids as the water is clean and shallow. Pedal boats are for rent here. On the rocky tip of the peninsula, a beautiful private beach is set below the ruins of the **Grotte di Catullo.** Fee. Ruins: Tues.–Sun. 9–6. Try the town's fresh fruit gelato.

Gardone Riviera has an air of Old World elegance. Be sure to visit Gabriele D'Annunzio's **Vittoriale,** a flamboyant home and garden. Annunzio was a true eccentric and his house is packed with objects from his outlandish life. You'll see a real airplane hanging from the ceiling, weapons, an enormous globe, and stairs that lead nowhere. The extravagance continues in the outdoor gardens, where a full-size navy ship is buried in the hillside amidst waterfalls and beautiful flowers. Fee. Mar.–Oct. daily 8–7.

LAKE COMO

Lago di Como (Lake Como) is Italy's version of Lake Tahoe—a water playground set against high alpine peaks and offering all types of sports at its many lakeside villages. En route from Bergamo, the reasonably priced lakefront resort of **Lecco** is highly recommended. Take the **funicular** up **Mt. Resegone** to **Piani d'Erna** for a view of the Alps. Kids will enjoy traversing Lake Como by paddle steamer, hydrofoil, or ferry. You can rent a covered fishing boat or motorboat at Navigazione sul Lago, Piazza Volta, 44, in the town of **Como,** or rent pedal boats at the harbor. Get off at any town that strikes your fancy. **Varenna** is a beautiful fishing village; **Tremezzo** has luxuriant gardens; **Cernobbio** is the lake's most up-scale resort; **Comacina** is the lake's only island and the site of late June's **Sagra di San Giovanni,** a week-long affair for which the island is illuminated and fireworks are set to create the illusion of the island's destruction. Tel. (031) 262091. The beach in the city of Como is not clean for swimming. From Como, take the **funicular** up to **Brunate** for great views.

LAKE MAGGIORE

Bordering the towering Alps of Switzerland, **Lago Maggiore (Lake Maggiore)** is the second largest Italian lake. Sailing, boating, canoeing, and swimming are all delightful on its temperate waters, while alpine pursuits are close by. Many lakefront towns offer a full range of accommodations, and there is an extensive network of ferries, hydrofoils, and steamers connecting you to cities as far north as Locarno in Switzerland.

Stresa is a good base for visiting the lake's **Borromean Islands.** The town's animal park and gardens at **Villa Pallavacini** have llamas, yaks, zebras, and other animals roaming free. There are even parrots who speak Italian! Fee. One-half km. from Stresa toward Arona. Mid-Sept.–Oct. daily 9–6. Tel. (0323) 32407. Take a short drive up to **Gignese** to see the **Umbrella Museum**'s collection of parasols and umbrellas from 1840 to 1940. Near Stresa's beach, where the ferries depart, a **funicular** will take you to the summit of **Monte Mottarone** for astounding views of Lake Maggiore's islands. Fee. Open daily. Last ride back at 5:50.

Off-season is the best time to visit Lake Maggiore's popular **Borromean Islands,** which can be reached by taking a short boat ride from Stresa or Switzerland's Lugano and Locarno. From Stresa, contact the Navigation Office at the center port [Tel. (0322) 46651]. You can travel to all three *isole* (islands) or get off at just one. We found **Isola Madre** to be the loveliest of the islands. It was the palace residence of Count Borromeo and has an exotic park with rare flowers and roaming parakeets and peacocks. In the island's **Palazzo Borromeo,** head to the **Sala delle Marionette** and the **Sala delle Bambole (Doll Room),** where there is a theater and stage set of puppets, skeletons, and animals. Fee. Late Mar.–Oct. Tues.–Sun. 9–12, 1:30–5:30. Tel. (0323) 31261.

Avoid touristy **Isola dei Pescatore**. **Isola Bella,** the island closest to Stresa, is the site of another lavish **Palazzo e Giardino Borromeo,** which looks like a palace from a Disneyland stage set. The island has rock jetties and great promenades for running, and the palace has a mazelike garden. Fee for palace. Late Mar.–Oct. Tues.–Sun. 9–12, 1:30–5:30. Tel. (0323) 30556.

LAKE ORTA

Of all the Italian lakes, **Lago d'Orta (Lake Orta),** at the foot of Monte Mottarone, is perhaps the most beautiful and the least touristy with luxurious villas and small villages lining its shores. Its principal town, *Orta San Giulio,* is a tranquil haven with shady piazzas. Take the boat or canoe out to the little island of **San Giulio,** where a 12th-century basilica and a melange of ancient buildings hang over the water. Boats depart from Orta San Giulio every half hour.

VENETO

To most people, the region of Veneto means Venice, one of the world's most unusual cities. With 400 bridges spanning its 160 canals, Venice is actually made up of 118 tiny islands. The image of a city built over waterways where everyone travels by boat, from police officers and mail carriers to those delivering groceries, will be permanently etched in the minds of your children. Side trips are easy to make from Venice to Verona, home of Romeo and Juliet, or to Strà, where you'll find Europe's largest hedge maze. The Alps dominate much of the region, which has numerous mountain resorts. Avoid swimming in the Adriatic near Venice as the water is not clean.

VENICE

If unusual transportation tops your kids' list of fun activities, then Venice will be the highlight of their trip to Italy. Cars are not allowed in the city and the only way to really get around is to take a boat. Venice is intoxicating and it appears unreal—like a stage set from some Italian opera. With beauty comes crowds, and tourism is synonomous with *Venezia,* especially during high-season. Take your kids anyway! They'll never forget it.

"Do Italians live here?" You'll feel like you are at an international summit conference when touring the city. Be sure to stray from the main tourist track, away from the areas around the Rialto Bridge and San Marco, and head for the Dorsoduro, San Polo, and Santa Croce, *sestieri* (city quarters) where you'll be sure to see Venetian families at play.

Pick up the English weekly *Un Ospite di Venezia (A Guest in Venice)*, which lists current events. Sites are typically open 10–12 and 2–5:30. In high-season, get to sites as early in the morning as possible to avoid crowds. The most helpful **tourist office** is at Piazza San Marco (Tel. 5226356). Venice's **telephone area code** is 041.

The Lay of the City

It is wise to purchase a good map that indicates the layout of the city's six *sestieri* and the *varporetti* (motorboat shops). The map provided by the tourist office is only helpful for getting a general feel for the city. The Grand Canal is Venice's main waterway and can be crossed on foot at its *ponti* (bridges) or by boat. There is not a logical sequence to the street numbers within the *sestieri*; have no fear, you will find your way around the winding streets and in the meantime you'll have fun exploring. Locals are used to being asked directions, and they will often escort you. Keep an eye out for the city's invaluable yellow signs indicating tourist destinations and the many signs for *Ferrovia* (where you catch a boat). For an introduction to the city, take *vaporetto accelerato* no. 1 or no. 4, which run the length of the Grand Canal from the train station all the way to the Lido. Your kids will love the ride.

Getting Around

If you're arriving by car, leave it in one of the garages near Piazzale Roma outside the city or in the car parks on the nearby island of Tronchetto. Then take a vaporetto into the city. Unlike San Francisco's cable cars, which are mainly used for the benefit of tourists, Venice's boats are used to cross the canals, especially when no bridge is in sight. For unlimited rides, purchase the economical 24-hour *biglietto turistico* at any of the main boat stations; for unlimited travel on all boats (except gondolas), including trips to Venice's outlying islands, there are 3-day passes available. Boats run 24 hours a day.

Your kids will enjoy sampling the variety of aquatic transportation: **Vaporetti** are the most common motorboat buses that traverse the canal; you can choose from the *accelerato*, which stops at every stop, or the faster *diretto*. **Traghetti** are ferry boats. **Gondolas** look just as they do in the movies, complete with accordion players and opera singers in blue-and-white-striped shirts. The going rate is about L50,000 for an hour, but you can bargain. If you're off the tourist track, a gondolier may take you for a short hop across the canal for a slight tip. Locals often traverse this way. If you visit Venice November through April, it is wise to check ahead to see whether high tides are flooding the city.

Where to Stay

It is difficult to obtain an **apartment** in the city because few agencies represent them. A studio or one-bedroom apartment for under $800 per week is a good value based on the high prices of hotels here. One option is to stay in a villa outside the city, which will cost considerably less, and commute in, which is easy. Try Cuendet; they have listings of villas about an hour away.

HOTELS

Note that in Venice's high-season (Apr.–Oct., Dec. 31–Jan. 2) prices can be as much as 30 percent higher than off-season. During February's Carnival, Venice is booked solid so plan ahead.

The very chic *Cipriani,* on Guidecca Island, has apartments, gardens, and an enormous pool. Isola della Guidecca, 10, 30133. Tel. 5207744. Fax 5203930. **Deluxe.**

The *Excelsior Palace,* with a pool and suites, is on a private stretch of the Lido. Lungomare Marconi, 41, 30126. Tel. 5260201. **Deluxe.**

The *Grand Hotel des Bains,* on the Lido Beach, has its own large park and pool. Lungomare Marconi, 17, 30126. Tel. 765921. **Expensive.**

La Fenice et des Artistes is a pension near San Marco with a garden, three-bedded rooms, suites, and small apartments. Campiello de la Fenice, 1936, 30124. Tel. 5232333. Fax 5203721. **Moderate.**

The *Pausania San Barnable* is in the Dorsoduro in a 14th-century palazzo with a large garden. Dorsoduro 2824, 30123. Tel. 5222083. **Moderate.**

The *Locanda Montin* is a budget find in the Dorsoduro on one of Venice's prettiest side streets. Its garden restaurant is one of the city's best for seafood and Adriatic specialties. Amy Carter ate here with her Dad after the summit; their pictures are all over the lobby. Book well in advance. Dorsoduro 1147, 30123. Tel. 5227151. **Inexpensive.**

Outside Venice, in Mirano, is the *Leon d'Oro,* which has a pool and is an easy commute into the city; its restaurant is recommended. Via Canonici, 3, 30035. Tel. 432777. **Inexpensive.**

CAMPGROUNDS

Marina di Venezia, in the Punta Sabbioni area (about 40 minutes from Venice by vaporetto), is popular with families. Via Hermada. Tel. 966146.

The *Litorale del Cavallino* is 25 minutes from San Marco by vaporetto no. 15 but is often crowded as it is on the beach.

Detour! What to See and Do

AROUND PIAZZA SAN MARCO

Magnificent **Piazza San Marco** is the heart of Venice and always draws a crowd, so get there bright and early. Buy corn for your children to feed the pigeons and they'll immediately attract a flock. The pigeons are so tame, you can pet them. An elevator ride up the piazza's **Campanile di San Marco** sweeps 325 feet to the top of the tower where there are telescopes alongside the giant bell. Fee. Daily 9:30 AM–9 PM. Tel. 5224064. Inside the **Basilica of San Marco** point out the glittering gold altarpiece inlaid with real gemstones. Fee. Mon.–Sat. 9:30–5, Sun. 1:30–5. Tel. 5225697. Climb the Golden Staircase to the top floor's **armor museum** in the piazza's grandiose **Palazzo Ducale**. A tour of the entire palace is too exhausting for kids; hunt for the huge globes on its second floor. From the east wing, follow the passageway to the covered **Bridge of Sighs,** which leads to the gloomy **prisons** that once held expatriates but where Casanova made a fantastic escape. The bridge was so named because condemned prisoners used to sigh before meeting their fate. Kids will want to see the torture chamber. Fee. Daily 8:30–7. Closed Sun. afternoons. Tel. 5224951. A short walk from Piazza San Marco will bring you to the **Acquario di Venezia,** with Adriatic fish and fauna. Fee. Follow the yellow sign at the right of the Torre del'Orologio. Calle dei Albamesi, 4260. Daily 9–9.

Where the Sidewalk Ends: Parks

Giardino Publico is a small park in front of the **Palazzo Reale** along the canal adjacent to Piazza San Marco. The park is full of cats who are fed by local feline lovers. Vaporetto no. 1 toward the Lido departs near the park. Stop at Piazzale Arsenale to visit the **Museo Storico Navale**'s maritime history exhibit with Venetian ships and small models of famous barges. Fee. Mon.–Fri. 9–1, Sat. 9–12. Tel. 5200276. The next stop on vaporetto no. 1 is Piazza Giardino, where you'll find another **park** and the site of Venice's famous biennial International Art Exhibition. The large overgrown garden is a nice picnic spot with benches and sculpture. Further down the canal is the **Parco delle Rimembranze,** a large grassy waterfront park under pine trees and a pleasant respite from the crowds of San Marco.

SAN POLO

Avoid the area immediately around the touristy **Rialto Bridge,** which is the entrance to this district, and head for the **Scuola Grande di San Rocco,** one of Venice's most famous guilds, which contains some of Tintoretto's most significant paintings. Point out to your kids the paintings of monsters at the bottom of the building's exterior columns. Behind the scuola along Rio de la Frescada dozens of whimsical **whirligigs** are suspended from windows along the canal. Your kids will delight in the colorful stars, moons, little houses, and daisies which dance in the wind.

DORSODURO

To experience the real Venice head to this charming neighborhood where children play and water laps the shores. We were captivated by a priest who made origami flying planes for our children to fly. **Campo S. Margarita** is the piazza where Venetian children hang out, especially during the *passeggiata*, around 5 PM. Your children can join in as their peers play hopscotch, jump rope, draw with chalk, and throw confetti.

The great Venetian **Palazzo Rezzonico** has a **Museum of the 18th Century** with an old pharmacy and a puppet theater. Fee. Mon.– Thurs. and Sat. 10–3:30, Sun. 9–12:30. Tel. 5224543. The **Collezione Peggy Guggenheim** is a wonderful museum of modern art. Peggy Guggenheim lived in this waterfront palace and in her bedroom are her young child Pegeen Vail's pastel drawings and paintings of brides and beach scenes. Colored-glass figurines line the bedroom windows through which you can see the canal. They were created following her youngster's design. In back of the museum there's a large garden area with contemporary sculpture and a tomb for all of Peggy Guggenheim's beloved dogs. Fee; Sat. 6–9 (free). Wed.–Sat. 12–9, Sun.–Mon. 12–6. Tel. 5206288.

VENETIAN LAGOON AND ISLANDS

The **Lido,** accessible by vaporetto no. 1 from San Marco, is a stretch of private beach with deluxe hotels.

The **Church of San Giorgio Maggiore,** a short ride in boat no. 5 or no. 8, stands on an island just across the lagoon from San Marco. Here is Tintoretto's renowned *Last Supper*. Kids will enjoy climbing the church **campanile,** which provides a great view of the lagoon. Fee. Summer daily 9–12:30, 2–6:30; off-season 9–12:30, 2–3:30.

The **Church of San Michele,** a 10-minute boat ride, occupies its own island. Your kids will enjoy the ride while you savor one of the city's most beautiful churches. The entrance through the 15th-century cathedral's cloister leads to shady trees and overgrown gardens.

The Venetian glassblowing center of *Murano* is a 10-minute ride in boat no. 5 from San Marco or no. 12 from Fondamenta Nuova. Kids can watch the glassblowing process at any of a number of *fornace* lining Fondamenta dei Vetrai. The town's **Museo Vetrario (Museum of Glass)** has photographs, diagrams, and tools that tell the whole story of how glass is made. Fee. Daily 10–4, Sun. 9–12:30. Closed Wed.

Burano, less than an hour away by boat no. 12, is a fishing village where you can watch the lace that is sold all over Venice being made by busy old ladies. The island, though touristy, has child-size canals and bridges, and each house is painted a different color. An hour's ride across the lagoon is *Torcello,* the most rural of the islands, with a beautiful cathedral, bell tower, and mosaics.

Special Events

Tel. for all, unless noted: (041) 5226356.

For the 10 days preceding Ash Wednesday in February, Venice goes wild for **Carnival,** which is one of the best in all of Italy. The city is transformed into a magical stage of figures in costumes; the masks are artworks in themselves.

Mid-July's **Festa del Redentore** is a must for those who love late-night fireworks displays. The following day features a procession from San Marco to the Church of Il Redentore over a temporary bridge made of boats.

On the first Sunday in September, the **Historical Regatta,** the city's most celebrated gondola race, takes place on the Grand Canal with costumed pageants.

NEAR VENICE

Europe's biggest and most complicated **hedge maze,** called **Il Labirinto (Labyrinth),** is found in *Strà,* in the elegant gardens of the **Villa Nazionale.** You and your kids are sure to get lost in its 4 miles of pathways. It had Napoleon totally confused when he visited in 1807, but there is a guard who rescues people today. The villa also houses a glorious optical-illusion frescoe by Tiepolo. About 30 km. south of Venice en route to Padua on the Brenta Canal. Fee. Tues.–Sun. 9–1:30. Tel. (049) 502074.

Boat excursions down the Brenta Canal in a "river stagecoach" from Venice to *Padua* are available. On its 7-hour one-way trip, the boat stops at grand villas, including the maze at Strà, along the way. The trip re-creates the historic trip of the *Burchiello,* a horse-pulled barge that used to escort royalty down the river. Fee. Apr.–Oct. Departs from Venice Tues., Thurs., Sat. or Padua Wed., Fri., Sun. and runs in both directions; you can take a short bus ride back to your original destination. Reserve at any travel agency or in Venice at C.I.T., Piazza San Marco, Tel. (041) 5285480, or in Padua at C.I.T., 12 Via Matteotti, Tel. (049) 663333.

VERONA

A visit to Verona, home to the tale of Romeo and Juliet, is not complete without visiting Juliet's ivy-covered balcony at the **House of Capulet** and the sweet teenager's **tomb.** Her house is on Via Capello, 23. Fee. Tues.–Sun. 8–6:30. Tel. (045) 38303. Her tomb is outside the old city walls in the Church of San Franceso. Fee. Via del Pontiere. Tues.–Sun. 7:30–7. And wherefore art thou, Romeo? Locals pay more attention to lovely Juliet, but you can hunt down her lover's **House of Montague** at Via Arche Scaligori, 2; it is now a cafe.

Kids can sample the perfect acoustics in the well-preserved 1st-century Roman **arena** in Verona's **Piazza Brà.** Though one of the world's largest (it seats 25,000), those in the last row are said to hear perfectly. Shakespearean plays are performed in the hilltop **Teatro Romano,** where there is also an **archaeology museum** and 19th-century **castle.** Fee. All open Tues.–Sun. 8–6:30; off-season 9–2. In mid-December, Verona holds a **toy fair** in Piazza Brà for the feast of Santa Lucia. Tel. (045) 592828.

Near Verona, in **Bussolengo-Pastrengo,** is a **Park of Dinosaurs** with reconstructions of prehistoric animals. Fee. Daily 9–6:30. Also in town is the **Autosafari del Garda,** a safari park. Fee. Daily 9–12, 1:30–6:30. Nearby **Castelnuovo del Garda**'s fun park, **Gardaland,** has a fun fair and games. Fee. Daily 9:30–6.

THE SOUTH

CAMPANIA

Mount Vesuvius looms over this rich region whose charm and mystery stirred the imaginations of the ancient Greeks. It was here amidst the smoke and fires of the volcanoes that they believed they had found the entrance to the underworld. The region's ancient sites, such as Pompeii and Herculaneum, can be easily explored using the area's resorts as a base. There are clean and beautiful beaches on the west coasts of the islands of Capri and Ischia and on most of the Gulf of Salerno.

NAPLES

High-spirited Naples, the region's principal city, is everything from fascinating to dirty to downright irritating, but the people are extremely friendly and the city has many compelling things for kids to do. Don't miss the old quarter, known as **Spacca Napoli,** to capture the feel of true Naples.

Detour! What to See and Do

Take the **funicular** up to the neighborhood of Vomero, where you'll find the **Museo di San Martino**. From the museum's balcony you can see Hohenstaufen's Castel dell'Ovo, the bay and its islands, and, on a clear day, Mount Vesuvius. Inside the museum, take a look at the presepi, Nativity crêches that are as significant to Neapolitan kids as Christmas trees are to ours; and don't miss the section of folklore, festival, and costumes. Via Torriaone di San Martino. Fee. Tues.–Sat. 9–2, Sun. 9–1. The museum's park, **Giardini del Museo di San Martino,** beckons for a picnic. Tues.–Sat. 9–2, Sun. 9–1. The funicular departs from Via Toledo across from the Galleria, from Piazza Madeo, and from Piazza Montesanto.

The **Museo e Gallerie di Capodimonte,** housed in an extravagant palace, has a marvelous collection of works by Titian, Botticelli, and Raphael. Your kids will appreciate its armor collection and most of all its grand park, the **Parco del Museo,** with century-old trees and grassy lawns. The view is heartstopping from the palace's terraces of the city and bay. Fee. Tondo di Capodimonte. Museum. July–Sept. Tues.–Sat. 9–7, Sun. 9–1; off-season Tues.–Sat. 9–2, Sun. 9–1. Park: daily 9-one hour before sunset.

Naples' exceptional **Museo Archeologico Nazionale** has many of the treasures excavated at Pompeii and Herculaneum. Fee. Piazza Museo. Mon.–Sat. 9–2, Sun. 9–1. Tel. (081) 440166.

Shhh . . . Churches

Naples' majestic **duomo** has many legends. Behind its high altar is a container said to hold the head of Saint Januarius and his congealed blood. Old folktales say if his blood does not turn to liquid on specific religious days, disaster will befall Naples. In historic center. Daily 8–1, 5–7:30. In mid-September locals gather to pray and await the miracle of the liquification. Tel. (081) 418744. Among the city's wealth of churches, the beautiful **Capella San Severo** is a must for both art lovers and young fans of the macabre, who can see two 16th-century corpses preserved in glass cases. Fee. Via de Sanctis. Mon.–Sat. 10–1:30, Sun. 11–1:30.

Where the Sidewalk Ends: More Parks

Villa Communale is a gracious waterfront park filled with fountains and sculpture. The park has Europe's oldest **aquarium,** with 200 species of fish and marine plants, all from the Bay of Naples. Fee. Center of park. Tues.–Sat. 9–5, Sun. 10–7. Tel. (081) 406222. The Mostra d'Oltremare is a large fairground that houses **Edenlandia,** a noisy, sticky, and fun amusement park. Fee. Entrance at Viale Kennedy. Open daily year-round. Tel. (081) 611182, or 619711. The fairground also has an Olympic-size **swimming pool,** a **children's theater,** and the **Naples Zoo.** Fee. Entrance from Viale Kennedy. Daily 9–5; summer until 7. Tel. (081) 615943.

NEAR NAPLES

The whole region west of Naples, the **Campi Flegrei (Phlegraean, or burning fields),** is of volcanic origin. Children will be fascinated with its smoking geysers, caves, grottoes, and strange craters, all of which can be explored from *Pozzuoli,* on the coast. The **Solfatara crater** still emits steam jets. Fee. Daily 9–one hour before sunset. Four kilometers from Pozzuoli is the huge crater of the **Lago d'Averno,** which was believed to be the doorway to Hell, as reported by Homer in the Odyssey. Some Italians still believe it to be true. Fee. Tues.–Sun. 9–two hours before sunset.

POMPEII/HERCULANEUM

Children have a short attention span for ruins but you can prepare them for the marvels of Pompeii and Herculaneum by taking them first to the still-active volcano of *Vesuvius.* Here they can begin to picture what the vicious lava did to these two communities 2,000 years ago as it submerged them in 30 feet of volcanic ash. It's a steep 1-hour climb to the top, where you can peer into the crater, but the views are worth every huff and puff. Fee. Guided tour up west and south faces.

Pompeii was a lavish city of 20,000 residents, with villas, a huge forum, baths, and a large commercial district, when it was buried in A.D. 79. Preserved in the volcanic ash were not only buildings but people who were stopped dead in their tracks. Pick up a free map at the tourist office near the east entrance and select a few sites to visit. Don't ruin the ruins for your kids by trying to see everything. To the west of the forum, in the **antiquarium,** there are plaster moldings of the people and animals caught in the attitudes in which they had died. Not for the squeamish. Fee. Tues.–Sun. 9–one hour before sunset.

The city of *Herculaneum* was also buried but the river of hot mud and lava shut out air and preserved the objects of its daily life much better than those at Pompeii. Herculaneum is less crowded than Pompeii and is more compact for sightseeing with youngsters. Although most of the objects have been placed in museums, kids can still see detailed traces of daily life 2,000 years ago: stoves with food cooking, a table set for dinner, a bakery with cookies, and even a sewing kit. Fee. Tues.–Sun. 9–one hour before sunset.

CAPRI, ISCHIA, AND PROCIDA

The Bay of Naples' islands of Capri, Ischia, and Procida are accessible by hydrofoil, steamer, or car ferry from Naples; Capri is also accessible from Sorrento. There is summer service between Salerno, Amalfi, Positano, and Capri. In summer, *Capri* can be a bit like crowded Waikiki; off-season it truly lives up to its name, the "Island of Dreams." Your kids will love the very touristy boat ride around the island and into the **Grotta Azzurra (Blue Grotto)** and its neighboring grottoes of Green, Yellow, Pink, and White. Their colors are caused by a phenomenon of light refraction. Fee. Boat departs regularly from the Marina Grande from 9 AM to 2 hours before sunset. Walk with your kids to the **Arco Naturale,** a gigantic arch rising above the sea, after visiting the excavations of Emperor Tiberius' **Villa Jovis. Marina Piccola** is a haven of beautiful beaches.

Kids will also enjoy the **funicular** from the port of Capri to the village of *Anacapri,* a less crowded part of the island. Or, you can take the stairs cut into the rock wall. Another cable car up from Anacapri's Piazza della Vittoria takes you to Capri's highest peak, Monte Solaro. Fee. Open 9:30–two hours before sunset. Don't miss Anacapri's **Villa San Michele** and its garden, which hangs over the sea. From the villa, kids can scamper down 800 steps to the harbor. The cleanest beaches are found on the island's west coast.

The "Emerald Island" of *Ischia* tends also to be overcrowded in the summer. Its pleasant year-round climate makes a June or September visit ideal. Unlike Capri, Ischia is of volcanic origin, and you can hike or take a donkey ride to the summit of its inactive volcano, **Mount Epomeo.** The cleanest beaches are on the island's west coast. The small island of **Procida** also has glorious beaches along its 14-kilometer coast and is less crowded.

AMALFI COAST: SORRENTO TO SALERNO

Sorrento has a nice beach at the **Punta di Sorrento,** while its park, the **Villa di Pollio,** has swimming amidst its ruins. The roller-coaster Amalfi Drive toward Salerno—breathtaking for both its spectacular scenery and dizzying hairpin curves (more than 1,000 of them!)—begins south of Sorrento and continues along the unrivaled Amalfi Coast.

Positano is a chic fishing-village-turned-resort built on high slopes spilling down to the sea. In neighboring *Amalfi,* visit the **Grotto dello Smeraldo (The Emerald Grotto),** where crystal clear water is illuminated by rays of sunlight, giving it an emerald glow. The light reveals stalactites and stalagmites down below. The grotto is reached by an elevator from the Positano-Amalfi road or by a spectacular boat ride inside the grotto. Fee. June–Sept. 8:30–5.

PAESTRUM AND ENVIRONS

Farther south along the coast is Paestrum, once a prosperous Greek colony in 600 B.C. Its miraculously preserved Greek ruins are said to be better than those found in Greece! Take a break from swimming at the beach east of the ruins to view the **Tempio (Temple) di Nettuno.** Tues.-Sun. 9-sunset. Farther south is *Palinuro,* near the ancient city of *Velia,* where there is a Club Méditerranée with kid's activities as well as many fine public beaches. Tel. 800-CLUB-MED.

APULIA

Show your kids a map of Italy. Calabria is the toe of the Italian boot; Basilicata is its instep; and Apulia is the boot's heel. All three, especially Apulia's Gargano Peninsula on the Adriatic, have some of Italy's most unspoiled and beautiful beaches, perfect for sizzling summer days.

GARGANO PENINSULA

On the Adriatic, the Gargano Peninsula has a spectacular coastline with miles of clean sandy beaches and dunes. Its main city is beautifully whitewashed *Vieste,* with a long sandy beach south of town. The water is crystal clear—you can see its sandy bottom miles offshore. Many Italian and German families vacation here in the summer. Kids will enjoy the boat excursions to the **Grotta Campana (Bell Grotto),** which depart regularly from Vieste in the summer. From Vieste you can also visit the delightful fishing and resort village of *Peschici* and the gorgeous *Tremiti Islands.* In the middle of the peninsula is the **Foresta Umbra,** a shade forest of beech and oak trees. No one knows how they grow here as these types of trees are totally uncharacteristic of the environment. You won't care. You'll delight in their cool, shady picnic spots. Close by is *Monte Sant'Angelo,* which has an unusual underground church. Climb down its eighty-six steps into a vast cave where you can see dazzling masterpieces of Byzantine art and a majestic church by candlelight. Daily 8–12, 3–8.

SICILY

The fertile Mediterranean island of *Sicily,* with its crystal-clear beaches, offshore islands, sizzling volcanoes, and majestic ruins that often surpass those of Greece, can be a perfect holiday spot for families. There are plenty of beaches and enough ruins to make it more than just a beach vacation. The beaches on the west and south coasts are the cleanest. The Sicilian landscape has been celebrated in myth and legend, and its small villages are still steeped in folklore, with costumes, singing, and dancing on feast day.

It is best to visit Sicily in early spring or fall, when the mountains are still snow-covered and the swimming is great. In the summer it is sweltering. You can fly to Sicily from all major Italian cities or take a ferry to its main port of Messina from Reggio di Calabria. Try to see one of Sicily's enchanting epic **puppet-theater performances.** You'll find performances in most Sicilian cities. Kids can pick up marionettes of the characters from the epic sagas at souvenir shops throughout the island. Don't forget to try Sicily's gelato specialty *cioccolata à la messinese,* a crunchy chocolate-rice delight.

MESSINA TO CEFALÙ

Messina is where you'll arrive by boat from Calabria. The town's **Piazza del Duomo**'s **campanile** has one of the world's largest **astronomical clocks** which performs daily at noon; a shorter show is held hourly at 15 minutes past the hour. When the clock strikes noon, a golden lion roars, a rooster flaps its wings, doves and angels fly. Messina's **Parade of the Giants,** held in mid-August, features the enormous statues of Mata and Grifone, the couple who founded their city. Tel. (090) 775356.

Midway between Messina and Palermo, on the Tyrrhenian Sea, is *Cefalù.* This seaside town of pastel-colored cottages has great swimming, delicious seafood, and lots of sunshine. Take a break from the beach and visit the town's spectacular 12th-century mosaic-laden **Norman cathedral** or climb up to **La Rocca,** a rock that towers over the town, for great views. Cathedral: daily 9–12, 3:30–7. The town has only a few hotels and is very popular so book ahead; Club Med has a big holiday village outside of town.

THE AEOLIAN ISLANDS

This small cluster of seven spectacular islands, all volcanic in origin, are off of Sicily's northern coast. Often called the Lipari Islands, they are very popular with Italian families. The black-lava beaches make a striking contrast with the clear azure water. The largest island is *Lipari.* Its main city of the same name has two terrific beaches as well as a Norman cathedral, a 16th-century Spanish citadel, and an archaeology museum. Lipari's waters are filled with exotic sea life such as seahorses and turtles. The island of *Stromboli* is the peak of a volcano that erupts daily and is considered the world's most active volcano. The flowing lava and flying red-hot rocks are especially impressive to kids at night when they look like a natural fireworks display. Older kids may enjoy the 3-hour hike up to the crater from the Point Labronzo Observatory on the island's north coast. Follow the "Trail of Fire." In summer there are boat trips to view the volcano from the sea; check with Lipari's tourist office on Corso Vittorio Emanuele. The island of *Vulcano* stinks! The sulfur from its three volcanic peaks emits quite an odor; the volcanoes also heat the water of its beaches. The island of *Filicudi* has a beautiful **Grotta del Bue Marino (Grotto of the Sea Ox),** while the small island of *Panarea* is a chic resort with prehistoric villages visible from its volcanic slopes. It is noted for its crystal-clear water which is great for undersea exploring.

PALERMO TO TRAPANI

Palermo, the capital of Sicily, is unkept and frenzied, yet its historic section is fascinating. Even among Sicilians, Palermo is noted for its crime, so proceed with caution. Its dazzling 12th-century chapel, the **Capella Palatina,** in the **Norman Palace,** is completely inlaid or painted; the effect is overpowering. The palace is behind the **Villa Bonnano,** a garden with palm trees. Palace: Mon. and Fri.–Sat. 9–12:30. Chapel: Mon–Tues. and Thurs.–Sat. 9–1, 3–5:30; Wed. and Sun. 9–1. One young park critic who traipsed this far south raved about the **Giardino Garibaldi,** a 15-minute walk from the Norman Palace. As you enter, take heed of the sign stating that adults are allowed in only if accompanied by children. The park has huge ficus trees that kids can climb into; locals claim they are 1,000 years old. Many of the park's trees have aerial roots that have spread into unusual formations. Via Emanuele. Free. Open daily 8–8.

Nearby is the **Museo delle Marionette,** a puppet museum with an extensive collection. Fee. Palazzo Fatta. Mon.–Sat. 10–1, 5–7; Sun. 10–1. Puppet shows Sat. 5:30 PM. Palermo has a **Puppet Festival** in November. More puppets, as well as traditionally decorated donkey carts, are on view at the **Museo Etnografico Pitrè,** where there's a free puppet show daily at 4. Fee. Mon.–Thurs. and Sat. 8:30–1, 3–5; Fri. 3–5; Sun. 9–12:30, 3–5. The museum is in the **Parco della Favorita,** the city's big spot of green. 3 km. north of city. With bones, skeletons, and over 8,000 mummies—some wearing robes—the **Catacombs of the Capuchin Monks** are very creepy. Not for the squeamish. Under the Cappuccini Convent; access by Via dei Cappuccini. Donation. Daily 9–12, 3–5.

In *Bagheria,* 16 kilometers from Palermo, is the **Villa Palagonia,** a palace decorated with grotesque monsters. You'll see images in stone of five-headed monsters, lions eating with napkins placed primly under their chins, and dwarfs riding on dolphins. The palace's eccentric patron, the hunchback Prince of Palagonia, had the ceiling of his villa painted with trompe l'oeil balustrades, animals, and flowers to fool us all. Fee. Open daily mornings and late afternoons.

Eighty kilometers southwest of Palermo is **Segesta**'s great Greek temple, which stands alone on a perch encircled by a deep ravine. The city, which sits above the beach town of **Marinella,** makes a great holiday spot. Even in spring, the beach is inviting. High above **Trapani** is the ancient town of **Erice,** which makes an unforgettable side trip. Climb to its **castle of Venus** for a view of the African Coast. The **Egadi Islands,** off the coast of Trapani, are idyllic, with grottoes, coral reefs, and some of Italy's cleanest beaches. The islands are accessible by ferry from Trapani.

AGRIGENTO

Further down the coast is Agrigento and its ancient city of the **Valle dei Templi (Valley of the Temples).** If you go to only one place in Sicily, go here! The valley stretches for more than 2 square miles. Amidst its array of gigantic ruins is a 25-foot-high statue of Atlas; his shoulders form the columns of the immense **Temple of Jupiter.** One of Sicily's most colorful celebrations is held here in late January. The **Festival of the Almond Blossoms** includes a pageant in historical costume as well as parades of Sicilian carts and fireworks. Tel. (0922) 20391.

SYRACUSE AND ENVIRONS

Syracuse (Siracusa) is on Sicily's east coast. The heart of this former Greek colony is the traffic-free island of **Ortigia,** with impressive Greek ruins and Gothic and Renaissance churches. A few kilometers away is the city's **archaeological park,** where kids enjoy the artificial cave, shaped like an earlobe, of the **Orecchio di Dionisio (Ear of Dionysus).** The cave's super acoustics accentuate even the tiniest of sounds. Whisper and it will sound like a rocket. Fee. Park: Mon.–Sat. 9–two hours before sunset.

One hundred kilometers from Syracuse are the snow-capped volcanic peaks of **Mt. Etna,** near **Catania.** Etna is Sicily's biggest tourist attraction as it is one of the world's most active volcanoes. You can walk along the moonscape of Etna's smoking cone and there are organized tours leading to the top; night-time tours are especially thrilling. Contact Catania's **tourist office** at Largo Paisiello, 5 [Tel. (095) 312124]. Due to numerous eruptions, all is subject to change.

The Netherlands

Water Laughter

The canals flow out to the ocean
flowing swift, soft, smooth
glowing with laughter.

Nicole Albert, age 8, while visiting Amsterdam

Water-logged and delirious, your children will adore Holland, the more familiar name for the Netherlands. The Dutch are children at heart and take play and fantasy very seriously. They've earnestly paid tribute to the American story *Hans Brinker and the Silver Skates*, about a young boy who sticks his finger in a dike to stop the country from flooding. A statue of Hans sits proudly in Spaarndam, and in Alkmaar there is a museum devoted to him.

In the book, Hans and his sister Gretel enter a race to win the coveted Silver Skates. They skate through harbors filled with brightly painted boats, past fisherman in baggy trousers and ladies in winged lace caps, to Haarlem, where they hear the Church of St. Bravo's gigantic organ which Mozart played as a boy. They visit Amsterdam and look at the great paintings of Vermeer and Rembrandt in the Rijksmuseum. Today, if you follow their trail, you'll find that hundreds of elaborate family play parks with miniature cities such as dazzling Madurodam, living fairy-tale forests, puppet shows, and children's circuses have been added to the landscape, even on the grounds of museums.

Have a great trip . . . *Dag Goede Reis!*

Preparing Your Children: Books and Art

Younger children: The Hole in the Dike by Norma Green, Cow Who Fell in the Canal by Phyllis Krasilovsky.

Older children: The Tinderbox by Hans Christian Andersen, Hans Brinker and the Silver Skates by Mary M. Dodge, The Diary of Anne Frank by Anne Frank, The Adventures of Mickey, Taggy, Puppo and Cica and How They Discover the Netherlands by Kati Rekai (see Chapter 4).

Art: Your children will encounter work by artists such as Rembrandt, Steen, Van Dyck, Van Gogh, and Vermeer. Although not native to the Netherlands, Frans Hals spent years working in Haarlem. Your library should have books with photographs of these artists' works.

Getting There

If you have time to kill at Amsterdam's Schiphol Airport, your kids will enjoy the **Nationaal Luchtvaart Museum Aviodôme,** which presents aviation and space travel from the past, present, and future. There's a fun flight simulator in which kids can play pilot. Fee. Westelijke Randweg 1. May–Sept. Mon.–Fri. 10–5, Sat.–Sun. 12–5; Oct.–Apr. Tues.–Fri. 10–5, Sat.–Sun. 12–5. Tel. (020)173640.

Wha'd'ya Wanna Do?

Among the most organized in the business, Holland's **national tourist offices** can send you information on bicycling, recreation parks, water sports, fishing, chartering a boat, special events, and accommodations. Once in the Netherlands, you'll find over 400 **local tourist offices**—the **VVV's**—which can assist you with everything from booking performances to baby-sitting referrals. Look for their trademark blue signs.

NATIONAL TOURIST OFFICES (NBT) OF HOLLAND
    U.S.A.–Chicago: National Tourist Office of Holland, 225 N. Michigan Ave., Suite 326, Chicago, IL 60601. Tel. 312-819-0300.
    U.S.A.–New York: National Tourist Office of Holland, 355 Lexington Avenue, New York, NY 10017. Tel. 212-370-7367.
    U.S.A.–San Francisco: National Tourist Office of Holland, 90 New Montgomery St., San Francisco, CA 94105. Tel. 415-543-6772.
    Canada–Toronto: National Tourist Office of Holland, 25 Adelaide St., East, Suite 710, Toronto, Ontario M5C 1Y2. Tel. 416-363-1577.

Elaborate *pretparken* (family recreation parks) are a Dutch specialty and you'll find them everywhere. They are typically in a wooded setting which makes them perfect for picnics and hikes.

Their lakes offer swimming and boating, and many have *speeltuinen* (fun fairs) with carousels, miniature lands, pony rides, and traffic parks. Museums and restaurants are often on the grounds as well. For a countrywide listing, request the free brochure "Children Love Holland" from the NBT. *Kinderboerderijen* (petting farms), where young ones can pet and feed farm animals, are widely found; they are typically part of a larger *dierenpark* (zoo) or a recreation park.

There are more than forty skilled *klompen* (wooden shoe) makers throughout the Netherlands. Handmade wooden shoes were designed to keep feet dry; they may look terribly uncomfortable but they aren't. Have your kids try them on.

Molen (windmills) are at their best in Kinderdijk, near Rotterdam, where nineteen 18th-century mills spin and twirl. It was wind power that pumped the water out of the country and kept it out until about 60 years ago, when electric pumps took over.

The wide, sandy **beaches** along the north and west coasts are great for swimming, although they can get crowded in July and August, when the Dutch are on vacation. Many locals, including families, enjoy swimming bare, and you'll find specially marked-off nude beaches.

Adults should consider the economical **Museumcard**, valid for 1 year, available from the NBT or from local VVV's. It is good for free or reduced admission to over 400 museums throughout the country. Children receive free entry to museums or are charged half price. Many museums provide frontpacks to carry babies.

Lights Out! Special Dutch Accommodations

Holland has a wide choice of self-catering **bungalows** and summer **houses,** from simple to luxurious, in all price ranges. Bungalow parks, often adjoining recreation areas with swimming and sports facilities, are widespread and inexpensive. The NBT's brochure "Bungalows" describes these accommodations, which can be booked through the Netherlands Reservation Center, P.O. Box 404, 2260 AK Leidschedam [Tel. (070) 3202500].

We have selected a few **hotels** in Amsterdam that are near parks, have a kitchen, or offer special amenities for families such as suites or connecting rooms. The Netherlands Reservation Center operates a free reservation service for many hotels; see the address above. Local VVV's supply free lists of accommodations and charge a small fee for bookings. Inexpensive family-run **bed-and-breakfast** establishments are found throughout the country. Local VVV's can provide listings.

Families can stay in Dutch *Jeugdherbergen* (youth hostels), which are widespread. A number are especially suited to families with kitchens, small "family bedrooms," children's beds, and high chairs. Contact the Dutch Youth Hostels Association, Prof. Tulpplein 4, 1018 GX Amsterdam [Tel. (020) 5513155].

Request the NBT's brochure "**Camping**," which lists 500 of the country's 2,000 sites. Sites can be reserved in advance through the Netherlands Reservation Center. *Kampeerterreinen* (camping) outside official sites is forbidden. For camping specifics, contact the Nederlands Toeristen Kampeer Club, 11 Dandelstraat, Den Haag, or local VVV offices.

Getting Around

Car travelers need a valid driver's license and proof of insurance, a first-aid kit, and a standard red triangle in the event of a breakdown. Car seats are regularly used and seat belts are required for all passengers. Children under 12 cannot sit in the front seat. The country has an excellent highway system, and there are no toll roads. Six-sided signs point out the country's most scenic routes. Kampeerautos (camper vans) are for rent in Amsterdam at ACC, Akersluisweg 4, 1069 MB [Tel. (020) 101819]; A-Point, Kollenbergweg 11, 1011 AR [Tel. (020) 964964] and Sprinter Campers, Motorkade 1, 1021 JP [Tel. (020) 230154].

If you intend to travel by **train** only in Holland, you should consider the economical **Gezinstoerkaart (Family Ranger Card),** which provides an entire family with unlimited travel for any 4 days out of 10 for June through August. Holland is as flat as its famous *pannekoeken* (pancakes), which makes **bicycling** the ideal and most popular way to get about. There are 14 million Dutch and 11 million bicycles in the country! An extensive country and citywide system of bike paths exists; bikes, including tandems, can be rented at train stations. It's best to reserve a day in advance. Car travelers should watch out for bicyclists who habitually ignore red lights.

Nuts and Bolts

Does anyone care what time it is? Shops are open weekdays from 8:30 or 9 AM to 5:30 or 6 PM, closing an hour earlier on Saturdays. They often have late-night shopping on Thursday or Friday evenings. Small shops close for lunch from 1 to 2. In addition, all shops close for a half-day each week, varying shop to shop. Banks are open weekdays from 9 AM to 4 PM, and generally on Thursday evenings from 6 to 8 PM or 7 to 9 PM.

National holidays: New Year's Day, Good Friday, Easter Monday, Queen's Day (April 30), Liberation Day (May 5), Ascension Day, Whit Monday, Christmas.

Can I have my allowance? Dutch currency is the *gulden* or *florin*, written as Fl. There are 1,000-, 250-, 100-, 50-, 25-, and 5-guilder notes.

Telephones: The country code for the Netherlands is 31. Long-distance and international calls are easy to make from any telephone booth or post office.

Useful nationwide phone numbers: Most operators speak English. Directory assistance is 008 for numbers within Holland and 060418 for numbers within Europe.

Embassies and consulates: The U.S. Consulate is at Museumplein 19, Amsterdam [Tel. (020) 6645661]; the U.S. Embassy is at Lange Voorhout 102, Den Haag [Tel. (070) 624911]; the Canadian Embassy is at Sophialiaan 7, Den Haag [Tel. (070) 614111].

Let's Eat

Dutch food is simple and hearty. Most restaurants have high chairs and half-price *kindermenus* (children's menus). International cuisine, especially Indonesian food, is very popular. Breakfast, almost always included in hotel prices, is typically rolls with cheese or cold meat, eggs, jam, and, yes, peanut butter (unusual for Europe). Dutch hot chocolate is renowned and hard for any child to resist.

For lunch, *broodjes*, or open-faced sandwiches, eaten in inexpensive shops called *broodjeswinkels*, are a whole meal for most children. A popular sandwich is a *uitsmijter* (a fried egg on buttered bread, topped with ham or roast beef). There are many traditional pancake restaurants where your kids will savor *poffertjes*, small round pancakes served with butter and sugar, or *pannekoeken*, crêpes with sweet or meat toppings. *Stroopwafels* are waffles; *siroopwafelen* are paper-thin waffles with gobs of sweet syrup. *Frites*, or french fries, with *fritesaus*, or mayonnaise, dolloped on top are a common fast-food snack. Of the fifty different varieties of Dutch cheese, Gouda and Edam are mild enough for most children's taste buds. Dinner is served early, around 6 or 7 in the evening, and is the big meal. Ask for the *dagschotel* or dish of the day. Have your kids try *bruine bonen met appelmoes*, a brown bean dish with apple sauce.

Desserts include delicious chocolates, such as Droste and Van Houten. At Christmas, kids can find their initials in chocolate, 10 inches tall. They'll love chocolates packaged in little wooden shoes or marzipan shaped to resemble windmills. *Ijs met slagroom* is ice cream with whipped cream; *pepernoten* are Dutch ginger cookies. *Taai-taai* is spiced honey cake, often cut in animal shapes, and served around St. Nicholaas Day (December 6). Saint Nicholaas arrives by steamship in the canals and rides a white horse into town. He drops presents for children through the chimney. Children put their shoes, filled with hay and carrots for his horse, in front of the chimney. It is a charming celebration.

Formula and Baby Food, Diapers and Baby Gear

Disposable diapers (weggooibare luiers) and baby wipes (natte wasdoekjes) are found in grocery stores or drugstores (drogisterij). Baby food (babyvoedsel) can also be found in a grocery store or in a pharmacy (apotheek). Rice cereal (rijstpap voor baby's), oatmeal (haverpap), and apple sauce (appel moes) are among the infant foods widely available.

Sidewalk Talk

bicycles *fiestsen*
canal *gracht*
cycle path *fiespad*
ice cream *ijs*
ice skates *schaatsen*
no *nee*
parks *parken*

playground *speelplaats voor kinderen*
please *alstublieft*
sea *zee*
swimming pool *zwembaden*
thank you *dank u wel*
yes *ja*

The Lay of the Land

The Holland of quaint villages, languid canals, tulip-filled meadows, and flat fields broken by windmills has been created by the tireless efforts of the Dutch in fighting off the sea. As the country's population grew, it became too crowded for its inhabitants, so huge dikes were built around sections of the sea. The water was then drained, creating dry land, called a *polder*, upon which towns were built. As you travel the polders, point out to your children that you are driving on the bottom of the sea! We have divided the country into its main provinces. Holland is very compact and most of these provinces are accessible from one another by car in only a few hours.

PROVINCE OF NORTH HOLLAND

AMSTERDAM

Amsterdam is a youthful city with a very liberal orientation. With more canals than Venice, your kids will enjoy traversing the narrow waterways by boat, seeing the circus, or visiting the great Artis zoo. For older children, a visit to the Anne Frank house may be the most riveting experience of their European journey.

The publication *Uitkrant* has a children's section called Jeugdagenda with listings of kid's entertainment and activities. *Amsterdam This Week*, in English, also lists what's happening. Both are available at newsstands. The tourist office's free brochure "Agenda" has a Kindervoorstellingen section with kid's performances. The **tourist office (VVV)** is at Stationsplein 10, in front of the Central Station, and there's a branch at Leidsestraat 106 (Tel. 266444). The city's **telephone area code** is 020.

The Lay of the City

A ring of canals, connected by many bridges, encircle Amsterdam's medieval center. The bustling main avenues of Damrak and Rokin lead to Dam Square, its main plaza. Both were once canals but have since been filled in. Many of the city's museums are along the three main canals west of Dam Square: Herengracht (Gentlemen's Canal), Keizersgracht (Emperor's Canal), and Prinsengracht (Prince's Canal). These canals are lined by streets of the same name. The Prinsengracht, one of the city's loveliest areas, is home to the Anne Frank House. Beyond is the Jordaan neighborhood, with narrow canals fun for wandering. The heart of Amsterdam is also close to the famous prostitution center, the Red Light District, a seedy area best avoided.

Getting Around

Amsterdam is an easy city for walking as it is very compact. Pick up the inexpensive map Falk Plan at the VVV. The city's public transportation network is efficient and its **trams** are a fun way for kids to get about. Free transit maps, an English guide to the ticketing system, and ticket passes are available at the GVB main city transit office, which is next door to the main VVV.

Glass-topped **boats** that travel through the canals of Amsterdam depart year-round opposite the Centraal Station, beside the Damrak, and near the Rijksmuseum. Kids love the 60- to 90-minute excursion under bridges and through narrow waterways. **Canal bikes** or **pedal boats** are another fun way to explore the city. Landing stages are on the Singelgracht, between the Rijksmuseum and the Heineken Brewery, on the Leidseplein by the American Hotel, on the Prinsengracht at the Westerkerk/Anne Frank House, and on the Keizersgracht junction with Leiderstraat. Apr.–Sept. Mon.–Sun. 9:30–7; summer Mon.–Sun. 9–11. Tel. 265574. The tourist office has a **museum boat** which will transport you from Centraal Station to the Anne Frank House, the Amsterdam Historical Museum, the Rijksmuseum, and more. Contact the VVV. Departs from Stationsplein 8. Apr.–Oct. Tues.–Sat. Tel. 256464 or 222181.

Where to Stay

HOTELS

Teens take note. The *Amsterdam Hilton* was where John and Yoko staged the 1969 Bed-In for peace. 138 Apollolaan. Tel. 780780. **Deluxe.**

The *Amsterdam Sonesta,* close to Dam Square, has apartments in restored 17th-century houses with hotel services. Kattengat 1, 1012. Tel. 212223. **Expensive.**

The *Ladbroke Park* is a stone's throw from Vondelpark. 25 Stadhouderskade, 1054 ES. Tel. 717474. **Expensive.**

The *Golden Tulip Barbizon* is within walking distance to Vondelpark. Children under 12 may stay in parents' room free of charge. 7 Stadhouderskade, 1054 ES. Tel. 851351. **Expensive.**

Casa 400 is a large modern hotel with a children's nursery, 10 minutes from the city center. Open June–September. 75 James Wattstraat, 1097 DL. Tel. 6651171. **Moderate.**

The *Hotel Weichmann* is in a restored canal house with triple and quadruple rooms. Prinsengracht 328-330. Tel. 268962. **Moderate.**

Prisen is on the edge of Vondelpark. Vondelstraat 36-38, 1054 GE. Tel. 162323. **Inexpensive.**

Hotel Van Ostade has free laundry service and a hearty breakfast. Van Ostadestraat 123. Tel. 793452. **Inexpensive.**

CAMPGROUNDS

Gaasper Camping is in a beautiful park with playgrounds, wading pools, and laundry facilities. It's accessible to the town center by a short metro or bus ride. Loosdrechatdreef 7. Tel. 967326.

Detour! What to See and Do

WEST OF DAM SQUARE

Lively **Dam Square** is a mecca for tourists, street musicians, and special events. On Wednesday and Saturday afternoons there are free **puppet shows** in the square, while in the summer, a *kermis* **(amusement park rides)** often makes an appearance. Tel. 5559221. The square's **bakery,** Kwekkeboom, has scrumptious sweets. The **Westerkerk,** on the Plaza Westermarkt, west of Dam Square, soars above the Prinsengracht Canal. Climb the church tower for a sweeping view. Tower: June–mid-Sept. Tues., Wed., Fri. and Sat. 2–5.

Look for the **small statue of Anne Frank** outside the Westerkerk. The **Anne Frank Huis** is a short walk from her statue; her story is especially moving to children. During the height of the Nazi occupation in Amsterdam in 1942, Anne and her Jewish family went into hiding with another family for 2 years in a tiny room just down the street from this church. They were separated from the world by a door disguised as a bookcase. In her diary, Anne described her life in this small room until the day her family was betrayed and the Gestapo took her away. She died of typhus just one week before the German surrender. One hundred thousand Dutch Jews died during the Nazi occupation. You can tour the attic where she hid; it remains just the way the family left it, with posters of Anne's favorite movie stars and pencil marks recording the children's heights. Fee. Prinsengracht 263. Sept.–May Mon.–Sat. 9–5, Sun. 10–5; June–Aug. Mon.–Sat. 9–7. Tel. 264533.

Another great climb is the church tower of the **Oude Kerk,** near Damrak and the city center. Ouderkerksplein 23. Tower: June–Sept. 15 Mon., Thurs. 2–5, Tues.–Wed. 11–2. Six blocks west of Dam Square is the **Nationaal Spaarpotten Museum** and its whimsical collection of 12,000 piggybanks. Pigs are obviously the most prevalent theme but you'll also see banks shaped like turtles and rats, primitive African money jars, a 19th-century clown who eats pennies, Santa Claus, and Rembrandt. Fee. Raadhuistraat 20. Mon.–Fri. 1–4. Tel. 5567400.

SOUTH OF DAM SQUARE

Walking south along the main commercial street, Kalverstraat, you reach the **Amsterdams Historisch Museum** with exhibitions of 13th-century life in Amsterdam. Kids like the play-it-yourself carillon, a large set of melodious bells. Fee. Kalverstraat 92. Tues.–Sat. 10–5. Tel. 5231822. A short hop away is **Madame Tussaud's** waxworks. Tour it after visiting Amsterdam's art museums so your children can see spoofs of various scenes from the life of Rembrandt or from paintings such as Hieronymous Bosch's *Garden of Delights* in wax. David Bowie, Michael Jackson, and Boy George complete the scene. Fee. Kalverstraat 156. Sept.–June daily 10–6; July–Aug. Mon.–Sat. 9–7, Sun. 10–7. Tel. 229949.

Further south is the city's green haven, **Vondelpark,** which is near three of the city's best museums. The 120-acre park has beautiful flowers, playgrounds, wading pools, and a lake with ducks. There are free outdoor performances for children in the summer. Right near Vondelpark are the Rijksmuseum, the Van Gogh Museum, and the contemporary Stedelijk, all clustered around Museumplein. The **Rijksmuseum** is a treasure trove with works by Rembrandt, Vermeer, Van Dyck, and other Dutch masters. Kids gravitate to the miniature skating scenes by Hendrik Avercamp and Jan Steen's *Feast of St. Nicholas* with bickering kids. There's always a crowd in the summer to see Rembrandt's *The Night Watch,* which was originally intended to be a look at a shady street; years of oxidation created its night aura.

The museum's ground floor has a wonderful array of doll houses. Fee; free with Museumcard. On Museumplein at Stadhouderskade 42. Tues.–Sat. 10–5, Sun. 1–5. Tel. 732121. The **Rijksmuseum Vincent Van Gogh** traces the artist's career with 200 of his magnificent paintings. Kids are most fascinated with the fact that the artist cut off part of his ear and then committed himself to an asylum in the south of France. You can see works from this period, such as the *Garden of St. Paul's Hospital.* Fee; free with Museumcard. Paulus Potterstr. 7. Tues.–Sat. 10–5, Sun. 1–5. Tel. 5705272.

The **Amsterdamse Bos** is a rural city park with playgrounds, a wading pool and lakes, indoor ice-skating, pony and horseback riding. Bison and buffalo roam in its reserve. There are miles of marked cycling trails; bikes can be rented March through October. The Bosbaan, north of the park, is a long canal for boating and swimming where you can rent canoes, canal bikes, and motorized boats. The **Bos Museum,** at the park entrance, provides park maps. Free. Koenenkade 56. Daily 10–5. Tel. 431414. A fun way to get to the Bos is by antique tram from the Tramline Museum (see "Museums").

EAST OF DAM SQUARE
The best city climb is up the tower of the **Zuiderkerk,** which has a magnificent city view. Zanstraat. Tower: Fee. June–Oct. 15 Wed. 2–5, Thurs.–Fri. 11–2, Sat. 11–4.

The **Tropenmuseum (Museum of the Tropics)** focuses on the life of people from the Third World with eye-opening exhibitions of daily life in a North African city, a house in Java, an Indian village, and an African market. Slums and shanties have been truthfully re-created with the sounds of traffic, dogs, and people arguing. Folk-art displays include tiny toothpick sculptures and rhythmic music performances. Fee. Linnaeusstraat 2. Mon.–Fri. 10–5, weekends 2–5. Tel. 5688200. Six- through 12-year-olds should head for its special children's museum, the **TM Kindermuseum,** which features many interactive exhibits and workshops designed to provide a glimpse of other cultures. Fee. Linnaeusstraat 2a. Open afternoons and weekends during school year. Tel. 5688300 Behind the museum is the peaceful **Oosterpark.**

Just One Look: More Museums

Lovers of the sea will want to visit the **Maritime Museum** to see models of sailing ships, maps, and weapons. Look through the museum's periscope for a city view. Fee. Kattenburgerplein 1. Tues.–Sat. 10–5, Sun. 1–5. The maritime history of Holland is related with model boats, globes, and instruments at the **Rijksmuseum Nederlands Scheepvaartmuseum.** Fee. Kattenburgerplein 1. Open Tues.–Sat. 10–5, Sun. 1–5.

In **Rembrandthuis,** the artist's former home, you'll see the master's tools, etching plates, and prints. Fee; Museumcard free. Jodenbreestr. 4–5. Mon.–Sat. 10–5, Sun. 1–5. Tel 249486.

The **Resistance Museum** documents how the Dutch resisted the Germans from 1940 to 1945. Kids can activate radio broadcasts by pushing buttons; realistic prison cells with sound effects recall the horrors of war. Fee. Lekstraat 63. Tues.–Fri. 10–5, weekends 1–5.

The **Tramline Museum** is literally a "moving museum" with examples of vintage trams. Kids can ride an antique tram to Amsterdamse Bos from the museum. Fee. Haarlemmermeerstation, Amsterlveenseweg 264. Late Mar.–Oct. and early July–Sept. Mon.–Fri. 10–6, Sat. 12–6. Tel. 737538.

The **Museum of Torture Instruments** is not for the squeamish. You'll see how people were punished in medieval times; don't sit on the chair of nails! Fee. Heiligweg 19. Mon.–Sat. 10–5.

De Klompenboer will allow children to get up close and watch the whole process of making **wooden shoes,** "step by step." Free. N. Z. Voorburgwal 20.

Where the Sidewalk Ends: Zoos and More Parks

The **Artis Zoo** has 6,000 animals, the largest aquarium in the Netherlands, a reptile house, a nocturnal animal house with flying squirrels and bats, and a children's petting farm. Its **Zeiss Planetarium** often has activities just for youngsters. The zoo's **museum** has a display of "parents and children" in the animal world. Fee. Plantage Kerklaan 40. Zoo: Mon.–Sat. 9–5. Planetarium: weekends 9:30–5:30, Wed. 12–5:30. Tel. for both: 262823.

Sports

Call Amsterdam's Sport Information Center for particulars on both spectator sports and activities (Tel. 850851). *Schaatsen* **(skating)** is very popular in winter and you'll find skates for rent everywhere. People zoom around the canals just like Hans Brinker. The small pond in Vondelpark is probably a safer bet if your children are not experienced skaters. De Mirandabad has indoor and outdoor *zwembaden* **(swimming pools)** with a deluxe wave machine and fun slides. De Mirandalaan 9. Tel. 428080.

Performing Arts

The tourist office's free brochure "Agenda" has listings of *kindervoorstellingen* (children's performances), which includes *poppentheaters* (puppet theaters), circuses, and *mimegroepen* (mime groups) where language is not a problem. Amsterdam's children's theater companies include **De Krakeling** (Tel. 245123), **Ostade Theater** (Tel. 795096), and **Polanentheater** (Tel. 821311) with repertoires for all ages. The puppeteers **Poppentheater Dirdas** [Hobbemakade 68 (Tel. 6621588] is known for its delightful marionette theater. **Cleyntheater** (Tel. 371815) is the city's mime troupe. The **Elleboog Circus** has children, ages 6–14, as performers (Tel. 269370). They perform throughout the country but are based in Amsterdam.

EXCURSIONS FROM AMSTERDAM

For swimming, *Zandvoort* is the closest **beach resort** to Amsterdam and a stone's throw from *Haarlem.* See the section covering environs of Alkmaar and Leiden for other easy-to-reach beaches.

HAARLEM AND ENVIRONS

Tulip-filled Haarlem is only a 10-minute train ride west of Amsterdam and yet has its own distinct character. The renowned **Frans Hals Museum,** housed where the Flemish artist spent his last years, is the city's treasure. While you admire the master's portraits, kids can hunt for the old pharmacy and original doll houses from 1750. Fee; free with Museumcard. Groot Heiligland 62. Mon.–Sat. 11–5, Sun. 1–5. Tel. (023) 319180. Near the city center of **Grote Markt** is the church **Grote Kerk of St. Bravo,** home of the Müller organ, one of the world's largest with over 5,000 pipes. Mozart played it when he was 11. Hans Brinker and his sister Gretel stopped to listen to it in the familiar tale. Fee. Mon.–Sat. 10–4. On Saturdays the Grote Markt explodes with color during its **weekly flower market,** where craft demonstrations take place from 9 to 4. Haarlem is host to a lavish **flower parade** on the last Saturday in April. **Tourist office (VVV):** Tel. (023) 319059.

A few kilometers north of Haarlam is *Spaarndam* and its statue of Pieter, the character from *Hans Brinker and the Silver Skates,* who saved Haarlem from flooding by poking his finger in the hole of a dike. The hamlet of *Spaarnwoude,* close by, has an extensive recreation area with canoeing, cycling, and play areas.

Southwest of Haarlem is the popular seaside resort of *Zaandvoort,* always packed with city sun seekers in the summer. Its **dolfirama** has dolphin shows, an underwater viewing area, and an aquarium. The **bulb fields,** which are dazzling in the spring, are found between Haarlem and Leiden. Late April brings daffodils, mid- to late-April welcomes hyacinths, and April through late May is tulip time.

SOUTH OF AMSTERDAM

Aalsmeer's **flower auction** is the world's largest, with millions of flowers and plants auctioned daily. Arrive early and stand above in the visitors gallery for a colorful view. Legmeerdijk 313. Mon.–Fri. 7:30–11:30. There is a **flower parade** in early September. Contact the **tourist office (VVV)** at 8 Stationsweg [Tel. (02977) 25374].

The **museum** in *Cruquius* is devoted to the topic of polder drainage! Sound dull? It's not. Housed in an antique steam-powered pumping station from 1850, the former boiler room is filled with models of windmills and steam engines. A room-size relief map of the country is flooded and drained at 10-minute intervals to illustrate the combined effect of the river flows and the North Sea tides. Fee. Cruquiusdijk 27. Apr.–Sept. Mon.–Sat. 10–5, Sun. 12–5; Oct.–Nov. Mon.–Sat. 10–4. Tel. (023) 285704.

Bennebroeck's **Linnaeushof Recreation Park** has broad appeal with over 300 attractions from water bikes to a mini-car track, a western village, a petting zoo, and a toddler's playground, all in a beautiful wooded landscape. An indoor play area with wooden shoe-making demonstrations is ideal for rainy days. Fee. Rijksstraatweg 4. Apr.–Sept. Mon.–Sun. 10–6.

Millions of tulips and hyacinths open into full color in the 66-acre showcase **Keukenhof Gardens** in the town of *Lisse.* Mar. 29–May 24 Mon.–Sun. 8–6:30.

NORTH OF AMSTERDAM

Along the IJsselmeer Sea directly north of Amsterdam is the Holland of tourist brochures: windmills, canals, costumes, and gabled houses. These quaint villages are packed with visitors in the summer. Everything in *Broek in Waterland* is built on a miniature scale. Its streets are so narrow, buses can't enter the town. The local clog makers are fun to watch. Havenrak 21. Mon.–Sun. 8–6.

The villages of *Marken* and *Volendam* are quaint and generally packed with tourists but the latter's **Goulde Kammer** is definitely worth a stop. Folk artist N. Molenaar worked for close to 15 years mosaicking the interior of his house with millions of golden cigarbands, creating intricate wall paintings. Quiz your kids to see if they can locate many of the sites you will have seen on your European tour, such as London's Big Ben or Venice's Piazza San Marco. Fee. Oudedraaipad 8. Daily 9–6. To please tourists, locals in Marken and Volendam still wear traditional regional costumes, including baggy pantaloons and red-and-white striped jackets for men and white lace bonnets with pointed wings for women.

A stone's throw from Volendam is cheese-famous and picture-perfect *Edam.* Houses decked with colorful flowers line its tranquil canals. Look for the funny portraits in its **Edams Municipal Museum** of 17th-century local characters. You'll see a giantess, a man with a 10-foot-long beard, and the fattest man in Dutch history. Weekdays 1:30–4:30, Sunday 10–12, 1:30–4:30.

Further north is the old whaling town of *Hoorn,* where a fun **folklore market** with locals in traditional costumes, folkdancing, and tasty food is held Wednesdays. Mid-June–Aug. In the town's **Noorderkerk** there's a miniature of Hoorn in the year 1650. Fee. Kleine Noord, near the station. Tel. (02290) 31128. The **Westries Museum** has charming dolls and doll houses from the 1800s. Fee. Rode Steen 1. Open Mon.–Fri. 11–5, weekends 2–5. Tel. (02290) 15597. Children will enjoy traveling by **historic steam train** from Hoorn through Medemblik to Enkhuizen. Departs Hoorn May 2–Sept. Tues.–Sun. Reserve: (031) 229014862.

Enkhuizen's **Rijksmuseum Zuiderzeemuseum** has close to 150 authentic Dutch houses with streets and gardens in its outdoor museum. Inside the museum, children can take a ride in a flat-bottomed boat along a simulated canal and watch sails and barrels being made. Fee. Wierdjk 18. Mar.–Oct. 22 daily 10–5. The town's **Sprookjeswonderland** is an enchanting fairy-tale park with Hansel and Gretel's house, "magic" toadstools, and life-size jigsaw puzzles of familiar stories to piece together. Kids can ride in horse-drawn carts with colorful court jesters, clowns, and magicians. Fee. Wilhelminaplantsoen. Mon.–Sat. 10–5:30, Sun. 1–5:30. Tel. (022) 8017853.

NORTHWEST OF AMSTERDAM

Zaandam is referred to as the "China of Holland" because its style of windmills and canals appear Asian. The nearby **Zaanse Schans,** an open-air old Dutch village, is a touristy look at the past but kids think it's fun, especially the wooden toy shops. Klaveringdijk. Mon.–Sun. 10–5; Oct.–Dec. weekends only 10–5.

Alkmaar is known for its lavish and very colorful **cheese market,** where buyers come to taste each cheese, shout at each other, and grumble about the price. Wheels and wheels of cheese, the size of bowling balls, are rolled down the street. Arrive early to avoid crowds. Mid-Apr.–mid-Sept. Fridays 10–12. Above the **Waggebouw (cheese-weighing house)** look for the clock's mechanical figures, which spell out the hour. In Waagplein. The **Hans Brinker Museum** is a skating museum in a 17th-century restored farmhouse. On view is a beautiful collection of sleds and skates from all over the world. Fee. Voordam 6. Apr.–Sept. daily 1–5; Oct.–Feb. Sun. 1–5. Check hours.

South of Den Helder, in *Broek op Langedijk,* the **Museum Broker**

Veiling holds a pretend auction of vegetables, fruits, and flowers where children can bid. The auction room is built on wooden piles over the water. Afterward take a cruise through the town's picture-postcard landscape of islands and windmills. Fee. Voorburggracht 20. May–Sept. Mon.–Fri. 10–5. Tel. (02260) 13807.

WADDENEILANDEN (WADDEN ISLANDS)

The five Wadden Islands, at the northern tip of Holland, attract many Dutch and German vacationers who come for its sandy beaches. The islands of **Texel** and **Terschelling** are most popular. For self-catering bungalows, contact the **tourist office (VVV)**, Texel Booking Department, P.O. Box 3, 1790 AA Den Gurg.

Texel, accessible by ferry from Den Helder, is noted for its abundant bird population; more than 300 species have been observed. Bikes are the best way to see its beautiful farmland and seascape. In its major seaside village, *De Koog,* set amidst the dunes, is the **Ecomare Zee Aquarium,** a natural history museum and bird sanctuary with exhibitions about the Wadden Islands. Kids can stroke a giant sperm whale, feed a seal, and view blue North Sea lobsters. Next to the aquarium is a large **dune park.** Fee. Ruyslaan 92. Mon.–Sat. 9–5. Seals feed daily at 11 and 3. Tel. (02228) 17741. Among the beachcombing displays at the **Maritiem en Jutters Museum** in *Oudeschild* are the findings of shipwrecks around the island. Fee. Barentszstraat 21. Mon.–Sat. 9–5. Tel. (02220) 4956. **Boat trips** set sail on the Waddensea from Oudeschild. Mon.–Sat. 10:30–2. Tel. (02220) 13806. Texel's least crowded beaches are south, toward *Den Hoorn.* Those south of marker 9 and south of *De Cocksdorp* are nude beaches. Others are "guarded beaches" with lifeguards, which are open June through August from 9 to 6. Den Hoorn has a children's farm with animals, play areas, and pony riding. Rommelpot 11. In season: daily 9:30–6. Tel. (02220) 19296. The four other Wadden islands, accessible by boat from Texel, are more deserted and have beautiful sand dunes and wildlife.

DEN HAAG (THE HAGUE), SCHEVENINGEN, AND ENVIRONS

Den Haag, with broad streets and stately architecture, is the country's seat of government. The **tourist office (VVV)** is in the Babylon Center, adjacent to the Central Station (Tel. 546200). The **telephone area code** for Den Haag and Scheveningen is 070.

Den Haag's prime children's attraction is **Madurodam,** a miniature version of a typical Dutch city meticulously re-created. Opened in 1952 in memory of a little boy who died in the Dachau concentration camp, it gives all proceeds to charity. Many of the models are animated, including a carnival, musicians at play, and planes getting ready to take off. After dark, 50,000 lights illuminate the small houses, churches, schools, and factories, reflecting sparkles on the water of the miniature canals and docks. This is one of Europe's best miniature villages, and one guaranteed to enchant your children. Fee. Haringkade 175. End Mar.–May Mon.–Sun. 9–10; June–Aug. 9–1:30; Sept. 9–9; Oct.–Dec. 9–6. Moonlight Miracle Sound and Light Show: May daily 10:30 PM, June–Aug. daily 11 PM; Sept. daily 9:30 PM. Tel. 3553900.

Just One Look: Museums

The **Rijksmuseum Gevangenpoort** will rank high for kids who are horror movie fans. Formerly the city prison and torture chamber, it is now a museum displaying how pain was inflicted from the 15th through 19th centuries with stretching racks; guillotines; hand, nail and thumb screws; branding irons; and more. The dark prison cells have been chillingly preserved. Fee. Bultenhof 33. Guided tours. Apr.–Sept. Mon.–Fri. 10–4, weekends 1–4; Oct.–Mar. Mon.–Fri. 10–4. Tel. 460861.

The **Museum Voor Het Poppenspel** has a charming collection of 1,000 puppets and marionettes from all over the world, some of which are 200 years old. Fee. Nassau Dillenburgstraat. Sun. 12–5. **Puppet performances** by the Guido van Deth Puppet Theater are held October–June on weekends at 2:30. Tel. 3280208.

The **Nederlands PTT Museum** chronicles the activities of the postal, telegraph, and telephone service. Every postal stamp that has ever been issued in Holland is on view. Fee. Zeestraat 82. Mon.–Sat. 10–5, Sun. 1–5. Tel. 3624531.

The **Panorama Mesdag**, the world's largest panoramic painting, depicts the seaside resort of Scheveningen in the 1800s. The painting surrounds you on all sides. Real sand has been set with objects you'd find at the beach so that it buts up to the painted sand, creating an unusual optical illusion which is enhanced by the taped sound track of seagulls. Fee. English tape available. Zeestraat 65. Mon.–Sat. 10–5, Sun. 12–5. Tel. 3642563.

The real *Scheveningen* is just northwest of Den Haag and, as the painting shows, is a popular beach resort. Its **tourist office (VVV)** is on the corner of Scheveningseslag and Gev. Deijnootweg (Tel. 546200). Kids will want to head to the **Pier Scheveningen,** where there's a 400-meter underwater walkway, aquarium, and amusement arcade. Strandweg 1. There are special children's attractions May–June and Sept. Mon.–Sun. 10–5; Oct.–Apr. Sun. 10–5; July–Aug. Mon.–Sun. 10–9. Fireworks explode from the pier every Friday night in July and August. Tel. 3543677. Kids can **make their own candles** in the age-old way next to the pier's **wave pool.** Fee. Strandweg 11. Tel. 3523486. In mid-June the beach hosts the **International Fokker Kite Flying Festival.**

North of Den Haag is *Wassenaar* and the **Duinrell Recreation Park.** Primarily a water park, it has a tropical wave pool called the Tiki Pool, four stomach-churning water slides said to be Europe's longest, and performances, including July and August's bloodcurdling stunts from international diving teams. Children can swing on "Super-roetsj," an old-fashioned whirligig, and get splashed in its fountains. The complex also has a room filled to the brim with brightly colored plastic balls to dive into, and pulleys that swing kids across a river into an animated world of giant insect puppets. Parents can relax in jacuzzis while their kids burn off steam. Camping is available; campers receive free admission to the attraction park and reduced rates to the Tiki Pool. Mar. 24–Oct. daily 9–5; July and Aug. until 9. Tel. (01751) 19212 or 19243.

Just west of Den Haag, in *Rijswijk,* is the **Recreation Park Drievliet,** a modern amusement park with water rafting, a thrilling roller coaster, a pirate ship, a vintage train called the Old 99, and the Hurricane Cave of Laughs. Not much charm, but kids will love it. Fee. Thijssenweg 16. End Mar.–beg. Apr., end Apr.–beg. Sept. Mon.–Sun. 10–6; Sept. weekends 10–6. Tel. (070) 999305.

PROVINCE OF SOUTH HOLLAND

LEIDEN AND ENVIRONS

Leiden, the birthplace of Rembrandt, is a university town with a youthful air and small-town feel. For a list of sports facilities stop at the **tourist office (VVV),** Stationsplein 210 [Tel. (071) 146846]. During the summer, **boat trips** on Leiden's canals depart from Beestenmarkt and Hoogstraat. Afternoon and evening windmill cruises sail to the Kagerplassen lakes. Tel. (071) 134938 or 413183.

From Leiden it's a short trip to the coastal resorts of *Katwijk* or *Noordwijk.* They are less crowded than those closer to Amsterdam and your kids will enjoy the chance to run on the sand and swim. Southeast of Leiden, in *Alphen aan de Rijn,* is the **Recreatie en Vogelpark Avifauna,** a beautifully landscaped tropical bird park with a recreation area, lakes, and fountains. You can take boat trips on the Brassemermeer Sea, and there are delightful activities for youngsters such as trampolines, pony rides, a toddler's carousel, and faithful replicas of Dutch buildings. Hoorn 65. Apr.–Sept. Mon.–Sun. 9–9; Oct.–Mar. Mon.–Sun. 9–6. Tel. (01720) 31109 or 31090.

ROTTERDAM AND ENVIRONS

Rotterdam's port is the world's largest and many of its sites are related to the sea. The **tourist office (VVV)**, Stadhuisplein 19 (Tel. 4136000), can inform you about local windmills, or diamond-cutting and craft demonstrations. The **telephone area code** for Rotterdam is 010.

Detour! What to See and Do

Ride the spiral elevator up to the revolving **Euromast Space Tower** for a great view of the harbor. Kids can play sailor on its ship wheel and there's a restaurant on top. Parkhaven 20. Mid-Mar–mid-Oct. Mon.–Sun. 10–9; mid-Oct.–mid-Mar. Mon.–Sun. 10–6. Space Tower: daily 11–4; Jan.–Feb. weekends only 11–4. Tel. 4364811.

There are boat tours of the port and trips to Deltawerken and Europort departing from the Willemsplein Dock. Contact **Spido** (Tel. 4135400). The **Maritiem Museum Prins Hendrik** is a boat lover's joy; its outdoor maritime museum has the ship *De Buffel*, which was built in 1868 and fully restored to its original state. Fee; under 17 free. Leuvehaven 1. Tues.–Sat. 10–5. Tel. 4132680.

The **Imax Theater** is a six-story high-tech science theater with shows about animals, how the human body functions, space, and time. Earphones for English translations. Fee. Leuvehaven 77. Shows: Tues.–Thurs. hourly 11–9; summer Mon.–Sun. hourly 11–9. Tel. 4048844.

The **Museum "Toy-Toy"** lives up to its name with antique dolls, miniatures, and mechanical toys. Fee. Wetering 41. Sun.–Thurs. 11–4. Tel. 4525941. More toys can be found at the **Museum De Dubbelle Palmboom,** which traces the town's history through exhibits of crafts and children's playthings. Fee; under 17 free. Voorhaven 12. Tues.–Sat. 10–5, Sun. 1–5. Tel. 5761533.

Where the Sidewalk Ends: Zoos and Parks

The **Blijdorp Dierentuin** is a zoo with a wide variety of animals, an aquarium, a lake, and an amusement area. Its Riviera Hall, a large covered garden with aquariums, crocodiles, apes, and elephants, makes for a great stop on a rainy day. Fee. Van Aerssenlaan 49. Nov.–Apr. Mon.–Sun. 9–5; May–Oct. 9–6. Tel. 4654333.

Plaswijck Park is a recreation park with domestic animals, an observation tower, playgrounds, miniature golf, a labyrinth, and a touring boat. Fee. C.N.A. Looslaan 23. Daily 9–6. Tel. 4181836. The **Tropicana** has swimming and wild water rapids. Fee. Maasboulevard 100. Mon.–Fri. 10–11; weekends 10–7.

Kinderdijk **(the Children's Dike),** a polder on the outskirts of Rotterdam, is so named because during a 15th-century flood, a cat jumped into the cradle of a drowning infant and by moving the cradle back and forth saved the child. Kinderdijk is the best place in the country to see **windmills.** Nineteen stately windmills line its canal; all are still in operating condition, draining the excess water from the Alblasserwaard polders. Every Saturday afternoon in July and August, the seventy-six mill sails are rigged and set to motion. During the second week in September, the mills are illuminated in the evening. May through October there are boat trips on the canal which provide a beautiful vantage point for windmill viewing. One is open to visitors. Apr.–Sept. Mon.–Sat. Tel. (01859) 14118.

DELFT

Delft has lost some of its charm to the tourists who swarm to buy its quaint blue and white pottery and admire its packaged prettiness of swan-filled canals and flower-decked bridges. Children will like the **horse-drawn streetcars** that depart from the town center or a climb up the tower of the **Nieuwe Kerk** for an expansive town view. Fee. Apr.–Oct. Mon.–Sat. 9–5; Oct.–Apr. Mon.–Fri. 10–12, 1:30–4. Tel. (015) 123025. Army buffs should visit the **Royal Netherlands Military and Weapons Museum,** which has an array of weapons and military attire from as early as the Spanish War. Fee. Kote Geer 1. Tues.–Sat. 10–5, Sun. 1–5. Tel. (015) 150500. Kids who have made ceramics at school will enjoy watching how the famous blue Delftware is created at the **De Delftse Pauw** factory. Free. Delftweg 133, north Delft. Apr.–mid-Oct. daily 9–4; mid-Oct.–Mar. Mon.–Fri. 9–4, weekends 11–1. **De Porceleyne Fles** has painting demonstrations. We were surprised to learn that the royal blue glaze is black when painted on. Rottersdamsweg 119, south Delft. Apr.–Oct. Mon.–Sat. 9–5, Sun. 10–4; Nov.–Mar. Mon.–Fri. 9–5, Sat. 10–4.

GOUDA AND ENVIRONS

Gouda plays host to a *kaas en handarbeid markt* **(cheese and craft market)** and to many tourist buses. The market is held every Thursday from 10–1 the last week of June through August. Even the town's church square, the Markt, is cheese-shaped! Look for the markt's Gothic **Stadhuis,** which has a carillon and animated figures built into its wall. The **Catarina Ziekenhuis,** now a municipal museum, was originally the town's hospital. Its eclectic display includes an apothecary, an old surgeon's room with medical instruments and a torture chamber (no, they are not the same thing!), an antique toy classroom, and the only isolation cell for the insane left in the

Netherlands. Fee. Oosthaven 9. Mon.–Sat. 10–5, Sun. 12–5. Tel. (01820) 13800.

Actually in the province of Utrecht but only 13 kilometers from Gouda is *Oudewater,* the home of bizarre **Heksenwaag,** a site not to miss. From 1497 to 1700, accused witches were weighed here to determine if they were truly witches and light enough to fly on broomsticks. Kids can receive a certificate after weighing in. Even if your children are light as a feather, they will still fail the test. Fee. Leeuweringerstraat 2. End Mar.–Oct. Tues.–Sat. 10–5, Sun. 12–5.

DORDRECHT

Dordrecht was the most important town in Holland until the 17th century, when Amsterdam was proclaimed the capital. For camping, sporting facilities, bicycle and boat rentals, stop by the **tourist office (VVV)** at Stationsweg 1 [Tel. (078) 132800]. Climb the 362 steps up the tower of Dordrecht's Gothic **Lage Church** for a view of the city's wide canals and gabled houses. Fee. May–Oct. Wed.–Sun. 1–4. Tel. (078) 144660. The **Museum Mr. Simon van Gijn** has a special **Toy House** with old trains, tin toys, magic lanterns, tea sets, board games, street toys, toy soldiers, and a boy's and girl's playroom from the 1700s. Fee. under 4 free. Nieuwe Haven 29. Museum: Tues.–Sun. 10–5, Sun. 1–5. Toy House: Wed. and weekends same hours as museum. Tel. (078) 133793. The puppet theater **Poppentheater Damiet** performs regularly for children at Buddinghplein 20. Tel. (078) 140342. There is a delightful children's farm at **Weizigtpark.** Fee. Mon.–Sun. 9–4:30. Tel. (078) 141900. **Wantijpark** has a miniature zoo and playground by the river Wantij.

Boat trips depart from the center of town for excursions on the Hollandse and to the beautiful water-filled **National Park De Biesbosch.** Departs July–Aug. Sun., Tues., Wed., and Thurs. Tickets are available from the VVV. The national park was formed by a great flood that turned the polder into an extensive water district. Once in the park, you can travel by canoe, pedal boat, or rowboat (available at visitor center) through its narrow creeks or swim, wind-surf, and fish. Camping sites abound.

CENTRAL HOLLAND

PROVINCE OF GELDERLAND

ARNHEM AND THE HOGE VELUWE NATIONAL PARK

The star attraction in Arnhem, 100 kilometers southeast of Amsterdam, is its **Nederlands Openluchtmuseum,** an 82-acre authentic old

Dutch landscape with over 50 meticulously re-created farms and windmills. There are paper-making demonstrations by people in authentic regional costumes, a horse-driven mill, and a bakery where you can taste currant buns baked in an oven fired by sticks. Special treasure hunts for children are held. Fee. Schelmseweg 89. Mar. 23– Oct. 22 weekdays 9–5, weekends 10–5. Tel. (085) 576111. Pack a picnic and head for **Sonsbeek,** a pleasant public park with duck ponds and fountains near the center of Arnhem.

Arnhem is close to the **Hoge Veluwe National Park,** a 13,000-acre preserve of forest and dunes that provides a pleasant break from the densely populated Dutch cities. Free bikes are distributed at the visitor center for riding through the park. As you walk or cycle there are many observation posts to view deer, wild sheep (called moufflon), and boar. Cross-country skiing and skating on outdoor ponds is available in winter. Park: 8–sunset. Camping and bungalows are available in the park. *Otterlo,* bordering the northwest side of the Hoge Veluwe Park, has a world-class museum set deep in a beautiful national park. The **Rijksmuseum Kröller Müller** has an astounding collection of over 200 works by Van Gogh as well as paintings by Seurat, Mondrian, and Gris. Contemporary sculpture by Henry Moore, Barbara Hepworth, and Jean Dubuffet line its beautiful **Beeldenpark.** Fee. Museum: Apr.–Oct. Tues.–Sat. 10–5, Sun. 11–5; Nov.–Mar. Tues.–Sun. 1–5. Sculpture garden: Apr.–Oct. Tues.–Sat. 10–4:30, Sun. 11–4:30. Tel. (08382) 1041. The museum is a 30-minute walk from any of the park's entrances; buses depart from Otterlo and from Arnhem's train station in the summer. Also in the national park is the **Kinderbos,** where an oak tree was planted for every child born in the Netherlands on April 26, 1985, the day the national park celebrated its 50th birthday. One and a half kilometers from Hoenderloo entrance. Kids enjoy feeding the carp in the pond in front of the park's **St. Hubert Hunting Lodge.** There's a playground with climbers in front of the terrace of the cafe Koperen Kop.

Near Arnhem, in *Burger's Bush,* is the 60-acre **Burgers Dieren-en Safaripark.** Its zoo has a safari park, wolves, chimpanzee center, "gorilla island," and tropical forest. Entrance fee includes a train trip through the safari park from which giraffes and zebras can be observed. Fee. Schelmseweg 85. Zoo: summer daily 9–8; winter until 9–6. Safari park: daily 9–5. Tel. (085) 424534.

NIJMEGEN AND ENVIRONS

Nijmegen may be far from Palestine but its 13-acre **Bijbels Open-luchtmuseum Heilig-Land Stichting** has brought the Middle East to Holland with models of 1st-century Palestinian monuments, buildings, caravans, tents, and actors in period dress. The intent is to realistically show how Christ lived in his day. Fee. Profetenlaan 2. Mid-Mar.–Oct. Mon.–Sun. 9–5:30. Tel. (080) 229829. While in town, drop into the **Velorama National Cycle Museum** with historic bicycles, accessories, and posters. Fee. Waalkade 107. Mon.–Sat. 10–5, Sun. 11–5. Tel. (080) 225851. Set in the woods, the **De Leemkuil** playground has a paddling pool, large fort, touring train, and pancake house. Fee. Luciaweg 32. May–Oct. daily 9:30–5:30; Nov.–Apr. daily 10:30–5. Tel. (080) 226811.

Just south of Nijmegen, in *Berg en Dal,* get a taste of Africa at the **Afrika Museum.** There are life-sized villages complete with thatched huts from North Ghana, two pile dwellings from Benin, a Mali village, native masks and crafts, and it's completely surrounded by a deer park. Fee. Postweg 6. Apr.–Oct. Mon.–Fri. 10–4:30, weekends 11–4:30. Tel. (08895) 42044.

APELDOORN AND ENVIRONS

Apeldoorn, one of Gelderland's largest cities, has preserved its small-town quality. Along the wide green avenues, surrounded by parks and ponds, there are grand villas built by prosperous Dutchmen. The city is surrounded by extensive nature reserves such as the **Koninklijke Houtvesterijen,** the former king's hunting grounds. **Koningin Juliantoren** recreation park has a tricky labyrinth, the "Bengali" grotto, a haunted house, and motorboat rides. Fee. Amersfoortsweg 35. End Mar.–Sept. Mon.–Sun. 10–6.

In the **Berg en Bos** park is the **Apenheul,** with more than 250 South African squirrel monkeys roaming free amongst visitors. Fee. J. C. Wilslaan 21. Apr.–June 9:30–5, July–Aug. 9:30–6, Sept.–Oct. 10–5. Tel. (055) 552556. In summer the park features gondola trips on its lake and **lumido,** a water and light spectacle. Park open daily. Take a trip on a **vintage steam train** from Apeldoorn through the woods of the Veluwe. Veluwsche steam trains depart Ascension Day, July–Aug. and Sept.

North of Apeldoorn, in *Vorchten,* is the **Puppetry Museum,** which chronicles the development of the puppet show from shadow play to puppet theater and hand puppets to marionettes. Fee. Kerkweg 38. July–Aug. Mon.–Wed. 2–5; rest of year by appointment. Tel. (05783) 1329.

EASTERN GELDERLAND

Zutphen's **Kruittoren** has old-fashioned toy soldiers ready for battle on display. Kids can set in motion a parade complete with marching music. Fee. Stationsplein 1. Apr.–Oct. 24 Wed and weekends 1:30–4:30. Tel. (05750) 14196. Just south of Zutphen, in *Vorden,* on a country estate, is the **Labyrinth Ruurlo,** one of the Netherland's largest hedge mazes. A tricky path leads to the central watchtower. Fee. Straatsabosbeheer. May–June, Sept.–Oct. weekends 1–5; summers Tues.–Fri. 11–5, weekends 1–5. Tel. (05752) 6451.

Doetinchem's **Land van Jan Klaasen** is a play farm for children up to 9 years old with a maze hall of mirrors, a crawl-through dragon, a large *gazenbord* (board game), and puppet shows. Fee. Havenstraat 78. Summer daily 10–4:30; rest of year Wed. and Sat. Puppet show at 3 only. Tel. (08340) 30878.

PROVINCE OF OVERIJSSEL

AROUND ZWOLLE AND GIETHOORN

Thirty-two kilometers north of Zwolle, in *Steenwijk,* is the **Kermis-en Circusmuseum,** with a jam-packed mini-circus. Kids will marvel at the acrobats, fat ladies, trapeze artists, merry-go-round, and carnival. Fee. Markt 64. Tues.–Fri. 10–12, 2–5; July–Aug. Tues.–Fri. 10–12, Sat. 10–12, 2–4.

Northeast of Zwolle, in *Slagharen,* visit the **Ponypark Slagharen,** a park with Shetland ponies and amusements such as a monorail, bumper boats, and an indoor swimming pool. Fee. Zwarte Dijk 39. End Mar.–mid-Sept. Mon.–Sun. 9:30–5:30; mid-Sept.–Oct. 12 weekends 9:30–5:30.

North of Zwolle is *Giethoorn,* a town that has remained virtually untouched through the centuries. Its houses all stand on their own islands and people travel from place to place by flat-bottomed boats; children travel this way to school, cows are transported by boat to pastures, even bridal parties travel via the canal.

DEVENTER AND ENVIRONS

Deventer's **Speelgoed-en-Blikmuseum** is a delight for kids as it is filled with hundreds of moving toys such as wind-up cars, electric trains, and planes dating as far back as 1870, as well as dolls, doll houses, and toy soldiers. The museum's star attraction is its collection of building blocks with unusual building elements such as pillars and buttresses. Hundreds were used to create the top floor's 3-foot-tall castle. Fee. Brink 46. Tues.–Sun. 10–5, Sun. 2–5.

Northeast of Deventer, in *Hellendoorn,* is **Avonturen park Hellendoorn,** a recreation complex with an enchanting fairy-tale park with elves and a maze and an amusement park that features a wild roller coaster, monorail, magnetic house, sea lion show, and a thrilling water chute with a free-fall section. Fee. Luttenbergerweg 22. End Mar.–early Oct. 9:30–5:30.

PROVINCE OF ZEELAND

In the southwest of Holland, Zeeland's coastline stretches for miles with wide beaches. For holiday cottages contact the provincial **tourist office,** (VVV) Zeeland, P.O. Box 123, 4330 AC Middelburg [Tel. (01180) 33051].

MIDDELBURG AND ENVIRONS

Middelburg's **Miniature Town of Walcheren** is a re-creation of the quaint island of Walcheren on a scale of 1/20 complete with dikes, windmills, trains, trees, and lakes. The real town was demolished in World War II and this park shows how well it has been reconstructed. Fee. Koepoortlaan 1, Molenwater. End Mar.–June and Sept.–Oct. Mon.–Sun. 9:30–5; July–Aug. Mon.–Sun. 9:30–6. Tel. (01180) 12525. Local women dressed in elaborate shell-shaped hats and traditional dress make the Thursday **market** in town a very colorful event.

SOUTHERN PROVINCES

BRABANT PROVINCE

DEN BOSCH (s'HERTOGENBOSCH) AND ENVIRONS

s'Hertogenbosch is a mouthful to pronounce (it means "in the Duke's Woods"), so locals have shortened the city's name to Den Bosch. Den Bosch has a colorful Wednesday and Saturday morning **market** in its beautiful central *markt*. Try *Bosse Bollen,* pastry balls covered with chocolate and smothered with whipped cream. In front of the town hall is a bronze statue of painter Hieronymus Bosch, who was a Den Bosch native. A carillon of 35 bells on top of the **Stadhuis** in the markt chimes every half hour. Look up at its clock tower to see a group of horsemen ride into view and spell out the time. In the center of Den Bosch stands the 13th-century Romanesque **St. Jan's Cathedral,** with a carillon of 50 bells. Its tower can be climbed in the summer. Kids enjoy walking the ancient town **fortifications,** where there is a moat and high ramparts. Free. Corner of Citadellaan and Zuid-Willemsvaart. **Punters,** or open boats, departing from Molenstraat near Visstraat, traverse the town's network of canals Tuesdays through Sundays in summer. There is sailing, wind surfing, and swimming in summer in the Zuiderplas and Oosterplas lakes.

Just outside of Den Bosh, in *Rosmalen,* the traffic park **Autotron** allows children to drive vintage cars from the days of Henry Ford. The park also has some thrilling tunnel slides for kids in need of a break from the "highway." Fee. Graafsebaan 133. End Mar.–June and Sept.

Mon.–Sun. 10–5; July–Aug. Mon.–Sun. 10–6. Tel. (04192) 19050.

West of Den Bosh, in **Drunen/Vlijmen,** is the **Het Land van Ooit,** a fantasy park on the grounds of the **D'Oultremont Castle.** Kids can roam through a land of giants and play in its children's playland while you take in the sculpture garden. Fee. Parklaan 40. End Apr.–end Oct. Mon.–Sun. 10–6. Tel. (04163) 77775.

TILBURG AND ENVIRONS

Tilburg, the heart of the province, serves as a convenient base for exploring the Brabant area. There is a program called "King Cyclist in the Heart of Brabant" that features **bicycle excursions** through the region's lovely, unspoiled, and *flat* (important!) terrain. The local VVV will provide you with bikes, maps, and suggested itineraries for 2- to 7-day excursions. Best of all, they will transport your luggage to your next overnight destination. The bike package includes meals and various accommodations in all price levels. Contact the **tourist office (VVV),** Spoorlaan 416a, 5038 Tilburg [Tel. (013) 351135]. The bike tours usually start in **Oisterwijk,** about 10 kilometers east of Tilburg, where you can stop to see the **Vogelpark Oisterwijk,** an exotic bird park in a beautiful forest. Gemullehoekenweg 147. Easter Sun.–mid-Oct. Mon.–Sun. 9–6.

Nearby, in **Hilvarenbeek,** is the **Strandpark De Beekse Bergen,** which has a lion safari park you can view by train, bumper boats, "Holland Island" in a lake, and a sightseeing plane. There's a maze to negotiate, a mini-traffic park, camping, and picnic facilities. Beekse Bergen 1. Apr.–June and Sept. Mon.–Sun. 10–5; July and Aug. Mon.–Sun. 10–6; Oct. 10–4. Tel. (013) 360035.

Near Tilburg is **Kaatsheuvel,** home to **De Efteling Park,** Europe's largest (375-acre) family amusement park. This is truly an exceptional place set amidst forests, lakes, and flowering meadows with multilingual parrots. Children will be enchanted with its steam-driven carousel, musical fountains, swinging pirate ship, and flying magic carpets. The park's highlight is the fairy-tale forest with a children's mushroom house where dwarfs perch on musical toadstools and dragons and animated fable characters perform. Thrill seekers can venture on the scariest roller coaster we've encountered or whirl on the Piranha, a spinning water ride. Litterbugs beware, the trash cans talk to you and say "Dank U" (thank you!). Fee includes all rides. Baby carriages and strollers available. Europaweg 1. End Mar.–Oct. Mon.–Sun. 10–6. Tel. (010) 314167.

Northeast of Tilburg is **Haaren'**s recreation park, which features **Il Grigio children's circus.** The performers, ages 7 through 16, give a wild performance at the Sporthal in July. Kerkstraat 15a. Afternoons. Call the Brabant VVV for details: Tel. (076) 225733.

EINDHOVEN AND ENVIRONS

Science buffs will enjoy Eindhoven's **Evoluon,** a museum of science and technology created in the shape of a large flying saucer. In a gracious park in the town center, Evoluon was founded by Holland's largest electrical company, the Philips Corporation. Although the displays are a bit out of date, kids will have fun with the push-button gadgets and interactive games to test their memory or determine color blindness. Most exhibits have English translations. Fee. Noordbrabantlaan. Mon.–Fri. 9:30–5:30, Sat. 10–5, Sun. 12–5. Stop for a picnic at **Philips-Van Lennep Park,** where you'll find a petting zoo. Another spot of green is the **Animal and Monkey Bird Park** on Roostenlaan 303. Fee. Daily 9–6. Tel. (040) 113738. There is a large indoor water park with swimming pools and kamikaze-style slides at the **Recreatiecentrum De Tongelreep.** Fee. Antoon Coolenlaan 1. Tel. (040) 123125.

Six kilometers north of Eindhoven, in *Best,* is the **Klompenmuseum de Platijn,** with examples of wooden shoes through the ages along with carving tools of the trade. We couldn't figure out how kids learned to walk in the tiny baby clogs. Fee. Broekdijk 16. Daily 10–5.

PROVINCE OF LIMBURG

MAASTRICHT AND ENVIRONS

The 2,000-year-old fortified town of Maastricht, capital of the province, is Holland's oldest city. Pick up "Maastricht Maandagenda," which has an English listing of events at the **tourist office (VVV),** Het Dinghuis, Kleine Straat 1 [Tel. (043) 252121]. Walk along Maastricht's **fortified ramparts,** which circle the city and once protected her from attacks. Below is a duck-filled moat; along the way you'll pass guard posts, cannons, and old gun barrels. The city's **parks** between Mass Boulevard and Prins Bisschopssingel have a duck pond, deer and small zoo. More animals are at the children's farm **De Zoonehof.** Romeinsebaan 200. Tues.–Fri. 10–12:30 and 2–5, Sun. 2–5. Tel. (043) 474786. There is a **playground** with a paddling pool and miniature golf at Fort Wilhem. Kastanjelaan 50. Easter Monday–Sept. 15 daily 10–6. Tel. (043) 211397. The **St. Pietersberg Pleasure Gardens** have boule courts, a toddler play area, and miniature golf. Luikerweg 78. Spring, summer, and fall 10–8. Tel. (043) 211729. The General House has a **children's theater** with puppet shows. Fee. Vrijthof Square. Sunday afternoons.

The enormous **Grotton St. Pietersberg** have resulted from centuries of excavating marl, a type of sandstone. The caves are a labyrinth with more than 20,000 passages. A 1-hour tour points out fossils of shells, shark's teeth, reptile bones, and a giant turtle. Fee. Slavante 1. Tour. Mid-May–beg. Sept. Mon.–Sun. hourly 10:45–3:45. Several **boat trips** on the river Meuse to the grottoes are led by Maastricht's Rederij Stiphout Bordertour. Good walkers only. Departs Maaspromenade 27. Tel. (043) 254151.

North of Maastricht, in *Stein,* is **Steinerbos,** a bucolic park with ducks and swan-filled ponds, a deer park, indoor and outdoor swimming pools with a water chute, pony rides, and more. Fee. Dieterenstraat 19. May–Sept. 14 daily 10–6. Tel. (04490) 32525.

VALKENBURG AND ENVIRONS

East of Maastricht is Valkenburg, once the home of ancient Romans who built houses of marl which they took from an extensive **underground network of caves** and corridors. These have since been spiced up with colored lights and hokey touring trains but kids get a kick out of it, especially cruising its subterranean lake by boat. Fee. Entrance at the foot of the Cauberg. Tel. (04406) 13364. Perched above the town are the ruins of its castle, inhabited from 1391 to 1661, with secret passages to the caves. Accessible by tourist train, the **Cauberg,** Valkenburg's highest hill, has many activities for children. A monorail or cable car will escort you up to the **Wilhelminatoren,** which is a fun tower to climb; an amusement hall and go-cart track is near the railway. The **Steenkolenmijn,** a replica coal mine hewn out of limestone, has original materials from the former South Limburg coal mines. Fee. Daalhmemerweg 31. Guided tours: Easter–Oct. daily 9–5; Nov.–Easter 1 tour per day. Tel. (04406) 12491.

Sprookjesbos Fairy-tale Park has moving storybook figures, a gnome's village, a water organ with aquatic concerts, a giant water chute, and a western show. Fee. Sibbegrubbe 1. Mid-May–Aug. Mon.–Sun. 10–6. Tel. (04406) 12985. The town's **Pretpark de Valkenier** has a "moon room" that takes you on a simulated ride to the moon, a rodeo hall, boating on its lake, and fairy-tale woods. Fee. Koningswinkelstraat 53. Apr.–Sept. Mon.–Sun. 10–6. Tel. (04406) 12682. Check with the **tourist office (VVV),** Th. Dorrenplein 5 [Tel. (04406) 13364], about local apartment hotels, camping, and bobsledding in Rotspark.

East of Valkenburg, in *Heerlerheide,* next to Heerlen, is the **Droomkasteel Fantastico (Fantastico Dream Castle).** Its beautiful castle park has sculptures of every imaginable fairy-tale character. Ganzeweide 113–115. Easter–Sept. daily 10–6. Tel. (045) 211767

THE NORTH

PROVINCE OF FRIESLAND

Locals in Friesland claim that children here are born with skates on their feet. During January's **Elfstedentocht,** Holland's greatest sporting event, skaters race 125 miles on frozen canals, across Friesland's eleven main towns. It only occurs when the winters are cold and the ice is strong. Sixteen thousand skaters have participated in recent years, achieving speeds of up to 30 miles an hour. Contact the **tourist office,** (VVV) Friesland-Leeuwarden, Stationsplein 1, Leeuwarden [Tel. (05100) 32224].

LEEUWARDEN AND ENVIRONS

The quaint canal-filled town of Leeuwarden, capital of the province, was home to the Dutch spy Mata Hari. Off the tourist track, Leeuwarden has maintained its fresh, clean, Dutch sheen. It has its own **leaning tower,** the 16th-century **Oldehove,** which tilts almost as much as the one in Pisa! Climb up on stairs that slant sideways. Fee. Tower: Mon.–Sat. 10–12 and 2–5, Sun. 2–5.

West of Leeuwarden is the small market town of *Franeker.* Its unusual **Planetarium Eise Eisinga** is in the original house of wool-comber Eise Eisinga, who built a realistic replica of the planetary system in his living room in the 1700s. Globes dangle from his ceiling and move on small tracks around the room, replicating the planets of the solar system as he knew them. Upstairs, through a wall opening, you can see how he engineered this ingenious feat. Working by candlelight, it took him 7 years. Fee. Eise Eisingastraat 3. Jan.–Apr., Sept.–Dec. Tues.–Sat. 10–12:30, 1:30–5; May–Aug. daily 1–5.

Northwest of Franeker, in *Sexbierum,* is the **Wind Attraction Park Aeolus.** A large park whose theme revolves around the wind, it has a wind tunnel, windmills, and wind games. Fee. Open end Mar.–Sept. Mon.–Sun. 10–6.

EASTERN FRIESLAND

In *Appelscha* the **Duinenzathe Recreation Park** has a fantasy park, amusement arcade, motor scooters, cakewalk, haunted house, carousel, and miniature cars to drive. Boerestreek 13. End Mar.–Sept. Mon.–Sun. 9:30–6. Tel. (05162) 2203. The neighboring **Miniaturpark Town Appelscha** provides a pint-sized look at Dutch village life. Boerestreek 7a. Same hours as recreation park. Tel. (05162) 2200.

Portugal

Portugal is one of the best bargains in Europe. With accommodations and food about one-third the price of those elsewhere in Europe, families can explore one of its most beautiful countries very inexpensively. The attractions for families are many: 500 miles of sandy beaches, harbors dotted with fishing boats painted in crayon-bright hues, castle-topped hillsides, old wooden carts pulled by donkeys, tile-fronted houses, and some of the most colorful folk festivals to be found.

Situated at the extreme southwestern edge of Europe, Portugal launched the great explorers who charted the New World. While the likes of Vasco da Gama and Magellan sailed the seas, pirates attacked Portugal's home shores, where a fascinating series of fortresses and castles were built in defense. Young modern-day explorers will love to investigate their ramparts and towers. The southern coast, the Algarve, has lost some of its charm to overdevelopment, but the western coast is still unspoiled, particularly in the north. And don't miss the chance to explore some of the country's inland towns and cities—Évora, Tomar, Coimbra, and many other fascinating destinations are filled with historical splendor and rich local traditions.

Have a great trip . . . Boa Viagem!

Wha'd'ya Wanna Do?

Request information on a wide variety of travel topics from:

PORTUGUESE NATIONAL TOURIST ORGANIZATION
U.S.A.: Portuguese National Tourist Organization, 590 Fifth Ave., New York, NY 10036. Tel. 212-354-4403.
Canada: Portuguese National Tourist Organization, 500 Sherbrooke West, Suite 930, Montreal, Québec PQH3A 3C6. Tel. 514-843-4623.

Local tourist offices, called **turismo,** are found in all big cities and most little towns. At the least they can provide you with maps and lists of accommodations, and many will make reservations for you and offer helpful suggestions.

Museums, churches, castles, and recreational activities charge entry fees much lower than those in the rest of Europe. Most are under $1 per adult, and many are just a few pennies. Lisbon and the Algarve are slightly more expensive than the rest of the country.

Festivals honoring a city or town's patron saint and celebrations for Carnival, Holy Week, and other religious holidays are lively affairs with processions, music, dancing, regional cuisine, and carnival rides. The tourist organization publishes an annual calendar of events listing dates for most of them. Try planning your itinerary to include at least one.

Quite different from the Spanish, Portuguese **bullfights** involve fanfare and flourishes rather than bloodshed. After flashy showmanship by *cavaleiros* (men on horseback) and *toureiros* (men on foot who pantomime with a sword), the bull is wrestled to the ground by eight *forcados.* This is the crowd's favorite part of the bullfight as it involves great agility and strength. Once this has been accomplished, the bull exits the ring. The bullfight season lasts from April through October, with most bullfights taking place during local festivals. Contact local tourist offices for schedules.

Lights Out! Special Portuguese Accommodations

Renting an **apartment** or a **villa** for stay of a week or more is more economical and convenient than staying in a hotel. Villa and apartment rentals are easy to find in the Algarve and in Lisbon and environs, but be sure to find out the proximity to the beach in resort areas. A list of companies specializing in apartment and villas rentals can be obtained through the national tourist organization.

Hotels are ranked by stars from one to five according to price and amenities. **Pensions** are much less expensive and are ranked from one to three stars, with a three-star pension similar in price to a one-star hotel. Room prices in Portugal are the least expensive in Europe. We have listed hotels in Lisbon and nearby Cascais. You can find even less expensive accommodations than those we've listed under "inexpensive," but they are often in much less desirable areas and without bathrooms. Hotels are less expensive away from big cities and resort areas. **Apartment hotels** with the conveniences of both hotels and apartments have become very popular in Portugal and are commonly found in resorts.

Pousadas are government-owned hotels similar to the paradors in Spain. Many are located in restored castles, palaces, monasteries, and convents in places of beauty throughout the country while others are modern. Care is taken to see that the pousadas reflect the culture and traditions of their region. They cost about the same as an expensive hotel but can be a memorable splurge. Particularly beautiful are those in Évora, Estremoz, and Óbidos. Their dining rooms feature local specialties as well as international cuisine and even if you can't afford to stay, you can have a drink or a meal. *Estalagems* are privately owned small hotels. The Portuguese National Tourist Organization publishes a brochure, "The Pousadas of Portugal," with names, addresses, and booking information.

Manor houses and elegant country homes have been opened to holiday guests. Most are in rural settings, quiet resorts, or old market towns. The tourist office can give you details.

The tourist office can send you a list of **youth hostels** that have family rooms. The list also indicates which hostels have kitchens, cafeterias, or bedding provided.

Campgrounds are often quite fancy, with supermarkets, swimming pools, and even indoor sports facilities. One hundred campgrounds exist and all are real bargains. Contact the tourist organization for their "Portugal Camping" brochure/map listing names and addresses.

Getting Around

Car travelers will need a current U.S. or Canadian driver's license and an insurance green card. Portugal has very few four-lane highways; most of the country is crisscrossed by two-lane roads, which can be slow going if you get stuck behind a truck or farm vehicle. If you rent a car in Portugal, it will not have back seat belts and children are not allowed to ride in the front seats.

Portugal's **trains** accept Eurailpasses. Trains with inexpensive fares provide an excellent network of services throughout the country. Children under 4 travel free and those 4 to 12 pay half-fare. A motorrail service between Opôrto, Lisbon, and Faro is available in summer months. There is a network of **buses** connecting the cities, villages, and hamlets of Portugal. Timetables are available from local tourist offices.

Nuts and Bolts

Does anyone care what time it is? Most businesses close at lunch for two hours. Stores generally open at 9 AM, close from 12:30 to 2:30 or 3 PM, and reopen at 7 PM. Supermarkets are open from 8 AM to 9 PM. Banking hours are generally 8:30 AM to 3 PM, Monday through Friday.

National holidays: New Year's Day (January 1), Carnival Tuesday, Good Friday, Liberty Day (April 25), Labor Day (May 1), National Day (June 10), São João (June 24), Corpus Christi, Assumption, First Republic Day (October 5), All Saints Day (November 1), Restoration of Independence (December 1), Feast of the Immaculate Conception, and December 24 and 25.

Can I have my allowance? The Portuguese currency unit is the *escudo*, divided into 100 *centavos*. Its symbol, $, is written between the escudo and centavo. Notes are issued in 5,000, 1,000, 500, and 100 denominations. Coins are issued for 50, 25, 20, 10, 5, 2$50, and 1 escudo.

Telephones: Portugal's **country code** is 351. You can make international calls from pay phones but have plenty of 25-escudo coins on hand. Post offices have phones where you can more conveniently place international calls and pay when you're finished.

Useful nationwide phone numbers: Emergency is 115.

Embassies and consulates: The U.S. Embassy is on Av. das Forças Armadas, Lisbon [Tel. (01) 725600]. Canada's is on Rua Rosa Araújo 2, 6th floor, Lisbon [Tel. (01) 563821].

Let's Eat!

Menus in restaurants are often translated into three or more languages, especially in tourist centers. The fixed price *ementa do dia* (menu of the day) or *prato do dia* (plate of the day) is often the best value, and you can order a *meia dose* (half-portion) for your kids or for yourself. Breakfast includes fresh bread, butter, jam, juice, and cheese. The mid-day meal is served between 12 and 2 and dinner is served between 8 and 10 PM. A snack, often eaten around 4 PM, is typically meat pastries or sweets.

Delicious fish is available everywhere. *Bacalhau* (cod), often salted, is one of the most commonly found. Kids usually enjoy *bacalhau à Brás* (fried in olive oil with onions, potatoes, and garlic); and *bacalhau à Gomes de Sá*, a casserolelike baked dish with potatoes, cod, onions, olives, and hard-boiled eggs. *Sardinhas assadas* (grilled sardines) are inexpensive and delicious and are served whole (watch out for the little bones). A *caldeirada* is similar to a Mediterranean bouillabaisse. *Frango assado* is delicious roast chicken, and *frango no churrasco* is barbecued and mouth-watering. Portuguese *sopas* (soups) are delicious and inexpensive. Many restaurants serve bread and olives and other goodies before your meal is served. Most charge for them by the amount eaten, so be careful. Portuguese *queijo* (cheese), especially *queijo da Serra*, is delicious. If all else fails, you can order *ovos mexidos* (scrambled eggs). Look out for the *enguias* (eels), a specialty of the north.

Pastries are substantial although some look more beautiful than they taste. Try *bolo de anjo* (angel food cake), delicious and easy-to-find *pudim flan* (creme caramel), and *arroz doce* (rice pudding). Ice cream stands are at every corner; our favorite was the "pintor," a pencil-shaped popsicle with a chocolate "lead" point.

Formula and Baby Food, Diapers and Baby Gear

Pharmacies *(Farmácias)* stock all kinds of baby items, with diapers *(fraldas)*, a wide selection of baby foods *(comida para bébé)*, toys and formula *(fórmula)* readily available. Supermarkets also stock diapers and baby food, as do some little neighborhood corner stores. Sugar *(açucar)* is often added to baby foods so read labels carefully. Chicken with rice is *frango com arroz;* mixed fruit is *frutas variadas;* applesauce is *sobremesa de maçã;* mixed vegetables are *legumes sortidos;* and peaches are *pêssego.* Rice cereals come ready to be mixed with milk or water. Cribs *(berço)* are available if you stay in four-star or deluxe hotels, but very few restaurants have high chairs. A stroller is a *carro de bébé.*

Sidewalk Talk

The Portuguese language is very difficult to pronounce and English is widely spoken in many regions. The tourist office publishes a brochure, ". . . And Here's How to Say it in Portuguese!" with a detailed explanation of pronunciations. It will give your children hours of entertainment trying to master the musical subtleties of the language.

bathroom *quarto de banho*	fireworks *fogo de artifício*
beach *praia*	girl *menina*
boat *barco*	ice cream *gelado*
boy *menino*	please *porfavor*
cake *bolo*	swimming *natação*
candy *rebuçado*	swimming pool *piscina*
children's bed *cama de criança*	thank you *obrigado*
children's playground *parque infantil*	toy *brinquedo*

The Lay of the Land

The capital city of Lisbon lies in the southern half of the country on the Atlantic coast. Its central location makes it a good starting point for trips to the north or the south of the country. The southern Algarve has the most popular beach resorts with the warmest waters, while the Costa de Prata and Costa Verde along the west coast have many good beaches and charming fishing villages. The inland southern plains *(planícies)* and northern mountain regions have many towns and villages undiscovered by the typical tourist.

LISBON

Lisbon has vintage trolley cars running up and down its seven hills, castles, fabulous art treasures, lively outdoor cafes, inexpensive museums, beautiful parks, and elaborate mosaic sidewalks. Every imaginable surface—walls of buildings, benches, fountains, and staircases—have been covered with glorious colorful tiles. Nearby beach resorts can be reached in less than an hour so you can easily intersperse city pursuits with seaside pleasures. Lisbon's main **tourist offices** are at Palácio Foz, Praça dos Restauradores (Tel. 3463643), Estação de Santa Apolónia, and (National Tourist Office) Aveni. António Ausgusto de Aguiar 86 (Tel. 575015). The **telephone area code** is 01.

The Lay of the City

Lisbon sits on seven hills on an estuary of the river Tagus. The old business district, the Baixa or Lower Town, is a grid of small streets. Avenida da Liberdade is a wide tree-lined boulevard that connects the Baixa with the newer business district. The Bairro Alto or Upper District has narrow streets and parks. The city's medieval quarter, the Alfama, with its maze of tiny streets and whitewashed houses, is built on the slopes of a hill topped by a castle.

Getting Around

Lisbon is served by three different **railway stations,** Estação de Santa Apolónia (international, northern, and eastern lines), Estação Cais do Sodré (for Estoril and Cascais), and Estação do Rossio (for Sintra and western lines). Its **subway** covers only part of the city but is fast and efficient, and you can buy economical books of ten tickets. **Streetcars** of every variety crisscross the city as do buses. Three **funiculars** connect the lower city with residential areas at the tops of the hills. **Taxis** are cheap and quick. If you park your car in town, remove all valuables. For a view of the city from the river, take a **boat trip** along the Tagus. Transportes Tejo (Transtejo) offers 2-hour trips. 181-4 Rua Áurea. Apr.–Oct. 3–5. Tel. 3469201.

Where to Stay

Lisbon has a full range of hotel and pension accommodations; we have listed a few best-suited to families. A better bet, if you want to be away from the city's hustle and bustle, is to stay in the beach town of Cascais, a 30-minute electric train ride from Lisbon. Its small-town atmosphere, sandy beaches, and broad esplanade make it great fun for children. (See "Cascais.")

HOTELS
Hotel Ritz overlooks Eduardo VII Park. Rua Rodrigo da Fonseca 88-A. Tel. 692020. Operated by Intercontinental Hotels. From U.S. Tel. 800-327-0200. **Deluxe.**

Hotel Lisbon Sheraton has a pool and health club. Rua Latino Coelho 2. Tel. 575757. From U.S. Tel. 800-327-0200. **Deluxe.**

Hotel Meridien also overlooks Eduardo VII Park. 149 Rua Catilho. Tel. 690900. **Expensive.**

Presidente Hotel has discounts for children under 9 and offers baby-sitting if arranged in advance. Guests can use the laundry facilities. 13 Rua Alexandre Herculano. Tel. 539501. **Moderate.**

Miraparque is close to the Eduardo VII Park and is a bargain for its location. 12 Av. Sidónio Pais. Tel. 578070. **Inexpensive.**

Albergaria Residencial Insulana is in the Rosa district close to the train station. Rua Assunção 52. Tel. 323131 or 327625. **Inexpensive.**

CAMPING
Parque Florestal de Monsanto, on the south bank of the Tagus, 10 minutes from Lisbon, is on a hilly tree-covered site with swimming pool, tennis courts, restaurant, and other amenities. Open year-round. Tel. 708384.

Detour! What to See and Do

THE ALFAMA
Lisbon's old town, the colorful **Alfama,** is full of narrow stepped streets with flower-filled balconies, tiny squares, open street markets, and patterned alleyways. Take your time wandering through this quarter, where wash and caged canaries hang from balconies and people still collect water from community fountains. High on the hilltop sits the **Castelo de São Jorge,** a castle used first by the Romans

and later by the Moors. From its top, the panorama of Lisbon, the river's mouth, and surrounding countryside is exceptional. In its gardens are ducks, peacocks, and deer. Its moat is filled with swans and ducks, and there is a tiny "zoo" with goats, peacocks, and other birds. Walk along the open parapets, climb on the cannons, and spend a moment at the small playground where local kids play soccer before wandering about on its many pathways. Get there by bus or taxi or walk the steep stairs and passageways through the Alfama. Free. Open 9 until sunset.

Santo António da Sé commemorates St. Anthony of Padua, a Franciscan monk who became the patron saint of Portugal. In order to erect the altar of this church, children of the Alfama built miniature altars with the saint's likeness on them to raise money. Known also as the protector of young brides, many come to light candles under his picture. St. Anthony's Day, on June 12 and 13, is a great celebration (see Lisbon's festivals below). **Fundação Espirito Santo Silva** is Lisbon's decorative arts museum. Filled with furniture and tapestries, it is good for a quick view of what 18th- and 19th-century life was like for Lisbon's upper-class residents. Free. Tues.–Sat. 10–1, 2:30–5. Visit the **Museu do Azulejo** in the Convento da Madre de Deus to see the striking Portuguese architectural decoration, the *azulejos*, or glazed, ornamental tiles. Rua Madre de Deus 4. Tues.–Sun. 10–5. The **Museu Militar** contains arms and armor from the 9th to the 20th century, including explorer Vasco da Gama's sword, coins, cannons, medallions, and other curiosities. Fee. In front of Estação Santa Apolónia. Tues.–Sat. 10–4, Sun. 11–5.

CIDADE BAIXA, THE LOWER TOWN

The city's bustling main square, the **Rossio,** was first a cattle market and later the site of public executions, bullfights, and carnivals. Little sidewalk cafes crowd this congested intersection. South of Rossio is the grid of shop-filled streets known as the Baixa, built after the earthquake and ensuing fire of 1755 devastated much of the town. Each street had a trade: cloth merchants on Rua Augusta, gold merchants on Rua do Ouro or Aurea, silver merchants on Rua da Prata. Some of the streets are pedestrian-only and sprinkled with sidewalk cafes and colorful umbrellas. Lisbon's busy main boulevard, the broad tree- and sidewalk-cafe-lined Avenida da Liberdade, traverses the lower town from the Rossio to the grand Parque Eduardo VII. Its shady center is a pedestrian promenade. The **Elevador da Glória** is actually a funicular that connects Praça dos Restauradores, north of Rossio, to the Bairro Alto. The elegant **Chiado** area is uphill to the west of the Rossio towards the Bairro Alto. Lisbon's famous glazed-tile maker, **Sant'Anna,** has a showroom at 95-97 Rua do Alecrim, where you can purchase splendid tiles and other tiled items.

BAIRRO ALTO, THE UPPER TOWN

Children adore the **Ascensor de Santa Justa (Santa Justa Elevator),** an ornate elevator in a tower that connects the Baixa to the remains of the Carmo Church. As you exit the elevator and walk along its pier to the hill, look down onto the colorful tops of cafe table umbrellas and take in the view of the entire city and Alfama. The church was partially destroyed in the earthquake of 1755 and its romantic ruins are now beautifully flood-lit at night. In the summer, free classical concerts take place. The Carmo is home to a number of cats who are cared for by local residents.

The **Praça do Príncipe Real** park has a pond, cafe, and sprawling tree whose gnarly limbs, held up by metal supports, provide a shady resting spot. **Jardim da Estrela** has flowers, ponds, fountains, grottoes, and two **playgrounds,** one for tiny tots and a "frontierland" for big kids. Paths meander through beautiful trees and landscapes to an outdoor cafe overlooking a shady pond where you can stop for lunch, ice cream, or hot and cold drinks. Locals play animated games of cards or chat and watch the world go by at this lovely park.

THE NEW CENTER OR NORTHERN DISTRICT

The northern stretch of Avenida da Liberdade ends at the Praça do Marquês de Pombal, from which the vast **Parque Eduardo VII** extends up a gradual slope. At its upper end is a terrace and greenhouses (the Estufa) with flamingos, ponds, and tropical gardens. Be sure to venture into its tree-lined perimeter, where several playgrounds are scattered. Outdoor fairs are often held in its grassy center. Free. Mon.–Sat. 9–7:30. Farther north is the **Jardim Zoológico (Zoo)** in the lovely gardens of the Parque das Laranjeiras (Park of the Orange Trees). It has a small "Jardim Infantil" with a merry-go-round, other rides, swings, and little houses. Pedal boats can be rented to sail amidst swans and ducks. The animal cages are sadly cramped. If you visit in late spring or early summer, be sure to see the enchanting baby baboons who are still small enough to slip through their cage bars and scramble about, never going too far from home. At the upper edge of the zoo is a funny pet cemetery with tombstones of Chu Chu, Popey, King, and Toy. Many have their portraits painted on tiles. Fee. Daily 9–6.

The **Gulbenkian Foundation**'s museums are surrounded by sculpture gardens. The modern **Museu Calouste Gulbenkian** contains the treasures from the private collection of oil magnate Calouste Gulbenkian. Here, miniature Persian paintings, Greek coins, ancient Egyptian scarabs, illuminated manuscripts, paintings by European masters, and other riches of the East and West add up to one of the best small museums in the world. Groups of schoolchildren come here on field trips dressed in school uniforms and matching hats.

Next door is the **Centro de Arte Moderna** which houses a lively collection of contemporary Portuguese art. Fee. Both open Tues. Thurs., Fri., and Sun. 10–5, Wed. and Sat. 2–7:30. Head outside to the lush **tropical gardens** for a break from viewing.

The **Bullring** and the **Museu Tauromáquico (Bullfighting Museum)** are near the Avenida da República. Remember, Portuguese bullfights are bloodless and more humane than those in Spain as the bulls are wrestled to the ground rather than killed. Praça de Touros do Campo Pequeno, Gate 20. Beyond the bullring lies the **Campo Grande** park with little outdoor cafes and boats.

BELÉM

Vasco da Gama, Ferdinand Magellan (Fernando Magalhães), and Bartholomew Dias (Bartolomeu Dias) started their voyages from Belém on their search for spices, new lands, and knowledge. As spices, gold, and diamonds began to pour back in, Belém prospered. Monuments were built, and two of them, the Tower of Belém and the Jerónimos Monastery, are among the few buildings left standing after the earthquake of 1755. Belém, originally a separate city, now houses many of Lisbon's major museums. Climb the tower of the sturdy yet fanciful 16th-century **Torre de Belém,** a wonderful example of the ornate architectural style called Manueline that characterizes many of Lisbon's buildings. Its narrow twisting steps lead to an expansive vista. Surrounded on three sides by the sea and accessible by a narrow spit of land, the tower was constructed as a monument to Portugal's Age of Discovery and to protect Lisbon from pirates and invaders and was later often used as a watery dungeon to hold political prisoners. Fee. Tues.–Sun. 10–6:30; winter until 5.

The 16th-century **Jerónimos Monastery** was also built as a monument to Portugal's great explorers. It contains the tomb of Vasco da Gama and other important Portuguese historical figures and monarchs. Move through quickly but be sure to see its interior courtyard/ cloister decorated with innumerable small gargoyles perched on the balcony surrounding a colorful formal garden and lion fountain. Fee. Summer 10–6:30; winter until 5. The **Praça do Império** gardens in front of the monastery have an illuminated fountain and formal gardens with flowers planted in the patterns of the coats of arms of all of Portugal's provinces.

Padrão dos Descobrimentos (Monument of the Discoveries), a narrow sweep of modern design, has an observation platform at the top, accessible by elevator. Look out to sea or back at the courtyard patterns.

The **Museu de Marinha** testifies to Portugal's past command of the seas with beautifully crafted and detailed models of fully rigged old sailing ships, 20th-century steamers, and warships. One side of the museum has full-size fishing boats and two royal barges from the 18th century with oarsmen in uniforms. Old maps, sextants, astronomical globes, and odd navigational tools complete the collection. Fee; free on Wed. Tues.–Sun. 10–5. The **Planetário C. Gulbenkian** across the square offers astronomy shows in English, French, and Portuguese.

Baroque coaches out of fairytales are among the carriages featured at the **Museu National dos Coches,** housed in the former Royal Riding School. Some are gilt and lavish; others are plain and functional. Litters, chaises, and pony carts are included in this world-famous collection. Fee. June.–Sept. Tues.–Sun. 10–6:30; rest of year 10–5. For a quick glimpse at the folk art of the country, visit the **Museu de Arte Popular,** with costumes, furniture, farm implements, and handicrafts from the various Portuguese provinces. Fee. Tues.–Sun. 10–12:30, 2–5.

Sports

Soccer is the Portuguese national sport and the season runs from May through September. Games are played at the Estádio da Luz and the Estádio José Alvalade. **Swimming** pools in town include Piscina do Areeior, Av. de Roma or Piscina dos Olivais, but better yet, head to one of the nearby beaches.

Special Events

The **Feast of St. Anthony** is held on June 12 and 13 with fireworks and festivities. The entire Alfama is decorated and singing, eating, and drinking last long into the night. Every little church in the city fills its plaza with food, bands, and dancing.

For the **Feast of St. John,** on June 23 and 24, there are parades with colorful costumes, songs, and bonfires scented with herbs. Part of the feast's tradition includes people leaping over the blazing bonfires.

The **Feast of St. Peter**, on June 29, the final celebration in the trio called the Festas dos Santos Populares, features a procession of boats, food, and dance.

The **Feira Popular** runs from May to September with carnival rides, bumper cars, merry-go-rounds, souvenirs, open-air bandstand performances, and great food in scores of little restaurants. Don't miss it if you visit Lisbon between those months, as it's a typically Portuguese event with lots of local families in attendance. Opposite the Entrecamps metro station toward the edge of town.

For more information on festivals, call the tourist office (Tel. 3463643).

NEAR LISBON

Just south of the city are the beaches of the *Costa da Caparica,* across the river Tagus bridge. Skip the town and take the narrow-gauge railway along the 8 kilometers of dunes; the earlier stops are the more family-oriented beaches but you can get off wherever you wish. Be aware that stop no. 19 is the nudist beach. Most of the beaches have cafes, restaurants, lounge chairs, and accessories. Pirates once used these beaches (*caparica* means "a cover for riches," named for the pirates who were believed to have buried their treasure in the sands), but the only risk in visiting them today is encountering an occasional gusty breeze.

ESTORIL AND CASCAIS

Estoril has long been known as the home of exiled royalty, and villas and luxury hotels are hidden throughout its hills. Stop here to visit the beachfront water slides or gardens that run from the beach to the casino and then head next door to the town of Cascais for the real fun.

Cascais is a lively and energetic resort town, small and pretty, with nearly everything you need in walking distance. We recommend you headquarter here and zip into Lisbon every other day on the 30-minute electric train into the Cais do Sodré station. Trains leave every 15 minutes. Stay in town, which will keep you out of the apartments beginning to creep up around its edges. Book in advance in July and August. The **tourist office** is in the town hall in the main square, Praça de Outubro [Tel. (01) 2868204].

Where to Stay

HOTELS

Estalagem do Farol is an elegant 4-star inn with a pool, tennis courts, disco, kiddie wading pool, parking, and an indoor-outdoor bar. Family suites are available. Rooms vary in size and furnishings. If the hotel is uncrowded, you can choose. Estrada da Boca do Inferno 7. Tel. (01) 280173. **Expensive.**

Residencial Itália, just up from the main square, has much charm with antique furnishings and a flower-filled outdoor cafe that serves lunch. It's quite small (5 rooms), so book in advance. Rua do Poço Novo 1. Tel. (01) 280151. **Moderate/Inexpensive.**

Quinta da Bicuda comes very highly recommended for families. Located just out of town in the countryside, it has small houses and apartments on an old family farm. A pool, horseback riding, outdoor cafe and restaurant make it an excellent choice. It is a quick taxi ride into town. Torre 2750 Cascais. Tel. (01) 2843233. **Inexpensive.**

Casa Pergola is an elegant tile-fronted villa with a colorful garden in the center of town. Av. Valbom 13. Tel. (01) 2840040. **Inexpensive.**

The *Pensão Residencial Palma* next door is also tile-fronted with lovely gardens. It's less expensive and a bit more tired than Casa Pergola. Av. Valbom 15. Tel. (01) 280257. **Inexpensive.**

CAMPGROUNDS

The nearest campsite is in Guincho. Tel. (01) 2850346.

Detour! What to See and Do

The beach is Cascais' main attraction, but be sure to wander along its picturesque mosaic-patterned streets and pedestrian avenues with sidewalk cafes, ice cream and espresso stands, pastry shops, and boutiques. Don't miss the **seaside promenade** between Cascais and Estoril with ice cream vendors and cafes overlooking the ocean. All kinds of water sports are available nearby. Lovely gardens with a playground and tree-lined pathways are in the trendy and up-scale **Parque do Marechal Carmona.** The town's stylish international visitors bring their kids, too, and your children will be playing with those from Scandinavia, Australia, England, and Germany. **Boca do Inferno (Mouth of Hell)** is a cliff in which the sea has hollowed out a number of caves and a wide hole. As the water crashes through, an impressive display of the power of the sea is unleashed. To complete the scene, a cafe and active street vending-scene is alongside. Follow the signs from Cascais. In July and August, the **Estoril Handicrafts Fair** comes to Cascais and Estoril with food, wines, crafts, and regional folklore.

SINTRA

An easy day trip from Lisbon or a delightful place to spend a few days wandering about, Sintra is a mountaintop village surrounded by a lush tangle of vegetation. The 14th-century **Palácio Nacional** was once the summer residence of the Portuguese royal family. Of interest to kids is the Sala das Pegas (Hall of the Magpies), where a flock of magpies was painted on the ceiling to satirize and admonish the gossipy women of the court. Fee. Tues.–Sun. 10–4. Close by (near the tourist office) is a small **Toy Museum** with dolls, tin cars, and complete little cast-metal armies from all periods of history set for battle. Fee. Outside, meander up to the ruins of a Moorish castle, or ascend a steep hill to **Pena Park** to see the domes, towers, and ramparts of

Palácio da Pena. It has been compared to Mad Ludwig of Bavaria's wild castles and its eccentric interior is a delight to tour. Some of it is so overdone, it looks like the set from a Hollywood spectacle. Fee. Tues.–Sun. 10–5. Plan to spend time wandering about the lovely walks and pathways through the woods and swan-filled ponds. The park is especially beautiful in spring, when camellias, azaleas, and rhododendrons bloom. Free. Daily 10–6. Above Pena, ascend to **Cruz Alta,** the highest point of Sintra.

MAFRA

Mafra's enormous **palace** practically bankrupted the country when it was built. Lavish in excess, it boasts 4,500 doors alone. Kids usually like the unsettling room that contains furniture constructed out of antlers and upholstered in animal skins. Lots of trompe l'oeil is evident here; have your children be on the lookout for phony painted doors, windows, curtains, ceilings, and architectural effects. Its two towers with bells from Antwerp play on Sundays.

COSTA DE PRATA: THE NORTHERN COASTLINE TO AVEIRO

The numerous forts and castles found along this stretch of coast were built to protect it from the many Algerian, Dutch, and English pirates who raided the towns or carried the Portuguese away to slave markets in North Africa and the Middle East. Towns kept watch and locked everything up tight. Many beautiful beaches are along this coast, but don't swim if you see a red or yellow flag. They indicate a dangerous undertow.

ÓBIDOS

The walled town of Óbidos, a medieval jewel of a town, has been declared a national monument city and indeed it has been polished to a sheen much smoother than it had in the Middle Ages. Its past is filled with tales of Moorish and Christian conquests and Portuguese kings and queens. Now the haunt of artists and tourists, its narrow streets are lined with flower-bedecked whitewashed houses and little shops. The many-towered **castle** overlooks the town. Climb its ramparts and walk around them for panoramic views of the town, rolling hills, and windmills. Its excellent **Pousada do Castelo** is housed in one corner of the former royal palace [Tel. (062) 95105]. A pottery workshop founded by the city hall allows children to try their hand at clay modeling. Contact the **tourist office** on Rua Direita (before

Praça de Santa Maria) Tel. (062)95231 for details. For souvenirs, look for miniature windmills.

PENICHE AND THE BERLENGA ISLANDS

Popular beaches and a well-preserved castle make *Peniche* an interesting stopover. On a rocky peninsula connected to the mainland by a narrow spit of sand, it has excellent beaches on either side. The northern beach is warmer while the southern beach is safer for swimming. The 16th-century **castle** was built to protect the peninsula and inland towns from attacks by pirates and slave traders and was later a popular spot for a prison. Just east of town is lighthouse-tipped **Cabo Carvoeiro** with breathtaking views of the wild surf crashing into elaborate rock formations hundreds of feet below the road. Climb the **lighthouse** for a magnificent view.

The rugged *Ilhas Berlengas* (Berlengas Islands) are masses of granite rising out of the ocean. Their transparent waters, underwater caves and reefs, and abundant marine life offer spectacular underwater viewing for skin divers. The archipelago's main island, *Berlenga,* now a bird preserve, can be reached by ferry boat from Peniche harbor during the summer months. A lighthouse crowns the highest point of the island, below which is the **São João Batista Fort.** Set on a tiny island, it is connected by a winding stone bridge across the sea. The island's resident monks first built it as a monastery, but in 1655 pirates forced them to turn it into a fortress. It is now an inn, the only public accommodations on the island. South of the castle is the **Furado Grande,** a natural tunnel leading to a tiny cove. Footpaths run around the island taking you to more caves, tunnels, and rocky coves.

NAZARÉ

A relatively "modern" city by Portuguese standards, Nazaré grew in the late 19th century from fishing and tourism. Take a funicular up to the cobbled streets and worn buildings of Sitio, the original old city. Nazaré is now one of the most popular and crowded resorts on the Atlantic and is to be avoided in July and August. Despite the influx of tourists, its old culture lives and fishing remains an important part of the economy. Be sure to see the brightly painted boats in the new harbor. The currents are so strong here that teams of oxen were once needed to pull the boats out of the water; today, tractors are used. Women still wear full skirts richly decorated with lace and supported by layers of petticoats while the men of Nazaré wear bright plaid pants, clashing patterned shirts, and floppy black stocking hats.

Fans of model boats should head to the **Museu Dr. Joaquim Manso** with miniature fishing boats and fishing artifacts. Exhibitions of **folk**

dancing take place throughout the town. Check with the **tourist office** at Rua de Mouzinho de Albuquerque 72 for details. Handicrafts from the region include dolls and miniature boats.

ALCOBAÇA

Set between the Alcoa and Baça rivers, Alcobaça is the heart of the largest area of orchards and vineyards in Portugal. Its most famous site is the **Real Abadia de Santa Maria de Alcobaça,** at one time one of the richest and most important religious houses in Portugal. There is much to see, but children should head for its kitchen with ovens where six oxen could be roasted at once. Monks washed their dishes and fished for trout and eels in a diverted underground stream running through it. The home cooking was so good and the monks were so plump that a special "weigh-in" door was constructed; those who failed to squeeze through had to fast until they could make it.

BATALHA

Between Lisbon and Coimbra is the famous **Batalha Abbey,** where Henry the Navigator is entombed. About 20 kilometers away, near the village of *Mira de Aire,* are some spectacular stalactite- and stalagmite-columned caves. Walk down the countless steps of the **Grutas dos Moinhos Velhos** to see their elaborate formations, fountains, lighting, and underground lake. Many formations have evocative names like Church Organ, Hell's Door, the Jellyfish, and the Chinese Hat. Rest assured, you can take the elevator back up. A bit farther away, near Alvados and San Antonio, the **Grutas de Alvados** have several small lakes in its many caverns; the Lake of Pearls is a favorite. **Grutas de Santo António** contain rows of weirdly shaped stalactites. Conducted tours. Fee. All open daily Oct.–Mar. 9–6; Apr.–June 9–7; July–Sept. 9–8.

FÁTIMA

The pilgrimage town of Fátima was made famous by three shepherd children, ages 10, 9, and 7, who sighted the Virgin Mary on six different occasions in 1917. It now attracts scores of pilgrims who journey to its little chapel, built on the spot where the Virgin appeared. On special pilgrimage days in May and October, the months of the first and last sighting, thousands travel on foot, bicycle, donkey cart, in cars, or even part way on their knees to the holy city, now a sprawling, modern religious complex. Be sure to find the original sanctuary built to honor the Virgin, set in a leafy park. Seeing the candle and torch-lit procession of the faithful on the holy days is beautiful, but keep in mind that accommodations are booked for miles around and the city is shoulder-to-shoulder with the faithful, many of whom camp out in the square. Accommodations are easy to find the rest of the year, and a wide variety of kitschy souvenirs will tempt your kids from every corner and shopfront. The small **Museu de Cera de Fátima (Wax Museum)** contains a tableau with the story of what put the town on the map. Fee. Rua Jacinta Marto. Daily Apr.–Oct. 9–8; Nov.–Mar. 9–5. Six kilometers away are the **Grutas da Moeda** at **São Mamede,** extensive caves with twisting stalactities and stalagmites that have been eerily illuminated. Fee. Daily 9 to 9.

COIMBRA

Halfway between Lisbon and Opôrto is Coimbra, a combination of narrow medieval streets and modern buildings. The city is crowned by the slender clock tower of its famous university. Founded in Lisbon in 1290, the university moved to Coimbra in 1634. The students wear black robes decorated with ribbons whose colors signify their fields of study. Beautiful parks and gardens are scattered throughout the town, such as the luxuriant **Santa Cruz Park,** commonly known as **Sereia Park (Mermaid Park)** because of its beautiful mermaid fountain. The 18th-century **Jardim Botânico** is a series of terraces with leafy avenues and imposing wrought-iron work, sculpture, and fountains. Next to it is the **Aqueduto S. Sebastião,** constructed to take water to Upper Coimbra.

There are many important historical sites, churches, and monuments in this fascinating town, but children will want to head right to **Portugal dos Pequeninos,** a miniature village with reproductions of major buildings, farmhouses, and the most famous monuments from all over Portugal and its former colonies. Kids can climb in and out of the miniature houses, Indian temple, palaces, and windmills. Small fee. Near the Santa Clara-a-Velha Convent, across the river from the main town. Daily Apr.–Sept. 9–7; rest of year 9–5:30. The city's campground, located in the municipal sports complex, has a swimming pool and tennis courts. Tel. (039) 72997.

FIGUEIRA DA FOZ

A popular seaside resort and important fishing center, Figueira da Foz's main attraction is its broad golden-sand beach, three-quarters of a mile wide in some places. A train once transported sunbathers to the water. Travelers with toddlers will wish it still did. A semipermanent rainbow can be found in the mists along the shore when the sun is close to the horizon in the afternoon. Stop here or head to *Buarcos* and try any of its beaches. The seafront promenade, large public pool, and campground with an olympic-size pool and tennis courts make it a popular family resort. The town hosts an international children's singing group competition in July, the **Gala Internacional dos Pequenos Cantores**. Contact the **tourist office** for details at Av. 25 de Abril [Tel. (033) 22610].

AVEIRO

Aveiro, called the Venice of Portugal, sits on a saltwater lagoon and is crosscrossed by canals covered by arched bridges. Look for the exquisite tiles on its houses facing the canals. Great salt flats are found along the shores of the lagoon with bridges on stilts crossing over it. Take a cruise on the lagoon to see the local fishermen in their distinctive boats, the *barcos moliceiros*, known for the pictures painted on their high prows and sterns. The boats are propelled by long poles or wails. Fishing for seaweed used for fertilizer continues to be an important industry. During the **Festa da Ria** in summer, the molicieiros sail in a regatta that features folk-dance festivals, boat races, handicraft stalls, and a competition for the boat with the best painting. Look for the miniature painted fishing boats for souvenirs. Contact the **tourist office** at Praça da República [Tel. (082) 23680] for details. There is a nature reserve in the **São Jacinto dunes** in front of the city. Behind the lagoon are hills filled with pine woods and the region's many lakes and rivers.

COSTA VERDE: FROM OPÔRTO TO THE SPANISH BORDER

The Costa Verde (Green Coast), the stretch of northern Portugal between Opôrto and the northern border with Spain, is a holiday center for the Portuguese due to its great scenic beauty, soft beaches, sand dunes, and rolling green hills. Much less visited than other parts of Portugal, its coastline and waters are not as warm or developed as those of the Algarve, and visitors are sparse until July. Inland, the green countryside is not widely explored by tourists. It is an area rich in folklore, with some of Portugal's finest crafts and most colorful traditional festivals.

OPÔRTO (PÔRTO) AND ENVIRONS

Portugal's second largest town, beautiful *Opôrto,* is situated on a rocky gorge cut by the Douro River. As early as Hellenistic times, there was a trading post here, with subsequent settlements of Romans, Visigoths, Moors, and Christians. Its large port is the outlet for most of the country's northern trade and consequently it's a busy industrial city as well as an historic town. Avoid driving here as traffic is terrible and the city's layout is confusing. The old town has many beautiful palaces, homes, churches, and buildings as it was a rich trade center for hundreds of years. If you walk it, you will encounter steep climbs; hire a taxi if your children tire easily. Be sure to explore the esplanade along the river. Opôrto's **tourist office** is at 25 Rua Clube Fenianos [Tel. (02) 312740].

For an overview of the city and surrounding countryside, climb the 240 steps of the baroque **Torre dos Clérigos,** once the tallest tower in Portugal. Small fee. 10:30–12, 3–5. Closed Wed., but hours can vary. The town's **Ethnological Museum** contains exhibits on the life and customs of the region, with farming implements, ancient toys, fishing equipment, ceramics, Roman coins, ship models, cannon balls, old spinning wheels, looms, and even a collection of 19th-century child-birth chairs. Free. In Largo São João Novo, in the Miragaia area. Tues.–Sat. 10–12, 2–5. The lovely park **Jardim do Palácio** plays host to a sprawling amusement park during summer months. During the **Festas de São Bartolomeu** in August, there is an odd parade for which people dress in paper costumes that satirize public figures. Led by "Neptune of the Sea" it culminates in a mock battle between the pirates and townspeople that ends when everybody jumps in the ocean.

Five kilometers from Opôrto is the suburb/beach resort of *São João da Foz,* whose palm-lined beach is called the **Douro Litoral.** Another popular beach is *Matosinhos.* South of Opôrto, at the chic resort of *Espinho,* you'll see oxen that are used to help pull in the fishing nets laden with fish. You can find charming carved miniatures of boats in the Monday market. Nearby, in *Penafiel,* the **Festival of Corpus Christi** in June brings fireworks, sword dances, mock battles between the Moors and Christians, and people dressed in traditional costumes.

AMARANTE

Inland on the Tâmega River is Amarante, which has a well-preserved old town with verandas hanging over the river and narrow cobblestone streets. You can rent boats if you wish to explore the river. The **Church of São Gonçala** has always been known as a healing center, and here in a side chapel you will find offerings from people whose maladies were cured by a prayer or votive offerings: wooden legs, jars filled with kidney stones, wax models of other body parts. From June to the end of October, there is a fiesta called the **Arrais de São Gonçalo** in the gardens of the **Casa da Calçada** on Thursday through Saturday evenings from 7 PM to 1 AM. Be sure to visit and sample the grilled chicken, sardines, or *caldo verde* (green cabbage soup) and enjoy fireworks, a parade of giants, and singing and folk dancing to local bands. Contact Hotel Navarras for details [Tel. (055) 424036]. **Festa e Romaria de São Gonçalo** takes place in early June with fireworks, a big fair with crafts, and much singing, dancing, and eating. Another large festival, the **Festa da Nossa Senhora dos Remédios,** takes place in **Lamego** from late August through mid-September with folk dancing, fireworks, parades with floats pulled by oxen, battles of flowers, sporting events, and exhibitions.

GUIMARÃES AND ENVIRONS

Known as the "Cradle of the Nation," *Guimarães* was Portugal's first capital and the birthplace of its first king, Afonso Henriques, in 1110. A well-preserved old town and a 10th-century castle are some of its attractions. Avoid its sprawling industrial perimeter and head for the old city. Walk the battlements of the **castle** and climb its eight towers for grand views from its ramparts. Free. Open 9 to 9. Wonderful handmade toys made from old cans are on sale opposite the castle. The **Festas Gualterianas,** in early August, have carnival rides, folk bands, dancing, and a medieval procession.

Six kilometers from the city is the town of *Caldas de Vizela,* used as a spa since Roman times with sulphurous hot springs. The lovely park along the river banks, where you can swim and hire rowboats, hosts a **Spa Week** at the end of August, with folk events, competitions, and contests. For an enchanting excursion, try **Penha Mountain,** with rocks and boulders given names such as the Shaking Rock, Bell Rock, Boat Rock, and Suspended Rock. There are caves, playgrounds, inns, restaurants, campgrounds, and wonderful picnic sites.

BRAGA

Braga, nicknamed "Portuguese Rome," has many fountains, churches (over 300), palaces, and gardens. Its **Cathedral Museum** houses an eclectic collection of chests whose secret compartments hid the church's treasures, centuries-old platform shoes, gold and silver objects, old keys, music boxes, a 17th-century organ, and much more. During the **Semana Santa (Holy Week Festival),** the streets are covered with flowers and lights, and many processions pass through. The **Festas de São João** at the end of June bring parades, religious processions, bands, singing, dancing, and bonfires. Contact Braga's **tourist office** at Av. Central 1 [Tel. (053) 22550].

The hilltop pilgrimage **Church of Bom Jesús do Monte,** 6 kilometers east of Braga, is famous for its long baroque staircase with hundreds of steps, zigzagging to the top. If your crew is feeling a bit tired, take the elevator to the top and climb down the steps, but keep in mind that many a devout pilgrim has climbed up on his or her knees. The top level's Stairway of the Five Senses has a sculptured fountain dedicated to each sense. Got a Kleenex? A man's nose runs a constant stream while another spits a jet of water. The Church draws thousands of pilgrims at Whitsun. Reach it by funicular from Braga, on foot, or by car. Three hotels are at the top, and if you continue up the mountain through grottoes, paths, and fountains, there is a lake with boats for hire and other sports facilities.

BARCELOS

Just west of Braga is Barcelos, home to fine handicrafts, one of the best weekly markets in Portugal, and the Barcelos cockerel (rooster), the tourist symbol of Portugal. Your children may have already purchased a hand-painted ceramic one to take home. Legend has it that a pilgrim traveling to Spain's Santiago de Compostela was wrongly accused of theft and condemned to hang. He claimed that the rooster dinner sitting on the judge's plate would leap up and crow to prove his innocence. Sure enough, just as the noose was tightened, the rooster crowed and the man was saved and acquitted.

The **Thursday market** in the enormous town square, Campo da República, offers everything from home-grown produce and oxen yokes to local pottery, eyelet lace, wooden toys, basketry, ceramic dolls, and brightly painted ceramic cockerels. When you tire of its hustle and bustle, head to the nearby flower-filled park, **Jardim das Barrocas.** The annual festival **Romaria das Cruzes,** held May 3, has a fun fair, parades, processions with giants, brass bands, and fireworks.

VIANA DO CASTELO

The former Greek trading post Viana do Castelo is now a popular resort with some of the north's best beaches. Its 14th-century **castle** above the town was built to defend it from pirates. Head for the old town center and avoid the overbuilt outskirts. **Praça da República** is a beautiful fountain-laden square at its center. Its Friday market is smaller than the one in Barcelos but worth a stop. There are playgrounds in **Jardim Marginal,** near the river and **Praça General Barbosa.** For the best view of the town, climb aboard a funicular (catch it behind the train station) to the top of **Monte de Santa Luzia.** Across the river is **Praia do Cabedelo** beach, the first of a series of excellent beaches.

Late August's pilgrimage of **Nossa Senhora da Agonia (Our Lady of Agony),** a 5-day affair, is internationally famous for its fireworks, regional costumes, handicrafts, and parades with giant heads, floats,

and pipe bands. Early August's **Festas de Santa Cristina** features a
fun fair with rides, music, dancing, and a parade with floats and
women in traditional dress. The **Santoinho** is a huge party held in
pavilions in Darque, across the river from Viana. One entrance fee
covers all you can eat and drink plus constant entertainment and
dancing. Old and young dance and enjoy themselves far into the
night. (Thurs. and Sat. in June, July, and Sept.; Sat. in May and Oct.;
Tues., Thurs. Sat. in Aug.) For information on festivals, contact the
tourist office at Praça da Erva [Tel. (058) 22620].

The **Peneda-Gerês Park,** the largest national park in Portugal, is
within easy reach. Consider staying close by in one of Portugal's
loveliest pousadas, **Pousada de São Bento,** situated between Cal-
deirinhas and Pontes do Rio Caldo. Its pool and surrounding countryside make it popular with families. Tel. (058) 57190.

COSTA AZUL

The Costa Azul (Blue Coast), stretching from Lisbon to the Algarve,
still has quaint fishing villages that have not been transformed into
tourist meccas. Take your time exploring and you will find unspoiled
beaches and little hamlets nestled along the sea.

The old town-center in the beach resort of *Sesimbra* still retains its
small-town atmosphere. Walk along the ruined battlements of the
Moorish castle perched above the town, have a look at the fleet of
colorful fishing boats moored in its harbor, or watch the frantic fish
auction when the fishing fleet returns to port.

Porto Covo, a small fishing village with stark white houses
trimmed in brilliant blue or red, has warm beaches along the foot of
jutting cliffs. Its two castles, one on shore and one on the island of
Pessegueiro, were built to protect the town from Algerian and Moroc-
can pirates. Scheduled excursions to the island fortification leave
from Sines, but it's common practice to negotiate with a fisherman to
take you over.

Continuing south, you'll come to pretty *Vila Nova de Milfontes,*
now a popular beach resort for Portuguese families and a good place
to base yourself while you explore the rest of the coast. Its castle,
originally built to protect the town from vicious Algerian pirates, is
now a hotel.

THE ALGARVE: FROM EAST TO WEST

Not too long ago, undiscovered beaches and coves dotted this warm
sparkling coastline. Now a favorite haunt of the English, Germans,
and Scandinavians, the Algarve is slowly being transformed into a
coastline of villa complexes and high-rise apartments. Children will

still enjoy a vacation here as there are beaches with warm waters, water parks galore, miniature golf, water sports, and every possible resort activity. Its sunny coastline, bordered by cliffs and long beaches, or its interior of gentle hills, dotted with little villages of stark white houses, makes it a popular stop to rest before heading off to Lisbon or other big cities.

THE EAST

Once the home of Prince Henry the Navigator's School of Navigation, *Sagres* was at one time inhabited by the finest astronomers, geographers, mapmakers, navigators, and shipbuilders in the land. Prominent explorers such as Magellan and Vasco da Gama studied here and launched their ships at its nearby beaches. After Henry died in 1460, the school was moved back to Lisbon but much of his archives were left, only to be destroyed by Sir Francis Drake and the earthquake and tidal waves of 1755. The ruins of his school, the **fortaleza,** are found on the windswept promontory projecting out into the sea. Within the walls is the large stone mariner's compass believed to have been used by the navigation school's students. The tourist office, now housed within it, offers personalized certificates to those who explore the fortress. Wind surfing is popular along this breezy coast, but beware of strong currents when you swim in its brisk waters. Beaches here can be much less crowded than in other parts of the Algarve. Those who sailed past **Cabo de São Vicente (Cape St. Vincent),** the southwesternmost point of continental Europe, were warned they would fall over the edge of the world into nothingness.

The ancient port town and old fishing village of *Lagos* was the capital of the Algarve from the 16th to the 18th centuries. Many ships built by Henry the Navigator's shipyards were launched from its port to explore distant points of the globe. Today its attractions are lovely sand beaches tucked into little coves sheltered by cliffs. In the oddball **Museu Regional de Lagos** there is a collection of cork carvings, costumes, coins, embroideries, replicas of distinctive Algarve chimney pots, and Roman mosaics. Fee. Tues.-Sun. 9:30-12:30, 2-5. Tel. (082) 62301. **Praia do Pinhão** and **Praia Dona Ana** are two of the most pleasant beaches near here. A boat leaves from Dona Ana on an informal grotto-viewing tour.

Silves is an inland city set back in the hills with peeling plaster and weathered doors that give it Old World charm. At one time a center of Moorish culture, it was filled with elegant palaces, gardens, and fountains. What the crusaders and other invaders didn't ruin was leveled in the series of earthquakes between the 14th and 18th centuries. It's fun to walk the partially restored castle's walls with their many lookout towers. During the summer the castle is illuminated at night. Stop for a bite to eat at one of Silves' small restaurants specializing in grilled sardines and chicken.

Portimão is a center for sardine canning and a big busy seaport with a famous beach, **Praia da Rocha,** nearby. Long popular with the British and other foreigners because of its cliff-backed golden-sand beaches, it has a picturesque seafront promenade with restaurants and viewpoints atop the cliffs. West of Portimão, on the main highway (N125), are two water parks: **The Big One** and **Slide and Splash.** Both have twisty water slides, swimming pools, wave pools, children's playgrounds, and water rides.

THE CENTRAL ALGARVE

Albufeira has struggled to retain its Moorish character and charm, and is a good and lively place to stay for kid-pleasing resort actitivies with an international twist. A short promenade and a tunneled-rock passageway to the beach, plus colorful fishing boats and an open-air market make it a delight. Its old town has narrow winding streets lined with sidewalk cafes and little shops that end at the Praça da República square. It can be very crowded in July and August. The edges of the old town are filled with new hotels, so stay in the center.

Avoid *Quarteira,* the blight of the Algarve, with concrete highrises parked side by side along the beach. Much of the central Algarve is filled with **"villa resorts,"** which are medium- and large-scale "planned communities" with villas, hotels, restaurants, stores, and recreational opportunities such as riding, bicycling, fishing, and miniature golf in one complex. They can provide a relaxing break from the bustle of travel. Except for the stark white architecture and distinctive Algarve chimney pots that look like little wedding cakes, these comfortable and well-done resorts could be anywhere—the Caribbean, Hawaii, Mexico, or Florida. Unwind in a villa here and then move on to a destination with a more Portuguese flair. Vale do Lobo and Quinta do Lago are two of the biggest, but others flourish nearby. We booked a smaller resort, Dunas Douradas, through Hideaways International and enjoyed our time swimming and sunbathing.

THE EASTERN ALGARVE

Faro's international airport paved the way for the overdevelopment of the Algarve, as it made this sun-drenched coastline a short flight away for northern Europeans needing a quick warm-up. Enter the town's old quarter, still partially walled, through large arched doorways. The **Ilha de Faro** is a long spit of land with the river on one side and the ocean on the other. Its white-sand beach has water sports, deck chair and umbrella rentals, and restaurants. When you need a break from the simple pleasures of the beach, explore the eerie **Capela dos Ossos (Chapel of Bones)** in the Igreja do Carmo. The chapel is completely paneled in the human bones and skulls of monks. The Latin plaque above the doorway reads: "Stop here and think of this fate that will befall you." The chapel is fascinating but not for those prone to nightmares. Daily 10–1, 3–5. The **Maritime Museum** has models of wooden boats, maps, and old fishing gear. Free. In the Departamento Marítimo do Sul (Harbor Master's Office). Mon.–Fri. 9:30–12:30 and 2–5:30, Sat. 9–1.

Olhão is the Algarve's largest fishing port whose once famous charms have sadly faded. The "amazing poodle of the Algarve" hails from here. This noble breed is web-footed, muscular, and hairy, and loves to swim so much that for centuries it helped guide fish into the nets and saved fishermen and sailors from drowning. Catch one of Olhão's ferries for far more lovely beaches on the island of *Armona.* Ferries leave from the jetty at the end of the municipal gardens. Only 15 minutes away, it has idyllic sandy beaches. *Tavira* is a picturesque medium-size fishing town and less developed as a beach resort. Its beaches are just out of town, hidden beyond a sand spit called the Ilha de Tavira. Come here for the day to explore a more typical Algarve fishing town.

THE INLAND PLAINS

From Lisbon to the Spanish border and from Tomar in the heart of Portugal to the Algarve, the expansive plains are some of the poorest areas in the country. Two regions make up this area—the Alentejo and the Ribatejo. Portugal is the largest exporter of cork in the world, and 90 percent of it comes from this region. Marble deposits have been excavated here since Roman times.

ÉVORA

This popular medieval university town, with its Roman and Moorish past, retains its provincial atmosphere with a tangle of narrow streets surrounded by gently rolling plains covered in olive and cork trees. Most of Évora's important monuments are clustered together above its old town. Believed to be one of the oldest trading posts on the Iberian peninsula, the city remained important as a political, cultural, and artistic center for centuries. Pick up the English version of the city map from the **tourist office** at the main square, Praça do Giraldo 73 [Tel. (066) 22671], as the city has a very confusing layout. To beat the heat, head for the **swimming pools** (open May–Sept.) and playground just outside of town. The tourist office will give you directions.

The 12th-century **Sé (cathedral)** contains a solid-gold chalice weighing about 8 pounds and a small crucifix with 850 diamonds, 400 rubies, 180 emeralds, and 2 huge sapphires. A statue of the Virgin Mary opens up at her tummy and shows off a triptych illustrating her life. Climb the dark spiral staircase to the top of the cathedral for a view of the town. Small fee. Tues.–Sun. 9–12, 2–5. The town's most important monument, the 4th-century **Roman Temple of Diana**, was used as a fortress in the Middle Ages and later as a slaughterhouse. Opposite the temple is one of the most beautiful of Portugal's government pousadas, **Pousada dos Lóios,** housed in the former 15th-century Convento do Lóios. It has rooms in the old monks' cells and a swimming pool. Even if you don't spend a night, wander through its cloisters or stop for a meal of regional specialties. Tel. (066) 24051. The **Capela dos Ossos (Chapel of the Bones)** in the **Church of São Francisco** is elaborately and gruesomely decorated with bones and skulls. Some claim they are the remains of 5,000 monks arranged neatly on the walls and pediments of the chapel. Others say they are the bones of plague victims and casualties of early wars. Above its main door is a Latin inscription that translates: "We bones that are here wait for yours." Very small fee. Daily 9–1, 2:30–6.

Head down the street to the town's lovely **Jardim Publico** garden to stroll through flowers and neatly trimmed hedges, past fountains and pools, before soaking up more of the city's past. The **Museu Artesanato Regional** has a collection of folk art, including a castle carved out of cork, wood carvings, costumes, colorfully painted clay figurines, pottery, weavings, and tapestries. Free. Praga Primero de Maio. Daily 10–12, 2–5. Purchase hand-crafted souvenirs in its small shop or head to the busy city market, which takes place Tuesday through Saturday mornings, to seek out handmade treasures. The **Feira de São João,** the largest fair in southern Portugal, has carnival rides, regional culinary specialties, folk dancing, bullfighting, fireworks, and booths selling the region's handicrafts. Last ten days of June.

ELVAS

The lovely frontier town of Elvas has some of the best-preserved fortifications anywhere in Europe. Known at one time as Queen of the Frontier, Elvas was once the strongest fortress-town in the country. As you enter the city, be sure to notice the **Aqueduto da Amoreira,** the five-tiered aqueduct that is Europe's largest and certainly one of its most beautiful. Plan to spend your time exploring its old town. The town's emblem, a warrior on horseback carrying a standard, is said to be João Pais Gago, who taunted the Spanish and bravely carried the standard back to Portugal. Local residents were afraid to let him in the city gates as he was pursued by a Spanish mob. Once caught he was fried in oil, but as he died he was heard to say, "The man dies but his fame lives on."

Be sure to climb the ramparts of the town's **Moorish castle** for a view of the town and surrounding countryside. May–Sept. Fri.–Wed. 9:30–12:30, 2:30–7; rest of year until 5:30. The thick walled **Forte da Graça** is 1 kilometer from town. Across town, the star-shaped **Forte de Santa Lucia** also protected the town with a vengeance. You can walk through the town's narrow cobblestone streets lined with canary cages and colorful flower boxes as you wander from one fortification to the next. Make a vision come true and stop along the way to sample the town's sweet specialty, candied sugar plums.

TOMAR AND ENVIRONS

In the center of Portugal, along the banks of the river Nabão, overlooked by a 12th-century castle, is Tomar. This beautiful city, a hodgepodge of rich architectural styles, contains many famous and striking churches, convents, and outdoor restaurants and cafes. Headquarter here as there are interesting hotels, an excellent campground, municipal swimming pool, and water sports along the river and nearby lake. Tomar's **tourist office** is on Avenida Dr. Cândido Madureira [Tel. (049) 313237].

The **castle** was built in 1160 on the site of previous Roman and Visigoth fortifications. Along with the magnificent **Convento de Cristo (Monastery of Christ),** it forms a complex which is set in gardens at the top of the hill, a 15-minute walk from town. Look carefully at the famous Chapter Windows, which are crammed with carvings of every sea motif imaginable: seaweed, anchors, nets, shells, lots of rope, and even the Old Man of the Sea. **Mouchão Park,** once a sandbank that was transformed into an elegant park in the 19th century, is now totally surrounded by the waters of the Nabão. A section of this glorious park has been set aside for picnicking. Children will enjoy seeing the large **wooden waterwheel** on the river which gathered water to carry to agricultural lands near the town. You can see many other waterwheels in the river in and near Tomar. Also in the park is the **Inn of Santa Iria,** a good place to stay the night. Tel. (049) 312427. Tomar's comfortable **campground** is near the stadium and the riverbank, with its shade trees, flowerbeds, a swimming pool, children's playground, restaurant, and water sports. Tel. (049) 313750.

The **Feira Nacional de Artesanato** takes place in June or July each year and features handicrafts from all over Portugal, dancing, and theater. The **Festas dos Tabuleiros (Feast of Trays)** is a famous festival that features a procession of young women dressed in white who are offering *tabuleiros* of bread. The tabuleiros are towers of thirty loaves of bread, stacked in columns of five or six, and topped with a white crown. The bread tower must be as high as the person carrying it and lavishly decorated with flowers, leaves, and blades of wheat. The bread is later distributed to the poor. The festival takes place every 2 or 3 years for 4 days in July; check with the tourist office for dates.

Thirteen kilometers from Tomar is **Lake Castelo do Bode,** a reservoir with swimming and water sports. Take a boat trip up the river from *Castelo do Bode* on the two-story Cristovão riverboat, complete with a restaurant. The government-run **Pousada de S. Pedro,** on the river bank overlooking the Castelo do Bode Dam, offers stunning views of the dam from its terrace, water sports, and a swimming beach. Moderate. Tel. (049) 381259/381175. Another good campground is in Castelo do Bode along the lake. Sprinkled here and there along the lake/dam are facilities for canoeing, water-skiing, rowing, fishing, sailing, and wind surfing. If you want to get away from it all, stay on the nearby tiny island **Ilha do Lombo** in Estalagem da Ilha do Lombo with a pool, boating, and fishing. Tel. (049) 371128/321106.

SANTARÉM

Historic *Santarém* sits high over the river Tagus on a rocky hilltop in the heart of grazing land used to raise the best fighting bulls and horses. The town's landmark, **Torre das Cabeças (Tower of the Gourds),** has an unusual clock with bells surrounded by sound boxes to increase its resonance. Its refreshing park and lookout point, **Portas do Sol,** is filled with flowers, tile fountains, shady walkways, and ponds with swans and statues. Planted on the grounds of the old castle, it offers an excellent view of the old town walls. Be sure to find the clock created from trimmed bushes which tells the day, month, and year. Santarém is famous for its festivals, the most important of which is the 2-week-long **Feira Nacional da Agricultura,** or **Ribatejo Fair,** with displays of agriculture and livestock, horse shows, eating, dancing, and bullfighting in late May and early June. Stuff yourselves silly at the **National Festival and Seminar of Gastronomy** in late October and early November. Each region of Portugal prepares a typical feast complete with local entertainment. The **tourist office** is on Rua Capelo Ivens, 63 [Tel. (043) 23140].

MADEIRA (ILHA DA MADEIRA)

Madeira, the lush, green main island of the small volcanic archipelago of the same name is endowed with a mild, subtropical climate and scenic beauty. Situated 535 miles southwest of Lisbon, it is actually closer to the coast of North Africa than Portugal. Madeira is an island of flowers, towering green peaks, sheer cliffs, terraces of farmland, vineyards, and a rocky coastline. Its architectural wealth and cultural heritage are due in part to the prosperity created by its sugar business and vineyards.

FUNCHAL

Its capital, Funchal, has recently had its old town restored. The **tourist office** is on Avenida de Arriaga, 18 [Tel. (091) 25658]. This main street has mosaic sidewalks and Jacaranda trees that bloom in spring. At one end, a stairway leads to the colorful park, **Parque Santa Catarina.** Avenida do Mar, the broad waterfront boulevard, is fun to stroll along. The **City Museum and Aquarium** houses land and aquatic animal life of the archipelago, including moray eels, loggerhead turtles, puffers, scorpion fish, and many bird species. Fee; free for children under 12. On the corner of Rua da Mouraria and Calçada de Santa Clara. Tues.–Fri. 10–8, Sat. and Sun. 12–6. Madeira may not have beaches but it does have plenty of swimming pools. The public **Complexo Balnear do Lido** has an olympic-size pool and a special plunge for children. The complex has sunbeds and umbrellas for rent, plus an ice cream parlor and cafe. Water sports such as wind surfing and water-skiing can be arranged from here if not from your hotel. Fees. Off Rua do Gorgulho. Summers 8–7; off-season 9–6.

Carnival in Funchal is celebrated with merrymakers in funny and fancy dress parading through the colorfully decorated main streets of the city. Funchal is beautifully illuminated for **Christmas** from mid-December through the start of the New Year. At midnight on **New Year's Eve,** all of the church bells in the city ring, and the sky is ablaze with fireworks.

NEAR FUNCHAL

Don't pass up a chance to travel to the top of *Monte,* about 4 miles from Funchal. Take a taxi or bus to the top, enjoy the views, and then ride down in a *carros de cesta,* a toboggan with a wicker frame and wooden runners. It depends on gravity for its locomotion and is controlled by ropes held by two men who run alongside. These were the main means of transportation in Monte from 1849 to 1942. The 2-

mile ride takes about 10 minutes. For a longer ride, start higher up at Terreiro da Luta. For an exceptional view down sheer cliffs, head up **Cabo Girão,** the second highest cliff in the world. You'll peer 2,000 feet down into the crashing surf below.

Spain

Spain is a land of contrasts. From the hot plains of Andalucía to the lush green countryside of Galicia, the north and south are about as different as their inhabitants. Spain's official language is Spanish, but there are three other regional languages as well: Euskera, spoken by the Basques; Gallego, spoken by those in Galicia; and Catalán, spoken by those in Barcelona and the surrounding region of Catalunya.

Barcelona is the jewel of Spain, sophisticated, colorful, high-spirited, and filled with unusual parks and wildly unconventional architecture designed by the eccentric and imaginative Antonio Gaudí. Sides of his buildings billow and swell, swirling wrought-iron balconies and doors almost jump out and grab you, and dazzling mosaic-tile patterns curve about rooftops and benches. This is the type of "fun-house" architecture that children can appreciate, but Barcelona has much more than just architecture to offer.

Granada has the Alhambra, a Moorish pleasure palace from the 13th century surrounded by colorful gardens filled with flowers, ponds, water courses, and fountains. It's a perfect blend of culture and the outdoors. Spend a day or two admiring it, and then move to the beach before exploring the ruined castles and whitewashed towns in hot, proud, Arab-influenced Andalucía.

To beat the heat of summer, head northwest to the Celtic-influenced region of Galicia, or for more cultural pursuits, to dramatic Madrid, whose abundance of artistic and historical treasures has always captivated visitors. A fascinating and varied culture awaits you.

Have a great trip. . . . ¡Feliz viaje!

411

Preparing Your Kids: Books and Art

Younger children: *The Story of Ferdinand the Bull* by Munro Leaf, *The Lieutenant Colonel and the Gypsy* by Frederico García Lorca, *For Pipita, An Orange Tree* by Claire Oleson, *The Riddle* by Adele Vernon.

Older children: *Don Quixote* by Miguel de Cervantes, *The Spanish Smile* by Scott O'Dell.

Art: Among the most famous Spanish artists whose works you will encounter are Dalí, Goya, El Greco, Miró, Murillo, Picasso, and Velásquez. Your library should have books with photographs of their works.

Wha'd'ya Wanna Do?

Most Spanish towns have a local tourist office, called the **Oficina de Turismo.** The Spanish National Tourist Office has a wide variety of brochures and publications to help you plan your trip.

SPANISH NATIONAL TOURIST OFFICES

   U.S.A.–Chicago: Spanish National Tourist Office, 845 N. Michigan Ave., Chicago, IL 60611. Tel. 312-642-1992.

   U.S.A.–Los Angeles: Spanish National Tourist Office, San Vicente Plaza Bldg., 8383 Wilshire Blvd., Suite 960, Los Angeles, CA 90211. Tel. 213-658-7188.

   U.S.A.–Miami: Spanish National Tourist Office, 1221 Brickell Ave., Suite 1850, Miami, FL 33131. Tel. 305-358-1992.

   U.S.A.–New York: Spanish National Tourist Office, 665 Fifth Ave., New York, NY 10022. Tel. 212-759-8822.

   Canada–Toronto: Spanish National Tourist Office, 102 Bloor St., West, 14th floor, Toronto, Ontario M4W 3B8, Canada. Tel. 416-961-3131.

Bullfights are an important tradition in Spain. They take place on Sunday afternoons March through mid-October in most major cities and in many towns during local fairs and festivals. The bloody spectacle, which culminates in the killing of the bull, can be upsetting to children and those adults who have not grown up understanding the history and symbolism of the bullfight.

As Easter approaches, much of Spain celebrates with the colorful **Semana Santa (Holy Week).** It is an elaborate affair, with candlelight processions winding through many of the cities' old quarters, bonfires, folk parades, and exhibitions of devotion. Each region's religious and artistic observance is different, but in many processions, ornate litters or floats, called *paseos*, holding images of Christ or Mary and decorated with flowers, candles, jewels, and banners are carried through the streets to the church. Seville's paseos are famous throughout Spain. The festivities combine solemn observances and riotous traditions and are worth attending. Contact the national tourist office for schedules.

Spain's fabulous, sun-soaked beaches on its **Mediterranean coast** are enjoyed by hundreds of thousands of foreign vacationers and by Spaniards trying to take a break from the fearsome inland summer heat. Parts of the Mediterranean coast have been exploited by highrise hotel developers. Quaint little fishing villages snuggled up against white sandy beaches have become harder to find. Kids still love the beach, especially since the water here is tropical; they'll most likely enjoy sharing a crowded beach as there will be other vacationing children. Popular beaches usually have pedal boats, ice cream stands, and wind surfing, with miniature golf, water slides, and other fun activities in the beach towns.

Lights Out! Special Spanish Accommodations

Apartments and villas can be rented in resort towns and a few major cities if you plan to stay for a week or more. The following companies can help you:

Interhome Inc., USA, 124 Little Falls Rd., Fairfield, NJ 04006. Tel. 201-882-6864.

International Lodging (Barcelona, Madrid, Costa del Sol, Costa Brava, Mallorca), 89-27 182 St., Hollis, NY 11423. Tel. 718-291-1342.

Overseas Connection (Ibiza, Madrid, Costa Brava to Costa del Sol, Barcelona), 70 West 71st St., Suite C, New York, NY 10023. Tel. 800-542-4007 or 212-769-1170.

Rent A Home International (Madrid, Barcelona, Costa del Sol, Costa Brava), 7200 34th Ave., NW, Seattle, WA 98117. Tel. 206-789-9377.

Rent A Vacation Everywhere (Madrid, Barcelona, Costa del Sol, Costa Brava), 328 Main St., Suite 526, Rochester, NY 14604. Tel. 716-454-6440.

Villas International (Madrid, Barcelona, Alicante, Valencia, Costa del Sol, Costa Brava, Balearic Islands), 71 West 23rd St., New York, NY 10010. Tel. 800-221-2260 or 212-929-7585.

Hotels are rated by one to five stars, depending on price and amenities. We have listed a few hotels in Madrid, Granada, and Barcelona that have special amenities for families such as kitchen facilities, swimming pools, or close proximity to parks. **Apartment hotels** are convenient for families as they combine the convenience and space of an apartment with the services of a hotel (maids, reception, etc.). **Hostales** are rated by one to three stars, which do not correspond to the star rating for hotels, as the hostales are much less expensive and simpler. **Fondas** are less expensive and simpler still.

Paradores are the most interesting and charming accommodations in Spain. Ancient monuments, old palaces, castles, and convents have been converted into three-, four-, and five-star hotels. For a listing with photos and descriptions, request the booklet "Paradores" from the national tourist office. Choose paradores that are remodeled historical sites rather than those in modern buildings. Most have excellent restaurants with traditional Spanish cuisine; some have pools, and the one in León has a day-care center. Even if you are on a budget, they are worth an occasional splurge. Reservations in the U.S. can be made through Marketing Ahead Inc., 433 Fifth Ave., New York, NY 10016 (Tel. 212-686-9213). The paradores in Granada and Toledo must be reserved months in advance.

Spanish **campgrounds** are often resortlike, with supermarkets, beauty parlors, swimming pools, playgrounds, and restaurants. The tourist office publishes *Guia de Campings (Guide to Campgrounds)*, a comprehensive guide to sites throughout the country.

Getting Around

Cars are most convenient, although if your time is limited and you want to see a lot of the country, consider flying or taking a fast train between major destinations and renting a car in each place. Much of Spain is crisscrossed by two-lane highways; four-lane toll freeways are found along the Mediterranean and in the North. Many travelers make the mistake of looking on a map and gauging the distance as we do here, only to find that it takes them almost twice as long to get anywhere. You'll need an International Driver's License, or you can submit your driver's license to the Spanish consulate and have it authorized before you go. The minimum driving age is 18. Gas is expensive and gas stations few and far between in the rural areas, so don't allow yourself to get too low on fuel. Rental cars are easy to spot and are often a target for thieves. Take your belongings out of your car when you stop for the night, especially in big cities. Don't leave anything in view that might tempt thieves, even for a short time.

Spain's extensive national railroad system, known as RENFE, ranges from efficient express **trains** between major cities to those that stop at every little town and village. Fares are inexpensive compared to those in the rest of Europe. The *talgo* speeds between major cities; the *electro* and *ter* stop more often; the *expreso* and *rápido* are slower still; and the *semidirecto* and *correo* stop at each station along the way. In addition to the Eurail Saverpass, those visiting only Spain can purchase a special pass for 8, 15, or 22 days on all of Spain's regular train routes. **Buses** can cost more than trains, but they service more isolated villages as well as most of the train stops.

Nuts and Bolts

Does anyone care what time it is? Business and shop hours are 9 AM to 2 PM and 5 PM to 8 or 9 PM. Spain closes for *siesta*, usually from 2 to 5 PM, although hours can vary considerably and tend to be longer in the hot south. **Banking hours** are 9 AM to 2 PM Monday to Friday and 9 AM to 1 PM on Saturdays.

National holidays: January 1, Epiphany (January 6), St. Joseph's (March 19), Good Friday, Easter Sunday and Easter Monday, May Day (May 1), Corpus Christi, Feast of Santiago (July 25), Assumption of the Virgin (August 15), National Day (October 12), All Saints Day (November 1), Constitution Day (December 6), Immaculate Conception (December 8), and Christmas Day. Be aware that there are many local holidays when everything in town closes down.

Can I have my allowance? Spain's currency is the *peseta*, and bills come in 10,000, 5,000, 2,000 1,000, 500, 200, and 100 peseta amounts. One hundred *centimos* equals 1 peseta, and coins are 1, 2, 5, 10, 25, 50, and 100, 200, and 500 pesetas.

Telephones: Spain's country code is 34. Telephones are coin-operated. *Cobra revertido* means "collect call"; *persona a persona* is a "person-to-person call."

Useful nationwide phone numbers: The operator is 009, international operator 07, medical emergencies 091.

Embassies and consulates: U.S. Embassy and Consulate, Serrano 75, Madrid 28006, [Tel. (091) 2763400] and Via Laietana, Barcelona [Tel. (093) 3199550]. Canadian Embassy, Núñez de Balboa 35, 30 Madrid 28001 [Tel. (091) 4314300].

Let's Eat!

Spaniards take their children out to eat regularly, and even the busiest waiters show little impatience in dealing with children. Breakfast is coffee with bread, rolls, or pastry. Kids can order hot chocolate or milk, but watch out, the milk is often served on a saucer accompanied by a packet or two of sugar! If you desire something heartier, order a *tortilla*, a delicious egg and potato dish similar to a frittata or a crustless quiche. Often called the Spanish potato omelet, they are served in pie slices and can be ordered for breakfast, lunch, or dinner in many cafes or bars. Our children loved them. *Churros* are long, donutlike pastries often served with a cup of hot chocolate for dipping. Each of Spain's regions has a distinctive way of cooking. Try fried fish and *gazpacho* (cold tomato vegetable soup) in Andalucia; *paella* (usually rice, vegetables, and seafood) in Valencia; *chanfaina* (a rice-based dish) in Salamanca; or *fabada* (a hearty stew of white beans with sausages or ham) in the north.

For **lunch,** be on the lookout for delicious *quesos* (cheeses), *pan* (bread), *manzanas* (apples), juicy *melocotónes* (peaches), *naranjas* (oranges), *plátanos* (bananas), *jamón serrano* (cured ham), *tomates* (tomatoes), and *pepinos* (cucumbers) at the local market. If you plan to picnic in a park, find a comfortable bench instead of a lawn, as picnicking on the grass is frowned upon.

Tapas are varied small appetizers traditionally served during the early part of the evening to tide the Spaniards over until dinner is served around 9 or 10 PM. Since many restaurants don't even open until 8 or 9 PM, skip dinner and feast on tapas during your children's regular dinner time at bars called *tascas, bodegas, cervecerías* and *tabernas.* Tapas are often displayed in the window or around the counter of a bar. Most can be ordered as *bocadillos* (sandwiches); they simply place the tapa between two pieces of roll.

Helados (ice cream) and frozen desserts are scrumptious and their whimsical presentation is especially enchanting to children. Popsicles are shaped as hands with pointing fingers, pink panthers, and slices of watermelon. Our favorite was the dark chocolate Dracula with a red middle. Order a double ice cream cone and you'll get a very wide cone with scoops side by side. A *polo* is a popsicle. A *pijama,* similar to an English trifle, has everything in it—ice cream, canned fruit, whipped cream, flan, little flags on top; it varies region to region. *Creme caramel* is flan, and *crème Catalana* is a rich creme caramel with a hard-sugar surface. Refreshing drinks include *granizado,* a drink of crushed ice, usually lemon- or coffee-flavored, and *horchata de chufa,* a cold, sweet milky drink made from chufa or earth almond.

Formula and Baby Food, Diapers and Baby Gear

Diapers, called *pañales,* are available in pharmacies, supermarkets, and some small markets. *Toallitas* are baby wipes. Pharmacies carry baby food, formula, and supplies such as bottles and thermometers. Three common baby food brands are Nutribén, Nestle, and Blevit. Isomil formula is available. Make an attempt to read the ingredients, as much of it comes with sugar. Look for those *sin azúcar* (without sugar). *Cereal al cacao* is, you guessed it, chocolate cereal. A few types of baby food you might want are *pollo con arroz* (chicken with rice), *zanhorias con arroz* (carrots with rice), *compota de manzana* (applesauce), *ternera con patatas* (veal with potatoes), and *meerluza con arroz* (fish with rice). If the pharmacies don't have what you want, look for stores with the sign Tienda Natural, Naturalista, or Dietetica, more like our natural food stores.

Sidewalk Talk

beach	*playa*	soft drink	*refresco*
boat	*bote*	suntan lotion	*aceite bronceador*
ok	*vale*	swimming pool	*piscina*
pedal boat	*bote de pedal*	thank you very much	*muchas*
playground	*parque infantil*		*gracias*
please	*por favor*	trampoline	*camas elásticas*
rowboat	*rodot*		("elastic jumping mattresses")

The Lay of the Land

We'll start with gracious Barcelona and the region of Catalunya, which edges up to the French border. To its south is a popular stretch of Mediterranean coastline and historic cities such as Valencia and Alicante. Colorful Andalucia, home of flamenco and heart of the bullfight, reflects Spain's Moorish influence and includes the Costa del Sol. Capital city Madrid is surrounded by the vast plains of Castilla la Mancha to the southwest. The castle-filled region of Castilla-León is to the north and west of Madrid amongst mountains and hot plains. The northern part of Spain includes the Basque country, the cooler Atlantic coastline, and the wet, green region of Galicia at the northwest corner of the country.

CATALUNYA

Catalunya is one of the most densely populated areas and one of the most forward-looking of the country's regions. Residents speak a different language, Catalán, and signs are in both Spanish and Catalán. TV shows are dubbed in Catalán, and much of the casual talk you hear in the rural areas as well as in sophisticated Barcelona is Catalán. The Catalán culture was suppressed during Franco's regime, when it was illegal to even speak the language, but now the culture is back full force. This fiercely proud region produced some of the country's most innovative artists—Gaudí, Dalí, and Miró—and examples of their extraordinary work can be seen throughout Barcelona and the surrounding area. We have listed most cities and sites using Catalán as it is more commonly found.

BARCELONA

Truly one of Europe's most beautiful cities, Barcelona is unusual in that its architecture challenges even a child's sense of proper proportion. Much of the city reflects the influence of architect and designer

Gaudí; his fantastic visions are right out of a child's wildest imagination. Sides of buildings undulate, rooftops drip with bright ornamentation, and stunning wrought-iron decorative details range from romantic Art Nouveau to that of a Gothic horror novel. Chic parks (most have playgrounds) and outdoor sculpture installations are also an important part of the city. Many of them are new, put in after Franco's demise, allowing the re-flowering of Catalán culture. And everything shines, spit and polish done for the 1992 Olympics and the 500th anniversary of Christopher Columbus' historic voyage.

Wha'd'ya Wanna Do?

The weekly magazine *Guia del Ocio* lists entertainment, movies, and restaurants in Spanish. *Vivir en Barcelona* is a monthly entertainment magazine that has some English copy in July and August. Both are available at the tourist office and most newsstands.

Try to catch a performance of the *sardana,* an old dance usually performed to the accompaniment of a *cobla* band of eleven instruments. Performances are held each Sunday from noon to 2 PM and Wednesday evenings on the cathedral steps and Plaça Sant Jaume Saturdays at 6:45 and Sundays at 6:30. **Tourist offices** are found in railway stations Estación Sants-Central and Estación Termino; at Plaça Portal de la Pau by the Columbus Monument (Tel. 3173041); in Plaça Sant Jaume (Tel. 3182525); on the Gran Via Corts Catalanes, 658 (Tel. 3017443); and inside the entrance of Pueblo Español (tel. 3250777). Barcelona's **telephone area code** is 093.

The Lay of the City

The city is wedged between the two hills of Montjüic and Tibidabo. Both peaks have amusement parks and stunning views of the city and port. The old part of town is bordered by the harbor and the Eixample. The geometrically arranged, gridlike Eixample has bold Art Nouveau buildings, swirling wrought-iron work, and beautifully patterned sidewalks. Walk through this area, along the elegant and chic Passeig de Gràcia or Diagonal, noticing the exceptional design detail. Barcelona's medieval Gothic quarter is at the heart of the old town. The Ramblas, with its lively pedestrian street scene of sidewalk cafes, newsstands, and plant and bird stands, runs between the harbor and the Plaça Catalunya, the heart of the city.

Getting Around

Barcelona's **Metro** system is extensive, clean, and convenient and will take you almost everywhere you want to go. It is supplemented by city **buses** whose routes are posted by the bus stop. Pick up a copy of the "Guia del Transport Públic" at tourist offices for a complete guide to metro and bus lines. Economical ten-ride passes for either the metro or metro-bus combination are available. Tourist bus 100 runs a continuous loop to the twelve most popular tourist sites in the city, stopping every half hour. It also entitles you to ride on the blue tram to Tibidabo or to take the funicular to Montjüic. Tickets, available for 1 or 3 days, provide unlimited use and are available during summer months only.

Where to Stay

Inexpensive accommodations can be hard to find in this elegant city. Inexpensive rooms are plentiful in the Gothic quarter and Ramblas area, but they tend to be unsafe at night.

HOTELS

Hotel Condes de Barcelona occupies a fascinating building designed in 1895 by a colleague of Gaudí. Passeig de Gràcia, 75. Tel. 2150616. **Deluxe.**

Hotel Regente is well-located with a rooftop pool and a parking garage. Rambla Cataluña, 76 Tel. 2152570. **Expensive.**

Hotel Ficus has one set of rooms with a communicating door. C. Mallorca, 163 Tel. 2533500. **Expensive.**

Aparthotel Senator has two-room apartments with kitchenettes and daily maid service. It's right next to a metro stop. Via Augusta, 167. Tel. 2011405. **Expensive.**

Hotel Wilson has a four-person family room and parking. Avda. Diagonal, 568. Tel. 2092511. **Moderate to expensive.**

Hotel Dante has a great location and a parking garage. C. Mallorca, 181. Tel. 3232254. **Moderate to expensive.**

Hostal Urbis has a four-person family room; it is a small, tired hotel but has a great location. Passeig de Gràcia, 23. Tel. 3172766. **Inexpensive.**

Residencia Montserrat is a very plain but serviceable fourth-floor hotel in the well-located Gràcia neighborhood. Passeig de Gràcia, 114. Tel. 2172700. **Inexpensive.**

CAMPGROUNDS

Cala-Gogo-El Prat, 7 kilometers from Barcelona, has a playground and pool and is near the beach. C-246 in Prat de Llobregat. Open Feb.–Nov. Tel. 3794600.

Detour! What to See and Do

THE LEGACY OF ANTONIO GAUDÍ

Plan to spend at least a half-day at **Parc Güell,** Gaudí's attempt at constructing a planned community. Financed by the Güells, a family of industrialists, it was intended to house sixty families but was turned into a park in 1923. Enter through the wacky gatehouse, which looks like something out of a Hieronymus Bosch vision. A huge mosaic lizard is part of a fountain that divides a stairway leading to a hall surrounded by crazy tilting pillars. Atop the hall is a plaza encircled by a curvy line of mosaic benches; each one is different and highly colorful. Grottoes, colonnades, prehistoric plants, and weird rock columns circle around the park. Free. May–Aug. daily 10–9; Sept.–Oct. 10–8; Nov.–Feb. 10–6; Mar.–Apr. 10–7. Gaudí's former house, **Casa-Museu Gaudí,** has a collection of furniture and personal memorabilia. Fee. Mon.–Thurs. 11–1:30 and 4:30–7:40, Fri. 11–1:30, Sun. 10–2, 4–7. Tel. 2046446.

The **Temple Expiatori de la Sagrada Familia**, with its soaring honeycomb spires, is one of the city's most famous landmarks; reassure your kids that this is no ordinary cathedral but a wildly decorative structure by a flamboyant and rule-breaking artist. Started by Francesc de Paula del Villar in 1882, it was taken over in 1891 and changed considerably by Gaudí, who worked on it for 43 years until his death. Work continues; Gaudí predicted it would take 200 years to finish his major *oeuvre*. The surface is so elaborately detailed that workmen, who have spent years constructing the church, admit that they still notice things for the first time. An elevator or worn spiral staircase leads to towers and a bridge from which you can see the entire work. The crypt has a model of the completed church. A debate rages among Barcelonians and designers over whether it is proper to continue work on the church without Gaudí. Some say absolutely not, while others say that it is what the artist intended. Fee. On C. Marina between C. Mallorca and C. de Provença. Daily 9–7. Tel. 2550247. A grassy park and pond are adjacent to the Sagrada Familia.

The dark and creepy **Palau Güell** is right out of a setting for *Dark Shadows*, with fabulous weird ironwork, huge light fixtures, and Gothic columns and arches. The only Gaudí building you can enter in the city (Sagrada Familia doesn't really have an interior), it houses the **Museu de l'Art de l'Espectacle,** a museum of 19th-and 20th-century theater memorabilia. Fee. Nou de la Rambla, 3–5. Mon.–Sat. 11–2, 5–8. Tel. 3173974. Gaudí's **Casa Míla**, at Passeig de Gràcia, 92, at the intersection of Provençal has an undulating facade of rough stone topped with a wavy roof of white marble mosiac and huge, sculptural "chimneys." The wrought-iron balconies are the wildest in the city. Not too far away is **Casa Batlló**, at Passeig de Gràcia, 43, another

Gaudí building, with a sinuous facade, mosaic surface, and floral dome. Kids love to walk past these two surrealistic buildings and marvel at the fact that they were built as homes.

MONTJÜIC

Perched above the city at one edge of the port is Montjüic, site of the Olympic stadium, lovely gardens, an amusement park, and a number of museums. Take a funicular or bus up to it, or walk from Plaça España up the many steps past the fountain, stopping halfway at the cafe for a rest and some refreshments. Its view of the city and the Mediterranean are spectacular.

At the top of the stairs is the **Palau Nacional**, which houses two museums. The **Museu de l'art de Catalunya** contains an excellent collection of Romanesque art from remote medieval chapels throughout Catalunya. Kids will inevitably gawk at the gruesome pictures of the tortured lives of the saints. The Museu de Cerámica's collection covers the history of Spanish ceramics. Both museums: Free. Tues.–Sun. 9–2. Tel. 3247199, 4238913. Take a break from the museums and visit the **Jardín Botánico** behind the Palau Nacional. Laid out in 1929, its plantings are arranged geographically. Fee. Mon.–Sat. 9–2, 3–7.

Even the youngest child can appreciate the stylish **Fundació Miró (Miro Museum)** with its explosion of bright colors, wiggly lines, and simple shapes. A second-floor patio sculpture garden and a chic outdoor cafe amidst the sculptures on a ground floor patio provide a refreshing break from indoor viewing. The well-stocked gift shop has paper-model kits of buildings found in Barcelona. Fee. Tues.–Sat. 11–5, Thurs. 11–9:30, Sun. 10:30–2:30. Tel. 3291908.

For a 360-degree view of the sea, port, city, and mountains, take a walk along the roof of the **Castell de Montjüic** fortress. Stop for lunch in its restaurant or continue to its **Military Museum** which contains weapons, uniforms, model castles, and dioramas with tin soldiers. Museum: Tues.–Sat. 10–2 and 4–8, Sun. 10–8. Tel. 4398613.

The **Parc d'Atracciones** with bumper cars, roller coaster, ferris wheel, house of horrors, glass maze, Pulpo the spinning green octupus, trampolines, wild mouse, and much more, as well as cafes on all levels, will be tops with your young set. Unlimited-ride tickets and/or entry fee to walk around. Late June–early Sept. Tues.–Fri. 6 PM-midnight, Sat. 6 PM–1:15 AM, Sun. noon–midnight; rest of year Tues.–Sun. noon–9 PM.

Walking through **Poble Espanyol** is like walking through a condensed course on Spanish architecture. Built in 1929 for the International Exhibition, it has reconstructions of buildings from every Spanish region crowded along narrow streets, squares, and patios. If you missed the chance to pick up a traditional craft souvenir in another part of Spain, you will probably find it here. The Catalán school kids we saw here were more interested in playing kick-the-can through the twisting cobblestone streets than in listening to their teacher. Your kids will probably feel the same way. Fee. Daily 9–8.

The **fuentes luminosas (illuminated fountains)** in Montjüic are at the end of Avenida Reina María Christina. The water- and light-show performances take place June–mid Sept. Thurs., Sat., Sun. 9–midnight, with music shows at 10; mid-Sept.–May Sat. and Sun. 8–11, with music shows at 9. Try to catch one of the music shows, as the fountains and lights play in time with the music.

BARRI GOTÌC: THE GOTHIC QUARTER AND THE RAMBLAS

The Barri Gotìc, originally called the Cathedral Quarter and the oldest part of the city, is marked by narrow winding streets now filled with a mixture of antique shops and garish tourist dreck. It's a popular site on most visitors' lists, but keep an eye on your pocketbook and avoid it at night. The wide ramblas are beautiful for strolling or for stopping at a sidewalk cafe for a horchata or café. Lined with stands selling newspapers, magazines, plants, and birds, they lead from Plaça Catalunya, the heart of the city, to the port and to the border of the Gothic Quarter. El Mercat de la Boqueria, a huge market selling fruits, vegetables, fresh meat and fish, and dried fruits, is midway down the ramblas and on the right as you head for the port. It's a perfect place to pick up supplies for a picnic.

The **Cathedral's** sky-bound spires can be seen throughout the city. Wander through its cool interior, and then head for the peaceful cathedral cloister, a charming garden with trees, flowers, a fountain, and swimming ducks. The best time to visit is on Sundays, when you can see the sardana danced in the square in front at noon. Cathedral and cloister: daily 7:30–1, 4–7:30. Tel. 3151554. No shorts allowed.

Take a break from the quiet of the cathedral and stroll around to the one-room **Museo Calzado** with its funny collection of antique and celebrity shoes. Kids like the exaggerated points on the 17th-century velvet roach killers, the huge clown shoe, the miniature shoes, and the wing-backed shoe. Adults appreciate the boots used to climb Mt. Everest and the shoes of Pau Casals. Small fee. Pl Sant Felip Neri. Tues.–Sun. 11–2.

The **Plaça de Sant Jaume** has been an important city square since Roman times. Today it is handsome but businesslike with few trees or shrubs to soften its cobblestone edge, where several government buildings stand. The sardana is danced here on Sundays. If you're looking for espadrilles, head for **La Manuel Alpargatera**. Its 100 styles for babies to big-foots are sewn by hand in the back. Salvador Dalí and Antonioni used to buy theirs here, and an autographed photo of Jack Nicholson implies that he did the same. C. Avinyó, off

Ferrar. Mon.–Sat. 9–1:30, 4:30–7:30. Tel. 3010172. **El Ingenio** is famous for its molded and painted masks, especially those of the giants used for the procession of the giants (see "Events") in the annual city festival. You'll find all kinds of other masks and accessories for the theater, but be sure to peek in the back room, where they are modeling and painstakingly painting the giants' heads. C. Raurich 6–8. Tel. 3177138.

The **Museu Picasso** contains drawings, paintings, and etchings from the artist's life, displayed chronologically, with an emphasis on his early years. Be sure to point out the works of art the gifted young Picasso created between the ages of 5 and 12. Fee. C. Montcada 15–17. Tues.–Sat. 9:30–1:30 and 4–8:30, Sun. 9:30–1:30. Tel. 3196310. **Museu Frederic Marés** contains a jumble of everyday objects from the 15th to the 20th century, such as playing cards, early cameras, ladies' fans, and folk art. All were collected by Marés, who built much of this collection by searching in flea markets and dusty little shops. Fee. Pl. de Sant Lu. Tel. 3105800.

If your kids can't pass up a wax museum, head for **Museu de Cera de Barcelona**, where over 300 wax figures from flamenco dancers to Star Wars characters will entertain them. Fee. Rambla de Santa Monica 4–6. Mon.–Fri. 11–2 and 4:30–8, Sat. 11–2 and 4:30–8:30. Tel. 3172649. The **Paulau de la Música Catalana**, designed by Gaudí's associate, Muntaner, is a beauty with lavish mosaic walls and columns, elaborate stained glass, and sculptures. Try to catch a concert just to see the interior. C. de Sant Pere mes Alt.

THE PORT AREA

You can spend a day here enjoying cool ocean breezes while you visit the port's attractions or tour by **horse-drawn carriage.** Be sure to negotiate price and select one of the carriages with the fringed umbrellas. Boat tours of the harbor are fun on one of the many **Las Golondrinas (the Swallows)**—double-decker motorboats.

In 1492, Columbus sailed the ocean blue, leaving from Barcelona on the *Pinta,* and *Niña,* and the *Santa María.* Tour a reproduction of the ***Santa María;*** your kids will marvel at how such a small boat could hold so many people. Make sure they see the crow's nest at the top. Fee. Open Tues.–Sat. 9–2, 3–sunset; Sun. 10–2. The **Monument a Colón (Columbus Monument),** erected in 1868, is a high column crowned with a bronze statue of the famous explorer. An elevator will take you to the top for a view of the port and the city. You'll see the rides at Montjüic on one end, the National Palace at the other, spires of the Sagrada Familia, and the cathedral tower. Elevator to top: Fee. July–Oct. daily 9–9; Nov.–June Tues.–Sun. 10:30–2, 3:30–6:30.

The **Museu Marítim** at the edge of the harbor was under extensive renovation when we visited but its new look can only improve an already excellent collection of ship's replicas, old sailing paraphernalia, maps from the days of Amerigo Vespucci, figureheads, reconstructed galleys, and full-size boats. Fee; free on Sunday. Tues.–Sun. 10–2, 4–7.

Take a ride across the harbor on the **funicular aéreo/aerial cable car** for a dizzying view of the inner city and harbor. It starts at the harbor on the Torre San Sebastian, stops midway at the Torre de Jaume I, and ends up near the Parc d'Atracciones at Montjüic. Fee. Daily 12–8.

TIBIDABO

Above Barcelona is the Tibidabo Mountain **amusement park** with a not-to-be-missed view on a clear day. Its trademark Red Baron airplane circles above the park on an attached arm. In addition to the merry-go-round, roller coasters, adventure playground, and typical amusement park fare, it has a **Museu de Automates** with beautiful old mechanical dolls, animated scenes, marionette theaters, and amusements from the past. One fee allows you to ride all rides, enter the museum, or simply walk around. Mid-Mar.–mid-Sept. Mon.–Fri. 10:30–8:30, Sat. and Sun. 10:30–9:30; rest of year weekends only. Tel. 2117942.

Museu de Ciéncia (Science Museum) is a hands-on museum with a planetarium and exhibits that have knobs to turn and dials to twist as you learn about optics, perception, and computers. Instructions are in Catalán and Spanish, so let your kids experiment or watch the other youngsters for instruction. Fee. C. Teodor Roviralta 55. Tues.–Sun. 10–8. Tel. 2126050.

More to See and Do

The **Museu de la Música** has elaborately painted Spanish dulcimers with scenes of sailing ships, carved and inlaid Spanish guitars, lutes, guitars of famous Spanish guitar players, animal-head horns, glass flutes from France, and old painted drums. One piano is a "piano-bureau"—a rolltop desk with a piano keyboard tucked into it. A giraffe piano from Vienna has, you guessed it, a long neck. Free. Diagonal 373, off P. de Gràcia. Tues.–Sun. 9–2. Tel. 2175517.

Cava bars serve champagne and chocolate truffles; many will admit children, allowing you to sip while they nibble. Check with the tourist office or your hotel for names and addresses.

Where the Sidewalk Ends: Zoos and More Parks

Parc de l'Espaňya Industrial has large amphitheaterlike steps cascading down to an artificial lake with rowboats for rent. Its two-story welded-steel dragon sculpture is actually a slide. Across the bridge and below is a children's playground and Ping-Pong tables. It's one of Barcelona's most unusual and attractive parks. C. Rector Triadó, 73. Near Sants station.

The **Parc de la Ciutadella** houses the Barcelona Zoo, Zoological Museum, Museum of Geology, and Museum of Modern Art. In addition to many winding pathways, there are several playgrounds designed for different ages and a lake with ducks and swans. The modern **zoo's** most famous resident is *Copital de Nieve* (Snowflake), the world's only captive albino gorilla, which has very pink skin and white fur, but 500 other species are also represented. There is a children's playground inside the zoo and dolphin and killer whale shows. Fee. Daily 9:30–7:30. Tel. 3092500.

Parc de la Creueta del Coll is dramatically built into a rugged hillside. Take the kids here for a swim in its large shallow pool. Water spills over a long concrete wall into the pool while a large sculpture is suspended along one edge. Small fee. Pl. Mare de Déu del Coll, 87.

Sports

La Barça, Barcelona's **soccer** team, plays at Camp Nou stadium off Avenida Diagonal. The other local team, Espanyol, plays nearby in Sarrià. **Swim** like an Olympian at the Piscina Picornell on Montjüic, near the Olympic stadium. Daily June–Sept. 15 10–5. (Tel. 3259281), or at Parc de La Creueta del Coll (see "Parks" above).

Events and Festivals

June 23 is **St. Joan's Day,** when the town comes alive with firecrackers, fireworks, flamenco displays, music, and dancing all night.

To celebrate **Mercè,** a festival in honor of the city's patron saint, there is a parade with giants, sporting events, bullfights, and other activities at the end of September.

Christmas time brings the twinkling lights of the **Fira de Santa Llúcia** markets, which convene outside the cathedral and in the Plaza de la Sagrada Familia to sell nativity figures.

NEAR BARCELONA

Sitges, just south of Barcelona, is a half-hour train ride from Barcelona from either Sants or Passeig de Gràcia station. The trains are filled with day-trippers on weekends. You can rent chairs or pedal boats while hawkers step around the tanning bodies selling drinks. If you tire of *la playa,* explore the castle and palace above the beach.

About 50 kilometers northwest of Barcelona is the famous monastery of **Montserrat** on a spectacular tall outcropping of craggy rock. It has been an important religious site since 888, when a lost statute of the La Moreneta (Black Virgin) mysteriously appeared, accompanied by visions and music. When a local bishop tried to remove it, it would not budge, and tales of its ever-increasing miracles began to spread. A chapel was built for it, and then monasteries were built and added onto until 1811, when Napoleon's forces destroyed the buildings. The cluster of buildings forming the monastery is a small town in itself, but only a few places are open. Kids will appreciate La Moreneta and the mummified crocodile in the **Museu de Montserrat** as well as the wax limbs that have been left in appreciation for healings. They'll want to ride the cable cars and funiculars that go to other religious sites, and to Sant Jeróni, the mountain's highest point, where you can see all the way to the Pyrenees on a clear day. Be sure to explore the well-marked paths leading to caves and deserted hermitages. The Escolaní Boys Choir, founded here in the 13th century, is famous throughout Europe. They sing at 1 PM and 7 PM but are on vacation in July. You can drive or take a train and aerial cable car from Barcelona (Plaça España). Check with the tourist office for details. Near the parking lot is an observation terrace with extensive views. For further information call the **tourist office** (English is spoken): Tel. (093) 8350251, ext. 162.

COSTA BRAVA

The "wild coast" extends from Barcelona to the French-Spanish border. A few towns are still unspoiled while others, especially Lloret de Mar, have become as overbuilt and overcrowded as the Costa del Sol. Ninety government-run campsites line the coast; they're cheap but often crowded.

Tossa de Mar, 83 kilometers north of Barcelona, is a popular beach resort with a renowned **vila vella,** the 12th-century mazelike old part of town, which sits high above the sea. Filled with cobblestone streets and flower boxes, it is protected as a national artistic monument. Both of the town's main beaches are set against a backdrop of the castle and the old village. **Es Codolar** is a small beach nestled on one side of the castle, and **Platja Gran** is a larger beach with a seafront promenade. Another beach, **Mar Menuda,** is nearby. These three are sandy; others in the area can be very rocky. Many of them are popular with snorkelers and skin divers and all varieties of aquatic sports are available. The **tourist office** is on Carretera de Lloret [Tel. (0972) 340108].

Nearby is **Aquadiver Parc Aquàtic** with crazy water slides, wave pools, boats, and play areas. Fee. In Platja d'Aro, Cntr. Circunvallació. Tel. (0972) 818732. **Parc Aquàtic** has the same. Fee. In Lloret de Mar, between Lloret-Vidreres km. 1, 2. Tel. (0972) 368613. **Marineland** has dolphin, sea lion, and parrot shows; a water park; children's playground; boating lake; and small zoo. Fee. Between Palafolls and Malgrat de Mar. Tel. (093) 7612802. Inland from Tossa de Mar, between Sant Feliu de Guíxols and Santa Cristina d'Aro, is the **rocking stone of Pedralta**, a granite block weighing over 80 tons. Balanced on an unstable base, it is a fascinating natural phenomenon.

Sant Feliu de Guíxols is another beautiful little coastal town frequented by tourists that has retained its fishing-village feel. If its beaches are crowded, head to nearby Platja de Sant Pol or La Conca. The **tourist office** is at Pl. d'España 6–9 [Tel. (0972) 320380].

Figueres' most famous native son, Salvador Dalí, made his imprint on the town with the **Teatro Museu Dalí,** one of Spain's most bizarre and frequently visited museums. Even the facade of the former theater has been altered, Dalí-style, with huge eggs on turrets and strange sculptural assemblages welcoming visitors. On view are his surreal drawings and paintings (some rather risqué), offbeat personal collections and constructions and parodies of virtually every movement in the history of art. A vintage black Cadillac acts as a base for a giant sculptured female "hood ornament" that accepts coins and then waters plants. Columns are made of automobile tires and TV sets while passengers in a taxi are covered with snails. Fee. Follow the many signs from town. July–Sept. daily 9–9, Oct.–June Tues.–Sun. 11:30–5:30. The light-filled **Museu de Joguets** has a collection of 3,000 old toys, such as tin soldiers, trains, cars, and doll houses, plus temporary exhibitions. Fee. Rambla 10 in the Hotel Paris. July–Aug. daily 10–12:30 and 4–7:30; Sept.–June Wed.–Mon only. Tel. (0972) 504585. The town's **castle** is used by the military but you can walk along its walls. Contact the **tourist office** at Plaça del Sol [Tel. (0972) 503155].

Cadaqués has held high-rise and condo development somewhat at bay thanks to the winding mountain road that separates it from the main highway. An artists' haven since the early 20th-century, it has been home to painters and writers such as André Breton, Paul Eluard, Max Ernst, and Dalí. Today's artists are committed to preserving its old village and skyline of whitewashed houses. The best beaches are just north of town, and water skiing, sailing, and skin diving are easy to arrange. For more information, contact the **tourist office** at Cotxe, 2-A [Tel. (0972) 258315].

ALONG THE COAST FROM VALENCIA TO ALICANTE

Warm water and hot sands characterize this stretch of coastline, which has beaches for all tastes—long and straight or secluded in coves. Sadly much of it has been overdeveloped, such as Benidorm, but there are still a few larger towns with a decidedly Spanish flair and a number of quaint villages. Mock fights between the Christians and the Moors celebrating the reconquest take place throughout the entire region, especially in the inland areas. They begin with a spectacular parade, followed by festivities, fireworks, and bonfires.

VALENCIA

Founded over 2,000 years ago, Valencia was first Roman, then Moorish, and later Christianized in the 13th century. The 15th century was one of Valencia's periods of cultural and economic splendor, and many buildings from this era have been preserved. Among them is the **Miguelet Tower,** a symbol of the city. Its 155-foot-high octagonal tower provides an expansive view. Small fee. Mon.–Sat. 10:30–12:30 and 5–7:30, Sun. AM only. The ornate rococo building **Palau del Marqués de Dos Aigües,** dripping with scrolls, flowers, people, and palm trees, houses the **Museu Cerámica,** which contains tiles, ceramics, and pottery from all over Spain. An eclectic collection of other items includes three 18th-century carriages on its bottom floor and a gallery of humorists. Fee. Tues.–Sat. 10–2, 4–6. Tel. (096) 3516392.

The city has some lovely parks: **Jardins dell Real,** on the north bank of the river next to Museu del Belles Artes, has a magnificent rose garden and a small zoo with cramped cages. Open 8 to sunset. **Monteforte Garden** is part of the National Art Treasure. Monforte. Free. Open 10–sunset.

The city's beach, **Malvarrosa,** is polluted, but there are other beaches in the seaside resort/suburbs of **El Cabañal** and **Nazaret. La Albufera,** a great lagoon that irrigates parts of Valencia's market gardens, is an important wildlife sanctuary outside of town. Along its shore is **El Saler,** which has a good beach. Boat trips can be hired on the lake from the dock area behind the town's main street.

Valencia is famous for **Les Falles,** a March celebration with parades, bullfights, street dancing, and most of all, glorious fireworks. The festivities culminate in the setting fire to hundreds of funny papier mâché effigies, *ninots,* that have been on display around the town. **Les Falles Museum** has an exhibition of ninots that were saved from burning, if you miss the real thing. Plaza 4 Monteolivete, 4. Tues.–Sun. 10–2, 4–7. Tel. (096) 3323336. Late July's **Fira de Juliol (July Fair)** has cultural events, more fireworks, and the Batalla de Flors, in which girls on floats parade through the streets throwing flowers at the crowd, which in turn, throws them back. The International Musical Bands Competition has been an important component for over 100 years. An international **Fireworks Festival** takes place in

October. Valencia's lovely Christmas fair, **La Fira de Nadal,** is especially designed for children. Contact the **tourist office** at Paz 48 [Tel. (096) 3733311], for more information.

Outside of town is **Aquasol,** a water park with slides, toboggans, pools, and a playground. Buses leave from Valencia daily at 10 A.M. Ctra. Valencia. Tel. (096) 1724949.

COSTA VALENCIA

Canet has a spacious beach with sand dunes. Many families vacation here; high-rise hotels are scarce, but vacation houses and villas are plentiful. *Olivia* has worked hard to preserve its old structure and the town's beaches have preserved their family atmosphere. They become crowded in the summer, but the limit on high-rise development makes this a charming spot. There are good beaches between Diamuz and Miramar, and Gardamar and the Bellereguard. **Safari Park Vergel** is a typical safari park with an added dolphin show, horseback riding, boating, trampolines, go-carts, aquatic scooters, and a children's amusement park. Fee. Summers daily 10–7:30; winter until 6. Tel. (096) 5750285.

COSTA BLANCA

Denia is a family resort that has thankfully avoided most of the high-rise hotel blight. Villas, houses, and campgrounds are available. Its beaches are lovely and its town charming. Its largest beaches, such as Les Marines, Les Bovetes, Els Palmars, and Les Deveses, are to the north. To the south, the beaches are more rugged, with cliffs and coves. Water skiing, wind surfing, sailing and fishing are popular here. The town is presided over by a castle and has a picturesque fishing quarter, Baix La Mar. Its old quarter, Les Roques, surrounds a Roman castle. Inland from Denia are the stalactite- and stalagmite-filled caves **Prehistórica Cueva de Las Calaveras.** Remains from humans who lived here 50,000 years ago and miscellaneous animal bones can be seen in its cavernous domes. Fee. On the road between Pedreguer and Benidoleig. Tel. (0965) 5583235.

Altea, a beautiful village with an artistic and cosmopolitan atmosphere, has an old quarter filled with stepped streets and whitewashed houses and crowned by a blue tile-domed church. An artificial sandy beach has been created in front of the town, or you can head south to the natural beach. Between Altea and Calpe is **Cactuslandia,** a rugged hanging garden with 1,500 different species of cacti, succulents, and exotic birds. Wander through steep terraces for views of the sparkling blue Mediterranean below. Fee. La Galera del Mar 27. Tel. (0965) 5842218.

ALICANTE

Alicante, a sizable city, is a refreshing change of pace from the high-rise–infested larger coastal towns nearby. If you're looking for a large, lively, and sophisticated resort town, especially if you have older kids who like action, this is a good choice. There's a little of everything: a broad sandy beach, wide tree-lined boulevards, a hill-top castle worth exploring, and an interesting old town. Its stately shorefront promenade, **Paseo Explanada de España,** is dotted with sidewalk cafes (even McDonald's has red and yellow umbrellas shading its chic outdoor tables) and booths selling colorful souvenirs and beach gear. The town's beach, **Playa Postiguet,** fills up fast in peak season but is loads of fun with pedal boats, vendors selling ice cream, and umbrellas and chairs for rent.

An elevator will take you straight up through a shaft cut in the hill to the **Castle of Santa Barbara** above the town. Roam around the various levels of the castle for breathtaking views of the coastline. Be sure to see its dungeon and the small museum next to the souvenir shop with its collection of painted clay replicas of award-winning floats from the **Fogueres de Sant Jordi.** Photographs show the scale of the enormous floats; other photos capture the mantilla-clad fiesta beauty queens from years past. Small fee. Summer daily 9–9; winter until 7. The festival itself takes place in late June with luminous jumping jacks and other fireworks, bonfires in the middle of the street, and a parade of floats. Just north of the town are the 10-kilometer-long beaches of San Juan. The **tourist office** is at Explanada de España, 2 [Tel. (0965) 200000].

NEAR ALICANTE

Twenty-four kilometers from Alicante, in the village of *Busot,* are the **Canalobre Caves.** With numerous candelabra-shaped stalactites, these caves are lavishly illuminated and resemble a huge cathedral. Fee. Apr.–Sept. 10:30–8:30; Oct.–Mar. 11–6:30. Tel. (0965) 5699250.

The biggest reward in touring the **Nougat and Costumes Museum** is at the end, when you get to sample the delicious nougat candy made from almonds and honey. Housed in the **Turrones El Lobo y 1880** nougat factory, it is a 13-kilometer hop from the caves in the city of *Jijona,* made famous by this candy. Free. Avda. de Alcoy, 62. Daily 9:30–1, 4–8. Tel. (0965) 610225 or 610250. A little farther inland, in *Penáguila,* is **Safari Park Aitana,** one of Europe's largest safari parks. In addition to lions, tigers, zebras, giraffes, and elephants, there are donkey-cart rides and a swimming pool. Fee. Summer daily 10–6:30; winter until 5. Contact Alicante tourist office for details.

Another safari park near Alicante is **Río Safari Elche,** on the Elche-Santa Pola road. With 6,000 palm trees, it resembles a tropical setting with hippos, monkeys, camels, rhinos, and the rest. Boats travel along a murky "river," and there is an elephant show, trampolines, and go-cart track. Fee. Open daily. Contact Alicante tourist office for details.

Just inland from Benidorm is the town of *Guadalest,* with one of the funniest museums we've found. The **Museo Mundial Miniaturas** bills itself as the world's largest collection of miniatures. Leonardo da Vinci's *Last Supper* is painted on a grain of rice; there's a collection of tiny shoes; a painting on a pin head; sculptures made from pieces of schoolroom chalk; and our favorites, the fancy-dress fleas. Microscopes are available for some of the displays—that's how small they are! Fee. Open daily at 10. Tel. (096) 5880808. The small town of Guadalest, constructed inside the ruins of a rocky castle, has **donkey rides** for children through its streets.

The **Europa Park Amusement Park** is in Benidorm, an overbuilt concrete-jungle of a city best avoided unless your children need a big-time amusement park fix. If water parks are more their style, **Aqualand** may fill the bill. Contact the **tourist office** for information [Tel. (0965) 853973].

ANDALUCÍA

Numerous civilizations have passed through Andalucía but it is the legacy of the Moors that gives it its distinctive flavor. In the three major cities of the Moors, Córdoba, Granada, and Seville, dazzling reminders of the past have been preserved. Small villages with whitewashed houses and flocks of sheep are set against the blazing blue sky and the hot summer sun. Eight provinces make up Andalucía's varied landscape of mountains, dry plains, fertile farmlands, and golden-sand beaches. Part of its coastline is occupied by the Costa del Sol, popular with vacationers but considerably overbuilt and crowded. If you are touring during the summer, air conditioning in your car and hotel is a must. Many monasteries and convents specialize in making and selling delicious sweets and baked goods. Most tourist offices carry the booklet "Gastronomic and Tourist Guide to Andalucía," which lists "sweetmeats" made famous by these religious establishments. Secular sweets are renowned, too. Colorful folklore and festivals abound. Pick up the English guide "Fairs and Festivals of Andalucía" at any tourist office for a detailed listing.

CÁDIZ

The province of Cádiz, whose coasts are washed by the Atlantic and Mediterranean seas, is hot in summer and mild in winter. The area is famous for horse breeding and the rearing of fighting bulls. Its capital city, Cádiz, was founded by the Phoenicians in 1100 B.C. and is Spain's oldest settlement. Still an important port, it gained prominence after the discovery of America, when it became headquarters for the Spanish treasure fleet. Wander through its fascinating maze-like old town, partially surrounded by walls, during the cooler part of the day and head to its beach, **Puerto de Santa María,** for a dip when the sun blazes overhead. For another good beach, cross the bay to one of the beaches in Puerto de Santa María or Chipona. **Marqués de Comillas** and **Alameda Apodaca Gardens** have broad avenues along the sea wall. **Carnaval** in Cádiz is joyous and colorful. The **tourist office** at C. Calderón de la Barca, 1 [Tel. (0956) 211313] can give you details.

BETWEEN CÁDIZ AND THE PORTUGUESE BORDER

The *Costa del Luz,* extending west of Cádiz to the Portuguese border, is not as overbuilt as the Costa del Sol. You'll find long stretches of sandy beaches and fishing villages with whitewashed houses interspersed with tourist developments.

El Rocío plays host to the colorful **Pilgrimage of the Rocío,** one of Spain's largest religious celebrations, which takes place annually at Pentecost. Thousands of Andalucians dressed in traditional costumes head toward the town on horseback, on foot, or in decorated ox carts to the accompaniment of guitars, castanets, fifes, and much partying and dancing. The festival culminates in the paseo of the Virgin of the Dew, who is thought to possess great fertility and magical powers.

Ayamonte is the last Spanish town before the Portuguese border. With 7 kilometers of sandy beaches, it can be a good place to stop for a dip if you're driving across to the Algarve, but the city's ferry crossing can have a very long line in summer.

JEREZ DE LA FRONTERA AND ENVIRONS

Jerez de la Frontera, 36 kilometers inland from Cádiz, is a town famous for its sherry, with a celebration in the fall honoring this smooth libation. More appropriate for your kids is May's **Feria del Caballo,** one of the oldest horse fairs in Spain, with shows, races, and carriage competitions featuring Jerez's famous horses. Visit the **Escuela de Arte Ecuestre (Andalusian School of Equestrian Art)** and try to catch a performance of "How the Andalusian Horses Dance."

Fee. Avda. Duque de Abantes. Tel. (0956) 311111. Its **flamenco festivals** take place in August and December, and if you miss those, wander through the **Museo de Flamenco.** Quintos. 1. Tel. (0956) 349702. The **Zoológico Alberto Durán** is a vast park with a zoo and botanical gardens. C. Taxdirt. Tues.–Sun. 10:30–6:30. Tel. (0956) 343347. Near Jerez is the **Circuito de velocidad de Jerez,** where the Spanish Formula 1 Gran Prix and other races are held. The **tourist office** is on Alameda Cristina, 7 [Tel. (0956) 331150].

Arcos de la Frontera is perched high on a hill with the river Guadalete flowing at its base and sharp ravines on all its sides. Its ancient castle stands at its highest point, above the maze of steep streets below. Some consider its fiesta at **Holy Week** to be the best in Spain.

SEVILLE (SEVILLA)

One of Spain's most beautiful cities and the site of Expo '92, Seville was the birthplace of painter Velásquez and Cervantes' famed character Don Quixote de la Mancha. More recently, the city has been plagued with economic difficulties and a resulting crime problem. Purse-snatching by riders on motorbikes and car break-ins (even while you are stopped at a traffic light) are common. Put all valuables in your trunk as you drive through this city and avoid carrying a purse or camera as you walk. The police have cracked down recently, but precautionary measures are wise. Plan to splurge on accommodations here and keep your valuables in the hotel safe. Or better yet, stay about an hour outside of the city in the magnificent Parador del Rey Don Pedro in Carmona (see below). The **tourist office** is at Avda. de le Constitución, 21 [Tel. (0945) 221404], and the police station is on Plaza de la Gavidia [Tel. (0945) 228840].

Dominating the skyline is Seville's most beautiful building, the **Giralda,** built by the Moors in the 12th century. Climb to the top of the bell tower for a view of the city and a close-up of the cathedral. Seville's world-famous 16th-century **cathedral,** the third largest church in the Christian world, took 100 years to build. The Patio de los Naranjos (Orange Tree Patio) used to be the patio of the mosque that originally stood there. Fee. Both open Mon.–Sat. 10:30–1 and 4:30–6:30, Sun. 10:30–1.

The magnificent gardens of **El Alcázar** are surrounded by walls and towers. Glazed tiles decorate its halls and altars. First built by Pedro the Cruel, it was later partially transformed by the Catholic monarchs. Its Casa Lonja houses the Archives of the Indies, which has a collection of maps, letters, and records from the Spanish conquests of the Americas. The **Plaza de España,** just east of the cathedral, has fountains, pools, and statues. Next door is **Parque de María Luisa**

(María Luisa Park), with more pools and fountains, lots of magnificent glazed tile work, a narrow boating lake, leafy paths, and horse-drawn carriage rides. Las Delicias gardens cover the area along the river near Guadalquivir. Just outside of the city, near the airport, is the Guadalpark–Parque Aquatico (water park), which bills itself as "La Playa de Sevilla" (the beach of Seville). Beat the sizzling summer heat and stop here to dip in one of its many pools, water slides or rapids courses.

Seville is the site of two of the largest festivals in Spain. Its Semana Santa (Holy Week), with elaborate processions of floats and masked penitents, culminates on Good Friday. April's Feria is a week-long festival during which sevillanas (rhythmically complex songs that are accompanied by the guitar, castanets, heel beat, and clapping movement of the dancer) are sung and danced. Displays of horsemanship by men in short jackets and broad hats and bullfights take place each afternoon. Part of the riverbank, the Real de la Feria, is transformed with canvas tents decorated with flowers, banners, and sparkling colored lights in which colorfully dressed flamenco dancers perform nightly.

CARMONA

The fortified town of *Carmona* is 33 kilometers from Seville. Its most famous sites include a Roman necropolis and amphitheater and a Moorish fortified gateway, but your kids will prefer the stunning tiled swimming pool and lush gardens of the town's exceptional Parador Alcázar del Rey Don Pedro. Built on the remains of a Moorish fortress, it was turned into a luxurious palace by Don Pedro the Cruel, and much later into a parador in the 1960s. It stands on the highest part of the town commanding a magnificent view of the surrounding countryside. Stay here and make day trips to Seville. Córdoba and Granada are within a 3- or 4-hour drive. Tel. (0954) 141010 or 140160.

CÓRDOBA

Córdoba, one of the country's oldest cities, was once the capital of Roman-occupied Spain and later of Muslim Spain. It is best known for its striking Mezquita (mosque), started in the 8th century and completed in the 10th century. Wander through its cool interior, filled with pillars and arches, making sure your children notice the intricately carved and colorfully painted ceilings and highly patterned details characteristic of Moorish design. Open hours vary considerably, but late afternoon and early evening hours stay somewhat firm at 3 to 7. The tourist office is at Plaza de Judá Leví [Tel. (0957) 471235].

Horse-drawn carriage rides are available near the **Juderia,** the fascinating old Jewish section of town, site of the Mezquita.

The **Alcázar** will be quite plain in comparison, but kids will enjoy climbing up its various *torreones* (towers) for a view of the cows grazing amidst flowers along the riverbank. Its lovely courtyard and the refreshing gardens are more fun than the tour of the interior. Children interested in bullfighting may enjoy the **Museo de Taurino,** with old costumes, journals, photos, posters, and stuffed bulls heads. A Manolete room includes the skin of the bull who killed him. Fee. In the Plazuela de Maimonides. Summer 9:30–1:30, 5–8; reduced hours in winter.

Two long and shady parks, **Jardines de la Victoria** and **Jardines Diego de Rivas,** run between the city's main street, and both have playgrounds. The **Parque Zoológico** has a rather depressing zoo and a good playground. The Cordoban sweet specialty is **pastel Cordobés,** a cake made of puff pastry and candied squash. The internationally renowned **Festival of Guitar,** held in early July, features classical, Latin American, and flamenco styles.

GRANADA

Granada is famous for one of the most beautiful sites in all of Spain, the Alhambra, which combines rich cultural experience with artistic beauty, fresh air, and the outdoors. Spare your kids a tour of the cathedral and Granada's many fascinating old churches and concentrate your stay on the Alhambra, with its lookouts, mazelike pathways, fountains, flowers, and magnificent tile work and architecture. Smiling Gypsies present you with flowers as you enter the Alhambra's walls. It's not part of the town's hospitality scheme; they ask a stiff price or to try to pick your pocket. A pleasant, but firm "No, gracias" will help discourage them. The **tourist office** is at Puerta del Vino. Alhambra [Tel. (0958) 229936].

Where to Stay

We strongly recommend that you stay inside the walls (although somewhat expensive) or as close as possible to the Alhambra. Reserve hotel accommodations in advance for July and August; the parador requires reservations months in advance any time of the year.

HOTELS INSIDE THE ALHAMBRA'S WALLS

Parador San Francisco is in a refurbished 14th-century Franciscan convent with views of the Alhambra's gardens. Be sure to visit its

Moorish outdoor patio/bar for a drink whether you stay or not for the stunning view of the Generalife. Alhambra 18009 Granada. Tel. (0958) 221493. **Deluxe.**

Hostal América has a shady patio lovely for eating home-cooked Spanish meals. Reserve as far in advance as possible. It's a good deal, as breakfast and dinner are included in the price. No credit cards. Real de la Alhambra, 53. Tel. 227471. **Expensive.**

HOTELS ALONGSIDE THE ALHAMBRA

The following hotels are a few steps from the Alhambra or near the shady walkway bordering it.

Hotel Alixares del Generalife has a pool, air conditioning, and a terrace for lunchtime barbecues. Alixares del Generalife. Tel. (0958) 225574/225575. **Moderate.**

Hotel Washington Irving has simple rooms, a dining room, and bar. Calle Carmen de los Mártires. Tel. (0958) 227550. **Moderate.**

Hotel Doña Lupe has an outdoor pool, quadruple room, 24-hour cafe, air conditioning, and a garage. Up the street from the Washington Irving. Tel. (0958) 221473. **Moderate.**

THE ALHAMBRA

The magnificent and romantic **Alhambra** has the perfect combination of qualities to make it an unbeatable attraction for children. Much of its beauty is out-of-doors, and city and country kids alike succumb to the enchantment of its spectacular gardens. Its palace will be unlike anything they see in the rest of Europe as it is North African-inspired and completely different from Western castles, palaces, or cathedrals. Experienced through the senses rather than through a textbook or guidebook, it encourages quiet contemplation—even by kids!

Three different sights are contained within the Alhambra. On the Hill of the Sun is the **Generalife,** with topiary-lined pathways surrounding beds of colorful flowers. Water runs through canals and pauses in lily-filled pools and fountains; groups of swallows circle above while well-fed cats groom themselves in the sun. Tall cypress trees cool those wandering through. The **Alcázar** is filled with painted tiles, delicately inscribed walls, intricate carvings, and keyhole archways. This was most likely the building that prompted Francisco de Icaza to utter, "There is nothing in life as sad as to be blind in Granada." The **Jardines del Partal** (Palace Gardens) are not as grand as those of the Generalife but with pools of fish and lily pads, shady gardens, and terraces of roses, are still lovely. The **Alcazaba,** the oldest part of the Alhambra, is not as refined as the Alcázar.

Children enjoy climbing up to its flag-bedecked lookout tower for a view of the Alhambra complex and the town below. One ticket entitles you to visit the Generalife, Alcázar, and Alcazaba; the rather dull (for kids) museums in the Palacio de Carlos V are separate. If you don't make it to all the sites, you can use your ticket the next day. Go early, at lunchtime, or late to avoid summer crowds. Daily 9:30–6:30.

Granada's old Arab quarter, the **Albaicín,** is a maze of steep, narrow alleyways with traditional Arab houses and flower-filled balconies. Its tourist shops are a good place to pick up souvenirs of the region.

Your best chance for seeing flamenco before 10 PM is at the touristy, but fun, **Cuevas Gitanas de Sacromonte (Sacromonte Gypsy Caves).** Gypsy families play guitars, castanets, and tambourines and dance flamenco. Years ago, thousands of Gypsies lived in these caves, but many were forced out by the floods of 1962. Take only as much money as you plan to spend on a performance and don't let the Gypsies talk you into a special private showing; it will cost! Instead, stick to the scheduled shows.

Granada's International Festival of Music and Dance features open-air performances in the breathtaking gardens of the Generalife and in the Renaissance palace mid-June through mid-July. For advance tickets, write Comisarie del Festival, Ancha de Santo Domingo, 1, Granada 18009. Their local office is at Calle Gracia, 21, 18002 Granada [Tel. (0958) 267442 or 267443].

THE COSTA DEL SOL

Running from Algeciras in the west to Almería in the north, the Costa del Sol is one of the most developed stretches of coastline on the entire Mediterranean. Sunseekers share the sand with thousands of other tourists against a backdrop of high-rise hotels; head elsewhere if it's local charm you're after.

Boat trips to Tangier (3 hours) depart from Algeciras. Across the bay is *Gibraltar* where you can take a **cable car** to the **Top of the Rock.** It leaves from the southern end of Main Street and stops at the **Ape's Den,** where a colony of wild Barbary apes roam as they have since the invasion of the Moors. Return by footpath or take the cable car down. Cable car: Fee. Mon.–Sat. 9:30–7:15. Near the cable-car station are **St. Michael's Caves,** which drip with stalactites, stalagmites, and weird rock formations colored with soft lights. Concerts are sometimes held in the cavernous chambers. Tour. Fee. Summer daily during 10–7; rest of year until 5:30.

Marbella, a chic and expensive villa-filled resort, has an interesting old part of town and popular beaches. Many families find it charming and very lively. Here *Club Med* has a vacation village with children's activity clubs for kids from 4 months to 11 years. From

U.S. Tel. 800-258-2633. One of the coast's most popular resorts is *Torremolinos,* with a 5-mile stretch of beach and hundreds of unattractive high-rise hotels, some of them priced somewhat reasonably.

Nerja is a late entry in the race to build the most high-rise hotels, so its Moorish past has been better preserved than that of other Costa del Sol cities. Its cliff-top promenade, the **Bálcon de Europa,** is fun for a stroll or snack. The **Cueva de Nerja (Cave of Nerja),** 5 kilometers from the town, was inhabited from 100,000 to 40,000 B.C. and lay undiscovered until 1959. It is filled with dripping stalactites and stalagmites made visible by colored lighting. Paths and stairways lead you through its ornate grottoes, chambers, and halls. A **Festival of Music and Dance** takes place in the caves in August, and there is a small museum showing artifacts discovered in the cave and a children's playground. Fee. May–Sept. 15 9–9; rest of year 10–2, 4–7. The **Parador Nacional de Nerja** is California bungalow-style with a big lawn, swimming pool, tennis courts, and an elevator to escort you to its beach below. It's expensive but worth the splurge if you plan to stay on this coast. Tel. (0952) 520050.

Almería and environs was a popular Hollywood film location for the spaghetti westerns of the 1960s. It's **Mini-Hollywood** and one of the sets constructed by Sergio Leone is now a tourist attraction. Kids will enjoy renting a costume and riding on horses through the town or viewing one of the staged bank-robbery performances. Other movies filmed here include *Lawrence of Arabia; The Good, the Bad, and the Ugly;* and *Reds.* Fee. On highway N340. Tel. (0951) 365236.

MADRID

Bustling Madrid has a park or playground at every turn. Most have been designed for locals to escape the heat of midday and for the evening strolls when families visit with their neighbors while their children play. Parks with lakes often have rowboats for rent, and many have little sidewalk cafes where you can stop for a cool and refreshing ice cream treat. *Guía del Ocio* is a weekly guide to what's happening in the city. Two monthly guides, *Tour Madrid* and *Madrid Visitor,* published in Spanish and English, list activities and events throughout the city. Madrid's **tourist offices** can be found at: Chamartin Railway Station (Central Hall, Gate 14); Calle Duque de Medinaceli, 2 (across from Palace Hotel); Torre de Madrid (the tallest building on Plaza España) Calle Princesa, 1 (Tel. 5412325); and at Plaza Mayor, 3 (Tel. 2665477). The **telephone area code** is 091.

The Lay of the City

The Puerta del Sol is considered the center of the old city, where many major streets intersect and an important metro center runs underneath. Six major freeways actually begin here, at what Spaniards call "kilometer zero." Calle Major, which runs southwest from Sol to the Royal Palace, is one of Madrid's oldest thoroughfares through the old part of the city. The Gran Vía is Madrid's major street. Two parks, Casa del Campo and Parque del Retiro, border the city center at the western and eastern edges, respectively.

The excellent **metro** system covers much of the city. Pick up a Plano del Metro (map) at the ticket booth when you buy your tickets. A ten-ride pass will save you money. **Buses** and **taxis** cover what the metro doesn't, but the bus system can be confusing to first-time users. Tourist offices can supply maps and information.

Where to Stay

HOTELS

Mindanao, which has several swimming pools, is in a residential neighborhood in the northwest part of town. San Francisco de Sales, 15. Tel. 4495500. **Deluxe.**

Alcalá is near Retiro Park. It has a garage and bar. Calle Alcalá, 66. Tel. 4351060. **Expensive.**

Novotel Madrid, which has a pool and garden, is on the outskirts of town for those who don't want to navigate the tricky streets of Madrid. Calle Albacete, 1. Tel. 4054600. **Expensive.**

The *Gran Hotel Victoria* is a very good value near Retiro Park, the Prado, and many good low-priced restaurants. Plaza de Angel, 7. Tel. 2316000 or 2314500. **Moderate.**

Zurbano offers very good value but is somewhat plain. Calle Zurbano, 79. Tel. 4415500. **Moderate.**

Hostal Don Diego has a triple room available and is very popular so reserve in advance. Calle Velásquez, 45, in Salamanca neighborhood. Tel. 4350760 or 4350829. **Inexpensive.**

Marbella is a small, very inexpensive older hotel. Plaza de Isabel II, 5. Tel. 2476148. **Inexpensive.**

CAMPGROUNDS

Both of the following offer laundry facilities, hot showers, swimming pools, children's playgrounds, supermarkets, and restaurants.

Camping Madrid is about 10 km. away on Nacional 1, Madrid–Burgos. Tel. 2022835.

Camping Osuna is 15 km. away near the airport (it can be noisy) on Avenida Logroño (Alameda de Osuna). Tel. 7410510.

Detour! What to See and Do

AROUND THE PRADO

The world-renowned **Museo del Prado** houses an art collection that is staggering in both quality and quantity. Kids seem to like best the mystical and slightly delirious paintings of Hieronymus Bosch, but be sure they view *Las Meninas*, a famous painting by 17th-century Spanish artist Diego Velásquez. They are bound to enjoy its subject matter—children, dogs, and dwarfs. Choose carefully from the rest of the works, as you may be able to wander endlessly from gallery to gallery feasting your eyes on the Goyas, El Grecos, Murillos, and Rubenses, but your kids will tire quickly. Fee. Paseo del Prado. Tues.–Sat. 9–7, Sun. 9–2. Tel. 4680950. Metro: Atocha or Banco España. Your ticket to the Prado will admit you to the **Legado Picasso,** which houses his enormous *Guernica* painting. Picasso donated the canvas to New York's Museum of Modern Art with the request that it be returned to Spain when the government he so strongly protested in the painting fell and democracy was restored. It was returned to Madrid in 1981. Still a controversial subject, visitors must pass through a metal detector before being allowed to view the glass-encased work. Tues.–Sat. 9–6:45, Sun. 9–1:45. Metro: same as Prado.

The vast **Parque del Retiro,** several blocks away from the Prado, has a huge rectangular lake, El Estanque, with ducks and statues and rowboats for rent from 8 AM to 8 PM. Bring along leftover bread for the ravenous fish. Walk along the many tree-lined avenues past the beautiful fountains or sit at the marble edge of the lake at an outdoor cafe. Retiro has three playgrounds, puppet shows, jugglers, clowns, and a street fair on weekends. Contact the tourist office for information on show times. In summer the rose garden is colorful and aromatic. On Sunday mornings during the summer, head toward the bandstand beside the lake for concerts. *Helados* (ice cream and popsicle) stands and outdoor cafes multiply in the summer. Don't picnic on the grass, but find a comfortable bench. Horse-drawn carriages will take you for a ride around the park. Metro: Retiro.

The **Museo del Ejército** contains guns, uniforms, medals, banners, model soldiers, and other military paraphernalia. Search out the Japanese armor in the excellent armor collection. Fee. Calle Méndez Núñez, 1. Tues.–Sat. 10–2, Sun. 10–3. Tel. 5314624. Metro: Banco de España.

At the **Museo Naval,** look for Juan de la Cosa's map of North America made in 1500. Young model enthusiasts will marvel at the intricately detailed models of ships. Several ship's cabins show how cozy life was on board in years past. Fee. Paseo del Prado, 5. Sept.–July Tues.–Sun. 10:30–1:30. Tel. 5210419. Metro: Banco de España.

THE ROYAL PALACE

The 2,800-room **Palacio Real** allows visitors to view the state apartments, reception room, tapestry gallery, armory, library, and royal pharmacy. Kids will head for the armory with helmets, shields, and lances. Much of the armor is child-size, which is fascinating when kids realize that the suits weren't made for children but rather for adults who were much smaller than people are today. Armor from all over the world is on display. Guided tours in English are available and are compulsory for the state apartments but are too long for most kids. Fee. Calle Bailén. Summer Mon.–Sat. 9:30–12:45 and 4–5:45, Sun. 9:30–12:30; winter Mon.–Sat. 9:30–12:45 and 3:30–5:15, Sun. 9:30–12:30. Tel. 2485350.

Beautiful gardens surround the palace. The **Plaza de Oriente** has a playground. Behind the palace, in the Campo del Moro gardens, is the **Museo de Carruajes Reales,** which has a collection of elegant and ornate carriages spanning 200 years. A few are still used for special state occasions. Small fee, included in ticket to Palacio Real. Mon.–Sat. 10–12:45 and 4–5:45, Sun. 10–12:45. Tel. 2487404. Metro: Norte.

Just One Look: Museums

At **Ciudade de los Niños (Children's City),** in Casa de Campo on Av. de Portugal, there are free workshops for children in radio, video, computers, photography, theater and art, plus outdoor games and sports facilities and a children's market on Saturdays. Theater performances and videos are organized throughout the year. The facility is open Saturdays, Sundays and public school holidays. For more information: Tel. 4635731.

The airy **Museo de Arte Contemporaneo** has a sculpture garden and fountain outside and brightly colored kid-pleasers by Dalí, Picasso, and Miró inside. Fee. Av. Juan de Herrera, 2. Tues.–Sat. 10–6, Sun. 10–3. Tel. 4497150. Metro: Moncloa or Ciudad Universitaria.

The **Museo de Figuras de Cera** has wax figures depicting scenes from Spanish history as well as 20th-century celebrities. Kids love the gory bullfight scene. A 30-minute "multivision" show takes you through Spain's history from the Phoenicians to the present day. Fee. Paseo de Recoletos, 41. Daily 10:30–1:30, 4–8:30. Tel. 4192649. Metro: Colón.

Museo Nacional de Ferroviario is housed in the city's first railway station, Estación de Delicias, and contains reproductions of old railway cars and the first steam engine that ran from Barcelona to Mataró. Also housed in the station is the **Museum of Science and Technology** and a **planetarium.** Fee. Paso de las Delicias, 61. Mon–Sat. 10–5, Sun. 10–2. Tel. 2273121.

The bullfighting memorabilia on display at the **Museo Taurino** includes everything from the costumes, capes, and hats of famous matadors to photographs, posters, and paintings. Go here for a dose of a Spanish bullfight if you'd rather not view the real thing. Fee. Calle Alcalá, 237, at Plaza de Toros de las Ventas. Tues.–Fri. and Sun. 9–2:30. Tel. 2551857. Metro: Ventas.

Where the Sidewalk Ends: Zoos and More Parks

Casa de Campo sprawls along the city's west side. Originally a royal hunting ground, it is now a park with horseback riding, a swimming pool, an amusement park, a zoo, and a lake filled with rowboats. If you're lucky, you might catch some apprentice bullfighters practicing early in the morning. At one edge of the park, accessible by cable car from Paseo de Rosales, is the **Parque de Atracciones** amusement park with merry-go-rounds, a glass maze, spinning rides, speedboats, little cars, and all. Its teatro offers a wide variety of free 1-hour shows. Try to catch the flamenco here (shows: May–Sept. 7:30 to 10:30) as other flamenco shows in town start after 10 PM. In the center is a tower with an elevator that will take you to the top for views of the city. Purchase individual-ride tickets or a pass that entitles you to ride as much as you want. Tel. 4632900. The **Zoo's** most popular animal is the giant panda; the many other animals are displayed by native continents. There is a small petting zoo and playground for children and there are trained bird and dolphin shows. Fee. Zoo. 10–sunset. Tel. for Zoo: 7119950. Metro for park: El Lago or El Batán. **Plaza Santa Ana** has a fun children's playground, as do many of the city's other parks and squares. **Parque Sindical** has a public pool and a skateboard ramp.

Sports

Bullfights are held daily during the Festival of St. Isidro in May and twice weekly during the season from April or May to September at the Plaza de Toros Monumental, Calle Alcalá, 231. Tel. 2462200. For **ice-skating,** try the Ciudad Deportiva del Real Madrid at Paseo de la Castellana, 259. Tel. 3150046. **Roller skaters** can head for the Rolling Disco, Estación de Chamartín. Tel. 3153000. Soccer *(futbol),* is a popular Spanish sport with games held almost every weekend of the year between September and May. Two teams, *Real Madrid* and *Atlético de Madrid* play in the city's two soccer stadiums. Check the local publications for listings. Throughout the city there are many municipal **sports complexes** with indoor and outdoor pools, playing fields, skating, and such. To find out what is available near you, call 4635498 or 4635563. **Swimming** pools are in abundance; check with the sports complex listing above or try the open-air pool at Casa de Campo Park.

Special Events

February's **Carnaval** is the occasion for wild parades of giants, bigheads, masked merrymakers, floats, and street dancers.

Cumbre Flamenca, which takes place in April, offers some of the best flamenco dancers and singers in Spain.

In mid-May, the city explodes with processions, concerts, puppet shows, a circus, and more during the **San Isidro Festival.** One of the best-known parts of the festival honoring Madrid's patron saint is 3 weeks of daily bullfights, considered the pinnacle of the art in Spain.

Fiestas in honor of the patron saint **Virgen del Carmen** take place during the month of July in various districts of the city.

In August, the celebrations of **San Lorenzo** (August 3), **San Cayetano** (August 5) and **Verbena de la Paloma** (August 15) are filled with much gaiety. The Verbena convenes around Puerta de Toledo with dancing, processions, ferris wheels, and barrel organs.

At **Christmas** and into the **New Year** the city is filled with a dazzling display of lights, trees, and nativity scenes. Plaza Major is filled with booths selling ornaments, nativity scenes, and other festive items. There is a children's festival and fair, **Juvenalia.** The season culminates on January 5, when the **Cabalgata de los Reyes Magos (Procession of the Three Kings)** winds through the town.

NEAR MADRID

In the township of *Aldea del Fresno,* on the outskirts of the city, is the **Safari Reserve El Rincón,** where free-range animals roam about. There are camel and horseback rides, water toboggans, a lake, and a restaurant. Fee. At km. 22 on the road from Navalcarnero to Villa del Prado. Tues.–Sun. 10–6. Tel. (091) 8620146.

Aranjuez, south of Madrid, was the spring and fall home of royalty. It's well-known today for its delicious *fresas* (strawberries), sold from roadside stands. The **Palacio Real,** set in romantic tree- and fountain-filled gardens, contains many exotic rooms, a few of which your kids may enjoy. The Salón de Porcelana is entirely covered in white porcelain painted with wreaths, Chinese motifs, and depictions of children's games. The **Museo de Trajes Reales** has a diverse collection of items such as royal robes, military uniforms, fans and children's games. Two small bridges lead to the wide avenues, lush foliage, and many stone and marble fountains of the man-made Jardines de la Isla and the shady river walks, ornamental lakes, arbors, fountains, and statues of the Jardines del Príncipe, site of the **Casa de Marinos (Boating Museum),** which houses a display of royal boats that once floated along the river. Free. Wed.–Mon. 10–1, 3:30–630. Cross the footbridge near the royal family's dock to the Arboleda on the other side of the river to rent **paddle boats.** The town's **Aquapark** is a cool and refreshing break from historical attractions. Head to Ctra. de Andalucía for water toboggans and slides. Tel. 8910641.

CASTILLA/LA MANCHA

This region borders Madrid on its western and southern edges.

TOLEDO

Toledo, once one of the great cultural centers of medieval Europe, is a fascinating blend of Arab, Jewish, Christian, and Roman influences. Its skyline has remained virtually unchanged since the 16th century. The capital of Spain until 1560, this National Monument City sits atop a hill overlooking vast plains and the Tagus River. Toledo's narrow twisting streets and alleys are difficult to navigate, even with a map; don't even attempt it in a car. Many of the most popular sites are on its central hill, while others are in the old Jewish quarter on the west side of town. Be sure to sample the city's famed **marzipán,** made from almonds and fruit.

Its ancient **cathedral,** the second largest in Spain, is filled with magnificent stained glass and elaborate ornamentation. In the Treasure Room point out the 16th-century 400-pound gold vessel supposedly fabricated from gold taken from the New World by Columbus. It is paraded through the streets during the annual Corpus Christi procession. Fee. 10:30–1, 3:30–7; winter until 6. No shorts allowed. The **Casa del Greco** is filled with the famous artist's paintings on El Greco's upper floor; kids may prefer looking through his home, which is furnished to show the way people lived in the 16th century. Fee. Calle Levi, 3. Tues.–Sat. 10–2 and 4–6, Sun. 10–2. The **Alcázar** gained world attention in 1936, when rebels telephoned the Nationalist colonel inside, telling him they would kill his captive son if the Nationalists didn't surrender the fortress. The general refused, so the structure was under siege for 3 months and then nearly destroyed. A transcript of the supposed conversation between the rebels and the colonel, translated into many languages, is on display in the colonel's office. The 13th-century structure has since been rebuilt and turned into an **Army Museum** with models, photos, and propaganda from the battle. Small fee. Daily 9:30–7; winter until 6.

CUENCA

The stunning medieval city of Cuenca, southeast of Madrid, is a tangle of narrow streets and odd corners surrounded by the rivers Júcar and Huécar. Overlooking the old city are las **Casas Colgadas.** Originally from the 14th century, these dramatic cliff-hanging structures are partially suspended over a gorge 60 feet below. Walk the wiggly suspension footbridge across from the houses for a first-rate view. For a gravity-defying experience, plan to have a meal in the restaurant housed in one of the structures or visit the **Spanish Abstract Art Museum** housed in another. Cuenca's **tourist office** is on Dalmacio García Izcara, 8 Tel. (0966) 222231.

The nearest parador, *Alarcón's* small **Parador Marques de Villena,** is housed in a restored Moslem castle/fortress. Your kids will think they are living in the romantic past, as this is an unforgettable medieval picture-book castle. It is well-situated for a number of interesting side trips and is only 6 kilometers from **Alarcón Lake,** where there are water sports and swimming. Tel. (0966) 331350. Several **campgrounds** are nearby.

About 36 kilometers northeast of Cuenca, past the gorges, caves, and waterfalls of the Trabaque River, is the **Ciudad Encantada (Enchanted City),** a huge field filled with weird rock formations modeled by the elements over the centuries. Some look like enormous misshapen mushrooms, others like huge animals or reclining people; you'll feel as if you are walking through a giant's sculpture garden.

The **Route of Don Quixote** goes from Cuenca (map available from the tourist office) to the old walled village of *Belmonte,* which has an exceptional mid-15th–century **castle,** and then to *Mota del Cuervo,* about 122 kilometers from Cuenca, which has a number of interesting **windmills.** Most of them have been rebuilt and are no longer in use, but they serve as reminders of the classic windmill battle scene in *Don Quixote.*

CASTILLA Y LEÓN

A region of mountains and hot plains north and west of Madrid, the kingdoms of Castilla and León were united in the 13th century. This new kingdom increased in power and prosperity through the 16th century and then gradually declined. Twelve provinces make up this castle- and religious-monument-filled region, which occupies about one-third of the territory of Spain. Religious festivals abound, particularly during Easter week.

SEGOVIA

The ancient city of *Segovia,* about 90 kilometers from Madrid, has narrow, winding streets and a fascinating fairy-tale castle, The **Alcázar.** Kids enjoy walking the battlements and will grimace as they imagine the castle's residents pouring boiling oil over the ramparts on their enemies below. Climb the circular stairway in the tower overlooking the drawbridge for a stunning view of the city. Be sure to see the collection of medieval armor. Small fee. Mon.–Sat. 10–2 and 4–6, Sun. 10–6. The **Roman aqueduct,** one of the world's best preserved Roman ruins, is a landmark of Segovia. It starts at the Plaza del Azoguejo, runs almost 800 yards, and has 167 arches. Thought to have been built in the 1st century A.D., it was partially destroyed by the Moors in 1072 and rebuilt by King Ferdinand and Queen Isabella.

ÁVILA

The walled city of *Ávila* is about 113 kilometers to the northwest of Madrid. Spain's highest city, it's fairly cool in summer months. Its well-preserved 11th-century walls, illuminated during the summer, have eighty-eight round watchtowers and several thousand battlements. Nine gates provide access. Ávila's most famous resident, St. Teresa, was born here in 1515. Deeply religious by the time she was 7, she later became a nun and was one of the most important figures of the Counter-Reformation. The town is filled with churches and places claiming an association with her, and the regional sweet **(yemas de Santa Teresa)** was named in her honor. Visit the **Convent of St. Teresa,** her birthplace, which contains her rosary beads and paintings of her celestial powers. Those who aren't squeamish can take a peek at the saint's withered finger. Free. Daily 9:30–1, 3:30–8. In mid-July the town celebrates with the **Fiestas de Verano** with fireworks, singing, and dancing. In October, the town honors her with a week-long **fiesta** of parades, open-air dances, competitions, and street entertainment. Contact the **tourist office** at Plaza de la Cathedral, 4 [Tel. (0918) 211387] for details.

SALAMANCA

Salamanca is home to Spain's oldest university, founded in 1218. Families with older children wishing to study Spanish often come to take advantage of its excellent summer language program and its temperate climate. The bustling Plaza Mayor, edged by ornate four-story buildings constructed of golden sandstone, is the center of town, where sidewalk cafes and restaurants abound. **Tunas** here are not fish but rather roving musicians dressed in traditional black costumes with white and red collars who entertain with song and dance.

While visiting the **universidad,** be sure to see the dark, airless 16th-century classroom with rough wooden benches; it's a far cry from your children's 20th-century schoolroom. The facade of the university is elaborately decorated, and in some of the flowery details hides a frog (hint: it's somewhere on the lower right side). Students say it brings them good luck on exams. Small fee. Summer Mon.–Sat. 9:30–1:30 and 4–7, Sun. 10–1; winter Mon.–Sat. 9:30–1:30, 4–6.

Wander through the **Cathedral Nueva ("New" Cathedral),** started in 1513 (free of charge), and then head to the 12th-century Romanesque **Cathedral Vieja (Old Cathedral)** next door. Point out the enormous stone that fell on top of a workman but didn't kill him—an event townspeople proclaimed a miracle. Small fee. Both open daily 10–1, 3:30–6; winter until 5.

Go to the south of the city on a cool day and walk across the beautiful 1,300-foot-long **Puente Romano (Roman Bridge),** Salamanca's oldest surviving monument. Restored many times, it offers a rewarding view of the city.

ARAGON AND BASQUE COUNTRY

The Basque countryside is as different from the rest of Spain as are its language and customs. The proud Basques have an autonomous regional government, collect their own taxes, and have signs in both Castillan and Basque. *Pelota,* or *jai-alai,* was invented here and is played with a passion.

SAN SEBASTIAN AND ENVIRONS

San Sebastian (Donostia), 18 kilometers from the French border, is a family resort with a large clean golden-sand beach. It's a popular summer retreat for Madrileños trying to beat the summer heat and lacks the overbuilt look of the Mediterranean coastline. Its old quarter is fascinating, and its newer parts, with wide boulevards, sidewalk cafes, and elegant shops, are worth exploring. Crescent-shaped **La Concha Beach** is partly surrounded by a promenade, and although crowded during peak summer months, it's a good spot to stretch out, swim, or nibble on one of the delectable prawns offered by walking food and drink vendors. At the smaller beach **Playa de Ondarreta,** there are pedal boats for rent and a wind-surfing school.

Take the funicular from the end of the Avenida de Satrústegui at the west end of the Concha Beach, to **Mount Igueldo's** amusement park, which offers bumper cars, donkey rides, little trains, and a breathtaking view of the city and curving bay. At the other end of the beach from Mount Igueldo is **Mount Urgull,** where you can take a winding footpath up to the ruined castle at its summit. At one edge near the harbor is the town's **aquarium,** which has a few fish and exhibits on the town's seafaring history. Fee. Daily 10–1:30, 3:30–7:30. Tel. (0943) 421905.

Kids may want to catch a game of **jai alai** or **pelota,** a popular Basque game played with wicker scoops, paddles, or a hand. Matches are regularly held in the Anoeta sports complex. **Grand Week,** in mid-August, includes a fireworks display on each of the festival's six nights. The **tourist office** is on Calle Andia, 13 [Tel. (0943) 426282]. Ride a boat out to **Isla de Santa Clara,** a small island in the bay, and take a picnic. During the summer boats leave from the port every half-hour until 8:30. The island is illuminated at night.

The ancient walled town of *Fuenterrabía (Hondarribía)* is 20 kilometers east of San Sebastian. Its old walls still bear some of the battle scars from past skirmishes, and it has a good **beach.** Its **Parador El Emperador** occupies a former 10th-century castle. Plaza de Armas del Castillo. Tel. (0943) 642140.

NAVARRE

The northern Province of Navarre has a rich variety of landscape and people.

PAMPLONA AND ENVIRONS

Pamplona, capital of the province, is best known for the **Running of the Bulls** in July, an event made famous by Ernest Hemingway. An old fortress-city, Pamplona has a very interesting old town with narrow streets and a citadel high above to explore. If you visit during the packed celebration of the town's patron saint, St. Fermín, you will see the daring young men chased by angry bulls as they race through the town. Arrive by 6 AM to get a view of the running of the bulls, which starts at 8 AM. That evening (around 6:30 PM), the same bulls appear in bullfights. To see a fight, purchase tickets by 6 AM for fights scheduled that night. There are fireworks and a fun fair near the citadel, and bands play throughout the city during the festival. Book accommodations a year in advance. Pamplona is filled with parks and gardens. **Taconera Park** is near the edge of the town walls, and shady **Media Luna Park** is along the river. Eight kilometers from town is the **Morea Lake** with sailing, swimming, and wind surfing. The **tourist office** is at Duque de Ahumada, 3 [Tel. (0948) 227200].

Bertiz, 45 kilometers from Pamplona, is a natural park with beech, oak, and chestnut woods that are home to foxes, otter, deer, and more.

The garden is embellished by waterfalls, ponds, ducks, peacocks, and pergolas. *Olite,* 42 kilometers south of Pamplona, has a magnificent old castle-palace right out of a child's fairytale that has been turned into the **Parador Príncipe de Viana,** Plaza de San Francisco [Tel. (0948) 740000].

ALONG THE ATLANTIC COAST

SANTANDER

A stylish Spanish seaside resort in the 19th century, *Santander* has plenty of popular beaches nearby. **El Sardinero** is an interesting older resort-suburb several kilometers out of town, and the beaches of *Santoña* to the east and *Suances* and *Comillas* to the west are also very nice. A fire destroyed the old part of Santander in the early 1940s; it was rebuilt along the same lines but with wide boulevards, a waterfront promenade, and sidewalk cafes and shops. The port has a free **maritime museum,** and if you spend time at **Playa de la Magdalena,** the town's beach, visit the small **zoo** in the gardens of the Magdalena Palace. The **International Festival of Music and Dance,** held in August, is one of Spain's best, and its summer language programs attract students throughout the summer. The **tourist office** is in Plaza de Velarde.

SANTILLANA DEL MAR

Twenty-six kilometers to the west of Santander is *Santillana del Mar,* which was populated in the Middle Ages by well-to-do noblemen. Because it has been so perfectly preserved, the entire town has been declared a historic monument. The town is small enough for children to appreciate. Strolling through it makes you feel as if you were going about your business a few centuries back. Souvenir shops serve up handicrafts from all over Spain. The town's **Parador Gil Blas** occupies a 400-year-old palace in the town. Plaza de Ramón Pelayo. Tel. (0942) 818000.

Just outside of town are the **Caves of Altamira,** some of the world's most famous prehistoric painted caves, with paintings of bison, red deer, bulls, and boars. Visitors used to tour them in great numbers, but their rapid deterioration because of human breath led the government to limit viewers to just a few each day. Eight tours of five people are allowed in daily; no children under 13 may participate. To request admission, write: Centro de Investigacíon y Museo de Altamira, 39330 Santillana del Mar, Spain. An admission-fee museum next to the caves' entrance has color photos and reproductions of the caves. Fee. Daily 10–1, 4–6. Tel. (0942) 818102. The **Santillana Zoo,** on the way to the Altamira Caves, contains a collection of animals found in Spain—bison, wolves, foxes, reptiles, and birds housed in rather cramped quarters. Fee. June–Sept. 10–8. Tel. (0942) 818125. *Comillas,* once a playground for 19th-century aristocracy, is worth a detour to see the crazy palace designed in the 1880s by architect Gaudí. Recently restored, it now houses a glamorous restaurant.

GALICIA

This green and heavily wooded area in the northwest corner of Spain has received tourists from all over Europe since the late Middle Ages, when pilgrims flocked to Santiago to see the tomb of St. James the Apostle. Tourists now travel to Santiago and other parts of Galicia for historical and scenic reasons as well as religious devotion. This area has strong Celtic influences which are reflected in its own language, Galego, and in its bagpipe music. Misty fiords mark its eastern coast, and the importance of the sea is seen throughout. If you have time, explore its many unspoiled fishing villages, battered rocky headlands, and deserted beaches; it's a lush and lovely part of Spain. Among the most original festivals found throughout this area is that of **La Rapa das Bestas (Marking of Wild Horses),** when wild horses are captured by their manes, marked, and sold.

SANTIAGO DE COMPOSTELA AND ENVIRONS

Santiago was the journey's end for pilgrims, rich and poor, after their arduous religious pilgrimage from all parts of Europe. In the Middle Ages they followed "The Pilgrim's Way," bringing with them new styles of architecture, culture, and ideas. Santiago is one of three cities in the world given the status of Holy City by the Vatican and more than half a million faithful pilgrims traveled here each year during the peak of its popularity in the 11th and 12th centuries. Why? To see the tomb of St. James the Apostle, discovered in 813 by a pious hermit who was led to it by a show of celestial light. This medieval National Monument City is built from golden-tone granite. One of the rainiest cities in Spain, it has abundant vegetation.

Its huge 11th-century **cathedral,** on the Plaza del Obradoiro, is thought to be one of Spain's most beautiful Romanesque buildings. As you enter the main door, press your hands into the holes at the roots of the Tree of Jesse, worn smooth from centuries of worshippers seeking indulgences. A silver urn in the crypt beneath the main altar contains the remains of St. James. Free. Open daily. Tel (0981) 583548. The **Museum of the Pilgrimages** may give you a deeper insight into this age-old excursion. Fee. San Miguel, 4. Tel. (0981) 581558. Summer 10–2, 5–8; winter 10–2.

Your kids may then want to unwind in the **Paseo de la Herradura** gardens southwest of the old part of town. The town's specialty dessert, *tarta compostelana*, is an almondy cake. Celebrations before and on **St. Jame's Day** (July 25) still take place with fireworks, religious parades, and ceremonies. When the saint's day falls on a Sunday (next in 1993), the "Year of Jubilee," the city receives a papal visit, which attracts streams of people visiting. The **tourist office** is on Rúa del Villar, 43 [Tel. (0981) 584081].

Vigo, an important port town, has a steep and winding old city with a park at the top. The best beaches are nearby on the rocky **Isles de Cíes,** where many Celtic remains have been discovered and rare birds make their homes. The island's beaches are uncrowded as there is a limit on the number of tourists allowed to visit. Mid-June through September boats leave six times each day from Vigo; plan to leave on an early boat to be guaranteed admission. Vigo has a small zoo. For details contact the **tourist office,** Jardines del Elduayen [Tel. (0981) 213057].

Parts of this coast, particularly **Costa de la Muerte,** have a long history of sea wrecks and their accompanying legends. Some claim that certain surnames in the region originate from the union of a sailor and a mermaid. The legends include a series of tips on how to uncover the identity of a mermaid when she is trying to pass as a real woman. How? She has no naval and the soles of her feet are as smooth as a baby's.

BALEARIC ISLANDS

This holiday island chain is extremely popular, especially with northern European sunseekers. Accommodations during high-season are scarce; reserve rooms and rental cars in advance as both can be in short supply. *Mallorca* is the largest and most popular of the chain, with *Ibiza* taking a close second. *Menorca,* with long stretches of sandy beaches, has suffered less from the impact of tourism and has more of its local color. Little *Formentera* mainly attracts day-trippers who come to enjoy its lovely beaches. To get to the islands, fly from Barcelona, Madrid, or Alicante, or take the seven- to nine-hour boat ride (some have postage-stamp-size swimming pools aboard) from Barcelona or Valencia. Once there, you can rent a car or bicycles to tour the island.

MALLORCA

The best beaches on this rugged but beautiful island are in the northeast and southeast, as the northwest is rocky and sprinkled with little coves. The capital city of *Palma* has the most tourist development, but other areas are becoming built up as well. The city is a bustling metropolis whose condo- and apartment-lined beaches stretch to the north and south. The old part of Palma, with its labyrinth streets, is much more interesting, as is the 14-century **Bellver Castle,** perched on a hill. The **tourist office** for all of the Balearic Islands is in Palma on Avenida Rey Jaime III, 10 [Tel. (0971) 712216].

Not too far from Palma, outside the city of *Porto Cristo,* is **Les Coves del Drach (Caves of the Dragon),** an underground grotto teeming with stalactites and stalagmites in all kinds of crazy shapes. Kids will love the boat ride across its large subterranean lake and the musicians who play Chopin from drifting boats. Try to plan your visit to coincide with one of the lakeside concerts held Monday through Friday at noon; the cave's acoustics are exceptional. Guided tours: May–Oct. Sun.–Fri. 11 AM, noon, 2 PM, and 3 PM; rest of year noon and 2 PM. Off the same road is an **aquarium** with magnifying tanks housing piranhas, electric eels, and other aquatic creatures. Not too far away is a **safari park** with a small but varied collection of wildlife. Both open daily 9–7.

Watchtowers preside over the terraced slopes and cliffs of *Banyalbufar,* on the northwest coast. At the quiet **beach** below the town is an inviting stop for a swim. Well-marked lookout points along the coast include the lookout point of Ses Ortigues and the lookout point of Las Ánimas. Near Banyalbufar is *Sa Granja,* an outdoor museum of Mallorcan life in times past. Guides dressed in traditional costumes lead you through arts and crafts exhibits and a farm. Kids can eat special *bunyols* (similar to donuts) while you sip homemade wine. There is folk dancing on certain days. Fee. Apr.–Oct. 10–7; Nov.–Mar. 10–5:30.

IBIZA

Third largest of the Balearic Islands, Ibiza shows clear signs of its popularity with expansive facilities for the thousands who descend upon it each year. *Ibiza* city is the island's capital and heaven for any teenage girl who loves lying on the beach perfecting her tan and dressing up for a night on the town. Others may disagree. The island's beaches range from those that are sardine-can packed to some that are somewhat deserted. Water sports of all varieties are found everywhere. The **tourist office** is at Vara de Rey, 13, Ibiza [Tel. (0971) 301900].

20

Switzerland

The Swiss are as orderly and efficient as their famous watches, which makes traveling through their country a breeze. Everything is punctual and well-organized. Days can be filled with hikes through alpine valleys where mountains rise like sheer walls, chilling dives into emerald lakes, picnics amidst wildflowers, and the sounds of cowbells. Your children will never forget dangling from alpine trams, dashing through the snow in horse-drawn sleighs, or taking a mouth-watering tour through a Swiss chocolate factory. The tricky puzzles and board and action games at the Swiss Museum of Games outside of Vevey or the Ice Palace atop the dizzying heights of the Jungfraujoch, with its glacial sculptures of furniture and Mickey Mouse, are only two of their possible Swiss journal entries. After a day of adventure you can all nestle into pillowy-plump down comforters, sip steaming cups of delicious hot chocolate, and fall exhausted to sleep. Does it sound like a scene from Heidi? It all really exists in Switzerland. In case you are concerned about leaving a superclean Swiss hotel room in a kid's state of disarray, the clever Swiss have eased your burden (or perhaps their own). They have devised a welcoming network of "happy family hotels."

Bon Voyage . . . gute Reise!

Preparing Your Children: Books and Art

Younger children: Piro and the Fire Brigade by Kurt Baumann; William Tell by Nina Bawden; The Pear Tree, the Birch Tree and the Barberry Bush by Alois Cariget; A Bell for Ursli, Florina and the Wild Bird, and The Snowstorm by Selina Chönz; and Ski Pup by Don Freeman.

453

Older children: A *Family in Switzerland* by Peter Jacobsen and Peban Kristensen, *The Adventures of Mickey, Taggy, Puppo and Cica and How They Discover Switzerland* by Kati Rekai, *Heidi* by Johanna Spyri, *William Tell* by Friedrich von Schiller.

Art: Your children will encounter artwork by Swiss artists such as Giacometti, Klee, Le Corbusier, and Jean Tinguely. Your library should have books with photographs of their works.

Getting There

Grateful parents will find sophisticated family facilities where they can leave their children in supervised, brightly decorated play areas at terminals A and B at the Zürich Airport and at the airports in Geneva and Basel. In Zürich, the moderately priced Novotel Zürich Airport hotel has an unsupervised children's playroom and kid's meals. Talackerstr. 21, 8152 Glarttbur. Tel. (01) 8103111.

Wha'd'ya Wanna Do

The **Swiss National Tourist Office** is very helpful and will send you information on home rentals, family hotels, camping, baby sitters, and sports.

SWISS NATIONAL TOURIST OFFICES (SNTO)
  U.S.A.–Chicago: Swiss National Tourist Office, 150 N. Michigan Ave., Chicago, IL 60601. Tel. 312-630-5840.
  U.S.A.–New York: Swiss National Tourist Office, 608 Fifth Ave., New York, NY 10020. Tel. 212-757-5944.
  U.S.A.–San Francisco: Swiss National Tourist Office, 260 Stockton St., San Francisco, CA 94108. Tel. 415-362-2260.
  Canada–Toronto: Swiss National Tourist Office, Commerce Court West, Toronto, Ontario M5L 1E8. Tel. 416-868-0584.

If your kids love the outdoors, they'll love Switzerland. In winter you'll find magnificent skiing for every level, skating, curling, tobogganing, sleigh rides, and horseback riding through the snow. Skiing in Switzerland is often less expensive than in North America. We have indicated many resorts with children's **ski schools** where kids get first-rate instruction and are attended by clowns, fairy-tale figures, and comic heroes.

Public pools or lakefront beaches, tennis courts, *Kinderparadies* (playground/recreation areas), and miniature golf are found in almost any town. Hiking through sparkling alpine valleys, mountaineering, high-altitude skiing, lake swimming, sailing, wind surfing, waterskiing, river rafting, and horseback riding are all available for summertime visitors. As you travel, look for posters advertising the delightful **Swiss National Knie Circus,** which performs regularly throughout the country.

Lights Out! Special Swiss Accommodations

Home rentals in villages and resorts are often called *chalets,* a word that can refer to either a private house or a building with apartments. City rentals are referred to as **apartments.** Prices vary considerably based on time of year and location, but you can plan on spending at least $500 per week during high-season for a simple chalet. Request the SNTO's free listing of agencies "Rental of Apartments, Chalets and Villas." The following agencies have rentals in the regions we profile:

Europa-Let, P.O. Box 3537, Ashland, OR 97520. Tel. 800-462-4486 or 503-482-5806.

Idyll Ltd., P.O. Box 405, Media, PA 19063. Tel. 215-565-5242

Interhome, Inc., 124 Little Falls Rd., Fairfield, NJ 04006. Tel. 201-882-6864.

Rent A Vacation Everywhere (RAVE), 328 Main St., East, Suite 526, Rochester, NY 14604. Tel. 716-454-6440.

Rent a Home International, 7200 34th Ave., NW, Seattle, WA 98117. Tel. 206-789-9377.

Swiss Touring, USA, 5537 N. Hollywood Ave., Milwaukee, WI 53217. Tel. 414-963-2020.

Vacation Home Rentals Worldwide, 235 Kensington Ave., Norwood, NJ 07648. Tel. 800-633-3284 or 201-767-9393.

Villas International, 71 West 23rd St., New York, NY 10010. Tel. 800-221-2260 or 212-929-7585.

We have suggested hotels in Zürich and Geneva that are either near parks or have apartment facilities or special amenities for families. Families traveling with children to Switzerland will be delighted to find a group of hotels specifically designed for them. The **Swiss Family Hotels** all meet certain "child-friendly" standards set by a private hotel association and fall into three categories. Found primarily in resort areas, the **Happy Family Swiss Hotels** have supervised playrooms, grass playgrounds, games, organized picnics and walks, cooking facilities for preparing baby food, kids' meals, high chairs, cribs, and cots. Many have apartments and all provide free child care at least 24 hours per week. The hotels are generally expensive or deluxe with the following price reductions given to kids who sleep in your room: Kids up to age 6 stay free of charge; 6- through 12-

year-olds are given 50 percent reductions; 12- through 16-year-olds receive a 30 percent reduction.

In addition, the **"Super" Happy Family Swiss Hotels** will care for kids 3 and over, free of charge, for at least 5 days a week, 8 hours per day. Infants are cared for by agreement. Those falling into the third category of Swiss Family Hotel have unsupervised children's playrooms and some are in the moderate price range. All are listed in the free guide "Hotels Specially Suitable for Families," available from the SNTO. We have provided a list of some of these hotels in the three most popular Swiss resort areas of the Bernese Oberland, the Valais, and the Grisons under "Where to Stay" and have profiled certain hotels where we stayed with our children.

For a list of **inexpensive hotels, inns, and pensions,** request the two brochures "Inexpensive Hotels and Country Inns" from the SNTO. In rural areas, **guest houses** or *Zimmer* are also a reasonable option. Always be on the lookout for *Zimmerfrei* (Room Free) signs.

Many youth **hostels** welcome families and have three- to four-bedded rooms. Request the Swiss Youth Hostel's guide from the SNTO.

Camping is a magnificent way to experience the outdoor splendor of Switzerland. The campgrounds in major cities that we have listed are often found outside of town. A complete listing of campgrounds, rated from one to five stars, is available from the Federation of Swiss Camping Clubs, Habsburgerstr. 35, 6000 Luzern, or from the SNTO.

Nurseries and Kindergartens

Switzerland has one of the most efficient child care systems for visitors. *Kindergartens* are not schools, but supervised child-care centers. *Kinderaufsicht* or *garderie* (nurseries) are also readily found for babies. All of the Happy Family Swiss Hotels provide these services and often make them available on a fee basis for nonresident guests.

We have indicated which major winter resorts have a nursery or kindergarten and how you can obtain further information. Kids will be cared for by trained *moniteurs* while they play, eat, and learn to ski. The Swiss National Tourist Office has compiled a very complete list of nurseries or kindergartens in most Swiss holiday resorts and towns. These facilities accept children for a full or half-day. Contact your nearest SNTO for their brochure "Nurseries." Many Swiss department stores have taken the pain out of shopping with young ones and have a *crèche,* or supervised playroom, where you can leave your child for a short while. Check in department stores in major cities such as Zürich or Berne.

Getting Around

The efficient Swiss have developed one of the world's best public transportation networks, which offers a wide variety of ways to get about. High-speed trains venture over jagged peaks, cog railways cling to sheer mountainsides, funicular railways travel through mountain passes, and dangling aerial cableways or chair lifts sweep you up through the clouds. Vintage paddle steamers traverse the country's many lakes and pedalboats can be rented for cruising.

In addition to the budget Eurail Saverpass (see Chapter 7), families traveling only in Switzerland should consider the **Family Card,** which provides free transportation to children under 16 if they are traveling with adults who have purchased a **Swiss Pass** or a **Swiss Card.** The Swiss Pass entitles adults to unlimited trips on nearly all of the Swiss travel system's private **trains, boats, and postal buses** and provides reductions on many mountain trains and cable cars. Eurail passes are unfortunately not valid on many of these. Passes are available for 4, 8, or 15 days or 1 month. The Swiss Card, valid for 1 month, entitles you to a round trip from the railroad station at Switzerland's border or from the airport to your Swiss destination. You then receive all other tickets (railroad, boat, or postal bus) at half-fare and a reduction on mountain railroads. Both passes are available from travel agents and must be purchased outside of Switzerland by non-Swiss residents.

Many fast-moving **Swiss Intercity (IC) trains** have a large **kindergarten car** with such amenities as colorful rocking horses, wooden-block castles, infants' changing areas, and game tables. **Car** travelers need only a passport, car registration papers, and a valid driver's license. Children under 12 must ride in the backseat and car seats or seat belts are required. Alpine roads are open from May until late fall. For breaks from autostrasse driving watch for Mövenpick restaurants (also found in almost every Swiss town), which feature children's menus, changing tables, and dinner-hour gifts. On Swiss public **cable cars, buses, and city trams,** children under 6 ride free, ages 6 through 15 pay half-price, and teens over 16 are charged full fare. **Bicycles** are for rent at most railroad stations and can be returned at any other station. Reservations must be made the day before by 6 PM.

Nuts and Bolts

Does anyone care what time it is? Shops are generally open from 8 AM to 12 PM and 1:30–6:30 PM Monday through Friday and close at 4 PM on Saturdays and all day Sunday. Shops are also closed in cities on Monday mornings. Typical banking hours are 8:30 AM to 4:30 or 5 PM.

National holidays: New Year's Day (January 1–2), Easter, Labor Day (May 1), Ascension Day, Whit Monday, Swiss National Day (August 1), and Christmas.

Can I have my allowance? The Swiss monetary unit is the Swiss *franc*. There are 10, 20, 50, 100, 500, and 1,000 *franc* notes and 1, 2, and 5 franc coins. Francs are divided into 100 *rappen*, called *centimes* in French-speaking Switzerland. There are 5, 10, 20, and 50 *rappen* coins.

Telephones: The country code for Switzerland is 41. You can direct-dial international calls from public phones, the post office, or a PTT office.

Useful nationwide phone numbers: English-speaking operator is 191; emergency is 117; ambulance is 144; for road conditions and mountain passes, dial 163; emergency road service is 140.

Embassies and consulates: The U.S. Consulate is at Zollikerstr. 14, Zürich [Tel. (01) 552566]; the U.S. Embassy is at Jubiläumstr. 93, Berne, [Tel. (031) 437011]; the Canadian Consulate is at Belpstr. 11, Berne [Tel. (031) 252261]; the Canadian Embassy is at Kirchenfeldstr. 88, Berne [Tel. (031) 446381].

Let's Eat

In the French and Italian cantons, breakfast is continental, while in the German- and Romansch-speaking cantons, all meals are heartier. Kids will enjoy starting their day with the delicious Swiss cereal called *Birchermüesli*, a blend of oats, fruits, nuts, and often yogurt. Children love a mug of *ovomaltine* hot chocolate (our Ovaltine) while you savor your coffee or tea.

The main Swiss meal is lunch, for which schoolkids come home and all is closed from noon to 1:30. Dinner is often a very light meal. Kids rave about the Swiss fast-food *Raclette*, a cheese and potato dish, and *fondue*, a bowl of melted cheese in which everyone dips bread, especially in the French-speaking cantons. *Hornli* and *Apfelmus* are small noodles served with applesauce. Delicious *Ramequins* are cheese pies served around Geneva and Lausanne, and *Roschti*, a Swiss version of hash-brown potatoes, are equally hard for kids to resist, especially around Neuchâtel. Fussy types can always get a *Wienerli* (hot dog) in the German-speaking cantons, where sandwiches are known as *Restbrot* or *Belegtes Brot*. The Swiss make great fizzy apple juice, called *Apfelsaft*, which our children called "kids' champagne." Swiss cheeses are delicious. Try *Appenzeller*, *Emmenthal* (what we call "Swiss cheese"), and *Gruyère* in their hometown cities.

No one can resist Swiss chocolate for dessert. Bring lots of dental floss and toothpaste for your taste tests of Lindt, Tobler, Suchard, and Cailler. *Bricelets* are wafer-thin cream biscuits from the French-speaking cantons; *cholermues* are special crêpes; *Rüeblitorte* is a scrumptious carrot cake, especially near Zürich. Meringues from the

Bernese Oberland and walnut pies in the Grisons are sinfully delicious.

Formula and Baby Food, Diapers and Baby Gear

Baby food and disposable diapers (*Papierwindeln* in German-speaking cantons, *couches á jeter* in French-speaking cantons, and *pannolini di carta* in Italian-speaking cantons) are always available in the Migros and Coop supermarket chains. Familiar brands such as Pampers are readily found. Formula can be purchased in pharmacies.

Sidewalk Talk

Switzerland has four national languages, although many Swiss speak English, too. French is the language of the west; Italian is spoken in the south; Romansch (a language that sounds a bit like Portuguese), is spoken in the Grisons and Engadin. The remaining 75 percent of the population speaks German. Refer to Germany, France, and Italy for helpful children's phrases.

The Lay of the Land

Switzerland has twenty-three cantons, three of which are divided into half-cantons. Each is a small sovereign state. We have divided the country into the German-, French-, Italian-, and Romansch-speaking cantons.

GERMAN-SPEAKING CANTONS

ZÜRICH

Zürich sits on the northern tip of the majestic swan-filled Zürichsee. Beautiful gardens line the lake, from which you can see distant, snow-capped peaks. Your kids will especially enjoy the streets around the Bahnhofstrasse, in the city's charming historic center, with its many toy stores and mouth-watering pastry shops. Stocking stuffers such as top-notch art supplies, puzzles, and fantasy dolls are among the wonderful selection at the Bahnhofstrasse's Franz Carl Weber Toy Store, which also has branches throughout the country.

Zürich is an easy city to explore on foot. Public **trams** are very efficient and serve all of the city. Purchase an inexpensive 24-hour pass, called a *tageskarte*. **Lake steamers** depart from the Bürkliplatz, on the southern end of the Bahnhofstrasse, for jaunts on the lake.

Trips down the Limmat River through the city depart from the Landesmuseum (see "Museums," below).

Wha'd'ya Wanna Do?

Pick up *Zürich News* at the **tourist office** at the main train station or at airport terminals A or B for listings of current events. Check with the tourist office for locations of **Freizeitanlagen,** "leisure facilities" where kids can do craft projects. In the summer there is swimming and sailing on the lake; the sandy shore of **Standbad Mythenquai** is the nicest beach for young children. Zürich's **telephone area code** is 01.

Where to Stay

HOTELS
The *Atlantis Sheraton* is a modern hotel with family suites, children's rooms with bunk beds and child-scale furniture, an indoor pool, and playroom 20 minutes outside of the town center. Dölschiweg 234. Tel. 4630000. **Deluxe.**

The *Nova-Park,* an enormous modern complex on the outskirts of town, has a kindergarten with activities and a pool. Locals call it the hotel with the TV bar as there are so many televisions in its lobby. Accessible by tram to central Zürich. Badesnerstr. 420. Tel. 4912222. **Expensive.**

The *Hotel Schiff,* 25 kilometers from the town center, has apartments, a pool, a children's playroom, and a kid's menu. Zürich-Ellikon. Tel. (052) 431741. **Moderate.**

The *Hotel Zürichberg* is near the zoo and is popular with families. Orellistr. 2, 8044. Tel. 2523848. **Moderate.**

The cozy *Foyer Hottingen,* for single women and families only, has a kitchen. Hottingerstr. 31. Tel. 479315. **Inexpensive.**

Outside of town the Schweizerische Familienherbergen, 4460 Gelterkinden [Tel. (061) 991747], rents very inexpensive weekly apartments. **Inexpensive.**

CAMPGROUNDS
Camping Seebucht is on the outskirts of town along the lake. Open May–Sept. Seestr. 559. Tel. 4821612.

Detour! What to See and Do

THE ALTSTADT

Most of the city's attractions are in the **Altstadt** (old city), between Bahnhofstrasse and the Burkliplatz, where the lake steamers depart. Save bread for the many swans and seagulls along its Limmat River. **Lindenhof Park,** a beautiful square with trees and a fountain overlooking the city, is popular with children and their families. It was the site of the Celtic and Roman settlements from which the city sprang. In June its lime trees bloom, filling the air with their sweet scent. Nearby in the square of St. Peterhofstatt is the **Peterskirche,** whose 13th-century church tower has what is said to be Europe's largest clock face: 28 feet wide!

Just One Look: Museums

The **Indianermuseum,** western Europe's only museum devoted to native American Indian culture, has an extensive collection of ritual objects, masks, jewelry, and real teepees. Fee. Schulhaus Feldstr. 89. Sat. 2–5, Sun. 10–12. Tel. 2410050. Tram 8 or bus 13.

Kulturama is a science museum with biology, anthropology, and paleontology presented in a novel way. Families of human skeletons go through the motions of day-to-day living. Special fossil-huntings for kids and adults and a painting competition called Dinosaur Days are among Kulturama's special events. Fee for museum and workshops. Espenhofweg 60. Mon.–Fri. and first Sun. of the month 10–5. Tel. 4932525. Tram 14 to Triemli.

The **Schweizerisches Landesmuseum** is one of the country's best museums devoted to folk culture, covering Switzerland from the 12th through the 19th century. Its top-floor costume display, collection of dolls, doll houses, and trains and its recreated craft workshops are favorites. There's a hall of weapons and an old apothecary's shop with a crocodile suspended from the ceiling. Free. Museumstr. 2, across from the train station on the Limmat River. Mid-June–mid-Sept. Tues.–Fri. and Sun. 10–5, Sat. 10–4; mid-Sept.–mid-June Tues.–Fri. and Sun. 10–12 and 2–5, Sat. 2–4. Tel. 2211010.

The **Museum Rietberg** is filled with objects from Indian, Chinese, and African cultures. Our Swiss friend brings drawing materials with her and has her kids draw those objects they like best while she takes in the exhibitions. They adore the masks. Fee. Galerstr. 15. Tues.–Sun. 10–5, Wed. until 9. Tel. 2024528. Adjacent to the museum is a wonderful park with old trees and a view of the lake and the lovely **Villa Wesendonk,** former home of Richard Wagner. The **Belvoir Park,** across the street from the Rietberg, on Seestrasse, has a merry-go-round of bicycles, which kids can rotate with their own energy.

In the center of town head for the **Zürcher Spielzeugmuseum** which houses the collection of toy-store maven Franz Carl Weber. You'll see miniature toy shops, trains, optical and mechanical toys, steam engines, dolls that speak many languages, and much more. Fee. Fortunagasse 15. Mon.–Fri. 2–5, Sat. 1–4. Tel. 2119305.

The **Wohnmuseum** shows how people lived back in the early 17th through 19th centuries. You'll see tiny baby clothes and a kid's play corner with dolls and toy soldiers. Its basement features an exhibition of dolls created by a local Swiss puppet artist in the 1920s. Free. Bärgengasse 22. Tues.–Fri. and Sun. 10–12 and 2–5, Sat. 10–12, 2–4. Tel. 2111716.

Where the Sidewalk Ends: Zoos and More Parks

The beautiful **Zürichhorn Gardens** above the city are filled with sculptures including the fun kinetic work *Heureka* by Jean Tinguely. The **Zoo Zürich**, in a large park atop the Zürichberg, has over 2,000 animals from all over the world. As you enter, note the sign that tells of the zoo's most recent births. Fee. Tram 5 from Paradeplatz. Summer 8–6; winter until 5. Tel. 2512500. En route to the zoo from the tram you'll find a miniature golf course, carousel, and the **Paradies der Alpenbahnen,** a miniature train directed by a robot stationmaster. The train transports children through a miniature Swiss landscape with mountains and lakes, villages and mills, all at a scale of 1/45. Daily 1:30–6:30. Tel. 2523830. From the city's **Botanical Gardens,** on Pelikanstrasse 40, take the funicular up to the summit of **Felsenegg,** where there's another carousel.

Special Events

Zürich welcomes the beginning of spring with **Sechseläuten,** a festival kicked off with a large **children's parade** and a show of wild, vintage costumes. At 6 PM at Sechseläutenplatz, the "Böögg," a snowman made of paper, is burned to bid farewell to the cold. Held on the third or fourth Sunday of April. Tourist office: Tel. 2114000.

NEAR ZÜRICH

Five kilometers south of Zürich, in *Kilchberg,* you can take a delicious tour of the **Lindt Chocolate Company.** The best part is the free samples. Free. Seestr. 204. Tours: Thurs. May–Oct. Reservations: Tel. 7162223. Further south is *Thalwil,* accessible by a 90-minute boat ride or a short drive down the Zürichsee. Its wonderful **playground** has a real ship set in sand where kids can play sailor. The lake is beautiful for swimming, and you can make campfires.

Uetliberg, Zürich's closest mountain, is about an hour outside the city. Once there, you can hike up a trail (45 minutes) or take a train to the summit, where there is a small restaurant, a large playground, and the **belvedere tower,** where children can play knights and queen. From the tower there is a spectacular view. Older kids will enjoy the hike at night, when the trail is illuminated. Trains depart from Zürich-Selnau Station.

Don't leave Zürich without visiting the small town of *Rapperswil,* south of the city, on the north shore of the lake. Its **Knie Kinderzoo (Children's Zoo)** is home to Switzerland's treasured **Knie National Circus,** which has assembled a heavenly park for young children. Kids can climb in Noah's Ark, visit a whale aquarium, and watch a dolphin show. There are elephants and ponies to ride, a tricky maze to negotiate, a gypsy caravan and a small train to tour the zoo. Fee. Mid-March–early November daily 9–6. Tel (055) 275222. Other stops in Rapperswil might include its regional **Heimatmuseum,** which features folklore collections; a massive 13th-century **castle** with round towers, armor, and falconry displays; and the town's **deer park** overlooking the lake.

East of Zürich, in *Pfäffikon,* kids can splash in the wave pool of the **Alpamare water park** and spa, whose highlight is the 1200-foot-long inner-tube ride down a swirling water slide, the **Alpabob Wildwasser.** Tel. (055) 472288, 483222.

THE EAST

APPENZELL AND ENVIRONS

A little narrow-gauge train will transport you from St. Gallen to the charming city of *Appenzell* in the canton of the same name. The canton has maintained a distinct sense of Swiss tradition. Quaint villages filled with painted, bracket-gabled houses are surrounded by soft undulating farmland. The mountains are not as high as those found near Lake Thun, but the gondola lift from *Schwäglp* to the peak of **Mount Säntis** is equally dramatic.

In the city of Appenzell, visit the **Volkskinde Museum** for a unique look at the folk culture and traditions of the region. Next door, you can watch the strong-smelling Appenzell cheese being made at the **Appenzeller Schaukäserei (Appenzell cheese dairy)** Fee. Museum: Tues.–Sun. 8–7. Cheese making: 9–3. Along the town's main street look for Appenzell cakes decorated with portraits of cow herders in their distinct yellow pants and red jackets. At festival time, you'll see local women wearing immense hats with tulle wings.

AROUND SCHAFFHAUSEN

Schaffhausen, north of St. Gallen on the Rhine, has preserved many of its medieval qualities. From the boat landing, climb the tower of its round fortress, the 16th-century **Schloss Munot,** for a great view of the town and the Rhine Valley. Its moat has been turned into a deer park.

Europe's most powerful waterfall is in *Neuhausen am Rheinfall,* a short bus ride south of Schaffhausen. The falls reach a height of nearly 70 feet. From the castle **Schloss Laufen am Rheinfall,** walk to a small platform overhanging the falls for dramatic (but damp) views. Older kids will enjoy the 40-minute walk on a riverside path from the castle along the Rhine, where they can cross the river on a bridge just over the falls. The falls are illuminated on summer nights. There's a small fee to view the falls from the castle. There are thrilling **boat trips** to a pool in the middle of the falls. Fee. May and Oct. daily 11–5. June–Aug. daily 10–6. Tel. (053) 222576.

A riverboat will carry you from Schaffhausen to the storybook medieval town of *Stein-am-Rhein.* On the houses around the old town square there are elaborate paintings and carvings, called *oriels,* depicting the theme of each house. Hunt for the House of the Pelican, House of the Red Ox, and Inn of the Sun. On the second floor of the **town hall** is a magnificent armor collection. From the tower of the town's 13th-century **Höhenklingen Castle** there's a view of the forests and farmland of Germany. 2 km. out of town. Switzerland's largest doll museum, the **Puppenmuseum,** has over 400 antique dolls. Fee. Schwarzhorngasse 136. Mid-Mar.–Oct. Tues.–Sun. 10–5.

AROUND THE BODENSEE (LAKE CONSTANCE)

The unspoiled landscape of the Rhine between Schaffhausen and Stein-am-Rhein is dotted with picturesque medieval villages along the Swiss and German lakeshores. Switzerland shares the **Bodensee (Lake Constance)** with Germany and Austria. The boat rides between Schaffhausen and *Constance/Kreuzlingen* are said to be among the most scenic in Europe, with a number of citadels and castles visible from the water. There is charming display of dolls in *Kreuzlingen* at the **Puppenmuseum Jeannine** at the Castle Grisberg. Fee. Monday, Sat., Sun. 2–6. Tel. (072)724655. North of Kreuzlingen is *Horn,* called the "Riviera of the Lake," which offers swimming, wind surfing, and water-skiing. Be sure to look for the topiary animals in the gardens on the lake's **Mainau Island,** which is accessible from Swiss ports in addition to lakefront ports in Germany. (See "Germany").

Southwest of Kreuzlingen, in *Lipperswil,* en route back toward Zürich, is **Conny-Land,** a kitschy amusement park your kids will adore. Its *delphinen*, with a dolphin and sea lion show, is tops, and the enormous rubber trampoline in the shape of a castle was a big hit. The Las Vegas Magic Show and Aquatic Bar for adults leaves a lot to be desired. Tel. (054) 632365

LUCERNE (LUZERN) AND CENTRAL SWITZERLAND

The cantons of Uri, Schwyz, Unterwalden, Zug, and Lucerne have spectacular alpine scenery, with emerald waters, forested mountains, green meadows, and peaks that ascend almost vertically from Lake Lucerne. This is William Tell country, where the legendary Swiss hero was forced to shoot an apple off the top of his son's head with a crossbow. Was this fact or fiction? No one will "tell."

LUCERNE (LUZERN)

Idyllic Lucerne, on the northwest end of the sparkling waters of the Vierwaldstättersee (Lake Lucerne), attracts more visitors than any other Swiss city. And for good reason. Steep funiculars, water sports, and boat trips in old Swiss paddle steamers along Lake Lucerne are a few of the many attractions the whole family will enjoy. Lucerne's **tourist office** is at Frankenstrasse 1 (tel. 517171). The city's **telephone area code** is 041.

Detour! What to See and Do

Head up to the medieval **Museggmauer (Musegg ramparts)** which along with its seven large watchtowers used to surround the city. Free. Daily Apr.–Oct. 8–7. Climb the **Schirmer, Mannli,** and **Zyt** towers for great vistas. May–Oct.

THE OLD TOWN AND ALONG THE LAKE

Lucerne's medieval quarter was at one time guarded by its hand-painted covered wooden bridges, which are now a symbol of the city. The 14th-century **Kapellbrücke (Chapel bridge)** spanning the Reuss River has on its triangular ceiling beams over 100 paintings of the city's historical events: William Tell, the plague, a fire, a murder, and various battles. "It's kind of like a comic strip," observed a friend's 9-year-old. Over 650 feet long, the bridge has at one end an octagonal water tower which at one time served as a prison and torture chamber. The forty-five painted panels illustrating the medieval morality play *The Dance of Death* on the **Spreuerbrücke** are a bit more macabre.

When observing the **Löwendenkmal,** Lucerne's mammoth 30-foot-high sculpture of a dying lion carved into a rock face, 9-year-old Julie agreed with fellow globe-trotter Mark Twain, who described the monument as the "saddest and most poignant piece of rock in the world." The lion, pierced by a spear, holding his paw over a shield, honors the Swiss guards who fought to defend Marie Antoinette in the French Revolution. Off Löwenstrasse. Adjacent to the lion sculpture is the amazing **Gletschergarten (glacier garden),** remnant of the huge layer of ice that covered Lucerne millions of years ago. The 30-foot-deep glacial potholes and spiral grooves are evidence of this past. Fossils of petrified palm leaves and seashells indicate that this area was a tropical landscape 20 million years ago. The garden's adjacent **museum** chronicles the miracle of the glaciers and has an enormous relief map of the Alps. Don't miss its labyrinth, which has a **maze** made out of mirrors. Fee. Denkmalstr. 4. May–Oct. 15 daily 9–6; Mar.–Apr. and mid.Oct.–mid-Nov. daily 9–5; mid-Nov.–Feb. Tues.–Sun. 10:30–4:30. Tel. 514340.

Another larger-than-life expression of the "wounds of war" is found in the **Great Panorama of Lucerne,** said to be the world's largest existing painting. The circular painting measures 12,000 square feet and brings the horrors of the Franco-Prussian War to life with thousands of full-sized people huddled in the fierce cold of winter. Löwenstr. 18. Fee. May, Apr., and Oct. daily 9–5; May–Sept. daily 9–6. Tel. 502250.

Just One Look: Museums

The **Trachtenmuseum (Costume Museum),** set in a park, has costumes and accessories from all over Switzerland and parts of Europe, including mementos from the Swiss Yodeling Association and life-size dolls in Swiss regional costume. Fee. Follow Dreilindenstr. for 1 km., and turn left on Basel Road to Utenberg Road. Daily Easter–late Apr. 9–5:30. Tel. 368058.

The **Verkehrshaus (Swiss National Transport Museum),** the world's largest transportation museum, contains models and examples of every imaginable mode of transportation and lots of push-button exhibits. You'll see a steam-driven snow plough from the 1800s, hot-air balloons, and a Mercury space capsule. Ride on the miniature steam railway in the Swiss Railway Room, talk to an office robot, or trace a letter from the time it is dropped into a mailbox to when it arrives. Adjacent to the museum's restaurant is an old paddle steamer whose machinery and steering mechanisms kids can operate. Fee. Lidostr. 4. Mar.–Oct. daily 9–6; Nov.–Feb. daily 10–4. Accessible by city bus, lake ship (get off at first stop), or 1/2-hour walk along the lakeside promenade from the town center. Tel. 314444.

ALONG LAKE LUCERNE

Boats or paddle steamers will glide you to lakefront towns and resorts where glorious mountains rise sharply from the shore. A complete lake trip takes 6 hours but you can disembark at any of a number of villages and catch the next boat back. Most of the resorts are also accessible by car or train and have facilities for sailing, fishing, water-skiing, riding, and tennis. Boats leave from the landing across from the train station.

Weggis is the "queen of the lake resorts," with boating, swimming, and daily concerts at 11:00 AM in its main park. Sweep up the cable car from Weggis to **Mt. Rigi,** accessible from the elegant resort of *Vitznau.* From Vitznau you can follow the trail of Mark Twain and climb the mountain by 1-1/4-hour rack-railway. Rigi's grassy summit is filled with cows in the summer. Children often yodel in the summit's Kulm restaurant. The mountain resort has a Swiss Family Hotel, the Hotellerie Rigi (Tel. 831616). From Mt. Rigi, there's a train down to *Arth-Goldau* and its **Bergsturzmuseum (Avalanche Museum).** The town was buried in an avalanche in the early 1800s, and the museum details the disaster. Fee. About 18 km. east of Lucerne. Parkstr. 46. Apr. 15–Oct daily 1:30–6. Tel. 821939. Goldau's **Zoopark** is in the area of the great avalanche. Designed for children, it invites them to feed baby deer and admire small bears and mountain goats. Fee. Nov.–Feb. daily 8–5; Mar.–Oct. daily 8–7. Another train will take you back to Lucerne.

MOUNT PILATUS AND ENGELBERG

Take the world's steepest funicular up 7,000 feet to the top of rugged **Mount Pilatus.** Its sharply defined peaks stand alone, offering a tremendous view of the Alps from the top of the funicular. Kids like roaming the tunnels at the top. The trip is expensive but well worth the price in clear weather. Fee: children half-price. Funicular open summer only; go early to avoid crowds. To get to Pilatus, take a train or boat from Lucerne to Alpnachstad. You can opt to return via two small cable cars (open year-round) to Kriens, a suburb of Lucerne, and then take a trolley back into town.

Take the hour train ride from Lucerne to *Engelberg* and then ride a series of four cable cars up to **Mt. Titlis'** glacier, where kids can throw snowballs in summer or ski in winter. This is central Switzerland's highest mountain and at 10,000 feet, the view from the summit is worthy of many postcards home. In summer, you can cool off in the glacial caves at the top. Gerschnialp is Engelberg's beginning ski area, whose ski school has a ski kindergarten program for 3- through 6-year-olds and instruction for 7- through 14-year-olds. The resort has ice-skating and horse-drawn sleighs. Engelberg has two Swiss Family Hotels, the Edelweiss [tel. (041) 941204] and the Sporthotel Truebsee [Tel. (041) 941371]. For ski information, contact the **tourist office** Kur-und-Verkehrsverein, CH-6390, Engelberg [Tel. (041) 941161].

One of Lucerne's best Christmas events, **Klausjagen (chasing Santa Claus)**, is held annually on December 5 in *Küssnacht am Rigi,* on the northern tip of the lake. Locals in white gowns wear enormous illuminated headdresses that have been adorned with detailed cut-outs covered with transparent colored paper. Inside the headdress candles glow. St. Nicholas is then chased through the lake's tiny villages.

In February, on the Monday after Ash Wednesday, Lucerne has a **Carnival** parade through the streets which includes the giving of fruit to the kids. Carnival extends into the following week. Contact the Lucerne tourist office: Tel. (041) 517171.

BASEL

Basel is in the northwest corner of the country where Switzerland, Germany, and France meet. The Rhine River divides the city into two halves which are linked by six bridges. To the west of the river you'll find the city's well-preserved historic section, the Altstadt. Basel's historic center has very little traffic and is easy to walk. Motorboat tours depart from the port to the point in the Rhine where France, Germany, and Switzerland meet. The ferry boats that cruise the Rhine in Basel are unusual in that they are attached to cables. At the western end of the **Mittlere Rheinbrücke,** the Rhine's middle bridge, stop for a look at the **Lällekönig (tongue king).** This sculpture of a king sticking his tongue out at the other half of the city mocks the industrial section of **Klein-Basel,** which is to the east of the river.

Wha'd'ya Wanna Do?

For a small city, Basel has many offbeat, specialized museums that will truly captivate your children. You'll find museums devoted exclusively to the topics of cats, sports, firefighting, cartoons, coaches, sleighs, and anatomy, to mention just a few. The **tourist office** is at Blumenrain 2 (Tel. 255050). The city's **telephone area code** is 061.

Detour! What to See and Do

THE ALTSTADT
The medieval town is gathered around **Marktplatz,** where there is a lively morning flower and vegetable market. Walk through the plaza

to the magnificent rose-colored Gothic **Münster** and ascend the cathedral's tower for a sweeping vista of the Rhine. Look for one of the cathedral's circular windows featuring "a wheel of fortune." Fee for tower. Cathedral: Mon.–Fri. 10–6, Sat. 10–12 and 2–5, Sun 1–5; Oct.–Easter daily 10–12, 2–4. Tower: Mar.–Oct. The **Basel Marionette Theater** gives performances in the Zehntenkeller, which is part of the cathedral, at Münsterplatz 8. Tickets are available at Musik Hug, Freie Str. 70 (Tel. 222323). The **Kunstmuseum,** down the street from the cathedral, is considered one of Switzerland's greatest art museums. Works of Picasso, Dalí, Klee, Kandinsky, Rodin, and Calder fill its rooms. Fee: Sun. free. St. Alban-Graban 16. Tues.–Sun. 10–5. Tel. 220828.

A short walk away is the **Augustinergasse,** which houses three museums. The **Naturhistorisches Museum** has dinosaurs compared with recent species. The **Schweizerisches Museum für Volkskunde** is a folk art museum with artifacts and ethnological displays from Asia, Africa, and Europe, including full-scale re-created rituals of African initiation scenes with strange totems and shells. Fee. Augustinergasse 2. Both open May–Oct. Tues.–Sun. 10–5; Nov.–Apr. Tues.–Sun. 10–12, 2–5. Tel. 258282. The adjacent **Swiss Museum of European Folklife** has delightful displays of Easter eggs, folk art, Christmas crèches, and masks from Basel's legendary Fasnacht (see "Events"). Münsterplatz 20. May–Oct. Tues.–Sun. 10–5; Nov.–Apr. Tues.–Sun. 10–12, 2–5. Tel. 258282.

Just One Look: More Museums

The **Anatomische Sammlung** features human skeletons, including a "beheaded prisoner" from the 16th century. Fee. Pestalozzistr. 20. Sun. 10–12 Tel. 570555.

Basel's collection of **ancient musical instruments** has all kinds of percussion and folk instruments. The sounds the instruments make can be heard on tape. Fee: free Sun. Leonhardstr. 8. Wed. and Fri. 2–5, Sun. 10–12, 2–5. Tel. 255722.

At the **Feuerwehrmuseum,** kids can see old fire devices such as medieval hand-operated spraying devices and a four-seated bicycle, a very early forerunner to today's fire engine. Kornhausgasse 18. Sun. 2–5. Tel. 232200.

Among the exhibits in the **Historisches Museum Barfüsserkirche** is a section devoted to the history of Basel, which contains kooky masks from the city's **Vogel Gryff** festival (see "Events"). Look for the 17th-century mask the Lällenkönig near the stairway where watchworks enable his tongue to stick out and his eyes to roll. Barfüsserplatz. Wed.–Mon. 10–5. Tel. 220505.

The **Historisches Museum Kirschgarten,** in an 18th-century house, has old clocks and toys, including doll houses, miniature carriages, and vintage boats. Elisabethenstr. 27. May–Oct. Tues.–Sun. 10–5; Nov.–Apr. Tues.–Sun. 10–12, 2–5. Tel. 221333.

In a mansion with a beautiful garden, the **Katzen Museum** has 10,000 cat-related objects assembled by two feline fanatics. You'll see cats as toys, cats on engravings, cat paintings and jewelry, cat postage stamps, and mummified Egyptian cats. No Garfields here. Suburb of Riehen, on Baselstr. 101. Tram 6 from downtown. Sun. 10–12, 2–5. Tel. 672694 or 259323.

The **Kunsthalle Basel** is devoted to contemporary art. It is set in a garden area with a restaurant amidst sculpture. Steinenberg 7. Daily 10–5, Wed. until 9:30. Tel. 234833. Nearby, Jean Tinguely's kinetic **Carnival Fountain,** made of miscellaneous found objects, is a favorite for locals as it seems to be doing a whimsical dance. You'll get soaked if you get too close!

The **Kutschen-und-Schlittensammlung (Collection of Coaches and Sleighs)** has 19th-century hunting carriages, dog carts, mail coaches, and even "one-horse open sleighs." The exhibition is in a barn in the **St. Jakob Botanical Gardens.** Free. Vorder-Brüglingen. Wed. and Sun. 2–5. Tel. 220505.

The **Basler Papiermühle,** housed in a 15th-century paper mill, has demonstrations of how paper is made. Kids can watch bookbinders at work. Its stamping mill is driven by water, as it was centuries ago. Fee. St. Alban-Tal 35–37. Tues.–Sun. 2–5. Tel. 239652.

The **Sammlung Karikaturen und Cartoons** features the cartoon drawings of 20th-century artists from all over the world. Accordingly, "Chuckling is permitted." Fee. St. Alban-Corstadt 9. Wed. and Sat. 4–6:30, Sun. 2–5. Tel. 221288.

Among the displays in the **Schweizerisches Sportmuseum** are bicycles from 1820 to the present. Displays include a trike without handlebars and hilarious photos of people falling off bikes, plus skates and skis from many eras. Kids can see examples of national games such as *schwingen* (a type of wrestling) and *hornussen* (a ball game). Free. Missionsstr. 28. Daily 2–5, except Sun. 10–12, 2–5. Tel. 251221.

The **Spielzeug-und-Dorfmuseum,** near the cat museum, features Swiss toys in a renovated 17th-century house. "Natural toys" made from bones and pine cones, "rural toys" created in mountainous regions, and "toys of diverse materials" such as tin, paper, or clay are on view. Nostalgic miniature worlds such as doll houses and kitchens have been set up. Its village museum has examples of old Swiss village cultures. In Riehen suburb, Baselstr. 34. Tram 6 from downtown. Wed. and Sat. 2–5, Sun. 10–12, 2–5. Tel. 672829.

Where the Sidewalk Ends: Zoos and Parks

Basel's **zoo,** said to be one of Switzerland's best, has 4,000 animals representing 600 different species in a magnificent park in the middle of the city. The zoo specializes in breeding animals that are endangered species. Head for the children's zoo to ride an elephant and pet young or newly born animals. New walkers can waddle amidst Mr. and Mrs. Penguin and their children, and there are trained elephant and sea lion performances. Fee. Next to the train station. Summer daily 8–6:30; off-season until 5:30.

Lange Erlenpark, an animal preserve, has a delightful carousel operating from April through October. A playground and ponds for sailing model boats are east of the animal park. Free. Fasanenstr. north of the city center. Open daily. **St. Jakob's Botanischer Garten** and park has a sports complex and the coach and sleigh museum (see "Museums"). You'll know you've arrived by the signature life-sized dinosaur that sits proudly on its hill.

Special Events

The Monday after Ash Wednesday's three-day **Fasnach (Carnival)** has locals in outlandish costumes swarming the streets to the sound of fifes and drums. There are even costume balls for children. For details, contact the tourist office. Tel. 25550.

BERNE (BERN)

In spite of the city's insignia **Child-Eater (Kindlifresserbrunnen)** fountain, which displays the figure of a giant enjoying a meal of young children, kids will immediately feel welcome in Berne. The city appears to be a page torn out of a fairytale with its turrets, towers, streets lined with miles of arcades, and hundreds of fountains, many of which are decked with flowers.

Ask any child who has visited the Swiss capital what he or she remembers the most. "The Bears" will inevitably be the response. Duke Berchtold V of Zähringen, the founder of Berne, claimed he would name the city after the first animal he slaughtered in a great chase. The animal he killed was a bear and thus Berne got its name. Locals take their mascot very seriously: The town's loving tribute to its emblem is the famous bear pit, a sunken cage where a dozen bears live in the center of the city. Another treasured memory will be the fact that Berne is the home of mouth-watering Toblerone chocolate. *This Week in Berne,* available from the **tourist office** at the Bahnhof (Tel. 227676), lists entertainment and special events. The city's **telephone area code** is 031.

Getting Around

Berne is a walkable city. Most sites are in the small hilly area of the old town. The city has a good system of trams and buses; for an unlimited number of rides, purchase the economical 24-hour season ticket or "tourist card," which enables you to travel for a number of days. Kids will enjoy the **Marzili Cogwheel Railway,** which runs from the Bundesterrasse down to the banks of the Aare River. The shortest railway in Europe, it is one of the few still operated by water.

Where to Stay

Berne is the urban gateway to the resorts of the Bernese Oberland, where **chalets** and **apartments** (as well as numerous Swiss Family Hotels and small inns) abound. If you are planning to spend more than a week in this area, rent a chalet and make easy day trips into Berne. **Camping Kappelenbrück,** 12 kilometers from town on the river, has modern facilities. Open mid-Jan.–Oct. 1. Tel. (031) 361007.

Detour! What to See and Do

AROUND MARKTGASSE

Start at the the **"child-eating" ogre fountain (Kindlifresserbrunnen)** on Kornhausplatz near Marktgasse, and remind your kids to *behave* or else . . . This peculiar 16th-century fountain depicts a giant with writhing infants in his arms munching on a child. Marktgasse, the old town's main street, bustles with activity. Kornhausplatz also boasts Berne's colorful **Zeitgloggeturm,** an astronomical clock with mechanical puppets who put on a charming performance every hour. You'll know it's about to begin when a rooster crows and lifts its wings. Watch the show from the corner of Kramgasse and Hotelgasse. Find a spot at least 10 minutes before the hour as the show starts 4 minutes before. Guided tours of the inside of the tower: May–Oct. at 4:30. Fee for tour. Tower tickets from tourist office: Tel. 227676.

The 270 steps of the tower of the magnificent Gothic **Münster** lead to a platform from which there are spectacular vistas of the towers and turrets of Berne, the river, and the Bernese Alps. Cathedral: Mon.–Sat. 10–12 and 2–5, Sun. 11–2, 2–5. Tower: Tues.–Fri. 10–11:30 and 2–3:30, Sat. 10–11:30 and 2–4:30, Sun. 11–11:30.

Cross the river via the Nydeggbrücke (Nydegg Bridge); on your left you'll find the **Bärengraben (Bear Pits).** The oldest town seal, dating from 1224, shows a bear as Berne's symbol and there is a city bear pit that dates from 1480. The dozen or so bears in this pit will perform all kinds of acrobatics for your kids if they dangle a snack above the bears' heads. No meat please; the bears are strict vegetarians. At

Easter, the newborn bear babies are introduced to visitors. Free. Pit: spring and summer daily 7–6; Oct.–Mar. 8:30–4.

Northwest of Marktgasse, along the river, is the **Kunstmuseum,** with the world's greatest collection of the works of Paul Klee. It's only a short walk from the museum to the **Botanischer Garten** via the bridge, the **Lorrainebrücke.** This vast garden has fountains, pools, and tropical plants. Museum: Fee. Children free. Hodlerstr. 8–12. Wed.–Sun. 10–5, Tues. 10–9. Tel. 220944. Garden: Free. Altenbergrain 21. Mon.–Fri. 7–6; Sat.–Sun. 8–5:30. Tel. 654911.

Just One Look: Museums

Across town is the plaza of Helvetiaplatz, where there is a number of city museums (take tram 3 or 5). The **Naturhistorisches Museum** has Europe's largest diorama display, but the real highlight for kids is Barry, a St. Bernard dog who saved people in the Alps. Fee. Berneastr. 15. Mon.–Sat. 9–12 and 2–5, Sun. 10–12, 2–5. Tel. 431839.

The **Bernisches Historisches Museum** has armor and re-created Swiss rooms in its collection. Look for the enormous scale on the second floor which weighed 2-ton cannons during the Berne arsenal. Fee. Children free; Sat. adults free. Helvetiaplatz 5. Tues.–Sun. 10–5. Tel. 431811.

The **Schweizerisches P.T.T. Museum** has stamps from around the globe and Swiss postal service paraphernalia; look for the first postal coach from 1832. Free. Helvetiaplatz 4. Mon. 2–5, Tues.–Sun. 10–12, 2–5. Tel. 449288.

Where the Sidewalk Ends: Parks and Zoos

Berne has been voted Europe's "most beautiful city of flowers" and you'll see why. Beyond Helvetiaplatz is the **Dählözi Städischer Tierpark (Zoological Garden),** which is home to European animals such as Przewalski's wild horse, musk-ox, seal, bison, and moose. There's also a vivarium, playground, and pony rides. Fee. Dalmaziquai 149. Bus 18, station Tierpark. Summer daily 8–6:30; winter daily 9–5. Tel. 430616.

At the far end of the Nydegg Bridge is a steep walk that leads you up to the sweet-scented **Rosengarten (Rose Gardens)** noted for their great city panorama. The view is especially spectacular at night, when the old part of Berne is illuminated daily from dusk until midnight. There are shady spots for picnics and life-sized chess games to watch.

Sports and Special Events

Pick up a listing of Berne's curling rinks, horseback riding facilities, fishing, ice-skating rinks, miniature golf clubs, and swimming pools at the tourist office. Ka-we-de is a **swimming pool** with artificial waves [Tel. 430175]. In summer good swimmers can swim in the Marzili River below the Bundeshaus. Tel. 220046.

On the fourth Monday in November, Berne hosts the enchanting **Zibelemärit (onion market)**, where you can find dolls and small animals made from onions. June's **Festival of Youth** has horse-drawn carts, puppet shows, and special activities for teens. For both, contact the tourist office: Tel. 227676.

THE BERNESE OBERLAND

With towering peaks, glaciers, and flower-filled valleys, the Bernese Oberland is the dramatic picture-postcard landscape that the name Switzerland evokes. This region has numerous lakefront and alpine holiday resorts. In summer you can picnic and hike in fields of wildflowers set against snow-capped mountains and thundering waterfalls, swim or sail on Lake Thun or Lake Brienz, or reach dizzying alpine heights in cable cars and aerial trams. Switzerland's highest ride up the Jungfraujoch sweeps you up through the clouds to a white glacial world. In winter, the ski resorts of Wengen, Grindelwald, Mürren and Gstaad all have a myriad of facilities for children. Request the holiday brochure **Familienferien** from the Berner Oberland **tourist office**, CH-3800 Interlaken: Tel. (036) 222621. It lists the region's hotels, restaurants, campgrounds, and summer or winter activities designed especially for families.

THE THUNERSEE

Majestic Thunersee is a perfect destination if you want beaches, water sports, castles, and easy access to the high Alps. Thunersee, said to be one of the most beautiful lakes for sailing, has a noted sailing school and several swimming beaches. For details, contact its **tourist office:** Tel. (036) 222121. At night, the lake is illuminated and elegant swans glide along its mirrored waters. Lake steamers connect all lakefront towns. Along the lake's north shore, en route to Interlaken, is a string of picturesque resorts with *Thun* at the northern tip of the lake. Kids will enjoy exploring the real dungeon in Thun's four-turreted castle, the **Schloss Thun**. The castle **museum** has displays on the Swiss army and firearms. Climb the corner turrets for a great view. Late March–Oct. 10–5. Tel. (033) 232001.

INTERLAKEN AND ENVIRONS

Interlaken, situated between the lakes of the Thunersee and the Brienzersee, is the main tourist base for the Bernese Oberland. Kids enjoy riding horse-drawn carriages through the center of town. Interlaken's **Casino Kursaal** has daily folk dancing, yodeling, and flag-tossing performances. It's very corny but kids love it. The casino also has a beautiful flower clock in its gardens. On the other side of the Aare River, there's an open-air **swimming pool** and **miniature golf course.** Take the funicular up to *Heimwehfluh,* where there's an **amusement park** with a bobsled run, model trains, a theater for children, and a wonderful playground. Departs near the Interlaken Ostbahnhof. Fee. At the top you'll have a beautiful alpine vista. In Interlaken you'll find three Swiss Family Hotels: the Du Lac [Tel. (036) 222922], Europe [Tel. (036) 227141], and the Splendid [Tel. (036) 227612].

Late June through early September, Interlaken attracts visitors to its outdoor performances of **Schiller's** *Wilhelm Tell,* with a cast of over 250 and herds of cows and horses which parade through town before the hoopla begins. Although in German, it's very colorful for children. Ticket information from Tellbüro, Bahnhofstr. 5 [Tel. (036) 223723] or from the **tourist office** at Höheweg 37, CH-3800 Interlaken [Tel. (036) 222121].

The **Bernese Oberland Railway** will take you up to *Wilderswil* for an amazing view of the **Jungfrau,** one of the most spectacular peaks in Europe. From Wilderswil you can climb for another hour by cogwheel to *Schynige,* where there's an alpine botanical garden and a view of lakes Thun and Brienz. Fee. Late June–mid-September. Seven kilometers east of Interlaken are the **St-Beatus Höhlen (St. Beatus Caves),** which were said to have been occupied by a dragon long ago. You'll see wax figures of prehistoric cave inhabitants amidst illuminated stalactites and underground pools. Fee. Wear rubber-soled shoes as the caves are slippery. Also accessible by boat on the Thunersee from Spiez. Caves: Palm Sunday–mid-Oct. daily 9:30–5. Tel. (036) 411643.

THE SCHILTHORN

The Jungfrau region, near Interlaken, consists of the towering peaks of the Jungfrau, Mönch, and Eiger mountains. A journey up the magnificent **Schilthorn** includes a train, funicular, and aerial cable car. From Interlaken, take the train to *Lauterbrünnen* to see a spectacular seven-level glacial waterfall, the **Trummelbach Falls,** which descend within a mountainous cave. Kids will get a thrill out of traveling the underground funicular near the falls. Fee. Apr.–Oct.

From **Lauterbrünnen** take the bus to *Stechelberg* to see **Mürrenbach,** Europe's highest waterfall. In Stechelberg take the four-stage cable car for 30 minutes to the summit of the Schilthorn, where you'll have a spectacular view of the Eiger, Mönch, and Jungfrau peaks. If the heights don't make you dizzy, the rotating restaurant at the top will. Note the restaurant window marked "007"; a James Bond movie was filmed on the Schilthorn. Cable car: Fee. Avoid it on weekends; it's packed. The cable car from Stechelberg operates every half hour in the summer.

THE JUNGFRAUJOCH

The most thrilling climb in all of Switzerland is that up the **Jungfraujoch,** the second highest of the Oberland peaks, to the highest train station in Europe. Check the weather before you leave, as it's only worth it on a clear day. Bring warm clothes, even if it's sunny and warm when you depart. From Interlaken's Ostbahnhof travel by train to *Lauterbrünnen* to catch a cogwheel to *Kleine Scheidegg.* The cogwheel stops at *Wengen,* a beautiful year-round mountaintop, traffic-free resort. With many easy slopes for children and a ski kindergarten for 3- to 7-year-olds, Wengen is the best ski resort in this area for families. Kids can also skate, toboggan, and take sleigh rides. Buggy sleds will take you through the charming town center. Wengen's Swiss Family Hotel is the Silberhorn [Tel. (036) 565131]. For resort information, contact the Wegen **tourist office,** CH-3823 [Tel. (036) 551414].

From Wengen the climb really begins. The Jungfrau Railway chugs earnestly for 40 minutes up a track chiseled out of the precipitous mountain before entering the Eiger Tunnel, which has been cut into the mountains. From Eigerwand you'll see Grindelwald and Lake Thun through small windows cut through the mountain's rock. The trip is unforgettable. Breathing may be difficult at this altitude, for the air is very thin. On top, visit the **Jungfraujoch Ice Palace,** accessible by an elevator. The palace is an ice maze carved out of a glacier and contains many ice sculptures from furniture to Mickey Mouse. For greater heights, visit the Jungfraujoch's **Sphinx Terrace,** Europe's highest scientific observatory. There's also a summer ski school at the top and short sleigh rides pulled by dogs. Expensive fee for rail up to Jungfraujoch; round trip takes all day. Ice palace and sphinx terrace: Free. Crowded on weekends. Tel. (036) 222621.

GRINDELWALD

On the way down from the Jungfraujoch you can take a train from Kleine Scheidegg to Grindelwald, a large year-round resort in the midst of countless jagged peaks. It's also accessible by car. The ski resort has some beginning slopes and a ski kindergarten for 3-through 7-year-olds. Kids can also ride sleds and skate in winter; horseback riding and swimming is available in summer. Grindelwald's **Firstbahn,** Europe's longest chair lift, scoots you up to a point called **The First** at 7,200 feet. The trip takes 1 hour each way. Grindelwald has two Swiss Family Hotels, the Belvedere [Tel. (036) 545434] and the Sans-Souci [Tel. (036) 534343]. From Grindelwald it's a 40-minute trip back down to Interlaken. For resort information, contact the Grindelwald **tourist office,** CH-3818 [Tel. (036) 531212].

GSTAAD AND ENVIRONS

South of Spiez are the mountain resorts of *Lenk, Gstaad, Adelboden,* and *Kandersteg,* all with year-round sporting activities. Adelboden's Swiss Family Hotel, the Parkhotel Bellevue [Tel. (033) 731621], is very special. The owner conducts a story time for children in ten languages! In summer, *Gstaad* has miniature golf, tennis, fishing, horseback riding, and swimming. In winter, this chic resort has great beginner and intermediate ski slopes. There's a ski school and a kindergarten for children and many of the local hotels have child-care centers. Other winter activities include ice-skating, swimming in its covered pool, and curling. Gstaad's Swiss Family Hotel is the Sporthotel Victoria [Tel. (030) 41431]. For resort information, write the Gstaad **tourist office,** CH-3780 [Tel. (030) 41055].

THE EASTERN WALLIS (VALAIS)

Extending along the upper Rhône valley, the eastern half of the Valais canton, or Wallis, as the German-speaking locals call it, contains many magnificent alpine resorts such as Saas-Fee and Zermatt. The French-speaking or western half of this canton is profiled in the chapter's next section.

ZERMATT AND THE MATTERHORN

What Swiss vacation would be complete without venturing up the **Matterhorn?** The famous winter resort of Zermatt is your destination and take-off point. To get there, take a thrilling 90-minute railway ride from Visp or Brig, where you leave your car. No autos are allowed in Zermatt; instead travel through the town in a horse-drawn carriage. If you arrive early or spend the night, you'll see a herd of goats parade through the town center each morning at 8:30 ringing their bells.

Zermatt is Switzerland's best-known ski resort with summer skiing. It has limited accommodations, so plan ahead. Two Swiss Family

Hotels are in town: the Schweizerhof [Tel. (028) 661155] and Nicoletta [Tel. (028) 661151]. If children can walk, they can enroll in Zermatt's ski school. The tourist office can provide you with information about local kindergartens. Other activities include a salt-water swimming pool, skating and riding, and many cable cars. For resort information, write the Zermatt **tourist office,** CH-3920 [Tel. (028) 661181].

At 14,690 feet, the Matterhorn is an awe-inspiring sight. Take Europe's highest open-air cogwheel railway, the **Gornergratbahn,** from Zermatt up to *Riffelberg.* Your family will not forget the climb or the view of the white glacial world from the top. Other excursions from Zermatt include the lift to the small lake of **Schwarzsee,** where you'll see mountain climbers at the Matterhorn hut before they make their ascent to the peak. A four-stage series of cable cars leads to **Klein Matterhorn,** Europe's highest peak (12,500 feet) served by aerial transportation. The trip takes about an hour each way.

SAAS-FEE

One valley east of Zermatt and surrounded by eighteen magnificently snow-capped peaks is Saas-Fee, another car-free summer and winter resort. Saas-Fee has felt the impact of tourism far less than Zermatt. Kids will enjoy the town's horse-drawn carriages; there's a parking area for your car outside of the town. The resort has a ski school for kids ages 5–12 years and you'll find a kindergarten in the village. The ski season extends into the summer. Saas-Fee has many cable cars, gondolas, and aerial cableways to lift you up to great heights. One unusual trip is the new combined gondola/underground lift which takes you up to the world's highest (11,500 feet) revolving restaurant. Back on the "ground floor" is the **Bielen Sports Center,** which has a kid's pool, and there are two Swiss Family Hotels in town: Beau-Site [Tel. (028) 571122] and Alphubel [Tel. (028) 571112]. For resort information, write the Saas-Fee **tourist office,** CH-3906 [Tel. (028) 571457].

NEAR BRIG

Thirty kilometers north of Brig is *Wiler,* where, on the Saturday before Mardi Gras in February, the town celebrates the **Parade of Ugly Masks.** Once intended to scare off ugly spirits, the masks, complete with shaggy manes and hideous features, are exhibited throughout the year in Wiler and its neighboring villages. Most homes have masks hanging outside, and you can buy one to take home in town. During the days before Shrove Tuesday, groups of young men wear these outrageous disguises for a competition and parade. Contact the regional **tourist office:** Tel. (027) 223161.

FRENCH-SPEAKING CANTONS

WESTERN VALAIS

Extending along the upper Rhône valley from Lac Léman to Sierre, the French-speaking or western part of the Valais boasts major ski resorts such as Crans-Montana and a myriad of summer alpine activities. The oldest of Switzerland's magnificent alpine pass roads, the **Great Saint Bernard Pass Road** connects the country with Italy. The Swiss road to the pass begins at Martigny near Verbier. At the road's highest point on the edge of a frozen lake is the **hospice** where for nine centuries mountaineering monks and St. Bernard dogs rescued lost travelers. In the hospice's **Musée du Grand St.-Bernard (St. Bernard Museum)** are mementos of the history of the pass, while in the kennel behind the nearby hotel, kids can pet the famous St. Bernards. The dogs have been replaced on the job by rescue helicopters. Museum: Fee. June 9–12, July–Aug. 9–6, Sept. 1–5. Tel. (026) 49236. Near the hospice, soar up the 9,500-foot **La Chenalette** mountain in a chair lift for a magnificent vista of Mont Blanc and the Grand Paradis. It's a 20-minute ride each way.

FRIBOURG, NEUCHÂTEL, AND THE SWISS JURA

FRIBOURG AND ENVIRONS

Although predominantly French, German is spoken in the eastern part of the canton. In the old walled city of Fribourg is the **Musée Suisse de la Marionnette,** where there are delightful performances for children featuring the **Théâtre des Marionnettes de Fribourg.** Fee. Rue de la Samaritaine, 34. Museum: Sun. 2–5. Tel. (037) 228513. Concerts designed for children are performed by the **Jeunesses Musicales de Fribourg.** Tickets and information are available from the **tourist office,** Square des Places, 1 [Tel. (037) 813175]. August's **International Folklore Festival** features parades and festivities with participants in native colorful costumes.

Gruyères, south of Fribourg, is a traffic-free storybook village with fountains and cobblestone streets. Its **castle** has a 13th-century dungeon and beautiful views from its ramparts. Daily June–Sept. 9–6; Mar.–May and Oct. 9–12, 1–5; Nov.–Feb. 9–12, 1–4:30. Kids can watch 77-pound wheels of Gruyère cheese being made at the **cheese dairy.** Daily 6–6. Tel. (029) 61410. Don't forget to try the town's scrumptious fondue. Gruyère also has a small **Musée de Cire (Wax Museum)** with famous Swiss historical figures. Kids enjoy its display of herdsmen making cheese. Fee. Daily 10:30–6. Tel. (029) 61170.

In **Broc,** just north of Gruyère, Nestlé gives a guided tour of their **chocolate factory** as well as ample samples. Feb.–Nov. Mon. afternoons, Tues. and Thurs. all day, Fri. mornings. Reservations: Tel. (029) 61212. For the "chocolate train" that takes you to Broc from Lake Geneva, see "Montreux."

NEUCHÂTEL

Northwest of Murten is the Swiss watchmaking capital of Neuchâtel. Stroll any of Lake Neuchâtel's many landscaped quais for stunning views of the jagged Alps and towering Mont Blanc. Village resorts line the lake's western shore. Its **Musée d'Art et d'Histoire** has Impressionist works, but its real draw for children is the display of 18th-century life-size automated dolls built by watchmakers. They move, play instruments, and draw pictures. Quai L.-Robert. Automatons perform only on the first Sunday of the month but you can call and see if they'll arrange a special showing. Museum: Tues., Wed., Fri.–Sun. 10–12 and 2–5; Thurs. 10–12, 2–9. Tel. (038) 251740. Don't miss the **Suchard-Tobler Chocolate Factory,** where kids can take a tour and consume delicious dark chocolate samples. Free. Rue de Tivoli, 5. Tues. afternoon guided tour. Reservations: Tel. (038) 212191. Neuchâtel celebrates its grape harvest, which is kicked off by a children's parade, the last week in September during the **Fête des Vendanges.**

SWISS JURA

The **Jura Mountains** are a short drive from Lake Neuchâtel's shore. This low mountain range with pastoral valleys, farms, and rolling hills stretches along the French border. Winter brings wonderful cross-country skiing and the thriving winter resorts are more affordable than their higher alpine neighbors. For information, contact the Jura **tourist office,** Pl. de la Gare, 12, CH-2800 Delémont. Tel. (066) 229977.

La Chaux-de-Fonds is an industrial city but its unrivaled **Musée International d'Horlogerie (International Clockwork Museum)** is well worth a stop. Also known as the "Man and Time Museum," it imaginatively traces the history of the measurement of time through a display of over 3,000 clocks. Kids can see sundials, primitive water clocks, and unique astronomical and musical clocks. Another section illustrates how clocks are made with craftsmen at work. The museum's showpiece is its carillon, an animated 15-ton clock in the adjoining **park.** A striking sculpture, the carillon consists of a master clock, numerical clock, electronic clock, tubular bells, and projectors, and performs musical acoustics, all to tell time. At night it provides a stunning light show. Fee. Rue des Musées, 29. Tues.–Sun.

10–12, 2–5. Tel. (039) 236263. Three other museums are in the same park or a short walk away: the **Museum of Fine Arts** {Tues.–Sun. 10–12, 2–5 [Tel. (039) 230444]}; **the History and Medal Museum** {Sat.–Sun. 10–12, 2–5 [Tel. (039) 235010]}; **Museum of Natural History,** which contains dioramas of African animals especially designed for children {Tues.–Sat. 2–5, Sun. 10–12, 2–5 [Tel. (039) 233976]}. While in town stop in the wooded **Bois du Petit Château** for a picnic at the small **Parc d'Acclimatation (zoo),** with over 400 animals, a vivarium, and playground. Free. Daily 6:30–dusk.

VAUD CANTON

Sparkling **Lac Léman (Lake Geneva)** at the foothills of the Vaud Alps and the slopes of the Jura is one of the main attractions in the Canton de Vaud. Paddle steamers, motorboats, and hydrofoils regularly traverse the lake, connecting Geneva, Vevey, Montreux, and Lausanne. We found a 1-hour trip was enough for children; schedules and fares are available from all lakefront tourist offices. Water sports are available from practically every town along the shore, especially between Montreux and Vevey. We'll start with the area south of Montreux and head west toward Geneva.

MONTREUX

Montreux is a peaceful and small city, except during early July's **Jazz Festival** and fall's **Classical Music Festival.** Its beautiful waterfront promenade is planted with exotic tropical flowers. Kids can tour the waterfront in **Le Petit Train.** There's miniature golf and steps leading down to the water for those who wish to feed its graceful resident swans. There's also a great **playground** at the promenade's Place du Marche, in the town center, with a tunnel slide, crazy climbers, and rocking horses. At sunset, the lake is magnificent. Take the mountain train from Montreux's main station up to the **Rochers de Naye.** At 6,700 feet you'll have a great view of Lac Léman and the Alps. There's skiing at the top December through April. Fee. 50-minute ride. Departs daily. Funiculars also depart from Montreux up to **Les Avants-Sonloup** or **Territ-Mont-Fleur.**
Five kilometers east of the city is the **Château de Chillon,** a restored 13th-century feudal castle with a moat, cannons, underground prison, a torture chamber and some very funny latrines. The castle, which inspired Lord Byron to write his noted poem "The Prisoner of Chillon" in 1816, forms an island surrounded by deep-blue water. There is a swimming beach nearby. Fee. Also accessible by boat from Montreux. Daily Apr.–June and Sept. 9–5:45; July–Aug. 9–6:15; Oct.–Feb. 10–12, 1:30–4. Tel. (021) 633911. Right next to Chillon is

the moderately priced **Hotel Masson,** which has a magnificent view of the lake and the castle. The hotel will make up family suites and has cribs and high chairs. Montreux-Veytaux, 1820. Tel. (021) 9638161.

Le train du chocolat will take fudge lovers from Montreux to the Nestlé Chocolate Factory in Broc (see "Fribourg, Neuchâtel, and the Swiss Jura"). Departs every Wed. Aug.–Sept. Depart Montreux 9:40, arrive Broc 2:34, return Montreux 5:30. It also stops in Gruyères. Tel. (021) 9635121.

NEAR MONTREUX

Thirty kilometers south of Montreux, in **Bex,** kids can travel great depths (for a change in Switzerland!) into the **Salt Mine** at Le Bouillet. An underground narrow-gauge train sweeps you down into the dark mine from where you'll walk through a maze of subterranean passages, shafts, stairways, and chambers with transparent salt deposits and both old and new mining equipment. Kids will learn how salt is tapped and processed. There's a restaurant down below; we wondered if they served unsalted food. Sit at the back of the train for the best view. Kids should be able sit through a film (very high-tech) and a 2-hour tour. Fee. Multilingual tours daily at 9, 2, and 3. Wear sturdy shoes and bring jackets. Apr.–Nov. 15. Reservations: Tel. (025) 632462.

VEVEY AND ENVIRONS

En route to Vevey from Montreux, you reach *La Tour-de-Peilz,* home to our favorite Swiss museum, the **Musée Suisse du Jeu (Swiss Museum of Games).** Children will immediately relate to the museum's stated philosophy, "Man is not fulfilled unless he plays," and you will have a hard time tugging them away from any one of the five rooms organized into educational games, strategic games, simulation games, games of skill, and games of chance. The museum is a unique hands-on games center designed to collect, research, and present games. You'll find tricky puzzles, playing cards, board games, and action games; its courtyard garden has hidden play areas and a life-size chessboard. Save your francs for the gift shop; the international assortment of toys is hard to resist. In the Château La Tour-de-Peilz on the lake. Fee; under 16 free. Tues.–Sun. 2–6. Tel. (021) 544050.

Vevey has many public beaches along its lakeshore and a colorful open-air market is held on the lake at the Grande-Place on Saturday mornings. The **Musée de L'Alimentation (Food Museum)** is a science museum designed by Nestlé to creatively educate us about food and nourishment "from the sun to the consumer." Kids like the "smell test," for which they dip small pieces of paper into the essence of food such as watermelon, hazelnut, cucumber, or asparagus and try to guess what they are smelling. There's a giant mouth to climb into with pillow-soft teeth where kids can watch a video about food and tooth decay. Fee. Quai Perdonnet and Rue du Léman, on the lake. Tues.–Sun, 10–12, 2–5. Tel. (021) 9244111.

LAUSANNE

Along the shore of Lac Léman and at the foot of the jagged Alps is urban and bustling Lausanne with a winding old medieval section and a busy lakeport where summer swimmers, water-skiers, and sailors crowd its colorful promenade. The streets of Lausanne are very steep so use its efficient public bus or the metro system to cross town quickly. Twenty-four-hour passes are available.

Pick up the indispensable English *Lausanne Official Guide* from the **tourist office** at Blvd. de Grancy, 20 (Tel. 275627), which has a section "For Your Children" with listings of theater, events, music, and sports. Lausanne has seven **Centres de Loisirs (leisure centers)** listed in the *Official Guide*, all with special activities such as sports or crafts for kids. The city's **telephone area code** is 021.

Detour! What to See and Do

For a view of the lake and the Alps, climb the 232 steps up the tower of the city's prized Gothic **cathedral,** in Lausanne's medieval section around Rue Cité Devant and Cité Derrière. On Saturday evenings, all Lausanne's church bells chime in tune with its carillon. Tower access is at the end of cathedral's south aisle. Tower: Mon.–Sat. 9–11:30, 1:30–6:30, Sun. 2–6:30; winter until 5.

Don't miss the **Collection de l'Art Brut ("raw" art),** a museum that displays art by "madmen and primitives" and those from society's fringes, such as eccentrics, hermits, and criminals. "Regular" folks, such as telephone operators and dental hygienists, are represented, too. All share a love for creating paintings, drawings, painted rocks, shell effigies, and masks without any sense of tradition or trend. For example, François Portrat gathered dinner plates from the flea markets of Paris which she used to create whimsical figures; another young man made contorted faces from bulbous shells. Fee. In the Château de Beaulieu. Av. des Bergiéres, 11, northwest of downtown. Tues.–Fri. 10–12 and 2–6, Sat. and Sun. 2–6. Tel. 375435.

The **Musée Olympique** recounts the history of the Olympic games. Lausanne is the headquarters for the International Olympics Committee. Free. Av. Ruchonnet, 18. Tues.–Sat. 9–12 and 2–6, Sun.–Mon. 2–6.

Where the Sidewalk Ends: Zoos and Parks

Take the funicular across from the central train station to **Ouchy,** Lausanne's lakeport, where, along its parklike esplanade, the Quai de Belgique, you'll find **le petit train** for touring (Easter and summer), boat rentals, and a hectic but fun scene. At the end of Quai d'Ouchy is the beautiful **Park de Denantou** with elaborate playgrounds, lawns, and ponds. Ouchy has many lakefront hotels.

Lausanne's other large park is **Bourget Park,** which has a bird sanctuary in the west, beyond the lakeport of **Vidy.** Vidy also boasts a narrow-gauge miniature train for kids. Mar.–Nov. Wed. and Sat. 2–6, Sun. 10–6. Tel. 279153. The port has a public beach and pedalboat rentals.

The **Vivarium** has one of Europe's largest collections of poisonous snakes as well as crocodiles, spiders, scorpions, and more. It's all in the small house of an eccentric reptile-loving man. We met his charming mother, who told us that his fascination began with worms at age 3. Fee. North of the city toward Servion Zoo (see below). Chemin de Boissonet, Mon., Wed., Thur., and Fri. 2–6:30; Sat.–Sun. 10–12, 2–6:30. Tel. 327294.

The **Zoo de Servion** is a bit run down but set in a beautiful pastoral park above the city. Highlights are its great playground and flamingos, which share quarters with a typical array of lions, tigers, and bears. Fee. Daily 9 AM until dusk. Easy to get to by taking bus 22 from the city terminal. Tel. 9311671.

Sports and Performing Arts

Check the tourist office's extensive sports listing in the *Lausanne Official Guide* for skating rinks, curling, ski schools, tennis, waterskiing, boat rentals, wind surfing, bowling, and horseback riding. **Bellerive Beach** has three swimming pools, including a kid's pool, expansive lawns, and beach access. Fee. Av. de Rhodanie, 23. May–Sept. Tel. 278131. The open-air **Montchoisi Swimming Pool** has a children's pool, shady lawn, heated water, and artificial waves. Av. du Servan, 30. May–Sept. Tel. 261062. Check to see what is being performed at Lausanne's children's theater, **le Théâtre pour Enfants de Lausanne** (Tel. 382261); language might not matter.

NEAR LAUSANNE

Lakefront *Pully,* toward Vevey, has a beach, a lakeshore swimming pool for children, and a kid's playground with a **miniature train** pulled by a small charcoal locomotive engine. Train runs Easter and summer season on weekends. Tel. 283320.

Forty kilometers north of Lausanne is *Lucens*. Its **Château de Lucens** has the **Musée Sherlock Holmes** with weapons used by gangsters at the end of the 19th century. The castle itself has plenty of room for children to run and a torture room with a resident "witch" puppet. The gift shop sells inexpensive models of the castle for children to glue and construct. Fee. Mar.–mid-June, mid-Sept.–Nov. weekends 10–5; mid-June–mid-Sept. Wed.–Sun. 10–6. Tel. 958032.

LAUSANNE TO GENEVA

About 20 kilometers west of Lausanne, in *Morges,* is the **Musée Militaire Vaudois,** housed in the town's 13th-century castle. Its twenty rooms are filled with cannons, swords, crossbows, and armor but the star attractions are the 8,000 hand-painted lead and pewter toy soldiers that trace all of Europe's military history up to 1939. Fee. Feb.–Dec. daily 10–12 and 1:30–5; weekends 1:30–5. During the first weekend in October, Morges celebrates the very popular **Wine Festival and Vintage Parade** with processions, floats, and parties.

Further toward Geneva, is the hilltop **park** in *Signal de Bougy,* a good rest stop. You'll find vast lawns with top-notch play areas for children, miniature golf, picnic areas, and a restaurant. Branch off Lausanne-Geneva motorway at Rolle or Aubonne and follow signs. Free. Mar.–Nov. daily 9 AM–10 PM. Tel. (021) 8085930.

In *Nyon* stop at the **Maison du Léman,** on the shore's beautiful promenade, where you'll find models of boats that have sailed the lake from all time periods. Fee. Apr.–Oct. Tues.–Sun. 9–12, 2–6; Nov.–Mar. Tues.–Sun. 2–5. Also by the shore is a large **outdoor pool complex** with separate pools for infants and older kids and a fun slide. The **Animal Park of La Garenne,** near Nyon, a noted Swiss breeding center for birds of prey, cares for young or injured birds until they can be released. There are also aquariums, an insectarium, and areas where kids can observe the breeding of rats, mice, rabbits, and guinea pigs. Fee. North of Nyon, west of St. Cergue. Summer daily 9–7; winter 9–dusk. Its cozy teahouse has a big central fireplace. Tel. (022) 661114.

GENEVA (GENÈVE)

Cosmopolitan Geneva is an international meeting ground and the European or global headquarters for almost every large organization, from multinational corporations to the Boy Scouts. Consequently, it is very expensive. Families may want to stay in the more reasonably priced French resorts near Annecy (see "France") and take a day trip into the city. The Rhône River divides the city into a right and left bank. Geneva's "kids-best" sections are the Vieille Ville (old city) around Place Neuve and the lakeshore. Parks with playgrounds are found everywhere.

Wha'd'ya Wanna Do?

The **tourist office** (Tel. 455200) in the Cornavin train station publishes the following free guides: Designed for children, *Guide du Moutard*, in French, has hundreds of listings and addresses of art workshops, sports, and excursions. The booklet "Quelques Bonnes Addresses Pour Vous et Vos Enfants" has listings of children's theater, *bibliothèques* (libraries), *ludothèques* (play centers), *place de jeux* (playgrounds), *garderies et crèches* (baby sitters and nurseries), *colonies de vacances* (camps), and *centres de loisirs* (activity centers with hands-on workshops). Their "List of Events" lets you know the special events in town. The city's **telephone area code** is 022.

The old section and lakeshore are easy to navigate on foot. The city has an efficient system of trams, trolleys, and buses. Tickets for unlimited rides for 1 hour and cards for six trips are available. Lac Léman **boat tours** and rides up the Rhône River depart for excursions from the Quai du Mont Blanc, 8. Boats also depart from the Jardin Anglais at the far end of the lake.

Where to Stay

HOTELS

Geneva's hotels are more expensive than those in other major Swiss cities and advance booking is necessary.

La Réserve, on the outskirts of town, has a pool and tennis, and is set in a lush park. Route de Lausanne, 301. Tel. 7741741. **Deluxe.**

Chateauvieux is a country inn in a beautiful garden 10 kilometers from Geneva. Suites (moderate) and apartments (expensive) are available. Peney-Dessus, 16, 1242, Satigny. Tel. 7531511. **Moderate.**

Le Petit Castel, 8 kilometers from the town center, has three- to four-bedded rooms, a large swimming pool, and tennis courts. Route de Thonon, 271, 1246, Corsier. Tel. 7512337. **Moderate.**

Rivoli, near the lake and swimming beach of Les Pâquis, has a garden and kitchenettes. Rue des Pâquis, 6. Tel. 7318550. **Moderate.**

De La Belotte, 5 kilometers from the town center along the lake, has three-bedded rooms and a garden terrace. Ch. des Pêcheurs, 1222, Vésenaz. Tel. 7521103. **Inexpensive.**

Le Manoir, 8 kilometers from the town center along the lake, has kitchenettes and a garden. Rue Armand-Dufaux, 1245 Collonge-Bellerive. Tel. 7522150. **Inexpensive.**

CAMPGROUNDS

Pointe-à-la-Bise (Tel. 7521296) and *Camping d'Hermance* (Tel. 7511483) are both near the lake and are open Apr.–Sept.

Detour! What to See and Do

Climb the north tower of the **Cathédrale de St-Pierre** for a superb view of the old town. Fee. Tower: June–Sept. daily 11:30–5:30; off-season 11:30–12, 2–5.

Geneva's **lakeshore** is magnificent. Stop at the end of a jetty on the far shore to view the **Jet d'Eau,** the world's tallest fountain, which in summer shoots water 476 feet into the sky. Stop in one of the delicious ice cream shops along Quai Gustave Ador and head to the nearby **Jardin Anglais** to see its large floral clock, the **Horloge Fleurie.** Pedalboats are for rent at Louge Léman, along the promenade, where there are two more parks: the **Parc de la Grange,** which has famous rose gardens, and the **Parc des Eaux-Vives,** both of which have good playgrounds. The swimming beach club **Genève Plage** (Tel. 7362482) is near the marina.

On the other side of the Rhône, across the Pont du Mont Blanc bridge, is the **Bains de Pâquis** swimming beach with pools. Tel. 7322974. Quai Wilson leads to the waterfront parks of **Mon Repos** (with a great playground), **Perle du Lac,** and **Villa Barton,** which are interconnected and beautifully landscaped.

The **Musée de l'Horlogerie** illustrates the history of time with sandclocks, sundials, and lots of offbeat clocks. Look for the musical watches. Free. Rue de Malagnou, 15. Bus 5 or 11. Tues.–Sun. 10–12, 2–6. Tel. 7367412.

The **Musée d'Instruments Anciens de Musique** has hundreds of 16th- to 19th-century musical instruments. Fee. Rue Lefort, 23. Tues. 3–6, Thurs. 10–12 and 3–6, Fri. 8–10 PM. Tel. 215670.

Where the Sidewalk Ends: More Parks

Giant chess games are among the attractions at **Promenade de Bastions Park,** where there are three 8-foot-square chessboards with knee-high plastic pieces. Its entrance is in front of Place Neuve. En route to the International Complex from the lake, is the highly manicured **Jardin Botanique** with a small zoo and a deer pen. 192, rue de Lausanne. Daily all day. Tel. 7326969. A tour of the **United Nations** may be interesting for social-studies buffs. Fee. End of Rue Montbrillant. July–Aug. daily 9–12, 2–6; Apr.–June and Sept.–Oct. daily 10–12, 2–4; Nov.–Mar. Mon.–Fri. 10–12, 2–4.

Performing Arts and Sports

The **Marionnettes de Genève**, Rue Rodo, 3 (Tel. 296759), and the **Marionnettes des 4 Seasons**, Av. des Communes Réunies, 68 (Tel. 7943085), have delightful repertoires where language may not make a difference. Our kids thoroughly enjoyed the Marionnettes de Genève's play, which included a concert piece performed by a violinist puppet. An extensive listing of children's theater and musical companies can be found in the *Guide du Moutard* under "Spectacles."

Check the *Guide du Moutard* for martial arts, badminton, basketball, bowling, bicycling, canoeing, horseback riding, gymnastics, go-carting, ice-skating, volleyball, skateboarding, swimming, and Ping-Pong facilities. The **Service des Sports de la Ville** (Tel. 923535) has hockey, skiing, and tennis classes for children and teens ages 4 through 17.

SOUTH CENTRAL SWITZERLAND: ITALIAN-SPEAKING

THE TICINO

The Italian-speaking Ticino canton is still decidedly Swiss in its un-Italian passion for order and efficiency. The region's magnificent Lake Maggiore and Lake Lugano, both of which border Italy, are prime attractions for children. Boats and steamers are slow but convenient links between Lugano and Locarno, the major resort towns, and the many idyllic lakefront villages. In the Ticino at Mardi Gras in February, a giant **Festa del Risotto** is held in most town squares. Refer to Italy's listings for Lake Como and Lake Maggiore for further activities that are a short boat ride or car journey away.

LUGANO AND ENVIRONS

Take the funicular from the hilltop train station down into Lugano, a relaxed but sophisticated semiurban resort town. A beautifully planted promenade with benches and fountains stretches along peaceful Lake Lugano, where kids can rent pedalboats and feed swans. **Lido Beach** is surrounded by spacious lawns and has both lake and pool swimming. Fee. June–Aug. 9–7. At the far end of the lake, the municipal **Parco Civico,** has sweet-scented Mediterranean flowers and open-air concerts. Life-size chess games are usually in full swing. Above the town, the **Parco Tassino** has a great view, deer, and one lonely Illama.

From Lugano's Paradiso quarter, take the 20-minute funicular ride up to **Monte Salvatore** for a lake and alpine view. March through November. A 30-minute funicular takes you up to the sunny summit of **Mount Brè.** Departs from Cassarte, operates all year. Journey to greater heights up the cogwheel train to **Monte Generoso.** At 5,600 feet, there's a far-reaching alpine panorama. Take a boat from Lugano to Capolago, and then the train. Tel. (091) 481105.

LAKE LUGANO EXCURSIONS

Boats depart every half-hour for a tour of the lake from the Giardino boat station along the promenade. The boat stop after *Gandria* is the small harbor of *Cantine de Gandria.* Kids will get a real kick out of its **Museo Dognale Svizzero (Smuggler's Museum).** The museum, which is only accessible by boat (about 1/2 hour from Lugano) and juts out onto the lake, has a beautiful small picnic area. Life-size mannequins re-create all sorts of attempts to trick the guards who patrol the Swiss-Italian border here on the lake. You'll see "I-Spy" smuggling devices like suitcases with false bottoms and an inflatable boat that once contained salami. Smuggled items such as gems that were hidden in loaves of bread or illegal purses made from cobra skins are all on display. Free. Apr.–Sept. daily 1:30–5:30. Tel. (091) 239843.

Boat service leaves in the morning and afternoon for the hour ride to *Morcote,* the "pearl of the lake"; the village is also accessible by car. Morcote's **Parco Scherrer** is a verdant park with fountains. Fee. Tel. (091) 692125. For a real treat, plan to stay in the village's deluxe Happy Swiss Family Hotel, the Olivella au Lac, set on the majestic lakeside. In addition to all sorts of water sports, you'll find rooms with separate sleeping areas for kids, apartment facilities, and swimming pools, including a shallow one for little guests. Book through Best Western International Hotels: From U.S. tel. 800-528-1234.

Melide, 7 kilometers south of Lugano, is home to **Swissminiatur,** where all the major Swiss sites and many familiar Swiss towns have been meticulously re-created. Kids will marvel at the tiny chalets, castles, ornate cathedrals, and snow-capped mountains, all at 1/25th their normal size. You'll see tiny people sunbathing, trains zooming, busy markets, boats, and aerial cable cars. The Swiss National Knie Circus even makes a doll-size appearance. The park has a children's playground with rope-climbing equipment and a small touring train. Fee. Mar. 12–Oct. 5 daily 8:30–6 (July 15–Aug. 13 until 10); Nov.– Mar. 15 Sun. only. Tel. (091) 687951.

LOCARNO AND ENVIRONS

Locarno, a less sophisticated resort than Lugano, is at the northern tip of Lake Maggiore. It has a more small-town feel as does its lakeshore neighbor, *Ascona.* Parks with the sweet smell of orange blossoms line the tranquil lake. From the center of Locarno take a funicular up to the town's landmark Madonna del Sasso sanctuary in *Orselina* for a splendid view. Travel up further via a cable car that swings you up to *Cardada,* where the views of the Alps and the lake are breathtaking. At the summit are pinewoods for picnics and hikes and a playground. Other lifts can take you up further to a full range of mountain-top destinations. Departs every 30 minutes. Locarno has four Swiss Family Hotels. We chose the Arcadia al Lago because of its ideal central location on the lake and its apartment facilities. Its children's playroom is out of a fun-filled preschool. There are outdoor swings, a climber, and a pool and balconies which look over the lake. Expensive. Casella postale 562. Tel. (093) 310282.

LAKE MAGGIORE EXURSIONS

Boats depart regularly for as far south as the Italian Borromean Islands (see "Italy"), a day-long journey. Shorter trips include a visit to the sandy swimming beach of *Vira* or the charming resort of *Ascona,* which is also accessible by car. Pedalboat rentals are available along Ascona's waterfront. The park near the boat landing has a playhouse and a contemporary wood sculpture of a prehistoric animal that serves double duty as a kid's climber. Many hotels line the water. On Lake Maggiore, between Locarno and Ascona, is the **Lido** beach club with swimming pools, an aquaslide, and play equipment. Further toward Locarno is a public beach and the Camping Segnale campground. Twelve kilometers east of Locarno, in *Verscio,* a world-renowned clown school gives hilarious German and Italian performances in the summer. Contact the Locarno **tourist office** at Viale F. Balli, 2 [Tel. (093) 318633].

SOUTHEASTERN SWITZERLAND: ROMANSCH/ MULTILINGUAL

GRAUBÜNDEN (GRISONS)

Graubünden (or Grisons), the largest and least-populated Swiss canton, has preserved its Old World traditions, which can be found in its many untouched mountain villages. Like the Bernese Oberland, this area of majestic Alps and 150 sparkling valleys is a favorite for winter and summer sports, all of which abound in the world-famous resorts of Arosa, Davos, Klosters, and St. Moritz. The language changes valley to valley. Half the canton speaks German, a third speak Romansch, and the rest speak Italian. In fact, locals from Graubünden joke that sometimes they don't even understand themselves.

Farm vacations are inexpensive and popular in the Grisons, as you have personal contact with friendly Swiss mountain families. Thirty different farms, some with apartments, are available. Request the "Farm Vacation" brochure from the Graubünden **tourist office,** Alexanderstr. 24, 7001 Chur [Tel. (081) 221360]. For **camping** request the brochure "Camping Graubünden" from the tourist office.

Wha'd'ya Wanna Do?

Every possible winter and summer sport is available in the Grisons. Some special summer activities include bicycling on the canton's extensive network of natural **bicycling paths** designed for those who may feel insecure on main roads. The canton's Rhaetian Railway has a service where bikes can be collected at the station of your choice and returned to any other station. Request the detailed brochure "Cycling in Upper Egadin" from the Graubünden tourist office. **River rafting** in inflatable dinghies down the breathtaking waters of the "Swiss Grand Canyon" or the Inn Gorge is a thrill. The only qualification needed is an ability to swim. The Graubünden tourist office can provide details.

AROSA AND ENVIRONS

If you head up the breathtaking **Schanfigg Valley** near Chur, you'll come to *Arosa,* a magnificent summer and winter resort. Every possible sport is available in winter, including horse-drawn sleigh rides. Beginning and intermediate skiers are comfortable here, and there are special programs for kids. Public kindergartens are available through hotels in the town; contact the tourist office for details. In summer you can swim or row in Arosa's lovely lakes, and there's an artificial ice-skating rink and horseback excursions through the valley. Ride the cable car up to Mount Weisshorn; at 7,000 feet the view is stupendous. Many accommodations, from apartments to hotels, are available in all price ranges. Swiss Family Hotels include the Hohenfels [Tel. (081) 310101], Prätschli [Tel. (081) 311861], Seehop [Tel. (081) 311541] and Anita [Tel (081) 311109]. Contact the Arosa **tourist office,** CH-7059. [Tel. (081) 311621].

North toward Lichtenstein is Heidi's hometown of *Maienfeld,* where children can see the landscape and homes from Johanna Spyri's classic 1881 Swiss fable. Heidi's home was set in the imaginary town of Dörfli, but Maienfeld locals argue that it was their town that inspired the author. Heidi's statue is a short walk up from the village square. Walk the bucolic **Der Heidi Wanderweg (Heidi Hiking Trail),** which starts at the main rail station, through glorious Swiss fairy-tale scenery, with wild strawberries and meadows and past houses like those in the story. A 90-minute trail leads to the **Heidihof**

Hotel, a mountain hut with menus inspired by the book. Try the Aunt Clara Platter. Tel. (085) 91195. A longer 3-hour uphill trail open May–Oct. leads to her grandpa's chalet.

KLOSTERS

Nestled in the next valley up from Arosa are the famous resorts of Klosters and Davos. *Klosters* is the most well-equipped resort for families in the Grisons. Its world-famous children's ski school draws families from all over the world. Discounts of 40 percent are given on all children's ski passes. The ski area of Madrisa has a child-care center at the top of the Madrisabahn which enables parents to enjoy a few hours of snow and skiing with or without kids. In town, the Hotel Vereina Klosters has a public kindergarten for ages 2–6, with care of infants provided upon request. All languages are spoken. Tel. (083) 41161.

In summer Klosters is a paradise for hikers in the valley of the Verein or the Silveretta refuge, accessible by the Madrisa gondola. The town has two children's playgrounds, one of which features a climbable tree house. A heated outdoor shallow children's pool set below the snow-capped Alps, summer children's free play afternoons, and fun fairs on Madrisa are available; contact the tourist office. Klosters has many chalet and apartment rentals. Request the brochure *Apartments and Private Rooms* from the Klosters **tourist office,** CH-7250 Klosters [Tel (083) 41877]. The town's Hotel Sport [Tel. (083) 42921] and Hotel Vereina [Tel. (083) 41161] have special programs for children; the Piz Bruin is a Swiss Family Hotel [Tel. (083) 48111].

DAVOS

The neighboring resort of *Davos* also features magnificent skiing and is renowned for its enormous ice-skating rink, the largest natural rink in Europe. Kids can skate October through June. Ski classes and ski races are held December through April for children. Three through 10-year-olds can attend the Pinocchio Kindergarten in Bünda and the Mickymaus Kindergarten in Bolgen, both of which are open December 25–April 21. For information contact the Swiss Ski School of Davos, Promenade 83, CH-7270 Davos Platz [Tel. (083) 37171]. Daily horse-drawn carriage rides will take you through the area, departing from the Davos Platz railway station. The town also has a **toy lending library,** which the tourist office can inform you about. January 7 and 14 bring an old Davos custom to town when local children participate in a **Children's Toboggan Procession.**

Summer in Davos features sailing, rowing, and wind surfing on the Davorsee. Kids can swim at the Davorsee's public beach or at the town's indoor and outdoor swimming pools. The resort's many summer funicular rides include the Schatzalp-Strela, Bramabuel-Jakobsen, Pischa, and Parsenn rides. In mid-July through the end of August Davos hosts the **International Cartoon Biennial.** Swiss Family Hotels in Davos are the Steigenberger Belvédère [Tel. (083) 21281], Morosani Posthotel [Tel. (083) 21161], Berghotel Schatzalp [Tel. (083) 35831], and the Derby [Tel. (083) 61166].

Davos-Weisen has Switzerland's first children's hotel, the Kinderhotel Muchetta, with an adventure playground, a water land, a fairy-tale room, a jumping room, a kids' library, a milk bar, and a Snow White playroom. Guests can choose a family apartment, a brother/sister room, or a room for three or more. Monelago Hotels, Golfhotel Waldhuus, 7270 Davos Platz. Tel. (083) 61131. For resort information contact the Davos-Platz **tourist office,** CH-7270 [Tel. (083) 35135].

ST. MORITZ AND ENVIRONS

St. Moritz is an elegant resort with primarily four- and five-star hotels. During the ski season, apartments are a popular and less expensive option. The resort's ski school teaches children ages 6–12. Off-the-slope activities include ice-skating, bobsledding, horseback riding, and dashing through the show on horse-drawn sleighs. Prices drop in summer, when you can hike or ride funiculars to gorgeous alpine vistas, pick wildflowers, and enjoy St. Mortiz's dazzling clear lake. Swimming, skating, summer skiing, sailing, and horseback riding will keep outdoor-loving families quite content. St. Moritz's Swiss Family Hotel is the Park-Hotel Kurhaus [Tel. (082) 22111]. Badrutt's Palace Hotel [Tel. (082) 37739] also has many amenities for families. Club Med has a winter village here with bilingual staffmembers and many kids' activities on and off the slopes. From U.S. Tel. 800 CLUB-MED. Contact the St. Moritz **tourist office,** CH-7500 [Tel. (082) 66488].

East of St. Moritz is *Pontresina,* a popular and more family-oriented winter playground with equally great skiing extending through the summer. For more fun there's an indoor swimming pool, a gymnasium, horseback riding, and trout fishing. Pontresina's Roseg Ice Rink has a playground, and there are beautiful horse-drawn carriage rides up the valley, the Val Roseg. Pontresina's mountain school offers 4-hour tours of the Diavolezza glacier. In summer, hikers can stay overnight in alpine huts. Pontresina has three Swiss Family Hotels: Grand Hotel Kronenhof [Tel. (082) 60111], the Atlas [Tel. (082) 66321], and the Engadinerhof [Tel. (082) 66212]. Contact the Pontresina **tourist office,** CH-7504 [Tel. (082) 66488].

Sampling of Unusual and Interesting Sites and Activities

A place-name index appears on page 497

Adventure playgrounds, 120, 133, 134, 136, 139, 140, 141, 147, 153–57, 163; *see also* Amusement parks; Theme parks
Africa museum, 214
Aircraft exhibits, 60, 104, 128, 204
Amusement parks: Austria, 31; Belgium, 47, 49, 50, 51; Denmark, 52, 53, 54, 56, 58, 60, 61; France, 74, 76, 77, 78, 88, 92, 98; Great Britain, 141; Ireland, 162, 163; Italy, 176, 186, 189, 198, 199; Netherlands, 207, 209–12, 215, 216, 218; Portugal, 229; Spain, 242, 243, 246, 247, 253, 256; Switzerland, 265, 270; West Germany, 99, 108, 111, 112; *see also* Adventure playgrounds; Theme parks
Aquariums: Denmark, 60, 62; France, 72, 73, 75, 79, 80, 81, 85, 90, 91, 97; Great Britain, 133, 141; Italy, 174, 190, 196, 199; Netherlands, 209, 210, 211, 212; Portugal, 235; Spain, 258; West Germany, 116
Aqueducts, Roman, 96, 255
Archeology museums and parks, 198, 199, 203
Armor: Austria, 30, 34, 39, 41; Denmark, 56; France, 73, 76; Great Britain, 126, 129, 132, 154; Italy, 181, 191, 192, 196, 199; Portugal, 223; Spain, 252, 255; Switzerland, 265, 269
Arms, *see* Weapons
Automobile museums, 45, 59, 60, 104, 135, 153, 165, 191
Automobile races, 90, 248

Balloons, hot-air, 136, 266
Banquets, 151; historic theme, 50; medieval, 109, 158, 166, 167
Barge trips, 86
Bat museum, 63
Battle sites, 47, 83, 254
Bear pits, 269
Beatles, exhibits related to the, 141
Beatrix Potter exhibits, 140, 143, 144
Bell towers, 70, 73, 180, 197
Bicycle museums, 165, 214, 268
Bicycle races, 77
Birds, 32, 95, 110, 140, 210, 212, 216, 227, 276, 277; aviary, 83, 156; falconry, 139, 140, 145
Blarney Stone, kissing the, 164
Boat exhibits, 143, 166, 224, 232, 244, 254; model, 227, 277; *see also* Maritime museums; Ships, old
Bottle museum, 62
Brass rubbings, 120, 128, 140, 142, 143, 151
Bread museums, 77, 109
Bridges, 94, 96, 127, 147, 196, 255, 266
Bullfights and bullfighting exhibits: Portugal, 219, 224, 233; Spain, 236, 244, 246, 249, 253, 256
Bulls, running of the, 256
Butterflies, 91, 98, 139, 152

Camogie competition, 162
Carillons, 42, 49, 50, 137, 208, 212, 216, 274, 276

Carnival(s): Belgium, 42; Great Britain, 134; Italy, 177, 181, 183, 189, 192, 198; Portugal, 235; Spain, 248, 254; Switzerland, 267, 268
Carousels: France, 72, 75, 76, 94, 97; Italy, 175; Netherlands, 212; Switzerland, 268; West Germany, 103, 114, 119
Carriages, *see* Coach collections
Cars, *see* Automobile museums; Automobile races
Cartoons, 268, 281
Castles: Austria, 32, 41; Denmark, 57, 58, 59, 60; France, 78, 79, 85, 86, 90, 94, 95, 97; Great Britain, 131–34, 138, 139, 141, 145, 146–47, 149, 151, 154–57; Ireland, 161, 163, 164, 166, 167; Italy, 198; Portugal, 223, 226, 227, 230, 231, 234, 235; Spain, 245, 255, 256, 258; Switzerland, 264, 265, 270, 273, 274, 276; West Germany, 108, 109, 111–12
Catacombs, 35, 76, 176, 202; *see also* Cemeteries; Mummies and preserved corpses
Cat festival and parade, 150
Cave exploring and cave art: Austria, 34, 36, 37, 38; Belgium, 51; Denmark, 63; France, 79, 80, 84–89, 96, 97; Great Britain, 132, 137, 148, 157; Ireland, 163–66; Italy, 199, 201, 203; Netherlands, 217; Portugal, 227–28; Spain, 246, 247, 250–51, 257, 258; Switzerland, 271
Cemeteries, 76, 80; for pets, 77; *see also* Catacombs; Mummies and preserved corpses
Chateaux, *see* Castles
Cheese making, 264, 273
Cheese markets, 210, 212
Chess games, 278
Chocolate factories, 78, 264, 273
Choirs, 28, 30, 111, 119, 244
Christmas-related events: Austria, 25, 33, 39; France, 77; Great Britain, 120; Italy, 173, 177, 187; Portugal, 235, 244; Spain, 246, 254; Switzerland, 267; West Germany, 99, 105, 109, 110, 118–19
Circuses, 57, 76, 90, 105, 118, 209, 215, 216, 254, 260, 264
Clocks: Austria, 29; France, 81, 82, 87; Great Britain, 126, 137; Italy, 184, 201; Netherlands, 210, 216; Portugal, 228, 235; Switzerland, 263, 269, 273–74, 277, 278; West Germany, 99, 108, 111, 116
Clowns, 61, 90, 94, 133, 252
Coach collections, 30, 126, 181, 253, 268
Concentration camp, 105
Copper mine, 145
Costumes: Austria, 30, 31, 38, 40; Belgium, 47; France, 73, 79, 80; Great Britain, 128, 129, 135, 136; Italy, 181, 188, 198; Portugal, 233; Spain, 247; Switzerland, 263, 266
Counterfeits, museum of, 74
Cowboys and Indians, 92, 95, 100, 109
Cricket (insect) festival, 182
Cricket (sport) matches, 130
Crystal factory, 163
Curling, 148–49

494

Place-Name Index

498 ◆ INDEX

Let Us Know . . .

If in your travels to Europe with your children you discover an out-of-the-way attraction, choice destination, or family-friendly accommodation that we did not mention in this book, please fill out this form and tell us about it. We will research your suggestions for possible inclusion in future editions of *Innocents Abroad: Traveling with Kids in Europe.*

What were your children's favorite places in Europe, and why?

What did they especially like that we didn't mention?

Did you find any accommodations that were especially comfortable for families? Please include address and phone number.

Have any of the places we've recommended changed for better or worse since this book was written?

Any tried-and-true travel tips to add?

Send to: Valerie Deutsch and Laura Sutherland
          c/o Plume
          Penguin USA
          375 Hudson Street
          New York, NY 10014